2ND EDITION
Invitation
to Computer
Science

Java Version

► G. Michael Schneider
Macalester College

► Judith L. Gersting
University of Hawaii, Hilo

Contributing author:
Keith Miller
University of Illinois, Springfield

THOMSON
COURSE TECHNOLOGY ™

Australia • Canada • Mexico • Singapore •
Spain • United Kingdom • United States

THOMSON

COURSE TECHNOLOGY

Invitation to Computer Science: Java Version, Second Edition
by G. Michael Schneider and Judith L. Gersting

Managing Editor:
Jennifer Muroff

Editorial Assistant:
Amanda Piantedosi

Marketing Manager:
Amy Yarnevich

Product Manager:
Alyssa Pratt

Associate Product Manager:
Mirella Misiaszek

Production Editor:
Kelly Robinson

Designer:
Terri Wright

Cover Design:
Joel Sadagursky

Senior Manufacturing Coordinator:
Trevor Kallop

Compositor:
Pre-Press Company, Inc.

Disclaimer
Course Technology reserves the right to revise this publication and make changes from time to time in its content without notice.

ISBN 0-534-41994-1

To my wife, Ruthann, and our children, Benjamin, Rebecca, and Trevor

G. M. S.

To my husband, John, and to our children, Adam and Jason

J. L. G.

BRIEF CONTENTS

CONTENTS

LEVEL 3   The Virtual Machine   232

LEVEL 6   Social Issues in Computing   656

PREFACE

This text is for a one-semester introductory course in computer science. It presents a breadth-first overview of the discipline while assuming no prior background in computer science, programming, or mathematics. It is appropriate for use in both a service course for students not majoring in computer science and at schools that implement their introductory sequence for majors using the breadth-first model described in the ACM/IEEE Computing Curricula 2001 Report. It would be quite suitable for high school courses as well. Previous editions of this text have been used in all these different types of courses.

The introductory computer science service course has undergone a number of changes in the past few years. In the 1970s and early 1980s, it was usually a course in FORTRAN, Pascal, or BASIC. At that time, it was felt that the most important skill a student could acquire was learning to program in a high-level language. In the mid–to late–1980s, a rapid increase in computer use caused the course to evolve into something called "computer literacy," in which students learned about new applications of computing in such fields as business, medicine, law, and education. With the growth of personal computers and productivity software, a typical early to mid–1990s version of this course would spend a semester teaching students to use word processors, databases, spreadsheets, presentation software, and electronic mail. The most recent change has been its evolution into a Web-centric course where students learn to design and implement Web pages using technology such as HTML, XML, and Java applets.

Many academics feel that it is time for the computer science service course to evolve once again. There are two reasons for this belief. First, virtually all students coming to college today are familiar with personal computers and productivity software. They have been using word processors since elementary school and are highly familiar with networks, bulletin boards, email, and the Web. Many have written Web pages and some even have their own Web sites. In today's world a course that focuses on these applications will be of little or no interest.

But a more important reason for rethinking the structure of this course, and the primary reason why we authored this book, is found in the following observation:

Most computer science service courses do not teach students about computer science!

We believe quite strongly that students in a computer science service course must receive a solid grounding in the central concepts of computer science as well as in the important uses of computing and information technology. The material in such a course would not be limited to "fun" applications such as Web page design and interactive graphics but would also cover such fundamental issues as algorithms, hardware design, computer organization, system software, language models, theory of computation, and social and ethical issues of computing. Exposure to these deeper and more complex core ideas introduces students to the richness and beauty of the field. It allows them not only to use computers and software effectively but to understand and appreciate the ideas underlying their creation and implementation.

This approach is consistent with most other scientific disciplines with respect to their introductory courses. For example, chemistry service courses typically focus on fundamental concepts (e.g., atoms, molecules, reactions) in addition to the uses and applications of chemistry. A beginning physics course spends the majority of time on a broad range of important theoretical concepts, such as elementary particles, force, matter, and energy.

A first course for computer science majors using the breadth-first curriculum model emphasizes an early exposure to many of the subdisciplines of the field rather than placing an exclusive emphasis on programming. This gives new majors a more complete and well-rounded understanding of their chosen field of study right from the start. As stated in the Curriculum 2001 Report, "[introductory] courses that emphasize only this one aspect [programming] fail to let students experience the many other areas and styles of thought that are part of computer science as a whole."

Our book—intended for both majors and nonmajors—is organized around this breadth-first approach, and it presents a wide range of subject matter drawn from many areas of computer science. However, to avoid drowning the student in a sea of seemingly unrelated facts and details, a breadth-first presentation must be woven into a fabric, a theme, a "big picture" that unifies the many topics and presents computer science as a single, integrated discipline. To achieve this, we have divided the study of computer science into a hierarchy of topics, with each layer in our hierarchy building and expanding upon concepts presented in earlier chapters.

The central theme of this book is that *computer science is the study of algorithms*. Our hierarchy utilizes this definition by first looking at the algorithmic basis of computer science and then moving upwards from this central theme to higher-level issues such as hardware, software, applications, and ethics. Just as the chemist starts from protons, neutrons, and electrons and builds up to atoms, molecules, and compounds, so too does our text build from such elementary concepts as algorithms, binary arithmetic, gates, and circuits to higher-level ideas such as computer organization, operating systems, high-level languages, compilation, applications, and the social, legal, and ethical issues of information technology.

The six levels in our computer science hierarchy are as follows:

Level 1.   The Algorithmic Foundations of Computer Science

Level 2.   The Hardware World

Level 3.   The Virtual Machine

Level 4.   The Software World

Level 5.   Applications

Level 6.   Social Issues in Computing

Following an introductory chapter, Level 1 (Chapters 2–3) introduces "The Algorithmic Foundations of Computer Science," the bedrock on which all other aspects of the discipline are built. It presents such important ideas as the design of algorithms, algorithmic problem-solving, abstraction, pseudocode, iteration, and efficiency. It illustrates these ideas using such well-known examples as searching a list, finding the largest element, sorting a list, and matching patterns. It also introduces the concepts of algorithmic efficiency and asymptotic growth and demonstrates that not all algorithms are, at least in terms of running time, created equal!

The discussions in Level 1 assume that our algorithms are executed by something called a "computing agent," an abstract concept for any entity that can effectively carry out the instructions in our solution. However, in Level 2 (Chapters 4–5), "The Hardware World," we want our algorithms to be executed by *real* computers to produce *real* results. Thus begins our discussion of hardware, logic design, and computer organization. The initial discussion introduces the basic building blocks of computer systems—binary numbers, Boolean logic, gates, and circuits. It then shows how these elementary concepts are used to construct a real computer using the classic Von Neumann architecture, including processor, memory, buses, and input/output. It presents a typical machine language instruction set and explains how the algorithms of Level 1 can be represented in machine language and run on the Von Neumann hardware of Level 2, conceptually tying together these two areas. It ends with a discussion of an important new direction in hardware design— massively parallel machines.

By the end of Level 2 students have been introduced to some basic concepts in logic design and computer organization, and they understand and appreciate the enormous complexity of these areas. This complexity is the motivation for Level 3 (Chapters 6–7), "The Virtual Machine." This section describes how system software produces a friendly, user-oriented problem-solving environment that hides many of the ugly hardware details just described. Level 3 looks at the same problem discussed in Level 2, encoding an algorithm and executing it, but shows how much easier this is in a virtual environment containing software tools like text editors, assemblers, and loaders. Level 3 also discusses the services and responsibilities of operating systems and introduces the different types of systems that exist. The section concludes by looking at one of the most important virtual environments in current use—networks of computers. It shows how systems such as the Ethernet, the Internet, and the Web are created from independent computers linked together via transmission media and communications software. This creates a virtual environment in which we are able to easily and effectively use not only the computers on our desks but computers located anywhere in the world.

Now that we have created a user-oriented virtual environment, what do we want to do? Most likely we will want to write programs to solve interesting problems. This is the motivation for Level 4 (Chapters 8–11), "The Software World." Although this book should not be viewed as a programming text, it contains a brief introduction to an object-oriented language and some important programming concepts—variables, data types, classes, objects, assignment, conditional instructions, iteration, and methods. This gives students an appreciation for the task of the programmer and the power of the problem-solving environment created by a modern high-level language. We also want students to know that there are language models in addition to object-oriented, so we provide a discussion of the functional, logic, and parallel paradigms as well as special-purpose languages such as SQL, HTML, and JavaScript. This level also describes the design and construction of a compiler and shows how these high-level languages can be translated into machine language for execution. This discussion ties together many of the ideas presented in earlier chapters as we show how an algorithm (Level 1) is translated into a high-level language (Level 4), compiled, and executed on a typical Von Neumann machine (Level 2), which makes use of the system software tools of Level 3. These "recurring themes" and frequent references to earlier concepts help to reinforce the idea of computer science as an integrated set of topics. At the conclusion of Level 4, we introduce the idea of computability and unsolvability. A formal model of computing (the Turing machine) is used to prove that there exist problems for which no general algorithmic solution can be found. That is, it shows students that there are indeed limits to what computers can do.

We now have a high-level programming environment in which it is possible to write programs to solve important problems. The question we must now ask ourselves is, What are the important problems that we want to address? In Level 5 (Chapters 12–14), "Applications," we take a look at a few of the important uses of computers in our modern society. There is no way to cover even a tiny fraction of the many applications of computers and information technology in a single section. Therefore, we focus on a relatively small set that demonstrates some of the important concepts, tools, and techniques of computer science. This includes applications drawn primarily from the sciences and engineering (simulation and modeling), business and finance (E-commerce, databases), and the social sciences (artificial intelligence). Our goal is not to try and provide encyclopedic coverage of modern computing usages. Instead, it is to show students that applications packages are not magic boxes whose inner workings are totally unfathomable, but rather they are the result of building on the core computer science concepts—algorithms, hardware, and languages—presented in previous chapters. We hope that our discussions in this section will encourage readers to seek out information on applications and software packages specific to their own areas of interest.

Finally, we reach the highest level of study, Level 6 (Chapter 15), "Social Issues in Computing," which addresses the social, ethical, and legal issues raised by the types of computer applications discussed in Level 5. This section (written by contributing author Professor Keith Miller of the University of Illinois at Springfield) examines such thorny problems as the ownership of intellectual property in the electronic age, national security concerns aggravated by information technology, and the erosion of individual privacy caused by the increasing use of online databases. This section does not attempt to provide quick solutions to these problems (as if such easy answers exist). Instead, it focuses on techniques that students can use in thinking about these ethical issues and reaching their own conclusions. Our goal in this final section is to make students aware of the enormous impact that information technology is having on everyone's lives and to give them tools that will allow them to make better and more informed ethical decisions.

This, then, is the hierarchical structure of our text. It begins with the algorithmic foundations of the discipline and works its way upward from low-level hardware concepts through virtual machine environments, languages, software, and applications to the social issues raised by computer technology. This organizational structure, along with the use of recurring themes, is one of the most important aspects of the book. It enables students to view computer science as a unified, integrated, and coherent field of study. While the social issues material in Chapter 15 can be presented at any time, the rest of the material is intended to be covered sequentially.

We have been enormously pleased with reactions to earlier versions of our book. In this new edition, we have made a number of significant changes and improvements from previous versions of the text. The most important changes are

- A totally rewritten "Applications" section that reflects important new uses of computing in our society. This includes a new Chapter 12, "Simulation and Modeling," and a new Chapter 13, "E-Commerce and Information Security," that includes a section on data encryption.

- A rewritten Chapter 7 on networking entitled "Computer Networks, the Internet, and the World Wide Web." It contains expanded coverage on such topics as the Web, HTTP, TCP/IP, and wireless computing.

- A revised Chapter 14, "Artificial Intelligence," that includes new sections on intelligent agents, expert systems, and swarm intelligence.

- A new Chapter 15 entitled "Making Decisions about Computers, Information, and Society." Rather than simply cataloging important ethical problems, this new chapter focuses on ways for students to think, reason, and make decisions about important ethical concerns.

- New material in Chapter 4 about the binary representation of sound and visual data and data compression.

- Moving the "History of Computing" section into Chapter 1 so that students can be introduced to the historical background of our field earlier in their studies.

Another important development in computer science education is the realization that, like physics, chemistry, and biology, computer science is an empirical, laboratory-based discipline in which learning comes not only through listening but also from doing and trying. Many complex ideas in computer science cannot be fully understood and appreciated until they are visualized, observed, and manipulated. Today, most computer science faculty consider laboratories to be an essential part of any introductory course. This development is fully reflected in our approach to teaching computer science.

Associated with this text is a laboratory manual and custom-designed laboratory software that enable students to experiment with many of the concepts that we present. The manual contains 23 laboratory experiences that are closely coordinated with the main text and cover all levels except Level 6. These labs give students the chance to observe, study, analyze, and/or modify an important idea or concept. For example, associated with Level 1 (the algorithmic foundations of computer science) are experiments that animate the algorithms in Chapters 2 and 3 and ask students to observe and discuss what is happening in these animations. There are also labs that allow students to measure the running time of these algorithms for different-sized data sets and discuss their observed behavior. Associated with Level 2 (the hardware world) are projects that let students design and analyze logic circuits as well as program a simulated Von Neumann machine identical to the one presented in the text. At the applications level, Level 5, there are new labs to run experiments using a restaurant customer/server simulation and an encryption algorithm.

Each of the 23 laboratories includes an explanation of how to use the software, a description of how to conduct the experiment, and discussion questions and problems for students to complete and hand in. To carry out these experiments students can work on their own or in teams, and the course may utilize either a closed-lab or an open-lab setting. The lab manual and software will coordinate well with all of these laboratory models.

To challenge the advanced students, each chapter includes, along with a regular set of exercises, some "Challenge Problems." These more complex questions can be used for longer assignments done either individually or by teams of students. Finally, if a student is interested in a topic and wants to go into it in more detail, there is a section at the end of each chapter entitled "For Further Reading" that has references to texts and Web sites containing additional material on the topic covered in that chapter.

Computer science is a young and exciting discipline, and we hope that the material in this text, along with the laboratory projects, will convey this feeling of newness and excitement. By presenting the field in all of its richness—algorithms, hardware, software, systems, applications, and social issues—we hope to give students a deeper appreciation for the many diverse and interesting areas of research and study within the discipline of computer science.

The following reviewers, along with the many users of previous editions who have provided helpful comments, have contributed to the writing of this new edition, and we want to thank them all.

Reviewer List

DANA ANGLUIN
Yale University

JULIA BENSON
Georgia Perimeter College

THOMAS BRENNAN
St. Thomas Aquinas College

MICHAEL COLLARD
Kent State University

KENDRA DINERSTEIN
Utah State University

JENNIFER GOLDBECK
Georgetown University

LIZ JOHNSON
Xavier University

CHE-CHEN LIOU
Caldwell College

MADELEINE SCHEP
Columbia College

SUSAN SELLS
Wichita State University

ZHIZHANG SHEN
Plymouth St. College

ALEXANDER SHIBAKOV
Tennessee Tech University

MARK TERWILLIGAR
Lake Superior University

WILLAM THACKER
Winthrop University

SCOTT VANDENBURG
Siena College

TERESA VITOLO
Gannon University

ARTHUR YANUSKA
Christian Brothers University

—G. Michael Schneider
   Macalester College
   schneider@macalester.edu

—Judith L. Gersting
   University of Hawaii—Hilo
   gersting@hawaii.edu

Invitation
to Computer Science

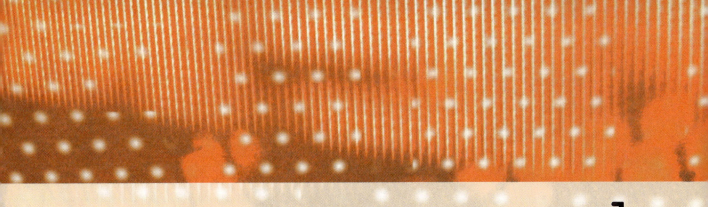

CHAPTER 1

An Introduction to Computer Science

1.1 Introduction

This text is an invitation to learn about one of the youngest and most exciting of scientific disciplines—**computer science.** Almost every day our newspapers, magazines, and televisions carry reports of new advances in computing, such as high-speed supercomputers that perform trillions of mathematical operations per second; networks that transmit high-definition images anywhere in the world in fractions of a second; and minute computers that can be embedded into our books, watches, clothing, and even our bodies. The next few years will see technological breakthroughs that, until a few years ago, existed only in the minds of dreamers and science fiction writers. These are exciting times in computing, and our goal in this text is to provide the reader with an understanding of computer science and an appreciation for the diverse areas of research and study within this important new field.

Despite its simple-sounding name, computer science is unusual in that many people do not have an intuitive feel for the types of problems studied by professionals in this area. The average person can produce a reasonably accurate description of most scientific fields, even if he or she did not study the subject in school. For example, you probably know that biology is the study of living organisms and that chemistry deals with the structure and composition of matter. However, you might not have the same intuitive understanding for the type of work that goes on in computer science. Before we describe what computer science is, let's look at a few common misconceptions about this field of study.

MISCONCEPTION 1: *Computer science is the study of computers.*

This apparently obvious definition is actually incorrect or, to put it more precisely, incomplete. For example, some of the earliest and most fundamental theoretical work in computer science took place during the period 1920–1940, years before the development of the first computer system. (This pioneering work was initially considered a branch of logic and applied mathematics, not the emergence of a new discipline. Computer science did not come to be recognized as a separate and independent field of scientific study until the late 1950s to early 1960s.) Even today, there are branches of computer science quite distinct from a study of "real" machines. In *theoretical computer science,* for example, researchers study the logical and mathematical properties of problems and their solutions. Frequently, these researchers investigate problems not with actual computers but rather with *formal models* of computation, which are easier to study and analyze mathematically. Their work involves pencil and paper, not circuit boards and disks.

This distinction between computers and computer science was beautifully expressed by computer scientists Michael R. Fellows and Ian Parberry in an article in the journal *Computing Research News*:

> Computer science is no more about computers than astronomy is about telescopes, biology is about microscopes, or chemistry is about beakers and test tubes. Science is not about tools. It is about how we use them and what we find out when we do.[1]

MISCONCEPTION 2: *Computer science is the study of how to write computer programs.*

For many people, their introduction to computer science involves learning to write programs in a language such as C++, Scheme, or Java. This almost universal use of programming as the entry to the discipline can create the misunderstanding that computer science is equivalent to computer programming. Again, this is a highly misleading point of view.

Programming is extremely important, but primarily as a tool by which researchers study new ideas and build and test new solutions. When a computer scientist has designed and analyzed a new approach to solving a problem or has created a new way to represent information, then he or she will implement that idea as a program in order to test it on an actual computer system. This permits the researcher to see how well these new ideas work and whether they perform better than previous methods.

For example, searching a list to locate a specific item is one of the most common applications of computers, and it is frequently applied to huge problems, such as finding one name among the approximately 20,000,000 listings in the New York City telephone directory. (We will solve this problem in the next chapter.) A more efficient lookup method would be quite useful to both the telephone company and its users by reducing the time that customers must wait for directory assistance. Assume that we have designed what we believe to be a "new and improved" search technique. After analyzing it theoretically, we would study it empirically. We would write a program to implement our new method, execute it on our computer, and measure its performance. These tests would demonstrate under what conditions our new method is or is not faster than the directory search procedures currently in use.

In computer science, it is not simply the construction of a high-quality program that is important but also the methods it embodies, the services it provides, and the results it produces. It is possible to become so enmeshed in writing code and getting it to run that we forget that a program is only a means to an end, not an end in itself.

MISCONCEPTION 3: *Computer science is the study of the uses and applications of computers and software.*

If one's introduction to computer science is not programming, then it may be a course on the application of computers and software. Such a course typically involves learning to use a number of popular packages, such as word

---

1 Fellows, M. R., and Parberry, I. "Getting Children Excited About Computer Science," *Computing Research News,* vol. 5, no. 1 (January 1993).

processors, database systems, imaging software, electronic mail, and a Web browser.

These packages are widely used by professionals in all fields. However, learning to use a software package is no more a part of computer science than driver's education is a branch of automotive engineering. A wide range of people *use* computer software, but the computer scientist is responsible for *specifying, designing, building,* and *testing* software packages as well as the computer systems on which they run.

Looking back at the previous discussion, we can see that these three views of computer science are not necessarily wrong; they are just woefully incomplete. Concepts such as computers, programming languages, software, and applications *are* part of the discipline of computer science, but individually they do not capture the richness and diversity of this field.

We have spent a good deal of time saying what computer science is *not*. What, then, is it? What are its basic concepts? What are the fundamental questions studied by professionals in this field? Is it possible to capture the breadth and scope of the discipline in a single definition? We answer these fundamental questions in the next section and, indeed, in the remainder of the text.

1.2   The Definition of Computer Science

There are many definitions of computer science, but the one that we feel best captures the richness and breadth of ideas embodied in this branch of science was first proposed by Professors Norman Gibbs and Allen Tucker.[2] As we will see from their definition, the central concept in computer science is the **algorithm,** and it is not possible to understand the field without a thorough understanding of this critically important idea. The Gibbs and Tucker definition of computer science follows.

DEFINITION

 Computer science   the study of algorithms, including

   1. Their formal and mathematical properties
   2. Their hardware realizations
   3. Their linguistic realizations
   4. Their applications

This definition says that it is the task of the computer scientist to design and develop algorithms to solve a range of important problems. This design process includes the following operations:

- Studying the behavior of algorithms to determine whether they are correct and efficient (their formal and mathematical properties)
- Designing and building computer systems that are able to execute algorithms (their hardware realizations)

---

2 Gibbs, N. E., and Tucker, A. B. "A Model Curriculum for a Liberal Arts Degree in Computer Science," *Comm. of the ACM,* vol. 29, no. 3 (March 1986).

- Designing programming languages and translating algorithms into these languages so that they can be executed by the hardware (their linguistic realizations)
- Identifying important problems and designing correct and efficient software packages to solve these problems (their applications)

Because it is impossible to appreciate this definition fully without knowing what an algorithm is, let's look more closely at this term. We first describe it informally and then, in the next section, examine this term much more rigorously. The dictionary defines the word *algorithm* as follows:

al • go • rithm   n. *A procedure for solving a mathematical problem in a finite number of steps that frequently involves repetition of an operation;* broadly: *a step-by-step method for accomplishing some task.*

Informally, an algorithm is an ordered sequence of instructions that is guaranteed to solve a specific problem. It is a list that looks something like this:

STEP 1:   Do something
STEP 2:   Do something
STEP 3:   Do something

    .   .
    .   .
    .   .

STEP N: Stop, you are finished

If you are handed this list and carefully follow its instructions in the order specified, then when you reach the end, you will have solved the task at hand.

The operations used to construct algorithms all belong to one of only three categories:

1. *Sequential operations*   A sequential instruction carries out a single well-defined task. When that task is finished, the algorithm moves on to the next operation. Sequential operations are usually expressed as simple declarative sentences.
   - Add 1 cup of butter to the mixture in the bowl.
   - Subtract the amount of the check from the current account balance.
   - Set the value of x to 1.
2. *Conditional operations*   These are the "question-asking" instructions of an algorithm. They ask a question and then select the next operation to be executed on the basis of the answer to that question.
   - If the mixture is too dry, then add one-half cup of water to the bowl.
   - If the amount of the check is less than or equal to the current account balance, then cash the check; otherwise, tell the person that the account is overdrawn.
   - If x is not equal to 0, then set y equal to $1/x$; otherwise, print an error message that says we cannot divide by 0.

3. *Iterative operations* These are the "looping" instructions of an algorithm. They tell us not to go on to the next instruction but, instead, to go back and repeat the execution of a previous block of instructions.

- Repeat the previous two operations until the mixture has thickened.
- While there are still more checks to be processed, do the following five steps.
- Repeat steps 1, 2, and 3 until the value of y is equal to $+1$.

We use algorithms (although we don't use that word) all the time—whenever we follow a set of instructions to assemble a child's toy, bake a cake, balance a checkbook, or go through the college registration process. A good example of an algorithm used in everyday life is the set of instructions shown in Figure 1.1 for programming a VCR to record a sequence of television shows. Note the three types of instructions in this algorithm: sequential (steps 2, 4, 5, 6, and 8), conditional (steps 1 and 7), and iterative (step 3).

Mathematicians use algorithms all the time, and much of the work done by early Greek, Roman, Persian, and Indian mathematicians involved the discovery of algorithms for important problems in geometry and arithmetic; an example is *Euclid's algorithm* for finding the greatest common divisor of two positive integers. (Exercise 7 at the end of the chapter presents this 2,300-year-old algorithm.) We also studied algorithms in elementary school, even if we didn't know it. For example, in the first grade we learned an algorithm for adding two numbers such as

$$
\begin{array}{r}
47 \\
+\ 25 \\
\hline
72
\end{array}
$$

The instructions our teacher gave were as follows: First add the rightmost column of numbers $(7 + 5)$, getting the value 12. Write down the 2 under the line and carry the 1 to the next column. Now move left to the next column, adding $(4 + 2)$ and the previous carry value of 1 to get 7. Write this value under the line, producing the correct answer 72.

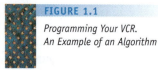

FIGURE 1.1

Programming Your VCR. An Example of an Algorithm

Algorithm for Programming Your VCR

Step 1   If the clock and calendar are not correctly set, then go to page 9 of the instruction manual and follow the instructions there before proceeding to step 2.

Step 2   Place a blank tape into the VCR tape slot.

Step 3   Repeat steps 4 through 7 for each program that you wish to record.

Step 4   Enter the channel number that you wish to record and press the button labeled CHAN.

Step 5   Enter the time that you wish recording to start and press the button labeled TIME-START.

Step 6   Enter the time that you wish recording to stop and press the button labeled TIME-FINISH. This completes the programming of one show.

Step 7   If you do not wish to record anything else, press the button labeled END-PROG.

Step 8   Turn off your VCR. Your VCR is now in TIMER mode, ready to record.

FIGURE 1.2

Algorithm for Adding Two m-digit Numbers

Algorithm for Adding Two *m*-Digit Numbers

Given: $m \geq 1$ and two positive numbers each containing m digits, $a_{m-1} \, a_{m-2,} \cdots a_0$ and $b_{m-1} \, b_{m-2,} \cdots b_0$
Wanted: $c_m c_{m-1} \, c_{m-2} \cdots c_0$, where $c_m c_{m-1} \, c_{m-2} \cdots c_0 = (a_{m-1} \, a_{m-2} \cdots a_0) + (b_{m-1} \, b_{m-2} \cdots b_0)$

Algorithm:

Step 1 Set the value of *carry* to 0.
Step 2 Set the value of *i* to 0.
Step 3 While the value of *i* is less than or equal to $m - 1$, repeat the instructions in steps 4 through 6.
Step 4   Add the two digits a_i and b_i to the current value of *carry* to get c_i.
Step 5   If $c_i \geq 10$, then reset c_i to $(c_i - 10)$ and reset the value of *carry* to 1; otherwise, set the new value of *carry* to 0.
Step 6   Add 1 to *i*, effectively moving one column to the left.
Step 7 Set c_m to the value of *carry*.
Step 8 Print out the final answer, $c_m \, c_{m-1} \, c_{m-2} \cdots c_0$.
Step 9 Stop.

Abu Ja' far Muhammad ibn Musa Al-Khowarizmi (A.D. 780–850?)

The word *algorithm* is derived from the last name of Muhammad ibn Musa Al-Khowarizmi, a famous Persian mathematician and author of the eighth and ninth centuries. Al-Khowarizmi was a teacher at the Mathematical Institute in Baghdad and the author of the book *Kitab al jabr w'al muqabala,* which in English means "Rules of Restoration and Reduction." It was one of the earliest mathematical textbooks, and its title gave us the word *algebra* (the Arabic word *al jabr* means "reduction").

In A.D. 825, Al-Khowarizmi wrote another book about the base-10 positional numbering system that had recently been developed in India. In this book he described formalized, step-by-step procedures for doing arithmetic operations, such as addition, subtraction, and multiplication, on numbers represented in this new decimal system. In the twelfth century this book was translated into Latin, introducing the base-10 Hindu-Arabic numbering system to Europe, and Al-Khowarizmi's name became closely associated with these formal numerical techniques. When written in Latin characters rather than Arabic, his last name became rendered as Algorismus, and eventually the formalized procedures that he pioneered and developed became known as *algorithms* in his honor.

Although as children we learned this algorithm informally, it can, like the VCR instructions in Figure 1.1, be written formally as an explicit sequence of instructions. Figure 1.2 shows an algorithm for adding two positive *m*-digit numbers. It expresses formally the operations informally described above. Again, note the three types of instructions used to construct the algorithm: sequential (steps 1, 2, 4, 6, 7, 8, and 9), conditional (step 5), and iterative (step 3).

Even though it may not look it, this is the same "decimal addition algorithm" that you learned in grade school; if you follow it rigorously, it is guaranteed to produce the correct result. Let's watch it work.

Add (47 + 25)

$m = 2$

$a_1 = 4$ $a_0 = 7$

$b_1 = 2$ $b_0 = 5$ } The input

STEP 1:   *carry* = 0.

STEP 2: $i = 0$.

STEP 3:   We now repeat steps 4 through 6 while i is less than or equal to 1.

First repetition of the loop (i has the value 0)

STEP 4:   Add $(a_0 + b_0 + carry)$, which is 7 + 5 + 0, so $c_0 = 12$.

STEP 5:   Because $c_0 \geq 10$, we reset **c_0 to 2** and reset *carry* to 1.

STEP 6:   Reset i to $(0 + 1) = 1$. Since i is less than or equal to 1, go back to step 4.

Second repetition of the loop (i has the value 1)

STEP 4:   Add $(a_1 + b_1 + carry)$, which is 4 + 2 + 1, so **$c_1 = 7$.**

STEP 5:   Because $c_1 < 10$, we reset *carry* to 0.

STEP 6:   Reset i to $(1 + 1) = 2$. Because i is greater than 1, do not repeat the loop but instead go to step 7.

STEP 7:   Set **$c_2 = 0$.**

STEP 8:   Print out the answer $c_2 \, c_1 \, c_0 = 072$ (see the **boldface** values).

STEP 9:   Stop.

We have reached the end of the algorithm, and it has correctly produced the sum of the two numbers 47 and 25, the three-digit result 072. (A slightly more clever algorithm would omit the unnecessary leading zero at the beginning of the number if the last carry value were a zero. We leave that modification as an exercise at the end of the chapter.) Try working through the algorithm shown in Figure 1.2 with another pair of numbers to be sure that you understand exactly how it functions.

The addition algorithm shown in Figure 1.2 is a highly formalized representation of a technique that most people learned in the first or second grade and that virtually everyone knows how to do informally. Why would we take such a simple task as adding two numbers and express it in so complicated a fashion? Why are formal algorithms so important in computer science? The answer is because of the following fundamentally important point:

If we can specify an algorithm to solve a problem, then we can automate its solution.

Once we have formally specified an algorithm, we can build a machine (or write a program or hire a person) to carry out the steps contained in the algorithm. The machine (or program or person) does not need to understand the concepts or ideas underlying the solution. It merely has to do step 1, step 2, step 3, . . . exactly as written. In computer science terminology, the machine, robot, person, or thing carrying out the steps of the algorithm is called a **computing agent.**

Thus computer science can also be viewed as "the science of algorithmic problem solving." Much of the research and development work in computer science involves discovering correct and efficient algorithms for a wide range of interesting problems, studying their properties, designing programming languages into which those algorithms can be encoded, and designing and building computer systems that can automatically execute these algorithms in an efficient manner.

At first glance, it may seem that every problem can be solved algorithmically. However, as we shall see, that is not true. Chapter 11 will present the startling result (first proved by the German logician Kurt Gödel in the early 1930s) that there are problems for which no generalized algorithmic solution can possibly exist. These problems are, in a sense, *unsolvable*. No matter how much time and effort is put into obtaining a solution, none will ever be found. Gödel's discovery, which staggered the mathematical world, effectively places a limit on the ultimate capabilities of computers and computer scientists.

There are also problems where it is possible to specify an algorithm but a computing agent would take so long to execute it that the solution is essentially useless. For example, to get a computer to play winning chess, we could use a *brute force* approach. Given a board position as input, the computer would examine every legal move it could possibly make, then every legal response an opponent could make to each initial move, then every response it could select to that move, and so on. This analysis would continue until the game reached a win, lose, or draw position. With that information the computer would be able to choose its next move optimally. If, for simplicity's sake, we assume that there are 40 legal moves from any given position on a chessboard, and it takes about 30 moves to reach a final conclusion, then the total number of board positions that our brute force program would need to evaluate in deciding its first move is

$$\underbrace{40 \times 40 \times 40 \times \ldots \times 40}_{\text{30 times}} = 40^{30}, \text{ which is roughly } 10^{48}$$

In the Beginning . . .

There is no single date that marks the beginning of computer science. Indeed, there are many "firsts" that could be used to mark this event. For example, some of the earliest theoretical work on the logical foundations of computer science occurred in the 1930s. The first general-purpose, electronic computers appeared during the period 1940–1946. (We will discuss the history of these early machines in Section 1.4.) These first computers were one-of-a-kind experimental systems that never moved outside the research laboratory and had little or no impact on society. The first commercial machine, the UNIVAC I, did not make its appearance until June 1951, a date that marks the real beginning of the computer industry. The first high-level (i.e., based on natural language) programming language was FORTRAN. Some people mark its debut in 1957 as the beginning of the "software" industry. The appearance of these new machines and languages created new occupations, such as programmer, numerical analyst, and computer engineer. To address the intellectual needs of these workers, the first professional society for people in the field of computing, the Association for Computing Machinery (ACM), was established in 1947. (The ACM is still the largest professional computer science society in the world. Its Web home page is located at www.acm.org.) To help meet the rapidly growing need for computer professionals, the first Department of Computer Science was established at Purdue University in October 1962. It awarded its first M.Sc. degree in 1964 and its first Ph.D. in computer science in 1966. An undergraduate program was begun in 1968.

Thus, depending on what you consider the most important "first," the field of computer science is somewhere between 40 and 70 years old. Compared to such classic scientific disciplines as mathematics, physics, chemistry, and biology, computer science is the new kid on the block.

If we could build a computer that evaluates one trillion (10^{12}) board positions per second (which is much too high at current levels of technology), it would take about 30,000,000,000,000,000,000,000,000,000 years for the computer to make its first move! Obviously, a computer could not use a brute force technique to play a real chess game.

In addition to problems that cannot be solved efficiently or that cannot be solved at all, there also exist problems that we do not yet know *how* to solve algorithmically. Many of these involve tasks that require a degree of what we term "intelligence." For example, after only a few days a baby recognizes the face of its mother from among the many faces it sees. In a few months it begins to develop coordinated sensory and motor control skills and can efficiently plan how to use them—how to get from the playpen to the toy on the floor without bumping into either the chair or the desk that are in the way. After a few years the child begins to develop powerful language skills and abstract reasoning capabilities.

We take these abilities for granted, but the operations just mentioned—sophisticated visual discrimination, high-level problem solving, abstract reasoning, natural language understanding—cannot be done well (or even at all) using the computer systems and software packages currently available. The primary reason is that researchers do not yet know how to specify these operations algorithmically. That is, they do not yet know how to specify a solution formally in a detailed step-by-step fashion. As humans, we are able to do them simply by using the "algorithms" in our heads. To appreciate this problem, imagine trying to describe algorithmically exactly what steps you follow when you are painting a picture, composing a poem, or formulating a business plan.

Thus, algorithmic problem solving has many variations. Sometimes solutions do not exist; sometimes a solution is too inefficient to be of any use; sometimes a solution is not yet known. However, discovering an algorithmic solution has enormously important consequences. As we noted earlier, if we can create a correct and efficient algorithm to solve a problem, and if we encode it into a programming language, then we can take advantage of the speed and power of a computer system to automate the solution and produce the desired result. This is what computer science is all about.

1.3 Algorithms

1.3.1 *The Formal Definition of an Algorithm*

The previous section discussed the central role that algorithms (creating them, analyzing them, representing them, executing them, and using them) play in computer science, and it provided an informal definition of what they are. This section provides a more thorough and formal definition of this critically important term.

> **DEFINITION**
>
> **Algorithm** a well-ordered collection of unambiguous and effectively computable operations that, when executed, produces a result and halts in a finite amount of time.

This is a rather imposing definition, and it contains a number of important ideas. Let's take it apart, piece by piece, and analyze each of its separate points.

. . . a well-ordered collection . . .

An algorithm is a collection of operations, and there must be a clear and unambiguous *ordering* to these operations. Ordering means that we know which operation to do first and that when we finish performing any one operation, we always know exactly what operation to do next. After all, we cannot expect a computing agent to carry out our instructions correctly if it is confused about which instruction it should be carrying out.

As an example of a set of operations that violates this ordering condition, consider the following "algorithm" that was taken from the back of a shampoo bottle and was intended as instructions on how to use the product.

Step 1: Wet hair
Step 2: Lather
Step 3: Rinse
Step 4: Repeat

At step 4, what operations should be repeated? If we go back to step 1, we will be unnecessarily wetting our hair. (It is presumably still wet from the previous operations.) If we go back to step 3 instead, we will not be getting our hair any cleaner because we have not reused the shampoo. The Repeat instruction in step 4 is ambiguous in that it does not clearly specify what to do next. Therefore, it violates the well-ordered requirement of an algorithm. (It also has a second and even more serious problem—it never stops! We will have more to say about this second problem shortly.) Statements such as

- Go back and do it again. (Do *what* again?)
- Start over. (From *where*?)
- If you understand this material, you may skip ahead. (How *far*?)
- Do either part 1 or part 2. (How do I decide *which* one to do?)

are ambiguous and can leave us confused and unsure about what operation to do next. We must be extremely precise in specifying the order in which operations are to be carried out. One possible way is to number the steps of the algorithm and use these numbers to specify the proper order of execution. For example, the ambiguous operations shown above could be made more precise as follows:

- Go back to step 3 and continue execution from that point.
- Start over from step 1.
- If you understand this material, skip ahead to line 21.
- If you are 18 years of age or older, do part 1 beginning with step 9; otherwise, do part 2 beginning with step 40.

. . . of unambiguous and effectively computable operations . . .

Algorithms are composed of things called "operations," but what do those operations look like? What types of building blocks can be used to construct an algorithm? The answer to these questions is that the operations used in an algorithm must meet two criteria—they must be *unambiguous,* and they must be *effectively computable*. Let's look at each of these two terms separately.

Here is a possible "algorithm" for making a cherry pie:

STEP 1:	Make the crust
STEP 2:	Make the cherry filling
STEP 3:	Pour the filling into the crust
STEP 4:	Bake at 350°F for 45 minutes

For a professional baker, this algorithm would be fine. He or she would understand how to carry out each of the operations listed above. Novice cooks, like most of us, would probably understand the meaning of steps 3 and 4. However, we would probably look at steps 1 and 2, throw up our hands in confusion, say we don't know what to do, and ask for clarification. We might then be given more detailed instructions.

STEP 1: Make the crust

    1.1 Take one and one-third cups flour

    1.2 Sift the flour

    1.3 Mix the sifted flour with one-half cup butter and one-fourth cup water

    1.4 Roll into two 9-inch pie crusts

STEP 2: Make the cherry filling

    2.1 Open a 16-ounce can of cherry pie filling and pour into bowl

    2.2 Add a dash of cinnamon and nutmeg, and stir

With this additional information most people, even inexperienced cooks, would understand what to do, and they could successfully carry out this baking algorithm. However, there may be some people, perhaps young children, who still do not fully understand each and every line. In that case, we must go through the simplification process again and describe the ambiguous steps in even more elementary terms.

For example, the computing agent executing the algorithm might not know the meaning of the instruction "Sift the flour" in step 1.2, and we would have to explain it further.

1.2 Sift the flour

    1.2.1 Get out the sifter, which is the device shown on page A-9 of your cookbook, and place it directly on top of a two-quart bowl

    1.2.2 Pour the flour into the top of the sifter and turn the crank in a counterclockwise direction

    1.2.3 Let all the flour fall through the sifter into the bowl

Now, even a child should be able to carry out these operations. But if that were not the case, then we would go through the simplification process yet one more time, until every operation, every sentence, every word was clearly understood.

An **unambiguous** operation is one that can be understood and carried out directly by the computing agent without needing to be further simplified or explained. When an operation is unambiguous, we call it a **primitive operation,** or simply a **primitive,** of the computing agent carrying out the algorithm. An algorithm must be composed entirely of primitives. Naturally, the primitive operations of different individuals (or machines) vary depending on their sophistication, experience, and intelligence, as was the case with the cherry pie recipe, which varied with the baking experience of the person following the instructions. Hence, what is an algorithm with respect to one computing agent may not be an algorithm with respect to another.

One of the most important questions we will be answering in this text is, What are the primitive operations of a typical modern computer system? What operations can a hardware processor "understand" in the sense of being able to carry out directly, and what operations must be further refined and simplified? We will answer these interesting questions in detail in the upcoming chapters.

However, it is not enough for an operation to be understandable. It must also be *doable* by the computing agent. If an algorithm tells me to flap my arms really quickly and fly, I understand perfectly well what it is asking me to do. However, I am incapable of doing it. "Doable" means there exists a computational process that allows the computing agent to complete that operation successfully. The formal term for "doable" is **effectively computable.**

For example, here is an incorrect technique for finding and printing the 100th prime number (a prime number is a whole number not evenly divisible by any numbers other than 1 and itself, such as 2, 3, 5, 7, 11, 13, . . .).

STEP 1:   Generate a list L of all the prime numbers: $L_1, L_2, L_3, \ldots$

STEP 2:   Sort the list L into ascending order

STEP 3:   Print out the 100th element in the list, L_{100}

STEP 4:   Stop

The problem with these instructions is in step 1, "Generate a list L of *all* the prime numbers. . . ." That operation cannot be completed. There are an infinite number of prime numbers, and it is not possible in a finite amount of time to generate the desired list L. No such computational process exists, and the operation described in step 1 is not effectively computable. Here are some other examples of operations that may not be effectively computable:

Write out the exact decimal value of π (π cannot be represented exactly.)
Set *average* to (*sum* $\div$ *number*). (If *number* = 0, division is undefined.)
Set the value of *result* to $\sqrt{N}$. (If $N < 0$, then *result* is undefined if you are using real numbers.)
Add 1 to the current value of x. (What if x currently has no value?)

This last example explains why we had to initialize the value of the variable called *carry* to 0 in step 1 of Figure 1.2. In step 4 the algorithm says, "Add the two digits a_i and b_i to the current value of *carry* to get c_i." If *carry* has no current value, then when the computing agent tries to perform the instruction in step 4, it will not know what to do, and this operation is not effectively computable.

. . . that produces a result . . .

Algorithms solve problems. In order to know whether a solution is correct, an algorithm must produce a result that is observable to a user, such as a numerical answer, a new object, or a change to its environment. This way the user can look at the result and determine whether it is indeed the desired one. Without some observable result, we would not be able to say whether the algorithm is right or wrong. In the case of the VCR algorithm (Figure 1.1), the result will be a tape containing recorded TV programs. The addition algorithm (Figure 1.2) produces an *m*-digit sum.

Note that we use the word *result* rather than *answer*. Sometimes it is not possible for an algorithm to produce the correct answer because for a given set of input, a correct answer does not exist. In those cases the algorithm may produce something else, such as an error message, a red warning light, or an approximation to the correct answer. Error messages, lights, and approximations, though not necessarily what we expected, are all observable results.

. . . and halts in a finite amount of time.

Another important characteristic of algorithms is that the result must be produced after the execution of a finite number of operations, and we must guarantee that the algorithm eventually reaches a statement that says, "Stop, you are done" or something equivalent. This was the second problem with the shampooing algorithm shown earlier. We have already pointed out that it was not well ordered because we did not know which statements to repeat in step 4. However, even if we knew which block of statements to repeat, the algorithm would still be incorrect because it makes no provision to terminate. It will essentially run forever, or until we run out of hot water, soap, or patience. This is called an **infinite loop,** and it is a common error in the designing of algorithms.

Figure 1.3(a) shows an algorithmic solution to the shampooing problem that meets all the criteria discussed in this section if we assume that we want to wash our hair twice. The algorithm of Figure 1.3(a) is well ordered. Each step is numbered, and the execution of the algorithm unfolds sequentially, beginning at step 1 and proceeding from instruction *i* to instruction *i* + 1 unless the operation specifies otherwise. (For example, the iterative instruction in step 3 says that after completing step 6, you should go back and start again at step 4 until the value of *WashCount* equals 2.) The intent of each operation is (we assume) clear, unambiguous, and doable by the person washing his or her hair. Finally, the algorithm will halt. This is confirmed by observing

FIGURE 1.3(a)

A Correct Solution to the Shampooing Problem

Algorithm for Shampooing Your Hair

STEP	OPERATION
1	Wet your hair
2	Set the value of *WashCount* to 0
3	Repeat steps 4 through 6 until the value of *WashCount* equals 2
4	Lather your hair
5	Rinse your hair
6	Add 1 to the value of *WashCount*
7	Stop, you have finished shampooing your hair

FIGURE 1.3(b)

Another Correct Solution to the Shampooing Problem

Another Algorithm for Shampooing Your Hair

STEP	OPERATION
1	Wet your hair
2	Lather your hair
3	Rinse your hair
4	Lather your hair
5	Rinse your hair
6	Stop, you have finished shampooing your hair

that *WashCount* is initially set to 0 in step 2. Step 6 says to add 1 to *Wash-Count* each time we lather and rinse our hair, so it will take on the values 0, 1, 2, ... However, the iterative statement in step 3 says stop lathering and rinsing when the value of *WashCount* reaches 2. At that point, the algorithm goes to step 7 and terminates execution with the desired result: clean hair. (Although it is correct, do not expect to see this algorithm on the back of a shampoo bottle in the near future.)

We should also mention that, as is true for any recipe or set of instructions, there is always more than a single way to write a correct solution. For example, the algorithm of Figure 1.3(a) could also be written as shown in Figure 1.3(b). Both of these are correct solutions to the shampooing problem. (Although they are both correct, they are not necessarily equally elegant. This point is addressed in Exercise 6 at the end of the chapter.)

 ### 1.3.2 *The Importance of Algorithmic Problem Solving*

The instruction sequences in Figures 1.1, 1.2, 1.3(a), and 1.3(b) are examples of the types of algorithmic solutions designed, analyzed, implemented, and tested by computer scientists, although they are much shorter and simpler. The operations shown in Figures 1.1 to 1.3 could be encoded into some appropriate language and given to a computing agent (such as a personal computer or a robot) to execute. The device would mechanically follow these instructions and successfully complete the task specified. Our device could do this without having to understand the creative processes that went into the discovery of the solution and without knowing the principles and concepts that underlie the problem. The robot simply follows the steps in the specified order (a required characteristic of algorithms), successfully completing each operation (another required characteristic), and ultimately producing the desired result after a finite amount of time (also required).

Just as the industrial revolution of the 19th century allowed us to construct machines to take over the drudgery of repetitive physical tasks, the "computer revolution" of the 20th and 21st centuries has enabled us to implement algorithms that mechanize and automate the drudgery of repetitive mental tasks, such as adding long columns of numbers, finding names in a telephone book, sorting student records by course number, and retrieving hotel or airline reservations from a file containing hundreds of thousands of pieces of data. This mechanization process offers the prospect of enormous increases in productivity. It also frees people to do those things that humans do much better than computers, such as creating new ideas, setting policy, doing high-level planning, and determining the significance of the results produced by a computer. Certainly, these operations are a much more effective use of that unique computing agent called the human brain.

1.4   A Brief History of Computing

Although the introduction to this chapter stressed that computer science is not simply a study of computers, there is no doubt that the field was formed and grew in popularity as a direct response to their creation and widespread use. Therefore, this section takes a brief look at the historical development of computer systems.

The appearance of some technologies, such as the telephone, the light bulb, and the first heavier-than-air flight, can be traced directly to a single place, a specific individual, and an exact instant in time. Examples include the flight of Orville and Wilbur Wright on December 17, 1903, in Kitty Hawk, North Carolina, and the famous phrase "Mr. Watson, come here, I want to see you" uttered by Alexander Graham Bell over the first telephone on March 12, 1876.

Computers were not like that. They did not appear in a specific room on a given day as the creation of some individual genius. Quite the contrary, the ideas that led to the design of the first computers evolved over a period of hundreds of years, with contributions coming from many people, each building on and extending the work of earlier discoverers. The following section highlights some of the major events that led to the development of the modern computer system.

 ### 1.4.1   The Early Period: Up to 1940

If this were a discussion of the history of mathematics and arithmetic instead of computer science, it would begin 3,000 years ago with the early work of the Greeks, Egyptians, Babylonians, Indians, Chinese, and Persians. All these cultures were interested in and made important contributions to the fields of mathematics, logic, and numerical computation. For example, the Greeks developed the fields of geometry and logic; the Babylonians and Egyptians developed numerical methods for generating square roots, multiplication tables, and trigonometric tables used by early sailors; Indian mathematicians developed both the base-10 decimal numbering system and the concept of zero; and in the ninth century the Persians developed algorithmic problem solving.

The first half of the seventeenth century saw a number of important developments related to automating and simplifying the drudgery of arithmetic computation. (The motivation for this work appears to be the sudden increase in scientific research during the sixteenth and seventeenth centuries in the areas of astronomy, chemistry, and medicine. This work required the solution of larger and more complex mathematical problems.) In 1614 the Scotsman John Napier invented **logarithms** as a way to simplify difficult mathematical computations. The early seventeenth century also witnessed the development of a number of new and quite powerful mechanical devices designed to help reduce the burden of arithmetic. The first **slide rule** appeared around 1622. In 1672 the French philosopher and mathematician Blaise Pascal designed and built one of the first **mechanical calculators** (named the **Pascaline**) that could do addition and subtraction. A model of this early calculating device is shown in Figure 1.4.

The famous German mathematician Gottfried Leibnitz (who, along with Isaac Newton, was one of the inventors of the calculus) was also excited by the idea of automatic computation. He studied the work of Pascal and others, and in 1674 he constructed a mechanical calculator called **Leibnitz's Wheel** that could do not only addition and subtraction but multiplication and division as well. Both Pascal's and Leibnitz's machines used interlocking mechanical cogs and gears to store numbers and perform basic arithmetic operations. Considering the state of technology available to Pascal, Leibnitz, and others in the seventeenth century, these first calculating machines were truly mechanical wonders.

These early developments in mathematics and arithmetic were important milestones because they demonstrated how mechanization could simplify and speed up numerical computation. For example, Leibnitz's Wheel enabled seventeenth-century mathematicians to generate tables of mathematical functions many times faster than had previously been possible by hand. (It is hard

FIGURE 1.4

The Pascaline. One of the Earliest Mechanical Calculators

Computer History Museum

to believe in our modern high-tech society, but in the seventeenth century the generation of a table of logarithms could represent a *lifetime's* effort of one person!) However, the slide rule and mechanical calculators of Pascal and Leibnitz, though certainly impressive devices, were not computers. Specifically, they lacked two fundamental characteristics:

- They did not have a *memory* where information could be stored in machine-readable form.
- They were not *programmable*. A person could not provide in *advance* a sequence of instructions that could be executed by the device without manual intervention.

Surprisingly, the first actual "computing device" to include both of these features was not created for the purposes of mathematical computations. Rather, it was a loom used for the manufacture of rugs and clothing. It was developed in 1801 by the Frenchman Joseph Jacquard. Jacquard wanted to automate the weaving process, at the time a painfully slow and cumbersome task in which each separate row of the pattern had to be set up by the weaver and an apprentice. Because of this, anything but the most basic style of clothing was beyond the means of the average person.

Jacquard designed an automated loom that used **punched cards** to create the desired pattern. If there was a hole in the card in a particular loca-

FIGURE 1.5

Drawing of the Jacquard Loom

© Bettmann/CORBIS

tion, then a hook could pass through the card, grasp a warp thread, and raise it to allow a second thread to pass underneath. If there was no hole in the card, then the hook could not pass through, and the thread would pass over the warp. Depending on whether the thread passed above or below the warp, a specific design was created. Each punched card described one row of the pattern. Jacquard connected the cards and fed them through his loom, and it automatically sequenced from card to card, weaving the desired pattern. A drawing of the **Jacquard loom** is shown in Figure 1.5. The rows of connected punched cards can be seen at the top of the device.

Jacquard's loom represented an enormously important stage in the development of computers. Not only was it the first programmable device, but it also showed how the knowledge of a human expert (in this case a master weaver) could be captured in machine-readable form and used to control a machine that accomplished the same task automatically. Once the program was created, the expert was no longer needed. The lowliest apprentice could load the cards into the loom, turn it on, and produce a finished, high-quality product, over and over again.

One of the major contributions of these pioneers was the enormous influence they had on the designers and inventors who came after them. One person strongly influenced by this early work was a mathematics professor at Cambridge University named Charles Babbage. Babbage was much interested in automatic computation. In 1823 he extended the ideas of Pascal and Leibnitz and constructed a working model of the largest and most sophisticated mechanical calculator of its time. This machine, called the **Difference Engine,** could do addition, subtraction, multiplication, and division to 6 significant digits, and it could solve polynomial equations and other complex mathematical problems as well. Babbage tried to construct a larger model of the Difference Engine that would be capable of working to an accuracy of 20 significant digits, but after 12 years of work he had to give up his quest. The technology available in the 1820s and 1830s was not sufficiently advanced to manufacture cogs and gears to the precise tolerances his design required. Like Galileo's helicopter or Jules Verne's atomic submarine, Babbage's ideas were fundamentally sound but years ahead of their time. (Interestingly, in 1991 the London Museum of Science, using Babbage's original plans, built an actual working model of the Difference Engine. It was 7 feet high, 11 feet wide, weighed 3 tons, and had 4,000 moving parts. It worked exactly as Babbage had planned.)

The Original "Technophobia"

The development of the automated Jacquard loom and other technological advances in the weaving industry was so frightening to the craft guilds of the early nineteenth century that in 1811 it led to the formation of a group called the **Luddites.** The Luddites, named after their leader Ned Ludd of Nottingham, England, were violently opposed to this new manufacturing technology, and they burned down factories that attempted to use it. The movement lasted only a few years and its leaders were all jailed, but their name lives on today as a pejorative term for any group that is frightened and angered by the latest developments in any branch of science and technology, including computers.

However, Babbage did not stop his investigations with the Difference Engine. In the 1830s he designed a more powerful and general-purpose computational machine that could be configured to solve a much wider range of numerical problems. His machine had four basic components: a **mill** to perform the arithmetic manipulation of data, a **store** to hold the data, an **operator** to process automatically the instructions contained on punched cards (Babbage was familiar with the work of Jacquard), and an **output unit** to put the results onto separate punched cards. Although it would be about 110 years before a "real" computer would be built, Babbage's proposed machine, called the **Analytic Engine,** is amazingly similar in design to a modern computer. The four components of the Analytic Engine are virtually identical in function to the four major components of today's computer systems:

Babbage's Term	Modern Terminology
mill	arithmetic/logic unit
store	memory
operator	processor
output	input/output

Babbage died before a working steam-powered model of his Analytic Engine could be completed. Although he did not live to see it become a reality, his ideas lived on to influence others, and many computer scientists consider the Analytic Engine the first "true" computer system, even if it existed only on paper and in Babbage's dreams.

Another person influenced by the work of Pascal, Jacquard, and Babbage was a young statistician at the U.S. Census Bureau named Herman Hollerith.

Charles Babbage (1791–1871)
Ada Augusta Byron, Countess of Lovelace (1815–1852)

Charles Babbage, the son of a banker, was born into a life of wealth and comfort in eighteenth-century England. He attended Cambridge University and displayed an aptitude for mathematics and science. He was also an inventor and "tinkerer" who loved to build all sorts of devices. Among the devices he constructed were unpickable locks, skeleton keys, speedometers, and even the first cow catcher for trains. His first and greatest love, though, was mathematics, and he spent the better part of his life creating machines to do automatic computation. Babbage was enormously impressed by the work of Jacquard in France. (In fact, Babbage had on the wall of his home a woven portrait of Jacquard that required the use of 24,000 punched cards.) He spent the last 30 to 40 years of his life trying to build a computing device, the Analytic Engine, based on Jacquard's ideas.

In that quest, he was helped by Countess Ada Augusta Byron, daughter of the famous English poet, Lord Byron. The countess was introduced to Babbage and was enormously impressed by his ideas about the Analytic Engine. As she put it, "We may say most aptly that the Analytic Engine weaves algebraic patterns just as the Jacquard Loom weaves flowers and leaves." Lady Lovelace worked closely with Babbage on specifying how instructions for the Analytic Engine would have to be organized to solve a particular mathematical problem. Because of that pioneering work, she is generally regarded as history's first computer programmer.

Babbage died in 1871 without being able to realize his dream. He also died quite poor because the Analytic Engine ate up virtually all of his personal fortune. His work was generally forgotten until the twentieth century when it became instrumental in moving the world into the computer age.

Because of the rapid increase in immigration to America at the end of the nineteenth century, officials estimated that doing the 1890 enumeration manually would take from 10 to 12 years. The 1900 census would begin before the previous one was finished. Something had to be done.

What Hollerith did was design and build programmable card processing machines that could automatically read, tally, and sort data entered on punched cards. (Like Babbage, Hollerith knew about the earlier work of Jacquard.) Census data were coded onto cards using a machine called a **keypunch.** The cards were taken either to a **tabulator** for counting and tallying or to a **sorter** for ordering alphabetically or numerically. Both of these machines were programmable (via wires and plugs) so that the user could specify in advance such things as which card columns should be tallied and in what order the cards should be sorted. In addition, the machines had a small amount of memory to store results. Thus, they had all four components described in Babbage's design of the Analytic Engine.

Hollerith's machines were enormously successful, and they were one of the first examples of the use of automated information processing to solve large scale "real-world" problems. Whereas the 1880 census required 8 years to be completed, the 1890 census was finished in about 2 years, even though there was a 30% increase in the U.S. population during that decade.

Although they were not really general-purpose computers, Hollerith's card machines were a very clear and very successful demonstration of the enormous advantages to be gained from automated information processing. This fact was not lost on Hollerith, who left the Census Bureau in 1902 to found the Computer Tabulating Recording Company to build and sell these machines. He planned to market his new product to a country that was just entering the Industrial Revolution and that, like the Census Bureau, would be generating and processing enormous volumes of inventory, production, accounting, and sales data. He was right—spectacularly so—and his punched card machines became the dominant form of data processing equipment during the first half of the twentieth century, well into the 1950s and 1960s. During this period, virtually every major U.S. corporation had data processing rooms filled with keypunches, sorters, and tabulators, as well as drawer upon drawer of punched cards. In 1924 Hollerith's tabulating machine company changed its name to IBM, and it eventually evolved into the largest computing company in the world.

We have come a long way from the 1640s and the Pascaline, the early adding machine constructed by Pascal. We have seen the development of more powerful mechanical calculators (Leibnitz), automated programmable manufacturing devices (Jacquard), a design for the first computing device (Babbage), and the initial applications of information processing on a massive scale (Hollerith). However, we have still not yet entered the "computer age." That did not happen until about 1940, and it was motivated by an event that, unfortunately, has fueled many of the important technological advances in human history—the outbreak of war.

 ### 1.4.2 *The Birth of Computers: 1940–1950*

The beginning of World War II created another, quite different set of information-based problems. Instead of inventory, sales, and payroll, the concerns of the 1940s became ballistics tables, troop deployment data, and secret codes. A number of research projects were started, funded largely by the military, to build automatic computing machines to perform these tasks and assist the Allies in the war effort.

Beginning in 1931, the U.S. Navy and IBM jointly funded a project at Harvard University under Professor Howard Aiken to build a computing device called Mark I. This was a general-purpose, electromechanical programmable computer that used a mix of relays, magnets, and gears to process and store data. The Mark I was the first computing device to use the base-2 binary numbering system that we will discuss in Chapter 4. It used vacuum tubes and electric current to represent the two binary values, off for 0, on for 1. Until then computing machines had used decimal representation, typically by having a 10-toothed gear, each tooth representing a digit from 0 to 9. The Mark I was completed in 1944 and is generally considered one of the first working general-purpose computers, about 110 years after Babbage's dream of the Analytic Engine. The Mark I had a memory capacity of 72 numbers, and it could be programmed to perform a 23-digit multiplication in the lightning-like time of 4 seconds. Although laughably slow by modern standards, the Mark I was operational for almost 15 years, and it carried out a good deal of important and useful mathematical work for the U.S. Navy during the war.

At about the same time, a much more powerful machine was taking shape at the University of Pennsylvania in conjunction with the U.S. Army. During the early days of World War II, the Army was producing many new artillery pieces, but it found that it could not produce the firing tables equally fast. These tables told the gunner how to aim the gun on the basis of such input as distance to the target and current values of temperature, wind, and elevation. Because of the enormous number of variables and the complexity of the computations (which use both trigonometry and calculus), these firing tables were taking more time to construct than the gun itself.

To help solve this problem, in 1943 the Army initiated a research project with J. Presper Eckert and John Mauchly of the University of Pennsylvania to build a completely electronic computing device. The machine, dubbed the ENIAC (*E*lectronic *N*umerical *I*ntegrator *A*nd *C*alculator), was completed in

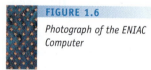

FIGURE 1.6

Photograph of the ENIAC Computer

From the Collections of the University of Pennsylvania Archives

1946 and was the first fully electronic general-purpose programmable computer. This pioneering machine is shown in Figure 1.6.

ENIAC contained 18,000 vacuum tubes and nearly filled a building; it was 100 feet long, 10 feet high, and weighed 30 tons. Because it was fully electronic, it did not contain any of the slow mechanical components found in Mark I. Consequently, it executed instructions much faster. The ENIAC could add two 10-digit numbers in about 1/5,000 of a second and could multiply two numbers in 1/300 of a second, a thousand times faster than the Mark I.

The Mark I and ENIAC are two well-known examples of early computers, but they are by no means the only ones of that era. For example, the ABC system (*Atanasoff-Berry Computer*), designed and built by Professor John Atanasoff and his graduate student Clifford Berry at Iowa State University, was actually the first electronic computer, constructed during the period 1939–1942. However, it never received the recognition it deserved because it was a more specialized computer than ENIAC. It was useful for only one task, solving systems of simultaneous linear equations. In England, a computer called Colossus was built in 1943 under the direction of Alan Turing, a famous mathematician and computer scientist whom we will meet again in Chapter 11. This machine, one of the first computers built outside the United States, was used to crack the famous German Enigma code that the Nazis believed to be unbreakable. Colossus has also not received as much recognition as ENIAC, this time because of the secrecy that shrouded the Enigma project. Its very existence was not known until many years after the end of the war.

Interestingly enough, at about the same time that Colossus was taking form in England, a German engineer named Konrad Zuse was working on a computing device for the German Army. The machine, code named Z1, was similar in design to the ENIAC—a programmable, general-purpose, fully electronic computing device. Fortunately for the allied forces, the Z1 project was not successfully completed before the end of World War II.

Although the machines just described—ABC, Mark I, ENIAC, Colossus, and Z1—were computers in the fullest sense of the word (they had memory and were programmable), they did not yet look quite like modern computer systems. One more step was necessary, and that step was taken in 1946 by the individual who was most instrumental in creating the computer as we know it today, John Von Neumann.

Von Neumann was not only one of the most brilliant mathematicians who ever lived but was a genius in many other areas as well, including experimental physics, chemistry, economics, and computer science. Von Neumann, who taught at Princeton University, had worked with Eckert and Mauchly on the ENIAC project at the University of Pennsylvania. Even though that project was completed successfully, he recognized a number of fundamental shortcomings in ENIAC. In 1946 he proposed a radically different computer design based on a model called the **stored program computer.** Until then, all computers were programmed *externally* using wires, connectors, and plugboards. The memory unit stored only data, not instructions. To solve a different problem on these computers, a user had to rewire virtually the entire machine. For example, the plugboards on the ENIAC contained 6,000 separate switches, and reprogramming the ENIAC involved specifying the new settings for all these switches—not a trivial task.

Von Neumann proposed that the instructions that control the operation of the computer be encoded as binary values and stored internally in the memory unit along with the data. To solve a different problem, you would not rewire the machine. Instead you would rewrite the sequence of instructions—

that is, create a new program. Von Neumann had invented programming as it is known today.

The model of computing proposed by Von Neumann included many other important features found on all modern computing systems, and to honor him this model of computation has come to be known as the **Von Neumann architecture.** We will study this architecture in great detail in Chapters 4 and 5.

Von Neumann's research group at the University of Pennsylvania implemented his ideas, and they built one of the first stored program computers, called EDVAC, in 1951. At about the same time, a stored program computer called EDSAC was built at Cambridge University in England under the direction of Professor Maurice Wilkes. The appearance of these machines, and others like them, ushers in the modern computer age. Even though they were much slower, bulkier, and less powerful than our current machines, EDVAC and EDSAC executed programs in a fashion surprisingly similar to the miniaturized and immensely more powerful computers of the 21st century. A commercial model of the EDVAC, called UNIVAC I, was built by Eckert and Mauchly and delivered to the U.S. Bureau of the Census on March 31, 1951—the first computer actually sold. (Interestingly enough, it ran for 12 years before it was retired, shut off for the last time, and moved to the Smithsonian Institute.) This date really marks the beginning of the "computer age."

The importance of Von Neumann's contributions to computer systems development cannot be overstated. Although his original proposals are almost 60 years old, virtually every computer built today is a Von Neumann machine in its basic design. A lot has changed in computing, and a powerful high-resolution graphics workstation and the EDVAC would appear to have little in common. However, the basic principles on which these disparate machines are

And the Verdict Is . . .

Our discussion of what was happening in computing from 1939 to 1946 showed that many groups were involved in designing and building the first computers—at places like Harvard, Pennsylvania, Iowa, and Princeton in the United States and England and Germany overseas. Therefore, it would seem that no one individual can be credited with the title Inventor of the Electronic Digital Computer.

Surprisingly, that is not true. In February 1964, the Sperry Rand Corp. (now UNISYS) was granted a U.S. patent on the ENIAC computer as the first fully electronic computing device, J. Presper Eckert and John Mauchly being its designers and builders. However, in 1967 a suit was filed in U.S. District Court in Minneapolis, Minnesota, to overturn that patent. The suit, *Honeywell vs. Sperry Rand*, was heard before U.S. Federal Judge Earl Larson, and on October 19,1973, his verdict was handed down. (Interestingly enough, this enormously important verdict was never given the media coverage it deserved because it happened in the middle of the Watergate hearings and on the very day that Vice President Spiro Agnew resigned in disgrace for tax fraud.) Judge Larson overturned the ENIAC patent on the basis that Eckert and Mauchly had been significantly influenced in their 1943–1944 work on ENIAC by earlier research and development work by John Atanasoff at Iowa State University. During the period 1939–1943 Mauchly had communicated extensively with Atanasoff and had even traveled to Iowa to see the ABC machine in person. In a sense, the verdict declared that Atanasoff is really the inventor of the first computer. This decision was never appealed. Therefore, the official honor of having designed and built the first electronic computer, at least in U.S. District Court, goes to Professor John Vincent Atanasoff.

On November 13, 1990, in a formal ceremony at the White House, Professor Atanasoff was awarded the National Medal of Technology by President George Bush for his pioneering contributions to the development of the computer.

constructed are virtually identical, and the same theoretical model underlies their operation. There is an old saying in computer science that "There is nothing new since Von Neumann!" This saying is certainly not true (much *has* happened), but it demonstrates the importance and amazing staying power of Von Neumann's original design.

 ### 1.4.3   *The Modern Era: 1950 to the Present*

Our historical review is now complete. We have reached the modern era of computing, and the stored program model on which the EDVAC and EDSAC are based, the Von Neumann architecture, is precisely the model in widespread use today. The last 50 or so years of computer development have involved taking this basic model and improving it in terms of both hardware and software. Since 1950 computer systems development has been primarily an *evolutionary* process, not a revolutionary one. The enormous number of changes in computers in the last half century have made them faster, smaller, cheaper, more reliable, and easier to use but have not drastically altered the basic ideas inherent in the Von Neumann architecture. However, the changes that have occurred are interesting, and this section briefly highlights some of these major developments.

The period 1950–1957 is often called the **first generation** of computing. (These dates are only rough approximations, and they should not be taken too literally.) This era saw the appearance of UNIVAC I, the first computer built for sale, and the IBM 701, the first computer built by the company that would soon become a leader in this new field. These early systems were similar in design to EDVAC, and they were bulky, expensive, slow, and unreliable. They used vacuum tubes for processing and storage, and they

John Von Neumann (1903–1957)

John Von Neumann was born in Budapest, Hungary. He was a child prodigy who could divide 8-digit numbers in his head by the age of 6. He was a genius in virtually every field that he studied, including physics, economics, engineering, and mathematics. At 18 he received an award as the best mathematician in Hungary, a country known for excellence in the field, and he received his Ph.D., summa cum laude, at 21. He came to the United States in 1930 as a guest lecturer at Princeton University and taught there for 3 years. Then, in 1933 he became one of the founding members (along with Albert Einstein) of the Institute for Advanced Studies, where he worked for the next 20 years.

He was one of the most brilliant minds of the twentieth century, a true genius in every sense, both good and bad. He could do prodigious mental feats in his head, and his thought processes usually raced way ahead of "ordinary" mortals who found him quite difficult to work with. One of his colleagues joked that "Johnny wasn't really human, but after living among them for so long, he learned to do a remarkably good imitation of one."

Von Neumann was a brilliant theoretician who did pioneering work in pure mathematics, operations research, game theory, and theoretical physics. He was also an engineer who was concerned about practicalities and real-world problems, and it was this interest in applied issues that led Von Neumann into the design and construction of the first stored program computer. One of the early computers built by the RAND Corp. in 1953 was affectionately called "Johnniac" in his honor, although Von Neumann detested that name. Like the UNIVAC I, it also has a place of honor at the Smithsonian Institute.

were extremely difficult to maintain. Just the process of turning the machine on could blow out a dozen tubes! For this reason, first-generation machines were used only by trained personnel and only in specialized locations such as large corporations, government and university research labs, and military installations, where this type of expensive support environment could be provided. These first-generation machines did not have much impact on the average person.

The **second generation** of computing, roughly 1957–1965, heralded a major change in the size and complexity of computers. In the late 1950s, the bulky vacuum tube was replaced by a single transistor only a few millimeters in size, and memory was now constructed using tiny magnetic cores only 1/50 of an inch in diameter. (We will introduce and describe both of these devices in Chapter 4.) These technologies not only dramatically reduced the size of computers but also increased their reliability and reduced costs. Suddenly, buying and using a computer became a real possibility for some small and medium-sized businesses, colleges, and government agencies that could not have considered it before. This was also the era of the appearance of FORTRAN and COBOL, the first **high-level** ("natural") **programming languages.** (We will study this type of programming language in Chapters 8 and 9.) Suddenly, it was no longer necessary to be an electrical engineer to solve a problem on a computer. One simply needed to learn how to write commands in a high-level language. The occupation called **programmer** was born.

Good Evening, This Is Walter Cronkite

In the earliest days of computing (1951–1952), few people knew what a computer was, and even fewer had seen or worked with one. Computers were the tool of a very small group of highly trained technical specialists in such fields as mathematics, physics, and engineering. In those days, the general public's knowledge of computer science was limited to the robots and alien computers of science fiction movies.

This all changed in November 1952, when millions of Americans turned on the television set (itself a relatively new technology) to watch returns from the 1952 presidential election between Dwight D. Eisenhower and Adlai Stevenson. In addition to seeing Walter Cronkite and TV reporters and analysts, viewers were treated to an unexpected member of the news staff—a UNIVAC I. CBS executives had rented a computer and installed it in the very center of their set, where it sat, lights blinking and tape drives spinning. They planned to use UNIVAC to produce election predictions quickly and scoop rival stations that did their analyses by hand. Ironically, UNIVAC correctly predicted early that evening, on the basis of well-known statistical sampling techniques, that Eisenhower would win the election, but nervous CBS executives were so skeptical about this new technology that they did not go on the air with the computer's prediction until it had been confirmed by old-fashioned manual methods.

It was the first time that millions of TV viewers had actually seen this thing called an electronic digital computer. The CBS staff, who were also quite inexperienced in computer technology, treated the computer as though it were human. They would turn toward the computer console and utter phrases like "UNIVAC, can you tell me who is currently ahead in Ohio?" or "UNIVAC, do you have any prediction on the final electoral vote total?" In actuality, the statistical algorithms had been programmed in, days earlier, by the Remington Rand staff, but it looked great on TV! This first public appearance of a computer was so well received that computers were used many more times in the early days of TV, primarily on quiz shows, where they reinforced the public's image of the computer as a "giant electronic brain."

This miniaturization process continued into the **third generation** of computing, which lasted from about 1965 to 1975. This was the era of the **integrated circuit.** Rather than using discrete electronic components, integrated circuits with transistors, resistors, and capacitors were photographically etched onto a piece of silicon, which further reduced the size and cost of computers. From building-sized to room-sized, computers now became desk-sized, and this period saw the birth of the first **minicomputer**—the PDP-1 manufactured by the Digital Equipment Corp. in 1963. It also saw the birth of the **software industry,** as companies sprang up to provide programs such as accounting packages and statistical programs to the ever-increasing numbers of computer users. By the mid–1970s, computers were no longer a rarity. They were being widely used throughout business, government, the military, and education.

The **fourth generation,** 1975–1985, saw the appearance of the first **microcomputer.** Integrated circuit technology had advanced to the point where a complete computer system could be contained on a single circuit board that you could hold in your hand. The desk-sized machine of the early 1970s now became a desktop machine, shrinking to the size of a typewriter. Figure 1.7 shows the Altair 8800, the world's first microcomputer, which appeared in January 1975.

It soon became unusual *not* to see a computer on someone's desk. The software industry exploded with all types of new packages—spreadsheets, databases, and drawing programs—to meet the needs of the burgeoning user population. This era saw the appearance of the first **computer networks,** as users realized that much of the power of computers derives not just from the numerical results of some program but also from an enhanced ability to communicate with other users. (We will look at networking in great detail in Chapter 7.) **Electronic mail** became an important application. Because so many users were novices who had never used a computer before, the concept of **user-friendly systems** evolved. This included new **graphical user interfaces** with pull-down menus, icons, and other visual aids to make computing

FIGURE 1.7

The Altair 8800, the World's First Microcomputer

easier and more fun. **Embedded systems** first appeared during this generation; these are systems that contain a computer inside them to control their operation. Computers were becoming small enough to be placed inside cars, thermostats, microwave ovens, and wristwatches.

The **fifth generation**, 1985–?, is where we are today. However, so much is changing so fast that most computer scientists believe that the concept of distinct generations of change has outlived its usefulness. In computer science, change is now a constant companion. Some of the recent developments in computer systems development include

- Massively parallel processors capable of trillions of computations per second
- Handheld devices and other types of personal digital assistants (PDAs)
- High-resolution graphics for imaging, movie making, and virtual reality
- Powerful multimedia user interfaces incorporating sound, voice recognition, touch, photography, video, and television
- Integrated global telecommunications incorporating data, television, telephone, FAX, the Internet, and the World Wide Web
- Wireless data communications
- Massive storage devices capable of holding hundreds of trillions of pieces of data
- Ubiquitous computing, in which miniature computers are embedded into our cars, kitchen appliances, home heating systems, and even the clothes we wear

The World's First Microcomputer

The Altair 8800, shown in Figure 1.7, was the first microcomputer when it made its debut on the cover of *Popular Electronics* in January 1975. Its developer, Ed Roberts, owned a tiny electronics store in Albuquerque, New Mexico. His company was in desperate financial shape when he read about a new microprocessor from Intel, the Intel 8080. Roberts reasoned that this new chip could be used to sell a complete personal computer in kit form. He bought these new chips from Intel at the bargain basement price of $75 each and packaged them in a kit called the Altair 8800 (named after a location in the TV series Star Trek), which he offered to hobbyists for $397. Roberts figured he might sell a few hundred kits a year, enough to keep his company afloat temporarily. He ended up selling hundreds of them a day! The Altair microcomputer kits were so popular that he could not keep them in stock, and legend has it that people even drove to New Mexico and camped out in the parking lot to buy their computers.

This is particularly amazing in view of the fact that the original Altair was difficult to assemble and had only 256 memory cells, no I/O devices, and no software support. To program it, the user had to enter binary machine language instructions directly from the console switches. But even though it could do very little, people loved it because it was a real computer, and it was theirs.

The Intel 8080 chip did have the capability of running programs written in the language called BASIC that had been developed at Dartmouth in the early 1960s. A small software company located in the state of Washington wrote Ed Roberts a letter telling him that it had a BASIC compiler that could run on his Altair, making it much easier to use. That company was called Microsoft—and the rest, as they say, is history.

In only 50–60 years, computers have progressed from the UNIVAC I, which cost millions of dollars, had a few thousand memory locations, and was capable of only a few thousand operations per second, to today's top-of-the-line workstation with a high resolution flat panel monitor, billions of memory cells, massive amounts of external storage, and enough processing power to execute over one billion instructions per second, all for well under $3,000. Changes of this magnitude have never occurred so quickly in any other technology. If the same rate of change had occurred in the auto industry, beginning with the 1909 Model-T, today's cars would be capable of traveling at a speed of 20,000 miles per hour, would get about a million miles per gallon, and would cost about $1.00!

Figure 1.8 summarizes the major developments that occurred during each of the five generations of computer development discussed in this section. As

FIGURE 1.8

Some of the Major Advancements in Computing

GENERATION	APPROXIMATE DATES	MAJOR ADVANCES
First	1950–1957	First commercial computers First symbolic programming languages Use of binary arithmetic, vacuum tubes for storage Punched card input/output
Second	1957–1965	Transistors and core memories First disks for mass storage Size reduction, increased reliability, lower costs First high-level programming languages First operating systems
Third	1965–1975	Integrated circuits Further reduction in size and cost, increased reliability First minicomputers Time-shared operating systems Appearance of the software industry First set of computing standards for compatibility between systems
Fourth	1975–1985	Large-scale and very-large-scale integrated circuits Further reduction in size and cost, increased reliability First microcomputers Growth of new types of software and of the software industry Computer networks Graphical user interfaces
Fifth	1985–?	Ultra-large-scale integrated circuits Supercomputers and parallel processors Laptops and handheld computers Wireless computing Massive external data storage devices Ubiquitous computing High-resolution graphics, visualization, virtual reality Worldwide networks Multimedia user interfaces

we have said before, underlying all of these amazing improvements, the theoretical model describing the design and construction of computers has not changed significantly in the last 50 years.

However, many people feel that significant and important structural changes are now on the way. At the end of Chapter 5 we will introduce models of computing that are fundamentally quite different from the Von Neumann architecture in use today. These totally new approaches (e.g., quantum computing) may possibly be the models that will be used in the 22nd century and beyond.

1.5   Organization of the Text

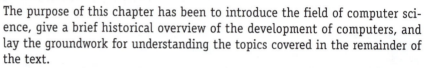

The purpose of this chapter has been to introduce the field of computer science, give a brief historical overview of the development of computers, and lay the groundwork for understanding the topics covered in the remainder of the text.

Certainly, the most important idea is the primacy and centrality of algorithms and algorithmic problem solving within the discipline of computer science. If we look back at the definition of computer science in Section 1.2, we see that it is the study of algorithms from a number of different viewpoints. In fact, the definition that began the chapter describes quite well the organization of the remaining sections and chapters of this text. This book is divided into six separate sections, called **levels,** each of which addresses one aspect of the definition of computer science. Let's repeat the definition and see how it maps into the sequence of topics to be presented.

> ### DEFINITION
>
> **Computer science**   the study of algorithms, including
>
> 1. Their formal and mathematical properties
> 2. Their hardware realizations
> 3. Their linguistic realizations
> 4. Their applications

Computer science is the study of algorithms, including

1. *Their formal and mathematical properties*   Level 1 of the text (Chapters 2 and 3) is entitled "The Algorithmic Foundations of Computer Science." It continues the discussion of algorithmic problem solving begun in Sections 1.2 and 1.3 by introducing important mathematical and logical properties of algorithms. Chapter 2 presents the development of a number of algorithms to solve important, real-world problems—certainly more "real-world" than shampooing your hair. It also looks at concepts related to the problem-solving process, such as how we discover and create good algorithms, what notation we can use to express our solutions, and how we can check to see whether our proposed algorithm correctly solves the desired problem.

Our brute force chess example showed that it is not enough simply to develop a correct algorithm; we also want a solution that is efficient and that produces the desired result in a reasonable amount of time. (After all, would you want to market a chess-playing program that takes 10^{48} years to make its first move?) Chapter 3 describes ways to compare the efficiency of different algorithms and select the best one to use to solve a given problem. The material in Level 1 provides the necessary foundation for a study of the discipline of computer science.

2. *Their hardware realizations*   Although our initial look at computer science investigated how an algorithm behaved when executed by some abstract "computing agent," we ultimately want to execute our algorithms on "real" machines to get "real" answers. Level 2 of the text (Chapters 4 and 5) is entitled "The Hardware World," and it looks at how to design and construct computer systems. It approaches this topic from two quite different viewpoints.

Chapter 4 presents a detailed discussion of the underlying hardware. It introduces the basic building blocks of computers—binary numbers, transistors, logic gates, and circuits—and shows how these elementary electronic devices can be used to construct components to perform arithmetic and logic functions such as addition, subtraction, comparison, and sequencing. Although it is both interesting and important, this perspective produces a rather low-level view of a computer system. It is difficult to understand how a computer works by studying only these elementary components, just as it would be difficult to understand human behavior by investigating the behavior of individual cells. Therefore, Chapter 5 takes a higher-level view of the study of computer hardware. It looks at computers not as a bunch of wires and circuits but as an integrated collection of subsystems called memory, processor, storage, input/output, and communications. It will explain in great detail the principles of the Von Neumann architecture introduced in Section 1.4.

However, a study of computer systems can be done at an even higher level. To understand how a computer works, we do not need to examine the functioning of every one of the thousands of components inside a machine. Instead, we need only be aware of a few critical pieces that are essential to our work. From the user's perspective, everything else is superfluous. This "user-oriented" view of a computer system and its resources is called a **virtual machine** or a **virtual environment.** A virtual machine is composed only of the resources that the user perceives rather than of all the hardware resources that actually exist.

This viewpoint is analogous to our level of understanding of what happens under the hood of our car. There may be thousands of mechanical components inside an automobile engine, but most of us concern ourselves only with the items reported on the dashboard—oil pressure, fuel level, engine temperature. This is our "virtual engine," and that is all we need or want to know. We are all too happy to leave the remaining details about engine design to our friendly neighborhood mechanic.

Level 3 (Chapters 6 and 7), entitled "The Virtual Machine," describes how a virtual environment is created using a component called the **system software**. Chapter 6 takes a look at the most important and widely used piece of system software on a modern computer system, the **operating system,** which controls the overall operation of a computer and makes it easier for users to access. Chapter 7 then goes on to describe how this virtual environment can extend beyond the boundaries of a single system as it examines how to interconnect individual machines into **computer networks and distributed systems** that provide users with access to a huge collection of computer systems and information as well as an enormous number of other users. It is the system software, and the virtual machine it creates, that makes computer hardware manageable and usable.

3. *Their linguistic realizations*   After studying hardware design, computer organization, and virtual machines, you will have a pretty good idea of the techniques used to design and build computers. In the next section of the text, we ask the question, How can this hardware be used to solve important and interesting problems? Level 4, entitled "The Software World" (Chapters 8–11), takes a look at what is involved in designing and implementing computer software. It investigates the programs and instruction sequences executed by the hardware, rather than the hardware itself.

Chapter 8 introduces some fundamental concepts related to the topic of computer programming. This one chapter is certainly not intended to make you a proficient programmer. That would require far more than a single chapter; instead, its purpose is to illustrate some basic features of modern programming languages and give you an appreciation for the interesting and challenging task of the computer programmer.

There are many programming languages such as C++, Scheme, Java, Perl, and Visual BASIC that can be used to encode algorithms. Chapter 9 overviews a number of different languages and language models in current use, including the functional and parallel models. Chapter 10 describes how a program written in a high-level programming language can be translated into the low-level machine language codes first described in Chapter 5. Finally, Chapter 11 shows that, even when we marshal all the powerful hardware and software ideas described in the first ten chapters, problems exist that cannot be solved algorithmically. Chapter 11 demonstrates that there are, indeed, limits to computing.

4. *Their applications*   By this point we have seen how to write programs to solve problems and how to execute them on a computer. However, most people are not computer scientists. They are concerned not with creating programs but simply with using programs, just as there are few automotive engineers but many, many drivers. In Level 5, entitled "Applications" (Chapters 12–14), we no longer care about *how* to build a program to solve a problem but look instead at *what* these programs can do.

Chapters 12 through 14 explore just a few of the many important and rapidly growing applications of computers, such as artificial intelligence, visualization, graphics, cryptography, simulation, and e-commerce. This section cannot possibly survey all the ways in which computers are being used today or will be used in the future. Indeed, there is hardly an area in our modern, complex society that information technology has not affected in some important way. Readers interested in other applications should search out readings specific to their own areas of interest.

Finally, there are individuals who are not concerned with building computers, creating programs, or using any of the applications just described. Instead, they are interested in the social and cultural impacts—both positive and negative—of this ever-changing technology. They do not care either how we build machines and programs or what problems we solve. They are interested in *why* we have chosen to implement this technology and in *what* the implications are for society.

To address this important perspective on computer science, we have added a sixth level to the structure of our text: the social implications of computer and information technology. This material was not part of the original definition of computer science but has become an important area of study. In Level 6, entitled "Social Issues" (Chapter 15), we move to the highest level of abstraction—the view furthest removed from the computer itself—to discuss social, ethical, legal, and professional issues related to computer and information technology. These ideas are of critical importance, because even individuals not directly involved in developing or using computers will be deeply affected by them, just as society has been drastically and permanently altered by such technological developments as the telephone, television, and automobile. This last chapter takes a look at such thorny and difficult topics as computer crime, information privacy, and the ownership of intellectual property. In these matters there are not always easy answers or even any answers at all. Our intent is simply to raise your awareness of these issues and give you some decision-making tools to help you reach your own conclusions.

The overall six-layer hierarchy of this text is summarized in Figure 1.9. The organizational structure diagrammed in Figure 1.9 is one of the most important aspects of this text. To describe a field of study, it is not enough to present a mass of facts or a huge amount of detail. For learners to absorb, understand, and integrate this information, there must be a theme, a relationship, a thread that ties together the various parts of the narrative—in essence, a "big picture." Our big picture is Figure 1.9.

We first lay out the basic foundations of computer science (Level 1). We then proceed upward through five distinct layers of abstraction, from extremely

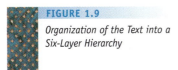

FIGURE 1.9

Organization of the Text into a Six-Layer Hierarchy

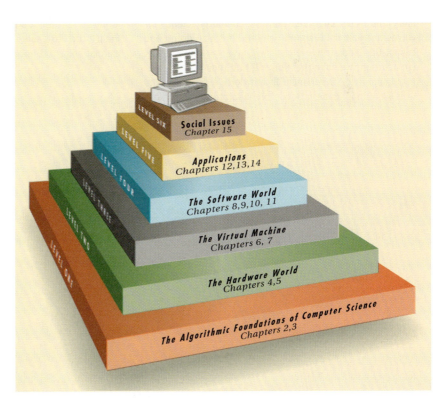

low-level machine details such as electronic circuits and computer hardware (Level 2), through intermediate levels that address virtual machines (Level 3), programming languages and software development (Level 4), to higher levels that investigate computer applications (Level 5) and address the use and misuse of information technology (Level 6). As the discussion of each level is completed, that material is used to help reveal the beauty and complexity of a higher and more abstract view of the discipline of computer science.

Just as a study of chemistry proceeds from protons, neutrons, and electrons to atoms, molecules, crystals, and finally chemical compounds, so too will we progress from transistors to circuits, components, computer systems, programs, applications, and finally social implications. We now begin that upward march and invite you to join us in our exploration of this fascinating field. In the next chapter, we start with Level 1 of our hierarchy and begin a study of the algorithmic foundations of computer science.

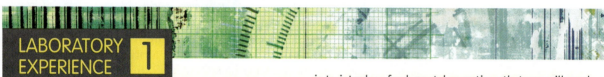

LABORATORY EXPERIENCE 1

Associated with this text is a laboratory manual that includes software packages and a collection of formal laboratory exercises. These laboratory experiences are designed to give you a chance to build, modify, play with, and experiment with the ideas discussed in the text. You are strongly encouraged to carry out these laboratories in order to gain a deeper understanding of the concepts presented in the chapters. Learning computer science involves not just reading and listening but also doing and trying. Our laboratory exercises will give you that chance. (In addition, we hope that you will find them fun.)

Laboratory Experience 1, entitled "A Glossary and Web Browsing," is an introductory laboratory. Its purpose is to introduce fundamental operations that you will need in all future labs—operations such as using menus, buttons, and windows and accessing pages on the Web. (In the text, you will find a number of pointers to Web pages containing a wealth of information that complements our discussions.) In addition, the lab will provide a useful tool that you may use during your study of computer science and in other courses as well. You will learn how to use a computer to build a *glossary* of important technical terms along with their definitions and locations in the text. Please turn to Laboratory Experience 1 in the laboratory manual and try it now.

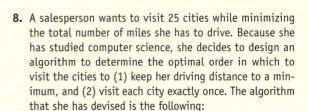

1. Come up with some algorithms, apart from VCR instructions and cooking recipes, that you encounter in your everyday life. Write them out in any convenient notation, and show that they meet all of the criteria for algorithms that were presented in this chapter.

2. In the VCR instructions of Figure 1.1, step 4 says, "Enter the channel number that you wish to record and press the button labeled CHAN." In your opinion, is that an unambiguous and well-defined operation? Explain why or why not.

3. Trace through the decimal addition algorithm of Figure 1.2 using the following input values:

$$m = 3 \quad a_2 = 1 \; a_1 = 4 \; a_0 = 9$$
$$b_2 = 0 \; b_1 = 2 \; b_0 = 9$$

   At each step, show the values for c_3, c_2, c_1, c_0, and *carry*.

4. Modify the decimal addition algorithm of Figure 1.2 so that it does not print out nonsignificant leading zeroes; that is, the answer to question 3 would appear as 178 rather than 0178.

5. Under what conditions would the well-known quadratic formula

$$Roots = \frac{-b \pm \sqrt{b^2 - 4ac}}{2a}$$

   not be effectively computable? (Assume that you are working with real numbers.)

6. Compare the two solutions to the shampooing algorithm shown in Figures 1.3(a) and 1.3(b). Which do you think is a better general-purpose solution? Why? (*Hint:* What if you wanted to wash your hair 1,000 times?)

7. Here is Euclid's 2,300-year-old algorithm for finding the greatest common divisor of two positive integers I and J.

Step	Operation
1	Get two positive integers as input. Call the larger value I and the smaller value J.
2	Divide I by J, and call the remainder R.
3	If R is *not* 0, then reset I to the value of J, reset J to the value of R, and go back to step 2.
4	Print out the answer, which is the value of J.
5	Stop.

   a. Go through this algorithm using the input values 20 and 32. After each step of the algorithm is completed, give the values of I, J, and R. Determine the final output of the algorithm.

   b. Does the algorithm work correctly when the two inputs are 0 and 32? Describe exactly what happens, and modify the algorithm so that it gives an appropriate error message.

8. A salesperson wants to visit 25 cities while minimizing the total number of miles she has to drive. Because she has studied computer science, she decides to design an algorithm to determine the optimal order in which to visit the cities to (1) keep her driving distance to a minimum, and (2) visit each city exactly once. The algorithm that she has devised is the following:

   > The computer would first list *all* possible ways to visit the 25 cities and then, for each one, determine the total mileage associated with that particular ordering. (Assume that the computer has access to a road map that provides the distances between all cities.) After determining the total mileage for each possible trip, the computer would search for the ordering with the minimum mileage and print out the list of cities on that optimal route, that is, the order in which the salesperson should visit her destinations.

   If a computer could analyze 10,000,000 separate paths per second, how long would it take the computer to determine the optimal route for visiting these 25 cities? On the basis of your answer, do you think this is a feasible algorithm? If it is not, can you think of a way to get a reasonable solution to this problem?

9. One way to do multiplication is by repeated addition. For example, 47×25 can be evaluated as $47 + 47 + 47 + \ldots + 47$ (25 times). Sketch out an algorithm for multiplying two positive numbers a and b by using this technique.

10. Go to the library and gather more detailed information about one of the early pioneers mentioned in this chapter—Pascal, Liebnitz, Jacquard, Babbage, Lovelace, Hollerith, Eckert, Mauchly, Aiken, Zuse, Atanasoff, Turing, or Von Neumann. Write a paper describing in detail that person's contribution to computing and computer science.

11. Get the technical specifications of the computer on which you are working (either from a technical manual or from your computer center staff). Determine its cost, its processing speed (in MIPS, millions of instructions per second), its computational speed (in MFlops, millions of floating point operations per second), and the size of its primary memory.

    Compare those values with what was typically available on first-, second-, and third-generation computer systems and determine the percentage improvement between your computer and the first commercial machines of the early 1950s.

12. One of the hot new areas of computer science is *ubiquitous computing*, in which a number of computers automatically provide services for a user without that user's

knowledge or awareness. An example might be a computer located in your car that contacts the garage door opener and tells it to open the garage door when the car is close to home. Read about this new model of computing and write a paper describing some of its applications. What are some of the possible problems that could be created?

CHALLENGE WORK

1. Assume we have a "computing agent" that knows how to do one-digit subtraction where the first digit is at least as large as the second (i.e., we do not end up with a negative number). Thus, our computing agent can do such operations as $7 - 3 = 4$, $9 - 1 = 8$, and $5 - 5 = 0$. It can also subtract a one-digit value from a two-digit value in the range 10–18 as long as the final result has only a single digit. This capability enables it to do such operations as $13 - 7 = 6$, $10 - 2 = 8$, and $18 - 9 = 9$.

   Using these primitive capabilities, design an algorithm to do *decimal subtraction* on two *m*-digit numbers, where $m \geq 1$. You will be given two unsigned whole numbers $a_{m-1} a_{m-2} \ldots a_0$ and $b_{m-1} b_{m-2} \ldots b_0$. Your algorithm must compute the value $c_{m-1} c_{m-2} \ldots c_0$, the difference of these two values.

$$
\begin{array}{r}
a_{m-1} \, a_{m-2} \cdots a_0 \\
- \, b_{m-1} \, b_{m-2} \cdots b_0 \\
\hline
c_{m-1} \, c_{m-2} \cdots c_0
\end{array}
$$

   You may assume that the top number ($a_{m-1} a_{m-2} \ldots a_0$) is greater than or equal to the bottom number ($b_{m-1} b_{m-2} \ldots b_0$) so that the result will not be a negative value. However, do not assume that each individual digit a_i is greater than or equal to b_i. If the digit on the bottom is larger than the digit on the top, then you will have to implement a *borrowing scheme* to allow the subtraction to continue. (*Caution*: It may have been easy to learn subtraction as a first grader, but it is devilishly difficult to tell a computer how to do it!)

2. Our definition of the field of computer science is just one of many that have been proposed. Because it is so young, people working in the field are still debating how best to define exactly what they do. Review the literature of computer science (perhaps some of the books listed in the next section) and browse the Web to locate other definitions of computer science. Compare these definitions with the one presented in this chapter and discuss the differences among them. Discuss how different definitions may give you a vastly different perspective on the field and what people in this field do. [*Note:* A very well-known and widely used definition of computer science was presented in "Report of the ACM Task Force on the Core of Computer Science," reprinted in the journal *Communications of the ACM*, vol. 32, no. 1 (January 1989).]

FOR FURTHER READING

Here are some books that will give you a good introduction to and overview of the field of computer science. Like this text, they survey many different aspects of the discipline.

Bierman, A. W. *Great Ideas in Computer Science,* 2nd ed. Cambridge, MA: MIT Press, 1997.

Brookshear, J. G. *Computer Science: An Overview,* 7th ed. Reading, MA: Addison Wesley, 2002.

Decker, R., and Hirshfield, S. *The Analytical Engine: An Introduction to Computer Science Using the Internet,* 3rd ed. Boston, MA: Brooks/Cole, 1998.

Dewdney, A. K. *The New Turing Omnibus.* New York: Freeman, 2001.

Dewdney, A. K. *Introductory Computer Science.* Boston, MA: Computer Science Press, 1996.

The following books provide an excellent overview of the historical development of both computers and software.

Broy, M., and Denert, E. *Software Pioneers*. Amsterdam: Springer-Verlag, 2002.

Cambell-Kelly, M., and Asprey, W. *Computers: A History of the Information Machine*. New York: Basic Books, 1997.

Ceruzzi, P. *A History of Modern Computing*. Cambridge, MA: MIT Press, 2000.

Ifrah, George. *The Universal History of Computing: From the Abacus to Quantum Computer*. New York: Wiley, 2000.

Wurster, C. *The Computer: An Illustrated History*. Cologne, Germany: Taschen, 2002

In addition, the Charles Babbage Institute at the University of Minnesota is an outstanding resource for information about the history of information technology and its impact on society. Its Web site is at www.cbi.umn.edu.

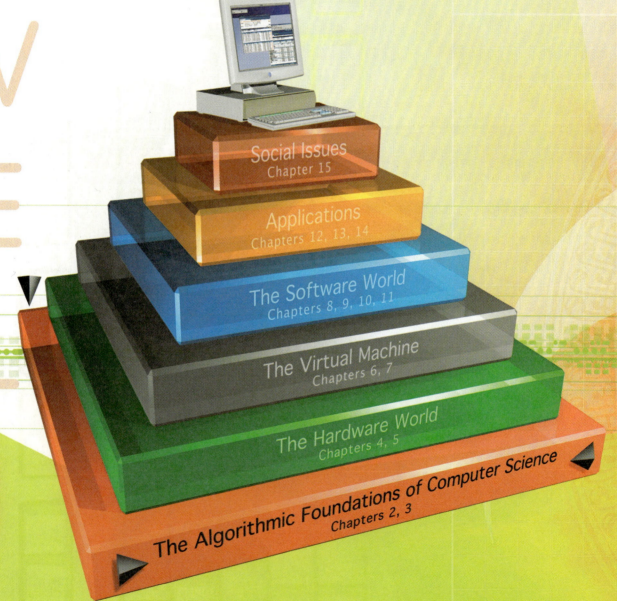

L
E
V
E
L
1

The Algorithmic Foundations of Computer Science

Social Issues
Chapter 15

Applications
Chapters 12, 13, 14

The Software World
Chapters 8, 9, 10, 11

The Virtual Machine
Chapters 6, 7

The Hardware World
Chapters 4, 5

The Algorithmic Foundations of Computer Science
Chapters 2, 3

LEVEL 1

Level 1 of the text continues our investigations into algorithms and algorithmic problem solving—essential material for studying any branch of computer science. It first introduces methods for designing and representing algorithms. It then uses these ideas to develop solutions to some interesting real-world problems, including an important application in medicine and biology.

When judging the quality of an essay or book report, we do not look only at such things as sentence structure, spelling, and punctuation. Although grammatical issues are important, we also evaluate the work's style, for it is a combination of correctness and expressiveness that produces a written document of high quality. So too for algorithms—correctness is not the only measure of "goodness." This section will present criteria for evaluating the quality and elegance of the algorithmic solutions that you develop.

CHAPTER 2

Algorithm Discovery and Design

2.1 Introduction

Chapter 1 introduced algorithms and algorithmic problem solving, two of the most fundamental concepts in computer science. Our introduction used examples drawn from everyday life, such as programming a VCR (Figure 1.1) and washing your hair (Figure 1.3). These are perfectly valid examples of algorithms, but as fascinating as they may be to shampoo makers and VCR manufacturers, they are not of immense interest to computer scientists. This chapter develops more fully the notions of algorithms and algorithmic problem solving and applies these ideas to problems that *are* of interest to computer scientists: searching lists, finding maxima and minima, and matching patterns. As we will see, these problems occur in many important applications.

2.2 Representing Algorithms

 ### 2.2.1 *Pseudocode*

Before presenting any algorithms, we must first make an important decision. How should we represent them? What notation should we use to express our algorithms so that they are clear, precise, and unambiguous?

One possibility would be **natural language,** the language we speak and write in our everyday lives. (In our case it is English, but it could be Spanish, Arabic, Japanese, Swahili, or any one of a thousand other languages.) This is an obvious choice because our own spoken and written language is the one with which we are most familiar. If we used natural language, then our algorithms would be written in much the same way as a term paper or an essay— a collection of pages divided into paragraphs and sentences. For example, when expressed in natural language, the addition algorithm of Figure 1.2 might look something like the paragraph given in Figure 2.1.

Comparing Figure 1.2 with Figure 2.1 illustrates the problems of using natural language to represent algorithms. Natural language can be extremely verbose, with the resulting algorithms ending up as rambling, unstructured paragraphs that are hard to follow. (Imagine reading 5, 10, or even 100 pages of text like Figure 2.1.) An unstructured, "free-flowing" writing style may be wonderful for essays, but it is horrible for algorithms. The lack of structure makes it difficult for the reader to locate specific sections of the algorithm, because they are buried deep inside the text. For example, on the eighth line

Initially, set the value of the variable *carry* to 0 and the value of the variable *i* to 0. When these initializations have been completed, begin looping as long as the value of the variable *i* is less than or equal to $(m - 1)$. First, add together the values of the two digits a_i and b_i and the current value of the carry digit to get the result called c_i. Now check the value of c_i to see whether it is greater than or equal to 10. If c_i is greater than or equal to 10, then reset the value of *carry* to 1 and reduce the value of c_i by 10; otherwise, set the value of *carry* to zero. When you are done with that operation, add 1 to *i* and begin the loop all over again. When the loop has completed execution, set the leftmost digit of the result c_m to the value of *carry* and print out the final result, which consists of the digits $c_m c_m -1 \ldots c_0$. After printing the result, the algorithm is finished, and it terminates.

of Figure 2.1 there is a phrase that says, " . . . and begin the loop all over again." To what part of the algorithm does this refer? Without any clues to guide us, such as indentation, line numbering, or highlighting, locating the beginning of that loop can be a daunting and time-consuming task. (For the record, the beginning of the loop corresponds to the sentence on the second line that starts, "When these initializations have been completed . . . ." It is certainly not easy to determine this from a casual reading of the text.)

A second problem is that natural language is too "rich" in interpretation and meaning. Natural language frequently relies on either context or a reader's experiences to give precise meaning to a word or phrase. This permits different readers to interpret the same sentence in totally different ways. This may be acceptable, even desirable, when writing poetry or fiction, but it is again disastrous when writing algorithms that should always execute in the same way and produce identical results. We can see an example of this problem in the sentence on lines 7 and 8 of Figure 2.1 that starts with "When you are done with that operation . . . ." When we are done with *which* operation? It is not at all clear from the text, and individuals may interpret the phrase *that operation* in different ways, producing radically different behavior. Given all of these problems, it is easy to see that natural languages do not provide the accuracy and precision needed to represent algorithms.

In place of natural languages we might be tempted to go to the other extreme. If we are ultimately going to execute our algorithm on a computer, why not write it out immediately as a computer program using a **high-level programming language** such as C++ or Java? If we adopt that approach, the addition algorithm of Figure 1.2 might start out looking like the program fragment shown in Figure 2.2.

As an algorithmic design language, this notation is also seriously flawed. During the initial phases of design, we should be thinking and writing at a highly abstract level. However, using a programming language to express our design forces us to deal immediately with detailed language issues such as punctuation, grammar, and syntax. For example, the algorithm in Figure 1.2 contains an operation that says, "Set the value of carry to 0." This is an easy statement to understand. However, when translated into a language like C++ or Java, that statement becomes

```
Carry = 0;
```

FIGURE 2.2

The Beginning of the Addition Algorithm of Figure 1.2 Expressed in a High-Level Programming Language

```
{
int i, m, Carry;
int[] a = new int[100];
int[] b = new int[100];
int[] c = new int[100];
m = Console.readInt();
for (int j = 0; j < =m−1; j++)    {
        a[j] = Console.readInt();
        b[j] = Console.readInt();
}
Carry = 0;
i = 0;
while (i < m)    {
        c[i] = a[i] + b[i] + Carry;
        if (c[i] > = 10)
        .
        .
        .
```

Is this operation setting Carry to 0 or asking if Carry is equal to 0? Why does a semicolon appear at the end of the line? Was it necessary to capitalize the letter C in Carry? These picky technical details clutter our thoughts, and at this point in the solution process, they are totally out of place. When creating algorithms, a programmer should no more worry about semicolons and capitalization than a novelist should worry about typography and cover design when writing the first draft!

If the two extremes of natural languages and high-level programming languages are both less than ideal, what notation should we use? What is the best way to represent the solutions shown in this chapter and the rest of the book?

Most computer scientists use a notation called **pseudocode** to design and represent algorithms. This is a special set of English language constructs modeled to look like the statements available in most programming languages. Pseudocode represents a compromise between the two extremes of natural and formal languages. It is simple, highly readable, and has virtually no grammatical rules. (In fact, pseudocode is sometimes called a programming language without any details.) However, because it contains only statements that have a well-defined structure, it is easier to visualize the organization of a pseudocode algorithm than one represented as long, rambling natural-language paragraphs. In addition, because pseudocode closely resembles many popular programming languages, the subsequent translation of the algorithm into a computer program is relatively simple. The algorithms shown in Figures 1.1, 1.2, and 1.3(a) and (b) are all written in pseudocode.

We will need to include pseudocode constructs for the three types of algorithmic operations introduced in Chapter 1: sequential, conditional, and iterative. In the following sections we will introduce a set of constructs that are among the most popular and easy to understand. However, keep in mind that pseudocode is *not* a formal language with rigidly standardized syntactic and semantic rules and regulations. On the contrary, it is an informal design notation used solely to express algorithms. If you do not like the specific constructs presented in the next two sections, feel free to modify them or select others that are more helpful to you in the design and development of algorithms. One of the nice features of pseudocode is its flexibility to adapt to your own personal way of thinking and problem solving.

 ### 2.2.2 *Sequential Operations*

Our pseudocode must include instructions to carry out the three basic sequential operations called **computation**, **input**, and **output**.

The instruction for performing a **computation** and saving the result looks like the following. (Words and phrases inside quotation marks represent specific elements that you must insert when writing an algorithm.)

> Set the value of "variable" to "arithmetic expression"

The meaning of this operation is to first evaluate the "arithmetic expression" and get a result. Then take that result and store it into the indicated "variable." A **variable** is simply a named storage location that can hold a data value. A commonly used analogy is that a variable is like a mailbox into which one can store a value and from which one can retrieve a value. Let's look at an example.

> Set the value of *carry* to 0

First, evaluate the arithmetic expression, which in this case is just the constant value 0. Then store that result into the variable called *carry*. If *carry* had a previous value, say 1, it will be discarded and replaced by the new value 0. Pictorially, you can view this operation as producing the following state:

Here is another example:

> Set the value of *Area* to (πr^2)

Assuming that the variable r has been given a value by a previous instruction in the algorithm, this statement evaluates the arithmetic expression πr^2 to produce a numerical result. This result is then stored in the variable called *Area*. If r does not have a value, an error condition occurs; this instruction is not effectively computable, and it cannot be completed.

We can see additional examples of computational operations in steps 4, 6, and 7 of the addition algorithm of Figure 1.2:

Step 4: Add the two digits a_i and b_i to the current value of *carry* to get c_i

Step 6: Add 1 to i, effectively moving one column to the left

Step 7: Set c_m to the value of *carry*

Note that these three steps are not written in exactly the format just described. If we had used that notation, they would have looked like this:

Step 4: Set the value of c_i to $(a_i + b_i + carry)$

Step 6: Set the value of i to $(i + 1)$

Step 7: Set the value of c_m to $carry$

However, in pseudocode it doesn't really matter exactly how you choose to write your instructions as long as the intent is clear and unambiguous. At this point in the design of a solution, we do not really care about the minor language differences between

Add a and b to get c

and

Set the value of c to $(a + b)$

As we noted earlier, pseudocode is not a precise set of notational rules to be memorized and rigidly followed. It is a flexible notation that can be adjusted to fit your own view about how best to express ideas and algorithms.

When writing arithmetic expressions, you may assume that the computing agent executing your algorithm has all the capabilities of a typical calculator. Therefore, it "knows" how to do all basic arithmetic operations such as $+$, $-$, $\times$, $\div$, square root, absolute value, sine, cosine, and tangent. It also knows the value of important constants such as π.

The final two sequential operations enable our computing agent to communicate with "the outside world," which means everything other than the computing agent itself:

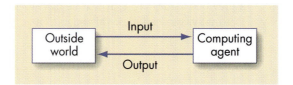

Input operations allow the computing agent to receive data values from the outside world that it may then use in later instructions. **Output** operations allow the computing agent to send results to the outside world for display. When the computing agent is a computer, communications with the outside world are done via the input/output equipment available on a typical computer system (e.g., keyboard, screen, mouse, printer, and a network). However, when designing algorithms, we generally do not concern ourselves with such details. We care only that data is given to us from somewhere (or somebody) when we request it and that results are sent to something (or someone) for presentation.

Our pseudocode instructions for input and output are expressed as follows:

Input: Get values for "variable", "variable", . . .

Output: Print the values of "variable", "variable", . . .

For example,

Get a value for r, the radius of the circle

When the algorithm reaches this input operation, it will wait until someone or something in the outside world provides it with a value for the variable r. (In a computer, this may be done by entering a value at the keyboard.) When the algorithm has received and stored a value for r, it will continue on to the next instruction.

Here is an example of an output operation:

Print the value of *Area*

Assuming that the algorithm has already computed the area of the circle, this instruction says to display that value to the "outside world." This display may be on a screen or printed on a printer. However, as we have said, that detail is not important right now.

Sometimes we use an output instruction to display a message rather than the desired results. This could happen, for example, if we were unable to complete a computation because of an error condition. In that case we might execute something like the following operation. (To avoid confusion, we will use 'single quotes' to enclose messages. This will distinguish them from such pseudocode constructs as "variable" and "arithmetic expression", which are enclosed in double quotes.)

Print the message 'Sorry, no answers were computed.'

Given the three sequential operations of computation, input, and output, we can now write some simple but useful algorithms. Figure 2.3 presents an algorithm to compute the average miles per gallon on a trip when given as input the number of gallons used and the starting and ending mileage readings on the odometer.

PRACTICE PROBLEMS

Write pseudocode versions of

1. An algorithm that gets three data values x, y, and z as input and outputs the *average* of those three values.

2. An algorithm that gets the radius r of a circle as input. Its output is both the circumference and the area of a circle of radius r.

3. An algorithm that gets the amount of electricity used in kilowatt-hours and the cost of electricity per kilowatt-hour. Its output is the total amount of the electric bill, including an 8% sales tax.

4. An algorithm that inputs your current credit card balance, the total dollar amount of new purchases, and the total dollar amount of all payments. The algorithm computes the new balance, which includes a 12% interest charge on any unpaid balance.

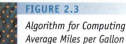

FIGURE 2.3

Algorithm for Computing Average Miles per Gallon

Average Miles per Gallon Algorithm (Version 1)

STEP	OPERATION
1	Get values for *gallons used, starting mileage, ending mileage*
2	Set value of *distance driven* to (*ending mileage – starting mileage*)
3	Set value of *average miles per gallon* to (*distance driven ÷ gallons used*)
4	Print the value of *average miles per gallon*
5	Stop

 2.2.3 *Conditional and Iterative Operations*

The average miles per gallon algorithm in Figure 2.3 performs a set of operations once and then stops. It does not have the ability to either select among alternative operations or perform a block of instructions more than once. A purely **sequential algorithm** of the type shown in Figure 2.3 is sometimes termed a **straight-line algorithm** because it executes its instructions in a straight line from top to bottom and then stops. Unfortunately, most real-world problems are not straight-line. They involve nonsequential operations such as branching and repetition.

To allow us to address these more interesting problems, our pseudocode needs two additional primitives to implement **conditional** and **iterative** operations. Together, these two types of operations are called **control operations**; they allow us to alter the normal sequential flow of control in an algorithm. As we saw in Chapter 1, control operations are an essential part of all but the very simplest of algorithms.

Conditional statements are the "question-asking" operations of an algorithm. They allow an algorithm to ask a question and, on the basis of the answer to that question, select the next operation to perform. There are a number of ways to phrase a question, but the most common conditional primitive is the *if/then/else*, which has the following format:

if "a true/false condition" is true then

first set of algorithmic operations

else (or otherwise)

second set of algorithmic operations

The meaning of this algorithmic primitive is as follows:

1. Evaluate the true/false condition on the first line to see whether it is true or false.

2. If the condition is true, then do the first set of algorithmic operations and skip the second set entirely.

3. If the condition is false, then skip the first set of operations and do the second set.

4. In either case, once the appropriate set of operations has been completed, continue execution of the algorithm with the operation that follows the if/then/else instruction.

Basically, the if/then/else operation allows you to select exactly one of two alternatives—either/or, this or that. We saw an example of this primitive in step 5 of the addition algorithm of Figure 1.2. (The statement has been reformatted slightly to highlight the two alternatives clearly, but it has not been changed.)

If ($c_i \geq 10$) then

    Set the value of c_i to ($c_i - 10$)

    Set the value of *carry* to 1

Else

    Set the value of *carry* to 0

The condition ($c_i \geq 10$) can be only true or false. If it is true, then there is a carry into the next column, and we must do the first set of instructions—subtracting 10 from c_i and setting *carry* to 1. If the condition is false, then there is no carry, and we skip over these two operations. Instead we perform the second block of operations, which simply sets the value of *carry* to 0.

Figure 2.4 shows another example of the if/then/else primitive. It extends the miles per gallon algorithm of Figure 2.3 to include a second line of output that says whether you are getting good gas mileage. Good gas mileage is defined to be a value for average miles per gallon greater than 25.0 mpg.

The last algorithmic primitive to be introduced allows us to implement a **loop**—the repetition of a block of instructions. The real power of a computer comes not from doing a calculation once but from doing it many, many times. If, for example, we needed to compute a single value of average miles per gallon, we would be foolish to convert an algorithm like Figure 2.4 into a computer program and execute it on a computer. That would take from a few minutes to an hour. It would be far faster to use a calculator, which could complete the job in a few seconds. However, if we needed to do the same computation 1,000,000 times, the power of a computer to repetitively execute a block of statements becomes quite apparent. If each computation of average miles per gallon takes 5 seconds on a hand calculator, then one million of them would require about 2 months, not allowing for such luxuries as sleeping and eating. Once the algorithm was developed and the program written, a computer could carry out that same task in less than 1 second!

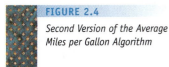

FIGURE 2.4

Second Version of the Average Miles per Gallon Algorithm

Average Miles per Gallon Algorithm (Version 2)

STEP	OPERATION
1	Get values for *gallons used, starting mileage, ending mileage*
2	Set value of *distance driven* to (*ending mileage – starting mileage*)
3	Set value of *average miles per gallon* to (*distance driven ÷ gallons used*)
4	Print the value of *average miles per gallon*
5	If *average miles per gallon* is greater than 25.0 then
6	Print the message 'You are getting good gas mileage'
	Else
7	Print the message 'You are NOT getting good gas mileage'
8	Stop

The first algorithmic primitive that we will use to express the idea of **iteration**, also called **looping**, is the **while** statement:

while ("a true/false condition") do step *i* to step *j*

step *i*:	operation
step *i* + 1:	operation
.	
.	
.	
step *j*:	operation

What this instruction means is that we initially evaluate the "true/false condition" to see if it is true or false. This condition is called the **continuation condition,** and its value is used to control execution of the loop. If the condition is true, we perform all operations from step *i* to step *j*, inclusive. This block of operations is called the **loop body.** (These operations should be indented so that it is clear to the reader of the algorithm which operations belong inside the loop.) When the entire loop body has finished executing, we again evaluate the continuation condition specified at the beginning of the loop. If it is still true, then the algorithm must execute the entire loop body, statements *i* through *j*, again. This looping process continues until the continuation condition evaluates to false, at which point execution of the loop body terminates and the algorithm proceeds to the statement immediately following the loop—step *j*+1 in the diagram shown above. If for some reason the continuation condition never becomes false, then we have violated one of the fundamental properties of an algorithm, and we have the error, first mentioned in Chapter 1, called an **infinite loop.**

Here is a simple example of a loop:

Step	Operation
1	Set the value of *count* to 1
2	While (*count* $\leq$ 100) do step 3 to step 5
3	Set *square* to (*count* x *count*)
4	Print the values of *count* and *square*
5	Add 1 to *count*

We initialize *count* to 1 in step 1 and get ready to begin the loop. We test whether (*count* $\leq$ 100), see that it is, and execute the loop body, which in this case includes the three statements in steps 3, 4, and 5. Those statements compute the value of *count* squared (step 3) and print out the value of both *count* and *square* (step 4). The last operation inside the loop body (step 5) adds 1 to *count* so that it now has the value 2. At this point we are at the end of the loop and must determine whether it should be executed again. We evaluate the continuation condition, (*count* $\leq$ 100), to see whether it is true or false. Because count is 2, the condition is true, and the algorithm must perform the loop body again. Looking at the entire loop, we can see that it will execute 100 times, producing the following output, which is a table of numbers and their squares from 1 to 100.

FIGURE 2.5

Third Version of the Average Miles per Gallon Algorithm

Average Miles per Gallon Algorithm (Version 3)

STEP	OPERATION
1	*response* = Yes
2	While (*response* = Yes) do steps 3 through 11
3	Get values for *gallons used, starting mileage, ending mileage*
4	Set value of *distance driven* to (*ending mileage – starting mileage*)
5	Set value of *average miles per gallon* to (*distance driven ÷ gallons used*)
6	Print the value of *average miles per gallon*
7	If average miles per gallon > 25.0 then
8	Print the message 'You are getting good gas mileage'
	Else
9	Print the message 'You are NOT getting good gas mileage'
10	Print the message 'Do you want to do this again? Enter Yes or No'
11	Get a new value for *response* from the user
12	Stop

1	1
2	4
3	9
.	
.	
.	
100	10,000

At the end of the 100th pass through the loop, the value of *count* will be incremented in step 5 to 101. When the continuation condition is evaluated, it will be false (because 101 is not less than or equal to 100), and the loop will terminate.

We can see additional examples of loop structures in steps 3 through 6 of Figure 1.2 and in steps 3 through 6 of Figure 1.3(a). Another example is shown in Figure 2.5, which is yet another variation of the average miles per gallon algorithm of Figures 2.3 and 2.4. In this modification, after finishing one computation, the algorithm asks the user whether he or she would like to do this calculation again. It waits until it gets a Yes or No response and repeats the entire algorithm until the response provided by the user is No. (Note that we must initialize the value of response to Yes, since the very first thing that the loop will do is test the value of this quantity.)

We conclude our discussion on control instructions by saying that there are many variations of this particular looping construct in addition to the While statement just described. For example, it is common to omit the line numbers from algorithms and simply execute them in order, from top to bottom. In that case we could use an End of Loop construct (or something similar) to mark the end of the loop rather than explicitly stating which steps are contained in the loop body. Using this approach, our loops would be written something like this:

```
While ("a true/false condition")
        operation
            .
            .
            .
        operation
End of the loop
```

In this case, the loop body is delimited not by explicit step numbers but by the two lines that read, "While . . ." and "End of the loop".

The type of loop described above is called a **pretest loop.** This means that the continuation condition is tested at the *beginning* of each pass through the loop, and therefore it is possible for the loop body never to be executed. (This would happen if the continuation condition were *initially* false.) Sometimes this can be inconvenient, as we saw in Figure 2.5. In that algorithm we ask the user if they want to solve the problem again, but we ask that at the very beginning of execution of the loop body. Therefore, we had to give the variable called *response* a "dummy" value of Yes so that the test would be meaningful when the loop was first entered.

A variation of the looping structure is the **posttest loop.** In this structure, we again use a true/false continuation condition to control execution of the loop. However, this time the test is done at the *end* of the loop body, not the beginning. The typical way to express this type of loop is using the **Do/While** primitive, which is usually written as follows:

```
Do
        operation
        operation
            .
            .
            .
While ("a true/false condition")
```

From Little Primitives Mighty Algorithms Do Grow

Although the set of algorithmic primitives shown in Figure 2.6 may seem quite "puny," it is anything but! In fact, an important theorem in theoretical computer science proves that the operations shown in Figure 2.6 are sufficient to represent *any* valid algorithm. No matter how complicated it may be, if a problem can be solved algorithmically, it can be expressed using only the sequential, conditional, and iterative operations just discussed. This includes not only the simple addition algorithm of Figure 1.2 but also the monstrously complex algorithms needed to fly NASA's space shuttles, run the international telephone switching system, and describe all the Internal Revenue Service's tax rules and regulations.

In many ways, building algorithms is akin to constructing essays or novels using only the 26 letters of the English alphabet, plus a few punctuation symbols. Expressive power does not always come from having a huge set of primitives. It can also arise from a small number of simple building blocks that can be combined in many interesting ways. This is the real secret of building algorithms.

This version of iteration first performs all the algorithmic operations contained in the loop body. Only then does it evaluate the true/false condition specified at the end of the loop. If this condition is false, the loop is terminated and execution continues with the operation following the loop. If it is true, then the entire loop body is executed again. Note that in the Do/While variation, the loop body must be executed at least once, while the While loop can execute 0, 1, or more times.

Figure 2.6 summarizes the algorithmic operations introduced in this section. These operations represent the **primitives** of our computing agent. These are the instructions that we assume our computing agent understands and is capable of executing without further explanation or simplification. In the next section we will use these operations to design algorithms that solve some interesting and important problems.

FIGURE 2.6

Summary of Pseudocode Language Instructions

COMPUTATION:

    Set the value of "variable" to "arithmetic expression"

INPUT/OUTPUT:

    Get a value for "variable", "variable". . .
    Print the value of "variable", "variable", . . .
    Print the message 'message'

CONDITIONAL:

    If "a true/false condition" is true then
        first set of algorithmic operations
    Else
        second set of algorithmic operations

ITERATIVE:

While ("a true/false condition") do step i through step j
    Step i: operation
      .
      .
      .
    Step j: operation

While ("a true/false condition") do
    operation
      .
      .
      .
    operation
End of the loop

Do
    operation
    operation
      .
      .
      .
While ("a true/false condition")

1. Write an if/then/else statement that sets the variable y to the value 1 if $x \geq 0$. If $x < 0$, then the statement should set y to the value 2. (Assume x already has a value.)

2. Write an algorithm that gets as input three data values x, y, and z and outputs the average of these values if the value of x is positive. If the value of x is either zero or negative, your algorithm should not compute the average but should print the error message 'Bad Data' instead.

3. Write an algorithm that inputs your current credit card balance, the total dollar amount of new purchases, and the total dollar amount of all payments. The algorithm computes the new balance, which this time includes an 8% interest charge on any unpaid balance below $100, 12% interest on any unpaid balance between $100 and $500, inclusive, and 16% on any unpaid balance above $500.

4. Write an algorithm that gets as input a single data value x and outputs the three values x^2, $\sin x$, and $1/x$. This process is repeated until the input value for x is equal to 999, at which time the algorithm terminates.

2.3   Examples of Algorithmic Problem Solving

 ### 2.3.1 Example 1: Looking, Looking, Looking

The first problem we will solve was mentioned in Chapter 1—searching for a particular person's name in a telephone book. This is just the type of simple and rather uninteresting repetitive mental task so well suited to computerization. (Many large telephone companies have implemented this application. Most of us have had the experience of dialing directory assistance and hearing the desired telephone number spoken in a computer-generated voice.)

Assume that we have a list of 10,000 names that we define as N_1, N_2, N_3, . . . , $N_{10,000}$, along with the 10,000 telephone numbers of those individuals, denoted as T_1, T_2, T_3, . . . , $T_{10,000}$. To simplify the problem, we will initially assume that all names in the book are unique and that the names need not be in alphabetical order. Essentially what we have described is a nonalphabetized telephone book of the following form:

Name	Telephone Number	
N_1	T_1	
N_2	T_2	
N_3	T_3	
.	.	} 10,000 (name, phone number) pairs
.	.	
.	.	
$N_{10,000}$	$T_{10,000}$	

Let's create an algorithm that allows us to input the name of any specific person, which we will denote as *NAME*. The algorithm will check to see if *NAME* matches any of the 10,000 names contained in our telephone book. If *NAME* matches the value N_j, where j is a value between 1 and 10,000, then the output of our algorithm will be the telephone number of that person: the value T_j. If *NAME* is not contained in our telephone book, then the output of our algorithm will be the message "I am sorry but this name is not in the directory." This type of lookup algorithm has many uses in addition to the telephone directory application described here. For example, it could be used to locate the zip code of a particular city, the seat number of a specific airline passenger, or the room number of a hotel guest.

The process of finding a solution to a given problem, such as this telephone book lookup, is called **algorithm discovery,** and it is the most challenging and creative part of the overall problem-solving process. Discovering a correct and efficient algorithm to solve a complicated problem can be difficult, and it can involve equal parts of intelligence, hard work, past experience, technical skill, and plain good luck. In this text we will develop solutions to a range of problems to give you experience in working with algorithms. Studying these examples, together with lots of practice, is by far the best way to learn how to do creative problem solving, just as experience and practice are the best ways to learn how to write essays, hit a golf ball, or repair cars.

For this particular problem, the names are not in alphabetical order, so there is no clever way to speed up the search. With a random collection of names, we cannot come up with any method that is more efficient than looking at all the names in the list, one at a time, until we either find what we are looking for or come to the end of the list. This rather simple and straightforward technique is called **sequential search,** and it is the standard algorithm for searching an *unordered* list of values. For example, this is how we would search a telephone book to see who lives at 123 Elm Street, because a telephone book is not sorted by address. It is also the way that we look through a shuffled deck of cards trying to locate one particular card. A first attempt at designing a sequential search algorithm to solve our search problem might look something like Figure 2.7.

The solution shown in Figure 2.7 is extremely long. At 66 lines per page, it would require about 150 pages to write out the 10,002 steps in the completed solution. The algorithm of Figure 2.7 would also be unnecessarily slow. If we are lucky enough to find *NAME* in the very first position of the telephone

FIGURE 2.7

First Attempt at Designing a Sequential Search Algorithm

STEP	OPERATION
1	Get values for *NAME*, N_1, ..., $N_{10,000}$, and T_1, ..., $T_{10,000}$
2	If *NAME* = N_1 then print the value of T_1
3	If *NAME* = N_2 then print the value of T_2
4	If *NAME* = N_3 then print the value of T_3
.	.
.	.
.	.
10,000	If *NAME* = $N_{9,999}$ then print the value of $T_{9,999}$
10,001	If *NAME* = $N_{10,000}$ then print the value of $T_{10,000}$
10,002	Stop

book, N_1, then we get the answer T_1 almost immediately at step 2. However, the algorithm does not stop at that point. Instead, even though it has already found the correct answer, it foolishly asks 9,999 more questions looking for *NAME* in positions $N_2, \ldots, N_{10,000}$. Of course, humans have enough "common sense" to know that when they find the answer they are searching for, they can stop. However, we cannot (and should not) assume common sense in a computer system. On the contrary, a computer will mechanically execute the entire algorithm from the first step to the last.

Not only is the algorithm excessively long and highly inefficient, it is also wrong. If the desired *NAME* is not in the list, this algorithm will simply stop (at step 10,002) rather than provide the desired result, a message that the name you requested is not in the directory. An algorithm is deemed correct only when it produces the correct result for *all* possible cases.

The problem with the first attempt shown in Figure 2.7 is that we are not using the powerful algorithmic concept called **iteration.** Instead of writing an instruction 10,000 separate times, it is far better to write it only once and indicate that it is to be repetitively *executed* 10,000 times, or however many times it takes to obtain the answer. As we noted in the previous section, much of the power of a computer comes from being able to perform a **loop**— the repetitive execution of a block of statements a large number of times. Virtually every algorithm developed in this text contains at least one loop and usually many. (This is the difference between the two shampooing algorithms shown in Figures 1.3(a) and (b). The algorithm in the former contains a loop; that in the latter does not.)

The algorithm in Figure 2.8 shows how we might write a loop to implement the sequential search technique. It uses a variable called i as an **index,** or **pointer,** into the list of all names. That is, N_i refers to the ith name in the list. The algorithm then repeatedly executes a group of statements using different values of i. The variable i can be thought of as a "moving finger" scanning the list of names and pointing to the one on which we are currently working.

The first time through the loop, the value of the index i is 1, so the algorithm checks to see whether *NAME* is equal to N_1, the first name on the list. If it is, then the algorithm writes out the result and sets *Found* to YES, which will cause the loop in steps 4 through 7 to terminate. If it is not the desired *NAME*, then i is incremented by 1 (in step 7) so that it now has the value 2, and the loop is executed again. The algorithm now checks (in step 4) to see whether *NAME* is equal to N_2, the second name on the list. In this way, the algorithm uses the single conditional statement "If *NAME* is equal to the ith

FIGURE 2.8

Second Attempt at Designing a Sequential Search Algorithm

STEP	OPERATION
1	Get values for *NAME*, $N_1, \ldots, N_{10,000}$, and $T_1, \ldots, T_{10,000}$
2	Set the value of i to 1 and set the value of *Found* to NO
3	While (*Found* = NO) do steps 4 through 7
4	If *NAME* is equal to the ith name on the list N_i then
5	Print the telephone number of that person, T_i
6	Set the value of *Found* to YES
	Else (*NAME* is not equal to N_i)
7	Add 1 to the value of i
8	Stop

name on the list . . ." to check up to 10,000 names. It executes that one line over and over, each time with a different value of i. This is the advantage of using iteration.

However, the attempt shown in Figure 2.8 is not yet a complete and correct algorithm because it still does not work correctly when the desired *NAME* does not appear anywhere on the list. This final problem can be solved by terminating the loop when we either find the desired name or we reach the end of the list. We can determine exactly what happened by checking the value of *Found* when the loop terminates. If the value of *Found* is NO, then the loop terminated because the index i exceeded 10,000, and we searched the entire list without finding the desired *NAME*. The algorithm should then produce the desired error message.

An iterative solution to the sequential search algorithm that incorporates this feature is shown in Figure 2.9. The sequential search algorithm shown in Figure 2.9 is a correct solution to our telephone book look-up problem. It meets all the requirements listed in Section 1.3.1: It is well ordered, each of the operations is clearly defined and effectively computable, and it is guaranteed to halt with the desired result after a finite number of operations. (In Exercise 12 at the end of this chapter you are asked to develop a formal argument that proves that this algorithm will always halt.) Furthermore, this algorithm requires writing out only 10 steps to produce the answer, rather than the 10,002 steps of the first attempt in Figure 2.7. As you can see, not all algorithms are created equal.

Looking again at the algorithm in Figure 2.9, our first thought may be that this is not at all how people search a telephone book by hand. When looking for a particular telephone number, we would never turn to page 1, column 1, and scan all names beginning with Aardvark, Alan—unless we happened to live in a *very* small community. Certainly, the New York City telephone company would not be satisfied with the performance of a directory search algorithm that always began on page 1 of its 2,000-page telephone book.

The reason we solved the problem in this fashion is that our telephone book was not alphabetized. Given this lack of organization, we really had no choice in the design of a search algorithm. However, in real life we can do much better than sequential search, because telephone books *are* alphabetized, and we can exploit this fact during the search process. For example, we know

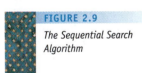

FIGURE 2.9

The Sequential Search Algorithm

Sequential Search Algorithm

STEP	OPERATION
1	Get values for *NAME*, $N_1, \ldots, N_{10,000}$, and $T_1, \ldots, T_{10,000}$
2	Set the value of i to 1 and set the value of *Found* to NO
3	While both (*Found* = NO) and ($i \leq 10,000$) do steps 4 through 7
4	If *NAME* is equal to the ith name on the list N_i then
5	Print the telephone number of that person, T_i
6	Set the value of *Found* to YES
	Else (*NAME* is not equal to N_i)
7	Add 1 to the value of i
8	If (*Found* = NO) then
9	Print the message 'Sorry, this name is not in the directory'
10	Stop

that *M* is about halfway through the alphabet, so when looking for the name Samuel Miller, we would open the telephone book somewhere in the middle rather than to the first page. We would see exactly where we were by looking at the first letter of the names on the current page, and then we would move forward or backward toward names beginning with *M*. This approach allows us to find the desired name much more quickly than searching sequentially beginning with the letter *A*.

This use of different search techniques points out a very important concept in the design of algorithms:

The selection of an algorithm to solve a problem is greatly influenced by the way the data for that problem are organized.

An algorithm is a method for processing some data to produce a result, and the way the data are organized has an enormous influence both on the algorithm we select and on how speedily that algorithm can produce the desired result.

In Chapter 3 we will expand on the concept of the efficiency and goodness of algorithms, and we will present an algorithm for searching *alphabetized* telephone books that is far superior to the one shown in Figure 2.9.

LABORATORY EXPERIENCE 2

This laboratory experience will introduce the concept of *algorithm animation*, in which you can observe an algorithm being executed and actually watch as data values are transformed into final results. "Bringing an algorithm to life" in this way can help greatly in understanding what it does and how it works. The first animation that you will work with is the sequential search algorithm shown in Figure 2.9.

 ### 2.3.2 *Example 2: Big, Bigger, Biggest*

The second algorithm we will develop is similar to the sequential search in Figure 2.9 in that it also searches a list of values. However, this time the algorithm will be searching not for a particular value supplied by the user but for the numerically largest value in a list of numbers. This type of "find largest" algorithm could be used to answer a number of important questions. (With only a single trivial change, the same algorithm also finds the smallest value, so a better name for it might be "find extreme values.") For example, given a list of examinations, which student received the highest (or lowest) score? Given a list of annual salaries, which employee earns the most (or least) money? Given a list of grocery prices from different stores, where should I shop to find the lowest price? All these questions could be answered by executing the algorithm that we will design.

In addition to being important in its own right, this algorithm can also be used as a "building block" for the construction of solutions to other problems. For example, the Find Largest algorithm that we will develop could be used to implement a *sorting algorithm* that puts an unordered list of numbers in ascending order. (Find and remove the largest item in list A and move it to the last position of list B. Now repeat these operations, each time moving the largest remaining number in A to the last unfilled slot of list B. We will develop and write this algorithm in Chapter 3.)

This concept of a "building-block" is a very important idea. The examples in this chapter may lead you to believe that every algorithm you write must be built from only the most elementary and basic of primitives—the sequential, conditional, and iterative operations shown in Figure 2.6. That is not always the case. Once an algorithm has been developed, it may itself be used in the construction of other, more complex algorithms, just as we will use "find largest" in the design of a sorting algorithm. This is similar to what a builder does when constructing a home from prefabricated units rather than bricks and boards. Our problem-solving task need not always begin at the beginning but can instead build upon ideas and results that have come before. Every algorithm that we create becomes, in a sense, a primitive operation of our computing agent and can be used as part of the solution to other problems. That is why a collection of useful algorithms, called a **library,** is such an important tool in algorithm design and development.

Formally, the problem we will be solving in this section can be defined as follows:

> Given a value $n \geq 1$ and a list containing exactly n unique numbers called $A_1, A_2, \ldots, A_n$, find and print out both the largest value in the list and the position in the list where that largest value occurred.

For example, if our list contained the five values

$$19, 41, 12, 63, 22 \quad (n = 5)$$

then our algorithm should locate the largest value, 63, and say that it occurred in the fourth position of the list. (*Note:* Our definition of the problem states that all numbers in the list are unique, so there can be only a single occurrence of the largest number. Exercise 15 at the end of the chapter asks how our algorithm would behave if the numbers in the list were not unique and the largest number could occur two or more times.)

When faced with a problem statement like the one just given, how do we go about creating a solution? What are the strategies that we can employ to discover a correct and efficient answer to the problem? One way is to ask ourselves how the same problem might be solved by hand. If we can understand and explain how we would approach the problem manually, we might be able to express that solution as a formal algorithm.

For example, what would we do if we were given a pile of papers each of which contained a single number and were asked to locate the largest number in the pile? (The following diagrams assume the papers contain the five values 19, 41, 12, 63, and 22.)

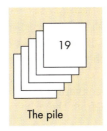

The pile

We might start off by saying that the first number in the pile (the top one) is the largest one that we have seen so far and then putting it off to the side where we are keeping the largest value.

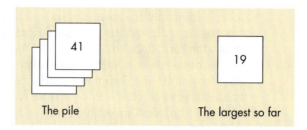

Now we might compare the top number in the pile with the one that we have called the largest one so far. In this case, the top number in the pile, 41, is larger than our current largest so far, 19, so we would want to make it the new largest so far. To do this, we would throw the value 19 into the wastebasket (or, better yet, into the recycle bin) and put the number 41 off to the side, because it is the largest value encountered so far.

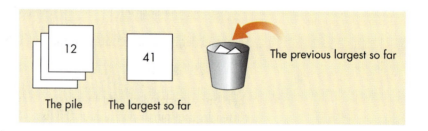

We now repeat this comparison operation, asking whether the number on top of the pile is larger than the largest value seen so far, now 41. This time the value on top of the pile, 12, is not larger, so we do not want to save it. We simply throw it away and move on to the next number in the pile.

This compare-and-save-or-discard process continues until our original pile of numbers is empty, at which time the largest so far will be the largest value in the entire list.

Let's see how we can convert this informal, pictorial solution into a formal algorithm that is built from the primitive operations shown in Figure 2.6.

We certainly cannot begin to search a list for a largest value until we have a list to search. Therefore, our first operation must be to get a value for n, the size of the list, followed by values for the n-element list $A_1, A_2, \ldots, A_n$. This can be done using our input primitive:

Get a value for n, the size of the list

Get values for $A_1, A_2, \ldots, A_n$, the list to be searched

Now that we have the data, we can begin to implement a solution.

Our informal description of the algorithm stated that we should begin by calling the first item in the list, A_1, the largest value so far. (We know that this operation is meaningful since we stated that the list must always have at least one element.) We can express this formally as

Set the value of *largest so far* to A_1

Our solution must also determine where that largest value occurred. To remember this value, let's create a variable called *location* to keep track of the position in the list where the largest value occurred. Because we have initialized *largest so far* to the first element in the list, we should initialize *location* to 1.

Set the value of *location* to 1

We are now ready to begin looking through the remaining items in list A to find the largest one. However, if we write something like the following instruction:

If the second item in the list is greater than *largest so far* then . . .

we will have made exactly the same mistake that occurred in the initial version of the sequential search algorithm shown in Figure 2.7. This instruction explicitly checks only the second item of the list. We would need to rewrite that statement to check the third item, the fourth item, and so on. Again, we are failing to use the idea of *iteration*, where we repetitively execute a loop as many times as it takes to produce the desired result.

To solve this problem let's use the same technique used in the sequential search algorithm. Let's not talk about the second, third, fourth, . . . item in the list but about the ith item in the list, where i is a variable that can take on different values during the execution of the algorithm. Using this idea, a statement such as

If $A_i > $ *largest so far* then . . .

can be executed with different values for i. This will allow us to check all n values in the list with a single statement. Initially, i should be given the value 2, because the first item in the list was automatically set to the largest value. Therefore, we want to begin our search with the second item in the list.

.
.
.

Set the value of i to 2
.
.
.

If A_i > *largest so far* then . . .

What operations should appear after the word *then*? When we find a new largest value, what do we want to do? A check of our earlier diagrams shows that we must reset the values of both *largest so far* and *location*.

If A_i > *largest so far* then
> Set *largest so far* to A_i
>
> Set *location* to i

If A_i is not larger than *largest so far*, then we do not want to do anything. To indicate this, our if/then instruction could include an else clause that looks something like

Else
> Don't do anything at all to *largest so far* and *location*

This is certainly correct, but instructions that tell us not to do anything are usually omitted from an algorithm because they do not carry any meaningful information.

Regardless of whether we do or do not reset the values of *largest so far* and *location*, we need to move on to the next item in the list. Our algorithm refers to A_i, the ith item in the list. So we can move to the next item by simply adding 1 to the value of i and repeating the if/then statement. The outline of this iteration can be sketched as follows:

> If A_i > *largest so far* then
> > Set *largest so far* to A_i
> >
> > Set *location* to i
>
> Add 1 to the value of i
> .
> .
> .

However, we do not want to repeat the loop forever. (Remember that one of the properties of an algorithm is that it must eventually halt.) What stops this iterative process? When do we display our answer and terminate execution?

The conditional operation "If A_i > *largest so far* then . . ." is meaningful only if A_i represents an actual element of list A. Because A contains n elements numbered 1 to n, the value of i must be in the range 1 to n. If $i > n$, then the loop has searched the entire list, and it is finished. The algorithm can now print the values of both *largest so far* and *location*. Using our looping primitive, we can describe this iteration as follows:

> While ($i \leq n$) do
>> If A_i > *largest so far* then
>>> Set *largest so far* to A_i
>>> Set *location* to i
>> Add 1 to the value of i
> End of the loop

We have now developed all the pieces of the algorithm and can finally put them together. Figure 2.10 shows the completed Find Largest algorithm. Figure 2.10 leaves out the numbering of the individual steps that was done in all previous examples. This omission is common, especially as algorithms get larger and more complex.

FIGURE 2.10

Algorithm to Find the Largest Value in a List

Find Largest Algorithm

Get a value for *n*, the size of the list
Get values for $A_1, A_2, \ldots, A_n$, the list to be searched
Set the value of *largest so far* to A_1
Set the value of *location* to 1
Set the value of *i* to 2
While ($i \leq n$) do
    If A_i > *largest so far* then
        Set *largest so far* to A_i
        Set *location* to *i*
    Add 1 to the value of *i*
End of the loop
Print out the values of *largest so far* and *location*
Stop

LABORATORY EXPERIENCE 3

This laboratory experience presents an animation of the Find Largest algorithm shown in Figure 2.10. Like the previous laboratory experience, it is intended to give you a deeper understanding of how this algorithm works by allowing you to visually observe its behavior during execution.

PRACTICE PROBLEMS

1. Modify the algorithm of Figure 2.10 so that it finds the smallest value in a list rather than the largest. Describe exactly what changes were necessary.

2. Describe exactly what would happen to the algorithm in Figure 2.10 if you tried to apply it to an empty list of length $n = 0$. Describe exactly how you could fix this problem.

3. Describe exactly what happens to the algorithm in Figure 2.10 when it is presented with a list with exactly one item, i.e., $n = 1$.

 ### 2.3.3 EXAMPLE 3: MEETING YOUR MATCH

The last algorithm to be developed in this chapter solves a common problem in computer science called **pattern matching.** As an example of this application, imagine that you have a collection of Civil War data files that you wish to use as resource material for an article on Abraham Lincoln. Your first step would probably be to search these files to locate every occurrence of the text patterns "Abraham Lincoln," "A. Lincoln," and "Lincoln." The process of searching for a special pattern of symbols within a larger collection of information is called pattern matching. Most good word processors provide this service as a menu item called FIND or something similar. Furthermore, most Web search engines work by trying to match your search keys to the keywords that appear on a Web page.

Pattern matching need not be done with only characters and textual information. The same character-based pattern-matching techniques that we will be discussing can be applied to almost any kind of information, including graphics, sound, and pictures. For example, an important medical application of pattern matching is to input an X-ray or CT scan image into a computer and then have the computer search for special patterns, such as dark spots, which represent conditions that should be brought to the attention of a physician. This can help speed up the interpretation of X-rays and avoid the problem of human error caused by fatigue or oversight. (Computers do not get tired or bored!)

One of the most interesting and exciting uses of pattern matching is to assist microbiologists and geneticists in studying and mapping the *human genome*, the basis for all human life. The human genome is composed of a sequence of approximately 3.5 billion *nucleotides*, each of which can be one of only four different chemical compounds. The names of these compounds are rather complex (adenine, cytosine, thymine, guanine), so these nucleotides are usually referred to by the first letter of their chemical names: A, C, T, and G. Thus, the basis for our existence turns out to be quite similar to a very large "text file" written in a four-letter alphabet.

. . . T C G G A C T A A C A T C G G G A T C G A G A T G . . .

Sequences of these nucleotides are called *genes*. There are about 25,000 genes in the human genome, and they determine virtually all of our physical characteristics—sex, race, eye color, hair color, and height, to name just a few.

Genes are also an important factor in the occurrence of certain diseases. When a nucleotide is either missing or changed, it can result in one of a number of extremely serious genetic disorders, such as Down syndrome or Tay-Sachs disease. To help find a cure for these diseases, researchers are attempting to map the entire human genome—to locate individual genes that when exhibiting a certain defect cause a specific malady. A gene is typically composed of thousands of nucleotides, and researchers generally do not know the entire sequence. However, they may know what a small portion of the gene—say, a few hundred nucleotides—looks like. Therefore, to search for one particular gene, they must match the sequence of nucleotides that they do know, called a *probe*, against the entire 3.5 billion-element genome to locate every occurrence of that probe. From this matching information, researchers hope to be able to isolate specific genes. For example,

Genome:	*...T C A G G C T A A T C G T A G G...*
Probe:	*T A A T C* a match

When a match is found, researchers can examine the nucleotides located before and after the probe to see whether they have located the desired gene and, if so, to see whether the gene is defective. If it is defective, physicians hope someday to be able to "clip out" the bad sequence and insert in its place a correct sequence.

We have discussed this application at some length in order to dispel the notion that algorithms such as sequential search (Figure 2.9), Find Largest (Figure 2.10), and pattern matching are nothing more than academic exercises—useless algorithms that serve as examples for introductory classes but have absolutely no role to play in solving real-world problems. That is not true. The algorithms that we have presented (or will present) *are* important, either in their own right or as building blocks for algorithms to be used by physical scientists, mathematicians, engineers, and social scientists.

Let's formally define the pattern-matching problem as follows:

You will be given some text composed of n characters that will be referred to as $T_1 T_2 \ldots T_n$. You will also be given a *pattern* of m characters, $m \le n$, that will be represented as $P_1 P_2 \ldots P_m$. The algorithm must locate every occurrence of the pattern within the text. The output of the algorithm is the location in the text where each match occurred. For this problem, the location of a match is defined to be the index position in the text where the match begins.

For example, if our text is the phrase "to be or not to be, that is the question" and the pattern for which we are searching is the word *to*, then our algorithm should produce the following output:

Text:	**to** *be or not to be, that is the question*
Pattern:	to
Output:	*Match starting at position 1.*

Text:	*to be or not* **to** *be, that is the question*
Pattern:	to
Output:	*Match starting at position 14. (The t is in position 14, including blanks.)*

The pattern-matching algorithm that we will implement is composed of two parts. In the first part, the pattern is aligned under a specific position of the text, and the algorithm sees whether there is a match at that given position. The second part of the algorithm "slides" the entire pattern ahead one character position. Assuming that we have not gone beyond the end of the text, the algorithm returns to the first part to check for a match at this new position. Pictorially, this algorithm can be represented as follows:

Repeat the following two steps.

STEP 1: The matching process: $T_1\ T_2\ T_3\ T_4\ T_5\ \ldots$
$P_1\ P_2\ P_3$

STEP 2: The slide forward: $T_1\ T_2\ T_3\ T_4\ T_5\ \ldots$
1-character slide → $P_1\ P_2\ P_3$

The algorithm involves repetition of these two steps beginning at position 1 of the text and continuing until the pattern has slid off the right-hand end of the text.

A first draft of an algorithm that implements these ideas is shown in Figure 2.11. Looking at Figure 2.11, we see that not all of the operations are expressed in terms of the basic algorithmic primitives of Figure 2.6. Whereas statements like "Set k, the starting location for the attempted match, to 1" and "Print the value of k, the starting location of the match" are just fine, the instruction that says, "Attempt to match every character in the pattern beginning at position k of the text" as well as the one that says, "Keep going until we have fallen off the end of the text" are certainly not primitives. On the contrary, they are both high-level operations that, if written out using only the operations in Figure 2.6, would expand into many instructions.

Is it okay to use high-level statements like this in our algorithm? Wouldn't their use violate the requirement stated in Chapter 1 that algorithms be constructed only from unambiguous operations that can be directly executed by our computing agent?

The answer is that it is perfectly acceptable, and even quite useful, to use high-level statements like this during the *initial phase* of the algorithm design process. When starting to design an algorithm, we may not want to think only in terms of elementary operations such as input, computation, output,

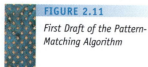

FIGURE 2.11

First Draft of the Pattern-Matching Algorithm

Get values for n and m, the size of the text and the pattern, respectively
Get values for both the text $T_1\ T_2 \ldots T_n$ and the pattern $P_1\ P_2 \ldots P_m$
Set k, the starting location for the attempted match, to 1
Keep going until we have fallen off the end of the text
    Attempt to match every character in the pattern beginning at
        position k of the text (this is step 1 from above)
    If there was a match then
        Print the value of k, the starting location of the match
    Add 1 to k, which slides the pattern forward one position (this is step 2)
End of the loop
Stop

conditional, and iteration. Instead, we may first want to express our proposed solution in terms of high-level and broadly defined operations that may represent dozens or even hundreds of primitive instructions. Here are some examples of these higher-level constructs:

- Sort the entire list into ascending order.
- Attempt to match the entire pattern against the text.
- Find a root of the equation.

Using instructions like these in an algorithm allows us temporarily to postpone worrying about how to implement that operation and lets us focus instead on other aspects of the problem. Eventually, we will come back to these statements and express them in terms of our available primitives, but we can do this at our convenience.

The use of high-level instructions during the design process is an example of one of the most important intellectual tools in computer science—the concept of **abstraction.** Abstraction means the ability to separate the high-level view of an entity or an operation from the low-level details of its implementation. It is abstraction that allows us to understand and intellectually manage any large, complex system, whether it is a mammoth corporation, a complex piece of machinery, or an intricate and very detailed algorithm. For example, the president of General Motors views the company in terms of its major corporate divisions and very high-level policy issues, not in terms of every worker, every supplier, and every car. Attempting to manage the company at that level of detail would drown him or her in a sea of detail.

In computer science we use abstraction a great deal because of the complexity of hardware and software. For example, abstraction allows us to view the hardware component called "memory" as a single, indivisible high-level entity without having to be aware of the billions of electronic devices that go into constructing a memory unit. (Chapter 4 examines how computer memories are built, and it makes extensive use of abstraction.) In the areas of algorithm design and software development, we use abstraction whenever we think of an operation at a high level, temporarily neglecting how we might actually implement that operation. This allows us to decide which details to address now and which to postpone. Viewing an operation at a high level of abstraction and fleshing out the details of its implementation at a later time constitute an important computer science problem-solving strategy called **top-down design.**

Ultimately, however, we have to describe how each of these high-level abstractions can be represented using the available algorithmic primitives. Let's do that now. The fifth line of the first draft of the pattern-matching algorithm shown in Figure 2.11 reads

Attempt to match every character in the pattern beginning at position k of the text.

When this statement is reached, the pattern is aligned under the text beginning with the kth character. Pictorially, we are in the following situation:

Text: $T_1 T_2 T_3 \cdots$ $T_k T_{k+1} T_{k+2} \cdots T_{k+(m-1)} \cdots$

Pattern: $P_1 P_2 \ P_3 \cdots \ P_m$

The algorithm must now perform the following comparisons:

Compare P_1 to T_k

Compare P_2 to T_{k+1}

Compare P_3 to T_{k+2}

.

.

.

Compare P_m to $T_{k+(m-1)}$

If the members of every single one of these pairs are equal, then there is a match. However, if even one pair is not equal, then there is not a match, and the algorithm can immediately cease all further comparisons at this location. Thus we must construct a loop that will execute until one of two things happens—it has either completed m successful comparisons (i.e., until we have matched the entire pattern) or until it has detected a mismatch. When either of these conditions occurs we stop; however, if both are still true, we must keep going. Algorithmically, this iteration can be expressed in the following way. (Remember that k is the starting location in the text where we are attempting to find a match.)

Set the value of i to 1

Set the value of *Mismatch* to NO

While both ($i \leq m$) and (*Mismatch* = NO)

    If $P_i \neq T_{k+(i-1)}$ then

        Set *Mismatch* to YES

    Else

        Increment i by 1 (to move to the next character)

End of the loop

When the loop has finished, we can determine whether there has been a match by examining the current value of the variable *Mismatch*. If *Mismatch* is YES, then there was not a match because at least one of the characters was out of place. If *Mismatch* is NO, then every character in the pattern matched its corresponding character in the text, and there is a match.

If *Mismatch* = NO then

    Print the message 'There is a match at position'

    Print the value of k

Regardless of whether or not there was a match at position k, we must add 1 to k in order to begin searching for a match at the next position. This is the "sliding forward" step diagrammed earlier.

The final high-level statement in Figure 2.11 that needs to be expanded is the loop on line 4.

Keep going until we have fallen off the end of the text

What does it mean to "fall off the end of the text"? Where is the last possible place that a match can occur? To answer these questions, let's draw a diagram in which the last character of the pattern, P_m, lines up directly under T_n, the last character of the text.

Text: $\quad T_1 \; T_2 \; T_3 \; \ldots \; T_{n-m+1} \; \cdots \; T_{n-2} \quad T_{n-1} \quad T_n$

Pattern: $\qquad\qquad\qquad\qquad\quad P_1 \quad \cdots \quad P_{m-2} \quad P_{m-1} \quad P_m$

We can determine from this diagram that the last possible place that a match could possibly occur is when the first character of the pattern is aligned under the character at position T_{n-m+1} of the text. We can see that by noting that P_m is aligned under T_n, P_{m-1} is under T_{n-1}, P_{m-2} is aligned under T_{n-2}, etc. Thus, P_1, which can be written as $P_{m-(m-1)}$, will be aligned under $T_{n-(m-1)}$, which is T_{n-m+1}. If we tried to slide the pattern forward any further, we would truly "fall off" the end of the right-hand end of the text. Therefore, our loop must terminate when k, the starting point for the match, strictly exceeds the value of $n-m+1$. We can express this as follows:

While $(k \leq (n - m+1))$ do

Again, we have all the pieces of our algorithm in place. We have expressed every statement in Figure 2.11 in terms of our basic algorithmic primitives and are ready to put it all together. The final draft of the pattern-matching algorithm is shown in Figure 2.12.

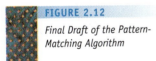

FIGURE 2.12

Final Draft of the Pattern-Matching Algorithm

Pattern-Matching Algorithm

Get values for n and m, the size of the text and the pattern, respectively
Get values for both the text $T_1 \; T_2 \ldots T_n$ and the pattern $P_1 \; P_2 \ldots P_m$
Set k, the starting location for the attempted match, to 1
While $(k \leq (n - m +1))$ do
    Set the value of i to 1
    Set the value of *Mismatch* to NO
    While both $(i \leq m)$ and (*Mismatch* = NO) do
      If $P_i \neq T_{k+(i-1)}$ then
        Set *Mismatch* to YES
      Else
        Increment i by 1 (to move to the next character)
    End of the loop
    If *Mismatch* = NO then
      Print the message 'There is a match at position'
      Print the value of k
    Increment k by 1
End of the loop
Stop, we are finished

1. Consider the following "telephone book."

Name	Number
Smith	555-1212
Jones	834-6543
Adams	921-5281
Doe	327-8900

   Trace the sequential search algorithm of Figure 2.9 using each of the following *NAME*s and show the output produced.

   a. Adams

   b. Schneider

2. Consider the following list of seven data values.

   22, 18, 23, 17, 25, 30, 2

   Trace the Find Largest algorithm of Figure 2.10 and show the output produced.

3. Consider the following text.

   Text: A man and a woman

   Trace the pattern-matching algorithm of Figure 2.12 using the 2-character pattern 'an' and show the output produced.

4. Explain exactly what would happen to the algorithm of Figure 2.12 if m, the length of the pattern, were greater than n, the length of the text.

2.4 Conclusion

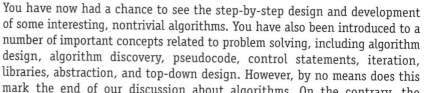

You have now had a chance to see the step-by-step design and development of some interesting, nontrivial algorithms. You have also been introduced to a number of important concepts related to problem solving, including algorithm design, algorithm discovery, pseudocode, control statements, iteration, libraries, abstraction, and top-down design. However, by no means does this mark the end of our discussion about algorithms. On the contrary, the development of a correct solution to a problem marks only the first step in creating a useful solution.

Designing a technically correct algorithm to solve a given problem is only part of what computer scientists do. They also must ensure that they have created an *efficient* algorithm that generates results quickly enough for its intended users. Chapter 1 described a brute force chess algorithm that would, at least theoretically, play perfect chess but that would be of no earthly use to anyone because it would take centuries to make its first move. Similarly, a directory assistance program that takes 10 minutes to locate a telephone number would be of little or no use. A caller would surely hang up long before the answer was found. This practical concern for efficiency and usefulness, in addition to correctness, is one of the hallmarks of computer science.

Therefore, after developing a correct algorithm, we must analyze it thoroughly and study its efficiency properties and operating characteristics. We must ask ourselves how quickly it will give us the desired results and whether it is better than other algorithms that solve the same problem. This analysis, which is the central topic of the next chapter, enables us to state that we have created not only a correct algorithm but an elegant, efficient, and useful one as well.

1. Write pseudocode instructions to carry out each of the following computational operations.

   a. Determine the area of a triangle given values for the base b and the height h.

   b. Compute the interest earned in 1 year given the starting account balance B and the annual interest rate I and assuming simple interest, that is, no compounding. Also determine the final balance at the end of the year.

   c. Determine the flying time between two cities given the mileage M between them and the average speed of the airplane.

2. Using only the sequential operations described in Section 2.2.2, write an algorithm that gets values for the starting account balance B, annual interest rate I, and annual service charge S. Your algorithm should output the amount of interest earned during the year and the final account balance at the end of the year. Assume that interest is compounded monthly and the service charge is deducted once, at the end of the year.

3. Using only the sequential operations described in Section 2.2.2, write an algorithm that inputs four numbers corresponding to scores received on three semester tests and a final examination. Your algorithm should compute and display the average of all four tests, weighting the final exam twice as heavily as a regular test.

4. Write an algorithm that inputs the length and width of a carpet (in feet) as well as the price in dollars (per square yard). The algorithm prints out the total cost of the carpeting, including a 6% sales tax.

5. Write an if/then/else primitive to do each of the following operations.

   a. Compute and display the value $x \div y$ if the value of y is not 0. If y does have the value 0, then display the message 'Unable to perform the division.'

   b. Compute the area and circumference of a circle given the radius r if the radius is greater than or equal to 1.0; otherwise, you should compute only the circumference.

6. Modify the algorithm of Exercise 2 to include the annual service charge only if the starting account balance at the beginning of the year is less than $1,000. If it is greater than or equal to $1,000, then no annual service charge is included.

7. Write an algorithm that uses a loop (1) to read in 10 pairs of numbers, where each pair represents the score of a football game with the Computer State University (CSU) score listed first, and (2) for each pair of numbers, determine whether CSU won or lost. After reading in

these 10 pairs of values, print out the won/lost/tie record of CSU. In addition, if this record is a perfect 10-0, then print out the message 'Congratulations on your undefeated season.'

8. Modify the test-averaging algorithm of Exercise 3 so that it inputs 15 test scores rather than 4. There are 14 regular tests and a final examination, which again counts twice as much as a regular test. Use a loop to input and sum the scores.

9. Modify the carpet computation algorithm of Exercise 4 so that after finishing the computation of one carpet, it starts on the computation of the next. This iterative process is repeated until we have located a carpet whose total cost is less than $1,000.

10. Write an algorithm that is given your electric meter readings (in kilowatt-hours) at the beginning and end of each month of the year. The algorithm determines your annual cost of electricity on the basis of a charge of 6 cents per kilowatt-hour for the first 1,000 kilowatt-hours of each month and 8 cents per kilowatt-hour beyond 1,000. After printing out your total annual charge, the algorithm also determines whether you used less than 500 kilowatt-hours for the entire year and, if so, prints out a message thanking you for conserving electricity.

11. Develop an algorithm to compute gross pay. The inputs to your algorithm will be the hours worked per week and the hourly pay rate. The rule for determining gross pay is to pay the regular pay rate for all hours worked up to 40, time-and-a-half for all hours over 40 up to 54, and double time for all hours over 54. Compute and display the value for gross pay using this rule. After displaying one value, ask the user whether he or she wants to do another computation. Repeat the entire set of operations until the user says no.

12. Develop a formal argument that "proves" that the sequential search algorithm shown in Figure 2.9 cannot have an infinite loop; that is, prove that it will always stop after a finite number of operations.

13. Modify the sequential search algorithm of Figure 2.9 so that it works correctly even if the names in the directory are not unique, that is, if the desired name may occur more than once. Your modified algorithm should find *every* occurrence of *NAME* in the directory and print out the telephone number corresponding to every match. In addition, after all the numbers have been displayed, your algorithm should print out how many occurrences of *NAME* were located. For example, if *NAME* occurred three times, the output of the algorithm might look something like this:

528-5638

922-7874

488-2020

A total of three occurrences were located.

14. Use the Find Largest algorithm of Figure 2.10 to help you develop an algorithm to find the median value in a list containing N unique numbers. The median of N numbers is defined as the value in the list in which approximately half the values are larger than it and half the values are smaller than it. For example, consider the following list of seven numbers.

26, 50, 83, 44, 91, 20, 55

The median value is 50 because three values (20, 26, and 44) are smaller and three values (55, 83, and 91) are larger. If N is an even value, then the number of values larger than the median will be one greater than the number of values smaller than the median.

15. With regard to the Find Largest algorithm of Figure 2.10, if the numbers in our list were not unique and therefore the largest number could occur more than once, would the algorithm find the first occurrence? The last occurrence? Every occurrence? Explain precisely how this algorithm would behave when presented with this new condition.

16. On the sixth line of the Find Largest algorithm of Figure 2.10 there is an instruction that reads,

While ($i \leq n$) do

Explain exactly what would happen if we changed that instruction to read as follows:

a. While ($i \geq n$) do

b. While ($i < n$) do

c. While ($i = n$) do

17. On the seventh line of the Find Largest algorithm of Figure 2.10 is an instruction that reads,

If A_i > largest so far then . . .

Explain exactly what would happen if we changed that instruction to read as follows:

a. If $A_i \geq$ largest so far then . . .

b. If $A_i <$ largest so far then . . .

Looking back over your answers to the previous two questions, what do they say about the importance of using the correct *relational operation* ($<$, $=$, $>$, $\geq$, $\leq$, $\neq$) when writing out either an iterative or conditional algorithmic primitive?

18. a. Refer to the pattern-matching algorithm in Figure 2.12. What is the output of the algorithm as it currently stands if our text is

Text: We must band together and handle adversity

and we search for the pattern "and"?

b. How could we modify the algorithm so that it finds only the complete word *and* rather than occurrence of the character sequence *a, n,* and *d* that are contained within another word, such as *band*?

19. Refer to the pattern-matching algorithm in Figure 2.12. Explain how the algorithm would behave if we accidentally omitted the statement on line 16 that says,

Increment k by 1

CHALLENGE WORK

1. Design an algorithm to find the *root* of a function $f(x)$, where the root is defined as a point x such that $f(x) = 0$. Pictorially, the root of a function is the point where the graph of that function crosses the x-axis.

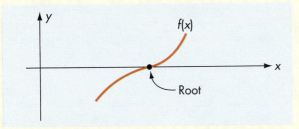

Your algorithm should operate as follows. Initially it will be given three values:

1. A starting point for the search

2. A step size

3. The accuracy desired

Your algorithm should begin at the specified starting point and begin to "walk up" the x-axis in units of step size. After taking a step, it should ask the question "Have I passed a root?" It can determine the answer to this question by seeing whether the sign of the function has changed from the previous point to the current point. (Note that below the axis the sign of $f(x)$ is negative; above the axis it is positive. If it crosses the x-axis, it must change sign.) If the algorithm has not passed a root, it should keep walking up the x-axis until it does. Pictorially,

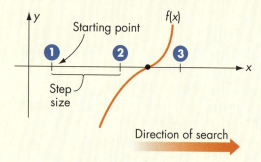

Starting point

Step size

Direction of search

When the algorithm passes a root, it must do two things. First, it should change the sign of step size so that it will start walking in the reverse direction, because it is now past the root. Second, it is going to multiply step size by 0.1, so our steps are $\frac{1}{10}$ as big as they were before. We now repeat the operation described above, walking down the x-axis until we pass the root.

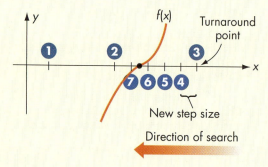

Turnaround point

New step size

Direction of search

Again, the algorithm changes the sign of step size to reverse direction and reduces it to $\frac{1}{10}$ of its previous size. As the diagrams show, we are slowly zeroing in on the root—going past it, turning around, going past it, turning around, and so forth. This iterative process stops when the algorithm passes a root and the step size is smaller than the desired accuracy. It has now bracketed the root within an interval that is smaller than the accuracy we want. At this point it should print out the midpoint of the interval and terminate.

There are many special cases that this algorithm must deal with, but in your solution you may disregard them. Assume that you will always encounter a root in your "travels" along the x-axis. After creating a solution, you may wish to look at some of these special cases, such as a function that has no real roots, a starting point that is to the right of all the roots, and two roots so close together that they fall within the same step.

2. One of the most important and widely used classes of algorithms in computer science is **sorting,** the process of putting a list of elements into a predefined order, usually

numeric or alphabetic. There are many different sorting algorithms, and we will look at some of them later in the book. One of the simplest sorting algorithms is called **selection sort,** and it can be implemented using only the tools that you have learned in this chapter. It is also one of the easiest to understand as it mimics how we often sort collections of values when we must do it by hand.

Assume that we are given a list named A, containing eight values that we want to sort into ascending order, from smallest to largest:

| A: | 23 | 18 | 66 | 9 | 21 | 90 | 32 | 4 |
| Position: | 1 | 2 | 3 | 4 | 5 | 6 | 7 | 8 |

We would first look for the largest value contained in positions 1 to 8 of list A. We can do this using something like the Find Largest algorithm that appears in Figure 2.10. In this case the largest value is 90, and it appears in position 6. Since this is the largest value in A, we will swap it with the value in position 8 so that it is in its correct place at the back of the list. The list is now partially sorted from position 8 to position 8:

| A: | 23 | 18 | 66 | 9 | 21 | 4 | 32 | 90 |
| Position: | 1 | 2 | 3 | 4 | 5 | 6 | 7 | 8 |

We now search the array for the second largest value. Since we know that the largest value is contained in position 8, we need to search only positions 1 to 7 of list A to find the second largest value. In this case the second largest value is 66, and it appears in position 3. We now swap the value in position 3 with the value in position 7 to get the second largest value into its correct location. This produces the following:

| A: | 23 | 18 | 32 | 9 | 21 | 4 | 66 | 90 |
| Position: | 1 | 2 | 3 | 4 | 5 | 6 | 7 | 8 |

The list is now partially sorted from position 7 to position 8, with those two locations holding the two largest values. The next search would go from position 1 to position 6 of list A, this time trying to locate the third largest value, and we would swap that value with the number in position 6. After repeating this process 7 times, the list will be completely sorted. (That is because if the last 7 items are in their correct place, the item in position 1 must also be in its correct place.)

Using the Find Largest algorithm shown in Figure 2.10 (which may have to be slightly modified) and the primitive pseudocode operations listed in Figure 2.6, implement the selection sort algorithm that we have just described. Assume that n, the size of the list, and the n-element list A are input to your algorithm. The output of your algorithm should be the sorted list.

3. Most people are familiar with the work of the great mathematicians of ancient Greece and Rome, such as Archimedes, Euclid, Pythagoras, and Plato. However, a great deal of important work in arithmetic, geometry, algebra, number theory, and logic was carried out by

scholars working in Egypt, Persia, India, and China. For example, the concept of zero was first developed in India, and positional numbering systems (like our own decimal system) were developed and used in China, India, and the Middle East long before they made their way to Europe. Read about the work of some mathematician (such as Al-Khowarizmi) from these or other places, and write a paper describing his or her contributions to mathematics, logic, and (ultimately) computer science.

FOR FURTHER READING

The classic text on algorithms is the three-volume series by Donald Knuth:

Knuth, D. *The Art of Computer Programming*, 3 vols. Reading, MA: Addison Wesley, 1997–1998. Volume 1: *Fundamental Algorithms*, 3rd ed., 1997. Volume 2: *Seminumerical Algorithms*, 3rd ed., 1998. Volume 3: *Sorting and Searching*, 2nd ed., 1998.

The following books provide additional information about the design of algorithms to solve a wide range of interesting problems.

Baase, S. *Computer Algorithms: Introduction to Design and Analysis*, 3rd ed. Reading, MA: Addison Wesley, 1999.

Cormen, T.; Leiserson, C.; Rivest, R.; and Stein, C. *Introduction to Algorithms*, 2nd ed. Cambridge, MA: MIT Press, 2001.

Harel, D. *Algorithmics: The Spirit of Computing*, 2nd ed. Reading, MA: Addison Wesley, 1992.

Michalewicz, Z., and Fogel, D. *How to Solve It: Modern Heuristics*. Amsterdam: Springer-Verlag, 1999.

Skiena, S. *The Algorithm Design Manual*. New York: Telos Press, 1997.

The following is an excellent introduction to algorithm design using the control of the motions and actions of a toy robot as a basis for teaching algorithmic problem solving.

Pattis, R.; Roberts, J.; and Stehlik, M. *Karel the Robot: A Gentle Introduction to the Art of Programming*, 2nd ed. New York: Wiley, 1994.

CHAPTER 3

The Efficiency of Algorithms

3.1   Introduction

Finding algorithms to solve problems of interest is an important part of computer science. Algorithms to perform a variety of tasks were discussed in the previous chapter. Suppose an algorithm has been developed to solve a specific problem. By definition, this algorithm will have certain required characteristics (see the formal definition in Chapter 1, Section 1.3.1), but are there other, desirable characteristics?

As an analogy, if we go to purchase an automobile, there are certain features that are part of the "definition" of an automobile, such as four wheels and an engine. These are the basics. However, we may also desire other things, such as ease of handling, style, and fuel efficiency. This analogy is not as superficial as it seems, because we will find that very similar properties are desirable for algorithms as well.

3.2   Attributes of Algorithms

First and foremost, we expect **correctness** from our algorithms. An algorithm intended to solve a problem must, again by formal definition, give a result and then halt. But this is not enough; we also have every right to demand the result be a correct solution to the problem. One could consider this an inherent property of the definition of an algorithm (like the car being capable of transporting us where we want to go), but it bears emphasizing. An elegant and efficient algorithm that is an example of creative and intellectual genius, but that gives wrong results for the problem at hand, is worse than useless. It can lead to situations that are enormously expensive or even fatal.

Determining that an algorithm gives correct results may not be as straightforward as it seems. For one thing, our algorithm may indeed be providing correct results—but to the wrong problem. This can happen when we design an algorithm without a thorough understanding of the real problem we are trying to solve, and it is one of the most common causes of "incorrect" algorithms. Then, once we understand the problem, the algorithm must provide correct results for all possible input values for the problem, not just for those values that we expect are the most likely to occur. Do we know ahead of time what all those correct results are? (Probably not, or we would not be writing an algorithm to solve this problem.) But there may be a certain standard against which we can check the result for reasonableness, thus giving us a way to determine when a result is obviously incorrect. In some cases, as noted in Chapter 1, the correct result may be an error message saying that there is no correct answer. There may be an issue of the accuracy of the result we are willing to accept as correct. If the "real" answer is π, for example, then we can only approximate its decimal value. Is 3.14159 close enough to be considered "correct?" Is 3.1416 close enough? What about 3.14? Computer scientists often summarize these two views of correctness by asking, Are we solving the right problem? Are we solving the problem right?

If an algorithm to solve a problem exists and has been determined, after all the considerations of the previous paragraph, to give correct results, what more can we ask? To many mathematicians, this would be the end of the matter. After all, once a solution has been obtained and shown to be correct, it is no longer of interest (except possibly for use in obtaining solutions to other problems). This is where computer science differs significantly from theoretical disciplines such as pure mathematics and begins to take on an "applied" character more closely related to engineering or applied mathematics. The algorithms developed by computer scientists are not merely of academic interest. They are also intended to be *used*.

Suppose, for example, that a road is to be built to the top of a mountain. An algorithmic solution exists that gives a correct answer for this problem in the sense that a road is produced: Just build the road straight up the mountain. Problem solved. But the highway engineer knows that the road must be usable by real traffic and that this constraint limits the grade of the road. Existence and correctness of the algorithm are not enough; there are practical considerations as well.

The practical considerations for computer science arise because the algorithms developed will be executed in the form of computer programs running on real computers to solve problems of interest to real people. Let's consider the "people aspect" first. A computer program is seldom written to be used only once to solve a single instance of a problem. It is written to solve many instances of that problem with many different input values, just as the sequential search algorithm of Chapter 2 would be used many times with different lists of names and different target *NAME* values. Furthermore, the problem itself does not usually "stand still." If the program is successful, people will want to use it for slightly different versions of the problem, which means they will want the program slightly enhanced to do more things. After a program is written, it will therefore need to be maintained, both to fix any errors that are uncovered through repeated usage with different input values and to extend the program to meet new requirements. Much time and much money are devoted to **program maintenance.** The person who has to modify a program, either to correct errors or to expand its functionality, often is not the person who wrote the original program. In order to make program maintenance as easy as possible, the algorithm the program uses should be easy to understand. **Ease of understanding,** clarity, "ease of handling"—whatever you want to call it—is a desirable characteristic for an algorithm.

On the other hand, there is a certain satisfaction in having an "elegant" solution to a problem. **Elegance** is the algorithmic equivalent of style. The classic example, in mathematical folklore, is the story of the German mathematician Karl Frederick Gauss (1777–1855) who was asked as a schoolchild to add up the numbers from 1 to 100. The straightforward algorithm of adding $1 + 2 + 3 + 4 + \ldots + 100$ by adding one number at a time can be expressed in pseudocode as

1. Set the value of *sum* to 0
2. Set the value of *x* to 1
3. While *x* is less than or equal to 100 do steps 4 and 5
4.   Add *x* to sum
5.   Add 1 to the value of *x*
6. Print the value of *sum*
7. Stop

This algorithm can be executed to find that the sum has the value 5,050. It is fairly easy to read through this pseudocode and understand how the algorithm works. It is also fairly clear that if we want to change this algorithm to one that adds the numbers from 1 to 1,000, we only have to change the loop condition to

3. While *x* is less than or equal to 1,000 do steps 4 and 5

However, Gauss noticed that the numbers from 1 to 100 could be grouped into 50 pairs of the form

$$1 + 100 = 101$$
$$2 + 99 = 101$$
$$\vdots$$
$$50 + 51 = 101$$

so that the sum equals $50 \times 101 = 5,050$. Now this is an elegant and clever solution, but is it easy to understand? If a computer program just said to multiply

$$\left(\frac{100}{2}\right)101$$

with no further explanation, we might guess how to modify the program to add up the first 1,000 numbers, but would we really grasp what was happening enough to be sure the modification would work? (The Practice Problems at the end of this section discuss this.) Sometimes elegance and ease of understanding work at cross-purposes; the more elegant the solution, the more difficult it may be to understand. If an algorithm has both characteristics—ease of understanding and elegance—at the same time, that's a plus.

Now let's consider the real computers on which programs will run. Although these computers can execute instructions very rapidly and have some memory in which to store information, time and space are not unlimited resources. The computer scientist must be conscious of the resources consumed by a given algorithm, and if there is a choice between two (correct) algorithms that perform the same task, the one that uses fewer resources is preferable. **Efficiency** is the term used to describe an algorithm's careful use of resources. In addition to *correctness, ease of understanding,* and *elegance,* we look for *efficiency* as an extremely desirable attribute of an algorithm. In light of this list of attributes, the computer scientist's job involves much more than simply "coming up with" an algorithm.

Because of the rapid advances in computer technology, today's computers have much more memory capacity and execute instructions much more rapidly than computers of just a few years ago. Efficiency in algorithms may seem to be a moot point; we can just wait for the next generation of technology and it won't matter how much time or space is used. There is some truth to this, but as computer memory capacity and processing speed increase, people find ever more complex problems to be solved, so the boundaries of the computer's resources continue to be pushed. Furthermore, we will see in this chapter that there are algorithms that consume so many resources that they will never be practical, no matter what advances in computer technology occur.

How shall we measure the time and space consumed by an algorithm to determine whether it is efficient? Space efficiency can be judged by the amount of information the algorithm must store in the computer's memory in order to do its job, in addition to the initial data on which the algorithm is operating. If it uses only a few extra quantities while processing the input data, the algorithm is relatively space-efficient. If the algorithm requires almost as much additional storage as the input data itself takes up, or even more, then it is relatively space-inefficient.

How can we measure the time efficiency of an algorithm? Consider the sequential search algorithm shown in Figure 2.9 for looking up a name in a telephone directory where the names are not arranged in alphabetical order. How about running the algorithm on a real computer and timing it to see how many seconds (or maybe what small fraction of a second) it takes to find a name or announce that the name is not present? The difficulty with this approach is that there are three factors in this problem, each of which can affect the answer to such a degree as to make whatever number of seconds we come up with rather meaningless.

1. On what computer will we run the algorithm? Shall we use a modest laptop or a huge supercomputer capable of doing many billions of calculations per second?

2. What telephone book (list of names) will we use, New York City or Mesquite, Nevada?

3. What name will we try to find? What if we pick a name that happens to be first in the list? What if it happens to be last in the list?

By just running our stopwatch, we are seeing the effects of variations in machine speed or variations due to input data rather than the efficiency (or lack thereof) inherent in the way the algorithm goes about solving the problem.

There is indeed a place for timing of the sort we have just described. For example, using the same input data (searching for Karlenski, say, in the New York City phone book) and timing the algorithm on different machines gives a comparison of machine speeds on identical tasks. Using the same machine and the same list of names, but trying a variety of names to search for, gives an indication of how the choice of *NAME* affects the algorithm's running time on that particular machine. These types of comparative timings are called **benchmarking.** They are useful for rating one machine against another with respect to one specific algorithm and for rating how sensitive a particular algorithm is with respect to variations in input on one particular machine.

However, what we mean by an algorithm's time efficiency is an indication of the amount of "work" required by the nature of the algorithm itself and the approach it uses. It is a measure of the inherent efficiency of the method, independent of the speed of the machine on which it is executing or the specific data on which it is working. Is the amount of work an algorithm does the same as the number of instructions it executes? Not all instructions do the same things, so perhaps they should not all be "counted" equally. Some instructions are carrying out work that is fundamental to the way the algorithm operates, whereas other instructions are carrying out peripheral tasks that must be done in support of the fundamental work. We will try to identify the fundamental unit or units of work of an algorithm. Once we have done this, it will be sufficient to count the number of instruction executions that do this work, because the total number of instructions executed will be proportional to that count.

Suppose we find two algorithms, A and B, that both do the same task (processing n items in some way) using the same fundamental unit of work. Suppose also that A has to execute many more of these work units than B. On a particular machine, each work unit takes a certain amount of time, and A will require more time than B. This time differential will not disappear, no matter what the speed of the machine. If we run these two algorithms on a machine that runs much faster than the previous machine, then the timing difference between algorithms A and B decreases. But if we use this faster machine to process a much larger quantity of input, the gap is just as bad as before. A faster machine can scale up the size of the input that produces the differential, but it cannot eliminate the differential. *It is the number of steps each algorithm requires, not the time the algorithm takes on a particular machine, that is important for comparing two algorithms that do the same task.*

PRACTICE PROBLEMS

1. Use Gauss's approach to find a formula for the sum of the numbers from 1 to n,

   $$1 + 2 + 3 + \ldots + n$$

   where n is an even number. Your formula will be an expression involving n.

2. Test your formula from Problem 1 for the following sums.

   a. $1 + 2$
   b. $1 + 2 + \ldots + 6$
   c. $1 + 2 + \ldots + 10$
   d. $1 + 2 + \ldots + 100$
   e. $1 + 2 + \ldots + 1000$

3. Now see if the same formula from Problem 1 works when n is odd; try it on

   a. $1 + 2 + 3$
   b. $1 + 2 + \ldots + 5$
   c. $1 + 2 + \ldots + 9$

Measuring Efficiency

The study of the efficiency of various algorithms is called the **analysis of algorithms,** and it is an important part of computer science. As a first example of the analysis of an algorithm, we'll look at the sequential search algorithm.

3.3.1 *Sequential Search*

The pseudocode description of the sequential search algorithm from Chapter 2 appears in Figure 3.1, where we have assumed that the list contains n entries instead of 10,000 entries.

The central unit of work seems to be the comparison of the *NAME* being searched for against a name in the list. The essence of the algorithm is the repetition of this task against successive names in the list until *NAME* is found or the list is exhausted. The comparison takes place at step 4, within the loop composed of steps 4 through 7. Peripheral tasks include setting the initial value of the index *i,* writing the output, adjusting *Found,* and moving the index forward in the list of names. Why can these be considered peripheral tasks?

Setting the initial value of the index and the initial value of *Found* requires execution of only a single instruction, done at step 2. Writing output requires executing only a single instruction, either at step 5 if *NAME* was in the list or at step 9 if *NAME* was not in the list. Note that instruction 5, although it is part of the loop, writes output at most once (if *NAME* equals N_i). Similarly, setting *Found* to YES occurs at most once (if *NAME* equals N_i) at step 6. We can ignore the small contribution of these single-instruction executions to the total work done by the algorithm.

Moving the index forward is done once for each comparison, at step 7. We can get a good idea of the total amount of work the algorithm does by simply counting the number of comparisons and then multiplying by some constant factor to take care of the index-moving task. Perhaps the constant factor should be 2 because we do one index move for each comparison, so we would double the work. Perhaps it should be less because it is less work to add 1 to i than it is to compare *NAME* letter by letter against N_i. We will see in the next section why we don't have to pay too much attention to the value of this constant factor.

FIGURE 3.1

Sequential Search Algorithm

1. Get values for *NAME, n,* $N_1, \ldots, N_n$ and $T_1, \ldots, T_n$
2. Set the value of *i* to 1 and set the value of *Found* to NO
3. While (*Found* = NO) and ($i \leq n$) do steps 4 through 7
4.   If *NAME* is equal to the *i*th name on the list, N_i, then
5.   Print the telephone number of that person, T_i
6.   Set the value of *Found* to YES
     Else (*NAME* is not equal to N_i)
7.   Add 1 to the value of *i*
8. If (*Found* = NO) then
9.   Print the message 'Sorry, this name is not in the directory'
10. Stop

Therefore, we will take the basic unit of work to be comparison of *NAME* against a list element. One comparison is done at each pass through the loop in steps 4 through 7, so we must ask how many times the loop is executed. Of course, this depends on when, or whether, we find *NAME* in the list.

The minimum amount of work is done if *NAME* is the very first name in the list. This will require only one comparison, because *NAME* has then been found and the algorithm exits the loop after only one pass. This would be called the **best case.** The **worst case,** requiring the maximum amount of work, occurs if *NAME* is the very last name in the list; in this case *NAME* must be compared against all n names in the list before the loop terminates because *FOUND* gets set to YES. If *NAME* is not in the list at all, the algorithm also compares *NAME* against all n names in the list before exiting the loop because the value of the index i exceeds n. Thus there are two conditions, each of which produces the worst-case behavior of the sequential search algorithm.

When *NAME* occurs somewhere in the middle of the list, it requires somewhere between 1 (the best case) and n (the worst case) comparisons. If we were to run the sequential search algorithm many times with random *NAME*s occurring at various places in the list and count the number of comparisons done each time, we would find that the average number of comparisons done is about $n/2$. (The exact average is actually slightly higher than $n/2$; see Exercise 4 at the end of the chapter.) It is not hard to explain why an average of approximately $n/2$ comparisons are done (or the loop is executed approximately $n/2$ times) when *NAME* is in the list. If *NAME* occurs halfway down the list, then roughly $n/2$ comparisons are required; random *NAME*s in the list will occur before the halfway point about half the time and after the halfway point about half the time, and these cases of less work and more work balance out.

This means that the average number of comparisons needed to find a *NAME* that occurs in a 10-element list is about 5, in a 100-element list about 50, and in a 1,000-element list about 500. On small values of n — say, a few hundred or a few thousand names—the values of $n/2$ (the average case) or n (the worst case) are small enough that a computer could execute the algorithm quickly and get the desired answer in a fraction of a second. However, computers are generally used to solve not tiny problems but very large ones. Therefore, we are usually interested not in the behavior of an algorithm on small problems but in its behavior as the size of a problem (n) gets very, very large. For example, in the New York City telephone directory, n may be as large as 20,000,000. If the sequential search algorithm were executed on a computer that could do 100,000 comparisons per second, it would require on the average about

$$\frac{20,000,000}{2} \text{ comparisons} \times \frac{1}{100,000} \text{ seconds/comparison} = 200 \text{ seconds}$$

or 3 1/3 minutes just to do the comparisons necessary to locate a specific name. Including the constant factor for advancing the index, the actual time needed would be even greater. It would require almost 7 minutes just to do the comparisons required to determine that a name was not in the directory! Sequential search does not seem to be sufficiently time-efficient for large values of n to be useful as a telephone directory lookup algorithm.

Information about the number of comparisons required to perform the sequential search algorithm on a list of n names is summarized in Figure 3.2. Note that the values for both the worst case and the average case in Figure

FIGURE 3.2

Number of Comparisons to Find
NAME *in a List of* n *Names*
Using Sequential Search

BEST CASE	WORST CASE	AVERAGE CASE
1	n	n/2

3.2 depend on *n,* the number of names in the list. The bigger the list, the more work must be done to search it. Few algorithms do the same amount of work on large inputs as on small inputs, simply because most algorithms require some sort of processing of the input data, and more data to process means more work to be done. The work an algorithm does is usually given in terms of a formula that depends on the size of the appropriate problem input. In the case of searching a list of names, the input size is the length of the list. For other tasks with other kinds of input, the size of the problem input may mean something different.

Finally, let's say a word about the space efficiency of sequential search. The algorithm stores the list of names and the target *NAME* as part of the input. The only additional memory required is storage for the index value *i* and the *Found* indicator. Two single additional memory locations are insignificant compared to the size of the list of names, just as executing a single instruction to initialize the value of *i* and *Found* is insignificant beside the repetitive comparison task. Therefore, sequential search uses essentially no more memory storage than the original input requires, so it is very space-efficient.

 ### 3.3.2   *Order of Magnitude—Order n*

When we analyzed the time efficiency of the sequential search algorithm, we glossed over the contribution of the constant factor for the peripheral work. As it turns out, we will be taking such a large-scale view that we can often ignore it! To see why this is the case, we need to understand a concept called *order of magnitude.*

The worst-case behavior of the sequential search algorithm on a list of *n* names requires *n* comparisons, or if *c* is a constant factor representing the peripheral work, it requires *cn* total work. Suppose that *c* has the value 2. Then the values of *n* and 2*n* are

n	2n
1	2
2	4
3	6

and so on

These values are shown in Figure 3.3, which illustrates how the value of 2*n,* which is the total work, changes as *n* changes. We can add to this graph to show how the value of *cn* changes as *n* changes, where *c* = 1 or *c* = 1/2 as well as *c* = 2 (Figure 3.4). These values of *c* are completely arbitrary. Figure 3.5 presents a different view of the growth rate of *cn* as *n* changes for these three values of *c.*

Both Figure 3.4 and Figure 3.5 show that the amount of work *cn* increases as *n* increases, but at different rates. The work grows at the same rate as *n*

FIGURE 3.3

Work = 2n

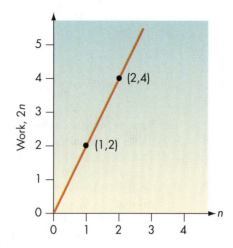

FIGURE 3.4

Work = cn for Various Values of c

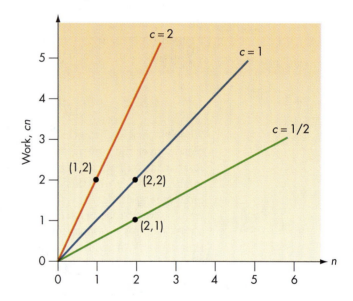

when $c = 1$, at twice the rate of n when $c = 2$, and at half the rate of n when $c = 1/2$. However, Figure 3.4 also shows that all of these graphs follow the same basic straight-line shape of n. Anything that varies as a constant times n (and whose graph follows the basic shape of n) is said to be of **order of magnitude n,** written $\Theta(n)$. All we are worried about is the straight-line shape; we don't care about the size of the constant factor. Sequential search is therefore an $\Theta(n)$ algorithm (an order-n algorithm) in both the worst case and the average case.

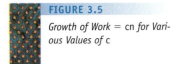

FIGURE 3.5

Growth of Work = cn *for Various Values of* c

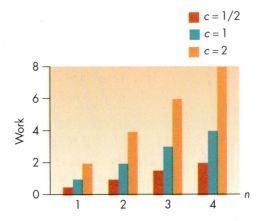

PRACTICE PROBLEM

Using the information in Figure 3.2, fill in the following table for the number of comparisons required in the sequential search algorithm.

n	Best Case	Worst Case	Average Case
10			
50			
100			
1,000			
10,000			
100,000			

▶ 3.3.3 Selection Sort

We have done an analysis of the sequential search algorithm and have learned that it is an $\Theta(n)$ algorithm in both the worst case and the average case. This algorithm solves a very common problem: **searching** a list of items (such as the names in a telephone directory) for a particular item. Another very common problem is that of **sorting** a list of items into order—either alphabetical order or numerical order. The registrar at your institution sorts students in a class by name, a mail-order business sorts its customer list by name, and the IRS sorts its tax records by Social Security number. In this section we'll examine a sorting algorithm and analyze its efficiency.

Suppose we have a list of numbers to sort into increasing order—for example, 5, 7, 2, 8, 3. The result of sorting this list would be the new list 2, 3, 5, 7, 8. We'll examine the **selection sort algorithm** to solve this task. The selection sort "grows" a sorted subsection of the list from the back to the front. We can look at "snapshots" of the progress of the algorithm on our example list, using a vertical line as the marker between the unsorted section at the front of the list and the sorted section at the back of the list in each case. At first the sorted subsection is empty; that is, the entire list is unsorted. This is how the list looks when the algorithm begins.

5, 7, 2, 8, 3|

Unsorted subsection (entire list)   Sorted subsection (empty)

Later, the sorted subsection of the list has grown from the back so that some of the list members are in the right place.

5, 3, 2, | 7, 8

Unsorted subsection   Sorted subsection

Finally, the sorted subsection of the list has grown to be the whole list; there are no unsorted numbers, and the algorithm stops.

| 2,3,5,7,8

Unsorted subsection (empty)   Sorted subsection (entire list)

At any point, then, there is both a sorted and an unsorted section of the list. A pseudocode version of the algorithm is shown in Figure 3.6.

Before we illustrate this algorithm at work, take a look at step 4. It consists of finding the largest number in some list of numbers. We developed an algorithm for this task in Chapter 2 (Figure 2.10). When we get to step 4 in Figure 3.6, we can just insert the pertinent instructions from that algorithm. New algorithms can be built up from "parts" consisting of previous algorithms. As an analogy, a recipe for pumpkin pie might begin with the instruction, Prepare crust for a one-crust pie. The recipe for pie crust is a previous algorithm that is now being used as one of the steps in the pumpkin pie algorithm.

Let's follow the selection sort algorithm. Initially, the unsorted section is the entire list, so step 2 sets the marker at the end of the list.

5, 7, 2, 8, 3 |

Step 4 says to select the largest number in the unsorted section—that is, in the entire list. This number is 8. Step 5 says to exchange 8 with the last number in the unsorted section (the whole list). In order to accomplish this exchange, it is necessary not only to know that 8 is the largest value but also to know the location in the list where 8 occurs. The Find Largest algorithm from Chapter 2 also provides this information. The exchange to be done is

5, 7, 2, 8, 3 |

FIGURE 3.6

Selection Sort Algorithm

1. Get values for *n* and the *n* list items
2. Set the marker for the unsorted section at the end of the list
3. While the sorted section of the list is not empty, do steps 4 through 6
4.   Select the largest number in the unsorted section of the list
5.   Exchange this number with the last number in the unsorted section of the list
6.   Move the marker for the unsorted section left one position
7. Stop

After this exchange and after the marker is moved left as instructed in step 6, the list looks like

5, 7, 2, 3 | 8

The number 8 is now in its correct position at the end of the list. It becomes the sorted section of the list, and the first four numbers are the unsorted section.

The unsorted section is not empty, so we repeat step 4 (find the largest number in the unsorted section); it is 7. Step 5 is to exchange 7 with the last number in the unsorted section, which is 3.

5, 7, 2, 3 | 8

After the marker is moved, the result is

5, 3, 2 | 7, 8

The sorted section is now 7, 8 and the unsorted section is 5, 3, 2.

Repeating the loop of steps 4 through 6 again, we find that the largest number in the unsorted section is 5. We exchange it with 2, the last number in the unsorted section.

5, 3, 2 | 7, 8

After we move the marker, we get

2, 3 | 5, 7, 8

Now the unsorted (as far as the algorithm knows) section is 2, 3. The largest number here is 3. Exchanging 3 with the last number of the unsorted section (which is also 3) produces no visible change. The marker is moved, giving

2 | 3, 5, 7, 8

When the only part of the list that is unsorted is the single number 2, there is also no visible change produced by carrying out the exchange. The marker is moved, giving

| 2, 3, 5, 7, 8

The unsorted section of the list is empty, and the algorithm terminates.

In order to analyze the amount of work the selection sort algorithm does, we must first decide on the unit of work to count. When we analyzed sequential search, the unit of work that we measured was a comparison between the name being searched for and the names in the list. At first glance there seem to be no comparisons of any kind going on in the selection sort. Ah, but remember that there is a subtask being done within the selection sort: the task of finding the largest number in the list. The algorithm from Chapter 2 for finding the largest value in a list begins by taking the first number in the list as the largest so far. The largest-so-far value is compared against successive numbers in the list; if a larger value is found, it becomes the largest so far.

When the selection sort algorithm begins, the largest-so-far value, initially the first number, must be compared to all the other numbers in the list. If there are n numbers in the list, $n - 1$ comparisons must be done. The next time through the loop, the last number is already in its proper place, so it is never involved in a comparison. The largest-so-far value, again initially the first number, must be compared to all the other numbers in the unsorted part of the list, which will require $n - 2$ comparisons. The number of comparisons keeps going down as the length of the unsorted section of the list gets smaller, until finally only one comparison is needed. The total number of comparisons is

$$(n - 1) + (n - 2) + (n - 3) + \ldots + 3 + 2 + 1$$

Reviewing our example problem, we can see that the following comparisons are done.

- To put 8 in place in the list 5, 7, 2, 8, 3 |
  Compare 5 (largest so far) to 7
    7 becomes largest so far
  Compare 7 (largest so far) to 2
  Compare 7 (largest so far) to 8
    8 becomes largest so far
  Compare 8 to 3
  8 is the largest
  Total number of comparisons: 4 (which is 5 − 1)

- To put 7 in place in the list 5, 7, 2, 3 | 8
  Compare 5 (largest so far) to 7
    7 becomes largest so far
  Compare 7 to 2
  Compare 7 to 3
  7 is the largest
  Total number of comparisons: 3 (which is 5 − 2)

- To put 5 in place in the list 5, 3, 2 | 7, 8
  Compare 5 (largest so far) to 3
  Compare 5 to 2
  5 is the largest
  Total number of comparisons: 2 (which is 5 − 3)

- To put 3 in place in the list 2, 3 | 5, 7, 8
  Compare 2 (largest so far) to 3
  3 is the largest
  Total number of comparisons: 1 (which is 5 − 4)

To put 2 in place requires no comparisons; there is only one number in the unsorted section of the list, so it is of course the largest number. It gets exchanged with itself, which produces no effect. The total number of comparisons is $4 + 3 + 2 + 1 = 10$.

FIGURE 3.7

Comparisons Required by Selection Sort

Length n of List to Sort	n^2	Number of Comparisons Required
10	100	45
100	10,000	4,950
1,000	1,000,000	499,500

The sum

$$(n - 1) + (n - 2) + (n - 3) + \ldots + 3 + 2 + 1$$

turns out to be equal to

$$\left(\frac{n - 1}{2}\right)n = \frac{1}{2}n^2 - \frac{1}{2}n$$

(You will recall from earlier in this chapter how Gauss computed a similar sum.) For our example with five numbers, this formula says that the total number of comparisons is (using the first version of the formula)

$$\left(\frac{5 - 1}{2}\right)5 = \left(\frac{4}{2}\right)5 = (2)5 = 10$$

which is the number of comparisons we had counted.

Figure 3.7 uses this same formula

$$\frac{1}{2}n^2 - \frac{1}{2}n$$

to compute the comparisons required for larger values of n. Remember that n is the size of the list we are sorting. If the list becomes 10 times longer, the work increases by much more than a factor of 10, it increases by a factor closer to 100, which is 10^2.

The selection sort algorithm not only does comparisons, it does exchanges. Even if the largest number in the unsorted section of the list is already at the end of the unsorted section, the algorithm exchanges this number with itself. Therefore, the algorithm does n exchanges, one for each position in the list to put the correct value in that position. With every exchange the marker gets moved. However, the work contributed by exchanges and marker moving is so much less than the amount contributed by comparisons that it can be ignored.

We haven't talked here about a best case, a worst case, or an average case for the selection sort. This algorithm does the same amount of work no matter how the numbers are initially arranged. It has no way to recognize, for example, that the list might already be sorted at the beginning.

A word about the space efficiency of the selection sort is in order. The original list occupies n memory locations, and this is the major space requirement. Some storage is needed for the marker between the unsorted and sorted sections and for keeping track of the largest-so-far value and its location in the list, used in step 4. Surprisingly, the process of exchanging two values at step 5 also requires an extra storage location. Here's why. If the two

FIGURE 3.8

An Attempt to Exchange the Values at X and Y

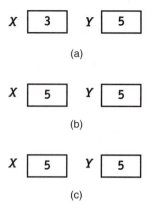

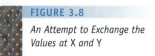

numbers to be exchanged are at position X and position Y in the list, we might think the following two steps will exchange these values:

1. Copy the current value at position Y into position X
2. Copy the current value at position X into position Y

The problem is that after step 1, the value at position X is the same as that at position Y. Step 2 does not put the original value of X into position Y. In fact, we don't even have the original value of position X any more. In Figure 3.8(a) we see the original X and Y values. At Figure 3.8(b), after execution of step 1, the current value of position Y has been copied into position X, writing over what was there originally. At Figure 3.8(c), after execution of step 2, the current value at position X (which is the original Y value) has been copied into position Y, but the picture looks the same as Figure 3.8(b).

Here's the correct algorithm, which makes use of one extra temporary storage location that we'll call T.

1. Copy the current value at position X into location T
2. Copy the current value at position Y into position X
3. Copy the current value at location T into position Y

Figure 3.9 illustrates that this algorithm does the job. In Figure 3.9(a), the temporary location contains an unknown value. After execution of step 1 (Figure 3.9b), it holds the current value of X. When Y's current value is put into X at step 2 (Figure 3.9c), T still holds the original X value. After step 3 (Figure 3.9d), the current value of T goes into position Y, and the original values of X and Y have been exchanged. (Step 5 of the selection sort algorithm thus stands for another algorithm, just as step 4 does.)

All in all, the extra storage required for the selection sort, over and above that required to store the original list, is slight. Selection sort is space-efficient.

FIGURE 3.9

Exchanging the Values at X and Y

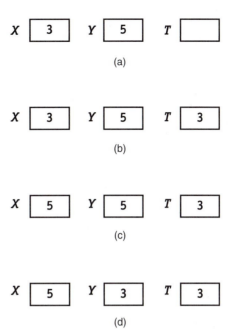

PRACTICE PROBLEM

1. For each of the following lists, perform a selection sort, and show the list after each exchange that has a visible effect.

   a. 4, 8, 2, 6
   b. 12, 3, 6, 8, 2, 5, 7
   c. D, B, G, F, A, C, E

▶ ### 3.3.4 *Order of Magnitude—Order n²*

We saw that the number of comparisons done by the selection sort algorithm does not grow at the same rate as the problem size n; it grows at approximately the *square* of that rate. An algorithm that does cn^2 work for any constant c is **order of magnitude n^2**, or $\Theta(n^2)$. Figure 3.10 shows how cn^2 changes as n changes, where $c = 1, 2,$ and $1/2$. The work grows at the same rate as n^2 when $c = 1$, at twice that rate when $c = 2$, and at half that rate when $c = 1/2$. But all three graphs in Figure 3.10 follow the basic shape of n^2, which is different from all of the straight-line graphs that are of $\Theta(n)$. Thus, we have come up with two different "shape classifications": one including all graphs that are $\Theta(n)$ and the other including all graphs that are $\Theta(n^2)$. The value of the constant factor does not affect the classification, which is why we can generally ignore it.

FIGURE 3.10

*Work = cn² for Various Values
of* c

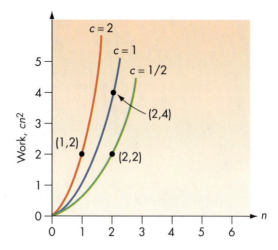

If it is not important to distinguish among the various graphs that make up a given order of magnitude, why is it important to distinguish between the two different orders of magnitude n and n^2? We can find the answer by comparing the two basic shapes n and n^2, as is done in Figure 3.11.

Figure 3.11 indicates that n^2 grows at a much faster rate than n. The two curves cross at the point (1,1), and for any value of n larger than 1, n^2 has a value increasingly greater than n. Furthermore, anything that is order of magnitude n^2 will eventually have larger values than anything that is of order n, no matter what the constant factors are. For example, Figure 3.12 shows that if we choose a graph that is $\Theta(n^2)$ but has a small constant factor to keep the values down, say $0.25n^2$, and a graph that is $\Theta(n)$ but has a larger constant factor to pump the values up, say $10n$, it is still true that the $\Theta(n^2)$ graph eventually has larger values. (Note that the vertical scale and the horizontal scale are different.)

FIGURE 3.11

A Comparison of n *and* n²

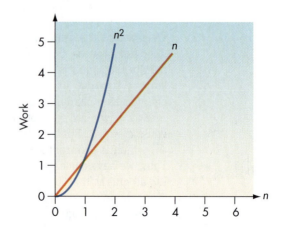

FIGURE 3.12

*For Large Enough n, 0.25n² Has
Larger Values Than 10n*

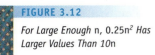

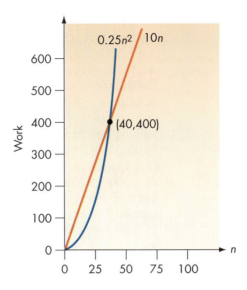

Selection sort is an $\Theta(n^2)$ algorithm (in all cases) and sequential search is an $\Theta(n)$ algorithm (in the worst case), so these two algorithms are different orders of magnitude. But because these algorithms solve two different problems, this is not necessarily surprising, and is somewhat like comparing apples and oranges. It's more interesting to compare two different algorithms that solve the same problem and count the same units of work.

Suppose that algorithm A does $0.0001n^2$ units of work to solve a problem with input size n and that algorithm B does $100n$ of the same units of work to solve the same problem. Here the factor of 100 that occurs with algorithm B is *one million times larger* than the factor of 0.0001 that occurs with algorithm A. Nonetheless, in the long run (when the problem gets large enough) the inherent inefficiency of algorithm A will cause it to do more work than algorithm B. Figure 3.13 shows that the "cross-over" point occurs at a value of 1,000,000 for n. At this point, the two algorithms do the same amount of work and therefore take the same amount of time to run. For larger values of n, the order-n^2 algorithm A will run increasingly slower than the order-n algorithm B. (Input sizes of 1,000,000 are not that uncommon—think of the New York City telephone list.)

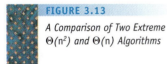

FIGURE 3.13

*A Comparison of Two Extreme
$\Theta(n^2)$ and $\Theta(n)$ Algorithms*

	NUMBER OF WORK UNITS REQUIRED	
	ALGORITHM A	ALGORITHM B
n	$0.0001n^2$	$100n$
1,000	100	100,000
10,000	10,000	1,000,000
100,000	1,000,000	10,000,000
1,000,000	100,000,000	100,000,000
10,000,000	10,000,000,000	1,000,000,000

As we have seen, if an $\Theta(n^2)$ algorithm and an $\Theta(n)$ algorithm exist for the same task, then for large enough n, the $\Theta(n^2)$ algorithm does more work and takes longer to execute, regardless of the constant factors for peripheral work. This is the rationale for ignoring constant factors and concentrating on the basic order of magnitude of algorithms. As an analogy, the two shape classifications $\Theta(n^2)$ and $\Theta(n)$ may be thought of as two different classes of transportation, the "walking" class and the "driving" class, respectively. The walking class is fundamentally more time-consuming than the driving class. Walking can include jogging, running, and leisurely strolling (which correspond to different values for c), but compared to any form of driving, these all proceed at roughly the same speed. The driving class can include driving a Geo and driving a Ferrari (which correspond to different values for c), but compared to any form of walking, these proceed at roughly the same speed. In other words, varying c can make modest changes within a class, but changing to a different class is a quantum leap.

Given two algorithms for the same task, we should usually choose the algorithm of the lesser order of magnitude, because for large enough n it will

The Tortoise and the Hare

One way to compare performance among different makes of automobiles is to give the number of seconds it takes each car to go from 0 to 60 miles per hour. One way to compare performance among different makes of computers is to give the number of arithmetic operations, such as additions or subtractions of real numbers, that each one can do in 1 second. These operations are called "floating-point operations," and computers are often compared in terms of the number of **flops** (floating-point operations per second) they can crank out. This is only one measure of a computer's performance, primarily related to "number crunching" applications. While this is the measure we will use here, other measures include the ability of the machine to handle multimedia, graphics, or multitasking (for example, how well can the machine run a virus checker in the background while you are playing a video game?).

As a comparison, a personal computer system based on the Intel Pentium 4 processor runs at about 837 megaflops (837 million floating-point operations per second). It sells for around $600. The Cray X1, a "parallel processor computing system" with up to 4,096 processors, can achieve top performance of 52.4 teraflops (52.4 trillion floating point operations per second). It is over 60,000 times faster than the Pentium machine. The Cray sells for a base price of $2.5 million, over 4,000 times the cost of the Pentium 4. The stage is set for the race between the tortoise and the hare.

Not fair, you say? We'll see. Let's suppose the Pentium machine is assigned to run an $\Theta(n)$ algorithm, whereas

the unfortunate Cray gets an $\Theta(n^2)$ algorithm for the same task. The work units are floating-point operations, and for simplicity, we'll take the constant factor to be 1 in each case. Here are the timing results:

n	Pentium 4	Cray X1
100,000	0.00012 sec	0.0000000002 sec
10,000,000	0.022 sec	0.0002 sec
1,000,000,000	2.15 sec	1.91 sec
100,000,000,000	215 sec = 3.58 min	19084 sec = 5.3 hr
1,000,000,000,000	2151 sec = 0.6 hr	1908397 sec = 22 days

Out of the gate—that is, for relatively small values of n such as 100 thousand or even 10 million—the Cray has a head start and takes less time. When n reaches 1 billion, the Pentium machine is only slightly slower than the Cray. And by the time n reaches 1 trillion, the Pentium has left the Cray in the dust. The difference in order of magnitude between the algorithms was enough to slow down the mighty Cray and let the Pentium machine creep past, chugging along doing its more efficient $\Theta(n)$ algorithm. Where would one need to perform 1 trillion operations? Complex problems involving weather simulations, biomedical research, and economic modeling might provide such number crunching applications.

The point of this little tale is obviously not to say that everyone who has bought a powerful computer system should have bought a PC instead! It is to note that the order of magnitude of the algorithm being executed can play a more important role than the raw speed of the computer.

always "win out." It is for large values of n that we need to be concerned about the time resources being used and, as we noted earlier, it is often for large values of n that we are seeking a computerized solution in the first place.

We should note, however, that for smaller values of n, the size of the constant factor is significant. In Figure 3.12, the $10n$ line stayed above the $0.25n^2$ curve up to the cross-over point of $n = 40$ because it had a large constant factor relative to the factor for n^2. Varying the factors would change the cross-over point. If $10n$ and $0.25n^2$ represented the work of two different algorithms for the same task, and if we could be sure that the size of the input was never going to exceed 40, then the $0.25n^2$ algorithm would be preferable in terms of time resources used. (To continue the transportation analogy, for traveling short distances—say, to the end of the driveway—walking will be faster than driving because of the overhead of getting the car started, and so on. But for long distances, driving is faster.)

However, making assumptions about the size of the input can be dangerous. A program designed to operate on small input size may be selected (perhaps because it seems efficient) to solve instances of the problem with large input size, at which point the efficiency may go down the drain! Sequential search may serve for directory assistance in Mesquite, Nevada, but it won't translate satisfactorily to New York City. Part of the job of **program documentation** is to make clear any assumptions or restrictions about the input size the program was designed to handle. But are there any tasks for which a choice of algorithms exists? Yes, as you will see in the next section, and in Laboratory Experience 4.

LABORATORY EXPERIENCE 4

Because sorting a list is such a common task, a lot of research has gone into finding good sorting algorithms. Selection sort is one sorting algorithm, but there are many others. One is the bubble sort, described in Exercises 8–10 at the end of this chapter. Others, such as insertion sort and quicksort, are described in the laboratory manual. This laboratory experience allows you to step through animations of these various sorting algorithms in order to understand how they work.

You may wonder why people don't simply use the one "best" sorting algorithm. It's not that simple. Some algorithms (unlike the selection sort) are sensitive to what the original input looks like. One algorithm may work well if the input is already close to being sorted, whereas another algorithm would work better if the input is rather random. An algorithm like selection sort has the advantage of being relatively easy to understand. If the size of the list, n, is fairly small, then an easy-to-understand algorithm may be preferable to one that is more efficient but more obscure.

PRACTICE PROBLEM

1. An algorithm does $14n^2 + 5n + 1$ units of work on input of size n. Explain why this is considered an $\Theta(n^2)$ algorithm even though there is a term that involves just n.

3.4.1 *Data Cleanup Algorithms*

In this section we'll look at three different algorithms that solve the same problem and then do an analysis of each. The problem is the *data cleanup problem*. Suppose a survey has been taken that includes a question about the age of the person filling out the survey. Some people will choose not to answer this question. When data from the survey are entered in the computer, there must be a way to show "no response" to this question. An entry of 0 will be used to denote "no response," because a legitimate value for age would have to be a positive number. As an example, we'll assume that the age data from 10 people who completed the survey are stored in the computer as the following 10-entry list, where the positions in the list range from 1 (far left) to 10 (far right).

0	24	16	0	36	42	23	21	0	27
1	2	3	4	5	6	7	8	9	10

In one use of the age data, the average age is to be computed. Because the 0 values are not legitimate data, including them in the average would produce too low a value. We want to perform a "data cleanup" and remove the 0 entries from the list before the average is computed. In our example, the cleaned-up data could consist of a 10-element list, where the seven legitimate elements are the first seven entries of the list, and some quantity—let's call it *legit*—has the value 7 to indicate that only the first seven entries are legitimate. An alternative acceptable result would be a 7-element list consisting of the seven legitimate data items, in which case there is no need for a *legit* quantity.

THE SHUFFLE-LEFT ALGORITHM. Algorithm 1 to solve the data cleanup problem works in the way we might solve this problem using a pencil and paper (and an eraser) to modify the list. We could proceed through the list from left to right, pointing with a finger on the left hand to keep our place, and passing over nonzero values. Every time we encountered a 0 value, we would squeeze it out of the list by taking each remaining data item in the list and copying it over one cell to the left. We could use a finger on the right hand to move along the list and point at what to copy next. The value of *legit*, originally set to the length of the list, would be reduced by 1 every time a 0 was encountered. (Sounds complicated, but you'll see that it is easy.)

The original configuration is

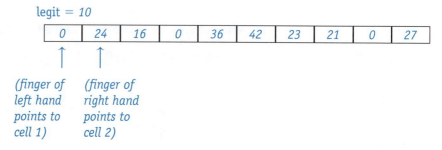

Because the first cell on the left contains a 0, the value of *legit* is reduced by 1, and all of the items to the right of the 0 must be copied one cell left. After the first such copy (of the 24), the situation looks like

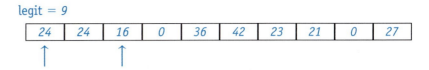

legit = 9

| 24 | 24 | 16 | 0 | 36 | 42 | 23 | 21 | 0 | 27 |

After the second copy (of the 16), we get

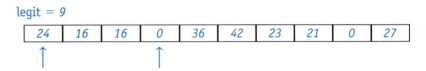

legit = 9

| 24 | 16 | 16 | 0 | 36 | 42 | 23 | 21 | 0 | 27 |

And after the third copy (of the 0),

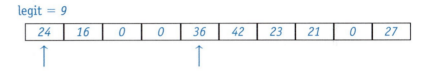

legit = 9

| 24 | 16 | 0 | 0 | 36 | 42 | 23 | 21 | 0 | 27 |

Proceeding in this fashion, we find that after we copy the last item (the 27), the result is

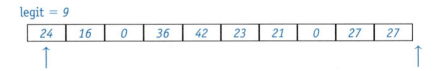

legit = 9

| 24 | 16 | 0 | 36 | 42 | 23 | 21 | 0 | 27 | 27 |

Because the right-hand finger has moved past the end of the list, one complete shuffle-left process has been completed. It required copying nine items. We reset the right-hand finger to start again.

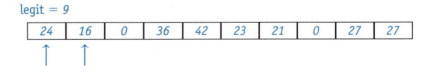

legit = 9

| 24 | 16 | 0 | 36 | 42 | 23 | 21 | 0 | 27 | 27 |

We must again examine position 1 for a 0 value, because if the original list contained 0 in position 2, it would have been copied into position 1. If the value is not 0, as is the case here, both the left-hand finger and the right-hand finger move forward.

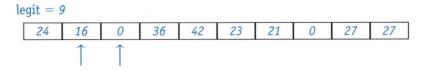

legit = 9

| 24 | 16 | 0 | 36 | 42 | 23 | 21 | 0 | 27 | 27 |

Moving along, we pass over the 16.

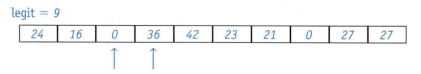

Another cycle of seven copies takes place to squeeze out the 0; the result is

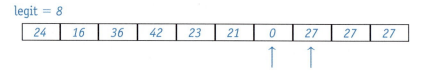

The 36, 42, 23, and 21 are passed over, which results in

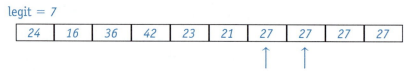

and then copying three items to squeeze out the final 0 gives

The left-hand finger is pointing at a nonzero element, so another advance of both fingers gives

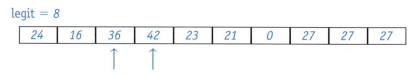

At this point we can stop because the left-hand finger is past the number of legitimate data items (*legit* = 7). In total, this algorithm (on this list) required examining all 10 data items, to see which ones were 0, and copying 9 + 7 + 3 = 19 items.

A pseudocode version of the shuffle-left algorithm to act on a list of n items appears in Figure 3.14. The quantities *left* and *right* correspond to the positions where the left-hand and right-hand fingers point, respectively. You should trace through this algorithm for the preceding example to see that it does what we described.

An analysis of the time efficiency of an algorithm must begin with identifying the units of work we are measuring. For the data cleanup problem, any algorithm must examine each of the n elements in the list to see whether they are 0. This gives a base of at least $\Theta(n)$ work units of examining numbers in the list.

The other unit of work in the shuffle-left algorithm is copying numbers. The best case occurs when the list has no 0 values because no copying is

FIGURE 3.14

The Shuffle-Left Algorithm for Data Cleanup

1. Get values for *n* and the *n* data items
2. Set the value of *legit* to *n*
3. Set the value of *left* to 1
4. Set the value of *right* to 2
5. While *left* is less than or equal to *legit* do steps 6 through 14
6.   If the item at position *left* is not 0 then do steps 7 and 8
7.   Increase *left* by 1
8.   Increase *right* by 1
9.   Else (the item at position *left* is 0) do steps 10 through 14
10.   Reduce *legit* by 1
11.   While *right* is less than or equal to *n* do steps 12 and 13
12.   Copy the item at position *right* into position (*right* − 1)
13.   Increase *right* by 1
14.   Set the value of *right* to (*left* + 1)
15. Stop

required. Conversely, a list with all 0 values is the worst case. If the first element is 0, this requires the remaining $n - 1$ elements to be copied one cell left and reduces *legit* from n to $n - 1$. After the 0 in position 2 gets copied into position 1, the first element is again 0, which again requires $n - 1$ copies and reduces *legit* from $n - 1$ to $n - 2$. This repeats until *legit* is reduced to 0, a total of n times. Thus there are n passes, during each of which $n - 1$ copies are done. The algorithm does

$$n(n - 1) = n^2 - n$$

copies. If we were to draw a graph of $n^2 - n$, we would see that for large n, the curve follows the shape of n^2. The second term can be disregarded, because as n increases, the n^2 term grows much larger than the n term; the n^2 term dominates and determines the shape of the curve. The shuffle-left algorithm is thus an $\Theta(n^2)$ algorithm in the worst case.

The shuffle-left algorithm is space-efficient because it only requires four memory locations to store the quantities *n, legit, left,* and *right* in addition to the memory required to store the list itself.

THE COPY-OVER ALGORITHM. The second algorithm to solve the data cleanup problem also works as we might using a pencil and paper if we decided to write a new list. It proceeds by scanning the list from left to right. Every legitimate value is copied into a new list that is being built. Zero values are not copied into the new list. After this algorithm is finished the original list still exists, but so does a new list in the desired form.

For our example, the result would be

0	24	16	0	36	42	23	21	0	27

24	16	36	42	23	21	27

Every list entry gets examined to see whether it is 0 (as in the shuffle-left algorithm), and every nonzero list entry gets copied once (into the new list), so a total of seven copies are done for this example. This is fewer copies than the shuffle-left algorithm requires, but a lot of extra memory space is

FIGURE 3.15

The Copy-Over Algorithm for
Data Cleanup

1. Get values for *n* and the *n* data items
2. Set the value of *left* to 1
3. Set the value of *newposition* to 1
4. While *left* is less than or equal to *n* do steps 5 through 9
5.   If the item at position *left* is not 0 then do steps 6 through 8
6.   Copy the item at position *left* into position *newposition* in new list
7.   Increase *left* by 1
8.   Increase *newposition* by 1
9.   Else (the item at position *left* is 0) increase *left* by 1
10. Stop

required because an almost complete second copy of the list is stored. Figure 3.15 shows the pseudocode for this copy-over algorithm.

The best case for this algorithm occurs if all elements are 0; no copies are done so the work is just the $\Theta(n)$ work to examine each list element and see that it is 0. No extra space is used. The worst case occurs if there are no 0 values in the list. The algorithm copies all *n* nonzero elements into the new list, and doubles the space required. Combining the two types of work units, we find that the copy-over algorithm is only $\Theta(n)$ in time efficiency even in the worst case, because $\Theta(n)$ examinations and $\Theta(n)$ copies still equal $\Theta(n)$ steps.

Comparing the shuffle-left algorithm and the copy-over algorithm, we see that no 0 elements is the best case of the first algorithm and the worst case of the second, while all 0 elements is the worst case of the first and the best case of the second. The second algorithm is more time-efficient at the expense of making it less space-efficient. This choice is called the **time/space tradeoff**—you win something by giving up something else. Seldom is one fortunate enough to obtain improvement in both dimensions at once, but our next algorithm will accomplish just that.

THE CONVERGING-POINTERS ALGORITHM. For the third algorithm, imagine that we move one finger along the list from left to right and another finger from right to left. The left finger slides to the right over nonzero values. Whenever the left finger encounters a 0 item, we reduce the value of *legit* by 1, copy whatever item is at the right finger into the left-finger position, and slide the right finger one cell left. Initially in our example

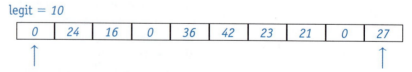

And because a 0 is encountered at position *left*, the item at position *right* is copied into its place, and both *legit* and *right* are reduced by 1. This results in

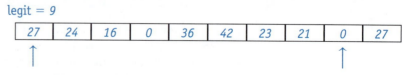

The value of *left* increases until the next 0 is reached.

legit = 9

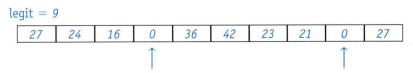

Again, the item at position *right* is copied into position *left,* and *legit* and *right* are reduced by 1.

legit = 8

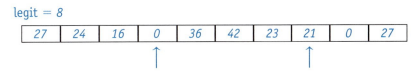

The item at position left is still 0, so another copy takes place.

legit = 7

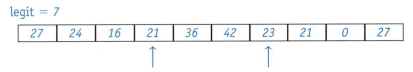

From here on, the left finger advances until it meets the right finger, which is pointing to a nonzero element, and the algorithm stops. Once again, each element was examined to see whether it equaled 0. A total of only three copies were done—fewer even than for algorithm 2 but requiring no more memory space than algorithm 1. The pseudocode version of this converging-pointers algorithm is given in Figure 3.16.

The best case for this algorithm, as for the shuffle-left algorithm, is a list containing no 0 elements. The worst case, as for the shuffle-left algorithm, is a list of all 0 entries. With such a list, the converging-pointers algorithm repeatedly copies the element at position *right* into the first position, each time reducing the value of *right*. *Right* goes from n to 1, with one copy done at each step, resulting in $n - 1$ copies. This algorithm is $\Theta(n)$ in the worst case. Like the shuffle-left algorithm, it is also space-efficient. Here

FIGURE 3.16

The Converging-Pointers Algorithm for Data Cleanup

1. Get values for *n* and the *n* data items
2. Set the value of *legit* to *n*
3. Set the value of *left* to 1
4. Set the value of *right* to *n*
5. While *left* is less than *right* do steps 6 through 10
6.   If the item at position *left* is not 0 then increase *left* by 1
7.   Else (the item at position *left* is 0) do steps 8 through 10
8.   Reduce *legit* by 1
9.   Copy the item at position *right* into position *left*
10.   Reduce *right* by 1
11. If the item at position *left* is 0, then reduce *legit* by 1
12. Stop

FIGURE 3.17

Analysis of Three Data Cleanup Algorithms

	1. SHUFFLE-LEFT		2. COPY-OVER		3. CONVERGING-POINTERS	
	Time	Space	Time	Space	Time	Space
Best case	$\Theta(n)$	n	$\Theta(n)$	n	$\Theta(n)$	n
Worst case	$\Theta(n^2)$	n	$\Theta(n)$	$2n$	$\Theta(n)$	n
Average case	$\Theta(n^2)$	n	$\Theta(n)$	$n \le x \le 2n$	$\Theta(n)$	n

we seem to have been able to beat the time-space tradeoff and obtain the best of both worlds. This was possible in part because the data cleanup problem puts no requirements on the order of the nonzero elements in the "clean" list; the converging-pointers algorithm moves these elements out of their original ordering.

It is hard to define what an "average" case might be for any of these algorithms; the amount of work done depends on how many 0 values there are in the list and perhaps on where in the list they occur. If we assume, however, that the number of 0 values is some percentage of n and that these values are scattered throughout the list, then it can be shown that the shuffle-left algorithm will still do $\Theta(n^2)$ work, whereas the converging pointers algorithm will do $\Theta(n)$. Figure 3.17 summarizes our analysis, although it doesn't reflect the three or four extra memory cells needed to store other quantities used in the algorithms, such as *legit, left,* and *right.*

Let's emphasize again the difference between an algorithm that is $\Theta(n)$ in the amount of work it does and one that is $\Theta(n^2)$. In an $\Theta(n)$ algorithm, the work is proportional to n. Hence if you double n, you double the amount of work; if you multiply n by 10, you multiply the work by 10. But in an $\Theta(n^2)$ algorithm, the work is proportional to the *square* of n. Hence if you double n, you multiply the amount of work by 4; if you multiply n by 10, you multiply the work by 100.

PRACTICE PROBLEMS

In the data cleanup problem, suppose the original data are

2	0	4	1

1. Write the data list after completion of algorithm 1, the shuffle-left algorithm.

2. Write the two data lists after completion of algorithm 2, the copy-over algorithm.

3. Write the data list after completion of algorithm 3, the converging-pointers algorithm.

4. Make up a data list such that step 11 of the converging-pointers algorithm (Figure 3.16) is needed.

This is probably a good place to explain why we worry about the difference between n and $2n$ when we are talking about space but simply classify n and $8000n$ as $\Theta(n)$ when we are talking about units of work. Units of work translate into time when the algorithm is executed, and time is a much more elastic resource than space. We want an algorithm to run in the shortest possible time, but in many cases we don't have a fixed deadline for the exact time that can be expended. There is, however, a fixed upper bound on the amount of memory that the computer has available to use while executing an algorithm, so we track space consumption more closely.

 ### 3.4.2   *Binary Search*

The sequential search algorithm searches a list of n items for a particular item; it is an $\Theta(n)$ algorithm. Another algorithm, the **binary search algorithm,** is more efficient but it works only when the list being searched is already sorted.

To understand how binary search operates, let us go back to the problem of searching for *NAME* in a telephone directory. When you go to look up the name Miranda in the telephone book, you do not do a sequential search beginning with the very first name in the directory and looking at each name in succession until you come to Miranda or the end of the directory! Instead you make use of the fact that the names in the directory have already been sorted into increasing (alphabetical) order. You open the phone book in a random place somewhere near the middle. If the name you see is Miranda, your search is over. If the name you see begins with *P,* you look farther toward the front of the book; if the name you see begins with *L,* you look farther toward the back of the book.

The binary search algorithm works in a similar fashion on a sorted list. It first looks for *NAME* at roughly the halfway point in the list. If the name there equals *NAME,* the search is over. If *NAME* comes alphabetically before the name at the halfway point, then the search is narrowed to the front half of the list, and the process begins again on this smaller list. If *NAME* comes alphabetically after the name at the halfway point, then the search is narrowed to the back half of the list, and the process begins again on *this* smaller list. The algorithm halts when *NAME* is found or when the sublist becomes empty.

Figure 3.18 gives a pseudocode version of the binary search algorithm on a sorted n-element list. Here *beginning* and *end* mark the beginning and end of the section of the list under consideration. Initially the whole list is considered, so at first *beginning* is 1 and *end* is n. If *NAME* is not found at the midpoint m of the current section of the list, then setting *end* equal to one less than the midpoint (step 9) means that at the next pass through the loop, the front half of the current section will be considered. Setting *beginning* equal to one more than the midpoint (step 10) means that at the next pass through the loop, the back half of the current section will be considered. Thus as the algorithm proceeds, the *beginning* marker can move toward the back of the list, and the *end* marker can move toward the front of the list. Should it ever happen that the *beginning* marker and the *end* marker cross over—that is, *end* becomes less than *beginning*—then the current section of the list is empty and the search terminates. Of course it also terminates if the name is found.

FIGURE 3.18

Binary Search Algorithm
(list must be sorted)

1. Get values for *NAME, n, N_1, ..., N_n* and *T_1, ..., T_n*
2. Set the value of *beginning* to 1 and set the value of *Found* to NO
3. Set the value of *end* to *n*
4. While *Found* = NO and *end* is less than *beginning* do steps 5 through 10
5. Set the value of *m* to the middle value between *beginning* and *end*
6. If *NAME* is equal to N_m, the name found at the midpoint between *beginning* and *end*, then do steps 7 and 8
7. Print the telephone number of that person, T_m
8. Set the value of *Found* to YES
9. Else if *NAME* precedes N_m alphabetically, then set *end* = *m* − 1
10. Else (*NAME* follows N_m alphabetically) set *beginning* = *m* + 1
11. If (*Found* = NO) then print the message 'I am sorry but that name is not in the directory'
12. Stop

Let's do an example, using seven names sorted into increasing (alphabetical) order. The following list shows not only the names in the list but also their locations in the list.

Ann	Bob	Cora	Devi	Grant	Nathan	Sue
1	2	3	4	5	6	7

Suppose we are searching this list for the name Cora. We set *beginning* to 1 and *end* to 7; the midpoint between 1 and 7 is 4. We compare the name at position number 4, Devi, with Cora. Cora precedes Devi alphabetically, so the algorithm sets *end* to 4 − 1 = 3 (step 9) in order to continue the search on the front half of the list,

Ann	Bob	Cora
1	2	3

The midpoint between *beginning* = 1 and *end* = 3 is 2, so we compare the name at position number 2, Bob, with Cora. Cora follows Bob alphabetically, so the algorithm sets *beginning* to 2 + 1 = 3 (step 10) in order to continue the search on the back half of this list, namely

Cora
3

At the next pass through the loop, the midpoint between *beginning* = 3 and *end* = 3 is 3, so we compare the name at position number 3, Cora, with the target name, Cora. We have found the name; the appropriate telephone number can be printed and *Found* changed to YES. Next the loop terminates, and then the algorithm terminates.

Now suppose we search this same list for the name Maria. As before, the first midpoint is 4, so Devi is compared with Maria. Maria follows Devi, so the search continues with *beginning* = 5, *end* = 7 on the back half:

Grant	Nathan	Sue
5	6	7

The midpoint is 6, so Nathan is compared with Maria. Maria precedes Nathan, so the search continues with *beginning* = 5, *end* = 5 on the front half:

Grant
5

The midpoint is 5, so Grant is compared with Maria. Maria follows Grant, so *beginning* is set to 6 in order to continue the search on the back half of this list. The algorithm checks the condition at step 4 to see whether to repeat the loop again and finds that *end* is less than *beginning* (*end* = 5, *beginning* = 6). The loop is abandoned, and the algorithm moves on to step 11 and notes that Maria is not in the list.

It is easier to see how the binary search algorithm operates if we list the locations of the names checked in a "tree-like" structure. The tree in Figure 3.19 shows the possible locations that will be searched for a 7-element list. The search starts at the top of the tree, at location 4, the middle of the original list. If the name at location 4 is *NAME*, the search halts. If *NAME* comes after the name at location 4 (as in our example with Maria), the right branch is taken and the next location searched is location 6. If *NAME* comes before the name at location 4 (as in our example with Cora), the left branch is taken and the next location searched is location 2. If *NAME* is not found at location 2, the next location searched will be either 1 or 3. Similarly, if *NAME* is not found at location 6, the next location searched will be either 5 or 7.

In Figure 3.18, the binary search algorithm, we assumed in step 5 that there is a middle position between *beginning* and *end*. This happens only when there is an odd number of elements in the list. Let us agree to define the "middle" of an even number of entries as the end of the first half of the list. With eight elements, for example, the midpoint position would be location 4.

1 2 3 4̲ 5 6 7 8

With this understanding, the binary search algorithm can be used on lists of any size.

Like the sequential search algorithm, the binary search algorithm relies

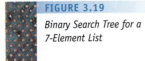

FIGURE 3.19

Binary Search Tree for a 7-Element List

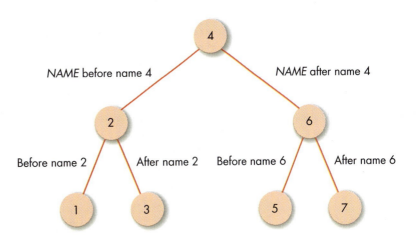

on comparisons, so to analyze the algorithm we will count the number of comparisons as an indication of the work done. The best case, as in sequential search, requires only one comparison—*NAME* is located on the first try. The worst case, as in sequential search, occurs when *NAME* is not in the list. However, we learn this much sooner in binary search than in sequential search. In our example of seven names, only three comparisons were needed to determine that Maria is not in the list. The number of comparisons needed is the number of circles in some branch from the top to the bottom of the tree in Figure 3.19. These circles represent searches at the midpoints of the whole list, half the list, one quarter of the list, and so on. This process continues as long as the sublists can be cut in half.

Let's do a minor mathematical digression here. The number of times a number *n* can be cut in half and not go below 1 is called the **logarithm of *n* to the base 2,** which is abbreviated lg *n* (also written in some texts as $\log_2 n$). For example, if *n* is 16, then we can do four such divisions by 2:

$$16/2 = 8$$
$$8/2 = 4$$
$$4/2 = 2$$
$$2/2 = 1$$

so lg 16 = 4. This is another way of saying that $2^4 = 16$. In general,

$$\text{lg } n = m \text{ is equivalent to } 2^m = n$$

Figure 3.20 shows a few values of *n* and lg *n*. From these, we can see that as *n* doubles, lg *n* increases by only 1, so lg *n* grows much more slowly than *n*. Figure 3.21 shows the two basic shapes of *n* and lg *n* and again conveys that lg *n* grows much more slowly than *n*.

Remember the analogy we suggested earlier about the difference in time consumed between $\Theta(n^2)$ algorithms, equivalent to various forms of walking, and $\Theta(n)$ algorithms, equivalent to various forms of driving? We carry that analogy further by saying that algorithms of $\Theta(\text{lg } n)$ are equivalent to various forms of flying. Changing the coefficients of lg *n* may mean that we go from a Piper cub to an F-14, but flying, in any form, is still a fundamentally different—and faster—category from driving or walking.

Now suppose we are doing a binary search on *n* names. In the worst case, as we have seen, the number of comparisons is related to the number of times the list of length *n* can be halved. Binary search does $\Theta(\text{lg } n)$ comparisons in the worst case (see Exercise 23 at the end of the chapter for an exact formula for the worst case). As a matter of fact, it also does $\Theta(\text{lg } n)$ comparisons in the average case to find a name that is in the list (although the exact value is a

FIGURE 3.20

Values for n and lg n

n	lg *n*
8	3
16	4
32	5
64	6
128	7

FIGURE 3.21

A Comparison of n *and* lg n

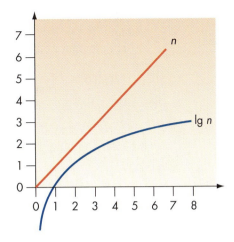

smaller number than in the worst case). This is because most of the names in the list occur at or near the bottom of the tree, where the maximum amount of work must be done; recall that it also took three comparisons to find that Cora was in the list. As Figure 3.19 shows, relatively few locations (where *NAME* might be found and the algorithm terminate sooner) are higher in the tree.

Both binary search and sequential search solve the telephone book search problem, but these algorithms differ in the order of magnitude of the work they do. Binary search is an $\Theta(\lg n)$ algorithm, whereas sequential search is an $\Theta(n)$ algorithm, in both the worst case and the average case. To compare the binary search algorithm with the sequential search algorithm, suppose there are 100 elements in the list. In the worst case, sequential search would require 100 comparisons, binary search 7 ($2^7 = 128$). In the average case, sequential search would require about 50 comparisons, binary search 6 or 7 (still much less work). The improvement in binary search becomes even more apparent as the list to be searched gets longer. For example, if $n = 100,000$, then in the worst case sequential search will require 100,000 comparisons, whereas binary search will require 17 ($2^{17} = 131,072$). If we wrote two programs, one using sequential search and one using binary search, and ran them on a computer that could do 1000 name comparisons per second, then to determine that a name is not in the list (the worst case) the sequential search program would use

$$100,000 \text{ comparisons} \times \frac{1}{1,000} \text{ seconds/comparison} = 100 \text{ seconds}$$

or 1.67 minutes, just to do the necessary comparisons, disregarding the constant factor for advancing the index. The binary search program would use

$$17 \text{ comparisons} \times \frac{1}{1,000} \text{ seconds/comparison} = 0.017 \text{ seconds}$$

to do the comparisons, disregarding a constant factor for updating the values of *beginning* and *end*. This is quite a difference.

Suppose our two programs are used with the 20,000,000 names we are assuming in the New York City phone book. On the average, the sequential search program would need about

$$\frac{20,000,000}{2} \text{ comparisons} \times \frac{1}{1,000} \text{ seconds/comparison} = 10,000 \text{ seconds}$$

(about 2.78 hours!) just to do the comparisons to find a name in the list, whereas the binary search program would need (because $2^{25} \approx 33,000,000$) about

$$25 \text{ comparisons} \times \frac{1}{1,000} \text{ seconds/comparison} = 0.025 \text{ seconds}$$

This is an even more impressive difference. Furthermore, it's a difference due to the inherent inefficiency of an $\Theta(n)$ algorithm compared to an $\Theta(\lg n)$ algorithm, which can be moderated but not solved by simply using a faster computer. If our computer does 50,000 comparisons per second, then the average times become about

$$\frac{20,000,000}{2} \text{ comparisons} \times \frac{1}{50,000} \text{ seconds/comparison} = 200 \text{ seconds}$$

or 3.33 minutes for sequential search and about

$$25 \text{ comparisons} \times \frac{1}{50,000} \text{ seconds/comparison} = 0.0005 \text{ seconds}$$

for binary search. The sequential search alternative is simply not acceptable. That is why analyzing algorithms, and choosing the best one, can be so important. We also see, as we noted in Chapter 2, that the way the problem data are organized can greatly affect the best choice of algorithm to solve the problem.

The binary search algorithm works only on a list that has already been sorted. If the list is not sorted, it could first be sorted and binary search then used, but sorting also takes a lot of work, as we have seen. If a list is to be searched only a few times for a few particular names, then it is more efficient to do sequential search on the unsorted list (a few $\Theta(n)$ tasks). But if the list is to be searched repeatedly—as in the daily use of an automated telephone directory for the foreseeable future—it is more efficient to sort it and then use binary search: one $\Theta(n^2)$ task and many $\Theta(\lg n)$ tasks, as opposed to many $\Theta(n)$ tasks.

PRACTICE PROBLEM

1. Suppose that, using the list of seven names from this section, we try binary search to decide whether Grant is in the list. What names would be compared to Grant?

As to space efficiency, binary search, like sequential search, requires only a small amount of additional storage to keep track of beginning, end, and midpoint positions in the list. Thus, it is space-efficient; in this case, we did not have to sacrifice space efficiency to gain time efficiency. But we did have to sacrifice generality—binary search works only on a sorted list whereas sequential search works on any list.

3.4.3 *Pattern Matching*

The pattern-matching algorithm from Chapter 2 involves finding all occurrences of a pattern of the form $P_1P_2 \ldots P_m$ within text of the form $T_1T_2 \ldots T_n$. Recall that the algorithm simply does a "forward march" through the text, at each position beginning an attempt to match each pattern character against the text characters. The process stops only after text position $n - m + 1$, when the remaining text is not as long as the pattern so that there could not possibly be a match. This algorithm is interesting to analyze because it involves two measures of input size: n, the length of the text string, and m, the length of the pattern string. The unit of work is comparison of a pattern character with a text character.

Surprisingly, both the best case and the worst case of this algorithm can occur when the pattern is not in the text at all. The difference hinges on exactly *how* the pattern fails to be in the text. The best case occurs if the first character of the pattern is nowhere in the text, as in

Text: *KLMNPQRSTX*

Pattern: *ABC*

In this case $n - m + 1$ comparisons are required, trying (unsuccessfully) to match P_1 with $T_1, T_2, \ldots, T_{n-m+1}$ in turn. Each comparison fails, and the algorithm slides the pattern forward to try again at the next position in the text.

The maximum amount of work is done if the pattern *almost* occurs everywhere in the text. Consider, for example, the following case:

Text: *AAAAAAAAA*

Pattern: *AAAB*

Starting with T_1, the first text character, the match with the first pattern character is successful. The match with the second text character and the second pattern character is also successful. Indeed $m - 1$ characters of the pattern match with the text before the mth comparison proves a failure. The process starts over from the second text character, T_2. Once again, m comparisons are required to find a mismatch. Altogether, m comparisons are required for each of the $n - m + 1$ starting positions in the text.

Another version of the worst case occurs when the pattern is found at each location in the text, as in

Text: AAAAAAAAA

Pattern: AAAA

This results in the same comparisons as are done for the other worst case, the only difference being that the comparison of the last pattern character is successful.

Unlike our simple examples, pattern matching is usually of interest only when the pattern length is short compared to the text length, that is, when m is much less than n. In such cases, $n - m + 1$ is essentially n. The pattern-matching algorithm is therefore $\Theta(n)$ in the best case and $\Theta(m \times n)$ in the worst case.

It requires somewhat pathological situations to create the worst cases we have described. In general, the forward-march algorithm performs quite well on text and patterns consisting of ordinary words. Other pattern-matching algorithms exist that are conceptually more complex but require less work in the worst case.

  ### 3.4.4 Summary

Figure 3.22 shows an order-of-magnitude summary of the time efficiency for the algorithms we have analyzed.

FIGURE 3.22

Order-of-Magnitude Time Efficiency Summary

PROBLEM	UNIT OF WORK	ALGORITHM	BEST CASE	WORST CASE	AVERAGE CASE
Searching	Comparisons	Sequential search	1	$\Theta(n)$	$\Theta(n)$
		Binary search	1	$\Theta(\lg n)$	$\Theta(\lg n)$
Sorting	Comparisons and exchanges	Selection sort	$\Theta(n^2)$	$\Theta(n^2)$	$\Theta(n^2)$
Data cleanup	Examinations and copies	Shuffle-left	$\Theta(n)$	$\Theta(n^2)$	$\Theta(n^2)$
		Copy-over	$\Theta(n)$	$\Theta(n)$	$\Theta(n)$
		Converging-pointers	$\Theta(n)$	$\Theta(n)$	$\Theta(n)$
Pattern matching	Character comparisons	Forward march	$\Theta(n)$	$\Theta(m \times n)$	

1. Use the first example pattern and text given in Section 3.4.3 for the worst case of the pattern-matching algorithm. What is m? What is n? What is $m \times n$? This algorithm is $\Theta(m \times n)$ in the worst case, but what is the exact number of comparisons done?

3.5 When Things Get Out of Hand

We have so far found examples of algorithms that are $\Theta(\lg n)$, $\Theta(n)$, and $\Theta(n^2)$ in time efficiency. Order of magnitude, as we know, determines how quickly the values grow as n increases. An algorithm of order $\lg n$ does less work as n increases than does an algorithm of order n, which in turn does less work than one of order n^2. The work done by any of these algorithms is no worse than a constant multiple of n^2, which is a polynomial in n. Therefore, these algorithms are **polynomially bounded** in the amount of work they do as n increases.

There are some algorithms that must do work that is not polynomially bounded. Suppose we consider four cities, A, B, C, and D, that are connected as shown in Figure 3.23 and ask the following question: Is it possible to start at city A, go through every other city exactly once, and end up back at A? Of course, we as humans can immediately see in this small problem that the answer is Yes and that there are two such paths: A-B-D-C-A and A-C-D-B-A. However, an algorithm doesn't get to "see" the entire picture at once, as we can; it has available to it only isolated facts such as "A is connected to B and to C," "B is connected to A and to D," and so on. If the number of *nodes* and connecting *edges* were large, even humans might not "see" the solution immediately. A collection of nodes and connecting edges is called a **graph.** A path through a graph that begins and ends at the same node and goes through all other nodes exactly once is called a **Hamiltonian circuit,** named for the Irish mathematician William Rowan Hamilton (1805–1865). If there are n nodes in the graph, then a Hamiltonian circuit, if it exists, must have exactly n links. In the case of the four cities, for instance, if the path must go through exactly A, B, C, D, and A (in some order), then there are five nodes on the path (counting A twice) and four links.

Our problem is to decide whether an arbitrary graph has a Hamiltonian circuit. An algorithm to solve this problem is to examine all possible paths through the graph that are the appropriate length to see whether any of them

FIGURE 3.23
Four Connected Cities

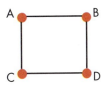

are Hamiltonian circuits. The algorithm can trace all paths by beginning at the starting node and choosing at each node where to go next. Without going into the details of such an algorithm, let's represent the possible paths with four links in the graph of Figure 3.23. Again, we will use a tree structure. In Figure 3.24, A is the tree "root," and at each node in the tree, the nodes directly below it are the choices for the next node. Thus, any time B appears in the tree, it has the two nodes A and D below it, because edges exist from B to A and from B to D. The "branches" of the tree are all the possible paths from A with four links. Once the tree has been built, an examination of the paths shows that only the two dark paths in the figure represent Hamiltonian circuits.

The number of paths that must be examined is the number of nodes at the bottom level of the tree. There is one node at the top of the tree; we'll call the top of the tree level 0. The number of nodes is multiplied by 2 for each level down in the tree. At level 1 there are 2 nodes, at level 2 there are 2^2 nodes, at level 3 there are 2^3 nodes, and at level 4, the bottom of the tree, there are $2^4 = 16$ nodes.

Suppose we were looking for a Hamiltonian circuit in a graph with n nodes and two choices at each node. The bottom of the corresponding tree would be at level n, and there would be 2^n paths to examine. If we take the examination of a single path as a unit of work, then this algorithm must do 2^n units of work. This is more work than any polynomial in n. An $\Theta(2^n)$ algorithm is called an **exponential algorithm.** Hence the trial-and-error approach to solving the Hamiltonian circuit problem is an exponential algorithm. (We could improve on this algorithm by letting it stop tracing a path whenever a repeated node different from the starting node is encountered, but it will still be exponential. If there were more than two choices at a node, the amount of work would be even greater.)

Figure 3.25 shows the four curves lg n, n, n^2, and 2^n. The rapid growth of 2^n is not really apparent here, however, because that curve is off the scale for values of n above 5. Figure 3.26 compares these four curves for values of n that are still small, but even so, 2^n is already far outstanding the other values.

FIGURE 3.24

Hamiltonian Circuits among All Paths from A in Figure 3.23 with Four Links

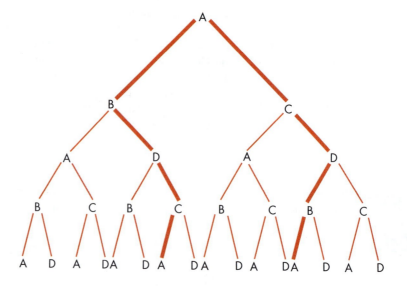

FIGURE 3.25

*Comparisons of lg n, n, n²,
and 2ⁿ*

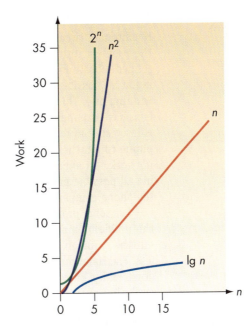

To appreciate more fully why the order of magnitude of an algorithm is important, let's again imagine that we are running various algorithms as programs on a computer that can perform a single operation (unit of work) in 0.0001 second. Figure 3.27 shows the amount of time it will take for algorithms of $\Theta(\lg n)$, $\Theta(n)$, $\Theta(n^2)$, and $\Theta(2^n)$ to complete their work for various values of n.

The expression 2^n grows unbelievably fast. An algorithm of $\Theta(2^n)$ can take so long to solve even a small problem that it is of no practical value. Even if we greatly increase the speed of the computer, the results are much the same. We now see more than ever why we added *efficiency* as a desirable feature for an algorithm and why such an issue is independent of future advances in computer technology. No matter how fast computers get, they will not be able to solve a problem of size $n = 100$ using an algorithm of $\Theta(2^n)$ in any reasonable period of time.

FIGURE 3.26

*Comparisons of lg n, n, n², and
2ⁿ for Larger Values of n*

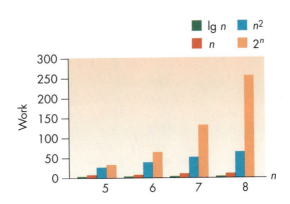

The algorithm we have described here for testing an arbitrary graph for Hamiltonian circuits is an example of a **brute force algorithm**—one that beats the problem into submission by trying all possibilities. In Chapter 1 we described a brute force algorithm for winning a chess game; it consisted of looking at all possible game scenarios from any given point on and then picking a winning one. This is also an exponential algorithm. Some very practical problems have exponential solution algorithms. For example, the telephone company is interested in routing its calls along the shortest possible path from one telephone to another through all the various switching points in the telephone network. An exponential algorithm to solve this problem would be to examine all possible paths and then use the shortest one. As you can imagine, the telephone company uses a better (more efficient) algorithm than this one!

For some problems, however, no polynomially bounded algorithm to solve the problem exists. Such problems are called **intractable**; they are solvable, but the solution algorithms all require so much work as to be virtually useless. The Hamiltonian circuit problem is suspected to be such a problem, but we don't really know for sure! No one has yet found a solution algorithm that works in polynomial time, but neither has anyone yet proved that such an algorithm does not exist. This is a problem of great interest in computer science. A surprising number of problems fall into this "suspected intractable" category. Here's another one, called the **bin-packing problem**: Given an unlimited number of bins of volume 1 unit and given n objects, all of volume between 0.0 and 1.0, find the minimum number of bins needed to store the n objects. A solution algorithm for this problem would be of interest to any manufacturer who ships sets of various items in standard-sized cartons or to anyone who wants to store image files on a set of CDs in the most efficient way.

Problems for which no known polynomial solution algorithm exists are sometimes attacked by **approximation algorithms.** These algorithms don't solve the original problem, but they provide a close approximation to the solution. For example, an approximation algorithm to solve the bin-packing problem is to take the objects in order, put the first one into bin 1, and stuff each remaining object into the first bin that can hold it. This (reasonable) approach may not give the absolute minimum number of bins needed, but it gives a first cut at the answer. (Anyone who has watched passengers stowing carry-on baggage in an airplane has seen this approximation algorithm at work.)

As an example, suppose a sequence of four objects with volumes of 0.3, 0.4, 0.5, and 0.6 are stored using the "first-fit" algorithm described above. The result would require three bins, which would be packed as shown in Figure 3.28. However, this is not the optimal solution (see Exercise 29 at the end of the chapter).

In this last section we've wandered rather far afield into the realm of problems that have algorithmic solutions but no known "fast" (polynomial)

FIGURE 3.27

A Comparison of Four Orders of Magnitude

			n	
ORDER	10	50	100	1,000
$\lg n$	0.0003 sec	0.0006 sec	0.0007 sec	0.001 sec
n	0.001 sec	0.005 sec	0.01 sec	0.1 sec
n^2	0.01 sec	0.25 sec	1 sec	1.67 min
2^n	0.1024 sec	3,570 years	4×10^{16} centuries	*Too big to compute!!*

solution algorithms. In Chapter 11, we will learn that there are problems with no algorithm at all to solve them, even if we are willing to accept an incredibly inefficient solution.

FIGURE 3.28

A First-Fit Solution to a Bin-Packing Problem

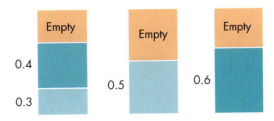

Empty

0.4

0.3

Empty

0.5

Empty

0.6

LABORATORY EXPERIENCE 6

The various sorting algorithms examined in Laboratory Experience 4 (selection sort, quicksort, etc.) do different amounts of work on the same data sets. In this laboratory experience, you can run these sorting algorithms and clock the time they take. This will enable you to make some comparisons of time efficiency on different sizes of input.

PRACTICE PROBLEMS

1. Consider the following graph:

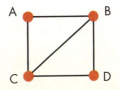

Draw a tree similar to Figure 3.24 showing all paths from A and highlighting those that are Hamiltonian circuits (these are the same two circuits as before). How many paths have to be examined?

2. The following tree shows all paths with two links that begin at node A in some graph. Draw the graph.

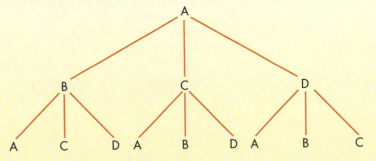

We defined computer science as the study of algorithms, so it is appropriate that Level 1 was devoted to exploring algorithms in more detail. In Chapter 2 we discussed how to represent algorithms using pseudocode. Pseudocode provides us with a flexible language in which to express the building blocks from which algorithms can be constructed. These building blocks include assigning a particular value to a quantity, choosing one of two next steps on the basis of some condition, or repeating steps in a loop.

We developed algorithmic solutions to three very practical problems: searching for a name in a list of names, finding the largest number in a list of numbers, and searching for a particular pattern of characters within a segment of text. In Chapter 3 we noted that computer scientists develop algorithms to be *used* and that this leads to a set of desirable properties for algorithms, such as ease of understanding, elegance, and efficiency, in addition to correctness. Of these, efficiency—which may be either time efficiency or space efficiency—is the most easily quantifiable.

A convenient way to classify the time efficiency of algorithms is by examining the order of magnitude of the work they do. Algorithms that are of differing orders of magnitude do fundamentally different amounts of work. No matter what the constant factor that reflects peripheral work and no matter how fast the computer on which these algorithms execute, for problems with sufficiently large input, the algorithm of the lowest order of magnitude will require the least time.

We analyzed the time efficiency of the sequential search algorithm and discovered that it is an $\Theta(n)$ algorithm in both the worst case and the average case. We found a selection sort algorithm that is $\Theta(n^2)$, we found a binary search algorithm that is $\Theta(\lg n)$, and we did an analysis of the pattern-matching algorithm from Chapter 2. Through examining the data cleanup problem, we learned that algorithms that solve the same task can indeed differ in the order of magnitude of the work they do, sometimes by employing a time/space trade-off. We also learned that there are algorithms that require more than polynomially bounded time to complete their work and that such algorithms may take so long, regardless of the speed of the computer on which they are run, that they provide no practical solution method. Some important and practical problems may be intractable, having no polynomially bounded solution algorithms at all.

Some computer scientists work on deciding whether a particular problem is intractable. Some work on finding more efficient algorithms for problems—such as searching and sorting—that are such common tasks that a more efficient algorithm would greatly improve productivity. Still others seek to discover algorithms for new problems. Thus, as we said, the study of algorithms underlies much of computer science. But everything we have done so far has been a pencil and paper exercise. In terms of the definition of computer science that we gave in Chapter 1, we have been looking at the formal and mathematical properties of algorithms. It is time to move on to the next part of that definition: the hardware realizations of algorithms. When we execute real algorithms on real computers, those computers are electronic devices. How does an electronic device "understand" an algorithm and carry out its instructions? We begin to explore these questions in Chapter 4 as we enter the hardware world.

1. a. Use Gauss's approach to find the sum

$$2 + 4 + 6 + \ldots + 100$$

  b. Use Gauss's approach to find a formula for the sum of the even numbers from 2 to $2n$,

$$2 + 4 + 6 + \ldots + 2n$$

  Your formula will be an expression involving n.

2. The **Fibonacci sequence** of numbers is defined as follows: The first and second numbers are both 1. After that, each number in the sequence is the sum of the two preceding numbers. Thus, the Fibonacci sequence is

$$1, 1, 2, 3, 5, 8, 13, 21, \ldots$$

If $F(n)$ stands for the nth value in the sequence, then this definition can be expressed as

$$F(1) = 1$$
$$F(2) = 1$$
$$F(n) = F(n - 1) + F(n - 2) \text{ for } n > 2$$

  a. Using the definition of the Fibonacci sequence, compute the value of $F(20)$.

  b. A formula for $F(n)$ is

$$F(n) = \frac{\sqrt{5}}{5}\left(\frac{1 + \sqrt{5}}{2}\right)^n - \frac{\sqrt{5}}{5}\left(\frac{1 - \sqrt{5}}{2}\right)^n$$

  Using the formula (and a calculator), compute the value of $F(20)$.

  c. What are your opinions on the relative clarity, elegance, and efficiency of the two algorithms (using the definition and using the formula) to compute $F(20)$? Would your answer change if you considered $F(100)$?

3. A tennis tournament has 342 players. A single match involves 2 players. The winner of a match will play the winner of a match in the next round, whereas losers are eliminated from the tournament. The 2 players who have won all previous rounds play in the final game, and the winner wins the tournament. What is the total number of matches needed to determine the winner?

  a. Here is one algorithm to answer this question. Compute $342 / 2 = 171$ to get the number of pairs (matches) in the first round, which results in 171 winners to go on to the second round. Compute $171 / 2 = 85$ with 1 left over, which results in 85 matches in the second round and 85 winners, plus the 1 left over, to go on to the third round. For the third round compute $86 / 2 = 43$, so the third round has 43 matches, and so on. The total number of matches is $171 + 85 + 43 + \ldots$. Finish this process in order to find the total number of matches.

  b. Here is another algorithm to solve this question.

Each match results in exactly one loser, so there must be the same number of matches as losers in the tournament. Compute the total number of losers in the entire tournament. (*Hint:* This isn't really a computation; it is a one-sentence argument.)

  c. What are your opinions on the relative clarity, elegance, and efficiency of the two algorithms?

4. We have said that the average number of comparisons needed to find a name in an n-element list using sequential search is slightly higher than $n/2$. In this problem we will find an exact expression for this average.

  a. Suppose a random list of names has an odd number of names, say 15. At what position is the middle name? Using sequential search, how many comparisons are required to find the middle name? Repeat this exercise with a few more odd numbers until you can answer the following question: If there are n names in the list and n is an odd number, write an expression for the number of comparisons required to find the middle name.

  b. Suppose a random list of names has an even number of names, say 16. At what positions are the two "middle" names? Using sequential search, how many comparisons are required to find each of these? What is the average of these two numbers? Repeat this exercise with a few more even numbers until you can answer the following question: If there are n names in the list and n is an even number, write an expression for the average number of comparisons required to find the two middle names.

  c. Noting that half the names in a list fall before the midpoint and half after the midpoint, use your answer to parts (a) and (b) to write an exact expression for the average number of comparisons done using sequential search to find a name that occurs in an n-element list.

5. Here is a list of seven names:

  Sherman, Jane, Ted, Elise, Raul, Maki, John

  Search this list for each name in turn, using sequential search and counting the number of comparisons for each name. Now take the seven comparison counts and find their average. Did you get a number that you expected? Why?

6. Perform a selection sort on the list 7, 4, 2, 9, 6. Show the list after each exchange that has a visible effect.

7. The selection sort algorithm could be modified to stop when the unsorted section of the list contains only one number, because that one number must be in the correct position. Show that this modification would have no effect on the number of comparisons required to sort an n-element list.

Exercises 8-10 refer to another algorithm, called **bubble sort,** to sort an n-element list. Bubble sort makes multiple passes through the list from front to back, each time exchanging pairs of entries that are out of order. Here is a pseudocode version:

1. Get values for n and the n list items
2. Set the marker U for the unsorted section at the end of the list
3. While the unsorted section has more than one element do steps 4 through 8
4.   Set the current element marker C at the second element of the list
5.   While C is has not passed U do steps 6 and 7
6.   If the item at position C is less than the item to its left then exchange these two items
7.   Move C to the right one position
8.   Move U left one position
9. Stop

8. For each of the following lists, perform a bubble sort, and show the list after each exchange. Compare the number of exchanges done here and in the Practice Problem at the end of Section 3.3.3.

   a. 4, 8, 2, 6

   b. 12, 3, 6, 8, 2, 5, 7

   c. D, B, G, F, A, C, E

9. Explain why the bubble sort algorithm above does $\Theta(n^2)$ comparisons on an n-element list.

10. Suppose selection sort and bubble sort are both performed on a list that is already sorted. Does bubble sort do fewer exchanges than selection sort? Explain.

11. Algorithms A and B perform the same task. On input of size n, algorithm A executes $0.003n^2$ instructions, and algorithm B executes $243n$ instructions. Find the approximate value of n above which algorithm B is more efficient. (You may use a calculator.)

12. Suppose a metropolitan area is divided into 4 telephone calling districts, 1, 2, 3, 4. The telephone company keeps track of the number of calls placed from one district to another and the number of calls placed within a district. This information is recorded per month in a 4×4 table as shown here. The entry in row 1, column 3, for example, shows the number of calls (314) placed from district 1 to district 3 for the month. The entry in row 1, column 1 shows the number of calls (243) placed from district 1 to district 1.

	1	2	3	4
1	243	187	314	244
2	215	420	345	172
3	197	352	385	261
4	340	135	217	344

Now suppose the telephone company serves n telephone districts, and maintains an $n \times n$ table.

   a. Write a pseudocode algorithm to print out the table, that is, to print each of the entries in the table. Write an expression for the number of print statements the algorithm executes.

   b. Write a pseudocode algorithm to print n copies of the table, one to give to each of the n district managers. Write an expression for the number of print statements the algorithm executes.

   c. What is the order of magnitude of the work done by the algorithm of Part b if the unit of work is printing a table element?

13. Write the data list that results from running the shuffle-left algorithm to clean up the following data. Find the exact number of copies done.

3	0	0	2	6	7	0	0	5	1

14. Write the resulting data list and find the exact number of copies done by the converging-pointers algorithm when it is executed on the data of Exercise 13.

15. Explain in words how to modify the shuffle-left data cleanup algorithm to reduce slightly the number of copies it makes. (*Hint:* Must item n always be copied?) If this modified algorithm is run on the data list of Exercise 13, exactly how many copies are done?

16. The shuffle-left algorithm for data cleanup is supposed to perform $n(n-1)$ copies on a list consisting of n 0s. Confirm this result for the following list:

   0 0 0 0 0 0

17. Consider the following list of names.

   Arturo, Elsa, JoAnn, John, Jose, Lee, Snyder, Tracy

   a. Use binary search to decide whether Elsa is in this list. What names will be compared to Elsa?

   b. Use binary search to decide whether Tracy is in this list. What names will be compared to Tracy?

   c. Use binary search to decide whether Emile is in this list. What names will be compared to Emile?

18. Use the binary search algorithm to decide whether 35 is in the following list:

   3, 6, 7, 9, 12, 14, 18, 21, 22, 31, 43

   What numbers will be compared to 35?

19. If a list is already sorted in increasing order, a modified sequential search algorithm can be used that compares against each element in turn, stopping if a list element exceeds the target value. Write a pseudocode version of this **short sequential search.**

20. This exercise refers to short sequential search (see Exercise 19).

   a. What is the worst-case number of comparisons of short sequential search on a sorted n-element list?

b. What is the approximate average number of comparisons to find an element that is in a sorted list using short sequential search?

c. Is short sequential search ever more efficient than regular sequential search? Explain.

21. For the 8-element list of Exercise 17, draw the tree structure that describes binary search on this list. What is the number of comparisons in the worst case? Give an example of a name to search for that would require that many comparisons.

22. Draw the tree structure that describes binary search on a list with 16 elements. What is the number of comparisons in the worst case?

23. We want to find an exact formula for the number of comparisons that binary search requires in the worst case on an n-element list. (We already know the formula is $\Theta(\lg n)$.)

a. If x is a number that is not an integer, then $\lfloor x \rfloor$, called the **floor function** of x, is defined to be the largest integer less than or equal to x. For example, $\lfloor 3.7 \rfloor = 3$ and $\lfloor 5 \rfloor = 5$. Find the following values: $\lfloor 1.2 \rfloor$, $\lfloor 23 \rfloor$, $\lfloor 8.9 \rfloor$, $\lfloor -4.6 \rfloor$.

b. If n is not a power of 2, then $\lg n$ will not be an integer. If n is between 8 and 16, for example, then $\lg n$ will be between 3 and 4 (because $\lg 8 = 3$ and $\lg 16 = 4$). Complete the following table of values:

n	$\lfloor \lg n \rfloor$
2	1
3	
4	2
5	
6	
7	
8	3

c. For $n = 2, 3, 4, 5, 6, 7, 8$, draw a tree structure similar to Figure 3.19 to describe the positions searched by binary search. For each value of n, use the tree structure to find the number of comparisons in the worst case, and complete the following table:

n	Number of compares, worst case
2	
3	
4	3
5	
6	
7	3
8	

d. Comparing the tables of Parts b and c, find a formula involving $\lfloor \lg n \rfloor$ for the number of comparisons binary search requires in the worst case on an n-element list. Test your formula by drawing trees for other values of n.

24. Using the tree of Figure 3.19, find the number of comparisons to find each of items 1–7 in a seven element list using binary search. Then find the average. Compare this with the worst case.

25. At the end of Section 3.4.2, we talked about the trade-off between using sequential search on an unsorted list as opposed to sorting the list and then using binary search. If the list size is $n = 100,000$, about how many worst-case searches must be done before the second alternative is better in terms of number of comparisons? (*Hint*: Let p represent the number of searches done.)

26. Suppose the pattern-matching problem is changed to require locating only the first instance, if any, of the pattern within the text.

a. Describe the worst case, give an example, and give the exact number of comparisons (of a pattern character with a text character) required.

b. Describe the best case, give an example, and give the exact number of comparisons required.

27. At about what value of n does an algorithm that does $100n^2$ instructions become more efficient than one that does $0.01(2^n)$ instructions? (Use a calculator.)

28. a. An algorithm that is $\Theta(n)$ takes 10 seconds to execute on a particular computer when $n = 100$. How long would you expect it to take when $n = 500$?

b. An algorithm that is $\Theta(n^2)$ takes 10 seconds to execute on a particular computer when $n = 100$. How long would you expect it to take when $n = 500$?

29. Find an optimal solution to the bin-packing problem described in Section 3.5.

30. In the data cleanup problem, we assumed that the items were stored in a list with a fixed number of positions. Each item could be examined by giving its position in the list. This arrangement of data is called an **array**. Here is an array of four items:

43	13	55	39
1	2	3	4

Another way to arrange items is to have a way to locate the first item and then have each item "point to" the next item. This arrangement of data is called a **linked list**. Here are the same four items in a linked list arrangement:

$$43 \longrightarrow 13 \longrightarrow 55 \longrightarrow 39$$

To examine any item in a linked list, one must start with the first item and follow the pointers to the desired item.

Unlike arrays, which are fixed in size, linked lists can shrink and grow. An item can be eliminated from a linked list by changing the pointer to that item so that it points to the next item instead.

a. Draw the linked list that results when item 13 is eliminated from the foregoing linked list.

b. Draw the linked list that results when data cleanup is performed on the following linked list.

$$19 \rightarrow 0 \rightarrow 53 \rightarrow 28 \rightarrow 0 \rightarrow 33$$

c. Describe (informally) an algorithm to do data cleanup on a linked list. You may assume that neither the first item nor the last item will have a value of 0, and you may assume the existence of operations such as "follow pointer" and "change pointer." If these operations are the unit of work used, show that your algorithm is an $\Theta(n)$ algorithm, where n is the number of items in the list.

CHALLENGE WORK

1. You are probably familiar with the children's song "Old MacDonald Had a Farm." The first verse is

   Old MacDonald had a farm, eee-eye, eee-eye, oh.
   And on that farm he had a cow, eee-eye,
       eee-eye, oh.
     With a moo-moo here and a moo-moo there,
     Here a moo, there a moo,
     Everywhere a moo-moo,
   Old MacDonald had a farm, eee-eye, eee-eye, oh.

   In successive verses, more animals are added, and the middle refrain gets longer and longer. For example, the second verse is

   Old MacDonald had a farm, eee-eye, eee-eye, oh.
   And on that farm he had a pig, eee-eye,
       eee-eye, oh.
     With an oink-oink here and an oink-oink there,
     Here an oink, there an oink,
     Everywhere an oink-oink,
     With a moo-moo here and a moo-moo there,
     Here a moo, there a moo,
     Everywhere a moo-moo,
   Old MacDonald had a farm, eee-eye, eee-eye, oh.

   a. Show that after n verses of this song have been sung, the total number of syllables sung would be given by the expression $22n(n + 1)/2 + 37n$

   (You may assume that all animal names and all animal sounds consist of one syllable, as in cow, pig, moo, oink, and so on.)

   b. If singing this song is the algorithm, and the work unit is singing one syllable, what is the order of magnitude of the algorithm?[1]

2. **Linear programming** involves selecting values for a large number of quantities so that they satisfy a set of inequalities (such as $x + y + z \leq 100$) while at the same time maximizing (or minimizing) some particular function of these variables. Linear programming has many applications in communications and manufacturing. A trial-and-error approach to a linear programming problem would involve guessing at values for these variables until all of the inequalities are satisfied, but this may not produce the desired maximum (or minimum) value. In addition, real-world problems may involve hundreds or thousands of variables. A common algorithm to solve linear programming problems is called the **simplex method**. Although the simplex method works well for many common applications, including those that involve thousands of variables, its worst-case order of magnitude is exponential. Find information on the work of N. Karmarkar of Bell Labs, who discovered another algorithm for linear programming that is of polynomial order in the worst case and is faster than the simplex method in average cases.

---

[1] This exercise is based on work found in Chavey, D., "Songs and the Analysis of Algorithms," *Proceedings of the Twenty-Seventh SIGCSE Technical Symposium* (1996), pp. 4–8.

FOR FURTHER READING

The first organized collection of algorithms was published as the following three-volume series, which is still quoted in computer science literature.

Knuth, D. *The Art of Computer Programming,* 3 vols. Reading, MA: Addison Wesley, 1997–1998. Volume 1: *Fundamental Algorithms,* 3rd ed., 1997. Volume 2: *Seminumerical Algorithms,* 3rd ed., 1998. Volume 3: *Sorting and Searching,* 2nd ed., 1998.

Other works on algorithms, their design, and their analysis include

Cormen, T. H.; Leiserson, C. E.; Rivest, R. L.; and Stein, C. *Introduction to Algorithms*. New York: McGraw-Hill, 2002.

Levitin, A. V. *Introduction to the Design and Analysis of Algorithms*. Reading, MA: Addison Wesley, 2003.

McConnell, J. *Analysis of Algorithms: An Active Learning Approach*. Boston: Jones and Bartlett, 2001.

Rawlins, G. *Compared to What? An Introduction to the Analysis of Algorithms*. New York: Freeman, 1992.

The following book offers a complete discussion on intractable problems (and those thought to be intractable) as of the date of its publication.

Garey, M. R., and Johnson, D. S. *Computers and Intractability: A Guide to the Theory of NP-Completeness*. New York: Freeman, 1979.

The Hardware World

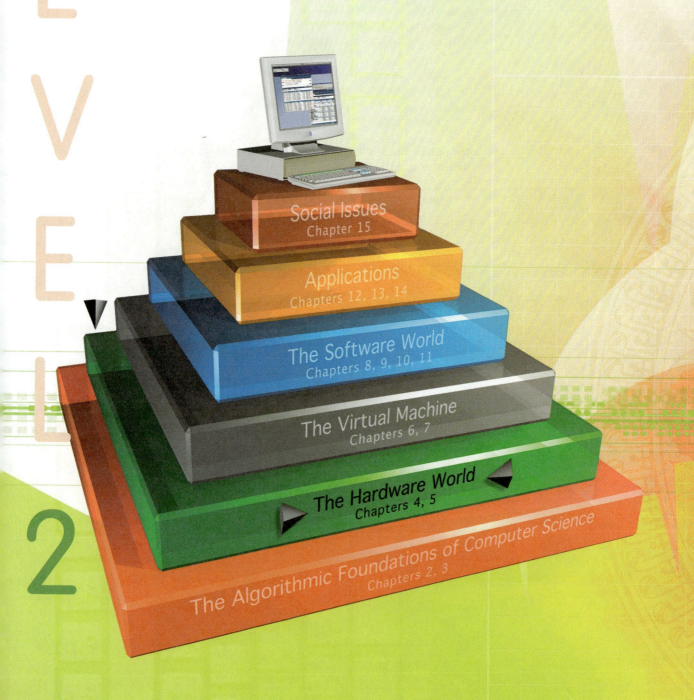

Social Issues
Chapter 15

Applications
Chapters 12, 13, 14

The Software World
Chapters 8, 9, 10, 11

The Virtual Machine
Chapters 6, 7

The Hardware World
Chapters 4, 5

The Algorithmic Foundations of Computer Science
Chapters 2, 3

LEVEL 2

LEVEL 2

Level 1 of the text developed a number of interesting algorithms such as sorting, searching, and pattern matching. It also described techniques for analyzing and studying the efficiency of these highly formalized solutions. For some computer scientists this is as far as it goes. They are interested only in the logical and mathematical properties of algorithms—the material presented in Level 1. However, for many others this is not enough. They are interested in discovering and studying a solution and *using* that solution to produce results more efficiently than was previously possible. They no longer want to think of their algorithm as being executed by an abstract entity called a computing agent. Instead, they want to execute it on a *real* computer.

Level 2 of the text launches our study of how to design and build computer systems, and it takes us into a fascinating new region of computer science, the hardware world.

CHAPTER 4

The Building Blocks:
Binary Numbers,
Boolean Logic, and Gates

4.1 Introduction

Level 1 of the text investigated the algorithmic foundations of computer science. It developed algorithms for searching tables, finding largest and smallest values, locating patterns, sorting lists, and cleaning up bad data. It also showed how to analyze and evaluate algorithms to demonstrate that they are not only correct but efficient and useful as well.

Our discussion assumed that these algorithms would be executed by something called a **computing agent,** an abstract concept representing any object capable of understanding and executing our instructions. We didn't care what that computing agent was—person, mathematical model, computer, or robot. In Level 1 we focused only on the creation of correct and efficient solutions to problems. However, in this section of the text we *do* care what our computing agent looks like and how it is able to execute instructions and produce results. In Level 2, "The Hardware World," we look at what is involved in designing and building real computers to solve "real-life" problems.

Level 2 is composed of two chapters, each of which takes a very different approach to this material. Chapter 4 begins our study of the hardware world by examining the fundamental building blocks used to construct computers. It discusses how to represent and store information inside a computer, how to use the principles of symbolic logic to design *gates,* and how to use gates to construct *circuits* that perform operations such as adding numbers, comparing numbers, and fetching instructions. These ideas are part of the branch of computer science known as **hardware design,** also called **logic design.**

The second part of Level 2, Chapter 5, investigates computer hardware from a higher-level perspective called **computer organization.** This chapter introduces the four major subsystems of a modern computer (memory, input/output, arithmetic/logic unit, and control unit), demonstrates how they are built from the elementary building blocks described in Chapter 4, and shows how these subsystems can be organized into a complete, functioning computer system. By way of analogy with the human body, Chapter 4 can be considered equivalent to a study of such elementary material as DNA, genes, cells, and tissues. Chapter 5 then demonstrates how our organs (e.g., heart, lungs) and bodily systems (e.g., circulatory, respiratory) are built from these basic biological units.

Our first concern with learning how to build computers is understanding how computers represent information. Their internal storage techniques are quite different from the way you and I represent information in our notebooks, desks, and filing cabinets.

 ### 4.2.1 Binary Representation of Numeric and Textual Information

People generally represent numeric and textual information (language differences aside) by using the following notational conventions:

a. The 10 decimal digits 0, 1, 2, 3, 4, 5, 6, 7, 8, 9 for numeric values such as 459.

b. *Sign/magnitude notation* for signed numbers—that is, a + or − sign placed immediately to the left of the digits; +31 and −789 are examples.

c. *Decimal notation* for real numbers, with a decimal point separating the whole number part from the fractional part; an example is 12.34.

d. The 26 letters A, B, C, . . . , Z for textual information (as well as lowercase letters and a few special symbols for punctuation).

These are the conventions for writing numbers and text to be read and understood by other persons. Therefore, it is tempting to believe that these well-known schemes are the same conventions that computers use to store information in memory. Surprisingly, this is not true.

When discussing the representation of information, we must distinguish between two types: The **external representation** of information is the way information is represented by humans and the way it is entered at a keyboard or displayed on a printer or screen. The **internal representation** of information is the way it is stored in the memory of a computer. This difference is diagrammed in Figure 4.1.

Externally, computers do use decimal digits, sign/magnitude notation, and the familiar 26-character alphabet. However, virtually every computer ever built stores data—numbers, letters, graphics, sound—internally using the **binary numbering system.**

Binary is a **base-2 positional numbering system** not unlike the more familiar decimal, or base-10, system used in everyday life. In these systems the value or "worth" of a digit depends not only on its absolute value but also on its specific position within a number. In the decimal system there are 10 unique digits (0, 1, 2, 3, 4, 5, 6, 7, 8, and 9), and the value of the positions in a decimal number is based on powers of 10. Moving from right to left in a number, the positions represent ones (10^0), tens (10^1), hundreds (10^2), thousands (10^3), and so on. Therefore, the decimal number 2,359 is evaluated as follows:

$$(2 \times 10^3) + (3 \times 10^2) + (5 \times 10^1) + (9 \times 10^0)$$
$$= 2,000 + 300 + 50 + 9$$
$$= 2,359$$

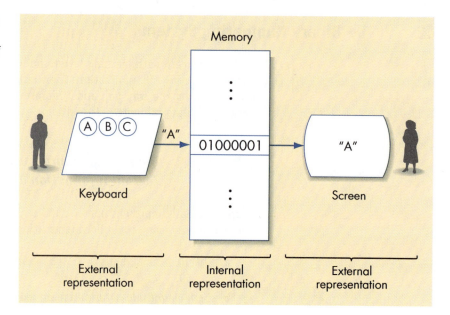

The same concepts apply to binary numbers except that there are only two digits, 0 and 1, and the value of the positions in a binary number is based on powers of 2. Again, moving from right to left, the positions represent ones (2^0), twos (2^1), fours (2^2), eights (2^3), sixteens (2^4), and so on. The two digits, 0 and 1, are frequently referred to as **bits,** a contraction of the two words *binary digits*.

For example, the 6-digit binary number 111001 is evaluated as follows:

$$111001 = (1 \times 2^5) + (1 \times 2^4) + (1 \times 2^3) + (0 \times 2^2) + (0 \times 2^1) + (1 \times 2^0)$$
$$= 32 + 16 + 8 + 0 + 0 + 1$$
$$= 57$$

As a second example, the 5-digit binary quantity 10111 is evaluated in the following manner:

$$10111 = (1 \times 2^4) + (0 \times 2^3) + (1 \times 2^2) + (1 \times 2^1) + (1 \times 2^0)$$
$$= 16 + 0 + 4 + 2 + 1$$
$$= 23$$

The evaluation of a binary number is quite easy, because 1 times any value is simply that value, and 0 times any value is always 0. Thus, when evaluating a binary number, use the following algorithm: Whenever there is a 1 in a column, add the positional value of that column to a running sum, and whenever there is a 0 in a column, add nothing. The final sum is the decimal value of this binary number. This is the procedure we followed in the previous two examples.

A binary-to-decimal conversion table for the values 0–31 is shown in Figure 4.2. You may want to evaluate a few of the binary values using this algorithm to confirm their decimal equivalents.

Any whole number that can be represented in base 10 can also be represented in base 2, although it may take more digits because a single decimal digit contains more information than a single binary digit. Note in the first example shown above that it takes only 2 decimal digits (5 and 7) to represent the quantity 57 in base 10, but it takes 6 binary digits (1, 1, 1, 0, 0, and 1) to express the same value in base 2.

In every computer there will always be a maximum number of binary digits that can be used to store an integer. Typically, this value is 16, 32, or 64 bits. Once we have fixed this maximum number of bits (as part of the design of the computer), we also have fixed the largest unsigned whole number that can be represented in this computer. For example, Figure 4.2 used at most 5 bits to represent binary numbers. The largest value that could be represented was 11111, not unlike the number 99999, which is the maximum mileage value that can be represented on a 5-digit decimal odometer. 11111 is the binary representation for the decimal integer 31. If there were 16 bits available, rather than 5, then the largest integer that could be represented is

$$1111111111111111$$

This quantity is $2^{15} + 2^{14} + \ldots + 2^2 + 2^1 + 2^0 = 65{,}535$. Unsigned integers larger than this cannot be represented with 16 binary digits. Any operation on this computer that produces an unsigned value greater than 65,535 will result in the error condition called **arithmetic overflow**. This is an attempt to represent an integer that exceeds the maximum allowable value. If this could be a problem, then the computer could be designed to use more than 16 bits to represent integers. However, no matter how many bits are ultimately used, there will always be a maximum value beyond which the computer cannot correctly represent any integer. This characteristic is one of the major differences between the disciplines of mathematics and computer science. In mathematics a quantity may usually take on any value, no matter how large. Computer science must deal with a finite—and sometimes quite limited—set of possible representations, and it must handle the errors that occur when those limits are exceeded.

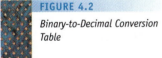

FIGURE 4.2

Binary-to-Decimal Conversion Table

BINARY	DECIMAL	BINARY	DECIMAL
0	0	10000	16
1	1	10001	17
10	2	10010	18
11	3	10011	19
100	4	10100	20
101	5	10101	21
110	6	10110	22
111	7	10111	23
1000	8	11000	24
1001	9	11001	25
1010	10	11010	26
1011	11	11011	27
1100	12	11100	28
1101	13	11101	29
1110	14	11110	30
1111	15	11111	31

Binary digits can be used to represent not only whole numbers but also other forms of data, including signed integers, decimal numbers, and characters. For example, to represent signed integers, we can use the leftmost bit of a number to represent the sign, with 0 meaning positive (+) and 1 meaning negative (−). The remaining bits are used to represent the magnitude of the value. This form of signed integer representation is termed **sign/magnitude notation**, and it is one of a number of different techniques for representing positive and negative whole numbers. For example, to represent the quantity −49 in sign/magnitude, we could use seven binary digits with one bit for the sign and six bits for the magnitude:

$$1\ 1\ 1\ 0\ 0\ 0\ 1$$

$$-\quad 49 \qquad (2^5 + 2^4 + 2^0 = 32 + 16 + 1 = 49)$$

The value +3 would be stored like this:

$$0\ 0\ 0\ 0\ 0\ 1\ 1$$

$$+\quad 3 \qquad (2^1 + 2^0 = 2 + 1 = 3)$$

You may wonder how a computer knows that the 7-digit binary number 1110001 shown in the first example above represents the signed integer value −49 rather than the unsigned whole number 113.

$$
\begin{aligned}
1110001 &= (1 \times 2^6) + (1 \times 2^5) + (1 \times 2^4) + (1 \times 2^0) \\
&= 64 + 32 + 16 + 1 \\
&= 113
\end{aligned}
$$

The answer to this question is that a computer does *not* know. A sequence of binary digits can have many different interpretations, and there is no fixed, predetermined interpretation given to any binary value. A binary number stored in the memory of a computer takes on meaning only because it is used in a certain way. If we use the value 1110001 as though it were a signed integer, then it will be interpreted that way and will take on the value −49. If it is used, instead, as an unsigned whole number, then that is what it will become, and it will be interpreted as the value 113. The meaning of a binary number stored in memory is based solely on the context in which it is used.

Initially this may seem strange, but we deal with this type of ambiguity all the time in natural languages. For example, in the Hebrew language, letters of the alphabet are also used as numbers. Thus the Hebrew character aleph (א) can stand for either the letter A or the number 1. The only way one can tell which meaning is appropriate is to consider the context in which the character is used. Similarly, in English the word *ball* can mean either a round object used to play games or an elegant formal party. Which interpretation is correct? We cannot say without knowing the context in which the word is used. The same is true for values stored in the memory of a computer system. It is the context that determines the meaning of a binary string.

Sign/magnitude notation is quite easy for people to work with and understand, but, surprisingly, it is used rather infrequently in real computer systems. The reason is the existence of the very "messy" and unwanted signed number: 10000 . . . 0000. Because the leftmost bit is a 1, this value is treated as negative. The magnitude is 0000 . . . 0000. Thus this bit pattern represents the numerical quantity "negative zero," a value that has no real mathematical meaning and should not be distinguished from the other representation for zero, 00000 . . . 0000. The existence of two distinct bit patterns for a single numerical quantity causes headaches for computer designers (e.g., does 1000 . . . 00 = 0000 . . . 00?). Therefore, they tend to favor integer representations that do not suffer from the problem of two zeroes. (A Challenge Work problem at the end of this chapter invites you to investigate one of these alternative representation techniques called **two's complement** notation.)

Decimal numbers, such as 12.34 and −0.001275, can also be represented in binary by using the signed-integer techniques we have just described. To do that, however, we must first convert the number to **scientific notation**:

$$\pm M \times B^{\pm E}$$

where M is the **mantissa,** B is the **exponent base** (usually 2), and E is the **exponent.** Let's work an example to illustrate these ideas. Assume we want to represent the decimal quantity +5.75. In addition, assume that we will use 16 bits to represent the number, with 10 bits allocated for representing the mantissa and 6 bits for the exponent. (The exponent base B is assumed to be 2 and is not explicitly stored.) Both the mantissa and the exponent are signed numbers, so we can use the sign/magnitude notation that we just learned to represent each of them. In each of the two fields, we will use the leftmost bit to represent the sign and the remaining bits to encode the magnitude.

In binary, the value 5 is 101. To represent the fractional quantity 0.75, we need to remember that the bits to the right of the decimal point (or binary point in our case) have the positional values r^{-1}, r^{-2}, r^{-3}, and so on, where r is the base of the numbering system used to represent the number. Because r is 2 in our case, the positional values of the digits to the right of the binary point are halves (2^{-1}), quarters (2^{-2}), eighths (2^{-3}), sixteenths (2^{-4}), and so on. Thus,

$$0.75 = 1/2 + 1/4 = 2^{-1} + 2^{-2} \text{ (which in binary is 0.11)}$$

Therefore, in binary 5.75 = 101.11. Using scientific notation, and an exponent base $B = 2$, we can write this value as

$$5.75 = 101.11 \times 2^0$$

Next, we must **normalize** the number so that its first significant digit is immediately to the right of the binary point. As we move the binary point, we adjust the value of the exponent so that the overall value of the number remains unchanged. If we move the binary point to the left one place (which makes the value smaller by a factor of 2), then we add 1 to the exponent (which makes it larger by a factor of 2). We do the reverse when we move the binary point to the right.

$$
\begin{aligned}
5.75 &= 101.11 \times 2^0 \\
&= 10.111 \times 2^1 \\
&= 1.0111 \times 2^2 \\
&= .10111 \times 2^3 \quad \text{(which is } (1/2 + 1/8 + 1/16 + 1/32) \times 8 = 5.75)
\end{aligned}
$$

We now have the number in the desired format and can put all the pieces together. We separately store the mantissa (excluding the binary point, which is assumed to be to the left of the first significant digit) and the exponent, both of which are signed integers and can be represented in sign/magnitude notation. The mantissa is stored with its sign—namely, 0, because it is a positive quantity—followed by the assumed binary point, followed by the magnitude of the mantissa, which in this case is 10111. Next we store the exponent, which is +3, or 000011 in sign/magnitude. The overall representation, using 16 bits, is

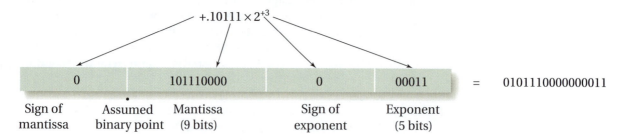

As a second example, let's determine the internal representation of the fraction $-5/16$.

$$
\begin{aligned}
-5/16 &= -(1/4 + 1/16) \\
&= -.0101 \times 2^0 \quad \text{(this is the value } -5/16 \text{ in scientific notation)} \\
&= -.101 \times 2^{-1} \quad \text{(after normalization)}
\end{aligned}
$$

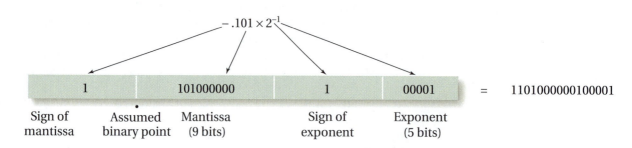

As our final example of the internal representation of numeric and textual information, let's look at how a computer is able to store *text*. To represent textual material in binary, the system assigns to each printable letter or symbol in our alphabet a unique number (this assignment is called a **code mapping**), and then it stores that symbol internally using the binary equivalent of that number. For example, here is one possible mapping of characters to numbers, which uses 8 bits to represent each character.

Symbol	Decimal Value	Binary Value (Using Eight Binary Digits)
A	1	00000001
B	2	00000010
C	3	00000011
D	4	00000100
⋮	⋮	⋮
Z	26	00011010
⋮	⋮	
@	128	10000000
!	129	10000001
⋮	⋮	⋮

To store the 4-character string "BAD!" in memory, the computer would store the binary representation of each individual character using the above 8-bit code.

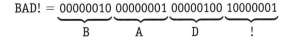

$$\text{BAD!} = \underbrace{00000010}_{B} \; \underbrace{00000001}_{A} \; \underbrace{00000100}_{D} \; \underbrace{10000001}_{!}$$

We have indicated above that the 8-bit numeric quantity 10000001 is interpreted as the character "!". However, as we mentioned earlier, the only way a computer knows that the 8-bit value 10000001 represents the symbol "!" and not the unsigned integer value 129 (128 + 1) is by the context in which it is used. If these 8 bits are sent to a display device that expects to be given characters, then this value will be interpreted as an "!". If, on the other hand, this 8-bit value is sent to an arithmetic unit that adds unsigned numbers, then it will be interpreted as a 129 in order to make the addition operation meaningful.

To facilitate the exchange of textual information, such as word processing documents and electronic mail, between computer systems, it would be most helpful if everyone used the same code mapping. Fortunately, this is pretty much the case. Currently the most widely used code for representing characters internally in a computer system is called **ASCII,** an acronym for the *American Standard Code for Information Interchange.* ASCII is an international standard for representing textual information in the majority of computers. It uses 8 bits to represent each character, so it is able to encode a total of $2^8 = 256$ different characters. These are assigned the integer values 0 to 255. However, only the numbers 32 to 126 have been assigned so far to printable characters. The remainder either are unassigned or are used for nonprinting control characters such as tab, form feed, and return. Figure 4.3 shows the ASCII conversion table for the numerical values 32–126.

However, a new code set called **UNICODE** is rapidly gaining in popularity due to the fact that it uses a 16-bit representation for characters rather than the 8-bit format of ASCII. This means that it is able to represent $2^{16} = 65,536$ unique characters instead of the $2^8 = 256$ of ASCII. It may initially seem like 256 characters are more than enough to represent all the textual symbols that we would ever need—for example, 26 upper case letters, 26 lower case letters, 10 digits, and a few dozen symbols, such as +=-{}][\:"?><.,;%$#@. Add that all together and it still totals only about 100 symbols, far less than the 256 that can be represented in ASCII. However, that is true only if we limit our work to Arabic numerals and the Roman alphabet. The world is rapidly growing more global—helped along by computers, networks, and the Web—and it is critically important that computers be able to represent and exchange textual information using alphabets other than these 26 letters and 10 digits. When we start assigning codes to symbols drawn from alphabets such as Russian, Arabic, Chinese, Hebrew, Greek, Thai, Bengali, and Braille, as well as mathematical symbols and special linguistic marks such as tilde, umlaut, and accent grave, we quickly see that we will not have nearly enough room to represent them all. However, UNICODE, with space for 65,000 symbols, is large enough to accommodate all these symbols and many more to come. In fact, UNICODE has defined standard code mappings for over 50,000 symbols from literally hundreds of alphabets, and it is a way for users around the world to share textual information regardless of the language in which they are writing. The UNICODE home page, which gives all the standard mappings that have been currently assigned, is located at www.unicode.org.

FIGURE 4.3

ASCII Conversion Table

Keyboard Character	Binary ASCII Code	Integer Equivalent	Keyboard Character	Binary ASCII Code	Integer Equivalent
(blank)	00100000	32	P	01010000	80
!	00100001	33	Q	01010001	81
"	00100010	34	R	01010010	82
#	00100011	35	S	01010011	83
$	00100100	36	T	01010100	84
%	00100101	37	U	01010101	85
&	00100110	38	V	01010110	86
'	00100111	39	W	01010111	87
(	00101000	40	X	01011000	88
)	00101001	41	Y	01011001	89
*	00101010	42	Z	01011010	90
+	00101011	43	[	01011011	91
'	00101100	44	\	01011100	92
−	00101101	45	]	01011101	93
.	00101110	46	^	01011110	94
/	00101111	47	_	01011111	95
0	00110000	48	`	01100000	96
1	00110001	49	a	01100001	97
2	00110010	50	b	01100010	98
3	00110011	51	c	01100011	99
4	00110100	52	d	01100100	100
5	00110101	53	e	01100101	101
6	00110110	54	f	01100110	102
7	00110111	55	g	01100111	103
8	00111000	56	h	01101000	104
9	00111001	57	i	01101001	105
:	00111010	58	j	01101010	106
;	00111011	59	k	01101011	107
<	00111100	60	l	01101100	108
=	00111101	61	m	01101101	109
>	00111110	62	n	01101110	110
?	00111111	63	o	01101111	111
@	01000000	64	p	01110000	112
A	01000001	65	q	01110001	113
B	01000010	66	r	01110010	114
C	01000011	67	s	01110011	115
D	01000100	68	t	01110100	116
E	01000101	69	u	01110101	117
F	01000110	70	v	01110110	118
G	01000111	71	w	01110111	119
H	01001000	72	x	01111000	120
I	01001001	73	y	01111001	121
J	01001010	74	z	01111010	122
K	01001011	75	{	01111011	123
L	01001100	76	:	01111100	124
M	01001101	77	]	01111101	125
N	01001110	78	~	01111110	126
O	01001111	79			

CHAPTER 4: The Building Blocks: Binary Numbers, Boolean Logic, and Gates

PRACTICE PROBLEMS

1. What is the value of the 8-bit binary quantity 10101000 if it is interpreted (a) as an unsigned integer and (b) as a signed integer represented in sign/magnitude notation?

2. What would the unsigned decimal value 99 look like in binary using 8 bits?

3. What would the signed integers −300 and +254 look like in binary using 10 bits?

4. What would the 3-character string "X+Y" look like internally using the 8-bit ASCII code given in Figure 4.3? What would it look like in 16-bit UNICODE? (Go to www.unicode.org to find the specific code mappings for these three characters.)

5. Using 10 bits to represent the mantissa (sign/magnitude) and 6 bits for the exponent (also sign/magnitude), show the internal representation of the following two values:

   a. +0.25
   b. −32 1/16

4.2.2 Binary Representation of Sound and Images

During the first 30 to 40 years of computing, the overwhelming majority of applications, such as word processing and spreadsheets, were text-based and limited to the manipulation of characters, words, and numbers. However, sound and images are now as important a form of representation as text and numbers due to the rapid growth of the Web, the popularity of digitally encoded music, the emergence of digital photography, and the almost universal availability of digital CD and DVD movies. Most of us, whether computer specialists or not, have probably had the experience of playing MP3 files or emailing vacation pictures to friends and family. In this section we take a brief look at how to represent sounds and images on a computer, using the same binary numbering system that we have been discussing.

Sound is analog information. This contrasts with the digital format used to represent text and numbers discussed in the previous section. In a **digital** representation, the values for a given object are drawn from a finite set, such as the letters {A, B, C, . . . , Z} or a subset of integers {0, 1, 2, 3, . . . , MAX }. In an **analog** representation, objects can take on any value. For example, in the case of sound, a tone is a continuous sinusoidal waveform that varies in a regular periodic fashion over time, as shown in Figure 4.4. (Note: This diagram shows only a single tone. Complex sounds, such as symphonic music, are composed of multiple overlapping waveforms. However, the basic ideas are the same.)

The **amplitude** (height) of the wave is a measure of its loudness—the greater the amplitude the louder the sound. The **period** of the wave, designated as T, is the time it takes for the wave to make one complete cycle. The **frequency** f is the total number of cycles per unit time measured in cycles/second, also called **hertz,** and defined as $f = 1/T$. The frequency is a measure of the

FIGURE 4.4

*Example of Sound Represented
as a Waveform*

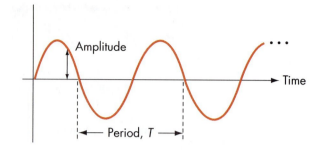

pitch, the highness or lowness of a sound. The higher the frequency the higher the perceived tone. A human ear can generally detect sounds in the range of 20 to 20,000 hertz.

To store a waveform such as the one in Figure 4.4 on a computer, the analog signal must first be **digitized**, that is, converted to a digital representation. This can be done using a technique known as **sampling**. At fixed time intervals, the amplitude of the signal is measured and stored as an integer value. The wave is thus represented in the computer in digital form as a sequence of sampled numerical amplitudes. For example, Figure 4.5(a) shows the sampling of the waveform of Figure 4.4.

FIGURE 4.5

Digitization of an Analog Signal

*(a) Sampling the Original
Signal
(b) Recreating the Signal from
the Sampled Values*

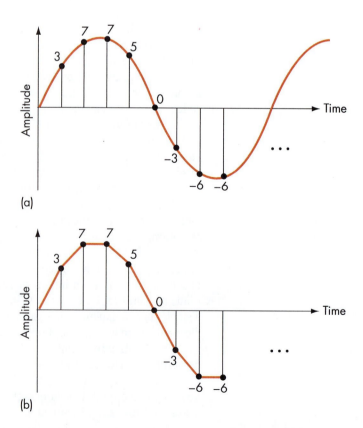

This signal can now be stored inside the computer as the series of signed integer values 3, 7, 7, 5, 0, −3, −6, −6, . . . , where each numerical value is encoded in binary using the techniques described in the previous section. From these stored digitized values the computer can recreate an approximation to the original analog wave. It would first generate an amplitude level of 3, then an amplitude level of 7, then an amplitude level of 7, and so on, as shown in Figure 4.5(b). These values would be sent to a sound-generating device, like stereo speakers, which would produce the actual sounds based on the numerical values received.

The accuracy with which the original sound can be reproduced is dependent on two key parameters—the sampling rate and the bit depth. The **sampling rate** measures how many times per second we sample the amplitude of the sound wave. Obviously, the more often we sample the more accurate the reproduction. Note, for example, that the sampling shown in Figure 4.5(a) completely missed the peak value of the wave since the peak occurred between two sampling intervals. Furthermore, the more often we sample, the greater the range of frequencies that can be captured. This can be seen by simply noting that if the frequency of a wave is greater than or equal to the sampling rate, we may not sample any points whatsoever on an entire waveform. For example, look at the following sampling interval t which is exactly equal to the period T of the wave being measured:

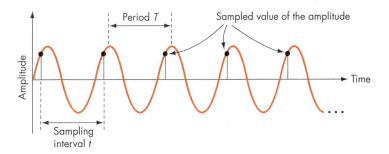

This rate of sampling produces a constant amplitude value, totally distorting the original sound. In general, a sampling rate of R samples/second will allow you to reproduce all frequencies up to about R/2 hertz. Since the human ear can normally detect sound up to about 20,000 hertz, a sampling rate of at least 40,000 samples per second is necessary to capture all audible frequencies.

The **bit depth** is the number of bits used to encode each sample. In the previous section we stated that ASCII is an 8-bit character code, allowing for 256 unique symbols. UNICODE expanded this to 16 bits, allowing for over 65,000 symbols and greatly increasing the number of symbols that can be represented. The same trend can be seen in sound reproduction. Initially, 8 bits per sample was the standard, but the 256 levels of amplitude that could be represented turned out to be insufficient for the sophisticated high-end sound systems being produced and marketed today. Most audio encoding schemes today use either 16 or 24 bits per sample level, allowing for either 65,000 or 16,000,000 distinct amplitude levels.

There are many audio-encoding formats in use today, including WAV, AU, Quicktime, and RealAudio. Probably the most popular and widely used digital audio format is **MP3,** an acronym for MPEG-1, Audio Level 3 Encoding. This is a digital audio encoding standard established by the Motion Picture Experts

Group (MPEG), a committee of the International Standards Organization (ISO) of the United Nations. MP3 samples sound signals at the rate of 44,100 samples/second, using 16 bits per sample. This produces high-quality sound reproduction, which is why MP3 is one of the most widely used formats for rock, opera, and classical music. For more details about the MPEG standards group and the MP3 audio standard, you can go to the MPEG home page at http://mpeg.telecomitalialab.com.

Similarly, it is possible to store visual images using binary representation. A graphical image, such as a photograph, is analog data just like the sound information just described. This means that it is represented as a continuous set of intensity and color values across its entire surface. However, it is possible to digitize an image by sampling the analog information, just as is done for sound. The sampling process, often called **scanning,** consists of measuring the intensity values of distinct points located at regular intervals across the image's surface. These points are called **pixels,** for picture elements, and the more pixels we use the more accurate is the encoding of the image. The average human eye cannot accurately discern components closer together than about 0.1 mm, so if the pixels, or dots, are sufficiently dense, they will appear to the human eye as a single contiguous image. For example, a high-quality digital camera stores about 3–5 million pixels per photograph. For a 3 in. $\times$ 5 in. image, this is about 250,000 pixels/in.^{2}, or 500 pixels per linear inch. This means the individual pixels are separated by about 1/500 of an inch, or 0.05 mm—too close together to be individually visualized. Figure 4.6 enlarges a small section of a digitized photograph to better see how it is stored internally as a set of discrete picture elements.

One of the key questions we need to answer is how much information is stored for each pixel. Suppose we want to store a representation of a black and white image. The easiest and most space-efficient approach is to mark each pixel as either white, stored as a binary 0, or black, stored as a binary 1.

Example of a Digitized Photograph

(a) Individual Pixels in the Photograph
(b) Photograph

(a)

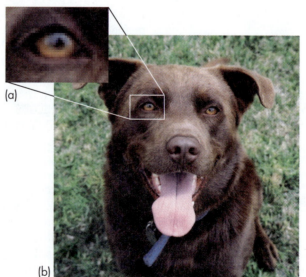

(b)

Photo by Maris Sidenstecker – Marine Biologist

FIGURE 4.7

An Eight-Level Gray Scale

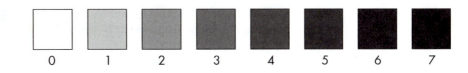

The only problem is that this produces a stark **black/white image,** with a highly sharp and unpleasant visual contrast. A much better way, though it takes more storage, is to represent black and white images using a **gray scale** of varying intensity. For example, if we use 3 bits per pixel, we can represent $2^3 = 8$ shades of intensity from level 0, pure white, to level 7, pure black. An example of this eight level gray scale is shown in Figure 4.7. If we wanted more detail than what is shown there, we could use 8 bits per pixel, giving us $2^8 = 256$ distinct shades of gray.

We now can encode our image as a sequence of numerical pixel values, storing each row of pixels completely, from left to right, before moving down to store the next row. Each pixel is encoded as an unsigned binary value representing its gray scale intensity. This form of image representation is called **raster graphics,** and it is widely used. It includes such well-known graphics standards as JPEG (Joint Photographer Experts Group), GIF (graphics interchange format), and BMP (bit mapped graphics).

Today, most images are not black and white but color. However, we can use the same digitization technique described above. We again measure the intensity value of the image at a discrete set of points, but this time we need to store more information about each pixel. The most common format for storing color images is the **RGB encoding scheme,** an acronym for Red-Green-Blue. This technique describes a specific color by capturing the individual contribution to a pixel's color of each of the three primary colors, red, green, and blue. It uses one **byte,** or 8 bits, for each color, allowing us to represent an intensity range of 0 to 255. The value 0 means that there is no contribution from this color, while the value 255 means a full contribution of this color.

For example, the secondary color yellow is produced from an equal mix of red and green. Therefore, an individual yellow pixel would be represented by the three numbers (255, 255, 0), which would be interpreted as

Red	*Green*	*Blue*
255	255	0

Similarly, the color magenta is an equal mix of pure red and blue, which would be encoded as (255, 0, 255):

Red	*Green*	*Blue*
255	0	255

Using three bytes, or 24 bits, of information per pixel allows us to represent 2^{24} distinct colors, about 16.7 million. For example, the color "hot pink" is produced by setting the three RGB values to Red = 255, Green = 105, Blue = 180, while "harvest gold" is rendered as Red = 218, Green = 165, and Blue = 32.

The 24-bit color-encoding scheme just described is often referred to as **True-Color,** and it provides an enormous range of shades and an extremely accurate color image reproduction. That is why it is the encoding scheme used in the JPEG imaging format. However, representing 16+ million colors requires a huge amount of memory space, and some image representation techniques reduce that value by using what is called a **color palette.** While theoretically supporting 16+ million different colors, they only allow you to use 256 (or some other small number) at any one time. (Just as a painter may have a lot of colors in his or her studio but puts only a few on the palette at a time.) With a palette size of 256, we can encode each pixel using only 8 bits rather than 24, since $2^8 = 256$, thus reducing storage space demands by almost 67%. Each of these 256 values does not represent an explicit RGB color value but rather an index into a palette, or a color table. This index specifies which color on the palette is to be used to draw this pixel. This is the technique used, for example, in the Graphics Interchange Format (GIF), which uses a palette that can hold as few as 2 colors or as many as 256.

This last discussion points out an important issue regarding the representation of sound and image data—it typically requires a huge amount of storage, far more than is required for the numbers and text discussed in Section 4.2.1. For example, a 300-page novel contains about 100,000 words. Each word has about 5 characters and, as discussed in the previous section, each character can be encoded into the ASCII code set using 8 bits. Thus, the total number of bits needed to represent this book will be roughly

100,000 words $\times$ 5 char/word $\times$ 8 bits/char = *4 million bits*

By comparison, 1 minute of sound recording encoded using the MP3 standard, which samples 44,100 times per second using a bit depth of 16 bits per sample, requires

44,100 samples/sec $\times$ 16 bits/sample $\times$ 60 sec/minute = *42 million bits*

It takes 10 times as much space to store the information in 1 minute of music as it does to store an entire 300-page book! Similarly to store a single photograph taken using a digital camera with 3 million pixels using 24-bit True-Color raster graphics requires:

3,000,000 pixels/photograph $\times$ 24 bits/pixel = *72 million bits*

A single photograph could require as much as 18 times more storage than an entire novel.

As these examples clearly show, the storage of analog information, such as sound, images, voice, and video, is enormously space-intensive, and an important area of computer science research—**data compression**—is directed at addressing just this issue. Data compression algorithms attempt to represent information in ways that preserve the accuracy of the information being encoded but using significantly less space.

For example, a simple compression technique that can be used on almost any form of data is **run-length encoding.** This method replaces a sequence of identical values $v_1, v_2, \ldots, v_n$ by a pair of values (v, n) which indicates that the value v is replicated n times. If both v and n require 1 byte of storage, then we have reduced the total number of bytes required to store this sequence from n down to 2. Using this method, we could encode the following 5×3 image of the letter E, where 0 = white, 255 = black:

```
255      255      255
255      0        0
255      255      255
255      0        0
255      255      255
```

like this:

(255, 4) (0, 2) (255, 4) (0, 2) (255, 3)

Run-length encoding reduced the number of bytes needed to store this image from 15, using the raster graphics representation, to the 10 bytes shown above. Compression schemes are usually evaluated by their **compression ratio,** which measures how much they have reduced the storage requirements of the data:

$$\text{compression ration} = \frac{\text{size of the uncompressed data}}{\text{size of the compressed data}}$$

For the example shown above, this ratio is

ratio $= 15/10 = 1.5$

meaning we have reduced the amount of space needed to store the image by 50%. Applied to a larger image, this might mean that a 4-million-bit representation could be reduced to about 2.7 million bits, quite a significant savings.

Another popular compression technique is **variable length code sets,** which are often used to compress text but can also be used with other forms of data. In Section 4.2.1 we showed that textual symbols, such as 'A', 'z', and '#' are represented internally by a code mapping that uses exactly the same number of bits for every symbol, either 8 (ASCII) or 16 (UNICODE). That is a wasteful approach as some symbols occur much more frequently than others. (For example, in English the letters E and A are much more common than J, Q, X, and Z.) If the codes representing commonly used symbols were shorter than the codes representing the less common symbols, this could result in a significant savings of space.

One of the most popular and widely used of the variable length codes is the **Huffman code,** and it is illustrated in Figure 4.8. Assume that we want to encode the Hawaiian alphabet, which contains only the 5 vowels A, E, I, O, and U, and the 7 consonants H, K, L, M, N, P, and W. If we were to store these characters using a fixed length code set, we would need at least 4 bits/symbol, since $2^4 = 16$. Figure 4.8(a) shows one possible encoding of these 12 letters using a fixed length, 4-bit encoding. However, if we knew that A and I were the most commonly used letters in the Hawaiian alphabet, with H and W next, we might opt to represent A and I using two bits, H and W using 3 bits, and the remaining letters using either 4, 5, 6, or 7 bits, depending on their frequency. However, we must be sure that if the 2-bit sequence s_1s_2 is used to represent an A, for example, then no other symbol representation can start with the same 2-bit sequence. Otherwise, if we saw the sequence s_1s_2 we would not know if it was an A or the beginning of another character.

One possible variable-length encoding for the Hawaiian alphabet is shown in Figure 4.8(b).

LETTER	4-BIT ENCODING	VARIABLE LENGTH ENCODING
A	0000	00
I	0001	10
H	0010	010
W	0011	110
E	0100	0110
O	0101	0111
M	0110	11100
K	0111	11101
U	1000	11110
N	1001	111110
P	1010	1111110
L	1011	1111111
	(a)	(b)

Now, to represent the 6-character word HAWAII using the fixed length 4-bit encoding scheme of Figure 4.8(a) requires $6 \times 4 = 24$ bits. Representing it with the variable length encoding shown in Figure 4.8(b) would produce the following:

H	A	W	A	I	I
010	00	110	00	10	10

This is a total of 14 bits, producing a compression ratio of $24/14 = 1.71$, a reduction in storage demand of over 70%.

The two techniques described above are examples of what are called **lossless compression** schemes. This means that no information is lost in the compression, and it is possible to reproduce exactly the original data. **Lossy compression** schemes compress data in a way that does not guarantee that all of the information in the original data can be fully and completely recreated. They trade a possible loss of accuracy for the opportunity for a higher compression ratio because the small inaccuracies that might occur to a sound or image are often undetectable to the human ear or eye. Many of the compression schemes in widespread use today, including MP3 and JPEG, use lossy techniques, which permit significantly greater compression ratios than would otherwise be possible. Using lossy JPEG, for example, it is possible to achieve

PRACTICE PROBLEMS

1. Using MP3, how many bits are required to store a 3-minute song in uncompressed format? If the information is compressed with a ratio of 4:1, how many bits are now required?

2. How many bits are needed to store a single uncompressed RGB image from a 2.1 megapixel digital camera? How many bytes of memory is this?

3. If we want the image in Exercise 2 to be able to fit into 1 megabyte of memory, what compression ratio is needed? If we want it to fit into 256 kilobytes of memory, what compression ratio is needed?

compression ratios of 10:1, 20:1, or more, depending on how much loss of detail we are willing to tolerate. This compares with the values of 1.5 and 1.7 we saw previously. Using these types of sophisticated compression schemes, that 72-megabit, high-resolution image mentioned earlier could possibly be reduced to only 2, 3, or 4 megabits, certainly a much more manageable value. Data compression schemes are an essential component in allowing us to represent multimedia information in a concise and manageable way.

 ### 4.2.3   *The Reliability of Binary Representation*

At this point there is a fundamental question that must be answered: Why are we bothering to use binary? Because people use decimal numbers to do their work, wouldn't it be more convenient to use a base-10 representation for both the external and the internal representation of information? If we did, then there would be no need to go through the time-consuming conversions diagrammed in Figure 4.1 and no need to learn the complex binary representation techniques discussed in the previous two sections.

There is absolutely no theoretical reason why one could not build a "decimal" computer or, indeed, a computer that stored numbers using base 3 (**ternary**), base 8 (**octal**), or base 16 (**hexadecimal**). The techniques described in the previous two sections apply to information represented in *any* base of a positional numbering system, including base 10.

Binary representation is used exclusively for building computers not for any theoretical reasons but for reasons of **reliability.** As we shall see shortly, computers store information using electronic devices, and the internal representation of information must be implemented in terms of electronic quantities such as currents and voltage levels.

Building a base-10 "decimal computer" requires finding a device with 10 distinct and stable energy states that can be used to represent the 10 unique digits (0, 1, . . . , 9) of the decimal system. For example, assume there exists a device that can store electrical charges in the range 0 to +45 volts. We could use it to build a decimal computer by letting certain voltage levels correspond to specific decimal digits:

Voltage Level	Corresponds to This Decimal Digit
+0	0
+5	1
+10	2
+15	3
+20	4
+25	5
+30	6
+35	7
+40	8
+45	9

Storing the 2-digit decimal number 28 requires two of these devices, one for each of the digits in the number. The first device would be set to +10 volts to represent the digit 2, and the second would be set to +40 volts to represent the digit 8.

However, although this is theoretically feasible, it is certainly not recommended. As electrical devices age they become unreliable, and they may slowly *drift*, or change their energy state, over time. What if the device representing the value 8 (the one set to +40 volts) lost about 6% of its voltage, not a huge amount for an old, well-used piece of equipment? The voltage would drop from +40 volts to about +37.5 volts. The question is whether the value +37.5 represents the digit 7 (+35) or the digit 8 (+40). It is impossible to say. If that same device lost another 6% of its voltage, it would drop from +37.5 volts to about +35 volts. Our 8 has now become a 7, and the original value of 28 has unexpectedly changed to 27. Building a reliable decimal machine can be an engineering nightmare.

The problem with a base-10 representation is that it needs to store 10 unique symbols, and therefore it needs devices that have 10 stable states. Such devices are extremely rare. Electrical systems tend to operate best in what is called a **bistable environment,** in which there are only two (rather than 10) stable states separated by a huge energy barrier. Examples of these bistable states include

- full on/full off
- fully charged/fully discharged
- charged positively/charged negatively
- magnetized/nonmagnetized
- magnetized clockwise/magnetized counterclockwise

In the binary numbering system there are only two symbols (0 and 1), so we can let one of the two stable states of our bistable device represent a 0 and the other a 1. This is a much more reliable way to represent information inside a computer.

For example, let's go back to our hypothetical electronic device that stored voltages in the range 0 to +45 volts. If we use binary rather than decimal to store the data, the representational scheme becomes much simpler:

    0 volts   = 0   (full off)
    +45 volts = 1   (full on)

Now a 6% or even a 12% drift causes no problem in interpreting the value being represented. In fact, it takes an almost 50% change in voltage level to create a problem in interpreting a stored value. The use of binary for the internal representation of data significantly increases the inherent reliability of a computer. This single advantage is worth all the time it takes to convert from decimal to binary for internal storage and from binary to decimal for the external display of results.

 ### 4.2.4 *Binary Storage Devices*

As we saw in the previous section, binary computers can be built out of any bistable device. This idea can be expressed more formally by saying that it is possible to construct a binary computer and its internal components using any hardware device that meets the following four criteria:

1. It has two stable energy states (one for a 0, one for a 1).
2. These two states are separated by a large energy barrier (so that a 0 does not accidentally become a 1, or vice versa).

3. It is possible to sense which state the device is in (to see whether it is storing a 0 or a 1) without permanently destroying the stored value.

4. It is possible to switch the state from a 0 to a 1, or vice versa, by applying a sufficient amount of energy.

There are many devices that meet these conditions, including some unexpected ones such as the familiar ON/OFF light switch. A light switch has two stable states (ON and OFF). These two states are separated by a large energy barrier so that a switch that is in one state will not accidentally change to the other. We can sense what state the switch is in by looking to see whether the label says ON or OFF (or just by looking at the light), and we can change the state of the switch by applying a sufficient amount of energy via our fingertips. Thus it would be possible to build a reliable (albeit very slow and bulky) binary computing device out of ordinary light switches and fingertips!

As you might imagine, computer systems are not built from light switches, but they have been built using a wide range of devices. This section reviews two of the most popular devices as examples of hardware technologies underlying the internal construction of computer systems. The first approach, magnetic cores, is no longer in use, but it is historically important. The second, transistors, is widely used and is a good example of the current state of computer technology.

Magnetic cores were used to construct computer memories for about 20 years. From roughly 1955 to 1975, this was by far the most popular storage technology, and it is not uncommon today to hear the memory unit of a computer referred to as **core memory** even though it has been decades since magnetic cores have been used.

A **core** is a small, magnetizable, iron oxide-coated "doughnut" about 1/50 of an inch in inner diameter with wires strung through its center hole. The two states used to represent the binary values 0 and 1 are based on the *direction* of the magnetic field of the core. When electric current is sent through the wire in one specific direction, say left to right, the core is magnetized in a counterclockwise direction.[1] This state could represent the binary value 0. Current sent in the opposite direction produces a clockwise magnetic field that could represent the binary value 1. These situations are diagrammed in Figure 4.9. Because magnetic fields do not change much over time, these two states are highly stable, and they form the basis for the construction of memory devices to store binary numbers.

In the early 1970s core memories were replaced by other technologies that were smaller and cheaper, required less power, and were easier to manufacture. One-fiftieth of an inch in diameter and a few grams of weight may not seem like much, but it can produce a bulky and unworkable structure when memory units are constructed containing millions or billions of bits. For example, a typical core memory from the 1950s or 1960s had about 500 cores/in^2. The memory in a modern computer typically has 512 MB (512 **megabytes** = 512 million bytes), which is over 4 billion bits. At the bit density of core memory, the memory unit would need about 8 million in^2, which is a square about 2,800 inches, or 230 feet, on a side. Built from cores, the memory unit would stand over 20 stories high!

---

1 The right-hand rule of physics says that if the thumb of your right hand is pointing in the direction of the electric current, then the fingers will be curled in the direction of the magnetic field.

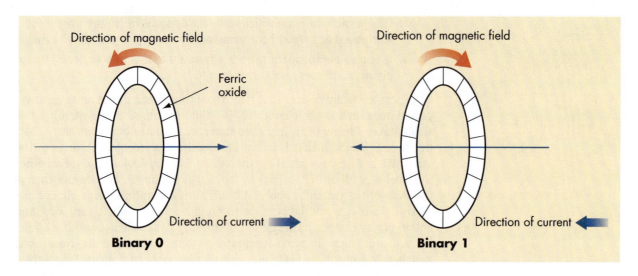

Direction of magnetic field

Ferric
oxide

Direction of current

Binary 0

Direction of magnetic field

Direction of current

Binary 1

FIGURE 4.9

*Using Magnetic Cores to
Represent Binary Values*

Today, the elementary building block for all modern computer systems is no longer the core but the transistor. A **transistor** is much like the light switch mentioned earlier. It can be in an OFF state, which does not allow electricity to flow, or in an ON state, in which electricity can pass unimpeded. However, unlike the light switch, a transistor is a solid-state device that has no mechanical or moving parts. The switching of a transistor from the OFF to the ON state, and vice versa, is done electronically rather than mechanically. This allows it to be fast as well as extremely small. Typically a transistor can switch states in a billionth of a second, and at current technology levels, 25 million or more transistors can fit into a space only 1 cm². (Furthermore, hardware technology is changing so rapidly that both these numbers may be out of date by the time you read these words.)

Transistors are constructed from special materials called **semiconductors**, such as silicon and gallium arsenide. A large number of transistors, as well as the electrical conducting paths that connect them, can be printed photographically on a wafer of silicon to produce a device known as an **integrated circuit** or, more commonly, a **chip.** The chip is mounted on a **circuit board**, which interconnects all the different chips (e.g., memory, processor, communications) needed to build a computer system. This circuit board is then plugged into the computer using a set of connectors located on the end of the board. The relationships among transistors, chips, and circuit boards is diagrammed in Figure 4.10. The use of photographic rather than mechanical production techniques has numerous advantages. Because light can be focused very sharply, these integrated circuits can be manufactured in very high densities—high numbers of transistors per square centimeter—and with a very high degree of accuracy. The more transistors that can be packed into a fixed amount of space, the greater the processing power of the computer and the greater the amount of information that can be stored in memory.[2]

2 The Power Mac G5 squeezes 58 million transistors onto a chip that is only 1.18cm².

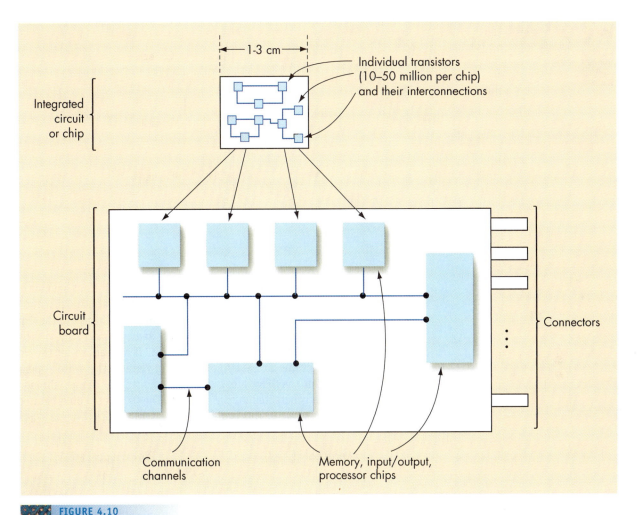

1-3 cm

Individual transistors
(10–50 million per chip)
and their interconnections

Integrated
circuit
or chip

Circuit
board

Connectors

Communication
channels

Memory, input/output,
processor chips

FIGURE 4.10

Relationships Among Transistors, Chips, and Circuit Boards

Another advantage of photographic production techniques is that it is possible to make a standard template, called a **mask,** that describes the circuit. This mask can be used to produce a virtually unlimited number of copies of that chip, much as a photographic negative can be used to produce an unlimited number of prints.

Together, these characteristics can result in very small and very inexpensive high-speed circuits. Whereas the first computers of the early 1940s, as seen in Figure 1.6, filled huge rooms and cost millions of dollars, the processor inside a modern workstation contains millions of transistors on a tiny chip just a few centimeters square, is thousands of times more powerful than those early machines, and costs just a few hundred dollars.

The theoretical concepts underlying the physical behavior of semiconductors and transistors, as well as the details of chip manufacture, are well beyond the scope of this book. They are usually discussed in courses in physics or electrical engineering. Instead, we will visualize a transistor in terms of the simplified model shown in Figure 4.11 and then use this model to explain its behavior. (Here is another example of the importance of abstraction in computer science.) In the model shown in Figure 4.11, each transistor contains three lines—two input lines and one output line. The first input line, called the **control** or the **base,** is used to open or close the switch inside the transistor. If we

FIGURE 4.11

Simplified Model of a Transistor

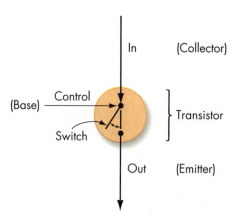

set the input value on the control line to a 1 by applying a sufficient amount of voltage, the switch closes and the transistor enters the ON state. In this state, voltage coming in from the **In** line, called the **Collector,** goes directly to the **Out** line, called the **Emitter,** and this voltage can be detected by a measuring device. This ON state could be used to represent the binary 1. If instead we set the input value of the control line to a 0 by not applying voltage, the switch opens and the transistor enters the OFF state. In this state no voltage can get through the transistor, so none is detected on the Out line. The OFF state could be used to represent the binary value 0. This is diagrammed as follows:

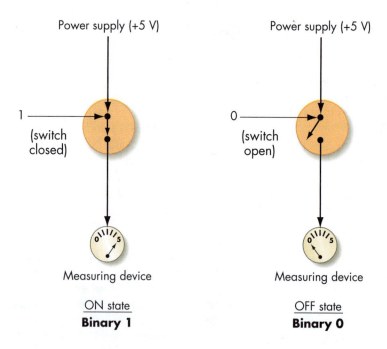

This solid-state switching device forms the basis for the construction of virtually all computers built today, and it is the fundamental building block for all high-level components described in the upcoming chapters. Remember, however, that there is no theoretical reason why we must use transistors as our "elementary particles" when designing computer systems. Just as cores

Dr.William Shockley was the inventor (along with John Bardeen and Walter Brattain) of the transistor. His discovery has probably done as much to shape our modern world as any scientific advancement of the 20th century. He received the 1956 Nobel Prize in Physics and, at his death, was a Distinguished Professor at Stanford University.

Shockley and his team developed the transistor in 1947 while working at Bell Laboratories. He left there in 1954 to set up the Shockley Semiconductor Laboratory in California—a company that was instrumental in the birth of the high-technology region called Silicon Valley. The employees of this company eventually went on to develop other fundamental advances in computing, such as the integrated circuit and the microprocessor.

However, although Shockley's work has been compared to that of Pasteur, Salk, and Einstein in importance,

his reputation and place in history have been forever tarnished by his outrageous and controversial racial theories. His education and training were in physics and electrical engineering, but Shockley spent the last years of his life trying to convince people of the genetic inferiority of blacks. He became obsessed with these ideas, even though he was ridiculed and shunned by colleagues who abandoned all contact with him. Although his work on the design of the transistor was of seminal importance, Shockley himself felt that his genetic theory on race and intelligence would ultimately be viewed as his most important contribution to science. By the time of his death in 1989, his intense racial bigotry prevented him from receiving the recognition that would otherwise have been his for monumental contributions in physics, engineering, and computer science.

were replaced by transistors, transistors may ultimately be replaced by some newer technology (perhaps molecular or biological) that is faster, smaller, and cheaper. The only requirements for our building blocks are those given in the beginning of this section—that they be able to represent reliably the two binary values 0 and 1. That's the beauty of the binary numbering system.

4.3 Boolean Logic and Gates

4.3.1 *Boolean Logic*

The construction of computer circuits is based on the branch of mathematics and symbolic logic called **Boolean logic.** This is the area of mathematics that deals with rules for manipulating the two logical values **true** and **false.** It is easy to see the relationship between Boolean logic and computer design when we realize that the truth value *true* could represent the binary value 1 and the truth value *false* could represent the binary value 0. Thus anything stored internally as a sequence of binary digits (which, as we saw in earlier sections, is everything stored inside a computer) can also be viewed as a sequence of the logical values true and false, and these values can be manipulated by the operations of Boolean logic.

Let us define a **Boolean expression** as any expression that evaluates to either true or false. For example, the expression $(x = 1)$ is a Boolean expression because it is true if x is 1, and it is false if x has any other value. Similarly, both $(a \neq b)$ and $(c > 5.23)$ are Boolean expressions.

In "traditional" mathematics (the mathematics of real numbers), the operations used to construct arithmetic expressions are $+$, $-$, $\times$, $\div$, and a^b, which map real numbers into real numbers. In Boolean logic, the operations

George Boole was an English mathematician and logician of the mid–19th century. He was the son of a shoemaker and had little formal education, having dropped out of school in the third grade. He taught himself mathematics and logic and mastered French, German, Italian, Latin, and Greek. He avidly studied the works of the great Greek and Roman philosophers such as Aristotle, Plato, and Euclid. He built upon their work in logic, argumentation, and reasoning and, in 1854, produced a book entitled *Introduction into the Laws of Thought*. This seminal work attempted to apply the formal laws of algebra and arithmetic to the principles of logic. That is, it treated reasoning as simply another branch of mathematics containing operators, variables, and transformation rules. He created a new form of logic containing the values *true* and *false* and the operators AND, OR, and NOT. He also developed a set of rules describing how to interpret and manipulate expressions that contain these values.

At the time of its development, the importance of this work was not apparent, and it languished in relative obscurity. However, 100 years later, Boole's ideas became the theoretical framework underlying the design of all computer systems. In his honor, these true/false expressions became known as **Boolean expressions,** and this branch of mathematics is called **Boolean logic** or **Boolean algebra.**

Even though he had very little formal schooling, Boole was eventually appointed Professor of Mathematics at Queens College in Cork, Ireland, and he received a gold medal from the Royal Mathematical Society. He is now universally recognized as one of the greatest mathematicians of the 19th century.

used to construct Boolean expressions are AND, OR, and NOT, and they map a set of (true, false) values into a single (true, false) result.

The rule for performing the AND operation is as follows: If a and b are Boolean expressions, then the value of the expression (a AND b), also written as ($a \cdot b$), is *true* if and only if both a and b have the value *true*; otherwise, the expression (a AND b) has the value *false*. Informally, this rule says that the AND operation produces the value *true* if and only if both of its components are true. This idea can be expressed using a structure called a **truth table,** shown in Figure 4.12.

The two columns labeled Inputs in the truth table of Figure 4.12 list the four possible combinations of true/false values of a and b. The column labeled Output specifies the value of the expression (a AND b) for the corresponding values of a and b.

As an example of the use of the AND operation, imagine that we want to check whether a test score S is in the range 90 to 100 inclusive. We wish to develop a Boolean expression that is true if the score is in the desired range and false otherwise. We cannot do this with a single comparison. If we test only that ($S \geq 90$), then a score of 105, which is greater than or equal to 90, will produce the result *true,* even though it is out of range. Similarly, if we test only that ($S \leq 100$), then a score of 85, which is less than or equal to 100, will also produce a *true,* even though it too is not in the range 90 to 100.

FIGURE 4.12

Truth Table for the AND Operation

INPUTS		OUTPUT a AND b
a	b	(ALSO WRITTEN a · b)
False	False	False
False	True	False
True	False	False
True	True	True

Instead, we need to determine whether the score S is greater than or equal to 90 *and* whether it is less than or equal to 100. Only if both conditions are true can we say that S is in the desired range. We can express this idea using the following Boolean expression:

$(S \geq 90)$ AND $(S \leq 100)$

Each of the two expressions in parentheses can be either true or false depending on the value of S. However, only if both conditions are true will the expression evaluate to *true*. For example, a score of $S = 70$ would cause the first expression to be false (70 is not greater than or equal to 90), whereas the second expression would be true (70 is less than or equal to 100). The truth table in Figure 4.12 shows that the result of evaluating (*false* AND *true*) is *false*. Thus, the overall expression is false, telling us (as expected) that 70 is not in the range 90 to 100. You might wish to check the value of the above expression for $S =135$ and $S = 95$ to confirm that it does indeed produce the correct results in all cases.

The second Boolean operation is OR. The rule for evaluating the OR operation is as follows: If a and b are Boolean expressions, then the value of the Boolean expression (a OR b), also written as ($a + b$), is *true* if a is *true*, if b is *true*, or if both are *true*. Otherwise, (a OR b) has the value *false*. The truth table for OR is shown in Figure 4.13.

As an example of the use of the OR operation, imagine that we have a variable called *major* that specifies a student's college major. If we want to know whether a student is majoring in either math or computer science, we cannot accomplish this with a single comparison. The test (*major* = math) omits computer science majors, whereas the test (*major* = computer science) leaves out the mathematicians. Instead, we need to determine whether the student is majoring in *either* math or computer science (or perhaps in both). This can be expressed as follows:

$(major = \text{math})$ OR $(major = \text{computer science})$

Now, if the student is majoring in either one or both of the two disciplines, then one or both of the two terms in the expression will be true. Referring to the truth table in Figure 4.13, we see that (*true* OR *false*), (*false* OR *true*), and (*true* OR *true*) all produce the value *true,* which lets us know that the student is indeed majoring in at least one of these two fields. However, if the student were majoring in English, both conditions would be false. Looking at Figure 4.13, we see that the value of the expression (*false* OR *false*) is *false,* which tells us that the student is not majoring in either math or computer science.

The last Boolean operator that we will introduce is NOT. Unlike AND and OR, which require two operands and are therefore called **binary operators,** NOT requires only one operand and is called a **unary operator,** like the square root operation in arithmetic. The rule for evaluating the NOT operation is as

FIGURE 4.13

Truth Table for the OR Operation

INPUTS		OUTPUT a OR b (ALSO WRITTEN a + b)
a	b	
False	False	False
False	True	True
True	False	True
True	True	True

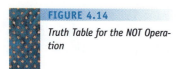

FIGURE 4.14

Truth Table for the NOT Operation

INPUT	OUTPUT
	NOT a
a	(ALSO WRITTEN ā)
False	True
True	False

follows: If *a* is a Boolean expression, then the value of the expression (NOT *a*), also written as ā, is *true* if *a* has the value *false,* and it is *false* if *a* has the value *true.* The truth table for NOT is shown in Figure 4.14.

Informally, we say that the NOT operation reverses, or **complements**, the value of a Boolean expression, making it true if currently false, and vice versa. For example, the expression (GPA > 3.5) is true if your grade point average is greater then 3.5, and the expression NOT (GPA > 3.5) is true only under the reverse conditions. That is, it is true only when your grade point average is less than or equal to 3.5.

AND, OR, and NOT are the three operations of Boolean logic that we will use in this chapter. (Note: There are other Boolean operators such as XOR, NOR, and NAND. We will mention them briefly but not make much use of them.) Why have we introduced these Boolean operations in the first place? The previous section talked about hardware concepts such as energy states, electrical currents, transistors, and integrated circuits. Now it appears that we have changed directions and are discussing highly abstract ideas drawn from the discipline of symbolic logic. However, as we shall see in the next section, there is a very close relationship between the hardware concepts of Section 4.2.4 and the operations of Boolean logic. In fact, the fundamental building blocks of a modern computer system (the objects with which engineers actually design) are not the transistors introduced in Section 4.2.4 but the gates that implement the Boolean operations AND, OR, and NOT. Surprisingly,

PRACTICE PROBLEMS

1. Assuming that $x = 1$ and $y = 2$, determine the value of each of the following Boolean expressions:

   a. $(x = 1)$ AND $(y = 3)$
   b. $(x < y)$ OR $(x > 1)$
   c. NOT $[(x = 1)$ AND $(y = 2)]$

2. What is the value of the following Boolean expression

   $(x = 5)$ AND $(y = 11)$ OR $([x + y] = z)$

   if $x = 5$, $y = 10$, and $z = 15$? Did you have to make some assumptions when you evaluated this expression?

3. Write a Boolean expression that is true if and only if x and y are both in the range 0 to 100 but x is not equal to y.

it is the rules of logic—a discipline developed by the Greeks 2,300 years ago and expanded by Boole 150 years ago—that provide the theoretical foundation for constructing modern computer hardware.

4.3.2 Gates

A **gate** is an electronic device that operates on a collection of binary inputs to produce a binary output. That is, it transforms a set of (0,1) input values into a single (0,1) output value according to a specific transformation rule. Although gates can implement a wide range of different transformation rules, the ones we will be concerned with in this section are those that implement the three Boolean operations AND, OR, and NOT introduced in the previous section. As shown in Figure 4.15, these gates can be represented symbolically, along with the truth tables that define their transformation rules.

Comparing Figures 4.12 through 4.14 with Figure 4.15 shows that if we consider the value 1 equivalent to *true* and the value 0 equivalent to *false,* then these three electronic gates directly implement the corresponding Boolean operation. For example, an AND gate will have its output line set to 1 (set to some level of current or voltage that represents a binary 1) if and only if both of its inputs are 1. Otherwise, the output line will be set to 0 (set to some level of current or voltage that represents a binary 0). This is functionally identical to the rule that says the result of (a AND b) is *true* if and only if both a and b are *true*; otherwise, (a AND b) is *false*. Similar arguments hold for the OR and NOT.

A NOT gate can be constructed from a single transistor, as shown in Figure 4.16, in which the collector is connected to the power supply and the emitter is grounded. If the control line is set to 1, then the transistor is in the ON state, and it passes the current through to the ground. In this case the output of the gate is 0. However, if the control line is set to 0, the transistor is in the OFF state, and it blocks passage of the current to the ground. Instead, the current is transmitted to the output line, producing an output of 1. Thus, the value appearing on the output line of Figure 4.16 will be the complement—the NOT—of the value appearing on the collector, or input line.

To construct an AND gate, we first connect two transistors **in series,** as shown in Figure 4.17(a), with the collector line of transistor 1 connected to the power supply and the emitter line of transistor 2 grounded. If both

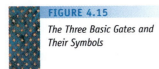

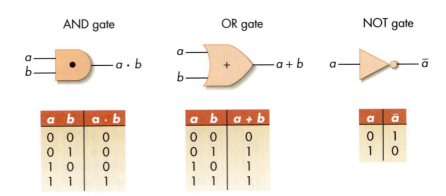

a	b	a · b
0	0	0
0	1	0
1	0	0
1	1	1

a	b	a + b
0	0	0
0	1	1
1	0	1
1	1	1

a	$\bar{a}$
0	1
1	0

FIGURE 4.16

Construction of a NOT Gate

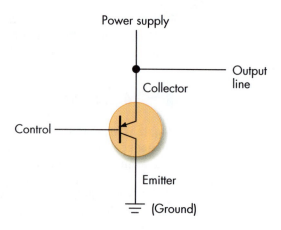

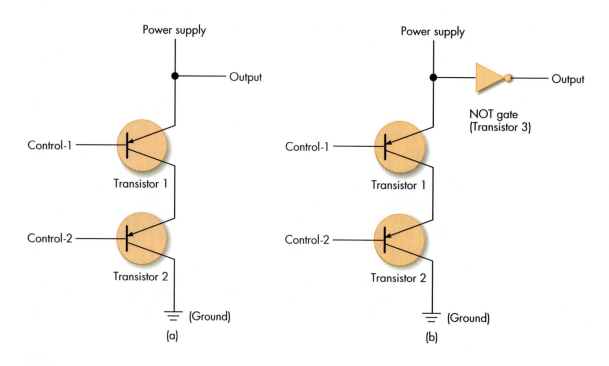

(a)

(b)

control lines, called Control-1 and Control-2 in Figure 4.17(a), are set to 1, then both transistors are in the ON state, and the current from the power supply is grounded, resulting in a value of 0 on the output line. If either (or both) Control-1 or Control-2 is a 0, then the corresponding transistor is in the OFF state, and it will not allow current to pass, resulting in a 1 on the output line. Thus, the output of the gate in Figure 4.17(a) is a 0 if and only if both inputs are a 1; otherwise, it is a 1. This is the exact *opposite* of the definition of AND, and Figure 4.17(a) represents a gate called NAND, an acronym for *NOT AND*. It produces the complement of the AND operation, and it is an important and widely used gate in hardware design.

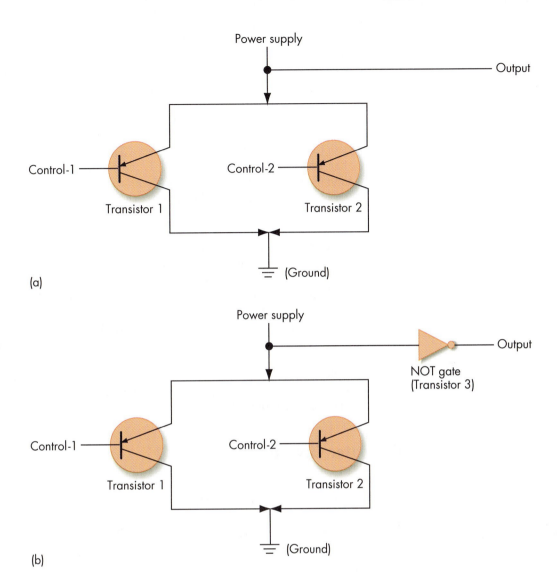

(a)

(b)

FIGURE 4.18

Construction of NOR and OR
Gates

(a) A Two-transistor NOR Gate
(b) A Three-transistor OR Gate

If, however, we want to build an AND gate, then all we have to do is add
a NOT gate (of the type shown in Figure 4.16) to the output line. This complements the NAND output and produces the AND truth table of Figure 4.12.
This gate is shown in Figure 4.17(b). Note that the NAND of Figure 4.17(a) requires two transistors while the AND of Figure 4.17(b) requires three. This is
one reason why NAND gates are more widely used to build computer circuits.

To construct an OR gate, we again start with two transistors. However,
this time they are connected **in parallel** rather than in series, as shown in
Figure 4.18(a).

In Figure 4.18(a) if either, or both, of the control lines Control-1 and
Control-2 are set to 1, then the corresponding transistor is in the ON state,
and current can pass from the power supply to the ground, producing an output value of 0. Only if both control lines are 0, effectively shutting off both
transistors, will the output line contain a 1. Again, this is the exact opposite

to the definition of OR given in Figure 4.13. Figure 4.18(a) is an implementation of a NOR gate, an acronym for *NOT OR*. To convert this to the OR gate we have been discussing, we do the same thing we did earlier—add a NOT gate to the output line. This gate is diagrammed in Figure 4.18(b).

Gates of the type shown in Figures 4.16 to 4.18 are not abstract entities that exist only in textbooks and classroom discussions. They are actual electronic devices that serve as the building blocks in the design and construction of modern computer systems. The reason for using gates rather than transistors is that a transistor is too elementary a device to act as the fundamental design component. It requires a designer to deal with such low-level issues as currents, voltages, and the laws of physics. Instead, transistors, grouped together to form more powerful building blocks called gates, allow us to think and design at a higher level. Instead of dealing with the complex physical rules associated with discrete electrical devices, we can use the power and expressiveness of mathematics and logic to build computers.

This seemingly minor change in viewpoint (from transistors to gates) has a profound effect on how computer hardware is designed and built. From this point on in our discussion of hardware design, we no longer need deal with anything electrical. We no longer require a knowledge of transistors, voltages, or currents, nor need we be physicists or electrical engineers. Instead, our building blocks will be AND, OR, and NOT gates, and our circuit construction rules will be the rules of Boolean logic. Here is another example of the importance of abstraction in computer science.

4.4 Building Computer Circuits

 ### 4.4.1 Introduction

A **circuit** is a collection of logic gates (1) that transforms a set of binary inputs into a set of binary outputs and (2) where the values of the outputs depend only on the current values of the inputs. (Actually, this type of circuit is more properly called a **combinational circuit**. We will use the simpler term *circuit* in this discussion.) A circuit C with m binary inputs and n binary outputs is represented as shown in Figure 4.19.

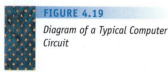
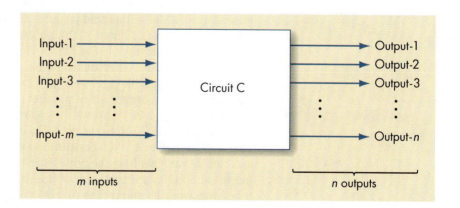

Internally, the circuit shown in Figure 4.19 is constructed from the AND, OR, and NOT gates introduced in the previous section. (*Note:* We will not be using the NAND and NOR gates diagrammed in Figure 4.17(a) and 4.18(a).) These gates can be interconnected in any way so long as the connections do not violate the constraints on the proper number of inputs and outputs for each gate. Each AND and OR gate must have exactly two inputs and one output. (Multiple-input AND and OR gates do exist, but we will not use them in our examples.) Each NOT gate must have exactly one input and one output. For example, the following is the diagram of a circuit with two inputs labeled a and b and two outputs labeled c and d. It contains one AND gate, one OR gate, and two NOT gates.

There is a direct relationship between Boolean expressions and **circuit diagrams** of this type. Every Boolean expression can be represented pictorially as a circuit diagram, and every output value in a circuit diagram can be written as a Boolean expression. For example, in the above diagram, the two output values labeled c and d are equivalent to the following two Boolean expressions:

$c = (a \text{ OR } b)$
$d = \text{NOT} ((a \text{ OR } b) \text{ AND } (\text{NOT } b))$

The choice of which representation to use depends on what we want to do. The pictorial view is better at allowing us to visualize the overall structure of the circuit, and it is often used during the design stage. A Boolean expression may be a more convenient representation for performing mathematical or logical operations, such as verification and optimization, on the circuit. We will use both representations in the following sections.

The value appearing on any output line of a circuit can be determined if we know the current input values and the transformations produced by each logic gate. (*Note:* There are circuits, called **sequential circuits,** that contain **feedback loops** in which the output of a gate is fed back as input to an earlier gate. The output of these circuits depends not only on the current input values but also on *previous* inputs. These circuits are typically used to build memory units because, in a sense, they can "remember" inputs. We will not discuss sequential circuits here.)

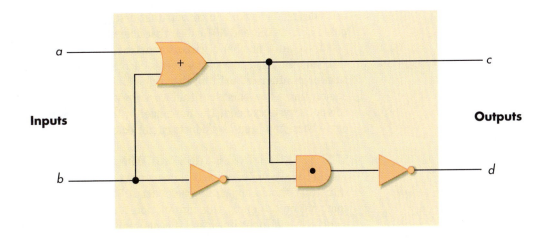

In the previous example, if $a = 1$ and $b = 0$, then the value on the c output line is 1, and the value on the d output line is 0. These values can be determined as follows:

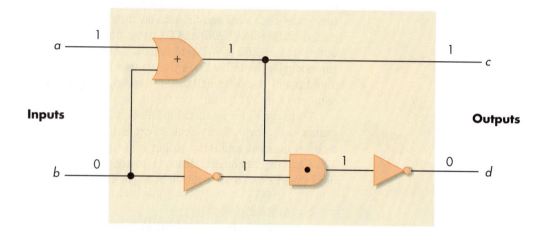

Note that it is perfectly legal to "split" or "tap" a line and send its value to two different gates. Here the input value b was split and sent to two separate gates.

The next section presents an algorithm for designing and building circuits from the three fundamental gate types AND, OR, and NOT. This will enable us to move to yet a higher level of abstraction. Instead of thinking in terms of transistors and electrical voltages (as in Section 4.2.4) or in terms of logic gates and truth values (Section 4.3.2), we can think and design in terms of circuits for high-level operations such as addition and comparison. This will make the task of understanding computer hardware much more manageable.

4.4.2   *A Circuit Construction Algorithm*

The circuit shown at the end of the previous section was simply an example, and it was not meant to carry out any meaningful operation. However, the circuits we want to build and study will perform useful arithmetic and logical functions. To create these important circuits, we need a way to take a description of a circuit's desired behavior and convert that description into a circuit diagram, composed of AND, OR, and NOT gates, that does exactly what we want it to do.

There are a number of **circuit construction algorithms** to accomplish this task, and the remainder of this section describes one such technique, called the **sum-of-products algorithm,** that will allow us to design circuits. Section 4.4.3 demonstrates how this algorithm works by constructing actual circuits that all computer systems need. The remainder of this section describes the operation of the four-step, sum-of-products circuit construction algorithm.

STEP 1: TRUTH TABLE CONSTRUCTION. First determine how the circuit should behave under all possible circumstances. That is, determine the binary value that should appear on each output line of the circuit for every possible combination of inputs. This information can be organized as a **truth table.** If a circuit has N input lines, and if each input line can be either a 0 or a 1, then there are 2^N combinations of input values, and the truth table will have 2^N rows. For each output of the circuit, we must specify the desired output value for every row in the truth table.

For example, if a circuit has three inputs and two outputs, then a truth table for that circuit will have $2^3 = 8$ input combinations and may look something like the following. (In this example, the output values are completely arbitrary.)

INPUTS			OUTPUTS		
a	b	c	OUTPUT-1	OUTPUT-2	
0	0	0	0	1	
0	0	1	0	0	
0	1	0	1	1	
0	1	1	0	1	$2^3 = 8$ input
1	0	0	0	0	combinations
1	0	1	0	0	
1	1	0	1	1	
1	1	1	0	0	

This circuit has two outputs labeled Output-1 and Output-2. The truth table specifies the value of each of these two output lines for every one of the eight possible combinations of inputs. We will use this example to illustrate the subsequent steps in the algorithm.

STEP 2: SUBEXPRESSION CONSTRUCTION USING AND AND NOT GATES.

Choose any one output column of the truth table built in step 1 and scan down that column. Every place that you find a 1 in that output column, you will build a Boolean *subexpression* that produces the value 1 (i.e., is true) for exactly that combination of input values and no other. The way you build this subexpression is to examine the value of each input for this specific case. If the input is a 1, use that input value directly in your subexpression. If the input is a 0, first take the NOT of that input, changing it from a 0 to a 1, and then use that **complemented** input value in your subexpression. You now have an input sequence of all 1s, and if all of these modified inputs are ANDed together (two at a time, of course), then the output value will be a 1. For example, let's look at the output column labeled Output-1 from the previous truth table.

INPUTS			OUTPUT-1	
a	b	c		
0	0	0	0	
0	0	1	0	
0	1	0	1	← case 1
0	1	1	0	
1	0	0	0	
1	0	1	0	
1	1	0	1	← case 2
1	1	1	0	

There are two 1s in the column labeled Output-1; they are referred to as case 1 and case 2. We thus need to construct two subexpressions, one for each of these two cases.

In case 1, the inputs a and c have the value 0 and the input b has the value 1. Thus we apply the NOT operator to both a and c, changing them from 0 to 1. Because the value of b is 1, we can use b directly. We now have three modified input values, all of which have the value 1. ANDing these three values together yields the Boolean expression $(\bar{a} \cdot b \cdot \bar{c})$. This expression produces a 1 only when the input is exactly $a = 0$, $b = 1$, $c = 0$. In any other case, at least one of the three terms in the expression will be a 0, and when the AND operation is carried out, it produces a 0. (Check this yourself by trying some other input values and seeing what is produced.) Thus the desired subexpression for case 1 is

$$(\bar{a} \cdot b \cdot \bar{c})$$

The subexpression for case 2 is developed in an identical manner, and it results in

$$(a \cdot b \cdot \bar{c})$$

This subexpression produces a 1 only when the input is exactly $a = 1$, $b = 1$, $c = 0$.

STEP 3: SUBEXPRESSION COMBINATION USING OR GATES.
Take each of the subexpressions produced in step 2 and combine them, two at a time, using OR gates. Each of the individual subexpressions produces a 1 for exactly one particular case where the truth table output is a 1, so the OR of the output of all of them will produce a 1 in each case where the truth table has a 1 and in no other case. Consequently, the Boolean expression produced in step 3 implements exactly the function described in the output column of the truth table on which we are working. In the example above, the final Boolean expression produced during step 3 is

$$(\bar{a} \cdot b \cdot \bar{c}) + (a \cdot b \cdot \bar{c})$$

STEP 4: CIRCUIT DIAGRAM PRODUCTION.
Construct the final circuit diagram. To do this, convert the Boolean expression produced at the end of step 3 into a circuit diagram, using AND, OR, and NOT gates to implement the AND, OR, and NOT operators appearing in the Boolean expression. This circuit diagram will produce the output described in the corresponding column of the truth table created in step 1. The circuit diagram for the Boolean expression developed in step 3 is shown in Figure 4.20.

We have successfully built the part of the circuit that produces the output for the column labeled Output-1 in the truth table shown in step 1. We now repeat steps 2, 3, and 4 for any additional output columns contained in the truth table. (In this example there is a second column labeled Output-2. We leave the construction of that circuit as a practice exercise.) When we have constructed a circuit diagram for every output of the circuit, we are finished. The sum-of-products algorithm is summarized in Figure 4.21.

This has been a formal introduction to one particular circuit construction algorithm. The algorithm is not easy to comprehend in an abstract sense. The next section clarifies this technique by using it to design two circuits that perform the operations of comparison and addition. Seeing it used to design actual circuits will make the steps of the algorithm easier to understand and follow.

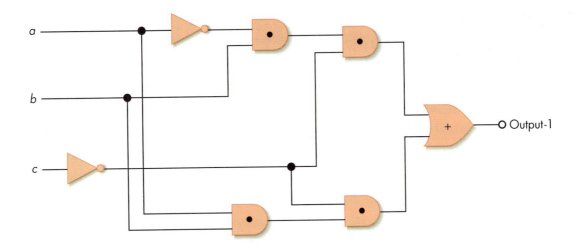

FIGURE 4.20

Circuit Diagram for the Output Labeled Output-1

We end this section by noting that the circuit construction algorithm just described does not always produce an **optimal** circuit, where *optimal* means that the circuit accomplishes its desired function using the smallest number of logic gates. For example, using the truth table shown on page 161, our sum-of-products algorithm produced the seven-gate circuit shown in Figure 4.20. This is a correct answer in the sense that the circuit does produce the correct values for Output-1 for all combinations of inputs. However, it is possible to do much better.

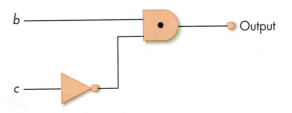

The preceding circuit also produces the correct result using only two gates instead of seven. This difference is very important because each AND, OR, and NOT gate is a physical entity that costs real money, takes up space on the chip, requires power to operate, and generates heat that must be dissipated.

FIGURE 4.21

The Sum-of-Products Circuit Construction Algorithm

Sum-of-Products Algorithm for Constructing Circuits

1. Construct the truth table describing the behavior of the desired circuit
2. While there is still an output column in the truth table, do steps 3 through 6
3.   Select an output column
4.   Subexpression construction using AND and NOT gates
5.   Subexpression combination using OR gates
6.   Circuit diagram production
7. Done

is a program that enables you to construct logic circuits from the AND, OR, and NOT gates just described. After you have constructed a circuit, this program allows you to test your circuit design by observing the outputs of the circuit you have built using any desired inputs.

To give you hands-on experience working with logic circuits, the first laboratory experience in this chapter introduces a software package called a **circuit simulator.** This

PRACTICE PROBLEMS

1. Design the circuit to implement the output described in the column labeled Output-2 in the truth table on page 161.

2. Design a circuit using AND, OR, and NOT gates to implement the following truth table.

a	b	Output
0	0	0
0	1	1
1	0	1
1	1	0

This is the **exclusive-OR** operation. It is true if and only if a is 1 or b is 1, but not both.

3. Build a circuit using AND, OR, and NOT gates to implement the following truth table.

a	b	c	Output
0	0	0	1
0	0	1	0
0	1	0	0
0	1	1	0
1	0	0	0
1	0	1	0
1	1	0	0
1	1	1	1

This is called a **full-ON/full-OFF** circuit. It is true if and only if all three of its inputs are OFF (0) or all three are ON (1).

Eliminating five unnecessary gates produces a real savings. The fewer gates we use, the cheaper, more efficient, and more compact will be our circuits and hence the resulting computer. Algorithms for **circuit optimization**—that is, for reducing the number of gates needed to implement a circuit—are an important part of hardware design. Challenge Work problem 1 at the end of the chapter invites you to investigate this interesting topic in more detail.

 ### 4.4.3 *Examples of Circuit Design and Construction*

Let's use the algorithm described in Section 4.4.2 to construct two circuits important to the operation of any real-world computer, a compare-for-equality circuit and an addition circuit.

A COMPARE-FOR-EQUALITY CIRCUIT. The first circuit we will construct is a **compare-for-equality circuit,** or CE circuit, which tests two unsigned binary numbers for exact equality. The circuit produces the value 1 (*true*) if the two numbers are equal and the value 0 (*false*) if they are not. Such a circuit could be used in many situations. For example, in the shampooing algorithm in Figure 1.3(a), there is an instruction that says,

> Repeat steps 4 through 6 until the value of *WashCount* equals 2

Our CE circuit could accomplish the comparison between *WashCount* and 2 and return a true or false, depending on whether these two values were equal or not equal.

Let's start by using the sum-of-products algorithm in Figure 4.21 to construct a simpler circuit called 1-CE, short for *1*-bit compare for *equality*. A 1-CE circuit compares two 1-bit values a and b for equality. That is, the circuit 1-CE produces a 1 as output if both its inputs are 0 or both its inputs are 1. Otherwise, 1-CE produces a 0. After designing 1-CE, we will use it to create a "full-blown" comparison circuit that can handle numbers of any size.

Step 1 of the algorithm says to construct the truth table that describes the behavior of the desired circuit. The truth table for the 1-CE circuit is

a	b	Output
0	0	1 ⟵ case 1
0	1	0
1	0	0
1	1	1 ⟵ case 2

Scanning down the output column of the truth table, we see that there are two 1 values, labeled case 1 and case 2, so step 2 of the algorithm is to construct two subexpressions, one for each of these two cases. The subexpression for case 1 is $(\overline{a} \cdot \overline{b})$ because this produces the value 1 only when $a = 0$ and $b = 0$. The subexpression for case 2 is $(a \cdot b)$, which produces a 1 only when $a = 1$ and $b = 1$.

We now combine the outputs of these two subexpressions with an OR gate, as described in step 3, to produce the Boolean expression

$$(\overline{a} \cdot \overline{b}) + (a \cdot b)$$

FIGURE 4.22

One-Bit Compare for Equality Circuit

1-CE Circuit

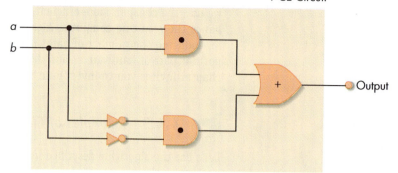

Finally, in step 4, we convert this expression to a circuit diagram, which is shown in Figure 4.22. The circuit shown in Figure 4.22 correctly compares two 1-bit quantities and determines whether they are equal. If they are equal, it outputs a 1. If they are unequal, it outputs a 0.

However, the numbers compared for equality by a computer are usually much larger than a single binary digit. We want a circuit that correctly compares two numbers that contain N binary digits. To build this "N-bit compare-for-equality" circuit, we will use N of the 1-CE circuits shown in Figure 4.22, one for each bit position in the numbers to be compared. Each 1-CE circuit produces a 1 if the two binary digits in its specific location are identical and produces a 0 if they are not. If every circuit produces a 1, then the two numbers are identical in every bit position, and they are equal. To check whether all our 1-CE circuits produce a 1, we simply AND together (two at a time) the outputs of all N 1-CE circuits. Remember that an AND gate produces a 1 if and only if both of its inputs are a 1. Thus the final output of the N-bit compare circuit is a 1 if and only if every pair of bits in the corresponding location of the two numbers is identical—that is, the two numbers are equal.

Figure 4.23 shows the design of a complete **N-bit compare-for-equality circuit** called CE. Each of the two numbers being compared, a and b, contains N bits, and they are labeled $a_{N-1} a_{N-2} \ldots a_0$ and $b_{N-1} b_{N-2} \ldots b_0$. The box labeled 1-CE in Figure 4.23 is the 1-bit compare-for-equality circuit shown in Figure 4.22. Looking at these figures, you can see that we have designed a very complex electrical circuit without the specification of a single electrical device. The only "devices" in those diagrams are gates to implement the logical operations AND, OR, and NOT, and the only "rules" we need to know in order to understand the diagrams are the transformation rules of Boolean logic. George Boole's "not very important" work is the starting point for the design of every circuit found inside a modern computer.

AN ADDITION CIRCUIT. Our second example of circuit construction is an addition circuit called ADD that performs binary addition on two unsigned N-bit integers. Typically, this type of circuit is called a **full adder.** For example, assuming $N = 6$, our ADD circuit would be able to perform the following 6-bit addition operation:

1 1	($\leftarrow$ the carry bit)
0 0 1 1 0 1	(the binary value 13)
+ 0 0 1 1 1 0	(the binary value 14)
0 1 1 0 1 1	(the binary value 27, which is the correct sum)

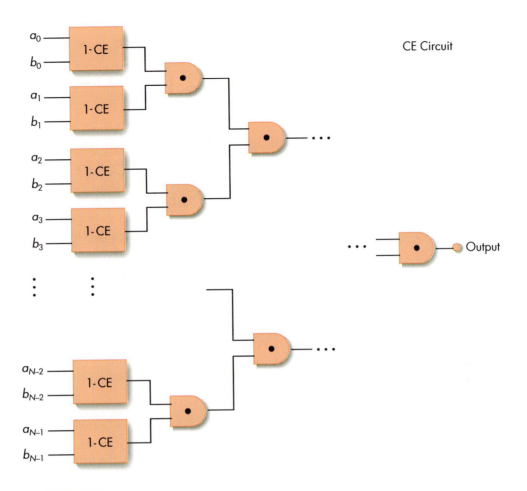

CE Circuit

FIGURE 4.23

N-*Bit Compare for Equality Circuit*

Just as we did with the CE circuit, we carry out the design of the ADD circuit in two stages. First, we use the circuit construction algorithm of Figure 4.21 to build a circuit called 1-ADD that adds a single pair of binary digits, along with a carry digit. We then interconnect N of these 1-ADD circuits to produce the complete N-bit full adder circuit ADD.

Looking at the addition example just shown, we see that summing the values in column i will require us to add three binary values—the two binary digits in that column, a_i and b_i, and the carry digit from the previous column, called c_i. Furthermore, the circuit must produce two binary outputs: a sum digit s_i and a new carry digit c_{i+1} that propagates to the next column. The pictorial representation of the 1-bit adder circuit 1-ADD and its accompanying truth table are shown in Figure 4.24.

Because the 1-ADD circuit being constructed has two outputs, s_i and c_{i+1}, we must use steps 2, 3, and 4 of the circuit construction algorithm twice, once for each output. Let's work on the sum output s_i first.

The s_i output column of Figure 4.24 contains four 1s, so we need to construct four subexpressions. In accordance with the guidelines given in step 2 of the construction algorithm, these four subexpressions are

Case 1: $\quad \overline{a}_i \cdot \overline{b}_i \cdot c_i$

Case 2: $\quad \overline{a}_i \cdot b_i \cdot \overline{c}_i$

FIGURE 4.24

The 1-ADD Circuit and Truth Table

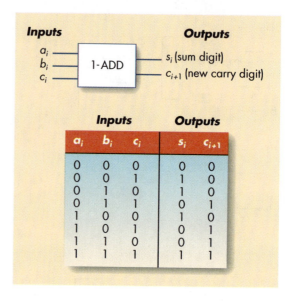

Inputs			Outputs	
a_i	b_i	c_i	s_i	c_{i+1}
0	0	0	0	0
0	0	1	1	0
0	1	0	1	0
0	1	1	0	1
1	0	0	1	0
1	0	1	0	1
1	1	0	0	1
1	1	1	1	1

Case 3: $a_i \cdot \overline{b_i} \cdot \overline{c_i}$

Case 4: $a_i \cdot b_i \cdot c_i$

Step 3 says to combine the outputs of these four subexpressions using three OR gates to produce the output labeled s_i in the truth table of Figure 4.24. The final Boolean expression for the sum output is

$$s_i = (\overline{a_i} \cdot \overline{b_i} \cdot c_i) + (\overline{a_i} \cdot b_i \cdot \overline{c_i}) + (a_i \cdot \overline{b_i} \cdot \overline{c_i}) + (a_i \cdot b_i \cdot c_i)$$

The logic circuit to produce the output whose expression is given above is shown in Figure 4.25. (This circuit diagram has been labeled to highlight the four separate subexpressions created during step 2, as well as the combining of the subexpressions in step 3 of the construction algorithm.)

We are not yet finished, because the 1-ADD circuit in Figure 4.24 has a second output—the carry into the next column. That means the circuit construction algorithm must be repeated for the second output column, labeled c_{i+1}.

The c_{i+1} column also contains four 1s, so we again need to build four separate subcircuits, just as for the sum output, and combine them using OR gates. The construction proceeds in a fashion similar to the first part, so we leave the details as an exercise for the reader. The Boolean expression describing the carry output c_{i+1} of the 1-ADD circuit is

$$c_{i+1} = (\overline{a_i} \cdot b_i \cdot c_i) + (a_i \cdot \overline{b_i} \cdot c_i) + (a_i \cdot b_i \cdot \overline{c_i}) + (a_i \cdot b_i \cdot c_i)$$

We have now built the two parts of the 1-ADD circuit that produce the sum and the carry outputs. The complete 1-ADD circuit is constructed by simply putting these two pieces together. Figure 4.26 shows the complete (and admittedly quite complex) 1-ADD circuit to implement 1-bit addition. To keep the diagram from becoming an incomprehensible tangle of lines, we have

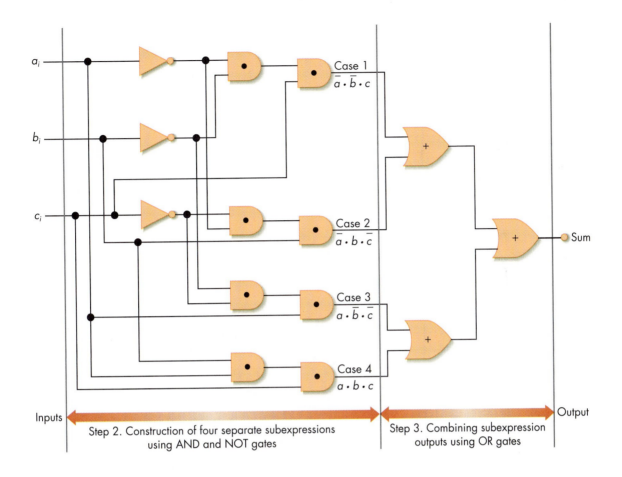

Case 1
$\overline{a} \cdot \overline{b} \cdot c$

Case 2
$\overline{a} \cdot b \cdot \overline{c}$

Case 3
$a \cdot \overline{b} \cdot \overline{c}$

Case 4
$a \cdot b \cdot c$

Sum

Inputs

Step 2. Construction of four separate subexpressions
using AND and NOT gates

Step 3. Combining subexpression
outputs using OR gates

Output

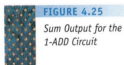

FIGURE 4.25

*Sum Output for the
1-ADD Circuit*

drawn it in a slightly different orientation from Figures 4.22 and 4.25. Everything else is exactly the same.

When looking at this rather imposing diagram, one should not become overly concerned with the details of every gate, every connection, every operation. The important concern reflected in Figure 4.26 is the *process* by which we were able to design such a complex and intricate circuit. We were able to transform the idea of 1-bit binary addition into an electrical circuit using the tools of algorithmic problem solving and symbolic logic.

How is the 1-ADD circuit shown in Figure 4.26 used to add numbers that contain N binary digits rather than just one? The answer is simple if we think about the way numbers are added by hand. (We discussed exactly this topic when developing the addition algorithm of Figure 1.2.) We add numbers one column at a time, moving from right to left, generating the sum digit, writing it down, and sending any carry to the next column. The same thing can be done in hardware. We use N of the 1-ADD circuits shown in Figure 4.26, one for each column. Starting with the rightmost circuit, each 1-ADD circuit adds a single column of digits, generates a sum digit that is part of the final answer, and sends its carry digit to the 1-ADD circuit on its left, which replicates this process. After N repetitions of this process, all sum digits have been generated, and the N circuits have correctly added the two numbers.

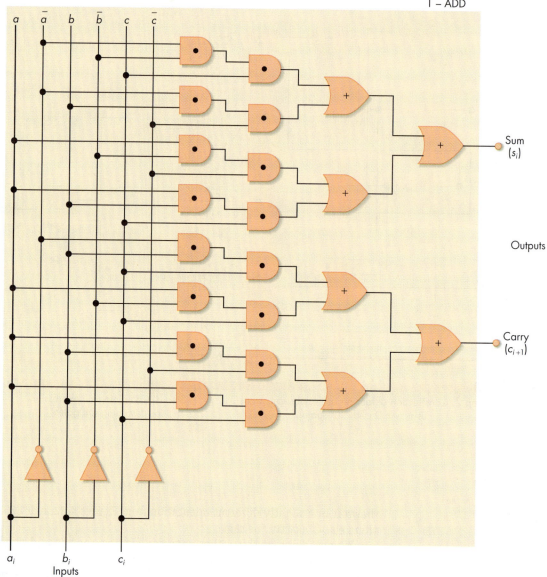

FIGURE 4.26

Complete 1-ADD Circuit for 1-Bit Binary Addition

The complete full adder circuit called ADD is shown in Figure 4.27. It adds the two N-bit numbers $a_{N-1} a_{N-2} \ldots a_0$ and $b_{N-1} b_{N-2} \ldots b_0$ to produce the $(N + 1)$ − bit sum $s_N s_{N-1} s_{N-2} \ldots s_0$. Because addition is one of the most common arithmetic operations, the circuit shown in Figure 4.27 (or something equivalent) would be one of the most important and most frequently used arithmetic components. Addition circuits are found in every computer, workstation, and handheld calculator in the marketplace. They are even found in computer-controlled thermostats, clocks, and microwave ovens, where they enable us, for example, to add 30 minutes to the overall cooking time.

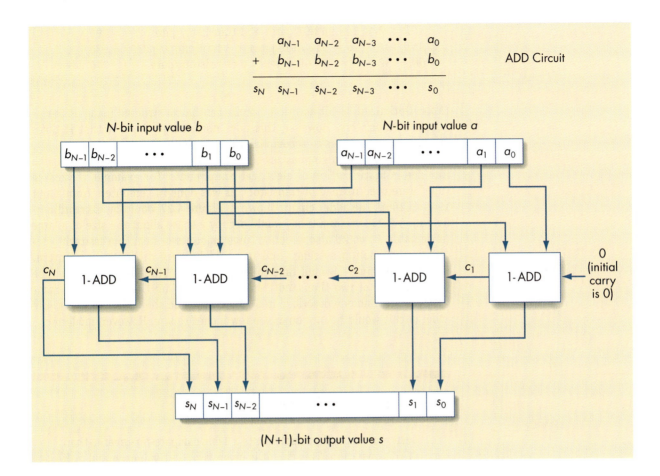

$$
\begin{array}{cccccc}
 & a_{N-1} & a_{N-2} & a_{N-3} & \cdots & a_0 \\
+ & b_{N-1} & b_{N-2} & b_{N-3} & \cdots & b_0 \\
\hline
s_N & s_{N-1} & s_{N-2} & s_{N-3} & \cdots & s_0
\end{array}
$$

ADD Circuit

N-bit input value *b*

N-bit input value *a*

b_{N-1} b_{N-2} $\cdots$ b_1 b_0

a_{N-1} a_{N-2} $\cdots$ a_1 a_0

c_N 1-ADD c_{N-1} 1-ADD c_{N-2} $\cdots$ c_2 1-ADD c_1 1-ADD 0 (initial carry is 0)

s_N s_{N-1} s_{N-2} $\cdots$ s_1 s_0

(*N*+1)-bit output value *s*

FIGURE 4.27

The Complete Full Adder ADD Circuit

Figure 4.27 is, in a sense, the direct hardware implementation of the addition algorithm shown in Figure 1.2. Although Figure 1.2 and Figure 4.27 are quite different, both represent essentially the same algorithm: the column-by-column addition of two *N*-bit numerical values. This demonstrates quite clearly that there are many different ways to express the same algorithm—in this case, pseudocode (Figure 1.2) and hardware circuits (Figure 4.27). Later chapters show additional ways to represent algorithms, such as machine language programs and high-level language programs. However, regardless of whether we use English, pseudocode, mathematics, or transistors to describe an algorithm, its fundamental properties are the same, and the central purpose of computer science—algorithmic problem solving—remains unchanged.

It may also be instructive to study the size and complexity of the ADD circuit just designed. Looking at Figure 4.27, we see that the addition of two *N*-bit integer values requires *N* separate 1-ADD circuits. Let's assume that *N* = 32, a typical value for modern computers. Referring to Figure 4.26, we see that each 1-ADD circuit uses 3 NOT gates, 16 AND gates, and 6 OR gates, a total of 25 logic gates. Thus the total number of logic gates used to implement 32-bit binary addition is 32 × 25 = 800 gates. Figures 4.16, 4.17(b), and 4.18(b) show that each AND and OR gate requires three transistors and each NOT gate requires one. Therefore, the total number of transistors needed to build a 32-bit adder circuit is over 2,200 transistors:

$$NOT: \quad 32 \times 3 = 96 \text{ NOT gates} \times 1 \text{ transistor/gate} \quad = \quad 96$$
$$AND: \quad 32 \times 16 = 512 \text{ AND gates} \times 3 \text{ transistors/gate} = 1{,}536$$
$$OR: \quad 32 \times 6 = 192 \text{ OR gates} \times 3 \text{ transistors/gate} \quad = \underline{\quad 576}$$
$$\text{Total} \quad = 2{,}208 \text{ transistors}$$

(*Note:* Optimized 32-bit addition circuits can be constructed using as few as 500–600 transistors. However, this does not change the fact that it takes many, many transistors to accomplish this addition task.)

This computation emphasizes the importance of the continuing research into the miniaturization of electrical components. For example, if vacuum tubes were used instead of transistors, as was done in computers from about 1940 to 1955, the adder circuit shown in Figure 4.27 would be extraordinarily bulky; 2,208 vacuum tubes would occupy a space about the size of a large refrigerator. It would also generate huge amounts of heat, necessitating sophisticated cooling systems, and it would be very difficult to maintain. (Imagine the time it would take to locate a single burned-out vacuum tube from a cluster of two thousand.) Using something on the scale of the magnetic core technology described in Section 4.2.4 and shown in Figure 4.4, the adder circuit would fit into an area a few inches square. However, modern cir-

PRACTICE PROBLEMS

1. Design a circuit that implements a 1-bit compare-for-greater-than (1-GT) operation. This circuit is given two 1-bit values, a and b. It outputs a 1 if $a > b$ and outputs a 0 otherwise.

2. Use the circuit construction algorithm just described to implement the NOR operation shown in Figure 4.18(a). Remember that the truth table for the NOR operation is:

a	b	(a NOR b)
0	0	1
0	1	0
1	0	0
1	1	0

LABORATORY EXPERIENCE 8

In the second laboratory experience of this chapter, you will again be using the circuit simulator software package. This time you will use it to construct circuits using the sum-of-products algorithm discussed in this section and shown in Figure 4.21. Using the simulator to design, build, and test actual circuits will give you a deeper understanding of how to use the sum-of-products algorithm to create circuits that solve specific problems.

cuit technology can achieve densities of over 25,000,000 transistors/cm². At this level, the entire ADD circuit of Figure 4.27 would easily fit in an area much smaller than the size of the period at the end of this sentence. That is why it is now possible to put powerful computer processing facilities not only in a room or on a desk but also inside a watch, a thermostat, or even inside the human body.

 ### 4.4.4 Summary

This section has been a brief introduction to the interesting but highly complex topic of circuit design. Our purpose here was not to make you experts in specifying and designing computer circuits but to demonstrate how it is possible to implement high-level arithmetic operations using only low-level electronic components such as transistors. We also demonstrated how it is possible to reorient our viewpoint and raise our level of abstraction. We changed the level of discussion from electricity to arithmetic, from hardware devices to mathematical behavior, from form to function. This is one of the first steps up the hierarchy of abstractions introduced in Figure 1.8. Succeeding chapters will take circuits like CE and ADD and use them as building blocks to construct yet higher-level abstractions such as functional units and complete computer systems.

4.5 Control Circuits

The previous section described the design of circuits for implementing arithmetic and logical operations. However, there are other, quite different, types of circuits that are also essential to the proper functioning of a computer system. This section briefly describes one of these other important circuit types, **control circuits.** These circuits are used not to implement arithmetic operations but to determine the order in which operations are carried out inside a computer and to select the correct data values to be processed. In a sense, they can be viewed as the sequencing and decision-making circuits inside a computer. These circuits are essential to the proper function of a computer because, as we noted in Chapter 1, algorithms and programs must be well ordered and must always know what operation to do next. The two major types of control circuits are called **multiplexors** and **decoders,** and, like everything else described in this chapter, they can be completely described in terms of gates and the rules of logic.

A **multiplexor** is a circuit that has 2^N **input lines** and 1 **output line.** Its function is to select exactly one of its 2^N input lines and copy the binary value on that input line onto its single output line. The way a multiplexor chooses one specific input is by using an additional set of N lines called **selector lines.** (Thus the total number of inputs to the multiplexor circuit is $2^N + N$.) The 2^N input lines of a multiplexor are numbered 0, 1, 2, 3, . . . , $2^N - 1$. Each of the N selector lines can be set to either a 0 or a 1, so we can use the N selector lines to represent all binary values from 000 . . . 0 (N zeroes) to 111 . . . 1 (N ones), which represent all integer values from 0 to $2^N - 1$. These numbers correspond exactly to the numbers of the input lines. Thus the binary number that appears on the selector lines can be interpreted as the identification number of the input line that is to be selected. Pictorially, a multiplexor looks like this:

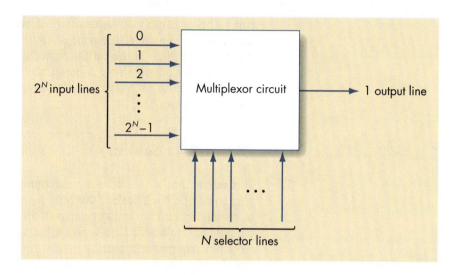

For example, if we had four (2^2) input lines (i.e., $N = 2$) coming into our multiplexor, numbered 0, 1, 2, and 3, then we would need two selector lines. The four binary combinations that can appear on this pair of selector lines are 00, 01, 10, and 11, which correspond to the decimal values 0, 1, 2, and 3, respectively (see Figure 4.2). The multiplexor selects the one input line whose identification number corresponds to the value appearing on the selector lines and copies the value on that input line to the output line. If, for example, the two selector lines were set to 1 and 0, then a multiplexor circuit would pick input line 2 because 10 in binary is 2 in decimal notation.

Implementing a multiplexor using logic gates is not difficult. Figure 4.28 shows a simple multiplexor circuit with $N = 1$. This is a multiplexor with two (2^1) input lines and a single selector line.

In Figure 4.28 if the value on the selector line is 0, then the bottom input line to AND gate 2 will always be 0, so its output will always be 0. Looking at AND gate 1, we see that the NOT gate will change its bottom input value to a 1. Because (1 AND a) is always a, the output of the top AND gate will be equal to the value of a, which is the value of the input from line 0.

FIGURE 4.28

A Two-Input Multiplexor Circuit

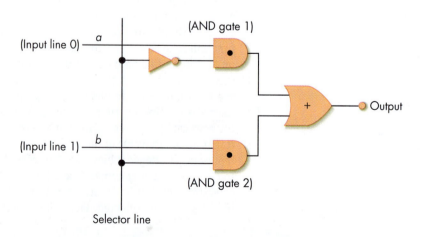

Thus the two inputs to the OR gate will be 0 and a. Because the value of the expression (0 OR a) is identical to a, by setting the selector line to 0 we have, in effect, selected as our output the value that appears on line 0. You should confirm that if the selector line has the value 1, then the output of the circuit in Figure 4.28 is b, the value appearing on line 1. We can design multiplexors with more than two inputs in a similar fashion, although they rapidly become more complex.

The second type of control circuit is called a **decoder** and it operates in the opposite way from a multiplexor. A decoder has N input lines numbered $0, 1, 2, \ldots, N - 1$ and 2^N output lines numbered $0, 1, 2, 3, \ldots, 2^N - 1$.

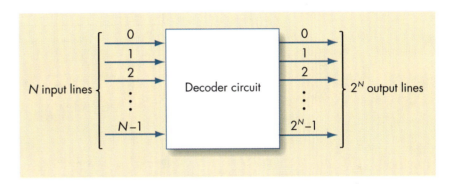

Each of the N input lines of the decoder can be set to either a 0 or a 1, and when these N values are interpreted as a single binary number, they can represent all integer values from 0 to $2^N - 1$. It is the job of the decoder to determine the value represented on its N input lines and then send a signal (i.e., a 1) on the single output line that has that identification number. All other output lines are set to 0.

For example, if our decoder has three input lines, it will have eight (2^3) output lines numbered 0 to 7. These three input lines can represent all binary values from 000 to 111, which is from 0 to 7 in decimal notation. If, for example, the binary values on the three input lines are 101, which is a 5, then a signal (a binary 1) would be sent out by the decoder on output line 5. All other output lines would contain a 0.

Figure 4.29 shows the design of a 2-to-4 decoder circuit with two input lines and four (2^2) output lines. These four output lines are labeled 0, 1, 2, and 3, and the only output line that will carry a signal value of 1 is the line whose identification number is identical to the value appearing on the two input lines. For example, if the two inputs are 11, then line 3 should be set to a 1 (11 in binary is 3 in decimal). This is, in fact, what happens because the AND gate connected to line 3 is the only one whose two inputs are equal to a 1. You should confirm that this circuit behaves properly when it receives the inputs 00, 01, and 10 as well.

Together, decoder and multiplexor circuits enable us to build computer systems that execute the correct instructions using the correct data values. As an example of their use, assume we have a computer that can carry out four different types of arithmetic operations—add, subtract, multiply, and divide. Furthermore, assume that these four instructions have code numbers 0, 1, 2, and 3, respectively. We could use a decoder circuit to ensure that the computer performs the correct instruction. We need a decoder circuit with two input lines. It receives as input the 2-digit code number (in binary) of the instruction that we want to perform: 00 (add), 01 (subtract), 10 (multiply), or 11

FIGURE 4.29

A 2-to-4 Decoder Circuit

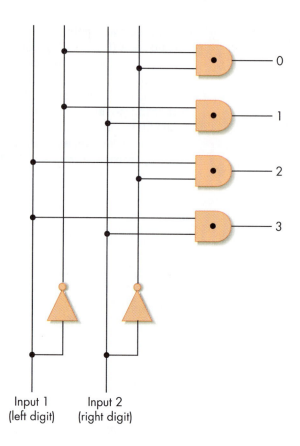

Input 1
(left digit)

Input 2
(right digit)

(divide). The decoder interprets this value and sends out a signal on the correct output line. This signal is used to activate the proper arithmetic circuit and cause it to perform the desired operation. This behavior is diagrammed in Figure 4.30.

While a decoder circuit can be used to select the correct instruction, a multiplexor can help ensure that the computer executes this instruction using the correct data. For example, suppose our computer has four special registers called R0, R1, R2, and R3. (For now, just consider a register to be a place to store a data value. We describe registers in more detail in the next chapter.) Assume that we have built a circuit called *test-if-zero* that can test whether any of these four registers contains the value 0. (This is actually quite similar to the CE circuit of Figure 4.23.) We can use a multiplexor circuit to select the register that we wish to send to the test-if-zero circuit. This is shown in Figure 4.31. If we want to test whether register R2 in Figure 4.31 is 0, we simply put the binary value 10 (2 in decimal notation) on the two selector lines. This selects register R2, and only its value will pass through the multiplexor and be sent to the test circuit.

This has been only a very brief illustration of how we can use electronic circuits to control the execution of operations within an algorithm. We will see many more examples of the use of control circuits in Chapter 5, which examines the execution of programs and the overall organization of a computer system.

FIGURE 4.30

Example of the Use of a Decoder Circuit

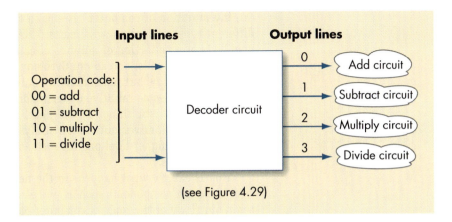

Input lines   **Output lines**

Operation code:
00 = add
01 = subtract
10 = multiply
11 = divide

Decoder circuit

0 → Add circuit
1 → Subtract circuit
2 → Multiply circuit
3 → Divide circuit

(see Figure 4.29)

FIGURE 4.31

Example of the Use of a Multiplexor Circuit

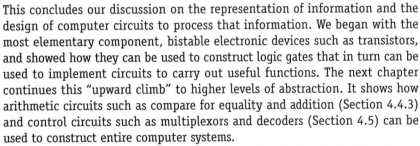

Registers

Input   **Output**

R0
R1
R2
R3

Multiplexor → Test-if-zero circuit

Selector lines

4.6   Conclusion

This concludes our discussion on the representation of information and the design of computer circuits to process that information. We began with the most elementary component, bistable electronic devices such as transistors, and showed how they can be used to construct logic gates that in turn can be used to implement circuits to carry out useful functions. The next chapter continues this "upward climb" to higher levels of abstraction. It shows how arithmetic circuits such as compare for equality and addition (Section 4.4.3) and control circuits such as multiplexors and decoders (Section 4.5) can be used to construct entire computer systems.

After reading this chapter, you may have the feeling that although you understand the individual concepts that were covered, you don't understand, in the grand sense, what computers are or how they work. You may feel that you can follow the details but can't see the "big picture." One possible reason is that this chapter looked at computers from a very elementary viewpoint.

Our investigation of computer systems in this chapter consisted of studying different types of specialized circuits. This is analogous to studying the human body as a collection of millions of cells of different types—blood cells, brain cells, skin cells, and so on. Cytology is certainly an important part of the field of biology, but understanding only the cellular structure of the human body provides no intuitive understanding of what people are and how we do such characteristic things as walk, eat, and breathe. Understanding these complex actions derives not from a study of molecules, genes, or cells, but from a study of higher-level organs, such as lungs, stomach, and muscles, and their interactions.

That is exactly what happens in the next chapter as we examine higher-level computer components such as processors, memory, and instructions and begin our study of the topic of computer organization.

1. Given our discussion of positional numbering systems in Section 4.2.1, see whether you can determine the decimal value of the following numbers.

    a. 133 (base 4)

    b. 367 (base 8, also called *octal*)

    c. 1BA (base 16, also called *hexadecimal*. B is the digit that represents 11; A is the digit that represents 10.)

2. In Exercise 1(c), we used the letters A and B as digits of the base 16 number. Explain why that was necessary.

3. Determine the decimal value of the following unsigned binary numbers.

    a. 11000   c. 1111111

    b. 110001   d. 1000000000

4. If a computer uses 18 bits to represent integer values, what is the largest unsigned value that can be represented?

5. Assume that the following 10-bit numbers represent signed integers using sign/magnitude notation. The sign is the leftmost bit and the remaining 9 bits represent the magnitude. What is the decimal value of each?

    a. 1000110001   c. 1000000001

    b. 0110011000   d. 1000000000

6. a. What is "unusual" about the 10-bit value shown in Exercise 5(d)? How could it cause problems on a computer system that used sign/magnitude notation? (*Hint:* Think about how it might affect the compare-for-equality circuit that we built.)

    b. Assume that we use 10 bits to represent signed integers, using sign/magnitude notation. What are the largest (in absolute value) positive and negative numbers that can be represented on our system?

7. Assume that our computer stores decimal numbers using 16 bits—10 bits for a sign/magnitude mantissa and 6 bits for a sign/magnitude base-2 exponent. (This is exactly the same representation used in the text.) Show the internal representation of the following decimal quantities.

    a. +7.5   b. −20.25   c. −1/64

8. Using the ASCII code set given in Figure 4.3, show the internal binary representation for the following character strings.

    a. AbC   c. $25.00

    b. Mike   d. (a+b)

9. How many binary digits would it take to represent the following phrase in ASCII code? In UNICODE? (Do not include the " " marks.)

    "Invitation to Computer Science"

10. How many bits would it take to store a 3-minute song using an audio encoding method that samples at the rate of 40,000 bits/second, has a bit depth of 16, and does not use compression? What if it used a compression scheme with a compression ratio of 5:1?

11. How many bits would it take to store an uncompressed 1,200 × 800 RGB color image? If we found out that the image actually took only 2.4 Mbits, what would be the compression ratio?

12. Show how we could use run-length encoding to compress the following text stream:

    xxxyyyyyyyzzzzAAxxxx

    What is the compression ratio?

13. Using the Huffman code shown in Figure 4.8, give the internal coding of the following Hawaiian words along with the amount of savings over the standard fixed-length four bit representation:

    a. KAI

    b. MAUI

    c. MOLOKAI

    Explain exactly what happened in this last example.

14. The primary advantage of using the binary numbering system rather than the decimal system to represent data is reliability, as we noted in Section 4.2.3. Describe two disadvantages of using binary rather than decimal notation for the internal representation of information.

15. Assume that $a = 1$, $b = 2$, and $c = 2$. What is the value of each of the following Boolean expressions?

    a. $(a > 1)$ OR $(b = c)$

    b. $[(a + b) > c]$ AND $(b \leq c)$

    c. NOT $(a = 1)$

    d. NOT $[(a = b)$ OR $(b = c)]$

16. Assume that $a = 5$, $b = 2$, and $c = 3$. What is the problem with attempting to evaluate the following Boolean expression?

    $(a = 1)$ AND $(b = 2)$ OR $(c = 3)$

    How can we solve this problem?

17. Using the circuit construction algorithm of Section 4.4.2, design a circuit using only AND, OR, and NOT gates to implement the following truth table.

a	b	Output
0	0	1
0	1	1
1	0	1
1	1	0

This operation is termed **NAND,** for *Not AND,* and it can be constructed as a single gate as shown in Figure 4.17(a).

18. Using the circuit construction algorithm of Section 4.4.2, design a circuit using only AND, OR, and NOT gates to implement the following truth table.

a	b	Output
0	0	1
0	1	1
1	0	0
1	1	1

This operation is termed **logical implication,** and it is an important operator in symbolic logic.

19. Build a **majority-rules circuit.** This is a circuit that has three inputs and one output. The value of its output is 1 if and only if two or more of its inputs are 1; otherwise, the output of the circuit is 0. For example, if the three inputs are 0, 1, 1, your circuit should output a 1. If its three inputs are 0, 1, 0, it should output a 0. This circuit is frequently used in **fault-tolerant computing**—environments where a computer must keep working correctly no matter what. An example is a computer on a deep-space vehicle where repairs would be impossible. In these conditions, we might choose to put three computers on board and have all three do every computation. We would then say that if two or more of the systems produce the same answer, we would accept it. Thus one

of the machines could fail and the system would still work properly.

20. Design an **odd-parity circuit.** This is a circuit that has three inputs and one output. The circuit outputs a 1 if and only if an even number (0 or 2) of its inputs are a 1. Otherwise, the circuit outputs a 0. Thus the sum of the number of 1 bits in the input and the output is always an odd number. (This circuit is used in error checking. By adding up the number of 1 bits, we can determine whether any single input bit was accidentally changed. If it was, the total number of 1s will be an even number when we know it should be an odd value.)

21. Design a **1-bit subtraction circuit.** This circuit takes three inputs—two binary digits a and b and a borrow digit from the previous column. The circuit has two outputs—the difference $(a - b)$, including the borrow, and a new borrow digit that propagates to the next column. Create the truth table and build the circuit. This circuit can be used to build N-bit subtraction circuits.

22. How many selector lines would be needed on a four-input multiplexor? On an eight-input multiplexor?

23. Design a **four-input multiplexor circuit.** Use the design of the two-input multiplexor shown in Figure 4.28 as a guide.

24. Design a **3-to-8 decoder circuit.** Use the design of the 2-to-4 decoder circuit shown in Figure 4.29 as a guide.

CHALLENGE WORK

1. **Circuit optimization** is a very important area of hardware design. As we mentioned earlier in the chapter, each gate in the circuit represents a real hardware device that takes up space on the chip, generates heat that must be dissipated, and increases costs. Therefore, the elimination of unneeded gates can represent a real savings. Circuit optimization investigates techniques to construct a new circuit that behaves identically to the original one but with fewer gates. The basis for circuit optimization is the transformation rules of symbolic logic. These rules allow you to transform one Boolean expression into an equivalent one that entails fewer operations. For example, the *distributive law* of logic says that $(a \cdot b) + (a \cdot c) = a \cdot (b + c)$. The expressions on either side of the = sign are functionally identical, but the one on the right determines its value using one less gate (one AND gate and one OR gate instead of two AND gates and one OR gate).

   Read about the transformation rules of binary logic and techniques of circuit optimization. Using these rules, improve the full adder circuit of Figure 4.27 so

that it requires less than 2,208 transistors. Explain your improvements and determine exactly how many fewer transistors are required for your "new and improved" full adder circuit.

2. Although this chapter described a signed-integer representation method called sign/magnitude, most computer systems built today use another technique called **two's complement representation** to represent signed integer values. This popular method is based on the concepts of *modular arithmetic,* and it does not suffer from the problem of two different representations for the quantity 0. Read about this integer representation technique, learn how signed integers are represented, and write a report describing how this method works, as well as the algorithms for adding and subtracting numbers represented in two's complement notation. In your report give the 16-bit, two's complement representation for the signed integer values +45, −68, −1, and 0. Then show how to carry out the arithmetic operations 45 + 45, 45 + (−68), and 45 − (−1).

3. In Section 4.2.2 we described lossless compression schemes, such as run-length encoding and Huffman codes. However, most interesting compression schemes in use today are lossy and only achieve extremely high rates of compression at the expense of losing some of the detail contained in the sound or image. Often they base their compression techniques on a specific knowledge of the characteristics of the human ear or eye. For example, it is well known that the eye is much more sensitive to changes in brightness (luminance) than to changes in color (chrominance). The JPEG compression algorithm exploits this fact when it is compressing a photographic image.

Read about the JPEG image compression algorithm in order to learn about how it is able to achieve compression ratios of 10:1 or even 20:1. A good place to start would be the JPEG home page, located at www.jpeg.org.

FOR FURTHER READING

This book offers an excellent discussion of the major topics covered in this chapter—the representation of information, logic gates, and circuit design. It is one of the most widely used texts in the field of hardware and logic design.

Patterson, D., and Hennessey, J. *Computer Organization and Design: The Hardware Software Interface,* 2nd ed. San Francisco: Morgan Kaufman, 1997.

> Chapter 4: "Arithmetic for Computers." This is an excellent introduction to the representation of information inside a computer.

> Appendix B: "The Basics of Logic Design."

Among the other excellent books about gates, circuits, hardware, and logic design are

Gajski, D. *Principles of Digital Design*. Englewood Cliffs, NJ: Prentice-Hall, 1997.

Mano, M. *Digital Design,* 3rd ed. Englewood Cliffs, NJ: Prentice-Hall, 2001.

Miano, J. *Compressed Image File Formats: JPEG, PNG, GIF, XBM, and BMP*. Reading, MA: Addison Wesley, 1999.

Reid, T. R. *The Chip: How Two Americans Invented the Microchip and Launched a Revolution*. New York: Random House, 2001.

Finally, a good reference text on the internal representation of numeric information and arithmetic algorithms is

Koren, I. *Computer Arithmetic Algorithms,* 2nd ed. Natick, MA: A. K. Peters, 2001.

CHAPTER 5

Computer Systems Organization

5.1 Introduction

This chapter takes a second look at the design and organization of computers, but in a rather different way from the discussion in Chapter 4. That chapter introduced the elementary building blocks of computer systems—transistors, gates, and circuits. This information is essential to understanding computer hardware, just as knowledge of atoms and molecules is necessary for any serious study of chemistry. However, as we noted at the end of the last chapter, this produces a very low-level view of computer systems, and even students who have mastered the material may still ask, OK, but how do computers *really* work? Gates and circuits operate on the most elemental of data items, binary 0s and 1s, whereas people reason and work with more complex units of information, such as decimal numbers, character strings, and instructions. To understand how computers process these types of information, we must look at higher-level components than the gates and circuits of Chapter 4. We must study computers as collections of **functional units** or **subsystems** that perform tasks such as instruction processing, information storage, computation, and data transfer. The branch of computer science that studies computers in terms of their major functional units and how they work is **computer organization,** and that is the subject of this chapter. This higher-level viewpoint will give us a much better understanding of how a computer really works.

All of the functional units introduced in this chapter are built from the gates and circuits of Chapter 4. However, those elementary components will no longer be visible because we will be adopting a different viewpoint, a different perspective, a different **level of abstraction.** This is an extremely important point, and as we have said, the concept of abstraction is used throughout computer science. Without it, it would be virtually impossible to study computer design because of its enormous complexity. In fact, it would be difficult to study any large, complex system.

For example, suppose that system S is composed of a large number of elementary components $a_1, a_2, a_3, \ldots$ interconnected in very intricate ways, as shown in Figure 5.1(a). This is equivalent to viewing a computer system as thousands or millions of individual gates. Although this may be an important way to view system S, it can overwhelm us with detail. To deal with this problem, we can redefine the primitives of system S. We group together the elementary components $a_1, a_2, a_3, \ldots$, as shown in Figure 5.1(b), and call these larger units (A, B, C) the basic building blocks of system S. A, B, and C are treated as nondecomposable elements whose internal construction is hidden from view. We care only about what functions these components perform and how they interact. This leads to the higher-level system view shown in Figure 5.1(c), which is certainly a great deal simpler than the viewpoint of

FIGURE 5.1

The Concept of Abstraction

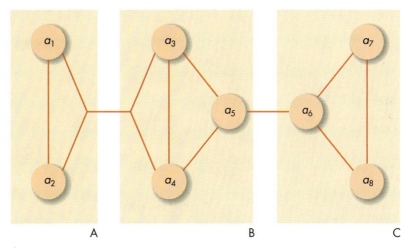

(a) Most detailed system view

(b) Grouping components

(c) Higher-level system view

(d) Highest-level system view

Figure 5.1(a), and that is how this chapter approaches the topic of computer hardware. Our primitives are much larger components, similar to A, B, and C, but internally they are still made up of the gates and circuits of Chapter 4.

This "abstracting away" of unnecessary detail can be done more than once. For example, at some later point in the study of system S of Figure 5.1, we may no longer care about the behavior of individual components A, B, and C. We may now wish to treat the entire system as a single primitive, nondecomposable entity whose inner workings are no longer important. This leads to the extremely simple system view shown in Figure 5.1(d), a view that we will adopt in later chapters.

Figures 5.1(a), (c), and (d) form what is called a **hierarchy of abstractions**. A hierarchy of abstractions of computer science forms the central theme of this text, and it was initially diagrammed in Figure 1.4. We have already seen this idea in action in Chapter 4 as transistors were grouped into gates and gates into circuits:

AND gate

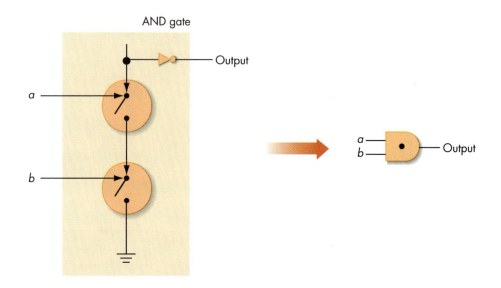

1-bit compare for equality

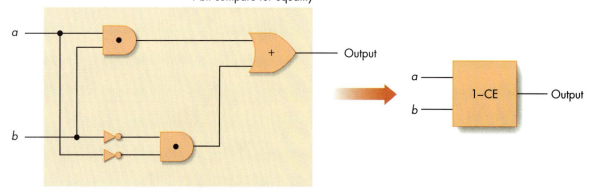

This process continues into Chapter 5, where we use the addition and comparison circuits of Section 4.4.3 to build an arithmetic unit and use the multiplexor and decoder circuits of Section 4.5 to construct a processor. These higher-level components then become our building blocks in all future discussions.

5.2   The Components of a Computer System

There are a huge number of computer systems on the market, manufactured by dozens of different vendors. There are $30-million supercomputers, million dollar mainframes, minicomputers, workstations, laptops, and tiny handheld "personal digital assistants" that cost only a few hundred dollars. In addition to size and cost, computers also differ in speed, memory capacity, input/output capabilities, and available software. The hardware marketplace is diverse, multifaceted, and ever-changing.

However, in spite of all these differences, virtually every computer in use today is based on a single design. Although a million-dollar mainframe and a thousand-dollar laptop may not seem to have much in common, they are based on the same fundamental principles.

An identical situation exists with automotive technology. Although a pickup truck, family sedan, and Ferrari racing car do not appear at all similar, "under the hood" they are all constructed using the same basic technology: a gasoline powered internal combustion engine turning an axle that turns the wheels. Differences among various models of trucks and cars are not basic theoretical differences but simply variations on a theme, such as a bigger engine, a larger carrying capacity, or a more luxurious interior.

What appear to be huge differences among computer systems are also simply variations on the same theme. The structure and organization of virtually all modern computers are based on a single theoretical model of computer design called the **Von Neumann architecture,** named after the brilliant mathematician John Von Neumann, who first proposed it in 1946. (We read a little about Von Neumann and his enormous contributions to computer science in the historical overview of Section 1.4.)

The Von Neumann architecture is a model for designing and building computers that is based on the following three characteristics:

- A computer constructed from four major subsystems called **memory, input/output,** the **arithmetic/logic unit** (ALU), and the **control unit.** These four subsystems are diagrammed in Figure 5.2.
- The **stored program concept,** in which the instructions to be executed by the computer are represented as binary values and stored in memory.
- The **sequential execution of instructions,** in which one instruction at a time is fetched from memory to the control unit, where it is decoded and executed.

This section looks individually at each of the four subsystems that make up the Von Neumann architecture and describes their design and operation. Then

FIGURE 5.2

Components of the Von Neumann Architecture

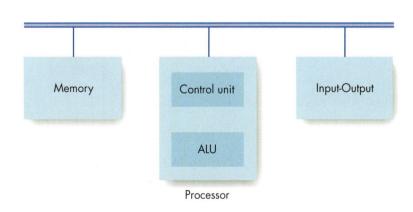

in the following section we put all these pieces together to show the operation of the overall Von Neumann model.

5.2.1 Memory and Cache

Memory is the functional unit of a computer that stores and retrieves the instructions and the data being executed. All information stored in memory is represented internally using the binary numbering system described in Section 4.2.

Computer memory uses an access technique called **random access,** and the acronym **RAM** (for *random access memory*) is frequently used to refer to the memory unit. A random access memory has the following three characteristics:

- Memory is divided into fixed-size units called **cells,** and each cell is associated with a unique identifier called an **address.** These addresses are the unsigned integers 0, 1, 2, . . . MAX.
- All accesses to memory are to a specified address, and we must always fetch or store a complete cell—that is, all the bits in that cell. The cell is the minimum unit of access.
- The time it takes to fetch or store a cell is the same for all the cells in memory.

(*Note:* **Read-only memory,** abbreviated **ROM,** is simply random access memory in which the ability to store information has been disabled. It is only possible to fetch information. In most computers a section of RAM is set aside as ROM to store essential system instructions where the user cannot overwrite them.) A model of a random access memory unit is shown in Figure 5.3.

As shown in Figure 5.3, the memory unit is made up of cells that contain a fixed number of binary digits. The number of bits per cell is called the **cell size** or the **memory width,** and it is usually denoted as W.

In earlier generations of computers there was no standardized value for cell size, and computers were built with values of $W = 6, 8, 12, 16, 24, 30,$

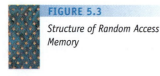

FIGURE 5.3

Structure of Random Access Memory

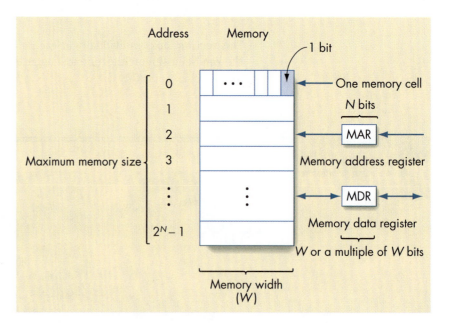

32, 36, 48, and 60 bits. However, computer manufacturers have now agreed on a standard cell size of 8 bits, and this 8-bit unit is universally called a **byte.** Thus, the generic term *cell* has become relatively obsolete, and it is more common now to refer to **memory bytes** as the basic unit. However, keep in mind that this is not a generic term but rather refers to a cell that contains exactly 8 binary digits.

With a cell size of 8 bits, the largest unsigned integer value that can be stored in a single cell is 11111111, which equals 255—not a very large number. Therefore, computers with a cell size of $W = 8$ use multiple memory cells to store a single data value. For example, many computers use 2 or 4 bytes (16 or 32 bits) to store one integer and either 4 or 8 bytes (32 or 64 bits) to store a single real number. This gives the range needed, but at a price. It may take several trips to memory, rather than one, to fetch a single data item.

Each memory cell in a RAM is identified by a unique unsigned integer address 0, 1, 2, 3, ... If there are N bits available to represent the address of a cell, then the smallest address is 0 and the largest address is a string of N 1s:

$$\underbrace{1111 \ldots 11}_{N \text{ digits}}$$

which is equal to the value $2^N - 1$. Thus the range of addresses available on a computer is $[0 \ldots (2^N - 1)]$, where N is the number of binary digits available to represent an address. This is a total of 2^N memory cells. The value 2^N is called the **maximum memory size** or the **address space** of the computer. Typical values of N in the 1960s and 1970s were 16, 20, 22, and 24. Today all computers have at least 32 address bits and sometimes as many as 40. (Remember that 2^N is the *maximum* memory size; a computer with N address bits does not necessarily come equipped with a memory capacity of 2^N cells, but its memory could potentially be expanded to 2^N.) Figure 5.4 gives the value of 2^N for each of these values of N.

Because numbers like 65,536 and 1,048,576 are hard to remember, computer scientists use a convenient shorthand to refer to memory sizes (and other values that are powers of 2). It is based on the fact that the values 2^{10}, 2^{20}, 2^{30}, and 2^{40} are quite close in magnitude to one thousand, one million, one billion, and one trillion, respectively. Therefore, the letters K (kilo, or thousand), M (mega, or million), G (giga, or billion), and T (tera, or trillion) are used to refer to these units.

$2^{10} = 1K\ (= 1{,}024)$	1 KB = 1 *kilobyte*
$2^{20} = 1M\ (= 1{,}048{,}576)$	1 MB = 1 *megabyte*
$2^{30} = 1G\ (= 1{,}073{,}741{,}824)$	1 GB = 1 *gigabyte*
$2^{40} = 1T\ (= 1{,}099{,}511{,}627{,}776)$	1 TB = 1 *terabyte*

FIGURE 5.4

Maximum Memory Sizes

N	MAXIMUM MEMORY SIZE (2^N)
16	65,536
20	1,048,576
22	4,194,304
24	16,777,216
32	4,294,967,296
40	1,099,511,627,776

Thus, a computer with $2^{16} = 65,536$ bytes of storage would be said to have 64 KB of memory, since $2^{16} = 2^6 \times 2^{10} = 64 \times 2^{10} = 64$ KB. This was a popular size for computers of the 1960s and early 1970s. Most computers today contain at least 256 MB of memory, and 512 MB to 1 GB is quite common, especially on larger machines. As memory technology advances and costs continue to drop, it will not be long before multi-gigabyte memories are common. The 32-bit address, which supports an address space of 4 GB, barely supports that level of expansion, and it is quite likely that we will soon begin to see 40-bit addresses that will be able to address directly 2^{40}, or 1 terabyte, of memory.[1]

When dealing with memory, it is important to keep in mind the distinction between an **address** and the **contents** of that address.

Address   *Contents*

42 | 1 |

The address of this memory cell is 42. The content of cell 42 is the integer value 1. As we will soon see, some instructions operate on addresses, whereas others operate on the contents of an address. A failure to distinguish between these two values can cause confusion about how some instructions behave.

The two basic memory operations are **fetching** and **storing,** and they can be described formally as follows:

- *value = Fetch(address)*

  Meaning: Fetch a copy of the contents of the memory cell with the specified *address* and return those contents as the result of the operation. The original contents of the memory cell that was accessed are unchanged. This is termed a **nondestructive fetch.** In terms of the preceding diagram, the operation Fetch(42) would return the number 1. The value 1 would also still be in address 42.

- *Store(address, value)*

  Meaning: Store the specified *value* into the memory cell specified by *address*. The previous contents of the cell are lost. This is termed a **destructive store.** The operation Store(42, 2) would store a 2 in cell 42, overwriting the previous value 1.

One of the characteristics of random access memory is that the time to carry out either a fetch or a store operation is the same for all 2^N addresses. At current levels of technology, this time, called the **memory access time,** is typically about 5–20 nsec (**nanosecond** = 1 nsec = 10^{-9} sec = 1 billionth of a second). Also note that fetching and storing are allowed only to an entire cell. If we wish, for example, to modify a single bit of memory, we first need to fetch the entire cell containing that bit, change the one bit, and then store the entire cell. The cell is the minimum accessible unit of memory.

---

1 Supercomputers today can perform computations at the rate of 35 teraflops, and there are storage devices capable of holding hundreds of terabytes. Therefore, we are getting close to needing the next metric unit after tera, which is peta. A petabyte is 1,000 trillion bytes or 10^{15} bytes—an almost unimaginably large value but one that is on the horizon!

When we talk about volumes of information such as megabytes, gigabytes, and terabytes, it is hard to fathom exactly what those massive numbers mean. Here are some rough approximations (say, to within an order of magnitude) of how much textual information corresponds to each of the storage quantities just introduced, as well as the next few on the scale.

Quantity in Bytes	Base-10 Value	Amount of Textual Information
1 byte	10^0	One character
1 kilobyte	10^3	One typed page
1 megabyte	10^6	Two or three novels
1 gigabyte	10^9	A departmental library or a large personal library
1 terabyte	10^{12}	The library of a major academic research university
1 petabyte	10^{15}	All printed material in all libraries in North America
1 exabyte	10^{18}	All words ever printed throughout human history
1 zettabyte	10^{21}	—

There is one component of the memory unit shown in Figure 5.3 that we have not yet discussed, the **memory registers.** These two registers are used to implement the fetch and store operations. Both operations require two operands: the *address* of the cell being accessed and *value,* either the value stored by the store operation or the value returned by the fetch operation.

The memory unit contains two special registers whose purpose is to hold these two operands. The **Memory Address Register** (MAR) holds the address of the cell to be fetched or stored. Because the MAR must be capable of holding any address, it must be at least N bits wide, where 2^N is the address space of the computer.

The **Memory Data Register** (MDR) contains the data value being fetched or stored. We might be tempted to say that the MDR should be W bits wide, where W is the cell size. However, as mentioned earlier, on most computers the cell size is only 8 bits, and most data values occupy multiple cells. Thus the size of the MDR is usually a multiple of 8. Typical values of MDR width are 32 and 64 bits, which would allow us to fetch, in a single step, either an integer or a real value.

Given these two registers, we can describe a little more formally what happens during the fetch and store operations in a random access memory.

- Fetch(address)
    1. Load the address into the MAR.
    2. Decode the address in the MAR.
    3. Copy the contents of that memory location into the MDR.

- Store(address, value)
    1. Load the address into the MAR.
    2. Load the value into the MDR.
    3. Decode the address in the MAR.
    4. Store the contents of the MDR into that memory location.

For example, to retrieve the contents of cell 123, we would initiate a fetch operation and (in binary, of course) load the value 123 into the MAR. When the operation is done, a copy of the contents of cell 123 will be in the MDR. To store the value 98 into cell 4, we initiate a store operation and load a 4 into the MAR and a 98 into the MDR.

The operation "Decode the address in the MAR" means that the memory unit must translate the N-bit address stored in the MAR into the set of signals needed to access that one specific memory cell. That is, the memory unit must be able to convert the integer value 4 in the MAR into the electronic signals needed to access *only* address 4 from all 2^N addresses in the memory unit. This may seem like magic, but it is actually a relatively easy task that applies ideas presented in the previous chapter. We can decode the address in the MAR using a **decoder circuit** of the type described in Section 4.5 and shown in Figure 4.29. (Remember that a decoder circuit has N inputs and 2^N outputs numbered 0, 1, 2, . . . , $2^N - 1$. The circuit puts the signal 1 on the output line whose number equals the numeric value on the N input lines.) We simply copy the N bits in the MAR to the N input lines of a decoder circuit. Exactly one of its 2^N output lines will be ON, and this will be the line whose identification number corresponds to the address value in the MAR.

For example, if $N = 4$ (the MAR contains 4 bits), then we would have 16 addressable cells in our memory, numbered 0000 to 1111 (that is, 0 to 15). We could use a 4-to-16 decoder whose inputs are the 4 bits of the MAR. Each of the 16 output lines would be associated with the one memory cell whose address is in the MAR and would enable us to fetch or store its contents. This situation is shown in Figure 5.5.

If the MAR contains the 4-bit address 0010 (decimal 2), then only the output line labeled 0010 in Figure 5.5 will be ON (that is, carry a value of 1).

FIGURE 5.5

Organization of Memory and the Decoding Logic

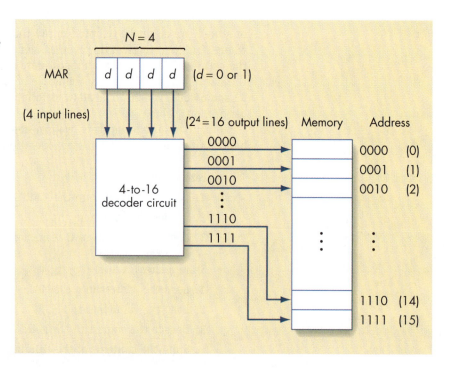

All others will be OFF. The output line 0010 is associated with the unique memory cell that has memory address 2, and the appearance of an ON signal on this line causes the memory hardware to copy the contents of location 2 to the MDR if it is doing a fetch, or to load its contents from the MDR if it is doing a store.

The only problem with the memory organization shown in Figure 5.5 is that it does not **scale** very well. That is, it could not be used to build a large memory unit. In modern computers a typical value for *N*, the number of bits used to represent an address, is 32. A decoder circuit with 32 input lines would have 2^{32} or more than 4 billion, output lines, which is totally unreasonable.

To solve this problem, memories are physically organized into a **two-dimensional** rather than a one-dimensional organization. In this structure, the 16-byte memory of Figure 5.5 would be organized into a two-dimensional 4×4 structure, rather than the one-dimensional 16×1 organization shown earlier. This two-dimensional layout is shown in Figure 5.6.

The memory locations are stored in **row major** order, with bytes 0–3 in row 0, bytes 4–7 in row 1 (01 in binary), bytes 8–11 in row 2 (10 in binary), and bytes 12–15 in row 3 (11 in binary). Each memory cell is connected to two selection lines, one called the **row selection line** and the other called the **column selection line**. When we send a signal down a single row selection line and a single column selection line, only the memory cell located at the *intersection* of these two selection lines will carry out a memory fetch or a memory store operation.

How do we choose the correct row and column selection lines to access the proper memory cell? The answer is that instead of using one decoder

FIGURE 5.6

Two-Dimensional Memory Organization

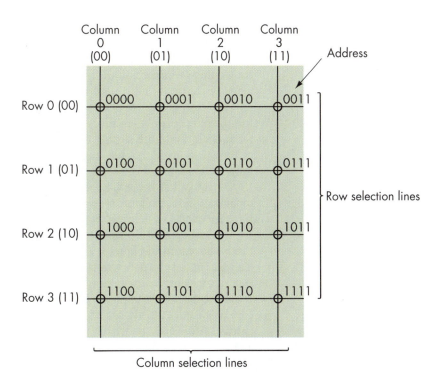

Column selection lines

circuit, we use two. Looking at the first two binary digits of the addresses in Figure 5.6, we see that they are identical to the row number. Similarly, looking at the last two binary digits of the addresses, we see that they are identical to the column number. Thus, we should no longer view the MAR as being composed of a single 4-bit address, but as a 4-bit address made up of two distinct parts—the leftmost 2 bits, which specify the number of the row containing this cell, and the rightmost 2 bits, which specify the number of the column containing this cell. Each of these 2-bit fields is input to a separate decoder circuit that pulses the correct row and column lines to access the desired memory cell.

For example, if the MAR contains the 4-bit value 1101 (a decimal 13), then the two **high-order** (leftmost) bits 11 are sent to the row decoder, while the two **low-order** (rightmost) bits 01 are sent to the column decoder. The row decoder sends a signal on the line labeled 11 (row 3), and the column decoder sends a signal on the line labeled 01 (column 1). Only the single memory cell in row 3, column 1 becomes active and performs the fetch or store operation. Referring to Figure 5.6, we see that the memory cell in row 3, column 1 is the correct one—the cell with memory address 1101.

The two-dimensional organization of Figure 5.6 is far superior to the one-dimensional structure in Figure 5.5, because it can accommodate a much larger number of cells. A memory unit containing 256 MB (2^{28} bytes) would be organized into a 16,384 $\times$ 16,384 two-dimensional array. To select any one row or column requires a decoder with 14 input lines ($2^{14} = 16,384$) and 16,384 output lines. This is a large number of output lines, but it is certainly more feasible to build two 14-to-16,384 decoders than a single 28-to-256 million decoder required for a one-dimensional organization. If necessary, we can continue this process and go to a three-dimensional memory organization, in which the address is broken up into three parts and sent to three separate decoders.

To control whether memory does a fetch or a store operation, our memory unit needs one additional device called a **fetch/store controller.** This unit determines whether we will put the contents of a memory cell into the MDR (a fetch operation) or put the contents of the MDR into a memory cell (a store operation). In a sense, the fetch/store controller is like a traffic officer controlling the direction in which traffic can flow on a two-way street. This memory controller must determine in which direction information will flow on the two-way link connecting memory and the MDR. In order to know what to do, this controller receives a signal telling it whether it is to perform a fetch operation (an F signal) or a store operation (an S signal). On the basis of the value of that signal, the controller causes information to flow in the proper direction and the correct memory operation to take place.

Putting all of these discussions together leads to a complete model of the organization of a typical random access memory in a Von Neumann architecture. The model is shown in Figure 5.7.

Let's complete this discussion by seeing how complex it would be to study the memory unit of Figure 5.7 not at the abstraction level presented in that diagram, but at the gate and circuit level presented in Chapter 4. Let's assume that our memory unit contains 2^{28} cells (256 MB), each cell containing 8 bits. There will be a total of about 2 billion bits of storage in this memory unit. A typical memory circuit used to store a single bit generally requires about 3 gates (1 AND, 1 OR, and 1 NOT) containing 7 transistors (3 per AND, 3 per OR, and 1 per NOT). Thus, our 256-MB memory unit would contain roughly 6 billion gates and 14 billion transistors, and this does not even include the circuitry required to construct the decoder circuits, the controller, and the MAR and MDR registers! These numbers should help you appreciate the power and advantages of abstraction. Without it, studying a memory unit like the one in Figure 5.7 would be a much more formidable task.

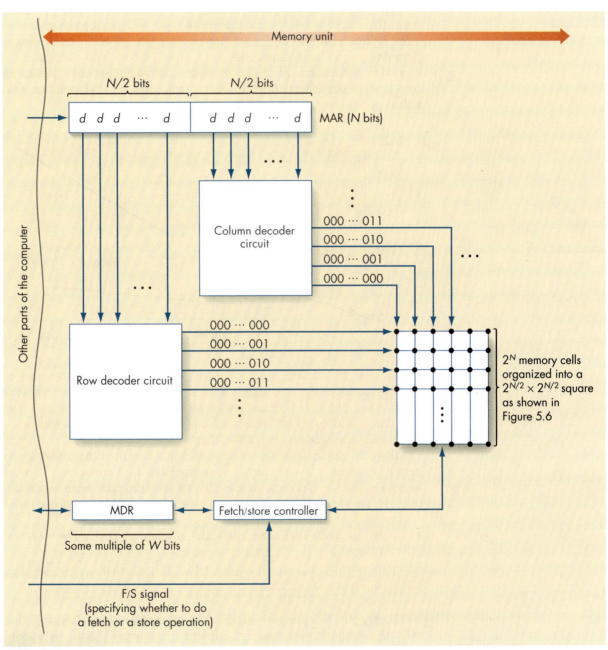

FIGURE 5.7

Overall RAM Organization

CACHE MEMORY. When Von Neumann created his idealized model of a computer, he included only a single type of memory. Whenever the computer needed an instruction or a piece of data, Von Neumann simply assumed it would get it from RAM using the fetch operation just described. However, as computers became faster, designers noticed that, more and more, the processor was sitting idle waiting for data or instructions to arrive. Processors were executing instructions so quickly that memory access was becoming a bottleneck. (It is hard to believe that a memory that can fetch a piece of data in a few billionths of a second could slow anything down, but it does.) As the following graph shows, during the period from 1980 to 2000, processors increased in performance by a factor of about 3,000 while memories speeded up by a factor of only about 10.[2] This led to a huge imbalance between the capabilities of the processor and the capabilities of memory.

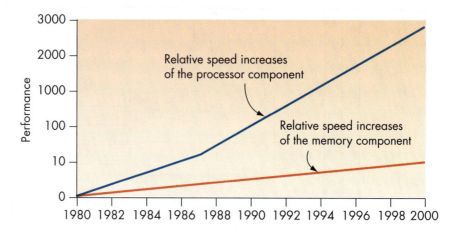

To solve this problem, designers needed to decrease memory access time to make it comparable with the time needed to carry out an instruction. It is possible to build extremely fast memory, but it is also quite expensive, and providing 256,000,000 or 1 billion of these ultra–high-speed memory cells would make the computer prohibitively expensive.

However, computer designers discovered that it really is not necessary to have *all* of memory be constructed from expensive, high-speed units in order to get a significant increase in speed. They observed that when a program fetches a piece of data or an instruction, there is a high likelihood that

1. It will access that same instruction or piece of data in the very near future.

2. It will likely access the instructions or data that are located near this one.

Simply put, this observation, called the **Principle of Locality,** says that when the computer uses something, it will probably use it again very soon, and it will probably use the "neighbors" of this item very soon. (Think about a loop in an algorithm that keeps repeating the same instruction sequence

---

2 From "Computer Architecture: A Quantitative Approach," 3rd Ed., J. Hennessy, D. Patterson, Morgan Kaufmann, 2002.

over and over.) To exploit this observation, the first time that the computer references a piece of data, it should move that data from regular RAM memory to a special, high-speed memory unit called **cache memory** (pronounced "cash," from the French word *cacher,* meaning "to hide"). It should also move the memory cells located near this item into the cache. A cache is typically 5 to 10 times faster than RAM but much smaller—on the order of hundreds of kilobytes of storage rather than hundreds of megabytes or gigabytes. However, this limited size is not a problem because the computer does not keep all of the data there, just those items that were accessed most recently and that, presumably, will be needed again immediately. The organization of the "two-level memory hierarchy" is as follows:

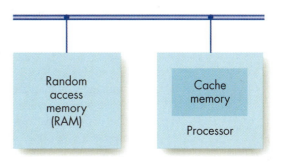

When the computer needs a piece of information, it does not immediately do the memory fetch operation described earlier. Instead, it carries out the following three steps:

1. Look first in cache memory to see whether the information needed is there. If it is, then the computer will be able to access it at the higher speed of the cache.
2. If it is not there, then access the desired information from RAM at the slower speed, using the fetch operation described earlier.
3. Copy the data just fetched into the cache along with the k immediately following memory locations. If the cache is currently full, then discard some of the older items that have not recently been accessed. (The assumption is that we will not need them again for a while.)

This algorithm can significantly reduce the average time to access information. For example, assume that the average access time of our RAM is 15 nsec, whereas the average access time of the cache is 5 nsec. Furthermore, assume that the information we need is in the cache 70% of the time, a value called the **cache hit rate.** In this situation, 70% of the time we will get what we need in 5 nsec. Thus 30% of the time we will have wasted that 5 nsec because the information is not in the cache, and we will have to get the desired information from RAM. Our overall average access time will now be

$$\text{Average access time} = (0.70 \times 5) + 0.30 \times (5 + 15) = 9.5 \text{ nsec}$$

which is a 37% reduction in access time. A higher cache hit rate can lead to even greater savings.

Assume that our memory unit was organized as a 1,024 × 1,024 two-dimensional array.

1. How big would the MAR register have to be?

2. How many bits of the MAR would have to be sent to the row decoder? To the column decoder?

3. If the average access time of this memory were 25 nsec and the average access time for cache memory were 10 nsec, what would be the overall average access time if our cache hit rate were 90%?

Surprisingly, a good analogy to cache memory is a home refrigerator. Without one we would have to go to the grocery store every time we needed an item; this corresponds to slow, regular memory access. Instead, when we go to the store we buy not only what we need now but also what we will need in the near future, and we put those items into our refrigerator. Now, when we need something, we do not immediately run to the store; instead we first check the refrigerator. If it is there, we can get it at a much higher rate of speed. We only need to go to the store when the food item we desire is not there.

Caches are found on every modern computer system today, and they are a significant contributor to the higher computational speeds achieved by new machines. Even though the formal Von Neumann model contained only a single memory unit, most computers built today have a multilevel hierarchy of random access memory.

 ### 5.2.2 *Input/Output and Mass Storage*

The **input/output** (I/O) units are the devices that allow a computer system to communicate and interact with the outside world as well as store information. The random access memory described in the previous section is **volatile** memory—the information disappears when the power is turned off. Thus, without some type of long-term, **nonvolatile** archival storage, information could not be saved between shutdowns of the machine. This nonvolatile storage is the role of **mass storage devices** such as disks and tapes.

Of all the components of a Von Neumann machine, the I/O and mass storage subsystems are the most ad hoc and the most variable. Unlike the memory unit, I/O does not adhere to a single well-defined theoretical model. On the contrary, there are dozens of different I/O and mass storage devices manufactured by dozens of different companies and exhibiting many alternative organizations, making generalizations difficult. However, two important principles transcend the device-specific characteristics of particular vendors—**I/O access methods** and **I/O controllers**.

Input/output devices come in two basic types: those that represent information in *human-readable* form for human consumption and those that store information in *machine-readable* form for access by a computer system.

The former include such well-known I/O devices as keyboards, screens, and printers. The latter group of devices, usually referred to as **mass storage systems,** includes floppy disks, hard disks, CD-ROMs, DVDs, and streaming tapes. Mass storage devices themselves come in two distinct forms, **direct access storage devices** (DASDs) and **sequential access storage devices** (SASDs).

Our discussion on random access memory in Section 5.2.1 described the fundamental characteristics of random access:

1. Every memory cell has a unique address.

2. It takes the same amount of time to access every cell.

A *direct access storage device* is one in which requirement number 2, equal access time, has been eliminated. That is, in a direct access storage device, every unit of information still has a unique address, but the time needed to access that information depends on its physical location and the current state of the device.

The best examples of DASDs are the different types of disks listed earlier: hard disks, floppy disks, CDs, DVDs, and so on. A disk stores information in units called **sectors,** each of which contains an address and a data block containing a fixed number of bytes:

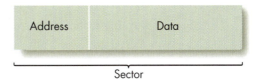

Sector

A fixed number of these sectors are placed in a concentric circle on the surface of the disk, called a **track:**

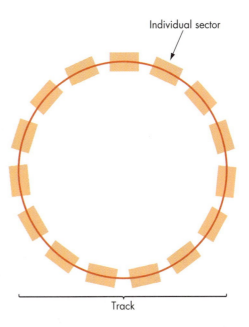

Individual sector

Track

Finally, the surface of the disk contains many tracks, and there is a single **read/write head** that can be moved in or out to be positioned over any track on the disk surface. The entire disk is rotating at high speed under the read/write head. This overall organization of a typical disk is shown in Figure 5.8.

The access time to any individual sector of the disk is made up of three components: seek time, latency, and transfer time. **Seek time** is the time needed to position the read/write head over the correct track; **latency** is the time for the beginning of the desired sector to rotate under the read/write head; **transfer time** is the time for the entire sector to pass under the read/write head and have its contents read into or written from memory. These values depend on the specific sector being accessed and the current position of the read/write head. Say we assume a disk drive with the following physical characteristics:

Rotation speed = 7,200 rev/min = 120 rev/sec = 8.33 msec/rev
(1 **msec** = 0.001 sec)

Arm movement time = 0.02 msec to move to an adjacent track

Number of tracks/surface = 1,000 (numbered 0 to 999)

Number of sectors/track = 64

Number of bytes/sector = 1,024

The access time for this disk can be determined as follows.

1. Seek Time   Best case = 0 msec (no arm movement necessary)

Worst case = 999 $\times$ 0.02 = 19.98 msec (move from track 0 to track 999)

Average case = 300 $\times$ 0.02 = 6 msec (assume that on the average, the read/write head must move about 300 tracks)

FIGURE 5.8

Overall Organization of a Typical Disk

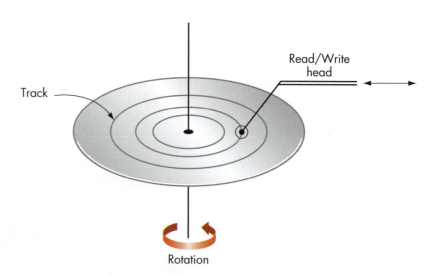

Track

Read/Write head

Rotation

2. Latency

Best case = 0 msec (sector is just about to come under the read/write head)

Worst case = 8.33 msec (we have just missed the sector and must wait one full revolution)

Average case = 4.17 msec (one-half a revolution)

3. Transfer

$1/64 \times 8.33$ msec = 0.13 msec (the time for one sector, or $1/64^{th}$ of a track, to pass under the read/write head)

The following table summarizes these access time computations (all values are in milliseconds).

	BEST	WORST	AVERAGE
Seek Time	0	19.98	6
Latency	0	8.33	4.17
Transfer	0.13	0.13	0.13
Total	0.13	28.44	10.3

The best-case time and the worst-case time to fetch or store a sector on the disk differ by a factor of more than 200—0.13 msec versus 28.44 msec. The average access time is about 10 msec, a typical value for current disk drive technology. Our summary table demonstrates the fundamental characteristic of all direct access storage devices, not just disks: They enable us to specify the address of the desired unit of data and go directly to that data item, but they cannot provide a uniform access time. Today, there is an enormous range of direct access storage devices in the marketplace, from tiny floppy disks that hold barely more than a megabyte, to hard disks and CDs that can store gigabytes, to massive online storage devices that are capable of recording and accessing terabytes of data.

The second type of mass storage device uses an access technique called **sequential access.** With a sequential access storage device (SASD), we eliminate the requirement that all units of data be identifiable via unique address. Now, to find any given data item, we cannot simply fetch the contents of some specific sector address because that address no longer exists. Instead, we must search all data sequentially, repeatedly asking the question, Is this what I'm looking for? If not, we move on to the next unit of data and ask the question again. Eventually we find what we are looking for or come to the end of the data.

A sequential access storage device behaves just like an audio cassette tape. To locate a specific song, we run the tape for a while and then stop and listen. This process is repeated until we find the desired song or come to the end of the tape. A direct access storage device is like a CD or DVD that numbers all the songs and allows you to select any one. (The song number is the address.) Direct access storage devices are generally much faster at accessing individual pieces of information, and that is why they are much more widely used for mass storage. However, sequential access storage devices can be useful in specific situations, such as sequentially copying the entire contents of memory or of a disk drive. This **backup** operation fits the SASD model well, and **streaming tape backup units** are common storage devices on computer systems.

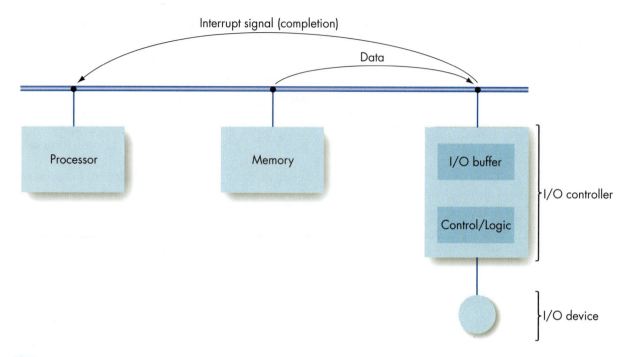

Interrupt signal (completion)

Data

Processor

Memory

I/O buffer

Control/Logic

I/O controller

I/O device

FIGURE 5.9

*Organization of an I/O
Controller*

One of the fundamental characteristics of many (though not all) I/O devices is that they are very, very *slow* when compared to other components of a computer. For example, a typical memory access time is about 10 nsec. The time to complete the I/O operation "locate and read one disk sector" was shown in the previous example to be about 10 msec.

Units such as nsec (billionths of a second), μsec (millionths of a second), and msec (thousandths of a second) are so small compared to human time scales that it is sometimes difficult to appreciate the immense difference between values like 10 nsec and 10 msec. The difference between these two quantities is a factor of 1,000,000—6 orders of magnitude. To give a better indication of these values, consider that this is the same relative difference as that between 1 mile and 40 complete revolutions of the earth's equator, or between 1 day and 30 centuries!

It is not uncommon for I/O operations such as reading a line on a monitor or printing a page on a printer to be 3, 4, 5, or 6 orders of magnitude slower than any other aspect of computer operation. If there isn't something in the design of a computer to account for this difference, components that operate on totally incompatible time scales will be trying to talk to each other, which will produce enormous inefficiencies. The high-speed components will sit idle for long stretches of time while they wait for the slow I/O unit to accept or deliver the desired character. It would be as though you could talk to someone at the normal human rate of 240 words/min (4 words/sec) but that person could respond only at the rate of 1 word every 8 hours—a difference of 5 orders of magnitude. You wouldn't get much useful work done!

The solution to this problem is to use a device called an **I/O controller.** An I/O controller is like a special-purpose computer whose responsibility is to handle the details of input/output and to compensate for any speed differences between I/O devices and other parts of the computer. It has a small amount of memory, called an **I/O buffer,** and enough **I/O control and logic**

Assume a disk with the following characteristics:

Number of sectors per track = 20
Number of tracks per surface = 50
Number of surfaces = 2 (called a **double-sided** disk)
Number of characters per sector = 1,024
Arm movement time = 0.4 msec to move 1 track in any direction
Rotation speed = 2,400 rev/min

1. How many characters can be stored on this disk?

2. What are the best-case, worst-case, and average-case access times for this disk? (Assume that the average seek operation must move 20 tracks.)

processing capability to handle the mechanical functions of the I/O device, such as the read/write head, paper feed mechanism, and screen display. It is also able to transmit to the processor a special hardware signal, called an **interrupt signal,** when an I/O operation is done. The organization of a typical I/O controller is shown in Figure 5.9.

Let's assume that we want to display one line (80 characters) of text on a screen. First the 80 characters are transferred from their current location in memory to the I/O buffer storage within the I/O controller. This takes place at the high-speed data transfer rates of most computer components—tens or hundreds of millions of characters per second. Once this information is in the I/O buffer, the processor can instruct the I/O controller to begin the output operation. The control logic of the I/O controller handles the actual transfer of these 80 characters to the screen. This transfer may be at a much slower rate—perhaps only hundreds or thousands of characters per second. However, the processor does not sit idle during this output operation. It is free to do something else, perhaps to work on another program. The slowness of the I/O operation now affects *only* the I/O controller. The inefficiency and wasted time of all other components have been eliminated. When all 80 characters have been displayed, the I/O controller sends an *interrupt signal* to the processor. The appearance of this special signal indicates to the processor that the I/O operation is finished.

 ### 5.2.3 *The Arithmetic/Logic Unit*

The **arithmetic/logic unit** (referred to by the abbreviation ALU) is the subsystem that performs such mathematical and logical operations as addition, subtraction, and comparison for equality. Although they can be conceptually viewed as separate components, in all modern machines the ALU and the control unit (discussed in the next section) have become fully integrated into a single component called the **processor.** However, for reasons of clarity and convenience, we will describe the functions of the ALU and the control unit separately.

The ALU is made up of three parts: the registers, the interconnections between components, and the ALU circuitry. Together these components are called the **data path.**

A **register** is a storage cell that holds the operands of an arithmetic operation and that, when the operation is complete, holds its result. Registers are quite similar to the random access memory cells described in the previous section, with the following minor differences:

- They do not have a numeric memory address but are accessed by a special **register designator** such as A, X, or R0.

- They can be accessed much more quickly than regular memory cells. Because there are few registers (typically, a few dozen up to a hundred), it is reasonable to utilize the expensive circuitry needed to make the fetch and store operations 2 to 10 times faster than regular memory cells of which there will be millions or billions.

- They are not used for general-purpose storage but for specific purposes such as holding the operands for an upcoming arithmetic computation.

For example, an ALU might have three special registers called A, B, and C. Registers A and B would hold the two input operands, and register C would hold the result. This organization is diagrammed in Figure 5.10.

In most cases, however, three registers would not be nearly enough to hold all the values that we might need. Therefore, a typical ALU has 16, 32, or 64 registers. To see why this many ALU registers are needed, let's take a look at what happens during the evaluation of the expression $(a\ /\ b) \times (c - d)$. After we compute the expression $(a\ /\ b)$, it would be nice to keep this result temporarily in a high-speed ALU register while evaluating the second expression $(c - d)$. Of course, we could always store the result of $(a\ /\ b)$ in a memory cell, but keeping it in a register allows the computer to fetch it

FIGURE 5.10

Three-Register ALU Organization

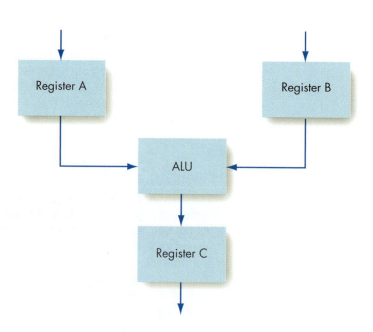

more quickly when it is ready to complete the computation. In general, the more registers available in the ALU, the faster programs run.

A more typical ALU organization is illustrated in Figure 5.11, which shows an ALU data path containing 16 registers designated R0 to R15. Any of the 16 ALU registers in Figure 5.11 could be used to hold the operands of the computation, and any register could be used to store the result.

To perform an arithmetic operation with the ALU of Figure 5.11, we first move the operands from memory to the ALU registers. Then we specify which register holds the left operand by connecting that register to the communication's path called "Left." In computer science terminology, a path for electrical signals (think of this as a wire) is termed a **bus.** We then specify which register to use for the right operand by connecting it to the bus labeled "Right." (Like RAM, registers also use nondestructive fetch so that when it is needed, the value is only copied to the ALU. It is still in the register.) The ALU is enabled to perform the desired operation, and the answer is sent to any of the 16 registers along the bus labeled "Result." (The destructive store principle says that the previous contents of the destination register will be

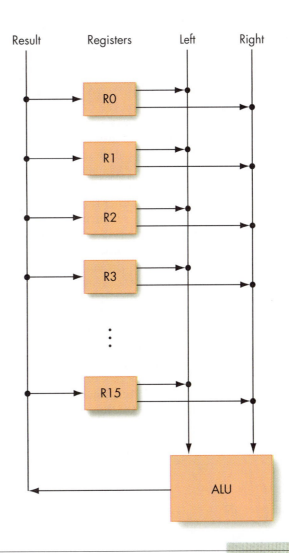

FIGURE 5.11

Multiregister ALU Organization

lost.) If desired, the result can be moved from an ALU register back into memory for longer-term storage.

The final component of the ALU to be described is the **ALU circuitry** itself. These are the circuits that carry out such operations as

$a + b$ (Figure 4.27)
$a = b$ (Figure 4.23)
$a - b$
$a \times b$
a / b
$a < b$
$a > b$
a AND b

Chapter 4 showed how circuits for these operations can be constructed from the three basic logic gates AND, OR, and NOT. The primary issue now is how to select the desired operation from among all the possibilities for a given ALU. For example, how do we tell an ALU that can perform the preceding eight operations that we want only the results of one operation, say $a - b$?

One possible approach is to use the **multiplexor** control circuit introduced in Chapter 4 and shown in Figure 4.28. Remember that a multiplexor is a circuit with 2^N input lines numbered 0 to $2^N - 1$, N selector lines, and 1 output line. The selector lines are interpreted as a single binary number from 0 to $2^N - 1$, and the input line corresponding to this number has its value placed on the single output line.

Let's imagine for simplicity that we have an ALU that can perform four functions instead of eight. The four functions are $a + b$, $a - b$, $a = b$, and a AND b, and these operations are numbered 0, 1, 2, and 3, respectively (00, 01, 10, and 11 in binary). Finally, let's assume that every time the ALU is enabled and given values for a and b, it automatically performs all four possible operations rather than just the desired one. These four outputs can be input to a multiplexor circuit as shown in Figure 5.12.

Now place on the selector lines the identification number of the one operation whose output we want to keep. The result of the desired operation appears on the output line, and the other three answers are discarded. Thus, for example, to select the output of the subtraction operation, we input the binary value 01 (decimal 1) on the selector lines. This puts the output of the subtraction circuit on the output line of the multiplexor. The outputs of the addition, comparison, and AND circuits are discarded.

The design philosophy in building an ALU is not to figure out how to perform only the correct operation. It is to have *every* circuit "do its thing" and then select only the desired answer.

Putting Figures 5.11 and 5.12 together produces the overall organization of the ALU of the Von Neumann architecture. This model is shown in Figure 5.13.

 ### 5.2.4 *The Control Unit*

The most fundamental characteristic of the Von Neumann architecture is the idea of a **stored program**—a sequence of machine language instructions stored as binary values in memory. It is the task of the **control unit** to

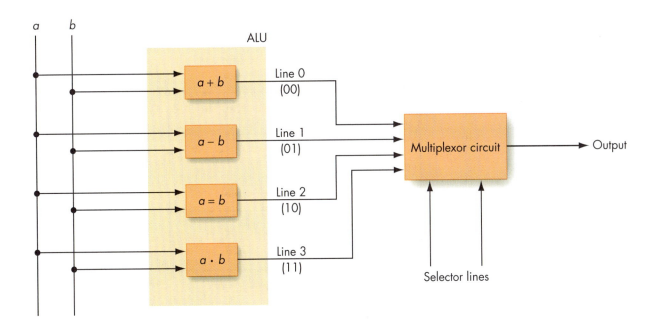

a b

ALU

a + b   Line 0 (00)

a − b   Line 1 (01)

a = b   Line 2 (10)

a · b   Line 3 (11)

Multiplexor circuit → Output

Selector lines

FIGURE 5.12

Using a Multiplexor Circuit to Select the Proper ALU Result

(1) **fetch** from memory the next instruction to be executed, (2) **decode** it—that is, determine what is to be done, and (3) **execute** it by issuing the appropriate command to the ALU, memory, and I/O controllers. These three steps are repeated over and over until we reach the last instruction in the program, typically something called HALT, STOP, or QUIT.

Thus, to understand the behavior of the control unit, we must first investigate the characteristics of machine language instructions.

MACHINE LANGUAGE INSTRUCTIONS. The instructions that can be decoded and executed by the control unit of a computer are in a representation called **machine language.** Instructions in this language are expressed in binary, and a typical format is shown in Figure 5.14.

The **operation code** field (referred to by the shorthand phrase **op code**) is a unique unsigned-integer code assigned to each machine language operation recognized by the hardware. For example, 0 could be an ADD, 1 could be a COMPARE, and so on. If the operation code field contains k bits, then the maximum number of machine language operation codes is 2^k.

The **address field(s)** are the memory addresses of the values on which this operation will work. If our computer has a maximum of 2^N memory cells, then each address field must be N bits wide to enable us to address every cell. That is because it takes N binary digits to represent all addresses in the range 0 to $2^N - 1$. The number of address fields in an instruction typically varies from 0 to about 3, depending on what the operation is and how many operands it needs to do its work. For instance, an instruction to add the contents of memory cell X to memory cell Y requires at least two addresses, X and Y. It could require three if the result were stored in a location different from either operand. In contrast, an instruction that tests the contents of memory cell X to see whether it is negative needs only a single address field, the location of cell X.

FIGURE 5.13

Overall ALU Organization

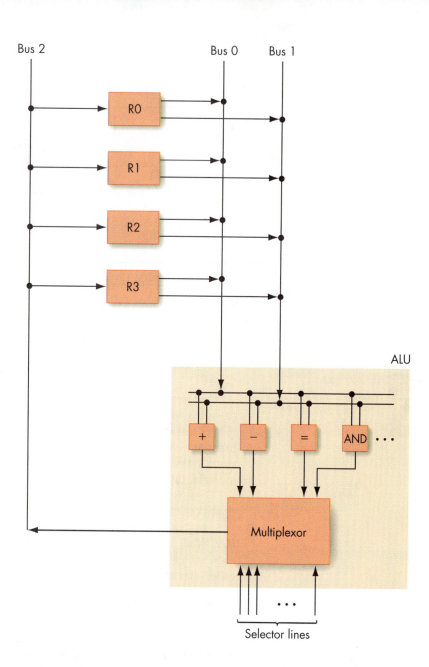

FIGURE 5.14

Typical Machine Language Instruction Format

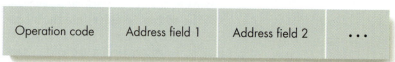

To see what this might produce in terms of machine language instructions, let's see what the following hypothetical instruction would actually look like when stored in memory.

ADD X, Y   Add contents of addresses X and Y and put the sum back into Y

Let's assume that the op code for ADD is a decimal 9, X and Y correspond to memory addresses 99 and 100 (decimal), and the format of instructions is

op code	address 1	address 2
8	16	16

bits →

A decimal 9, in 8-bit binary, is 00001001. Address 99, when converted to a 16-bit binary value, is 0000000001100011. Address 100 is 1 greater: 0000000001100100. Putting these values together produces the representation of the instruction ADD X, Y as it would appear in memory:

00001001   0000000001100011   0000000001100100

op code   address 1   address 2

Somewhat cryptic to a person, but easily understood by a control unit.

The set of all operations that can be executed by a processor is called its **instruction set,** and the choice of exactly what operations to include or exclude from the instruction set is one of the most important and difficult decisions in the design of a new computer. There is no universal agreement on this issue, and the instruction sets of processors from different vendors are completely different. This is one reason why a computer that uses a Macintosh G5 processor cannot directly execute programs written for a system that contains an Intel Pentium 4. The operation codes and address fields that these two processors recognize, understand, and carry out are different and completely incompatible.

The machine language operations on most machines are quite elementary, and each one typically performs a very small and simple task. The power of a processor comes not from the sophistication of the operations in its instruction set but from the fact that it can execute each instruction very quickly, typically in a few billionths of a second.

One approach to designing instruction sets is to make them as small and as simple as possible, say with as few as 30–50 instructions. Machines with this sort of instruction set are called **reduced instruction set computers** or **RISC machines.** This approach minimizes the amount of hardware circuitry (gates and transistors) needed to build a processor. The extra space on the chip can be used to optimize the speed of the instructions and allow them to execute very quickly. The philosophy behind the RISC design is that a program for a RISC processor may require more instructions to solve a problem (because the instructions are very simple), but this will be compensated for by the fact that each instruction runs much faster so the overall running time is less. The opposite philosophy, common on the computers of the 1970s, 1980s, and 1990s, is to include a much larger number, say 300–500, of very powerful instructions in the instruction set. These types of processors are called **complex instruction set computers,** or **CISC machines.** The philosophy here is that you want your instruction set to directly provide all of the features you will need when you write programs to solve problems. Of course, CISC machines will be more complex, more expensive, and more difficult to build. Like most things in life (including computing), it turns out that compromise is the best path. Most modern processors have some of the features of both the RISC and the CISC approaches, and are a mix of the two design philosophies.

A little later in this chapter we will present an instruction set for a hypothetical computer in order to examine how machine language instructions are executed by a control unit. To maximize the clarity of our discussion, we will not display these instructions in binary, as we did earlier. Instead, we will write out the operation code in English (for example, ADD, COMPARE, MOVE), use the capital letters X, Y, and Z to symbolically represent binary memory addresses, and use the letter R to represent an ALU register. Remember, however, that this notation is just for convenience. All machine language instructions are stored internally using binary representation.

Machine language instructions can be grouped into four basic classes called data transfer, arithmetic, compare, and branch.

1. *Data Transfer*   These are operations that move information between or within the different components of the computer—for example:

   Memory cell → ALU register

   ALU register → memory cell

   One memory cell → another memory cell

   One ALU register → another ALU register

   All data transfer instructions follow the nondestructive fetch/destructive store principle described earlier. That is, the contents of the **source cell** (where it now is) are never destroyed, only copied. The contents of the **destination cell** (where it is going) are overwritten, and its previous contents are lost.
   Examples of data transfer operations include

OPERATION	MEANING
LOAD X	Load register R with the contents of memory cell X.
STORE X	Store the contents of register R into memory cell X.
MOVE X,Y	Copy the contents of memory cell X into memory cell Y.

2. *Arithmetic*   These are operations that cause the arithmetic/logic unit to perform a computation. Typically, they include arithmetic operations like $+$, $-$, $\times$, and $/$, as well as logical operations such as AND, OR, and NOT. Depending on the instruction set, the operands may reside in memory or they may be in an ALU register.
   Examples of possible formats for arithmetic operations include the following. (Note: The notation CON(X) means the contents of memory address X.)

OPERATION	MEANING
ADD X,Y, Z	Add the contents of memory cell X to the contents of memory cell Y and put the result into memory cell Z. This is called a **three-address instruction,** and it performs the operation CON(Z) = CON(X) + CON(Y)
ADD X,Y	Add the contents of memory cell X to the contents of memory cell Y. Put the result back into memory cell Y. This is called a **two-address instruction,** and it performs the operation CON(Y) = CON(X) + CON(Y)

ADD X   Add the contents of memory cell X to the contents of register R. Put the result back into register R. This is called a **one-address instruction,** and it performs the operation R = CON(X) + R (Of course, R must be loaded with the proper value before executing the instruction.)

Other arithmetic operations such as SUBTRACT, MULTIPLY, DIVIDE, AND, and OR could be structured in a similar fashion.

3. *Compare*   These operations compare two values and set an indicator on the basis of the results of the compare. Most Von Neumann machines have a special set of bits inside the processor called **condition codes** (or a special register called a **status register** or **condition register**), and it is these bits that are set by the compare operations. For example, let's assume there are three 1-bit condition codes called GT, EQ, and LT that stand for greater than, equal to, and less than, respectively. The operation

COMPARE X,Y   Compare the contents of memory cell X to the contents of memory cell Y and set the condition codes accordingly.

would set these three condition codes in the following way:

CONDITION	HOW THE CONDITION CODES ARE SET
CON (X) > CON (Y)	GT =1 EQ =0 LT = 0
CON (X) = CON (Y)	GT =0 EQ =1 LT = 0
CON (X) < CON (Y)	GT =0 EQ =0 LT = 1

4. *Branch*   The normal mode of operation of a Von Neumann machine is *sequential*. After completing the instruction in address i, the control unit executes the instruction in address $i + 1$. (*Note:* If each instruction occupies k memory cells rather than 1, then after finishing the instruction starting in address i, the control unit executes the instruction starting in address $i + k$. In the following discussions, we assume for simplicity that each instruction occupies one memory cell.) The **branch instructions** alter this normal sequential flow of control.

Typically, the decision whether or not to branch is based on the current settings of the condition codes. Thus, a branch instruction is almost always preceded by either a compare instruction or some other instruction that sets the condition codes. Typical branch instructions include

OPERATION	MEANING
JUMP X	Take the next instruction unconditionally from memory cell X.
JUMPGT X	If the GT indicator is a 1, take the next instruction from memory cell X. Otherwise, take the next instruction from the next sequential location.

(JUMPEQ and JUMPLT would work similarly on the other two condition codes.)

JUMPGE X	If *either* the GT or the EQ indicator is a 1, take the next instruction from memory location X. Otherwise, take the next instruction from the next sequential location.

(JUMPLE and JUMPNEQ would work in a similar fashion.)

HALT	Stop program execution. Don't go on to the next instruction.

These are some of the typical instructions that a Von Neumann computer can decode and execute. (The second challenge question at the end of this chapter asks you to investigate the instruction set of a real processor found inside a modern computer and compare it with what we have described here.)

The instructions that we have presented are quite simple and easy to understand. The power of a Von Neumann computer comes not from having thousands of complex built-in instructions but from the ability to combine a great number of simple instructions into large, complex programs that can be executed extremely quickly. Figure 5.15 shows examples of how these simple machine language instructions can be combined to carry out some of the high-level algorithmic operations first introduced in Level 1 and shown in Figure 2.6. (The examples assume that the variables *a, b,* and *c* are stored in memory locations 100, 101, and 102, respectively, and that the instructions occupy one cell each and are located in memory locations 50, 51, 52, ...)

Don't worry if these "mini-programs" are a little confusing. We treat the topic of machine language programming in more detail in the next chapter.

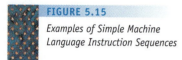

FIGURE 5.15

Examples of Simple Machine Language Instruction Sequences

Address	Contents
100	Value of *a*
101	Value of *b*
102	Value of *c*

Algorithmic notation   **Machine Language Instruction Sequences**

		Address	Contents	(Commentary)
			⋮	
1.	Set *a* to the value *b* + *c*	50	LOAD 101	Put the value of *b* into register R.
		51	ADD 102	Add *c* to register R. It now holds *b* + *c*.
		52	STORE 100	Store the contents of register R into *a*.
2.	If *a* > *b* then	50	COMPARE 100, 101	Compare *a* and *b* and set condition codes.
	set *c* to the value *a*	51	JUMPGT 54	Go to location 54 if *a* > *b*.
	Else	52	MOVE 101, 102	Get here if *a* ≤ *b*, so move *b* into *c*
	set *c* to the value *b*	53	JUMP 55	and skip the next instruction.
		54	MOVE 100, 102	Move *a* into *c*.
		55	• • •	Next statement begins here.

Assume that the variables *a, b, c,* and *d* are stored in memory locations 100, 101, 102, and 103, respectively. Using any of the sample machine language instructions given in this section, translate the following pseudocode operations into machine language instruction sequences. Have your instruction sequences begin in memory location 50.

1. Set *a* to the value $b + c + d$

2. If $(a = b)$ then set *c* to the value of *d*

3. If $(a \leq b)$ then

   Set *c* to the value of *d*

   Else

   Set *c* to the value of 2*d* (that is, $d + d$)

4. Initialize *a* to the value *d*

   While $a \leq c$

   Set *a* to the value $(a + b)$

   End of the loop

For now, we simply want you to know what machine language instructions look like so that we can see how to build a control unit to carry out their functions.

CONTROL UNIT REGISTERS AND CIRCUITS. It is the task of the control unit to fetch and execute instructions of the type shown in Figures 5.14 and 5.15. To accomplish this task, the control unit relies on two special registers called the **Program Counter (PC)** and the **Instruction Register (IR)** and on an **instruction decoder circuit.** The organization of these three components is shown in Figure 5.16.

The program counter holds the address of the *next* instruction to be executed. It is like a "pointer" specifying which address in memory the control unit must go to in order to get the next instruction. To get that instruction, the control unit sends the contents of the PC to the MAR in memory and executes the Fetch(address) operation described in Section 5.2.1. For example, if the PC holds the value 73 (in binary, of course), then when the current instruction is finished, the control unit will send the value 73 to the MAR and fetch the instruction contained in cell 73. The PC gets incremented by 1 after each fetch, because the normal mode of execution in a Von Neumann machine is sequential. (Again, we are assuming that each instruction occupies one cell. If an instruction occupied *k* cells, then the PC would be incremented by *k*.) Therefore, the PC frequently has its own incrementor (+ 1) circuit to allow this operation to be done quickly and efficiently.

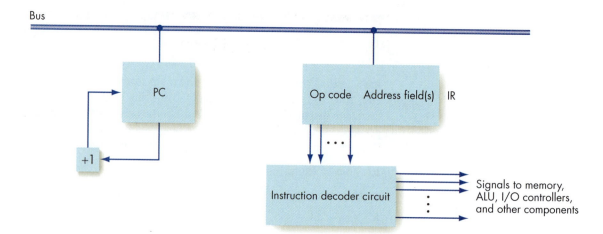

FIGURE 5.16

Organization of the Control Unit Registers and Circuits

The **instruction register (IR)** holds a copy of the instruction fetched from memory. The IR holds both the op code portion of the instruction, abbreviated IR_{op}, and the address(es), abbreviated IR_{addr}.

To determine what instruction is in the IR, the op code portion of the IR must be decoded using an **instruction decoder.** This is exactly the same type of decoder circuit discussed in Section 4.5 and used in the construction of the memory unit (Figure 5.7). The k bits of the op code field of the IR are sent to the instruction decoder, which interprets them as a numerical value between 0 and $2^k - 1$. Exactly one of the 2^k output lines of the decoder will be set to a 1—specifically, the output line whose identification number matches the operation code of this instruction. Figure 5.17 shows a decoder that accepts a 3-bit op code field and has $2^3 = 8$ output lines, one for each of the eight possible machine language operations.

The three bits of the IR_{op} are fed into the instruction decoder, and they are interpreted as a value from 000 (0) to 111 (7). If the bits are, for example, 000, then line 000 in Figure 5.17 will be set to a 1. This line enables the circuitry that will carry out the ADD operation because the operation code for ADD is 000. The appearance of a 1 on this line will cause the following four things to happen: (1) fetch the two operands of the add and send them to the ALU, (2) have the ALU perform all of its possible operations, (3) select the output of the adder circuit, discarding all others, and (4) move the result of the add to the correct location. These are the four steps needed to carry out the ADD operation.

If the op code bits are 001 instead, then line 001 in Figure 5.17 will be set to a 1. This time the LOAD circuitry will be enabled, because the operation code for LOAD is the binary value 001. Instead of performing the previous four steps, the hardware will carry out the following three operations: (1) send the value of IR_{addr} to the memory unit, (2) fetch the contents of that address and put it in the MDR, and (3) copy the contents of the MDR into ALU register R. This is what is needed to perform a LOAD operation correctly.

For every one of the 2^k machine language operations in our instruction set, there will exist the circuitry needed to carry out, step by step, the function of that operation. The instruction decoder has 2^k output lines, and each output line enables the circuitry that performs the desired operation.

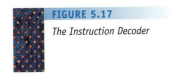

FIGURE 5.17

The Instruction Decoder

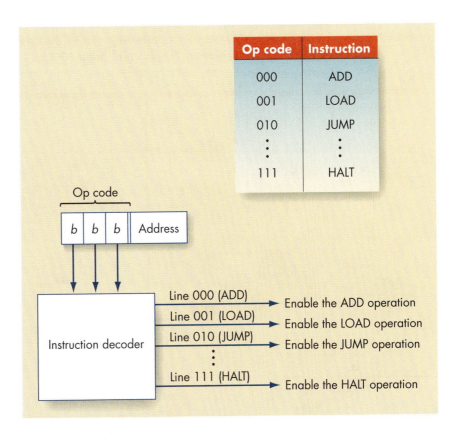

Op code	Instruction
000	ADD
001	LOAD
010	JUMP
⋮	⋮
111	HALT

Op code

| b | b | b | Address |

Instruction decoder

Line 000 (ADD) → Enable the ADD operation
Line 001 (LOAD) → Enable the LOAD operation
Line 010 (JUMP) → Enable the JUMP operation
⋮
Line 111 (HALT) → Enable the HALT operation

5.3 Putting All the Pieces Together—the Von Neumann Architecture

We have now described each of the four components that make up the Von Neumann architecture:

- Memory (Figure 5.7)
- Input/output (Figure 5.9)
- ALU (Figure 5.13)
- Control unit (Figures 5.16, 5.17)

This section puts all these pieces together and shows how the entire model functions. The overall organization of a Von Neumann computer is shown in Figure 5.18. Although highly simplified, this diagram is quite similar in structure to virtually every computer ever built!

In order to see how the Von Neumann machine of Figure 5.18 would execute instructions, let's pick a hypothetical instruction set for our system. The instruction set that we will use is shown in Figure 5.19. We will use the same instruction set in the laboratory experiences for this chapter and again in Chapter 6 when we introduce and study assembly languages. (*Reminder*: CON(X) means the contents of memory cell X; R stands for an ALU register; and GT, EQ, and LT are condition codes that have the value of 1 for ON and 0 for OFF.)

The execution of a program on the computer shown in Figure 5.18 proceeds in three distinct phases called **fetch, decode,** and **execute.** These

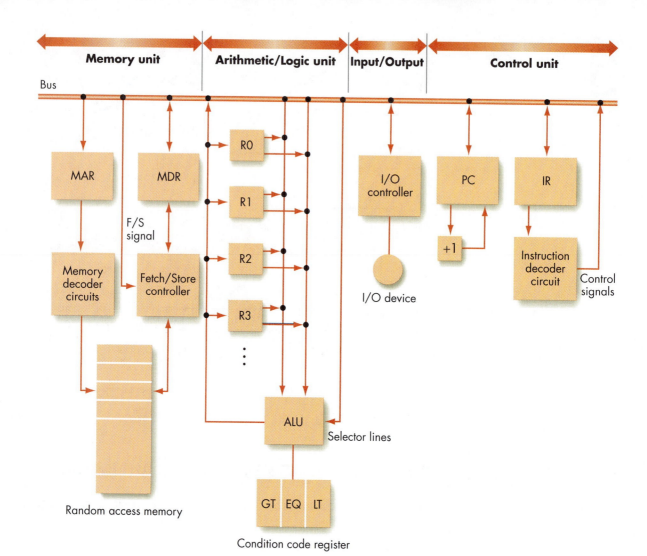

Memory unit | Arithmetic/Logic unit | Input/Output | Control unit

Bus

MAR

MDR

F/S signal

Memory decoder circuits

Fetch/Store controller

Random access memory

R0

R1

R2

R3

ALU

Selector lines

GT EQ LT

Condition code register

I/O controller

I/O device

PC

+1

IR

Instruction decoder circuit

Control signals

FIGURE 5.18

The Organization of a Von Neumann Computer

three steps are repeated for every instruction, and they continue until either the computer executes a HALT instruction or there is a fatal error that prevents it from continuing (such as an illegal op code, a nonexistent memory address, or division by zero). Algorithmically the process can be described as follows:

While we do not have either a HALT instruction or a fatal error

Fetch phase

Decode phase

Execute phase

End of the loop

This repetition of the fetch/decode/execute phase is called the *Von Neumann cycle*. To describe the behavior of our computer during each of these three phases, we will use the following notational conventions:

FIGURE 5.19

Instruction Set for Our Von Neu-
mann Machine

Binary Op Code	Operation	Meaning
0000	LOAD X	CON(X) → R
0001	STORE X	R → CON(X)
0010	CLEAR X	0 → CON(X)
0011	ADD X	R + CON(X) → R
0100	INCREMENT X	CON(X) + 1 → CON(X)
0101	SUBTRACT X	R − CON(X) → R
0110	DECREMENT X	CON(X) − 1 → CON(X)
0111	COMPARE X	if CON(X) > R then GT = 1 else 0
		if CON(X) = R then EQ = 1 else 0
		if CON(X) < R then LT = 1 else 0
1000	JUMP X	Get the next instruction from memory location X.
1001	JUMPGT X	Get the next instruction from memory location X if GT = 1.
1010	JUMPEQ X	Get the next instruction from memory location X if EQ = 1.
1011	JUMPLT X	Get the next instruction from memory location X if LT = 1.
1100	JUMPNEQ X	Get the next instruction from memory location X if EQ = 0.
1101	IN X	Input an integer value from the standard input device and store into memory cell X.
1110	OUT X	Output, in decimal notation, the value stored in memory cell X.
1111	HALT	Stop program execution.

CON(A) The *contents* of memory cell A. An instruction occupies 1 cell.

A → B Send the value stored in register A to register B. The following abbreviations refer to the special registers and functional units of the Von Neumann architecture introduced in this chapter:

PC The program counter

MAR The memory address register

MDR The memory data register

IR The instruction register, which is further divided into IR_{op} and IR_{addr}

ALU The arithmetic/logic unit

R Any ALU register

GT, EQ, LT The condition codes of the ALU

+ 1 A special increment unit attached to the PC

FETCH Initiate a memory fetch operation (that is, send an F signal on the F/S control line of Figure 5.18).

STORE Initiate a memory store operation (that is, send an S signal on the F/S control line of Figure 5.18).

ADD Instruct the ALU to select the output of the adder circuit (that is, place the code for ADD on the ALU selector lines shown in Figure 5.18).

SUBTRACT   Instruct the ALU to select the output of the subtract circuit (that is, place the code for SUBTRACT on the ALU selector lines shown in Figure 5.18).

A. *Fetch Phase* During the fetch phase, the control unit gets the next instruction from memory and moves it into the IR. The fetch phase is the same for every instruction and consists of the following four steps.

1. PC $\rightarrow$ MAR	Send the address in the PC to the MAR register.
2. FETCH	Initiate a fetch operation using the address in the MAR. The contents of that cell are placed in the MDR.
3. MDR $\rightarrow$ IR	Move the instruction in the MDR to the instruction register so that we are ready to decode it during the next phase.
4. PC + 1 $\rightarrow$ PC	Send the contents of the PC to the incrementor and put it back. This points the PC to the next instruction.

The control unit now has the current instruction in the IR and has updated the program counter so that it will correctly fetch the next instruction when the execution of this instruction is completed. It is ready to begin decoding and executing the current instruction.

B. *Decode Phase* First it must decode the instruction. This is simple because all that needs to be done is to send the op code portion of the IR to the instruction decoder, which determines its type. The op code is the 4-bit binary value in the first column of Figure 5.19.

1. $IR_{op} \rightarrow$ instruction decoder

The instruction decoder will generate the proper control signals to activate the circuitry to carry out this particular instruction.

C. *Execution Phase* The actions that occur during the execution phase are obviously different for each instruction in the instruction set. The control unit circuitry generates the necessary sequence of control signals and data transfer signals to the other units (ALU, memory, and I/O) to accomplish the purpose of the instruction. The following are examples of what signals and transfers would take place during the execution phase of some of the instructions in Figure 5.19 using the Von Neumann model of Figure 5.18.

a) LOAD X   Load register R from memory cell X.

1. $IR_{addr} \rightarrow$ MAR	Send address X (currently in IR_{addr}) to the MAR.
2. FETCH	Fetch contents of cell X and place that value in the MDR.
3. MDR $\rightarrow$ R	Copy the contents of the MDR into register R.

b) STORE X   Store register R into memory cell X.

    1. $IR_{addr} \rightarrow MAR$ Send address X (currently in IR_{addr}) to the MAR.

    2. $R \rightarrow MDR$ Send the contents of register R to the MDR.

    3. STORE   Store the value in the MDR into memory cell X.

c) ADD X   Add the contents of cell X and register R and put the result back into register R.

    1. $IR_{addr} \rightarrow MAR$ Send address X (currently in IR_{addr}) to the MAR.

    2. FETCH   Fetch the contents of cell X and place it in the MDR.

    3. $MDR \rightarrow ALU$ Send the two operands of the ADD to the ALU.

    4. $R \rightarrow ALU$

    5. ADD   Activate the ALU and select the output of the add circuit as the desired result.

    6. $ALU \rightarrow R$ Copy the selected result into the R register.

d) JUMP X   Jump to the instruction located in memory location X.

    1. $IR_{addr} \rightarrow PC$ Send address X to the PC so the instruction stored there will be fetched during the next fetch phase.

e) COMPARE X   Compare to see whether $CON(X) < R$, $CON(X) = R$, or $CON(X) > R$, and set condition codes to GT, EQ, and LT, respectively. (Assume all codes are initially 0.)

    1. $IR_{addr} \rightarrow MAR$ Send address X to the MAR.

    2. FETCH   Fetch the contents of cell X and place it in the MDR.

    3. $MDR \rightarrow ALU$ Send the contents of address X and register R to the ALU.

    4. $R \rightarrow ALU$

    5. SUBTRACT   Evaluate $CON(X) - R$. Don't save the result. Do it only so that the condition codes are set. If $CON(X) - R > 0$, then $CON(X) > R$ and set GT to 1. If $CON(X) - R = 0$, then they are equal and set EQ to 1. If $CON(X) - R < 0$, then $CON(X) < R$ and set LT to 1.

f) JUMPGT X   If GT condition code is 1, jump to the instruction in location X. Otherwise, continue to the next instruction.

    1. IF GT = 1   Send the address X to the PC only if the GT condition code is set to 1. Otherwise, nothing happens.

      THEN $IR_{addr} \rightarrow PC$

These are six examples of the sequence of signals and transfers that would occur during the execution phase of the fetch/decode/execute cycle. There will be a unique sequence of actions for each of the 16 instructions in the sample instruction set of Figure 5.19 and for the 50–300 instructions in the instruction set of a typical Von Neumann computer. When the execution of one instruction is done, the control unit fetches the next instruction, starting the cycle all over again. That is the fundamental sequential behavior of the Von Neumann architecture.

These six examples clearly illustrate the concept of abstraction at work. In Chapter 4 we built complex arithmetic/logic circuits to do operations like addition and comparison. Using these circuits, this chapter describes a computer that can execute machine language instructions such as ADD X and COMPARE X,Y. A machine language instruction such as ADD X is a complicated concept, but it is quite a bit easier to understand than the enormously detailed full adder circuit shown in Figure 4.27, which contains 800 gates and over 2,000 transistors.

Abstraction has allowed us to replace a complex sequence of gate-level manipulations with the single machine language command ADD, which does addition without our having to know how—the very essence of abstraction.

An Alphabet Soup of Speed Measures— MIPS, MFLOPS, MHz, and GHz

It is easy to identify the fastest car, plane, or train—just compare their top speeds in miles/hour (or km/hr) and pick the greatest. However, in the computer arena things are not so simple, and there are many different measures of speed.

The unit you may be most familiar with is *clock speed*, measured in either millions of cycles per second, called megahertz (MHz) or billions of cycles per second, called gigahertz (GHz). The actions of every computer are controlled by a central clock, and the "tick" rate of this clock is one possible speed measure. Processors today have clock rates of 500 MHz up to 2–3 GHz. However, clock speed can be misleading as a machine's capability depends not only on the tick rate but also on how much work it can do during each tick. If machine A has a clock rate twice as fast as machine B, but each instruction on machine A takes twice as many clock cycles as machine B to complete, then there will be no observable speed difference.

Therefore, a more accurate measure of machine speed is *instruction rate*, measured in MIPS, an acronym for *millions of instructions per second*. This measures how many machine language instructions of the type listed in Figure 5.19 (e.g., LOAD, STORE, COMPARE, ADD) can be fetched, decoded, and executed in one second. If a computer completed one instruction for every clock cycle, then the in-struction rate would be identical to the clock rate. However, many instructions require multiple clock ticks, while parallel computers can often complete multiple instructions in a single tick. Thus, MIPS is a better measure of performance because it tells you how much work is actually being done, in terms of completed instructions, in a given amount of time.

Finally, some people are not interested in how fast a computer executes all of its instructions, but in only the subset of instructions most important to their applications. For example, scientific programs do an enormous amount of floating point (i.e., decimal) arithmetic, so the computers that execute these programs must be able to execute arithmetic instructions as fast as possible. For these machines, a better measure of speed might be the *floating-point instruction rate,* measured in MFLOPS—for millions of floating point instructions per second. This is like MIPS, except the instructions we focus most closely on are those for adding, subtracting, multiplying, and dividing real numbers. Modern processors can perform at a rate of about 500–1,000 MFLOPS.

So, as you can see, there is no universal measure of computer speed, and that is what allows different computer vendors all to stand up and claim, My machine is the fastest!

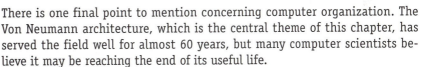

The next laboratory experience introduces a software package that simulates the behavior of a Von Neumann computer. It will give you a chance to work with and observe the behavior of a Von Neumann machine quite similar to the one shown in Figure 5.18. Our simulated computer contains the same functional units introduced in this section, including memory, registers, arithmetic/logic unit, and control unit, and it uses the instruction set shown in Figure 5.19. The simulator will allow you to observe the step-by-step execution of machine language instructions and watch the flow of information that occurs during the fetch, decode, and execute phases. It will also allow you to write and execute your own machine language programs.

Well, why should we stop here? Machine language commands, though better than hardware, are hardly user-friendly. (Some might even call them "user-intimidating.") Programming in binary and writing sequences of instructions such as

    010110100001111010100001

is cumbersome, confusing, and very error-prone. Why not take these machine language instructions and make them more user-oriented and user-friendly? Why not give them features that allow us to write correct, reliable, and efficient programs more easily? Why not develop **user-oriented programming languages** designed for people, not machines? This is the next level of abstraction in our hierarchy, and we introduce that important concept in Level 3 of the text.

5.4   The Future: Non–Von Neumann Architectures

There is one final point to mention concerning computer organization. The Von Neumann architecture, which is the central theme of this chapter, has served the field well for almost 60 years, but many computer scientists believe it may be reaching the end of its useful life.

The problems that computers are being asked to solve have grown significantly in size and complexity since the appearance of the first-generation machines in the late 1940s and early 1950s. Designers have been able to "keep up" with these larger and larger problems by building faster and faster Von Neumann machines. Through advances in hardware design, manufacturing methods, and circuit technology, computer designers have been able to take the basic sequential architecture described by Von Neumann in 1946 and improve its performance by 3 or 4 orders of magnitude. First-generation machines were able to execute about 10,000 machine language instructions per second. By the second generation, that had grown to about 1 million instructions per second. Today, even a desktop PC can perform about 300–500 million instructions per second, and larger workstations can execute instructions at the rate of 1,000–2,000 MIPS. Figure 5.20 shows the changes in computer speeds from the mid-1940s to the present. (*Note:* This graph is logarithmic. Each unit on the vertical axis is 10 times the previous one.) Note that the

FIGURE 5.20

Graph of Processor Speeds,
1945 to the Present

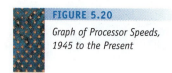

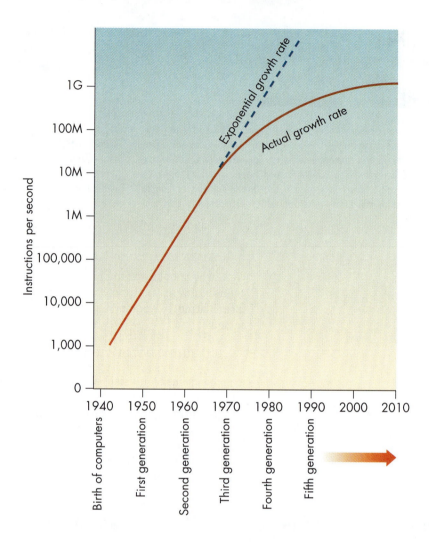

period from about 1945 to about 1970 was characterized by exponential increases in computation speed. However, as Figure 5.20 shows, even though computer speeds are increasing, the rate of improvement appears to be slowing down.

This slowdown is due to many things. One important limit on increased processor speed is the inability to place gates closer and closer together on a chip. Today's high-density chips contain tens of millions of transistors separated by distances less than 0.0001 cm, and it is becoming difficult to accurately place components any closer together. However, if we cannot get them any closer, then the time it takes to send data between two devices, such as the memory and the ALU, will become a limiting factor in the ultimate speed of our computer, because electronic signals cannot travel faster than the speed of light—299,792,458 meters per second.

Even though the rate of increase in the performance of newer machines is slowing down, the size of the problems that researchers are attempting to solve is not slowing down; in fact, it is increasing dramatically. New applications in such areas as computational modeling, real-time graphics, and bioinformatics are rapidly increasing the demands placed on new computer systems. (We will look at some of these applications in Level 5, Chapters 12–14.) For example, to have a computer generate and display animated images without flicker it must generate 30 new frames each second. Each frame may contain as many as $1,500 \times 1,500$ picture points (**pixels**) whose position, color, and intensity must be recomputed. This means that 67,500,000 pixel computations need to be completed every second. Each of those computations may require the execution of a few dozen instructions. (Where does this point move to in the next frame? How bright is it? Is it visible or hidden behind something else?) If we assume that it requires about 100 computations per pixel to answer these questions (a reasonable approximation), then doing real-time computer animation requires a computer capable of executing $67,500,000 \times 100 = 6.75$ billion computations per second. This is well beyond the abilities of current processors, which are limited to about 0.5–3 billion instructions per second. The inability of the sequential one-instruction-at-a-time Von Neumann model to handle today's large-scale problems is called the **Von Neumann bottleneck,** and it is a major problem in computer organization.

To solve this problem, computer engineers are rethinking many of the fundamental ideas presented in this chapter, and they are studying nontraditional approaches to computer organization called **non–Von Neumann architectures.** They are asking the question, Is there a different way to design and build computers that can solve problems 10 or 100 or 1,000 times larger than what can be handled by today's computers? Fortunately, the answer is a resounding, Yes!

One of the most important areas of research in these non–Von Neumann architectures is based on the following fairly obvious principle:

If you cannot build something to work twice as fast, do two things at once. The results will be identical.

From this truism comes the principle of **parallel processing**—building computers not with one processor as shown in Figure 5.18, but with tens, hundreds, or even thousands. If we can keep each processor occupied with meaningful work, then it should be possible to speed up the solution to large problems by 1, 2, or 3 orders of magnitude and overcome the Von Neumann bottleneck. For example, in the graphical animation example discussed earlier, we determined that we needed a machine that could execute 6.75 billion operations/second, but today's processors are limited to about 500 million to 3 billion operations/second. If we take about 4–16 processors and get them all to work together on this one problem, then we should (in theory!) have a sufficiently powerful system to solve our problem.

There are two fundamentally distinct approaches to designing parallel processing systems. The first technique is termed **SIMD parallel processing** (SIMD stands for *single instruction stream/multiple data stream*). It is diagrammed in Figure 5.21.

In the SIMD model there is a single program whose instructions are fetched/decoded/executed in a sequential manner by one control unit, exactly as described earlier. However, the ALU (circuits and registers) is replicated many times, and each ALU has its own local memory where it may keep private data. When the control unit fetches an instruction (such as a LOAD, ADD, or STORE), it **broadcasts** that instruction to every ALU, which executes

FIGURE 5.21

A SIMD Parallel Processing System

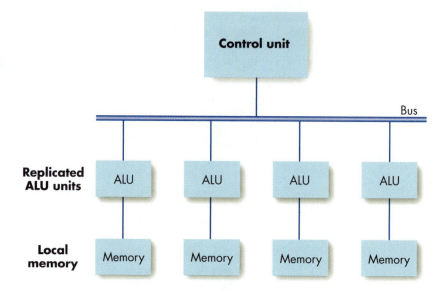

it in parallel on its own local data. Thus, if we have 100 replicated ALUs, we can perform 100 parallel additions by having every ALU simultaneously execute the instruction

ADD X   Add memory cell X to the contents of register R

on its own local value of X, using its own personal copy of register R.

A good analogy to SIMD parallel processing is the way the game of Bingo is played. There is one caller (control unit) calling out a single number (the instruction) to the entire room. In the room listening are many people (ALUs) who simultaneously cover that number on their own private Bingo cards (local memories).

This style of parallelism is especially useful in operations on mathematical structures called **vectors** and **arrays.** A vector V is simply an ordered collection of values. For example, here is a six-element vector V, whose elements are termed $v_1, v_2, \ldots, v_6$.

	v_1	v_2	v_3	v_4	v_5	v_6
V	1	8	−13	70	9	0

Many operations on vectors match the SIMD parallel model quite well. For example, to add the constant value +1 to a vector, you add it to every individual element in the vector; that is, you simultaneously compute $v_1 + 1$, $v_2 + 1, \ldots$. Thus the operation $V + 1$, when applied to the previous vector, produces the new vector 2, 9, −12, 71, 10, 1. On a SIMD machine, this vector addition operation can be implemented in a single step by distributing one element of the vector to each separate ALU. Then in parallel, each arithmetic unit executes the following instruction:

INC v v is an element of the vector V. This instruction increments the contents of that location by $+1$.

In one time unit, we will update all six elements of the vector V. In the traditional Von Neumann machine, we would have to increment each element separately in a sequential fashion, so it would take six instructions:

INC $v1$

INC $v2$

⋮

INC $v6$

Our parallel vector addition operator runs six times as fast. Similar speedups are possible with other vector and array manipulations.

SIMD parallelism was the first type of parallel processing put into widespread commercial use. It was the technique used to achieve breakthroughs in computational speeds on the first **supercomputers** of the early 1980s.

A more interesting and much more widely used form of parallelism is called **MIMD parallel processing** (*multiple instruction stream/multiple data stream*). In MIMD parallelism we replicate entire processors rather than just the ALU, and every processor is capable of executing its own separate program in its own private memory at its own rate. This model of parallel processing is diagrammed in Figure 5.22.

Each processor/memory pair in Figure 5.22 is a Von Neumann machine of the type described in this chapter. Each one is executing its own program in its own local memory at its own rate. However, rather than each having to solve the entire problem by itself, the problem is solved in a parallel fashion by all processors simultaneously. Each of the processors tackles a small part of the overall problem and then communicates its result to the other processors via the **interconnection network** that allows processors to exchange messages and data.

A MIMD parallel processor would be an excellent system to help us speed up the New York Telephone Directory lookup problem discussed in Chapter 2. In the sequential approach that we described, the single processor doing the work had to search all 20,000,000 entries from beginning to end (or until the desired name was found). The analysis in Chapter 3 showed that using sequential search and a computer that can examine 50,000 names per second, this lookup operation takes an average of 3.5 minutes to find a particular name—much too long for the typical person to wait.

If we use 100 processors instead of one, however, the problem is easily solved. We just divide the 20,000,000 names into 100 equal-sized pieces and assign each piece to a different processor. Now each processor searches *in parallel* to see whether the desired name is in its own section. If it finds the name, it broadcasts that information to the other 99 processors so that they can stop searching. Each processor needs only to look through a list of 200,000 names, which is 1/100 the amount of work it had to do previously. Instead of requiring an average of 3.5 minutes, we will now get our answer in

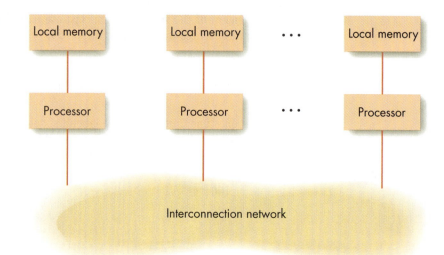

FIGURE 5.22

Model of MIMD Parallel Processing

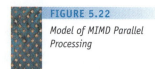

Local memory   Local memory   ···   Local memory

Processor   Processor   ···   Processor

Interconnection network

1/100 the time—about 2 seconds. Parallel processing has elegantly solved our problem.

MIMD parallelism is an exciting computational model because in addition to making possible massive speedups, it is also a scalable architecture. **Scalability** means that, at least theoretically, it is possible to match the number of processors to the size of the problem. If 100 processors are not enough to

Speed to Burn

The first computer to achieve a speed of 1 million floating point operations per second, 1 **megaflop,** was the Control Data 6600 in the mid-1960s. Modern microprocessors, such as the Pentium 4, can typically perform computations at about 600–800 megaflops. The first machine to achieve 1 billion floating point operations per second, 1 **gigaflop,** was the Cray X-MP in the early 1980s. Large multiprocessor Web servers and supercomputers often have computing speeds in the range of 1–100 gigaflops. In 1996 the Intel Corporation announced that its ULTRA computer had successfully become the world's first **teraflop** machine. This $55 million computer contained 9,072 Pentium Pro processors, and on December 16, 1996 it achieved a sustained computational speed of 1 trillion computations per second.

However, even that is not enough to handle today's unbelievably massive computational problems. The Earth Simulator, completed by a group of Japanese engineers in March 2002, contains 5,120 processors and is one of the most powerful supercomputers ever built. It runs at more than 35 trillion calculations per second. To get an idea of how unimaginably fast this is, consider that if all 6 billion people in the world worked together on a single problem, each person would have to carry out 6,000 computations/second to equal the speed of this one machine! The Earth Simulator was designed for a single purpose: to create an accurate computational model of the entire Earth—climate, environment, ecology, ocean currents, land formation, everything. Located at a vast, newly built facility in Yokohama, Japan, the Earth Simulator is the size of four tennis courts. Its price tag: $350 million.

And just so you don't think computer designers are now sitting around relaxing, there already exists a major effort to design and build the first **petaflop** machine, a computer capable of one thousand trillion (10^{15}) computations per second. Project Blue Gene, an initiative of the IBM Corp., is directed at building a 1-million-processor petaflop computer by the year 2006. The machine will be used to study the problem of protein folding, the biochemical process by which complex molecules in the human body are constructed by instructions carried in our DNA.

solve the telephone book lookup problem, then 200 or 500 can be used instead, assuming the interconnect network can provide the necessary communications. (Communications can become a serious bottleneck in a parallel system.) In short, the resources applied to a problem can be in direct proportion to the amount of work that needs to be done. **Massively parallel** MIMD machines containing over 8,000 independent processors have achieved solutions to large problems thousands of times faster than was possible using a single processor. (For an up-to-date listing of the fastest parallel computers, take a look at the home page of the *Performance Database,* a list of the most powerful computers in the world. Its URL is www.netlib.org/performance/html/PDStop.html.)

The real key to using massively parallel processors is to design solution methods that effectively utilize the large number of available processors. It does no good to have 1,000 processors available if only 1 or 2 are doing useful work while 998 or 999 are sitting idle, waiting for something to do. That would be equivalent to having a large construction crew at a building site but having the roofers, painters, and plumbers sitting around waiting for one person to put up the walls. The field of **parallel algorithms,** the study of techniques that make efficient use of parallel architectures, is an important branch of research in computer science. Advances in this area will go a long way toward speeding the development and use of large-scale parallel systems of the type shown in Figures 5.21 and 5.22.

In order to solve the complex problems of the 21st century, the computers of the 21st century will probably be organized much more like the parallel processing systems of Figures 5.21 and 5.22 than like the 55-year-old Von Neumann model of Figure 5.18.

5.5   Summary of Level 2

We have now seen the basic principles underlying the design of a modern computer system. In Chapter 4 we looked at the basic building blocks of computers: binary codes, transistors, gates, and circuits. This chapter examined the standard model for computer design, called the Von Neumann architecture. It also discussed some of the shortcomings of this sequential model of computation and described briefly how parallel computers may be designed and built in the 21st century.

At this point in our hierarchy of abstractions, we have created a fully functional computer system capable of executing an algorithm encoded as sequences of machine language instructions. The only problem is that the machine we have created is enormously difficult to use and about as unfriendly and unforgiving as it could be. It has been designed and engineered from a machine's perspective, not a person's. Sequences of binary encoded machine language instructions such as

    1011010000001011
    1001101100010111
    0000101101011001

give a computer no difficulty, but they cause people to throw up their hands in despair. We need to create a friendlier environment—to make the computer and its hardware resources less intimidating and more accessible. Such an environment would be more conducive to developing correct solutions to problems and satisfying a user's computational needs.

The component that creates this kind of friendly, problem-solving environment is called **system software.** It is an intermediary between the user and the hardware components of the Von Neumann machine. Without it, a Von Neumann machine would be virtually unusable by anyone but the most technically knowledgeable computer experts. We examine these ideas in the next level of our investigation of computer science.

1. What would be the advantages and disadvantages of using a very large memory cell size, say, $W = 64$ instead of the standard size, $W = 8$? If each integer occupies *one* 64-bit memory cell and was stored using sign/magnitude notation, what are the largest (in terms of absolute value) positive and negative integers that could be stored? What if *two* cells are used to store integers?

2. At a minimum, how many bits would be needed in the MAR with each of the following memory sizes?
   a. 1 million bytes
   b. 10 million bytes
   c. 100 million bytes
   d. 1 billion bytes

3. A memory unit that was said to be 640 KB would actually contain how many memory cells? What about a memory of 512 MB?

4. Explain what use a read-only memory (ROM) could possibly serve in the design of a computer system. What type of information might be kept in a ROM, and how could that information originally get into the memory?

5. Assuming the square two-dimensional memory organization shown in Figure 5.6, what are the dimensions of a memory containing 1 MB (2^{20}) bytes of storage? How large would the MAR be? How many bits would be sent to the row and column decoders? How many output lines would these decoders have?

6. Assume a 24-bit MAR that is organized as follows:

row select lines	*column select lines*
12 bits	12 bits

   What is the maximum size of the memory unit on this machine? What are the dimensions of the memory, assuming a square two-dimensional organization?

7. Assume that our MAR contains 20 bits, enabling us to access up to 2^{20} memory cells, which is 1 MB, but our computer has 4 MB of memory. Explain how it might be possible to address all 4 MB memory cells using a MAR that contains only 20 bits.

8. Do you think that our human memory unit, the brain, does or does not follow the random access model described in Section 5.2.1? If you think not, state why and explain in what ways the brain might differ from RAM.

9. Assume that we have an arithmetic/logic unit that can carry out 20 distinct operations. Describe exactly what kind of multiplexor circuit would be needed to select exactly one of those 20 operations.

10. Assume that a floppy disk has the following characteristics:

   Rotation speed = 7,200 rev/min

   Arm movement time = 0.5 msec fixed startup time + 0.05 msec for each track crossed (The startup time is a constant no matter how far the arm moves.)

   Number of surfaces = 2 (a **double-sided** floppy disk. A single read/write arm holds both read/write heads.)

   Number of tracks per surface = 500

   Number of sectors per track = 20

   Number of characters per sector = 1,024

   a. How many characters can be stored on a single floppy disk?

   b. What are the best-case, worst-case, and average case access times for this disk?

11. In general, information is stored on a disk not at random but in specific locations that help to minimize the time it takes to retrieve that information. Using the specifications given in Exercise 10, where would you store the information in a 50 Kbyte file on the disk to speed up subsequent access to that information?

12. Assume that our disk unit had one read/write head per *track* instead of only one per surface. (A **head-per-track disk** is sometimes referred to as a **drum**.) Using the specifications given in Exercise 10, what are now the best-case, worst-case, and average case access times? How much have the additional read/write heads helped reduce access times?

13. Discuss some situations wherein a sequential access storage device such as a tape could be a useful form of mass storage.

14. Assume that we are receiving a message across a network using a modem with a rate of 56,000 bits/second. Furthermore, assume that we are working on a workstation with an instruction rate of 500 MIPS. How many instructions can the processor execute between the receipt of each individual bit of the message?

15. Consider the following structure of the instruction register.

op code	*address-1*	*address-2*
6 bits	18 bits	18 bits

   a. What is the maximum number of distinct operation codes that can be recognized and executed by the processor on this machine?

   b. What is the maximum memory size on this machine?

   c. How many bytes are required for each operation?

16. Assume that the variables *v, w, x, y,* and *z* are stored in memory locations 200, 201, 202, 203, and 204, respectively. Using any of the machine language instructions in

Section 5.2.4, translate the following algorithmic operations into their machine language equivalents.

a. Set v to the value of $x - y + z$. (Assume the existence of the machine language command SUBTRACT X, Y, Z that computes $CON(Z) = CON(X) - CON(Y)$.)

b. Set v to the value $(w + x) - (y + z)$

c. If $(v \geq w)$ then

  set x to y

Else

  set x to z

d. While $y < z$ do

  Set y to the value $(y + w + z)$

  Set z to the value $(z + v)$

End of the loop

17. Explain why it would be cumbersome to translate the following algorithmic operation into machine language, given only the instructions introduced in this chapter:

Set x to the value of $y + 19$

Can you think of a way to solve this problem?

18. Describe the sequence of operations that might go on inside the computer during the execution phase of the following machine language instructions. Use the notation shown in Section 5.2.5.

a. MOVE X, Y Move the contents of memory cell X to memory cell Y

b. ADD X, Y Add together the contents of memory cells X and Y. Put the result back into memory cell Y

CHALLENGE WORK

1. It is easy to write a sequential algorithm that sums up a 100-element vector:

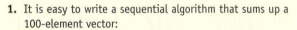

$$Sum = a_1 + a_2 + a_3 + \ldots + a_{100}$$

It would look something like

  Set i to 1

  Set Sum to 0

  While $i < 101$ do the following

    $Sum = Sum + a_i$

    $i = i + 1$

  End of the loop

  Write out the value of Sum

  Stop

It is pretty obvious that this algorithm will take about 100 units of time, where a unit of time is equivalent to the time needed to execute one iteration of the loop. However, it is not so easy to see how we might exploit the existence of *multiple* processors to speed up the solution to this problem.

Assume that instead of having only a single processor, you have 100. Design a parallel algorithm that utilizes these additional resources to speed up the solution to the previous computation. Exactly how much faster would your **parallel summation algorithm** execute than

the sequential one? Did you need all 100 processors? Could you have used more than 100?

2. In this chapter we described the Von Neumann architecture in broad, general terms. However, "real" Von Neumann processors, such as the Pentium 4, the G5 used in the Apple Macintosh, and the SUN SPARC, are much more complex than the simple model shown in Figure 5.18. Pick one of these processors (perhaps the processor inside the computer you are using for this class) and take an in-depth look at its design. Specifically, examine such issues as

• Its instruction set and how it compares with the instruction set shown in Figure 5.19

• The collection of available registers

• The existence of cache memory

• Its computing speed in MIPS and MFLOPS

• How much primary memory it has and how memory is addressed in the instructions

• Memory access time

• In what size "chunks" can memory be accessed

Write a report describing the real-world characteristics of the processor you selected.

FOR FURTHER READING

In the area of computer organization and machine architecture:

Patterson, D., and Hennessey, J. *Computer Organization and Design: The Hardware/Software Interface,* 3rd Ed. San Francisco: Morgan Kaufmann, 2002.

Stallings, W. *Computer Organization and Architecture,* 6th ed. Englewood Cliffs, NJ: Prentice-Hall, 2002.

Tanenbaum, A. *Structured Computer Organization,* 4th ed. Englewood Cliffs, NJ: Prentice-Hall, 1998.

A fascinating and thoroughly enjoyable nontechnical book that explores some of the issues involved in designing and building a computer is

Kidder, T. *The Soul of a New Machine.* San Francisco: Back Bay Books, 2000.

In the area of parallel processing:

Dongarra, J. *Sourcebook of Parallel Computing.* San Francisco: Morgan Kaufman, 2002.

Jordan, H. F. *Fundamentals of Parallel Computing.* Englewood Cliffs, NJ: Prentice-Hall, 2002.

The Virtual Machine

LEVEL 3

LEVEL 3

Level 3 It has been said that computer science is "the science of building pretend worlds." What that rather unusual comment means is that the underlying hardware structure of a computer can be so difficult to work with that we must create more friendly and more usable "virtual worlds" in which to work and solve problems. Without that layer of abstraction between us and the machine, we would be relegated to solving problems by applying only the ideas and capabilities studied in Level 2—binary numbers, digital circuits, absolute memory addresses, and machine language instructions. That is not a very comforting thought.

In this part of the text we will learn how to create these user-friendly "microworlds" and produce an environment in which efficient and productive problem solving is possible.

CHAPTER 6

An Introduction to System Software and Virtual Machines

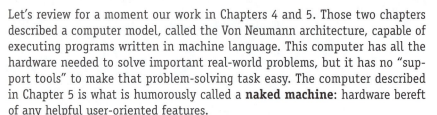

Let's review for a moment our work in Chapters 4 and 5. Those two chapters described a computer model, called the Von Neumann architecture, capable of executing programs written in machine language. This computer has all the hardware needed to solve important real-world problems, but it has no "support tools" to make that problem-solving task easy. The computer described in Chapter 5 is what is humorously called a **naked machine**: hardware bereft of any helpful user-oriented features.

Imagine what it would be like to work on a naked machine. To solve a problem, you would have to create hundreds or thousands of cryptic and highly confusing machine language instructions that looked like this:

      1011010011010001110011110000100

and you would have to do that without making a single mistake. To execute properly, a program must be error-free, for even one minor mistake can cause it to behave incorrectly. Imagine the likelihood of writing a perfectly correct program containing thousands of instructions like the one shown above. Even worse, imagine trying to locate an error buried deep inside that incomprehensible mass of 0s and 1s. That is a truly depressing thought.

On a naked machine the data as well as the instructions must be represented in binary. For example, a program cannot refer to the decimal integer +9 directly but must express it as

      0000000000001001   (the binary representation of +9 using 16 bits)

You cannot use the symbol *A* to refer to the first letter of the alphabet but must represent it using its 8-bit ASCII code value, which is decimal 65:

      01000001   (the 8-bit ASCII code for *A*. See Figure 4.3.)

As you can imagine, writing programs for a naked machine is no joy.

Even if you are lucky enough to get the program written correctly, your work is still not done. A program for a Von Neumann computer must be stored in memory prior to execution. Therefore, you must now take the program and store its instructions into sequential cells in memory. On a naked machine there is no assistance provided for this task, so the programmer must do it, one instruction at a time. Assuming that each instruction occupies one memory cell, the programmer loads the first instruction into address 0, the second instruction into address 1, the third instruction into address 2, and so on, until all have been stored.

Finally, what starts the program running? A naked machine does not do this automatically. (As you are probably coming to realize, a naked machine does not do *anything* automatically, except fetch, decode, and execute machine language instructions.) The programmer must initiate execution by storing a 0, the address of the first instruction of the program, into the program counter (PC) and pressing the START button. This would begin the fetch/decode/execute cycle described in Chapter 5. The control unit fetches from memory the contents of the address in the PC, currently 0, and executes that instruction. The program continues sequentially from that point while the user prays that everything works, because he or she cannot bear to face a naked machine again!

We have painted a bleak picture but an honest one. Working directly with the underlying hardware is a virtually impossible task for a human being. The functional units described in Chapter 5 were built from the standpoint of what is easy for hardware to do, not what is easy for people to do.

To make a Von Neumann computer usable, we must create an **interface** between the user and the hardware. This interface would do many things:

- Hide from the user the messy and unnecessary details of the underlying hardware
- Present information about what is happening in a way that does not require in-depth knowledge of the internal structure of the system
- Allow easy user access to the resources available on this computer
- Prevent accidental or intentional damage to hardware, programs, and data

By way of analogy, let's look at how people use another common tool—an automobile. The internal combustion engine is a complex piece of technology, and very few people really understand how it works. For most of us, the functions of carburetors, distributors, and camshafts are a total mystery. However, most people find driving a car quite easy. This is because the driver does not have to lift the hood and interact directly with the hardware; that is, he or she does not have to drive a "naked automobile." Instead, there is an interface, the **dashboard,** which simplifies things considerably. The dashboard hides the details of engine operation that a driver does not need to know. What *is* important—things such as oil pressure, fuel levels, and vehicle speed—are presented in a simple, "people-oriented" way: oil indicator warning light on or off, fuel gauge empty or full, speed in miles per hour. Access to the engine and transmission is achieved in terms of a few simple operations: a key to start and stop, pedals to speed up or slow down, a shift lever to go forward and backward.

We need a similar interface for our Von Neumann machine. This "computer dashboard" would eliminate most of the hassles of working on a naked machine and let us view the hardware resources of Chapter 5 in a much friendlier way. Such an interface does exist, and it is called the **system software.** That is our focal point in this chapter.

6.2.1   *The Virtual Machine*

System software is a collection of computer programs that manage the re-sources of a computer and facilitate access to those resources. It is important to remember that we are describing software, not hardware. There are no black boxes wired to a computer and labeled "system software." Software consists of sequences of instructions—namely, programs—that solve a problem. However, instead of solving *user* problems, such as looking up names in a telephone book, system software has the responsibility of making a computer and its many resources easier to access and use.

System software acts as an *intermediary* between the users and the hardware, as shown in Figure 6.1. System software presents the user with a set of services and resources across the interface labeled A in Figure 6.1. These resources may actually exist, or they may be simulated by the software to give the user the illusion that they exist. The set of services and resources created by the software and seen by the user is called a **virtual machine** or a **virtual environment.** The system software, not the user, interacts with the actual hardware (that is, the naked machine) across the interface labeled B in Figure 6.1.

The system software has responsibilities similar to those of the dashboard of an automobile:

- Hide messy and unimportant details of the internal structure of the Von Neumann architecture
- Present important information to the user in a way that is easy to understand
- Allow the user to access machine resources in a simple and efficient way
- Provide a secure and safe environment in which to operate

For example, to add two numbers, it is much easier to use simple notation such as $a = b + c$ than to worry about (1) loading ALU registers from memory cells b and c, (2) activating the ALU, (3) selecting the output of the addition

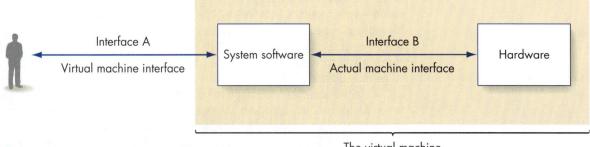

The virtual machine

FIGURE 6.1

The Role of System Software

circuit, and (4) sending the result to memory cell *a*. The programmer should not have to know about registers, addition circuits, and memory addresses but instead should see a virtual machine that "understands" the symbols + and =.

After the program has been written, it should automatically be loaded into memory without the programmer having to specify where it should be placed or having to set the program counter. Instead, he or she should be able to issue one simple command (or one set of mouse clicks) to the virtual machine that says, Run my program. Finally, when the program is running and generating results, the programmer should be able to instruct the virtual machine to send the program's output to the printer in Room 105. The messy I/O details related to I/O controllers, interrupt signals, and code sets should be the farthest thing from our mind.

All the useful services just described *are* provided by the system software available on any modern computer system, making it much easier to do problem solving on a virtual machine than on a real one. The following sections show how this friendly, user-oriented environment is created.

 ### 6.2.2 *Types of System Software*

System software is not a single monolithic entity but a collection of many different programs. The types found on a typical computer are shown in Figure 6.2.

The program that controls the overall operation of the computer is the **operating system,** and it is the single most important piece of system software on a computer. It is the operating system that communicates with the user, determines what he or she wants, and activates other system programs, applications packages, or user programs to carry out that request. The software packages that might handle these requests include

- *User Interface.* All modern operating systems provide a powerful **graphical user interface (GUI)** that gives the user an intuitive visual overview as well as graphical control of the capabilities and services of the computer.
- *Language services.* These programs, called **assemblers, compilers,** and **interpreters,** allow you to write programs in a high-level, user-oriented language rather than the machine language of Chapter 5 and

FIGURE 6.2

Types of System Software

to execute these programs easily and efficiently. They often include components such as text editors and debuggers that assist you in getting the program working.

- *Memory managers.* These programs allocate memory space for programs and data and retrieve this memory space when it is no longer needed.

- *Information managers.* These programs handle the organization, storage, and retrieval of information on mass storage devices such as the disks, CD-ROMs, and tapes described in Section 5.2.2. They allow you to organize your information in an efficient hierarchical manner, using directories, folders, and files.

- *I/O Systems.* These software packages allow you to easily and efficiently use the many different types of input and output devices that exist on a modern computer system.

- *Scheduler.* This system program keeps a list of programs ready to run on the processor, and it selects the one that will execute next. This is the package that allows you to have a number of different programs active at a single time, for instance, to surf the Web while you are waiting for something to finish printing.

- *Utilities.* These are collections of library routines that provide useful services either to a user or to other system routines. Text editors, on-line help routines, drawing programs, and control panels are examples of utility routines. Sometimes these utilities are organized into collections called **program libraries.**

These system routines are used during every phase of problem solving on a computer, and it would be virtually impossible to get anything done without them. Let's go back to the problem described at the beginning of this chapter—the job of writing a program, loading it into memory, running it, and printing the results. On a naked machine this job would be formidable. On the virtual machine created by system software, it is much simpler:

Step   Task
1   Use a *text editor* to create program P written in a high-level, English-like notation rather than binary.

2   Use the *file system* to store program P on the hard disk in your home directory

3   Use a *language translator* to translate program P from a high-level language into a machine language program M.

4   Use the *scheduler* to load, schedule, and run program M. The scheduler will itself use the *memory manager* to obtain memory space for program M.

5   Use the *I/O system* to print the output of your program on printer R.

6   If the program did not complete successfully, use a *debugger* to help locate the error. Use the text editor to correct the program and the file system to store the newly modified program.

Furthermore, most of these operations will be invoked via the graphical user interface provided by the operating system.

On a virtual machine, the messy details of machine operation are no longer visible, and a user can concentrate on higher-level issues: writing the program, executing the program, and saving and analyzing results.

There are many types of system software, and it would be impossible to cover them all in this section of the text. Instead, in this chapter we will investigate two types of system software, and use these as representatives of the entire group. Section 6.3 treats assemblers, and Section 6.4 looks at the design and construction of operating systems. These two packages create a friendly and usable virtual machine. Then, in Chapter 7, we extend that virtual environment from a single computer to a collection of computers. That chapter will look at the software required to create one of the most important and widely used virtual environments—a computer network

6.3 Assemblers and Assembly Language

 ### 6.3.1 Assembly Language

One of the first places where we need a more friendly virtual environment is in our choice of programming language. Being designed from a machine's point of view, not a person's, machine language is complicated and difficult to understand. What specifically is wrong with machine language, and what needs to be changed? Many things.

- It uses binary. There are no natural language words, mathematical symbols, or other convenient mnemonics to make the language more readable to people.
- It allows only numeric memory addresses. A programmer cannot name an instruction or a piece of data and refer to it by name.
- It is difficult to change. If we insert or delete an instruction, all memory addresses following that instruction will change. For example, if we place a new instruction into memory location 503, then the instruction previously in location 503 is now in 504. All references to address 503 must be updated to point to 504. There may be hundreds of such references.
- It is difficult to create data. If a user wishes to store a piece of data in memory, he or she must compute the internal binary representation for that data item. These conversion algorithms are complicated and time consuming.

The individuals who programmed on those early first-generation computers quickly realized the shortcomings of machine language. They developed a new language, called **assembly language,** designed for people as well as computers. Assembly languages created a more productive, user-oriented environment, and assemblers were one of the first pieces of system software to be widely used. When assembly languages first appeared in the early 1950s, they were one of the most important new developments in programming—so important, in fact, that they were considered an entirely new generation of language, analogous to the new generations of hardware described in Section 1.4.3. Assembly languages were termed **second-generation languages** to distinguish them from machine languages, which were viewed as **first-generation languages.**

Today, assembly languages are more properly viewed as **low-level programming languages,** which means they are closely related to the machine language of Chapter 5. Each symbolic assembly language instruction is translated into exactly *one* binary machine language instruction.

This contrasts with languages like C++ and Java, which are **high-level programming languages**. High-level languages are more user-oriented, they are not machine-specific, and they use both natural language and mathematical notation in their design. A single high-level language instruction is typically translated into *many* machine language instructions, and the virtual environment created by a high-level language is much more powerful than the one produced by an assembly language. We discuss high-level languages in detail in Chapters 8 and 9.

Figure 6.3 shows a "continuum of programming languages," from the lowest level (closest to the hardware) to the highest level (most abstract, farthest from the hardware).

The machine language of Chapter 5 is the most primitive; it is the language of the hardware itself. Assembly language, the topic of this chapter, represents the first step along the continuum from machine language. High-level programming languages like C++ and Java are much closer in style and structure to natural languages and are quite distinct from assembly language. Natural languages, such as English, Spanish, and Japanese, are the highest level; they are totally unrelated to hardware design.

A program written in assembly language is called the **source program;** it uses the features and services provided by the language. However, the processor does not "understand" assembly language instructions, in the sense of being able to fetch, decode, and execute them as described in Chapter 5. The source program must be translated into a corresponding machine language program, called the **object program.** This translation is carried out by a piece of system software called an **assembler.** (Translators for high-level languages are called **compilers**. They are discussed separately in Chapter

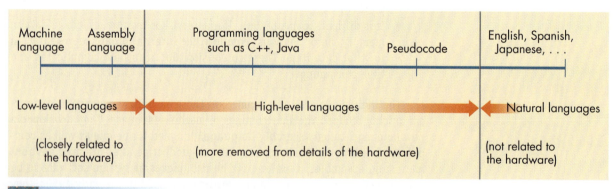

FIGURE 6.3

The Continuum of Programming Languages

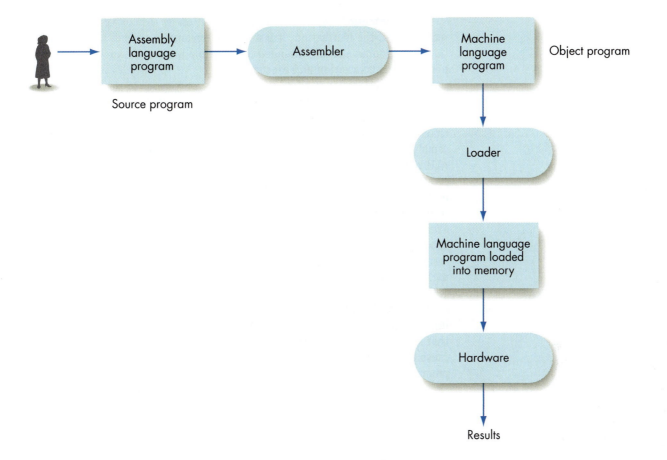

FIGURE 6.4

The Translation/Loading/ Execution Process

10.) Once the object program has been produced, its instructions can be loaded into memory and executed by the processor exactly as described in Section 5.3. The complete translation/loading/execution process is diagrammed in Figure 6.4.

What are the services that an assembler provides? What are the advantages of writing in assembly language rather than machine language? There are three major advantages:

- Use of symbolic operation codes rather than numeric (binary) ones
- Use of symbolic memory addresses rather than numeric (binary) ones
- Pseudo-operations that provide useful user-oriented services such as data generation

This section describes a simple, but nonetheless realistic, assembly language that demonstrates these three advantages.

Our hypothetical assembly language is composed of instructions in the following format:

label: op code mnemonic   address field   --comment

The **comment** field, preceded in our notation by a double dash, --, is not really part of the instruction. It is a helpful explanation added to the instruction by a programmer and intended for someone reading the program. It is ignored during translation and execution.

Assembly languages allow the programmer to refer to op codes using a symbolic name, called the **op code mnemonic,** rather than by a number. We can write op codes using meaningful words like LOAD, ADD, and STORE rather than obscure binary codes like 0000, 0011, and 0001. Figure 6.5 shows an assembly language instruction set for a Von Neumann machine that has a single ALU register R and three condition codes GT, EQ, and LT. Each numeric op code, its assembly language mnemonic, and its meaning are listed. This table is identical to Figure 5.19, which summarizes the language used in Chapter 5 to introduce the Von Neumann architecture and explain how instructions are executed. (However, Chapter 5 was describing binary machine language and used symbolic names only for convenience. In this chapter we are describing assembly language, where symbolic names such as LOAD and ADD are actually part of the language.)

Another advantage of assembly language is that it lets programmers use **symbolic addresses** instead of numeric addresses. In machine language, to jump to the instruction in location 17, you must refer directly to address 17; that is, you must write JUMP 17 (in binary, of course). This is cumbersome, because if a new instruction is inserted anywhere within the first 17 lines of the program, the location where you wish to jump will change to 18. The old refer-

FIGURE 6.5

Typical Assembly Language Instruction Set

BINARY OP CODE	OPERATION	MEANING
0000	LOAD X	CON(X) → R
0001	STORE X	R → CON(X)
0010	CLEAR X	0 → CON(X)
0011	ADD X	R + CON(X) → R
0100	INCREMENT X	CON(X) + 1 → CON(X)
0101	SUBTRACT X	R − CON(X) → R
0110	DECREMENT X	CON(X) − 1 → CON(X)
0111	COMPARE X	if CON(X) > R then GT = 1 else 0
		if CON(X) = R then EQ = 1 else 0
		if CON(X) < R then LT = 1 else 0
1000	JUMP X	Get the next instruction from memory location X.
1001	JUMPGT X	Get the next instruction from memory location X if GT = 1.
1010	JUMPEQ X	Get the next instruction from memory location X if EQ = 1.
1011	JUMPLT X	Get the next instruction from memory location X if LT = 1.
1100	JUMPNEQ X	Get the next instruction from memory location X if EQ = 0.
1101	IN X	Input an integer value from the standard input device and store into memory cell X.
1110	OUT X	Output, in decimal notation, the value stored in memory cell X.
1111	HALT	Stop program execution.

ence to 17 is incorrect, and the address field must be fixed. This makes modifying programs very difficult, and even small changes become big efforts. It is not unlike identifying yourself in a waiting line by position—as, say, the tenth person in line. As soon as someone in front of you leaves (or someone cuts into line ahead of you), that number is incorrect. It is far better to identify yourself using a characteristic that does not change as people enter or exit the line. For example, you are the person wearing the green suit with the orange and pink shirt. Those characteristics won't change (though maybe they should).

In assembly language we do exactly the same thing. We can attach a symbolic **label** to any instruction or piece of data in the program. The label becomes a permanent identification for this instruction or data, regardless of where it appears in the program or where it may be moved in memory. A label is a name (followed by a colon to identify it as a label) placed at the beginning of an instruction.

LOOPSTART: LOAD X

The label LOOPSTART has been attached to the instruction LOAD X. This means that the name LOOPSTART is *equivalent to* the address of the memory cell that holds the instruction LOAD X. If, for example, the LOAD X instruction ends up being stored in memory cell 62, then the name LOOPSTART is equivalent to address 62. Any use of the name LOOPSTART in the address field of an instruction is treated in exactly the same way as though the user had written the numeric address 62. For example, to jump to the load instruction shown above, we do not need to know that it is stored in location 62. Instead, we need only write the instruction

JUMP LOOPSTART

Symbolic labels have two advantages over numeric addresses. The first is **program clarity.** As with the use of mnemonics for op codes, the use of meaningful symbolic names can make a program much more readable. Names like LOOPSTART, COUNT, and ERROR carry a good deal of meaning and help people to understand what the code is doing. Memory addresses such as 73, 147, and 2001 do not. A second advantage of symbolic labels is **maintainability.** When we refer to an instruction via a symbolic label rather than an address, we no longer need to modify the address field when instructions are added to or removed from the program. Consider the following example:

```
          JUMP      LOOP
            :       ←point A
LOOP:     LOAD      X
```

Say a new instruction is added to the program at point A. When the modified program is translated into machine language, all instructions following point A are placed in a memory cell whose address is 1 higher than it was before (assuming that each instruction occupies one memory cell). However, the JUMP refers to the LOAD instruction only by the name LOOP, not by the address where it is stored. Therefore, neither the JUMP nor the LOAD instruction needs to be changed. We need only retranslate the modified program. The assembler determines the new address of the LOAD X instruction, makes the label LOOP equivalent to this new address, and places this new address into the address field of the JUMP LOOP instruction. The assembler does all the messy bookkeeping previously done by the machine language programmer. That is the beauty of system software and the virtual machine environment that it creates.

The final advantage of assembly language programming is **data generation.** In Section 4.2.1 we showed how to represent in binary data types such as unsigned and signed integers, floating point values, and characters. When writing in machine language, the programmer must do these conversions. In assembly language, however, the programmer can ask the assembler to do them.

To make this request, we use a special type of assembly language op code called a **pseudo-op.** A pseudo-op (preceded in our notation by a period to indicate its type) does not generate a machine language instruction like other operation codes. Instead, it invokes a service of the assembler. One of these services is generating data in the proper binary representation for this system. There are typically assembly language pseudo-ops to generate integer, character, and (if the hardware supports it) real data values. In our example language, we will limit ourselves to one data generation pseudo-op called .DATA that builds signed integers. This pseudo-op converts the signed decimal integer in the address field to the proper binary representation. For example, the pseudo-op

```
FIVE:     .DATA      +5
```

tells the assembler to generate the binary representation for the integer +5, put it into memory, and make the label "FIVE" equivalent to the address of that cell. If a memory cell contained 16 bits, and the next available memory cell was address 53, then this pseudo-op would produce

address	contents
53	0000000000000101

and the name FIVE would be equivalent to memory address 53. Similarly, the pseudo-op

```
NEGSEVEN: .DATA      -7
```

might produce the following 16-bit quantity, assuming sign/magnitude representation:

address	contents
54	1000000000000111

and the symbol NEGSEVEN would be equivalent to memory address 54.

We can now refer to these data items by their attached label. For example, to load the value +5 into register R, we can say

```
LOAD      FIVE
```

This is equivalent to writing LOAD 53, which would load register R with the contents of memory cell 53—that is, the integer +5. Note that if we had incorrectly said

```
LOAD     5
```

the *contents* of memory cell 5 would be loaded into register R. This is not what we intended, and the program would be wrong. Here is a good example of why it is so important to distinguish between the address of a cell and its contents.

To add the value −7 to the current contents of register R, we would write

```
ADD      NEGSEVEN
```

The contents of R (currently +5) and the contents of address NEGSEVEN (address 54, whose contents are −7) are added together, producing −2. This becomes the new contents of register R.

When generating data values, we must be careful not to place them in memory locations where they could be misinterpreted as instructions. In Chapter 4 we said that the only way a computer can tell that the binary value 01000001 is the letter *A* rather than the decimal value 65 is by the context in which it appears. The same is true for instructions and data. They are indistinguishable from each other, and the only way a Von Neumann machine can determine whether a sequence of 0s and 1s is an instruction or a piece of data is by how we use it. If we attempt to execute a value stored in memory, then that value *becomes* an instruction whether we meant it to be or not.

For example, if we incorrectly write the sequence

```
LOAD     X
.DATA    +1
```

then, after executing the LOAD X command, the processor will fetch, decode, and attempt to execute the "instruction" +1. This may sound meaningless, but to a processor, it is not. The representation of +1, using 16 bits, is

```
0000000000000001
```

Because this value is being used as an instruction, some of the bits will be interpreted as the op code and some as the address field. If we assume a 16-bit, one-address instruction format, with the first 4 bits being the op code and the last 12 bits being the address field, then these 16 bits will be interpreted as follows:

0000	000000000001
op code	*address*

The "op code" is 0, which is a LOAD on our hypothetical machine (see Figure 6.5), and the "address field" contains a 1. Thus, the data value +1 has accidentally turned into the following instruction:

```
LOAD     1          --Load register R with the contents of memory cell 1
```

This is obviously incorrect, but how is the problem solved? The easiest way is to remember to place all data at the end of the program in a section where they cannot possibly be executed. One convenient place that meets this criterion is after a HALT instruction because the HALT prevents any further execution. The data values can be referenced; they just cannot be executed.

1. Assume that register R and memory cells 80 and 81 contain the following values:

   R: 20   memory cell 80: 43   memory cell 81: 97

   Using the instruction set shown in Figure 6.5, determine what value will end up in register R and memory cells 80 and 81 after each of the following instructions is executed. Assume that each question begins with the values shown above.

   a. LOAD 80   d. ADD 81
   b. STORE 81   e. IN 80
   c. COMPARE 80   f. OUT 81

2. Assume that memory cell 50 contains a 4 and label L is equivalent to memory location 50. What value would each of the following LOAD instructions load into register R?

   a. LOAD 50   c. LOAD L
   b. LOAD 4   d. LOAD L+1 (Assume that this is legal.)

A second service provided by pseudo-ops is **program construction.** Pseudo-ops that mark the beginning (.BEGIN) and end (.END) of the assembly language program specify where to start and stop the translation process, and they do not generate any instructions or data. Remember that it is the HALT instruction, not the .END pseudo-op, which terminates execution of the program. The .END pseudo-op ends the translation process. Figure 6.6, which shows the organization of a typical assembly language program, helps explain this distinction.

6.3.2 *Examples of Assembly Language Code*

This section looks at how to use assembly language to translate algorithms into programs that can be executed on a Von Neumann computer. Today, virtually no one does software development in assembly language except for special-purpose tasks; most prefer to use one of the higher-level languages mentioned in Figure 6.3 and described in detail in Chapters 8 and 9. Our pur-

FIGURE 6.6

Structure of a Typical Assembly Language Program

```
.BEGIN      --This must be the first line of the program.
   ⋮        --Assembly language instructions like those in Figure 6.5.
   HALT     --This instruction terminates execution of the program
   ⋮        --Data generation pseudo-ops such as
            --.DATA are placed here, after the HALT.
.END   --This must be the last line of the program.
```

pose in offering these examples is to demonstrate how system software, in this case an assembler, can create a user-oriented virtual environment that supports effective and productive problem solving. The use of symbolic operation codes, symbolic addresses, and convenient data representations makes problem solving a far simpler task than it would be in the naked machine environment described at the beginning of this chapter.

One of the most common operations in any algorithm is the evaluation of arithmetic expressions. For example, the sequential search algorithm of Figure 2.9 contained the following arithmetic operations:

Set the value of i to 1 (line 2).

⋮

Add 1 to the value of i (line 7).

These algorithmic operations can be translated quite easily into assembly language as follows:

```
        LOAD        ONE     --Put a 1 into register R.
        STORE       I       --Store the constant 1 into i.

          ⋮

        INCREMENT I         --Add 1 to memory location i.

          ⋮

I:      .DATA       0       --The index value. Initially it is 0.
ONE:    .DATA       1       --The constant 1.
```

Note how readable this code is, compared to machine language, because of such op code mnemonics as LOAD and STORE and the use of descriptive labels such as I and ONE.

As a second example, here is the assembly language translation of the arithmetic expression $A = B + C - 7$. (Assume that B and C have already been assigned values.)

```
        LOAD        B       --Put the value B into register R.
        ADD         C       --R now holds the sum (B + C).
        SUBTRACT    SEVEN   --R now holds the expression (B + C - 7).
        STORE       A       --Store the result into A.

          ⋮                 --These data should be placed after the HALT.

A:      .DATA       0
B:      .DATA       0
C:      .DATA       0
SEVEN:  .DATA       7       --The constant 7.
```

Another important algorithmic operation involves testing and comparing values. The comparison of values and the subsequent use of the outcome to decide what to do next are termed a **conditional** operation, which we first saw in Section 2.2.3. Here is a conditional that outputs the larger of two values x and y. Algorithmically, it is expressed as follows:

Input the value of x

Input the value of y

If x ≥ y then

    Output the value of x

Else

    Output the value of y

In assembly language, this conditional operation could be translated as follows:

```
            IN        X         --Read the first data value
            IN        Y         --and now the second.
            LOAD      Y         --Load the value of Y into register R.
            COMPARE   X         --Compare X to Y and set the condition codes.
            JUMPLT    PRINTY    --If X is less than Y, jump to PRINTY.
            OUT       X         --We get here only if X ≥ Y, so print X.
            JUMP      DONE      --Skip over the next instruction and continue.
PRINTY:     OUT       Y         --We get here if X < Y, so print Y.
DONE:       :                   --The program continues here.

            :

                                --The following data go after the HALT.
X:          .DATA     0         --Space for the two data values.
Y:          .DATA     0

            :
```

Another important algorithmic primitive is **looping,** which was also introduced in Section 2.2.3. The following algorithmic example contains a while loop that executes 10,000 times.

Step	Operation	Explanation
1	Set i to 0	Start the loop counter at 0.
2	While the value of $i < 10,000$ do lines 3 through 9.	
3–8	:	Here is the loop body that is to be done 10,000 times.
9	Add 1 to the value of i	Increment the loop counter.
10	End of the loop	
11	Stop	

This looping construct is easily translated into assembly language.

```
            LOAD      ZERO      --Initialize the loop counter to 0.
            STORE     I         --This is step 1 of the algorithm.
LOOP:       LOAD      MAXVALUE  --Put 10,000 into register R.
            COMPARE   I         --Compare I against 10,000.
```

	JUMPEQ	DONE	--If $I = 10{,}000$ we are done (step 2).
	:		--Here is the loop body (steps 3–8).
	INCREMENT	I	--Add 1 to I (step 9).
	JUMP	LOOP	--End of the loop body (step 10).
DONE:	HALT		--Stop execution (step 11).
ZERO:	.DATA	0	--This is the constant 0.
I:	.DATA	0	--The loop counter. It goes to 10,000.
MAXVALUE:	.DATA	10000	--Maximum number of loop executions.
	:		

As a final example, we will show a complete assembly language program (including all necessary pseudo-ops) to solve the following problem:

Read in a sequence of non-negative numbers, one number at a time, and compute a running sum. When you encounter a negative number, print out the sum of the non-negative values and stop.

Thus, if the input is

8
31
7
5
−1

then the program should output the value 51, which is the sum (8 + 31 + 7 + 5). An algorithm to solve this problem is shown in Figure 6.7, using the pseudocode notation of Chapter 2. Our next task is to convert the algorithmic primitives of Figure 6.7 into assembly language instructions. A program that does this is shown in Figure 6.8.

Of all the examples in this chapter, the program in Figure 6.8 demonstrates best what is meant by the phrase *user-oriented virtual environment*. Although it is not as clear as natural language or the pseudocode of Figure 6.7, this program can be read and understood by humans as well as computers.

FIGURE 6.7

Algorithm to Compute the Sum of Numbers

STEP	OPERATION
1	Set the value of Sum to 0
2	Input the first number N
3	While N is not negative do
4	Add the value of N to Sum
5	Input the next data value N
6	End of the loop
7	Print out Sum
8	Stop

FIGURE 6.8

Assembly Language Program
to Compute the Sum of
Nonnegative Numbers

```
         .BEGIN                   --This marks the start of the program.
         CLEAR      SUM           --Set the running sum to 0 (line 1).
         IN         N             --Input the first number N (line 2).
--The next three instructions test whether N is a negative number (line 3).
AGAIN:   LOAD       ZERO          --Put 0 into register R.
         COMPARE    N             --Compare N and 0.
         JUMPLT     NEG           --Go to NEG if N < 0.
--We get here if N ≥ 0. We add N to the running sum (line 4).
         LOAD       SUM           --Put SUM into R.
         ADD        N             --Add N. R now holds (N + SUM).
         STORE      SUM           --Put the result back into SUM.
--Get the next input value (line 5).
         IN         N
--Now go back and repeat the loop (line 6).
         JUMP       AGAIN
--We get to this section of the program only when we encounter a negative value.
NEG:     OUT        SUM           --Print the sum (line 7)
         HALT                     --and stop (line 8).
--Here are the data generation pseudo-ops
SUM:     .DATA      0             --The running sum goes here.
N:       .DATA      0             --The input data are placed here.
ZERO:    .DATA      0             --The constant 0.
--Now we mark the end of the entire program.
         .END
```

Tasks such as modifying the program and locating an error are significantly easier on the code of Figure 6.8 than on its machine language equivalent.

The program in Figure 6.8 is an important milestone in that it represents a culmination of the algorithmic problem-solving process. Earlier chapters introduced algorithms and problem solving (Chapters 1, 2, 3), discussed how to build computers to execute algorithms (Chapters 4, 5), and introduced system software that enables us to code algorithms into a language that computers can translate and execute (Chapter 6). The program in Figure 6.8 is the end product of this discussion. That program can be input to an assembler, translated into machine language, loaded into a Von Neumann computer, and exe-

LABORATORY EXPERIENCE 10

This section of Chapter 6 has introduced assembly language instructions and programming techniques. However, as mentioned before, one does not learn programming and problem solving by reading and watching but rather by doing and trying. In this laboratory experience you will be programming in an assembly language that is virtually identical to the one shown in Figure 6.5. You will be able to design and write programs like the one shown in Figure 6.8 and execute them on a simulated Von Neumann computer. You will observe the effect of individual instructions on the functional units of this machine and produce results. This experience should give you a deeper understanding of the concepts of assembly language programming and the Von Neumann architecture.

1. Using the instruction set in Figure 6.5, translate the following algorithmic operations into assembly code. Show all necessary .DATA pseudo-ops.

   a. Add 1 to the value of x
   b. Add 50 to the value of x
   c. Set x to the value y + z − 2
   d. If x > 50 then output the value of x, otherwise input a new value of x

2. Using the instruction set in Figure 6.5, write a complete assembly language program (including all necessary pseudo-ops) that reads in numbers and counts how many inputs it reads until it encounters the first negative value. The program then prints out that count and stops.

   For example, if the input data were 42, 108, 99, 60, 1, 42, 3, −27, then your program would output the value 7 because there are seven nonnegative values before the appearance of the negative value −27.

cuted to produce answers to our problem. This **algorithmic problem-solving cycle** is one of the central themes of computer science.

6.3.3 Translation and Loading

What happens to the assembly language program in Figure 6.8? What must be done so that it can be executed on a processor? Figure 6.4 shows that before our source program can be run, we must invoke two system software packages called an **assembler** and a **loader.**

The job of an **assembler** is to translate a symbolic assembly language program, such as the one in Figure 6.8, into machine language. We usually think of translation as an extremely difficult task. In fact, if two languages differ greatly in vocabulary, grammar, and syntax, it can be quite formidable. (This is why a translator for a high-level programming language is a very complex piece of software.) However, machine language and assembly language are very similar, and an assembler is a relatively simple piece of system software.

An assembler must perform the following four tasks, none of which is particularly difficult.

1. Convert symbolic op codes to binary.
2. Convert symbolic addresses to binary.
3. Perform the assembler services requested by the pseudo-ops.
4. Put the translated instructions into a file for future use.

Let's see how these operations would be carried out using the hypothetical assembly language of Figure 6.5.

The conversion of symbolic op codes such as LOAD, ADD, and SUBTRACT to binary makes use of a structure called the **op code table.** This is an alphabetized list of all legal assembly language op codes and their binary equivalents. An op code table for the instruction set of Figure 6.5 is shown in Figure 6.9. (The table assumes that the op code field is 4 bits wide.)

The assembler looks up the operation code mnemonic in column 1 of the table and, when it has been found, replaces the characters with the 4-bit binary value in column 2. (If the mnemonic is not found, then the user has written an illegal op code, which will result in an error message.) Thus, for example, if we use the mnemonic SUBTRACT in our program, the assembler will convert it to the binary value 0101.

An interesting question is what algorithm to use to look up the op code in the op code table. We could select the sequential search algorithm introduced in Chapter 2 and shown in Figure 2.9. However, if we choose this algorithm, translation of our program may be slowed down significantly. The analysis of the sequential search algorithm in Chapter 3 showed that locating a single item in a list of N items takes, on the average, $N/2$ comparisons if the item is in the table and N comparisons if it is not. In Chapter 5 we stated that modern computers may have as many as 500 machine language instructions in their instruction set, so the size of the op code table of Figure 6.9 could be as large as $N = 500$. This means that using sequential search, we will perform an average of $N/2$, about 250, comparisons for every op code in our program. If our assembly language program contains 10,000 instructions (not an unreasonably large number), the op code translation task will require a total of 10,000 instructions $\times$ 250 comparisons/instruction = 2.5 million comparisons. That is a lot of searching, even for a computer.

We can do much better by realizing that the op code table of Figure 6.9 is sorted alphabetically. This enables us to use the more efficient **binary search** algorithm discussed in Section 3.4.2 and shown in Figure 3.18. On the average, the number of comparisons needed to find an element using binary search is not $N/2$ but $(\log_2 N)$, the logarithm of N to the base 2. [*Note:* $(\log_2 N)$ is the value k such that $2^k = N$.] For a table of size $N = 500$, $N/2$ is 250, whereas $(\log_2 N)$ is approximately 9 ($2^9 = 512$). This says that on the average, we will be able to find an op code in the table in about 9 comparisons rather than 250. If our assembly language program contains 10,000 instructions, then the op code translation task requires only about 10,000 $\times$ 9 = 90,000 comparisons rather than 2.5 million, a reduction of 2,410,000. By

FIGURE 6.9

Structure of the Op Code Table

Operation	Binary Value
ADD	0011
CLEAR	0010
COMPARE	0111
DECREMENT	0110
HALT	1111
⋮	
STORE	0001
SUBTRACT	0101

selecting a better algorithm, we have achieved a speed-up of about 96%, quite a significant reduction!

This example demonstrates why algorithmic analysis, introduced in Chapter 3, is such a critically important part of the design and implementation of system software. The clever replacement of a slow algorithm by a faster one can turn an "insoluble" problem into a solvable one and a worthless solution into a highly worthwhile one. Remember that, in computer science, we are looking not just for correct solutions but for efficient ones as well.

After the op code has been converted into binary, the assembler must perform a similar task on the address field. It must convert the address from a symbolic value, such as X or LOOP, into the correct binary address. This task is more difficult than converting the op code, because the assembler itself must determine the correct numeric value of all symbols used in the label field. There is no "built-in" address conversion table equivalent to the op code table of Figure 6.9.

In assembly language a symbol is defined by appearing in the label field of an instruction or data pseudo-op. Specifically, the symbol is given the value of the address of the instruction to which it is attached. Assemblers usually make two passes over the source code, where a **pass** is defined as the process of examining and processing every assembly language instruction in the program, one instruction at a time. During the **first pass** over the source code, the assembler looks at every instruction, keeping track of the memory address where this instruction will be stored when it is translated and loaded into memory. It does this by knowing where the program begins in memory and knowing how many memory cells are required to store each machine language instruction or piece of data. It also determines whether there is a symbol in the label field of the instruction. If there is, it enters the symbol and the address of this instruction into a special table that it is building called a **symbol table.**

We can see this process more clearly in Figure 6.10(a). The figure assumes that each instruction and data value occupies one memory cell and that the first instruction of the program will be placed into address 0.

The assembler looks at the first instruction in the program, IN X, and determines that when this instruction is translated, it will go into memory cell 0. Because the label LOOP is attached to that instruction, the name LOOP is

FIGURE 6.10

Generation of the Symbol Table

LABEL	CODE		LOCATION COUNTER	SYMBOL TABLE	
				SYMBOL	ADDRESS VALUE
LOOP:	IN	X	0	LOOP	0
	IN	Y	1	DONE	7
	LOAD	X	2	X	9
	COMPARE	Y	3	Y	10
	JUMPGT	DONE	4		
	OUT	X	5		
	JUMP	LOOP	6		
DONE:	OUT	Y	7		
	HALT	8			
X:	.DATA	0	9		
Y:	.DATA	0	10		

(a)   (b) made equivalent to address 0. The assembler enters the (name, value) pair (LOOP, 0) into the symbol table. This process of associating a symbolic name with a physical memory address is called **binding,** and the two primary purposes of the first pass of an assembler are (1) to bind all symbolic names to address values and (2) to enter those bindings into the symbol table. Now, any time the programmer uses the name LOOP in the address field, the assembler can look up that symbol in column 1 of the symbol table and replace it with the address value in column 2, in this case address 0. (If it is not found, the programmer has used an undefined symbol, which will produce an error message.)

The next six instructions of Figure 6.10(a), from IN Y to JUMP LOOP, do not contain labels, so they do not add new entries to the symbol table. However, the assembler must still update the counter it is using to determine the address where each instruction will ultimately be stored. The variable used to determine the address of a given instruction or piece of data is called the **location counter.** The location counter values are shown in the third column of Figure 6.10(a). Using the location counter, the assembler can determine that the address values of the labels DONE, X, and Y are 7, 9, and 10, respectively. It will bind these symbolic names and addresses and enter them in the symbol table, as shown in Figure 6.10(b). When the first pass is done, the assembler will have constructed a symbol table that it can use during pass 2. The algorithm for pass 1 of a typical assembler is shown (using an alternative form of algorithmic notation called a **flowchart**) in Figure 6.11.

During the **second pass,** the assembler translates the source program into machine language. It has the op code table to translate mnemonic op codes to binary, and it has the symbol table to translate symbolic addresses to binary. Therefore, the second pass is relatively simple, involving two table look-ups and the generation of two binary fields. For example, if we assume that our instruction format is a 4-bit op code followed by a single 12-bit address, then given the instruction

SUBTRACT   X

the assembler will

1. Look up SUBTRACT in the op code table of Figure 6.9 and place the 4-bit binary value 0101 in the op code field.
2. Look up the symbol X in the symbol table of Figure 6.10(b) and place the binary address value 0000 0000 1001 (decimal 9) into the address field.

After these two steps, the assembler will have produced the 16-bit instruction

0101 0000 0000 1001

which is the correct machine language equivalent of SUBTRACT X.

When it is done with one instruction, the assembler moves on to the next and translates it in the same fashion. This continues until it sees the pseudo-op .END, which terminates translation.

The other responsibilities of pass 2 are also relatively simple.

- Handle data generation pseudo-ops (only .DATA in our example).
- Produce the object file needed by the loader.

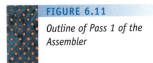

FIGURE 6.11

Outline of Pass 1 of the Assembler

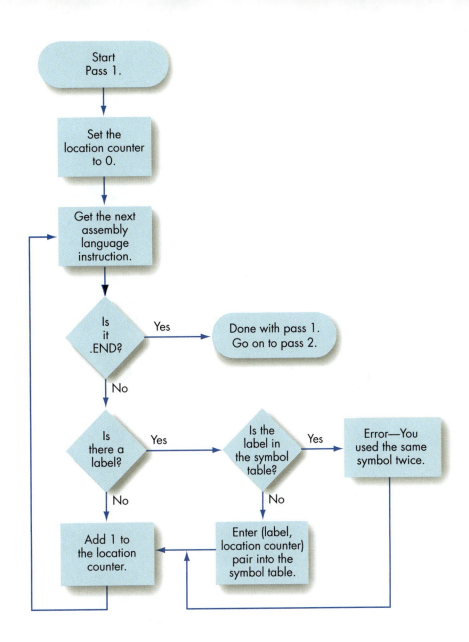

The .DATA pseudo-op asks the assembler to build the proper binary representation for the signed decimal integer in the address field. To do this, the assembler must implement the sign/magnitude integer representation algorithms described in Section 4.2.

Finally, after all the fields of an instruction have been translated into binary, the newly built machine language instruction and the address of where it is to be loaded are written out to a file called the **object file.** (On Windows machines, this is referred to as a .EXE file.) The algorithm for pass 2 of the assembler is shown in Figure 6.12.

After completion of pass 1 and pass 2, the object file contains the translated machine language **object program** referred to in Figure 6.4. One possible object program for the assembly language program of Figure 6.10(a) is shown in Figure 6.13. (Note that a real object file contains only the address and instruction fields. The meaning field is included here for clarity only.)

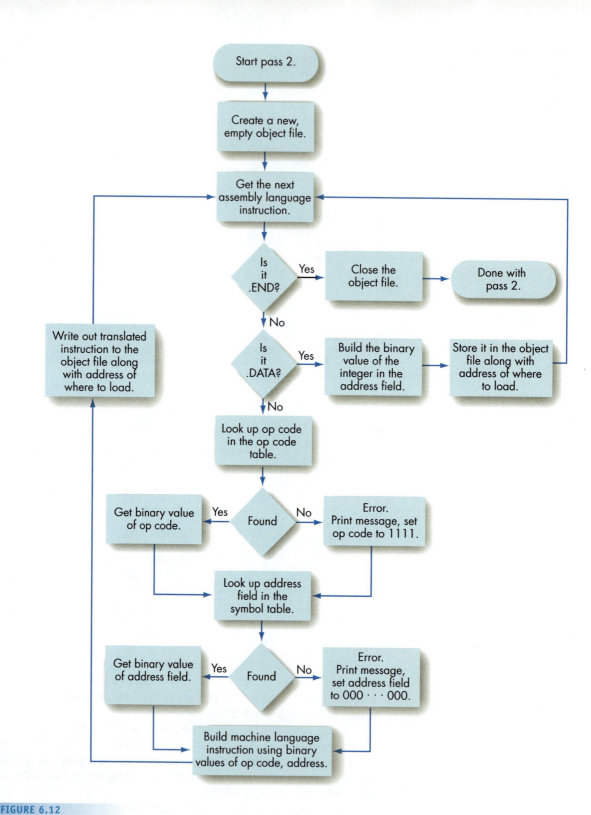

FIGURE 6.12

Outline of Pass 2 of the Assembler

FIGURE 6.13

Example of an Object Program

INSTRUCTION FORMAT: OP CODE   ADDRESS

                               4 bits   12 bits

OBJECT PROGRAM:

Address	Machine Language Instruction	Meaning
0000	1101 000000001001	IN X
0001	1101 000000001010	IN Y
0010	0000 000000001001	LOAD X
0011	0111 000000001010	COMPARE Y
0100	1001 000000000111	JUMPGT DONE
0101	1110 000000001001	OUT X
0110	1000 000000000000	JUMP LOOP
0111	1110 000000001010	OUT Y
1000	1111 000000000000	HALT
1001	0000 000000000000	The constant 0
1010	0000 000000000000	The constant 0

PRACTICE PROBLEMS

1. Translate the following algorithm into assembly language using the instructions in Figure 6.5.

Step	Operation
1	Set *Negative Count* to 0
2	Set *i* to 1
3	While $i \leq 50$ do lines 4 through 6
4	Input a number *N*
5	If $N < 0$ then increment *Negative Count* by 1
6	Increment *i* by 1
7	End of the loop
8	Output the value of *Negative Count*
9	Stop

2. What would be the machine language representation of each of the following instructions? Assume the symbol table values shown in Figure 6.10(b) and the instruction format of Figure 6.13.

   a. COMPARE   Y
   b. JUMPNEQ   DONE
   c. DECREMENT   LOOP

3. What is wrong or inconsistent with the instruction that is shown in Problem 2(c)?

4. Take the assembly language program that you developed in Problem 1 and determine the physical memory address associated with each label in the symbol table. (Assume the first instruction is loaded into address 0 and that each instruction occupies one cell.)

The object program shown in Figure 6.13 would become input to yet another piece of system software called a **loader.** It would be the task of the loader to read instructions from the object file and store them into memory for execution. To do this, it reads an address value—column 1 of Figure 6.13—and a machine language instruction—column 2 of Figure 6.13—and stores that instruction into the specified memory address. This operation is repeated for every instruction in the object file. When loading is complete, the loader places the address of the first instruction (0 in this example) into the program counter (PC) to initiate execution. The hardware, as we learned in Chapter 5, then begins the fetch, decode, and execute cycle starting with the instruction whose address is located in the PC, namely the beginning of this program.

6.4 Operating Systems

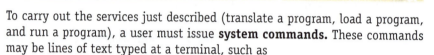

To carry out the services just described (translate a program, load a program, and run a program), a user must issue **system commands.** These commands may be lines of text typed at a terminal, such as

>assemble MyProg (Invoke the assembler to translate a program called MyProg.)

>run MyProg (Load the translated MyProg and start execution.)

or they may be menu items displayed on a screen and selected with a mouse and a button, using a technique called **point-and-click.**

Regardless of how it is done, the important question is what program examines these commands? What piece of system software waits for requests and activates other system programs like a translator or loader to service these requests? The answer is the **operating system,** and, as shown in Figure 6.2, it is the "top-level" system software component on a computer. This section takes a look at the services provided by an operating system and traces how these services have evolved over the last 50 years.

 ### 6.4.1 Functions of an Operating System

An operating system is an enormously large and complex piece of software that has many responsibilities within a computer system. This section examines five of the most important tasks that it performs.

THE USER INTERFACE. The operating system is executing whenever no other piece of user or system software is using the processor. Its most important task is to wait for a user command delivered via the keyboard, mouse, or other input device. If the command is legal, the operating system activates and schedules the appropriate software package to process the request. In this sense, the operating system acts like the computer's *receptionist* and *dispatcher.*

Operating system commands usually request access to hardware resources (processor, printer, communication lines), software services (translator, loader, text editor, application program), or information (data files, date, time). Examples of typical operating system commands are shown in Figure 6.14. Dozens or even hundreds of different commands are available on a modern operating system.

After a command is entered, it is analyzed to see which software package needs to be loaded and put on the schedule for execution. When that package has completed execution, control returns to the operating system, which waits for a user to enter the next command. This **user interface** algorithm is diagrammed in Figure 6.15.

The user interfaces on the operating systems of the 1950s, 1960s, and 1970s were text-oriented. The system would display a **prompt character** on the screen to indicate that it was waiting for input, and then it would wait for something to happen. The user could then enter a command in a special, and sometimes quite complicated, **command language.** For example, on the UNIX operating system, widely used on personal computers and workstations, the following command asks the system to list the names and access privileges of the files contained in the home directory of a user called mike.

> ls -al /usr/mike/home   (">"is the prompt character)

As you can see, commands were not always easy to understand, and learning the command language of the operating system was a major stumbling block for new users. Unfortunately, until you learned some basic commands, no useful work could be done.

Because users found text-oriented command languages very cumbersome, virtually all modern operating systems now include a **graphical user interface,** abbreviated **GUI.** To communicate with a user, a GUI supports visual aids and point-and-click operations entered via a mouse, rather than textual commands. The interface uses **icons, pull-down menus, scrolling windows,** and other visualizations and graphical metaphors that make it much easier for a user to formulate requests.

For example, in Figure 6.16 we see a window listing the folders on the hard disk called mike. One of these is a folder called home. To list all the files contained in this folder, a user points-and-clicks on it, and the list of its files appears in a new window. Compare the clarity of that operation with the preceding UNIX command that does virtually the same thing.

FIGURE 6.14

Some Typical Operating System Commands

- Translate a program
- Run a program
- Save information in a file
- Retrieve a file previously stored
- List all the files for this user
- Print a file on a specified device
- Delete or rename a file
- Copy a file from one I/O device to another
- Let the user set or change a password
- Establish a network connection
- Tell me the current time and date

FIGURE 6.15

User Interface Responsibility of the Operating System

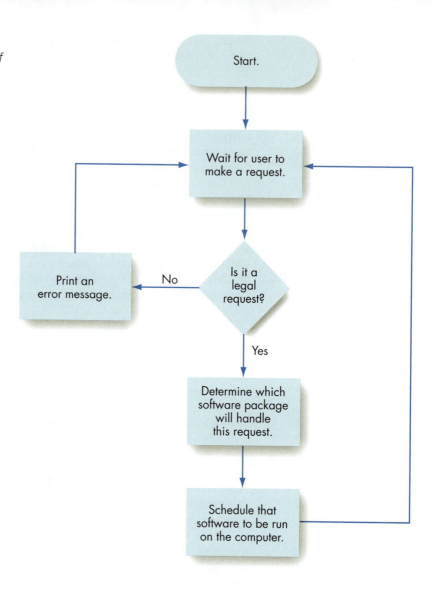

Graphical interfaces are a good example of the high-level virtual machine created by the operating system. A GUI hides a great deal of the underlying hardware and software, and it makes the computer appear very easy to use. In reality, the computer that produces the elegant windowing environment shown in Figure 6.16 is the same Von Neumann machine described in Chapters 4 and 5.

SYSTEM SECURITY AND PROTECTION. In addition to being a receptionist, the operating system also has the responsibilities of a *security guard*—controlling access to the computer and its resources. It must prevent unauthorized users from accessing the system and prevent authorized users from doing unauthorized things.

At a minimum, the operating system must not allow people to access the computer if they have not been granted permission. In the "olden days" of computing (the 1950s and 1960s), security was implemented by physical

FIGURE 6.16

Example of a Graphical User Interface

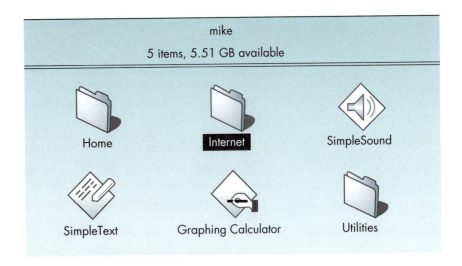

means—putting walls and locked doors around the computer and stationing security guards at the door to prevent unauthorized access. However, when telecommunications networks appeared on the scene in the late 1960s and 1970s (we will discuss them in detail in the following chapter), access to a computer by telephone became possible from virtually anywhere in the world, and responsibility for access control migrated from the guard at the door to the operating system inside the machine.

In most operating systems, access control is handled by requiring a user to enter a legal **user name** and **password** before any other requests are accepted. For example, here is what a user sees when logging on to the central computer at Macalester College:

> ***Welcome to the Macalester College Computing Center.***
> ***Please enter your User Name and Password in the appropriate boxes:***
> *User Name:* [_____]
> *Password:* [_____]

If an incorrect user name or password is entered, the operating system will not allow access to the computer. Similar security measures are implemented on Windows NT, Windows XP, Macintosh, UNIX, and Linux machines.

It is also the operating system's responsibility to safeguard the **password file** that stores all valid user name/password combinations. It must prevent this file from being accessed by any unauthorized users, because that would compromise the security of the entire system. This is analogous to putting a lock on your door but also making sure that you don't lose the key. (Of course, some privileged users, called **superusers,** must be able to access and maintain this file. They are usually computer center employees or system administrators.) To provide this security, the operating system may choose to **encrypt** the password file using an encoding algorithm that is extremely difficult to crack. A thief must steal not only the encrypted text but also the algorithm to change the encrypted text back to the original clear text. Without this information the stolen password file is useless. Operating systems use encryption algorithms whenever they must provide a high degree of security for sensitive information. We will learn more about these encryption algorithms in Chapter 13.

Even when valid users gain access to the system, there are things they should not be allowed to do. The most obvious is that they should access only their own personal information. They should not be able to look at the files or records of other users. Therefore, when the operating system gets a request such as

> open filename (Open up a file and allow this user to access it.)

(Or the user clicks on Open in the File menu.)

it must check to see who is the owner of the file—that is, who created it. If the individual accessing the file is not the owner, then it will usually reject the request. However, most operating systems allow the owner of a file to provide a list of additional authorized users or a general class of authorized users, such as all students or all faculty. Like the password file, these **authorization lists** are highly sensitive files, and an operating system would probably store them in an encrypted format.

Most modern operating systems not only determine whether you are allowed to access a file, they also check what operations you are permitted to do on that file. The following hierarchically ordered list shows the different types of operations that users may be permitted to do on a file:

- Read the information in the file but not change it
- Append new information to the end of the file but not change existing information

A Machine for the Rest of Us

In January 1984, Apple Computer launched its new line of Macintosh computers with a great deal of showmanship: a TV commercial at the 1984 NFL Superbowl Game. The company described the Macintosh as a computer that anyone could understand and use—"a machine for the rest of us." People who saw and used it quickly agreed, and in the early days, its major selling point was that "a Macintosh is much easier to use than an IBM PC." However, the Macintosh and IBM PC were extremely similar in terms of hardware, and they both looked a great deal like the architecture of Figure 5.18. Both systems used Von Neumann-type processors, and these processors executed similar sets of machine language instructions exactly as described in Chapter 5. It certainly was not the underlying hardware that created these huge differences in ease of use.

What made the Macintosh easier to use was its radically new graphical user interface, created by two system software packages called the *Finder* and the *System*. They produced a sophisticated visual environment that most users found much easier to understand than the text-oriented interface of *MS-DOS*, the most popular PC-based operating system of the 1980s and early 1990s. IBM users quickly realized the importance of having a powerful user interface and in the early and mid-1990s began to switch to Microsoft *Windows*, which provided a windowing environment similar to the Macintosh. Newer versions of these systems, such as *Mac OS X*, *Windows NT*, and *Windows XP* all represent attempts at creating an even more powerful and easy to use virtual environment.

We can see now that it was wrong for Apple to say that "a Macintosh is easier to use than a PC." What they should have said is that "the virtual machine environment created by the Macintosh operating system is easier to use than the virtual machine environment created by the IBM PC operating system." However, maybe that was just a little too wordy!

- Change existing information in the file
- Delete the entire file from the system

For example, the grade file GRADES of a student named Smith could have the authorization list shown in Figure 6.17

The authorization list of Figure 6.17 says that Smith, the student whose grades are in the file, has the right to access his or her own file, but only to read the information.

Jones, a clerk in the administration center, can read the file and can append new grades to the end of the file at the completion of the term. Adams, the school's registrar, can read and append information and is also allowed to change the student's grades if an error was made. Doe, the director of the computer center, can do all of these operations as well as delete the file and all its information.

Permission to look at information can be given to a number of people. However, changing information in a file is a sensitive operation (think about changing a payroll file), and permission to make such changes must be limited. Deleting information is the most powerful and potentially damaging operation of all, and its use must be restricted to people at the highest level. It is the operating system's responsibility to help ensure that individuals are authorized to carry out the operation they request.

Unfortunately, today, a large number of programs attempt to supercede these security measures, either for profit or fun. A **virus** is a computer program that was written to intentionally damage computer systems and the information they contain. One of the most common virus types is a program that illegally accesses files and deletes the entire contents of that file, causing the loss of valuable information.

EFFICIENT ALLOCATION OF RESOURCES. Section 5.2.2 described the potentially enormous difference in speed between a processor and an I/O unit: up to 5 orders of magnitude. To handle that difference, we created a hardware device called an I/O controller (Figure 5.9) that frees the processor to do useful work while the I/O operation is being completed. What useful work can a processor do in this free time? What keeps it busy and ensures that this valuable resource is used efficiently? Again, it is the operating system's responsibility to see that the resources of a computer system are used efficiently as well as correctly.

To ensure that a processor does not sit idle if there is useful work to do, the operating system keeps a **queue** (a waiting line) of programs that are ready to run. Whenever the processor is idle, the operating system picks one

FIGURE 6.17

Authorization List for the File GRADES

File: GRADES

NAME	PERMITTED OPERATIONS
Smith	R (R = Read only)
Jones	RA (A = Append)
Adams	RAC (C = Change)
Doe	RACD (D = Delete)

Every new technology develops its own set of "undesirables"—those who see a new technology in terms not of potential benefits but of increased opportunities for misuse, just as automobiles brought wonderful benefits but also car thieves and drunk drivers. In computer science our abusive subculture goes by the name **hackers.**

Originally, the word *hacker* did not have a negative connotation. It was a mildly complimentary term for people who knew how to get things done on a computer—those somewhat strange and quirky individuals who seemed to know all the incomprehensible details about how computers worked, in essence, computer enthusiasts. They were the "tinkerers" and "fixers" who could enter some weird sequence of commands that miraculously cured whatever was wrong with our system.

As computers became more and more important to the functioning of society, and as computer networks increased the number of machines that could be accessed by individuals, the term *hacker* began to take on a different meaning. It became associated with individuals who *abuse* information technology for purposes of profit, revenge, or just plain fun, the computer equivalent of joyriding in a stolen automobile. Hackers are especially fond of figuring out how to override security measures to gain unauthorized access to other computers. Once in the machine, they could make changes to data or steal valuable information. More often than not, they only do such things as browse through files and leave anonymous messages. (Recently, the term **cracker** has been used to indicate someone who intentionally damages a computer system, while the term hacker is limited to its original meaning—a knowledgeable and enthusiastic user of computers.)

Only recently has the legal system begun, through new laws and tougher enforcement, to deal with the issue of information abuse. Just as vandalism is not considered a harmless prank, the misuse of information technology is no longer viewed as the harmless intellectual play of "computer jockeys." It is seen for what it is—a serious crime with serious consequences and very severe penalties. We will examine the legal and ethical issues related to hacking in Chapter 15.

---

of these ready jobs and assigns it to the processor. This guarantees that the processor always has something to do.

To see how this algorithm might work, let's define the following three classes of programs:

Running	The one program currently executing on the processor
Ready	Programs that are loaded in memory and ready to run but are not yet executing
Waiting	Programs that cannot run because they are waiting for an I/O operation (or some other time-consuming event) to complete

Here is how these three lists might look at some instant in time:

Waiting	*Ready*	*Running*
	B	A
	C	
	D	

There are four programs, called A, B, C, and D, in memory. Program A is executing on the processor; B, C, and D are ready to run and are in line waiting their turn. Assume that program A performs the I/O operation "read a sector from the disk." (Maybe it is a word processor, and it needs to get another piece of the document on which you are working.) We saw in Section 5.2.2 that, relative to processing speeds, this operation takes a long time, about 10 msec or so. While it is waiting for this disk I/O operation to complete, the processor has nothing to do, and system efficiency plummets.

To solve this problem, the operating system can do some shuffling. It first moves program A to the waiting list, because it must wait for its I/O operation to finish before it can continue. It then selects one of the ready programs (say B) and assigns it to the processor, which starts executing it. This leads to the following situation:

Waiting	Ready	Running
A	C	B
	D	

Instead of sitting idle while A waits for I/O, the processor works on program B and gets something useful done. Perhaps B also does an I/O operation. The operating system repeats the same steps. It moves B to the waiting list, picks any ready program (say C) and starts executing it, producing the following situation:

Waiting	Ready	Running
A	D	C
B		

As long as there is at least one program that is ready to run, the processor will always have something useful to do.

At some point, the I/O operation that A started will be completed, and the "I/O completed interrupt signal" described in Section 5.2.2 will be generated. The appearance of that signal indicates that program A is now ready to run, but it cannot do so immediately because the processor is currently assigned to C. Instead, the operating system moves A to the ready list, producing the following situation:

Waiting	Ready	Running
B	D	C
	A	

Programs cycle from running to waiting to ready and back to running, each one using only a portion of the resources of the processor.

PRACTICE PROBLEM

Assume that programs spend about 25% of their time waiting for I/O operations to complete. If there are two programs loaded into memory, what is the likelihood that both programs will be blocked waiting for I/O and there will be nothing for the processor to do? What percentage of time will the processor be busy? (This value is called **processor utilization.**) By how much does processor utilization improve if we have four programs in memory instead of two?

In Chapter 5 we stated that the execution of a program was an unbroken repetition of the fetch/decode/execute cycle from the first instruction of the program to the HALT. Now we see that this view may not be completely accurate. For reasons of efficiency, the history of a program may be a sequence of starts and stops—a cycle of execution, waits for I/O operations, waits for the processor, followed again by execution. By having many programs loaded in memory and sharing the processor, the operating system can use the processor to its fullest capability and run the overall system more efficiently.

THE SAFE USE OF RESOURCES. Not only must resources be used *efficiently*, they must also be used *safely*. That doesn't mean an operating system must prevent a user from sticking his or her finger in the power supply and getting electrocuted! It means that it is the job of the operating system to prevent programs or users from attempting operations that could cause the computer system to enter a state where it is incapable of doing any further work—a "frozen" state where all useful work comes to a grinding halt.

To see how this could happen, imagine a computer system that has one laser printer, one data file called D, and two programs A and B. Program A wants to load data file D and print it on the laser printer. Program B wants to do the same thing. Each of them makes the following requests to the operating system:

Program A	*Program B*
Get data file D.	Get the laser printer.
Get the laser printer.	Get data file D.
Print the file.	Print the file.

If the operating system satisfies the first request of each program, then A will "own" data file D and B will have the laser printer. When A now requests ownership of the laser printer, it will be told that the printer is being used by B, and it will have to wait. Similarly, B will be told that it will have to wait for the data file until A is finished with it. Each program will be waiting for a resource to become available that never will become free. This situation is called a **deadlock.** Programs A and B are in a permanent waiting state, and if there is no other program ready to run, all useful work on the system will cease.

More formally, deadlock means that there is a set of programs, each of which is waiting for an event to occur before it may proceed, but that event can be caused only by another waiting program in the set. Everybody is waiting, and nothing happens. As another example of deadlock, imagine a telecommunication system in which program A sends messages to program B, which acknowledges their correct receipt. Program A cannot send another message to B until it knows that the last one has been correctly received.

Program A	*Program B*
Message →	
	← Acknowledge
Message →	
	← Acknowledge
Message →	

At this point, B sends an acknowledgment, but let's say it gets lost. (Perhaps there was static on the line, or a lightning bolt jumbled the signal.) What happens? Program A is stopped, waiting for receipt of an acknowledgment from B. Program B is stopped, waiting for the next message from A. Deadlock! Neither side can proceed, and unless something is done, all communication between the two will cease.

How does an operating system solve these problems and handle deadlock conditions? There are two basic approaches, called **deadlock prevention** and **deadlock recovery.** In deadlock prevention, the operating system uses resource allocation algorithms that prevent deadlock from occurring in the first place. In the example of the two programs simultaneously requesting the laser printer and the data file, the problem was caused by the fact that each program had a portion of the resources needed to solve its problem, but neither had all that it had requested. To prevent this, the operating system could use the following algorithm:

> *If a program cannot get all the resources that it needs, it must give up all the resources it currently owns and issue a completely new request.*

Essentially, this resource allocation algorithm says, If you cannot get everything you need, then you get nothing. If we had used this algorithm, then after program A acquired the laser printer but not the data file, it would have had to relinquish ownership of the printer. Now B could get everything it needed to execute, and no deadlock would occur. (It could also work in the reverse direction, with B relinquishing ownership of the data file and A getting the needed resources. Which scenario unfolds depends on the exact order in which requests are made.)

In the telecommunications example, one possible deadlock prevention algorithm is to insist that messages and acknowledgments never get garbled or lost. Unfortunately, that is impossible. Real-world communication systems (telephone, microwave, satellite) do make errors, so we are powerless to guarantee that deadlock conditions can never occur. Instead we must detect them and recover from them when they do occur. This is typical of the class of methods called **deadlock recovery algorithms.**

For example, here is a possible algorithmic solution to our telecommunications problem:

> *Sender:* Number your messages with the nonnegative integers 0, 1, 2, . . . and send them in numerical order. If you send message number i and have not received an acknowledgment for 30 seconds, send message i again.

> *Receiver:* When you send an acknowledgment, include the number of the message you received. If you get a duplicate copy of message i, send another acknowledgment and discard the duplicate.

Using this algorithm, here is what might happen:

Program A	Program B
Message (1) →	
	← Acknowledge (1)
Message (2) →	
	← Acknowledge (2)
	(Assume this acknowledgment is lost.)

At this point we have exactly the same deadlock condition described earlier. However, this time we are able to recover in a relatively short period. For 30 seconds nothing happens. However, after 30 seconds A sends message (2) a second time. B acknowledges it and discards it (because it already has a copy), and communication continues:

```
(Wait 30 seconds.)
Message (2) →        (Discard this duplicate copy but acknowledge)
                     ← Acknowledge (2)
Message (3) →
```

We have successfully recovered from the error, and the system is again up and running.

Regardless of whether we prevent deadlocks from occurring or recover from those that do occur, it is the responsibility of the operating system to create a virtual machine in which the user never sees deadlocks and does not worry about them. The operating system should create the illusion of a smoothly functioning, highly efficient, error-free environment—even if, as we know from our glimpse behind the scenes, that is not always the case.

SUMMARY. In this section we have highlighted some of the major responsibilities of the critically important software package called the operating system:

- User interface management (a receptionist)
- Program scheduling and activation (a dispatcher)
- Control of access to system and files (a security guard)
- Efficient resource allocation (an efficiency expert)
- Deadlock detection and error detection (a traffic officer)

The Open Source Movement

The design and development of an operating system like Windows XP or Mac OS X is an enormous undertaking that can take thousands of person-years to complete. Furthermore, the likelihood of getting everything correct is quite small. (We have all had the experience of being frustrated by the freezes, errors, and crashes of our operating system.) One of the ways that people are attempting to address this issue is via the *Open Source Movement*. This is a worldwide movement of people who feel that the best way to develop efficient and bug-free software is to enlist the cooperation of interested, skilled, and altruistic programmers who are willing to work for free. They are inspired simply by the goals of producing high-quality software and of working cooperatively with similarly minded individu-

als. The software is distributed to anyone who wants to use it. Furthermore, that person is allowed to modify it, improve it, and change it. This is quite different from the proprietary approach to software development within a corporation such as IBM or Microsoft. In this environment, the development process is kept secret, and the source code is not shared with anyone else.

Essentially, the Open Source Movement encourages contributions to the development process from anyone in the world, the idea being that the more open the process and the more eyes examining the code, the more likely it is that errors or invalid assumptions will be located and corrected. Both the LINUX operating system and the Apache Web server package were developed using the open source model.

These are by no means the operating system's only responsibilities, which can also include such areas as input/output processing, allocating priorities to programs, swapping programs in and out of memory, recovering from power failures, managing the system clock, and literally dozens of other tasks, large and small, essential to keeping the computer system running smoothly.

As you can imagine, given all these responsibilities, an operating system is an extraordinarily complex piece of software. An operating system for a large network of computers can require millions of lines of code, take thousands of person-years to develop, and cost as much to develop as the hardware on which it runs. Even operating systems for personal computers and workstations (e.g., Windows-XP, LINUX, Mac OS X) are huge programs developed over periods of years by teams of dozens of computer scientists. Designing and creating a high-level virtual environment is a difficult job, but without it, computers would not be so widely used nor anywhere near as important as they are today.

 ### 6.4.2 *Historical Overview of Operating Systems Development*

Like the hardware on which it runs, system software has gone through a number of changes, or generations, since the earliest days of computing. The functions and capabilities of a modern operating system described in the previous section did not appear all at once but evolved over many years.

During the **first generation** of system software (roughly 1945–1955, but again these dates are only approximate), there really were no operating systems and there was very little software support of any kind—typically just the assemblers and loaders described in Section 6.3. All machine operation was "hands-on." Programmers would sign up for a block of time and, at the appointed time, show up in the machine room carrying their programs or punched cards or tapes. They had the entire computer to themselves, and they were responsible for all machine operation. They loaded their assembly language programs into memory along with the assembler and, by punching some buttons on the console, started the translation process. Next they loaded their program into memory and started it running. Working with first-generation software was a lot like working on the naked machine described at the beginning of the chapter. It was attempted only by highly trained professionals intimately familiar with the computer and its operation.

System administrators quickly realized that this was a horribly inefficient way to use an expensive piece of equipment. (Remember that these early computers cost millions of dollars.) A programmer would sign up for an hour of computer time, but the majority of that time was spent analyzing results and trying to figure out what to do next. During this "thinking time," the system was idle and doing nothing of value. Eventually, the need to keep machines busy led to the development of a **second generation** of system software called **batch operating systems** (1955–1965).

In second-generation batch operating systems, rather than operate the machine herself, a programmer would hand the program, typically entered on punched cards, to a trained computer operator, who grouped it into a "batch"—hence the name. After a few dozen programs were collected, the operator would carry this batch of cards to a small I/O computer that would put these programs

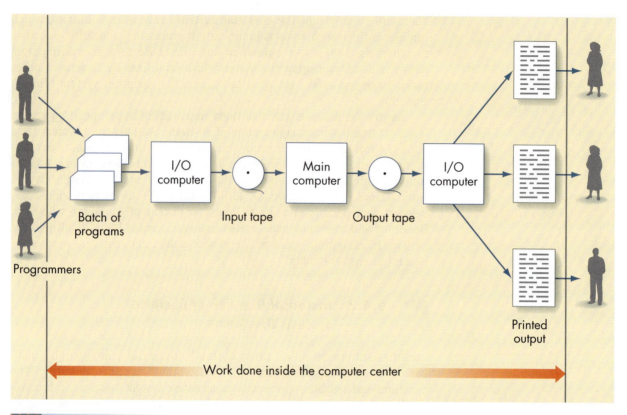

Work done inside the computer center

FIGURE 6.18

Operation of a Batch Computer System

on tape. This tape would be carried into the machine room and loaded onto the "big" computer that would actually run the users' programs, one at a time, writing the results to yet another tape. During the last stage, this output tape would be carried back to the I/O computer to be printed and handed to the programmer. The entire cycle is diagrammed in Figure 6.18.

This cycle may seem cumbersome and, from the programmer's point of view, it was. (Every programmer who worked in the late 1950s or early 1960s has horror stories about waiting many hours—even days—for a program to be returned, only to discover that there was a missing comma.) From the computer's point of view, however, this new batch system worked wonderfully, and system utilization increased dramatically. No longer were there delays while a programmer was setting up to perform an operation. There were no long periods of idleness while someone was mulling over what to do next. As soon as one job was either completed normally or halted because of an error, the computer went to the input tape, loaded the next job, and started execution. As long as there was work to be done, the computer was kept busy.

Because programmers no longer operated the machine, they needed a way to communicate to the operating system what had to be done, and these early batch operating systems were the first to include a **command language,** also called a **job control language.** This was a special-purpose language in which users wrote commands specifying to the operating system (or the human operator) what operations to perform on their programs. These commands were interpreted by the operating system, which initiated the proper action. The

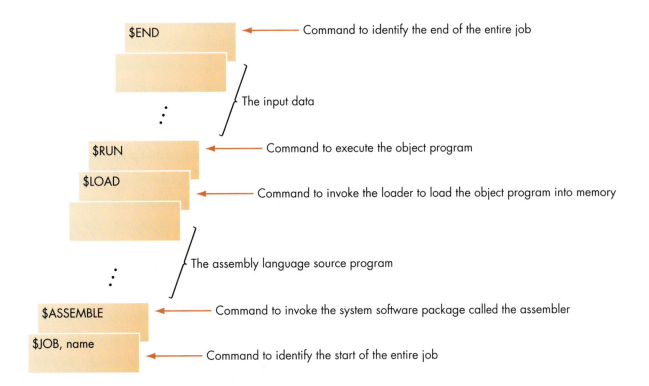

$END   ◄——— Command to identify the end of the entire job

⋮   The input data

$RUN   ◄——— Command to execute the object program

$LOAD   ◄——— Command to invoke the loader to load the object program into memory

⋮   The assembly language source program

$ASSEMBLE   ◄——— Command to invoke the system software package called the assembler

$JOB, name   ◄——— Command to identify the start of the entire job

FIGURE 6.19

Structure of a Typical Batch Job

"receptionist/dispatcher" responsibility of the operating system had been born. A typical batch job was a mix of programs, data, and commands, as shown in Figure 6.19.

By the mid-1960s, the use of integrated circuits and other new technologies had boosted computational speeds enormously. The batch operating system just described kept only a single program in memory at any one time. If that job paused for a few milliseconds to complete an I/O operation (such as read a disk sector or print a file on the printer), the processor simply waited. As computers became faster, designers began to look for ways to use those idle milliseconds. The answer they came up with led to a **third generation** of operating systems called **multiprogrammed operating systems** (1965–1985).

In a multiprogrammed operating system, there are many user programs simultaneously loaded into memory, rather than just one:

Memory
Operating System
Program 1
Program 2
Program 3

If the currently executing program pauses for I/O, one of the other ready jobs is selected for execution so that no time is wasted. As we described earlier, this cycle of running/waiting/ready states led to significantly higher processor utilization.

In order to make this all work properly, the operating system had the new responsibility of protecting user programs (and itself) from damage by other programs. When there was a single program in memory, the only user program that could be damaged was your own. Now, with many programs in memory, an erroneous instruction in one user's program could play havoc with any of the others. For example, the seemingly harmless instruction

STORE 1000   --Store the contents of register R into memory cell 1000.

should not be executed if the physical address 1000 is not located within this user's program. It could wipe out an instruction or piece of data in someone else's program, causing unexpected behavior and (probably) incorrect results.

These third-generation operating systems would keep track of the upper and lower address bounds of each program in memory:

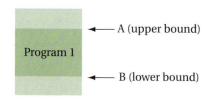

and insure that no program ever attempted a memory reference outside this range. If it did, then the system would cease execution of that program, produce an error message, remove that program from memory, and begin work on another ready program.

Similarly, the operating system could no longer permit any program to execute a HALT instruction, because that would shut down the processor and prevent it from finishing any other program currently in memory. These third-generation systems developed the concept of **user operation codes** that could be included in any user program and **privileged operation codes** whose use was restricted to the operating system or other system software. The HALT instruction became a privileged op code that could be executed only by a system program, not by a user program.

These multiprogrammed operating systems were the first to have extensive protection and error detection capabilities, and the "traffic officer" responsibility began to take on much greater importance than in earlier systems.

During the 1960s and 1970s, computer networks and telecommunications systems developed and grew rapidly. (We will discuss these concepts in great detail in the next chapter.) Another form of third-generation operating system evolved to take advantage of this new technology. It was called a **time-sharing** system, and it is a variation of the multiprogrammed operating system just described.

As before, many programs can be stored in memory rather than just one. However, instead of requiring the programmer to load all system commands, programs, and data in advance, a time-sharing system allows them to be entered **online**—that is, entered dynamically by users sitting at terminals

FIGURE 6.20

*Configuration of a Time-Shared
Computing System*

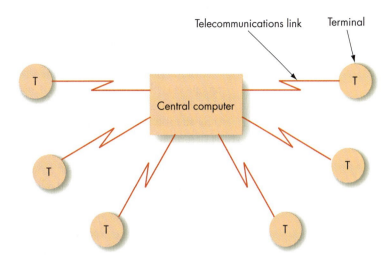

and communicating interactively with the operating system. This configuration is shown in Figure 6.20.

The terminals are connected to the central computer via communication links and can be located anywhere. This new system design freed users from the "tyranny of geography." No longer did they have to go to the computer to hand in their deck of cards; the services of the computer were delivered directly to them via their terminal. However, now that the walls and doors of the computer center no longer provided security and access control, the "security guard/watchman" responsibility became an extremely important part of operating system design.

In a time-sharing system, a user would sit down at a terminal, log in, and initiate a program or make a request by entering a command:

>run MyJob

In this example, the program called MyJob would be loaded into memory and would compete for the processor with all other ready programs. When the program was finished running, the system would again display a prompt (">") and wait for the next command. The user could examine the results of the last program, think for a while, and decide what to do next, rather than having to determine the entire sequence of operations in advance. For example, say there was a mistake in the program and we want to correct it using a text editor. We can enter the command

>edit MyJob

which will load the text editor into memory, schedule it for execution, and cause the file system to load the file called MyJob.

However, one minor change was needed to make this new system work efficiently. In a "true" multiprogrammed environment, the only event, other than termination, that causes a program to be **suspended** (taken off the processor) is the execution of a slow I/O operation. What if the program currently executing is heavily **compute-bound**? That is, it does mostly computation and little or no I/O (for example, computing the value of π to a million decimal places).

It could run for minutes or even hours before it is suspended and the processor is given to another program. During that time, all other programs would have to sit patiently in the ready queue, waiting their turn. This is analogous to being in line at a bank behind someone depositing thousands of checks.

In a noninteractive environment this situation may be acceptable because no one is sitting at a terminal waiting for output. In fact, it may even be desirable, because a compute-bound job keeps the processor heavily utilized. In a time-sharing system, however, this waiting would be disastrous. There *are* users sitting at terminals communicating directly with the system and expecting an immediate response. If they do not get some type of response soon after entering a command, they may start banging on the keyboard and, eventually, hang up the phone. (Isn't that what you would do if the party at the other end of a telephone did not respond for several minutes?)

Therefore, to design a time-sharing system, we must make the following change to the multiprogrammed operating system described earlier. A program can keep the processor until *either* of the following two events occurs:

- It initiates an I/O operation.
- It has run for a maximum length of time, called a **time slice.**

Typically, this time slice is on the order of about a tenth of a second. This may seem like a minuscule amount of time, but it isn't. As we saw in Chapter 5, a typical time to fetch and execute a machine language instruction is about 2 nsec. Thus, in the 0.1-second time slice allocated to a program, a modern processor could execute roughly 50 million machine language instructions.

The basic idea in a time-sharing system is to service many users in a circular, round-robin fashion, giving each user a small amount of time and then moving on to the next. If there are not too many users on the system, the processor can get back to a user before he or she even notices any delay. For example, if there are five users on a system and each one gets a time slice of 0.1 second, a user will wait no more than 0.5 second for a response to a command. This delay would hardly be noticed. However, if 40 or 50 users were actively working on the system, they might begin to notice a 4- or 5-second delay and become irritated. (This would be an example of the "virtual environment" created by the operating system *not* being helpful and supportive!) The number of simultaneous users that can be serviced by a time-sharing system depends on (1) the speed of the processor, (2) the time slice given to each user, and (3) the type of operation each user is doing (i.e., how many use the full time slice, and how many stop before that).

Time sharing was the dominant form of operating system during the 1970s and 1980s, and time-sharing terminals sprouted throughout government offices, businesses, and campuses.

The early 1980s saw the appearance of the first personal computers, and in many business and academic environments the "dumb" terminal began to be replaced by these newer PCs. Initially, the PC was viewed as simply another type of terminal, and during its early days it was used primarily to access a central time-sharing system. However, as PCs became faster and more powerful, people soon realized that much of the computing being done on the centralized machine could be done much more conveniently and at far less cost by the microcomputers sitting on their desktops.

During the late 1980s and the 1990s computing rapidly changed from the centralized environment typical of batch, multiprogramming, and timesharing systems to a **distributed environment** in which much of the computing was done remotely in the office, laboratory, classroom, and factory. Computing moved from the computer center out to where the real work was actually being done. Initially, the operating systems available for early personal computers were simple **single-user operating systems** that gave one user total access to the entire system. Because personal computers were so cheap, there was really no need for many users to share their resources, and the time-sharing and multiprogramming designs of the third generation became less important.

Although personal computers were relatively cheap (and were becoming cheaper all the time), many of the peripherals and supporting gear—laser printers, large disk drives, tape back-up units, and specialized software packages—were not. In addition, electronic mail was growing in importance, and standalone PCs were unable to communicate easily with other users and partake in this important new application. The personal computer era required a new approach to operating system design. It needed a virtual environment that supported both *local computation* and *remote access* to other users and shared resources.

This led to the development of a **fourth-generation** operating system called a **network operating system** (1985–present). A network operating system manages not only the resources of a single computer but also the capabilities of a telecommunications system called a **local area network,** or **LAN** for short. (We will take a much closer look at these types of networks in the next chapter.) A LAN is a network that is located in a geographically contiguous area such as a room, a building, or a campus. It is composed of personal computers, workstations, and special shared resources called **servers,** all interconnected via a high-speed link made of **coaxial** or **fiber-optic cable.** A typical LAN configuration is shown in Figure 6.21.

The users of the individual computers in Figure 6.21, called **clients,** can perform local computations, oblivious to the existence of the network. In this mode, the operating system provides exactly the same services described earlier: loading and executing programs and managing the resources of this one machine.

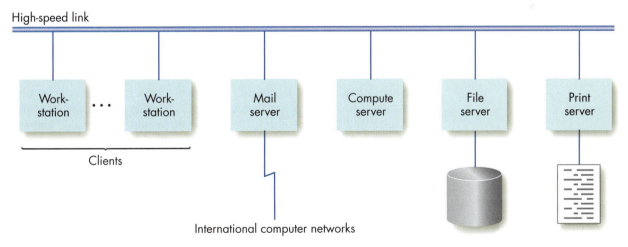

FIGURE 6.21

A Local Area Network

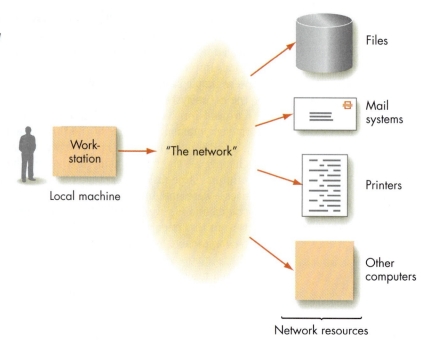

Network resources

However, a user can also access any one of the shared network resources just as though it were local. These resources are provided by a computer called a *server* and could include a special high-quality color printer, a shared file system, or access to an international computer network. The system software will do all the work needed to access that resource, hiding the details of communication and competition for this shared resource with other nodes. These technical issues are of no concern to the network user who is working in a high-level virtual environment.

Network operating systems create a virtual machine that extends beyond the boundaries of the local system on which the user is working. They let us see a huge pool of resources—computers, servers, users—all accessible exactly as though they were connected to our own computer. These fourth-generation virtual environments, exemplified by modern operating systems such as Windows NT, Windows XP, Mac OS X, and LINUX, is diagrammed in Figure 6.22.

One important variation of the network operating system is called a **real-time operating system.** During the 1980s and 1990s, computers got smaller and smaller, and it became common to place them inside other pieces of equipment to control their operation. These types of computers are called **embedded systems;** examples include computers placed inside automobile engines, microwave ovens, thermostats, assembly lines, airplanes, and watches.

For example, a Boeing 777 jet plane contains hundreds of embedded computer systems inside its engines, braking system, wings, landing gear, and cabin. The central computer controlling the overall operation of the airplane is connected by LAN to these embedded computers that are monitoring system functions and sending status information. Now imagine that the central computer receives two requests. The first request is from a cabin monitoring system, which says that it is too cool in the cabin and that it wants the central system to raise the temperature a little for passenger comfort. The second message says that another plane is approaching on the same flight path, and there is about to be a mid-air collision. It would like the central computer to take evasive action. Which request should be serviced next? Of course, the collision detection message, even though it arrived second. In all the operating systems described, we have implied that the system satisfies requests for services and resources in the order received. In some systems, however, certain requests are much more important than others, and when these important requests arrive, we must drop everything else to service them. Other examples include the need to attend immediately to a chemical reaction that is overheating and about to explode and the need for a microwave oven to shut off exactly when it is supposed to.

A real-time operating system manages the resources of embedded computers that are controlling ongoing physical processes and that have requests that must be serviced within fixed time constraints. This type of operating system guarantees that it can service these important requests within that fixed amount of time. For example, it may guarantee that, regardless of what else it is currently doing, if a collision detection message arrives, the software to implement collision avoidance will be activated and executed within 50 milliseconds. The way that this is typically done is that all requests to a real-time operating system are **prioritized.** Instead of being handled in first-come, first-served order, they are handled in priority sequence, from most important to least important, where "importance" is defined in terms of the time-critical nature of the request. A real-time operating system lets passengers be uncomfortably cool for a few more seconds while it handles the problem of avoiding a crash.

 ### 6.4.3 *The Future*

The discussions in this chapter have shown that, just as there have been huge changes in hardware over the last 50 years, there have been equally huge changes in system software during the same period. We have progressed from a first-generation environment in which a user personally managed the computing hardware, using a complicated text-oriented command language, to current fourth-generation systems in which users can request services from anywhere in a network, using enormously powerful and easy-to-use graphical user interfaces.

And just as hardware capabilities are continuing to improve, there is also no reason to believe that the evolution of system software has ended. On the contrary, there is a good deal of computer science research directed at further improvements in the high-level virtual environment created by a modern fourth-generation operating system, and a fifth-generation operating system is certainly not far off.

These next generation systems will have even more powerful user interfaces that incorporate not only text and graphics but photography, touch, sound, fax, video, and TV as well. These **multimedia user interfaces** will interact with users and solicit requests in a variety of ways. Instead of point-and-click, a fifth generation system might allow you to speak the command, "Please display my meeting schedule for May 6." The visual display may include separate windows for a verbal reminder about an important event and a digitally encoded photograph of the person with whom you are meeting. Just as text-only systems are now viewed as outmoded, today's text and graphics system may be viewed as too limiting for high-quality user/system interaction.

A fifth-generation operating system will typically be a **parallel processing operating system** that can efficiently manage computer systems containing tens, hundreds, or even thousands of processors. Users do not want to be bothered with knowing the technical details of MIMD or SIMD parallel processing described in Chapter 5. They simply want their programs to run faster; how that is accomplished is the task of the system, not the user. The operating system will need to recognize opportunities for parallel execution, send the separate tasks to the appropriate processor, and coordinate their concurrent execution, all in a transparent way. On this virtual machine, a user would be unaware that multiple processors even existed, except for the fact that programs run 10, 100, or 1,000 times faster. Without this type of software support, a massively parallel system would be a "naked parallel processor" just as difficult to work with as the "naked machine" discussed at the beginning of this chapter.

Finally, new fifth-generation operating systems will create a truly **distributed computing environment** in which users do not need to know about the location of a given resource within the network. In current network operating systems, the details of how the communication is done are hidden, but not the existence of separate nodes in the network (see Figure 6.22). The user is aware that a network exists and must specify the network node where the work is to be done. In a typical fourth-generation network operating system, a user issues the following types of commands:

- Access file F on file server S and copy it to my local system.
- Run program P on machine M.
- Save file F on file server T.
- Print file F on print server Q.

Compare these commands with how the manager of a business gives instructions to an assistant: "Get this job done. I don't care how or where. Just do it, and when you are done, give me the results." The details of how and where to get the job done are left to the underling. The manager does not want to be bothered with those details and is concerned only with results.

In a truly **distributed operating system,** the user is the manager and the operating system the assistant, and the user does not care where or how the system satisfies a request as long as it gets done correctly. The users of a distributed system would not see a network of distinct sites or "local" and "remote" nodes. Instead, they would see a single logical system that provides resources and services. The individual nodes and the boundaries between them would no longer be visible to the user, who would think only in terms of *what* must be done, not *where* it will be done or *which* node will do it. This situation is diagrammed in Figure 6.23.

Now the very existence of both a telecommunication system and separate computer systems is hidden from view. In a distributed operating system, the commands shown earlier might be expressed as follows:

- Access file F wherever it is located.
- Run program P on any machine currently available.
- Save file F wherever there is sufficient room.
- Print file F on any laser printer with 400 dpi resolution that is not in use.

This is certainly the highest and most powerful virtual environment we have yet described, and an operating system that could create such an environ-

FIGURE 6.23

Structure of a Distributed
System

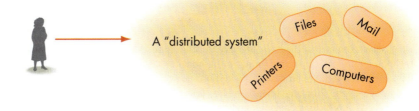

ment would significantly enhance the productivity of all its users. These "fifth-generation dashboards" would make using the most powerful and most complex computer system as easy as driving a car—perhaps even easier. Surfing the Web can give us a good indication of what it will be like to work on a distributed system. When we click on a link we have no idea at all where that information is located and, moreover, we don't care. We simply want that page to appear on our screen. To us, the Web behaves like one giant logical system.

Figure 6.24 summarizes the historical evolution of operating systems, much as Figure 1.8 summarized the historical development of computer hardware.

FIGURE 6.24

Some of the Major Advances in Operating Systems Development

GENERATION	APPROXIMATE DATES	MAJOR ADVANCES
First	1945–1955	No operating system available Programmers operated the machine themselves
Second	1955–1965	Batch operating systems Improved system utilization Development of the first command language
Third	1965–1985	Multiprogrammed operating systems Time-sharing operating systems Increasing concern for protecting programs from damage by other programs Creation of privileged instructions and user instructions Interactive use of computers Increasing concern for security and access control First personal computer operating systems
Fourth	1985–present	Network operating systems Client-server computing Remote access to resources Graphical user interfaces Real-time operating systems Embedded systems
Fifth	??	Multimedia user interfaces Massively parallel operating systems Distributed computing environments

1. What serves the role of the user interface in other high-technology devices commonly found in the home or office, such as a VCR, stereo system, television, copier, or microwave oven? Pick one specific device and discuss how well its interface is designed and how easy it is to use. Does the device use techniques of computer system interfaces, such as menus and icons?

2. Can you think of situations where you might *want* to see the underlying hardware of the computer system? That is, you want to interact with the actual machine, not the virtual machine. How could you accomplish this? (Essentially, how could you bypass the operating system?)

3. Assume that you write a letter in English and have a friend translate it into Spanish. In this scenario, what is equivalent to the source program of Figure 6.4? The object program? The assembler?

4. Assume that memory cells 60 and 61 and register R currently have the following values:

   > Register R: 13
   >
   > 60: 472
   >
   > 61: −1

   Using the instruction set in Figure 6.5, what will be in register R and memory cells 60 and 61 after completion of each of the following operations? Assume that each instruction starts from the above conditions.

a. LOAD 60	d. COMPARE 61
b. STORE 60	e. IN 61 (Assume that the user enters a 50.)
c. ADD 60	f. OUT 61

5. Assume that memory cell 79 contains the value +6. In addition, the symbol Z is equivalent to memory location 79. What would be placed in register R by each of the following load commands?

a. LOAD 79	c. LOAD Z
b. LOAD 6	d. LOAD Z + 1 (Assume that this is allowed.)

6. Say we accidentally execute the following piece of data:

   > .DATA 16387

   Describe exactly what would happen. Assume that the format of machine language instructions on this system is the same format shown in Figure 6.13.

7. What is the assembly language equivalent of each of the following binary machine language instructions? Assume the format described in Figure 6.13 and the numeric op code values shown in Figure 6.5.

   a. 0101001100001100

   b. 0011000000000111

8. Is the following data generation pseudo-op legal or illegal? Why?

   > THREE: .DATA 2

9. Using the instruction set shown in Figure 6.5, translate the following algorithmic primitives into assembly language code. Show all necessary .DATA pseudo-ops.

   a. Add 3 to the value of K

   b. Set K to $(L + 1) - (M + N)$

   c. If $K > 10$ then output the value of K

   d. If $(K > L)$ then output the value of K and increment K by 1

   otherwise output the value of L and increment L by 1

   e. Set K to 1

   Repeat the next two lines until $K > 100$

   Output the value of K

   Increment K by 1

   End of the loop

10. What, if anything, is the difference between the following two sets of instructions?

LOAD X	INCREMENT X
ADD TWO	INCREMENT X
.	
.	
.	
TWO: .DATA 2	

11. Look at the assembly language program in Figure 6.8. Is the statement CLEAR SUM on line 2 necessary? Why or why not? Is the statement LOAD ZERO on line 4 necessary? Why or why not?

12. Modify the program in Figure 6.8 so that it separately computes and prints the sum of all positive numbers and all negative numbers and stops when it sees the value 0. For example, given the input

    > 12, −2, 14, 1, −7, 0

your program should output the two values 27 (the sum of the three positive values 12, 14, and 1) and −9 (the sum of the two negative numbers −2 and −7) and then halt.

13. Write a complete assembly language program (including all necessary pseudo-ops) that reads in a series of integers, one at a time, and outputs the largest and smallest values. The input will consist of a list of integer values containing exactly 100 numbers.

14. Assume that we are using the 16 distinct op codes in Figure 6.5. If we write an assembly language program that contains 100 instructions and our processor can do about 50,000 comparisons per second, what is the maximum time spent doing operation code translation using:

a. Sequential search (Figure 2.9)

b. Binary search (Figure 3.19).

In this case, which one of these two algorithms would you recommend using? Would your conclusions be significantly different if we were programming in an assembly language with 300 op codes rather than 16? If our program contained 50,000 instructions rather than 100?

15. What value will be entered in the symbol table for the symbols AGAIN, ANS, X, and ONE in the following program? (Assume that the program is loaded beginning with memory location 0.)

```
        .BEGIN
        --Here is the program.
        IN          X
        LOAD        X
AGAIN:  ADD         ANS
        SUBTRACT    ONE
        STORE       ANS
        OUT         ANS
        JUMP        AGAIN
        --Here are the data.
ANS:    .DATA       0
X:      .DATA       0
ONE:    .DATA       1
        .END
```

16. Look at the assembly language program in Figure 6.8. Determine the physical memory address associated with every label in the symbol table. (Assume that the program is loaded beginning with memory location 0.)

17. Is the following pair of statements legal or illegal? Explain why.

```
LABEL:  .DATA    3
LABEL:  .DATA    4
```

If it is illegal, will the error be detected during pass 1 or pass 2 of the assembly process?

18. What are some drawbacks in using passwords to limit access to a computer system? Describe some other possible ways for an operating system to limit access. In what type of application might these alternative safeguards be appropriate?

19. Why are authorization lists so sensitive that they must be encrypted and protected from unauthorized change? What kind of damage is possible if these files are modified in unexpected or unplanned ways?

20. Assume that any individual program spends about 50% of its time waiting for I/O operations to be completed. What percentage of time is the processor doing useful work (called **processor utilization**) if there are three programs loaded into memory? How many programs should we keep in memory if we want processor utilization to be at least 95%?

21. Here is an algorithm for calling a friend on the telephone:

Step	Operation
1.	Dial the phone and wait for either an answer or a busy signal
2.	If the line is not busy then do steps 3 and 4
3.	Talk as long as you want
4.	Hang up the phone, you are done
5.	Otherwise (the line is busy)
6.	Wait exactly 1 minute
7.	Go back to step 1 and try again

During execution this algorithm could get into a situation where, as in the deadlock problem, no useful work can ever get done. Describe the problem, explain why it occurs, and suggest how it could be solved.

22. Explain why a batch operating system would be totally inadequate to handle such modern applications as airline reservations and automatic teller machines.

23. In a time-sharing operating system, why is system performance so sensitive to the value that is selected for the time slice? Explain what type of system behavior we would be likely to observe if the value selected for the time slice were too large? Too small?

24. As hardware (processor/memory) costs became significantly cheaper during the 1980s and 1990s, time-sharing became a much less attractive design for operating systems. Explain why this is the case.

25. See whether the computer system on which you are working is part of a local area network. If it is, determine what servers are available and how they are used. Is there a significant difference between the ways you access local resources and remote resources?

26. The following four requests could come in to an operating system as it is running on a computer system:

- The clock in the computer has just "ticked," and we need to update a seconds counter.

- The program running on processor 2 is trying to perform an illegal operation code.

- Someone pulled the plug on the power supply, and the system will run out of power in 50 msec.

- The disk has just read the character that passed under the read/write head, and it wants to store it in memory before the next one arrives.

In what order should the operating system handle these requests?

CHALLENGE WORK

1. In Chapter 2 we wrote a number of algorithms that assumed the ability to specify a list of values. That is, our algorithm contained statements such as

Get values for $A_1, A_2, \ldots, A_N$ the list to be searched

Here we are thinking not only of individual data items such as A_1 and A_2 but also of a collection of such items, the list. A collection of related data items is called a **data structure.** High-level programming languages like C++ and Java provide users with a rich collection of data structures that go by such names as arrays and lists. We can program with these structures just as though they were an inherent part of the hardware of the computer. However, the discussions in the previous two chapters have shown that data structures such as lists of numbers do *not* exist directly in hardware. There are no machine language instructions that could carry out the type of algorithmic command shown above. When you write an instruction that uses a structure such as a list, the language translator (that is, the compiler) must map it into what is available on the hardware—the machine language instruction set shown in Figure 5.19 and the sequential addresses in our memory. (This is another good example of the virtual environment created by a piece of system software.)

Write an assembly language program to sum up a list of 50 numbers that are read in and stored in memory. Here is the algorithm you are to translate:

Read in 50 numbers $A_1, A_2, \ldots, A_{50}$

Set *Sum* to 0

Set *i* to 1

While the value of *i* is less than or equal to 50

    Sum = Sum + A_i

    i = i + 1

End of the loop

Write out the value of Sum

Stop

To implement this algorithm, you will have to simulate the concept of a list of numbers using the assembly language resources that are available. (*Hint:* Remember that in the Von Neumann architecture there is no distinction between an instruction and a piece of data. Therefore, an assembly language instruction such as LOAD A can be treated as data and modified by other instructions.)

Here are some excellent introductory texts on the design and implementation of operating systems. Most of them also include a discussion of some specific modern operating system such as LINUX, Mac OS X, or Windows NT.

Silbershatz, A.; Galvin, P.; and Gagne, G. *The Design of Operating Systems,* 6th ed. New York: Wiley, 2001.

Stallings, W. *Operating Systems,* 4th ed. Englewood Cliffs, NJ: Prentice-Hall, 2000.

Tanenbaum, A. S., and Woodhull, A. *Operating Systems: Design and Implementation,* 2nd ed. Englewood Cliffs, NJ: Prentice-Hall, 1997.

For a discussion of future directions in operating system design, especially network and distributed operating systems, here are a couple of excellent references:

Coulouris, G.; Dollimore, J.; and Kindberg, T. *Distributed Systems: Concepts and Design,* 3rd ed. Reading, MA: Addison Wesley, 2000.

Tanenbaum, A. *Distributed Systems: Principles and Paradigms.* Englewood Cliffs, NJ: Prentice-Hall, 2002.

Finally, here is an excellent general reference on system software:

Clarke, D., and Merusi, D. *System Software: The Way Things Work*. Englewood Cliffs, NJ: Prentice-Hall, 1998.

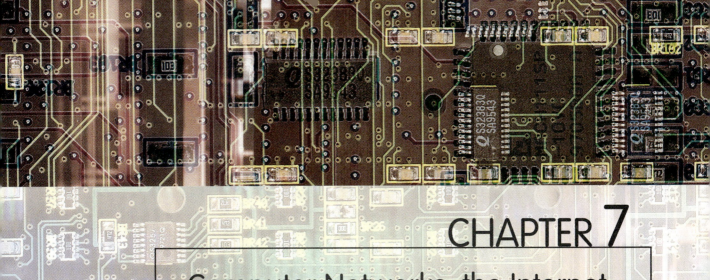

CHAPTER 7

Computer Networks, the Internet, and the World Wide Web

7.1 Introduction

Every once in a while there occurs a technological innovation of such importance that it forever changes a society and the way its people live, work, and communicate. The invention of the printing press by Johannes Gutenberg in the mid-15th century was one such development. The books and manuscripts it produced helped fuel the renewed interest in science, art, and literature that came to be called the Renaissance, an era that influenced Western civilization for over 500 years. The Industrial Revolution of the 18th and early 19th centuries made consumer goods such as clothing, furniture, and cooking utensils affordable to the middle class and changed European and American societies from rural to urban and from agricultural to industrial. In our own century, we are certainly aware of the massive social changes, both good and bad, wrought by inventions like the telephone, automobile, television, and computer.

Many people feel that we are witnessing yet another breakthrough, one with the potential to make as great a change in our lives as those just mentioned. This innovation is the *computer network*—computers connected together for the purpose of exchanging resources and information. During the early stages of network development, the only information exchanged was text such as email, database records, and technical papers. However, the material sent across a network today can be just about anything—television and radio signals, voice, graphics, handwriting, photographs, and movies, to name just a few. If information can be represented in the 0s and 1s of binary (as described in Section 4.2), it can be transmitted across a network.

The possibilities created by this free flow of data are enormous. Networks can equalize access to information and eliminate the concept of "information haves" and "information have-nots." Students in a small, poorly funded school would no longer be handicapped by an out-of-date library collection. A physician practicing in an emerging economy would be able to transmit medical records, test results, and X-ray images to specialists anywhere in the world and have immediate access to the online databases and reference works of major medical centers. Researchers would have the same ability to communicate with experts in their discipline whether they were in New York, New Delhi, or New Guinea. Small business owners could use the network to locate suppliers and customers on an international scale.

Networking also offers the potential to foster the growth of democracy and global understanding by providing unrestricted access to newspapers, magazines, radio, and television, as well as supporting the unfettered exchange of diverse and competing thoughts, ideas, and opinions. Because we live in an increasingly information-oriented society, network technology contains the seeds of massive social and economic change. It is no surprise that during civil uprisings political leaders who wish to prevent the dissemination of opposing ideas often move quickly to restrict Internet access.

In the last chapter we saw how system software can create a user-friendly "virtual machine" on top of the raw hardware of a single computer. In today's world computers are seldom isolated stand-alone devices, and the modern view of a "virtual machine" has expanded into a worldwide collection of resources. In this chapter we take a detailed look at the technology of computer networks—what they are, how they work, and the benefits they can bring. We also examine in detail the most widely used network, the Internet, and its most important application, the World Wide Web.

7.2   Basic Networking Concepts

A **computer network** is a set of independent computer systems connected by telecommunication links for the purpose of sharing information and resources. The individual computers on the network are referred to as **nodes, hosts,** or **end systems,** and they can range from PDAs and tiny laptops to the massively parallel supercomputers introduced in Chapter 5. In this section we describe some of the basic characteristics of a computer network.

 ### 7.2.1   *Communication Links*

The communication links used to build a network vary widely in physical characteristics, error rate, and transmission speed, and in the approximately 35 years that networks have existed, telecommunications facilities have undergone enormous change.

In the early days of networking, the most common way to transmit data was via **switched, dial-up telephone lines,** the same telephone lines you use to talk with friends and family. The terms "switched, dial-up" mean that when we dial a telephone number, a **circuit** (i.e., a path) is temporarily established between the caller and callee. This circuit lasts for the duration of the call, and when we hang up it is terminated.

The voice-oriented dial-up telephone network is (at least in part) an **analog** medium. As we first explained in Chapter 4, this means that the physical quantity used to represent information, usually voltage level, is continuous and can take on any value. An example of this is shown in Figure 7.1(a). Although analog is fine for transmitting the human voice, which varies continuously in pitch and volume, a computer produces **digital** information—specifically, a sequence of 0s and 1s, as shown in Figure 7.1(b).

In order for the binary signals of Figure 7.1(b) to be transmitted on a switched dial-up telephone line, the signal must be restructured into the analog representation of Figure 7.1(a). The device that accomplishes this is a **modem,** because it modulates, or alters, a standard analog signal called a **carrier** so that it encodes binary information. The modem modifies the physical characteristics of the carrier wave, such as amplitude or frequency, so that it is in one of two distinct states, one state representing 0 and the other state representing 1. Figure 7.2 shows how a modem could modulate the amplitude (height) of a carrier wave to encode the binary signal 1010.

FIGURE 7.1

Two Forms of Information Representation

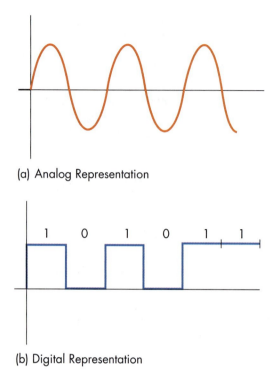

(a) Analog Representation

(b) Digital Representation

At the other end of the transmission line, a modem performs the inverse operation, which is called demodulation. (Modem is a contraction of the two terms *mo*dulation and *dem*odulation.) It takes the received waveform, separates the carrier from the encoded digital signal, and passes the digital data on to the computer.

Initially, these analog encoding and decoding operations could not be done very quickly because of the high error rate and low capacity, or **bandwidth,** of a switched telephone line. In the early days of telecommunications—the 1970s and 1980s—the rate at which information could be sent and received via a phone line was limited to about 1,200–9,600 bits per second (bps). Advances in modem design have produced devices that now transmit at 56,000 bps, or 56 Kbps, an order-of-magnitude increase. However, this is still considered insufficient to handle the transmission of multimedia-based documents such as Web pages, MP3 files, and streaming video.

The dial-up telephone system is still used today for remote access to networks, and most computers are equipped with a built-in 56 Kbps modem. However, their limited speed makes dial-up phone links inconvenient for applications where speed is vital or we are sending large volumes of data.

In the last few years a technology called **broadband** has slowly been replacing modems and analog phone lines for data communications to and from our homes, schools, and offices. The term broadband refers to any communication link with a transmission rate exceeding 128,000 bps. In the case of home users, there are currently two broadband options widely available—digital subscriber lines (DSL) and cable modems.

A **digital subscriber line** uses the same wires that carry regular telephone signals into your home, and therefore it is a service provided by either

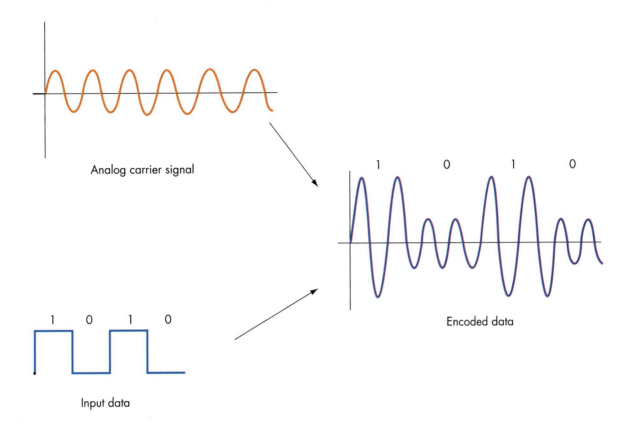

Analog carrier signal

1   0   1   0

Encoded data

1   0   1   0

Input data

FIGURE 7.2

*Modulation of a Carrier to
Encode Binary Information*

your local telephone company or someone certified to act as their intermediary. Although it uses the same wires, a DSL signal uses a different set of frequencies, and it transmits digital rather than analog signals. Therefore, the voice traffic generated by talking with a friend on the phone does not interfere with a Web page being simultaneously downloaded by someone else in the family. Furthermore, unlike the modem where you must explicitly establish a connection (dial a number) and end a connection (hang up), a DSL is a permanent, "always-on" link, which eliminates the aggravating delay of dialing and waiting for the circuit to be established.

A digital subscriber line is often **asymmetric.** This means that it does not have the same transmission speed in the download direction (from the network to your computer) as in the upload direction (from your computer to the network). That is because most users consume much more data than they generate. For example, to obtain a Web page, your computer sends a request message to the machine with that page. (It does this by sending the address of that page, such as www.macalester.edu.) This request message is small and contains only a few dozen characters. However, in return, you get a Web page—complete with applets, graphics, and plug-ins—containing possibly millions of bits. To handle this imbalance, a DSL provides greater bandwidth coming into your computer than going out. Typical DSL speeds are 1–2 million bits per second (Mbps) for downloads and 100,000–200,000 bits per second for uploads—still much more than is available from a modem.

The second option for broadband communications is a **cable modem.** This technology makes use of the links that deliver cable TV signals into your home, so this service is offered by cable TV providers. Some of the link capacity previously allocated for TV signals is now used for data communications. Like a DSL, a cable modem also provides an "always-on" link and offers download speeds of about 1–2 million bits per second.

In the commercial and office environment, the most widely used broadband technology is the **Ethernet.** Its high-speed links provide dedicated data transmission throughout a building or a campus at rates of either 10 Mbps or 100 Mbps—1,800 times faster than a 56K modem!

The Ethernet was developed in the mid-1970s by computer scientists at the Xerox PARC research center in Palo Alto, California. It was originally designed to operate at 10 Mbps using coaxial cable. However, even 10 Mbps may be too slow for some applications, so in the early 1990s researchers developed a "new and improved" version, called **Fast Ethernet,** which transmits at 100 Mbps across either coaxial cable, fiber optic cable, or regular twisted-pair copper wire. Many classrooms and office buildings today are wired to support 100 Mbps Fast Ethernet communications. In addition, most PCs today come with a built-in Ethernet interface, and even new homes and dorm rooms are often equipped with Ethernet links.

Even 100 Mbps may not be fast enough for multimedia applications, and computer science researchers are actively investigating the concept of **gigabit networking**—networks with transmission lines that support speeds in excess of 1 billion bits per second (Gbps). In the early 1990s the U.S. government funded a long-term research project called NREN, the *National Research and Education Network*. Its goal was to investigate wide-area gigabit data networks and to have demonstration networks up and running within 10 years. The project is on schedule, and a number of gigabit networks are now being tested. (To read more about NREN, go to their home page at www.nren.nasa. gov.) Furthermore, a new *gigabit Ethernet* standard was adopted which supports communication on an Ethernet cable at 1,000 Mbps, 100 times faster than the original standard.

One might wonder why anyone would need to transmit information at billions of bits per second. Do there exist applications that truly need this level of performance? To answer that question, let's determine how long it takes to transmit a high-resolution color image, such as a CAT scan, satellite image, or a single movie frame, at different transmission speeds. As described in Section 4.2, a high-resolution color image contains about 5 million picture elements (pixels), and each pixel is encoded using 8–24 bits. If we assume 16 bits per pixel, then a single uncompressed image would contain 80,000,000 bits of data. If the image is compressed before it is sent, and the compression ratio is 10:1 (see Section 4.2 for a definition of compression ratio), then we must transmit a total of 8 million bits in order to send this one image. Figure 7.3 shows the time needed to send this amount of information at the speeds discussed in this chapter.

Figure 7.3 clearly demonstrates the need for high-speed communications to support visual applications such as video on demand, medical imaging, and virtual reality. Receiving an 8 Mb image using a 56 Kbps modem takes 2.4 minutes, an agonizingly long time. (You have probably had the experience of waiting for what seemed like forever as a Web page s-l-o-w-l-y appeared on your screen.) That same 8 Mb image can be received in 4 seconds using a DSL or cable modem with a download speed of 2 Mbps, 0.8 second using a 10 Mbps Ethernet, and a blazing 0.08 second with 100 Mbps Ethernet.

However, even 0.08 second may not be fast enough if an application requires the rapid transmission of either multiple images or a huge amount of

LINE TYPE	SPEED	TIME TO TRANSMIT 8 MILLION BITS (ONE COMPRESSED IMAGE)
Dial-up phone line	56 Kbps	2.4 minutes
DSL line, cable modem	2 Mbps	4 seconds
Ethernet	10 Mbps	0.8 second
Fast Ethernet	100 Mbps	0.08 second
Gigabit Ethernet	1 Gbps	0.008 second

data in a short period of time. For example, to watch a real-time video image without flicker or delay, you need to send at least 24 frames per second. Any less and the human eye will notice the time delay between frames. If each frame contains 8 Mb, you need a bandwidth of 8,000,000 × 24 = 192 Mbps. This is well beyond the speed of modems, DSL, cable modems, and the Ethernet, but it is achievable using gigabit networks. The NREN research project mentioned earlier envisions using gigabit networking for exchanging 3D medical images, transmitting weather satellite data, and supporting collaboration between researchers working on the Human Genome Project.

A relatively recent development in telecommunications is the growth of **wireless data communication** using radio, microwave, and infrared signals. In the wireless world, users no longer need to be physically adjacent to a wired network to access data, just as cellular phones liberated users with regard to voice communications. Using wireless, one can be in the backyard, a car, at the beach, or on the factory floor and still send and receive email, access online databases, or surf the Web. This ability to deliver data to users regardless of where they are located is termed **mobile computing.**

There are two forms of wireless data communications. In a **wireless local access network,** a user transmits from his or her computer to a local wireless **base station**—the receiving unit—that is no more than a few hundred feet away. This base station is then connected into a traditional wired network, such as a DSL or cable modem. This is the type of wireless configuration typically found in a home, conference room, office, or coffee shop. It is cheap,

Ubiquitous Computing

The rapid growth of wireless communications, along with the availability of extremely cheap microprocessors, has led to an exciting new area of computer science research called **ubiquitous computing,** also called **pervasive computing.** In the early days of computing, a single large mainframe served many users. In the PC era, a single desktop machine served a single user. In the ubiquitous computing model, many computers work together to serve a single user, and rather than being perched on a desktop, they become nearly invisible. The idea is that computers will become so commonplace that they will blend into the background and disappear from our consciousness, much as electricity has today. The goal is to create a system that is embedded in the environment, providing its service in a seamless, efficient manner.

Computers will be located inside our phones, appliances, furnaces, lights, clocks, and even clothing in order to provide useful services in a transparent fashion. Topics of research in this area include such things as **wearable computing** and **smart homes.** As described by Mark Weiser of Xerox, "ubiquitous computing is invisible, *everywhere* computing that does not sit on the desktop but lies deep inside the woodwork."

1. Show how the 4-bit digital value 0110 would be converted to an analog signal by a modem that modulated the *frequency* of a carrier wave, rather than its amplitude.

2. Assume an uncompressed 1,200 × 780 image, with each pixel stored using an 8-bit gray scale representation. If we want to transmit the entire image in under 1 second, what is the minimum acceptable transmission speed?

simple, low powered, and easy to install, but it cannot provide mobile access if you are in a car, out of doors, or not adjacent to your local base station.

The second type of wireless networking is the **wireless wide-area access network.** In this case the computer transmits its message to a remote base station provided by a telecommunications company, which may be located many miles away. In this case, the base station is usually a large antenna placed on top of a tower or building. This is similar to the way that cellular phone service is provided.

Although wireless data communication is an exciting prospect, it is not without problems that must be studied and solved. For example, some forms of wireless such as microwaves are line-of-sight, traveling only in a straight line. Because of the curvature of the earth, transmitters must be placed on top of hills or tall buildings, and they cannot be more than about 10 to 50 miles apart, depending on height. Other types of wireless media suffer from environmental problems; they are strongly affected by rain and fog, cannot pass through obstacles such as buildings or large trees, and have a higher error rate than wired communication. In addition, wireless is often much slower than wired communications (hundreds of Kbps rather than Mbps), which may make it inappropriate for the transfer of large amounts of data.

However, the computer science research community is addressing these issues, and in the near future mobile computing will certainly become a more important form of data access. Surfing the Web via mobile phone or sitting in your backyard using a wireless laptop will soon become as common as talking on a cell phone. In the meantime, most computer networking is done via wired networks, as discussed in the next two sections.

 ### 7.2.2 *Local Area Networks*

There are two types of computer networks. A **local area network,** abbreviated **LAN,** connects hardware devices such as computers, printers, and storage devices that are all in close proximity. (A diagram of a LAN was given in Figure 6.21.) Examples of LANs include the interconnection of machines in one room, in the same office building, or on a single campus. An important characteristic of a LAN is that the owner of the computers is also the owner of the means of communications. Because a LAN is located entirely on private property, the owner is free to install whatever telecommunications facilities he or she wants without having to purchase services from a third-party provider such as a phone or cable company.

Wired LANs can be constructed using a number of different interconnection strategies, as seen in Figure 7.4. In the **bus** topology, Figure 7.4(a), all nodes are connected to a single shared communication line, and if two or more nodes use the link at the same time, the messages collide and are unreadable. With a bus, therefore, nodes must take turns, and they must back off when another node is using the line. The cable modem technology described in Section 7.2.1 is based on a bus topology. A number of homes are all connected to the same shared coaxial cable. If two users want to download a Web page at the exact same time, then the effective transmission rate will be lower than expected, since one of them will have to wait.

The **ring** topology of Figure 7.4(b) connects the network nodes in a circular fashion, with messages circulating around the ring in either a clockwise or counter clockwise direction until they reach their destination. Finally, the **star** network, Figure 7.4(c), has a single central node that is connected to all other sites. This central node can route information directly to any other node in the LAN. To send a message, we first send it to the central site, which then forwards it on to the correct location.

There are many different LAN technologies available in the marketplace, but the most widely used is the **Ethernet** introduced in the previous section. It is the model that we will use to describe the general behavior of all LANs.

The Ethernet uses the bus topology of Figure 7.4(a). To send a message, a node places the message, including the destination address, on the cable. Since the line is shared, the message is received by every other node (assuming no one else sent at the exact same time and garbled our data). Each node looks at the destination address to see if it is the intended recipient. If so, it accepts the message; if not, it discards it.

There are two ways to actually construct an Ethernet LAN. In the first method, called the **shared cable,** a wire (such as twisted-pair copper wire, coaxial cable, or fiber optic cable) is literally stretched around and through a

FIGURE 7.4

Some Common LAN Topologies

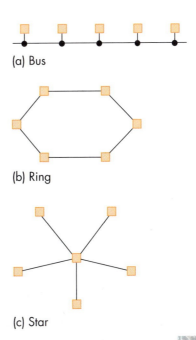

(a) Bus

(b) Ring

(c) Star

FIGURE 7.5

*An Ethernet LAN Implemented
Using Shared Cables*

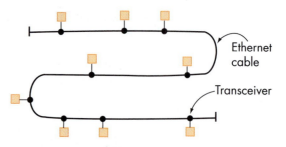

(a) Single Cable Configuration

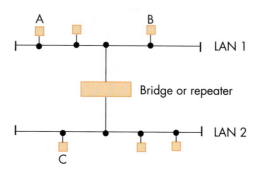

(b) Multiple Cable Configuration

building. Users tap into the cable at its nearest point using a device called a **transceiver,** as shown in Figure 7.5(a). Because of technical constraints, an Ethernet cable has a maximum allowable length. For a large building or campus it may be necessary to install two or more separate cables and connect them via a hardware device called either a repeater or a bridge.

A **repeater** is a device that simply amplifies and forwards a signal. In Figure 7.5(b), if the device connecting the two LANs is a repeater, then every message on LAN1 is forwarded to LAN2, and vice versa. Thus, when two Ethernet LANs are connected by a repeater, they function exactly as if they were a single network.

A **bridge,** also called a **switch,** is a "smarter" device that has knowledge of the nodes located on each separate network. It examines every message sent to see if it should or should not be forwarded from one network to another. For example, if node A is sending a message to node B, both of which are on LAN1, then the bridge will not do anything with the message. However, if node A on LAN1 is sending a message to node C on LAN2, then the bridge will copy the message from LAN1 onto LAN2 so node C will be able to see it and read it.

In the second approach to constructing an Ethernet LAN, there is no shared cable strung throughout the building. Instead, there is a box called a **hub** located in a room called a **wiring closet.** The hub contains a number of **ports,** with a wire leading from each port to an Ethernet interface in the wall of a room in the building. To connect to the network, we first activate that port, typically by flipping a switch, and then simply plug our machine into the wall socket. It is no longer necessary to climb into the ceiling or crawl through ductwork looking for the cable. The shared cable is located inside the hub instead of inside the building walls. That is why hubs are the most widely used technique for constructing local area networks. This approach is diagrammed in Figure 7.6.

FIGURE 7.6

An Ethernet LAN Implemented
Using a Hub

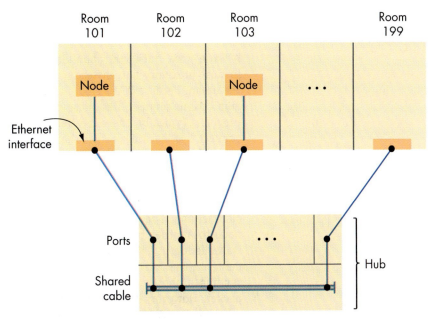

PRACTICE PROBLEMS

1. Explain why we would or would not have collisions occurring on local area networks that used the ring topology of Figure 7.4b or the
   star topology of Figure 7.4c.

2. What changes, if any, would have to be made to our description of
   the Ethernet protocol to allow a message to be sent by node A on
   a local area network to *every other* node on that same LAN? This
   operation is called **broadcasting.**

3. Assume you are given the following configuration of three local area
   networks, called LAN1, LAN2, and LAN3, connected by bridges B1
   and B2.

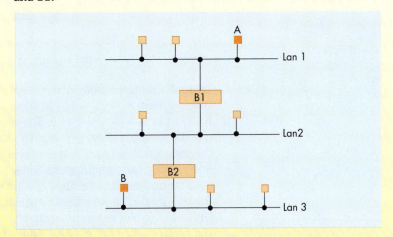

Explain exactly how node A on LAN1 would send a message to node
B on LAN3.

▶ 7.2.3 Wide Area Networks

A **wide area network,** abbreviated **WAN,** connects devices that are not in close proximity but, instead, are across town, across the country, or across the ocean. Because WANs cross public property, users must purchase telecommunications services, like those described in Section 7.2.1, from an external provider. Typically, these are **dedicated point-to-point** lines that directly connect two machines rather than the shared channels found on a LAN such as the Ethernet. The typical structure of a wide area network is shown in Figure 7.7.

Most WANs use a **store-and-forward, packet-switched** technology to deliver messages. Unlike a LAN, in which a message is broadcast on a shared channel and is received by all nodes, a WAN message must "hop" from one node to another to make its way from source to destination. The unit of transmission in a WAN is a **packet**—an information block with a fixed maximum size that is transmitted through the network as a single unit. If you are sending a short message, then it can usually be transmitted as a single packet. However, if you are sending a long message, the source node may "chop" it into N separate packets (such as the first 1,000 characters, the next 1,000 characters, and so on) and send each packet independently through the network. When the destination node has received all N packets, it will reassemble them into a single message.

For example, assume the following 6-node WAN:

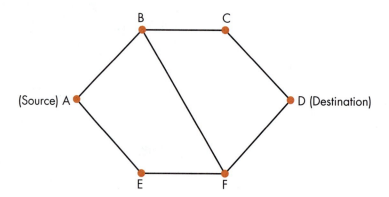

To send a message from source node A to destination node D, the message could go from A → B → C → D. Alternately, the message may travel via A → B → F → D or A → E → F → D. The exact route is determined by the network, not the user, based on which path can deliver the message most quickly. If the message is large, it may be broken up into multiple packets, with each one possibly taking a different route.

One of the nicest features of a store and forward network is that the failure of a single line or a single node does not necessarily bring down the entire network. For example, assume the line connecting node B to node C in the previous diagram crashes. Nodes B and C can still communicate via the route B → F → D → C. Similarly, if node F fails completely, nodes E and D, lo-

FIGURE 7.7

Typical Structure of a Wide Area Network

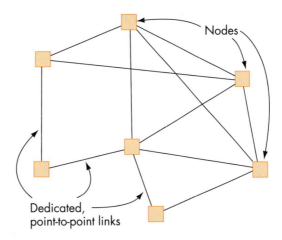

cated on either side of F, can still exchange messages. However, instead of talking via node F, they now use the route E → A → B → C → D.

Reliability and fault tolerance were the reasons that wide-area networks were first studied in the late 1960s and early 1970s. The U.S. military was interested in communication systems that could survive and function even if some of its components were destroyed, as might happen in time of war or civil unrest. Their research ultimately led to the creation of the Internet. (We will have much more to say about the history of networking and the Internet later in this chapter.)

7.2.4 *Overall Structure of the Internet*

We have defined two classes of networks, LANs and WANs, but all real-world networks, including the Internet, are a complex mix of both network types.

For example, a company or a college would typically have one or more LANs connecting its local computers, for example, a computer science department LAN, a humanities building LAN, an administration building LAN, and so forth. These individual LANs might then be interconnected into a wide-area "company network" that allows users to send email to other employees in the company and access the resources of other departments. These individual networks would be interconnected via a device called a **router.** Like the bridge of Figure 7.5(b), a router transmits messages between two distinct networks. However, unlike a bridge that connects two identical types of networks, routers can transmit information between networks using totally different communication techniques—much as an interpreter would be placed between two people who speak different languages. For example, a router, not a bridge, would be used to send messages from an Ethernet LAN to a packet-switched, store-and-forward WAN. We can see this type of interconnection structure in Figure 7.8(a).

The diagram in Figure 7.8(a) is fine for allowing the employees of a single company or the students of a single college to communicate with each

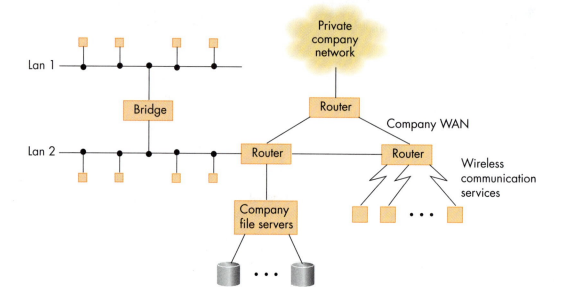

Structure of a Typical Company Network

other, or access local resources, but how do these people reach users outside their institution or access remote resources such as Web pages that are not part of their own network? Furthermore, how does an individual home user who is not part of any company or college network access the larger community? The answer is that a user's individual computer or a company's private network is connected to the world through an **Internet Service Provider**, or **ISP**. An ISP is a wide-area network whose purpose is to provide a pathway from a specific network to other networks, or from an individual to other networks, as shown in Figure 7.8(b).

An ISP typically provides many ways for a user to connect to it, from 56 Kbps modems to dedicated broadband telecommunication links with speeds in excess of hundreds of millions of bits per second.

However, the scope of networking worldwide is so vast, a single ISP cannot possibly hope to directly connect a single campus, company, or individual to every other computer in the world, just as a single airport cannot directly serve every possible destination. Instead, ISPs are hierarchical, interconnecting to each other in multiple layers, or tiers, that provide ever expanding geographic coverage. This hierarchical structure is diagrammed in Figure 7.8(c).

An individual or a company network will connect to a local ISP, the first level in the hierarchy. This local ISP will typically connect to a regional or national ISP that interconnects all local ISPs in a single geographic region or country. Finally, a regional or national ISP might connect into an international ISP, also called a tier-1 network or an **Internet backbone** that provides global coverage. This hierarchy is similar to the standard telephone system. When you place a call to another country, the telephone line from your home or office connects to a local phone switching center, which establishes a connection to a regional switching center, which establishes a connection to a national switching center. This national center has high-speed connections

FIGURE 7.8(b)

Structure of a Network Using an ISP

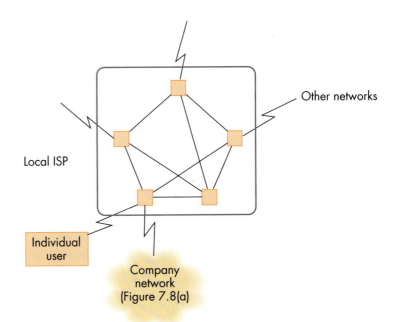

Other networks

Local ISP

Individual user

Company network (Figure 7.8(a))

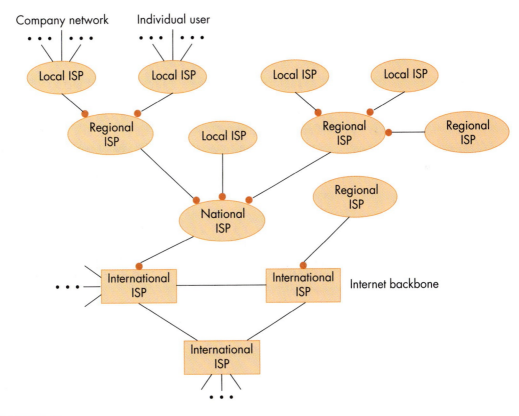

Company network

Individual user

Local ISP

Local ISP

Local ISP

Local ISP

Local ISP

Regional ISP

Local ISP

Regional ISP

Regional ISP

National ISP

Regional ISP

International ISP

International ISP

Internet backbone

International ISP

FIGURE 7.8(c)

Hierarchy of Internet Service Providers

FIGURE 7.9

Internet Domain Host Survey Count Graph

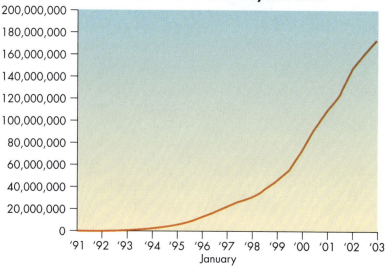

Internet domain survey host count

Source: Internet Software Consortium (http://www.isc.org/)

to similar national switching centers in other countries, which are connected, in turn, to a regional and then a local switch to establish a connection to the phone you are calling.

The diagram in Figure 7.8(c) is a good pictorial representation of that enormously complex telecommunications entity we call the **Internet.** The Internet is not a single computer network; instead, it is a huge interconnected "network of networks" that includes nodes, LANs, WANs, bridges, routers, and multiple levels of ISPs. As of early 2003, there were about 170 million nodes (hosts) and hundreds of thousands of separate networks located in over 225 countries. A graph of the number of host computers on the Internet over the last 12 years is shown in Figure 7.9. (This figure is really an undercount, since there are numerous computers located behind protective firewalls that will not respond to any external attempts to be counted.)

How does something as massive as the Internet actually work? How is it possible to get 170 million or more machines around the world to function efficiently as a single system? We answer that important question in the next section.

7.3 Communication Protocols

Again, an analogy with the telephone system is appropriate. When you talk on the phone, there is a set of procedures that you follow. When you answer the phone you say, Hello, and then remain silent, waiting for the individual on the other end to respond. The conversation continues until someone says, Good Bye, at which time both parties hang up. You might call this "telephone etiquette," and the existence of these conventions is what allows orderly exchanges to take place. Imagine what would happen if someone were unaware of them. For example, he or she might answer the phone but not say anything. Hearing silence, the person on the other end would be totally confused, think the call did not get through, and hang up.

The same is true for computer networks. To have meaningful communications we need a set of procedures that specify how the exchanges will take place. However, rather than calling this "network etiquette," these procedures are called network protocols.

In the network arena, a **protocol** is a mutually agreed upon set of rules, conventions, and agreements for the efficient and orderly exchange of information. Even though the Internet has hundreds of millions of machines made by dozens of manufacturers and located in hundreds of countries, they can all exchange messages correctly and efficiently for one simple reason: they all agree to use the same protocols to govern that exchange.

You might think that something as massive and international as the Internet would be managed by either the governments of the major industrialized nations or an international agency like the United Nations. Surprisingly, that is not the case. The Internet is operated by the **Internet Society,** a nonprofit, nongovernmental, professional society composed of more than 150 worldwide organizations (e.g., foundations, educational institutions, companies) united by the common goal of maintaining the viability and health of the Internet. It is this group, along with its subcommittees, the Internet Architecture Board (IAB) and the Internet Engineering Task Force (IETF), that establish and enforce network protocol standards. (Perhaps the fact that the Internet developed outside the scope of governmental bureaucracies and their "red tape" is exactly what has allowed it to become so enormously successful!) To learn more about the Internet Society and its activities, check out its home page at www.isoc.org.

The protocols that govern the operation of the Internet are set up as a multilayered hierarchy, with each layer addressing one aspect of the overall communications task. They are structured in this way because of the volatility of telecommunications and networking. By dividing the protocols into separate, independent layers, a change to the operation of any one layer will not cause a change to other layers, making maintenance of the Internet much easier.

The Internet **protocol hierarchy,** also called a **protocol stack,** has five layers, and their names and some examples are listed in Figure 7.10. This hierarchy is also referred to as **TCP/IP,** after the names of two of its most important protocols.

In the following sections we briefly describe the responsibilities of each of the five layers in the hierarchy of Figure 7.10.

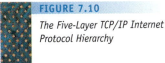

FIGURE 7.10

The Five-Layer TCP/IP Internet Protocol Hierarchy

Layer	Name	Examples
5	Application	HTTP, SMTP, FTP
4	Transport	TCP, UDP
3	Network	IP
2b	Logical Link Control	PPP, Ethernet ⎫ Data Link Layer
2a	Medium Access Control	Ethernet ⎬
1	Physical	Modem, DSL, Cable Modem

7.3.1 Physical Layer

The **physical layer protocols** are the rules governing the exchange of binary digits across a physical communication channel, such as a fiber optic cable, copper wire, or wireless radio channel. These protocols specify such things as

- How do we know when a bit is present on the line?
- For how much time will that bit remain on the line?
- Will the bit be in the form of a digital or an analog signal?
- What voltage levels will be used to represent a binary 0 and a binary 1?
- What is the shape of the connector between the computer and the transmission line?

The goal of the physical layer is to create a "bit pipe" between two computers, such that bits put into the pipe at one end can be read and understood by the computer located at the other end, as shown in Figure 7.11.

Once you have selected a physical layer protocol, by purchasing a modem, getting a digital subscriber line, or using a mobile phone with wireless data capabilities, you have the ability to transmit binary signals across a physical channel. From this point on in the protocol stack, you no longer need be concerned about such engineering issues as voltage levels, wavelengths, or radio frequencies. These details are hidden inside the physical layer, which provides all of the necessary bit transmission services. From now on all you need to know about the communication channel is that when you ask the physical layer to send a bit, it does so, and when you ask the physical layer to get a bit, it presents you with a 0 or a 1. How it does this is not important, and that is the beauty of the layered model of network protocols.

7.3.2 Data Link Layer

The physical layer protocols create a bit pipe between two machines connected by a communications link. However, this link is not an error-free channel, and due to interference or weather or any number of other reasons, it can introduce errors into the transmitted bit stream. The bits that come out may not be an exact copy of the bits that went in. This creates what is called the **error detection and correction** problem—how do we detect that an error has occurred and, if so, how do we correct it?

Furthermore, we are not really interested in receiving a raw stream of bits. We want to receive complete *messages*. Therefore, we need to know which bits in the incoming stream belong together; that is, we need to iden-

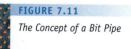

FIGURE 7.11

The Concept of a Bit Pipe

100111 ⟶   ⟶ 100111

Bit pipe

tify the start and the end of a message. This is called the **framing** problem. It is the job of the **data link protocols** to address and solve these two issues— error handling and framing. This process is done in two stages called layer 2a, **medium access control,** and layer 2b, **logical link control.** Together these two services form the layer 2 protocol called the data link layer.

In Section 7.2.1 we described how local area networks use a channel in which many machines are connected by a single shared link. In this type of environment, a necessary first step in transmitting a message is determining how to allocate this shared line among the competing machines. The **medium access control protocols** are the rules for determining how to arbitrate ownership of a shared line when multiple nodes want to send at the same time. In a sense, we are saying that before we can transmit a message from a source to a destination, we must first determine *who* is the source and *who* is the destination.

This could be done in a *centralized* manner by creating a single master control node responsible for determining who gets ownership of the line at any instant in time. Although easy to do, centralized control is rarely used. One reason is that it can be slow. Each node sends its request to the master, who must decide which node gets the line, and then inform every other node of its decision. This will take a good deal of time, making the network highly inefficient. Another problem is that centralized control is not fault tolerant. If the master node fails, the entire network is inoperable.

Instead, most medium access control protocols, including the Ethernet, use a *contention-based* approach in which there is no central authority and all nodes compete equally for access to the line. When a node wants to send a message, it first listens to the line to see whether or not it is currently in use. If the line is idle, then the node transmits immediately. However, if the line is busy the node wishing to send continually monitors the status of the line and, as soon as it becomes idle, it transmits. This situation is diagrammed in Figure 7.12(a). In that diagram, node B wants to send but notices that A is using the line. B listens and waits until A is finished, and as soon as that occurs, B is free to send.

However, there is still a problem. If two or more users want to send a message while the line is in use, then both will be monitoring its status. As soon as the line is idle, both will transmit at exactly the same time. This is called a **collision,** and it is a not uncommon occurrence in contention-based networks like the Ethernet. When a collision occurs, all information is lost. This scenario is shown in Figure 7.12(b). According to the Ethernet protocols, when a collision occurs, the colliding nodes immediately stop sending, wait a random amount of time, and then attempt to resend. Because it is unlikely that both nodes will select the exact same random waiting period, one of them should be able to acquire the line and transmit while the other node must wait a little longer. This situation is diagrammed in Figure 7.12(c).

One reason why the Ethernet is so popular is that control is *distributed*. Responsibility for network operation is shared by all nodes in the network rather than centralized in a single master controller. Each node makes its own decisions about when to listen, when to send, and when to wait. That means that the failure of one node will not affect the operation of any other node in the network.

If our network uses point-to-point links like those in Figure 7.7, rather than shared lines, we do not need the medium access control protocols just described since we always know the identity of the two machines that will

FIGURE 7.12

The Medium Access Control Protocols in the Ethernet

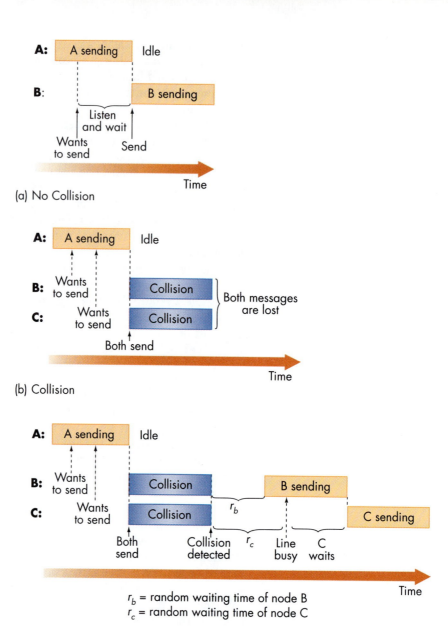

(a) No Collision

(b) Collision

(c) Collision and Retransmission

r_b = random waiting time of node B
r_c = random waiting time of node C

exchange a message—the two machines connected by this dedicated line. Therefore, regardless of whether we are using a shared channel or a point-to-point link, we now have a sender and a receiver directly connected by a channel who want to exchange a single message. It is the job of the layer 2b **logical link control protocols** to ensure that the message traveling across this channel from source to destination arrives correctly.

How is it possible to turn an inherently error-prone bit pipe like the one in Figure 7.11 into an error-free channel? The answer is that we cannot entirely eliminate errors, but we can detect that an error has occurred and retransmit a new and unblemished copy of the original message. This is called the **ARQ algorithm,** for *a*utomatic *r*epeat re*q*uest, and it is the basis for all data link control protocols in current use.

FIGURE 7.13

A Message Packet Sent by the
Data Link Protocols

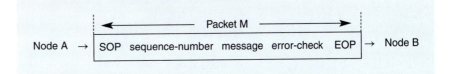

Remember that at this point, nodes A and B are directly connected by a physical link. When A wishes to send a message to B, it first adds some additional information to form what is called a **packet.** It inserts a sequence number (1, 2, 3, . . .) uniquely identifying this packet, and it adds some error checking bits that will allow B to determine if the packet was or was not corrupted during transmission. Finally, it adds a start of packet (SOP) and end of packet (EOP) delimiter to allow node B to determine exactly where the packet begins and ends.

Thus, the packet M sent from A to B looks like Figure 7.13. This packet is sent across the communication channel, bit by bit, using the services of the physical layer protocols described in the previous section. When B receives the packet, it examines the error check field to determine if the packet was transmitted correctly.

The thing that makes the ARQ algorithm work is that node A maintains a *copy* of the packet after it has been sent. If B correctly receives the packet, it acknowledges that fact by returning to A a special **acknowledgment message,** abbreviated ACK, containing the sequence number of the correctly received packet. Node A now knows that this packet was correctly received and can discard its local copy. It is now free to send the next message:

A	B	
M(1) →		Send the first packet from A to B
	← ACK(1)	B says to A, "I got it," A can discard it
M(2) →		Send the second packet from A to B
	← ACK(2)	B says to A, "I got it," A can discard it
⋮		

If B does not correctly receive the packet (or the packet is lost entirely), then A will not receive the ACK message from B. After waiting a reasonable amount of time, A will resend the message to B using the copy stored in its memory:

A	B	
M(1) →		Send the first packet from A to B
	← ACK(1)	B says to A, "I got it," A can discard it
M(2) →		Send the second packet from A to B
		No response. Wait for a while
M(2) →		and resend the second packet from A to B
	← ACK(2)	B says to A, "I got it," A can discard it
⋮		

Node A and node B are exchanging messages using the ARQ algorithm described in this section. State what action node B should take in each of the following situations:

Node A		Node B
1. M(3)	→	
	←	ACK(3)
M(3)	→	
		?
2. M(3)	→	
	←	ACK(3)
M(4)	→	
		?
3. M(3)	→	
	←	ACK(3)
M(5)	→	
		?

The ACK for a correctly received packet is itself a message and can be lost or damaged during transmission. If an ACK is lost, then A will incorrectly assume that the original packet was lost and will retransmit a copy. However, B will know this is a copy since it will have the same sequence number as the correct packet received earlier. It simply acknowledges the duplicate and discards it. This ARQ algorithm guarantees that every message sent will (eventually) be correctly received at the destination.

Thus, we can think of the data link layer protocols as creating an error-free "message pipe," in which messages go in one end and always come out the other end correct and in the proper order.

• • • M(3) M(2) M(1) ⟶ ▬▬▬▬▬▬ ⟶ • • • M(3) M(2) M(1)

Message pipe

▶ 7.3.3 Network Layer

The first two layers of our protocol stack together give us the ability to transmit a message from node A to node B, but only if these two nodes are directly connected by a physical link. If we look back at the model of a wide-area network shown in Figure 7.7, we see that the great majority of nodes are *not* directly connected. It is the job of the end-to-end **network layer** protocols to deliver a message from the site where it was created to its ultimate destination. As part of this delivery task, every node must agree to use the same node addressing scheme so that everyone is able to identify that ultimate destination. Thus, the two critical responsibilities of the network layer are

- Creating a universal addressing scheme for all network nodes
- Delivering messages between any two nodes in the network

Every node in the network must run the identical network layer protocol, and it is one of the most important parts of the protocol stack. It is often said that the network layer is the "glue" that holds the entire network together. The network layer in the Internet is called **IP**, for **Internet Protocol**, and it is the protocol that we will describe in this section.

You have almost certainly been exposed to the host naming scheme used by the Internet, as you use it in all your email and Web applications. For example, the machines of the two authors of this book have the following names:

macalester.edu

hawaii.edu

However, these symbolic **host names** are not the actual names that nodes use to identify each other in IP. Instead, nodes identify each other using a 32-bit **IP address**, often written as four 8-bit numeric quantities in the range 0–255, each grouping separated by a dot.[1] For example, the machine referred to as macalester.edu has the 32-bit IP address 141.140.1.5. In binary it appears as follows:

10001101 10001100 00000001 00000101
   141   *140*   *1*   *5*

and this is the actual destination address that would be placed inside the message as it makes its way through the Internet. Looking at the numeric address shown above, it is easy to understand why people prefer symbolic names. While it is easy for humans to remember mnemonic character strings, imagine having to remember a sequence of 32 binary digits. (This is reminiscent of the benefits of assembly language over machine language.)

It is the task of a special Internet application called the **Domain Name Service,** abbreviated **DNS,** to convert from a symbolic host name such as

---

1 The people who assign IP addresses are actually starting to run out of numbers. The new standard for IP calls for increasing the size of the address field from 32 to 128 bits. This would provide enough IP addresses for every atom in the universe. They are determined not to run out of numbers this time!

macalester.edu to its 32-bit IP address 141.140.1.5. The DNS is a massive data-base, distributed over literally thousands of machines that, in total, contain the host name-to-IP address mappings for the 170 million or so host computers on the Internet. When you use a symbolic host name, such as mySchool.edu, this character string is forwarded to a computer called a **local name server** that checks to see if it has a data record containing the IP address for this symbolic name. If so, it returns the corresponding 32-bit value. If not, the local name server forwards it on to a remote name server (and possibly another, and another, . . .) until it locates the name server that knows the correct IP address.

Let's use the diagram shown earlier to see how the network layer operates:

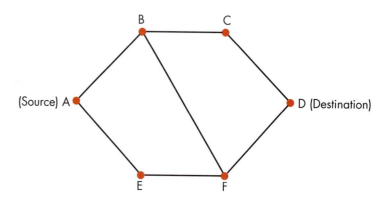

Assume A wishes to send a message to D. First, node A uses the DNS to obtain the IP address of node D, which it inserts into its message. Since there is no direct path from A to D, the message will be sent along a multi-hop path reaching from A to D. (Each of these direct machine-to-machine hops uses the data link layer protocols described in the previous section.) In this example there are four possibilities—ABCD, AEFD, ABFD, and AEFBCD—and the process of selecting one specific path is called **routing**.

Routing algorithms are highly complex because of the massive volume of data that must be maintained and the enormous amount of processing required to determine the optimal route, called the **shortest path**. The shortest path between two nodes is not necessarily the physically shortest path in length, but the path through which the message can travel the fastest. To determine the shortest path between every pair of nodes, we need to know the time delay between every connected pair of nodes in the network. In the example above, this would be the time to get from A to B, from B to C, from A to E, and so on. For small networks this is feasible, but for networks like the Internet, with hundreds of millions of nodes and links, this is an unimaginably huge amount of data to obtain and keep current.

Even if we were somehow able to collect all this data, we are still not finished. Now we must determine exactly which path to select. One possible algorithm is to determine the time required to send a message along *every* path from a source to a destination and then pick the one with the smallest delay. For example, to determine the optimal path from A to D, we could start out by summing the individual delays from A to B, B to C, and C to D, which would give us the time to get from A to D using the route A → B → C → D. We now repeat this process for every other path from A to D and pick the smallest.

However, in Section 3.5 we showed that these types of "brute force" algorithms grow exponentially in the time needed to solve the problem, and it is infeasible for any but the tiniest networks. Fortunately, there are much better algorithms that can solve this problem in $O(N^2)$ time, where N is the number of nodes in the network. (The Internet uses a method called **Dijkstra's shortest path algorithm.**) For large networks, where $N = 10^7$ or 10^8, an $O(N^2)$ algorithm might require on the order of 10^{14} or 10^{16} calculations to determine the best route from any node to another—still a lot of work.

There are additional problems that make routing so difficult. One complication is *topological change.* The Internet is not static but, instead, highly dynamic, with new links and new nodes added on an almost daily basis. Therefore, a route that is optimal now may not be optimal in a couple of days or even a couple of hours. For example, the optimal route from A to B in our diagram may currently be A → B → C → D. However, if a new line is added connecting nodes E and D, this might change the shortest path to A → E → D. Because of frequent changes, routing tables must be recomputed often, which further magnifies the amount of work.

There is also the question of *network failures.* It may be that when everything is working properly, the optimal route from A to D is A → B → C → D. But what if node B fails? Rather than have all communications between A and D suspended, it would be preferable for the network to switch to an alternative route that does not pass through node B, such as A → E → F → D. This ability to dynamically reroute messages would allow a WAN to continue operating even in the presence of node and link failures.

This has been only a brief overview of the network layer; it has many other responsibilities not mentioned here, including network management, broadcasting, and locating mobile nodes that move around the network. The network layer is truly a complex piece of software.

With the addition of the network layer to our protocol stack, we no longer have just a bit pipe or a message pipe, but a true "network delivery service" in which messages are delivered between any two nodes in the network, regardless of where they are located:

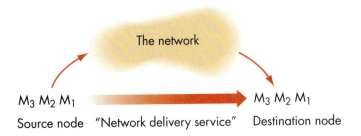

$M_3 \; M_2 \; M_1$ $M_3 \; M_2 \; M_1$

Source node   "Network delivery service"   Destination node

It may seem that we are now finished, as our message has reached the correct destination. Unfortunately, that is not the case. You will see what is left as we discuss the last two layers in our protocol stack.

Imagine that 123 Main St. is a large, multistory office building with thousands of tenants. When you address a letter to one of these tenants, it is not enough to write:

Joe Smith

123 Main St.

My Town, Minnesota

This identifies the correct building, but how will the people in the central mailroom locate "Joe Smith" from among the thousands of people who work

PRACTICE PROBLEMS

Given the following 6-node wide-area network where the numbers attached to the links are a measure of the "delay" in using that link (e.g., some lines could be more heavily used than others, and there is more waiting), answer the following questions:

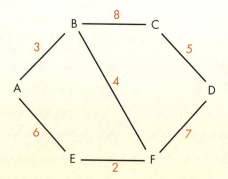

1. What is the shortest path from node A to node D, where shortest path is defined as the path with the smallest sum of the delays on each individual link? Explain exactly how you went about finding that path.

2. Do you think the algorithm you used in Problem 1 would work if we redrew the graph so it had 26 nodes rather than 6 and about 50 links rather than 10? Why or why not?

3. What if the link connecting node F to node D fails? What is now the shortest path from node A to node D? Could the failure of any one link in this network prevent nodes A and D from communicating?

in this building? The answer is that we need to provide a more descriptive address, one that not only identifies the correct building but also exactly where inside this building Mr. Smith works:

Joe Smith

Acme Services Inc., Suite 2701

123 Main St.

MyTown, Minnesota

The same situation exists on the Internet. Every host computer has an IP address that uniquely identifies it. However, there may be many application programs running on that one machine, each one "doing its own thing." When a message comes in, how will we know which application program it is for and where to deliver it?

The answer is that we need a second level of address that identifies not only a specific machine but also a specific program running on that machine. This "program identifier," usually just a small integer value, is called a **port number,** and it serves the same role as the address line "Acme Services Inc., Suite 2701" shown above. Assigning port numbers to programs and remembering which program goes with which port, is a part of the **transport layer protocols**. While each host computer has one IP address, it may at any instant in time have many active ports.

The relationship between these two address types is shown in Figure 7.14. This diagram shows two hosts: Host A whose IP address is 1.2.3.4, and Host B with IP address 5.6.7.8. Host A is currently running two programs called W and X, with port numbers 12 and 567 respectively, while Host B is executing two programs named Y and Z, with port numbers 44 and 709.

It is the job of the transport layer protocols to create a "program-to-program" delivery service, in which we don't simply move messages from one host to another, but from a specific program at the source to a specific program at the destination.

In the example of Figure 7.14, it would be the job of the network layer protocol to deliver the message from the host with IP address 1.2.3.4 to the host with IP address 5.6.7.8, at which point its responsibilities would be over. The transport protocol at the destination node would now examine the message that just arrived to determine which program should get it, based on the

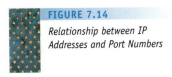

FIGURE 7.14

Relationship between IP Addresses and Port Numbers

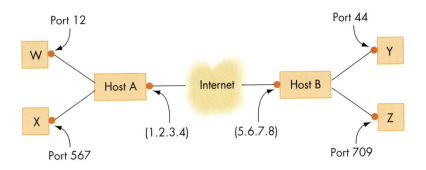

port number field inside the message. For example, if the port number field were 709, then the information in the message would be forwarded to application program Z. (What program Z does with this information and exactly what that message means are not part of the transport protocols but rather the application protocols discussed in the next section.)

How does a program learn the port number of a program running on a remote machine somewhere out in the network? The answer is that all important applications on the Internet use **well-known port numbers.** Just as everyone in the U.S. knows that directory service is located at 555-1212 and police and fire emergencies are reported to 911, fixed integer values are assigned to certain applications, and those values are made known to every machine on the Internet. For example, the HTTP protocol, which allows us to access remote Web pages (and which we will discuss in the next section), always uses port 80. If you wish to get a Web page from another machine, you simply need to talk to the program that is listening for messages on port 80.

Figure 7.16 (in the next section) lists the port numbers of some common Internet applications. A list of all well-known port assignments is contained in the report entitled *Assigned Numbers on the Internet* (RFC 1700) available over the Internet[2]. The only time you would need to get a new port number is when you are developing a new application.

The other primary responsibility of the transport layer has to do with errors and reliability. When we introduced the data link layer in Section 7.3.2, we said that one of its tasks was to take the inherently unreliable physical channel underneath it and turn it into an efficient and error free channel. That same type of relationship exists between the transport layer and the layer underneath it, namely the network layer.

The network layer of the Internet, IP, is an inherently unreliable communication channel. IP uses what is called a *good faith* transmission model. That means that it tries very hard to deliver a message from source to destination, but it does not guarantee delivery. In this sense, IP is like the post office. The post office does a very good job of delivering mail, and the overwhelming majority of letters do get through. However, they do not guarantee that absolutely every letter you send will arrive, and they do not guarantee that letters will arrive either within a specific time period or in exactly the same order that they were originally posted. If you need these features you have to use some type of "special handling" service such as Registered Mail or Express Mail.

In a sense, the transport layer represents just this type of "special handling" service. Its job is to create a high-quality, error free, order preserving end-to-end delivery service on top of the unreliable delivery services provided by IP. On the Internet, the primary transport protocol is **TCP,** an acronym for *Transport Control Protocol.* (There is another transport protocol called **UDP** for *User Datagram Protocol.* We will not be discussing it here.)

To provide its services, TCP requires that the two programs at the source and destination node initially establish a **connection.** That is, they must first

---

2 RFCs, as we will mention in the Challenge Work section, are technical documents that describe virtually all aspects of Internet behavior. They are all available online at www.rfc-editor.org/rfc.html.

FIGURE 7.15

Logical View of a TCP Connection

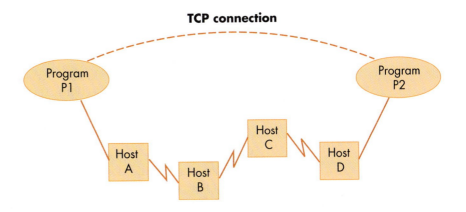

inform each other of their desire to exchange messages, and they must describe the "quality of service" they wish to receive. This connection does not exist in a hardware sense, and there is no "wire" stretched between the two nodes. Instead, it is a logical connection that exists only as entries in tables. However, TCP can make this logical connection behave exactly as if there were a real connection directly between these two programs. This logical view of a TCP connection is shown in Figure 7.15.

Once this connection has been established, messages can be transmitted along it from the source program to the destination program. Programs P1 and P2 will appear to have a direct, error free link between them. In reality, however, their communications will go from P1 to A, B, C, D, and finally to P2.

TCP uses the same ARQ algorithm described in our discussion of the data link level. The receiving program must acknowledge every message correctly received. Therefore, if a message is lost in the network and does not arrive, the sending program will not receive an acknowledgment. After waiting a while, a copy can be resent. Thus, every single message will ultimately be delivered to the application program waiting for it and, from its point of view, this TCP connection does appear to be an error-free channel.

Furthermore, every message sent on this TCP connection contains a sequence number—1, 2, 3, ... If messages are received out of order (say message 3 comes in before message 2 because of errors along the route), then TCP will simply hold the later message (number 3) until the earlier one (number 2) correctly arrives. At that time it can deliver both messages to the application program in the proper order, first 2 then 3. From the destination's point of view, this TCP connection always delivers messages in the proper order.

After describing four layers of protocol, we have a complete end-to-end delivery service. The network is able to transmit a message from a program anywhere in the network to another program anywhere in the network, and do it both correctly and efficiently. The only thing left to specify is the *content* of those messages; that is, what does a program want to say to another program? Essentially we are asking, What types of applications do we want to give to our network users and exactly how do we implement them? We answer that question as we look at the very top layer of our protocol stack—the application layer.

▶ 7.3.5 Application Layer

The **application layer protocols** are the rules for implementing the end-user services provided by a network, and they are built on top of the four protocol layers described in previous sections. These services are the reason that networks exist in the first place, and it has been the appearance of exciting new applications (often called "killer apps") that has fueled the rapid growth of networking and the Internet—email in the 70s, chat rooms in the 80s, the Web and E-commerce in the 90s and the 21st century. Figure 7.16 lists a few of the important application protocols on the Internet.

It is not possible in this one section to discuss all the protocols listed in Figure 7.16. Instead, we will briefly overview the HTTP protocol used by the World Wide Web to access and deliver Web pages. This explanation will serve as a general model for how application layer services are typically built on top of the TCP/IP protocol stack that we have introduced.

A single Web page is identified by a symbolic string called a **Uniform Resource Locator,** abbreviated **URL.** URLs have three parts, and they look like this:

> *protocol://host address/page*

The first part, *protocol*, indicates the type of information contained in this page. The most common format is hypertext information, and we access it using the **hypertext transfer protocol** called "HTTP." The Web is designed to accept and transfer other types of information as well. Thus, we could use the protocol identifier "news" to obtain information from bulletin boards and news groups, or "mailto," which allows us to send and receive email documents via the Web. The second part of the URL is the *host address* of the machine where the page is stored. This is the symbolic host name first discussed in Section 7.3.3. Finally, the third and last part of the URL is the *page* identification, which is usually a file stored on the specified machine. Thus, a typical URL might look like the following:

> *http://www.macalester.edu/about/history.html*

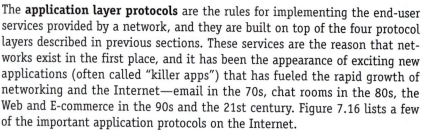

FIGURE 7.16

Some Popular Application Protocols on the Internet

Acronym	Name	Application	Well-known Port
HTTP	Hypertext Transfer Protocol	Accessing web pages	80
SMTP	Simple Mail Transfer Protocol	Sending electronic mail	25
POP3	Post Office Protocol	Receiving electronic mail	110
IMAP	Internet Mail Access Protocol	Receiving electronic mail	143
FTP	File Transfer Protocol	Accessing remote files	21
TELNET	Terminal Emulation Protocol	Remote terminal access	23
DNS	Domain Name Service	Translating symbolic host names to 32-bit IP addresses	42

This identifies a hypertext ("http") document stored in a file called /about/history.html located on a host computer whose symbolic name is www.macalester.edu. (Note: "http" is the assumed default if the protocol field is omitted. Thus, the previous URL can also be written as simply www.macalester.edu/about/history.html.)

Before we can use the HTTP protocol to transfer the desired page, we must first establish a connection between the HTTP client program (the Web browser being run by the user) and port 80, the port number of the HTTP Web server located at the node where the Web page resides, namely www.macalester.edu. The network uses the TCP protocol described in Section 7.3.4 to establish this connection. Thus, we can clearly see how the "HTTP" application protocol is built on top of the TCP/IP protocol stack just described.

Once we have established this connection, we then use the HTTP application protocol to access the desired Web page. An HTTP **request message** is sent on the TCP connection from the client to the server, specifying the name of a Web page. A second HTTP message type, called a **response message,** is returned from the server to the client along the same TCP connection. The response contains a status code specifying whether or not the request was successful and, if so, it includes the requested page.[3]

Let's illustrate how these pieces work together using a simple example. Imagine that you are using a Web browser and have just clicked on the following URL:

http://www.macalester.edu/about/history.html

The following sequence of events will take place:

1. Your browser scans the URL and extracts the host name of the machine to which it must connect—www.macalester.edu. (Let's disregard the issue of how this symbolic name is converted to its corresponding 32-bit IP address.)

2. Your browser asks TCP to establish a connection between itself and port 80 (the Web server) of the machine called www.macalester.edu.

3. When the TCP connection between your browser and the Web server is successfully established, the browser scans the URL on which you clicked to determine the identify of the page you want to access. In this case it is /about/history.html. The browser constructs an http GET message, which requests the contents of that Web page. This GET message will look something like the following:

   GET   /about/history.html   HTTP /1.1

   Host: www.macalester.edu

   Accept-language: English

   This message says that we want a copy of the English language page /about/history.html located at www.macalester.edu, and it

---

3 We have probably all had the experience of seeing return code 404: Page Not Found, which means the requested document does not exist on this server.

should be accessed using the HTTP protocol, version 1.1. (An actual GET message is a bit more complex and includes a number of additional fields not shown here.)

4. The http GET message in step 3 is transmitted across the Internet from the client's Web browser program at the source node to the Web server at the destination node using the services of TCP/IP as well as the data link and physical layer protocols.

5. When the GET message arrives, it is delivered to the Web server (since it is the one listening on port 80). The Web server locates the file named in the GET message and creates a response message containing a copy of the contents of that file. This response message looks something like the following:

HTTP/1.1   200 OK

Connection: close

Date: Thursday, 24 Mar 2004

Content Length: 53908

Content Type: text/html

. . . (the contents of the Web page go here) . . .

This response message says that the server successfully found the file (code 200), and it contains 53,908 bytes of text. It also says that after the Web page has been sent, the TCP connection between the browser and the server will be closed. Finally, there is a copy of the entire Web page. (Again, some fields in the response message have been omitted for clarity.)

6. This HTTP response message in step 5 is transmitted across the Internet from the Web server back to the port of the client's Web browser using the services of TCP/IP as well as the data link and physical layer protocols.

7. The message is delivered to your browser, and the page is displayed on the screen. The TCP connection between the two programs is terminated.

Something similar to this will be followed every time we click on a new URL. This sequence of events is diagrammed in Figure 7.17.

LABORATORY EXPERIENCE 11

We have just completed a rather long and complex discussion of how a network functions. In this laboratory experience, we illustrate these ideas using a network simulator package. This simulator allows you to observe and control many of the technical concepts introduced in this section, concepts such as packets, messages, error detection, error correction, and routing. By simulating the behavior of a wide-area network, many of these technical concepts should become much more clear and understandable.

FIGURE 7.17

Behavior of the HTTP Application-Level Protocol

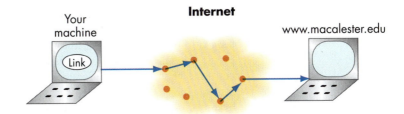

Internet

Your machine

Link

www.macalester.edu

Link = www.macalester.edu

(a) Using TCP/IP to establish a connection to the destination machine

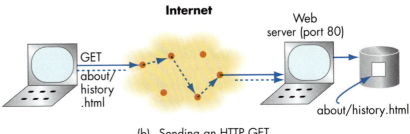

Internet

GET about/ history .html

Web server (port 80)

about/history.html

(b) Sending an HTTP GET message to the destination to fetch the desired page

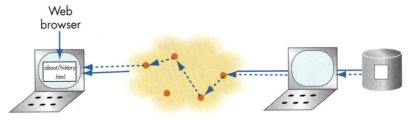

Web browser

about/history .html

(c) Returning a copy of the page using a response message and displaying it using the web browser

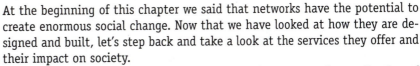

7.4   Network Services and Benefits

At the beginning of this chapter we said that networks have the potential to create enormous social change. Now that we have looked at how they are designed and built, let's step back and take a look at the services they offer and their impact on society.

Electronic mail (email) has been the single most popular application of networks for the last 30 years. When the Internet was first developed, its designers thought that it would be an ideal way to access advanced, high-performance hardware and software. Instead, what they found was that it was a wonderfully effective way to reach other people, and email rapidly became the dominant application.

Email is *convenient*. You can send a message whenever you want, and it will wait for the recipient to log on and read it at his or her convenience.

Email is *fast*. A message from the United States will typically arrive anywhere in the world in less than a minute, even though it may have to pass through 15 or 20 nodes along the way (using the packet-switched protocols described in the previous section). Email supports *multimedia*. The contents of your electronic messages are not limited to characters but can also include a wide range of *attachments*, including photographs, text, graphics, and sound. Finally, email is a *broadcast medium*. A computer can send a letter to a thousand recipients as easily as it can send it to one (which may, in fact, be a detriment rather than an advantage as we see in the box labeled "Spam").

An interesting application related to email is **bulletin boards** and **news groups.** A bulletin board is a shared public file where anyone can post messages and everyone is free to browse and read the postings of others. It is an electronic version of the bulletin boards commonly seen in grocery stores, cafes, and public libraries. Most bulletin boards are associated with a particular topic or special area of interest. These specialized bulletin boards, called **news groups,** are a wonderful way to create a community of individuals who share a common interest and want to exchange ideas and opinions. Some news groups support **chat rooms**—the real-time exchange of messages. Rather than posting a message to a file that is read at a later time, what the sender types appears immediately on the screen of one or more individuals, allowing for the direct exchange of ideas.

In addition to allowing people to interact, another important network service is **resource sharing,** the ability to share *physical resources*, such as a printer or storage device, as well as *logical resources*, such as software and information.

The prices of computers and peripherals have been dropping for many years, so it is tempting to think that everyone should buy their own I/O or storage devices. However, that is not a cost-effective way to configure computer systems. For example, a high-quality color printer may be used rather

Spam

Spam is electronic "junk mail"—unsolicited email sent to thousands, even millions, of network users without their permission or knowledge. It is not certain where the term *spam* came from, but the best guess is from the famous Monty Python comedy routine in which the word *spam* is repeated over and over. Thus, spam is a synonym for the seemingly endless repetition of silly or worthless words.

Junk mail in the form of advertising flyers and political brochures has been a staple of surface mail for many years. But there is a natural cap on its volume—the sender has to pay the post office to deliver it. So, unless

that person feels that a mailing will produce a profitable return or have a worthwhile purpose, it will not be sent.

However, email does not have that built-in cap, and it is beginning to clutter our electronic mail boxes and consume large amounts of bandwidth. Since the Internet is a public facility, there is not a lot that can be done to regulate spam. A number of companies have developed **mail filters** that attempt to determine which emails are useful and which are spam. Unfortunately, as soon as a filter is developed and released, the "spammers" quickly figure out a way to beat it and get their email through to your machine. Probably the best filter developed so far (and for the near future) is the DELETE button on your keyboard!

FIGURE 7.18

The Client-Server Model of
Computing

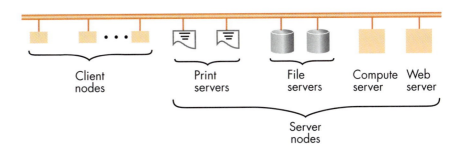

Client
nodes

Print
servers

File
servers

Compute
server

Web
server

Server
nodes

infrequently. Buying everyone in the office his or her own printer would leave
most of them idle for long periods of time. It is far more efficient to have a
few shared printers, called **print servers**, which can be accessed whenever
needed. Similarly, if a group of users require access to a data file or a piece of
software, it makes sense to keep a single copy on a shared network disk,
called a **file server.** A network file server can also be a cost-effective way to
provide shared backup services to multiple sites.

The style of computing wherein some nodes provide services while the
remaining nodes are users (or clients) of those services is called, naturally
enough, **client-server computing.** We have seen two examples—print
servers and file servers—but there are many others, such as mail servers,
name servers, compute servers, and Web servers. The philosophy behind the
client-server model is that we use a network to share resources that are too
widespread, too expensive, or used too infrequently to warrant replication at
every node. A diagram of the client-server model of computing is shown in
Figure 7.18.

Information sharing is another important service, and a network is an
excellent way to access scientific, medical, legal, and commercial data files
stored on systems all over the world. (In fact, it was a desire to share information efficiently among hundreds of physicists that led to the development
of the World Wide Web in the early 1990s.) For example, information can be
distributed among the geographically dispersed sites of a multinational corporation and shared as needed, using a **distributed database.** Web pages can
be exchanged between remote systems. Files can be transmitted anywhere in
the world using the FTP protocol discussed in the previous section, and online databases can be accessed by anyone regardless of location.

Many network sites now provide a service called an **information utility.**
These nodes contain massive amounts of information that can be electronically searched for specific facts or documents. Frequently the site contains
highly specialized information about a single topic, such as geopolitical data,
current stock prices, real estate records, or information on case law and legal
precedents. Nowadays it is more common for students, scientists, businesspeople, and politicians to search for information at their monitor than in the
stacks of a library.

Another important network service is the ability to support collabora-
tive group efforts in producing a shared document such as a user's manual,
grant application, or design specification. Workers on a project can communicate via the network, electronic calendars can be checked and meetings

scheduled automatically, and documents in progress can be shared, discussed online, and jointly reviewed and edited. A rapidly growing network application is **groupware**—software that facilitates the simultaneous efforts of individuals connected by a network and working on a single shared project.

Electronic commerce (or just **e-commerce**) is a general term applied to any use of computers and networking to support the paperless exchange of goods, information, and services in the commercial sector. The idea of using computers and networks to do business has been around for some time; the early applications of e-commerce include (1) the automatic deposit of paychecks, (2) automatic teller machines (ATMs) for handling financial transactions from remote sites, and (3) the use of scanning devices at check-out counters to capture sales and inventory information in machine-readable form.

More recently interest has focused on the use of the Internet and the World Wide Web to advertise and sell goods and services online. Initially, the Internet was used mostly by scientists and engineers. However, the business world soon came to appreciate the potential of a communications medium that could cheaply and reliably reach millions of people around the world. In the last 5–10 years, traffic on the Internet has changed from primarily academic and professional to heavily commercial. For example, as of early 2003, there were about 41,000,000 host computers in the .com (U.S. commercial) domain, while fewer than 8,000,000 were in the .edu domain (U.S. educational institutions).

We will have much more to say about electronic commerce and commercial uses of the Internet in Chapter 13.

7.5   A Brief History of the Internet and the World Wide Web

In the preceding sections we have discussed the technical characteristics and services of networks in general. However, to most people, the phrase *computer network* isn't a generalized term but a very specific one—the global Internet and its most popular component, the World Wide Web.

In this section we highlight the history, development, and growth of the Internet and the World Wide Web. Much of the information in the following pages is taken from the 1997 article "A Brief History of the Internet," written by its original designers and available on the World Wide Web.[4]

In the words of its designers, "The Internet has revolutionized the computer and communications world like nothing before. It is at once a worldwide broadcasting capability, a mechanism for information dissemination, and a medium for collaboration and interaction between individuals and their computers without regard for geographic location." This statement is most accurate, for the Internet has indeed changed the way that people learn and study, access information, exchange ideas, and do business.

---

4 Leitner, B., Cerf, V., Kahn, R., Kleinrock L., Lynch, D., Postel, J., Roberts, L., and Wolff, S., "A Brief History of the Internet," www.isoc.org/internet-history/, February 20, 1997.

7.5.1   *The Internet*

Surprisingly, the Internet is not a recent development but an idea that has been around for more than 35 years. The concept first took shape during the early and mid-1960s and was based on the work of computer scientists at MIT and the RAND Corporation in the United States and the NPL Research Laboratory in Great Britain. The first proposal for building a computer network was made by J. C. R. Licklider of MIT in August 1962. He wrote his colleagues a memo entitled (somewhat dramatically) "The Galactic Network," in which he described a globally interconnected set of computers through which everyone could access data and software. He convinced other researchers at MIT of the validity of his ideas, including Larry Roberts and Leonard Kleinrock. From 1962 to 1967 they and others investigated the theoretical foundations of wide area networking, especially such fundamental technical concepts as protocols, packet switching, and routing.

In 1966 Roberts moved to the Advanced Research Projects Agency (ARPA), a small research office of the Department of Defense charged with developing technology that could be of use to the U.S. military. ARPA was interested in packet-switched networking because it seemed to be a more secure form of communications during wartime. (Traditional dial-up telephones were considered too vulnerable because the failure of the central phone switch would completely cut all voice communications. As we described earlier, a WAN can automatically route around a failed line or node in order to maintain communications.)

ARPA funded a number of network-related research projects, and in 1967 Roberts presented the first research paper describing ARPA's plans to build a wide area packet-switched computer network. For the next two years, work proceeded on designing the network hardware and software. The first two nodes of this new network, called the ARPANET, were constructed at UCLA and the Stanford Research Institute (SRI), and in October 1969, the first computer-to-computer network message was sent. Later that same year two more nodes were added (UC Santa Barbara and the University of Utah), and by the end of 1969, the budding 4-node network was off the ground.

The ARPANET grew quickly during the early 1970s, and it was formally demonstrated to the scientific community at an international conference in 1972. It was also in late 1972 that the first "killer app" (critically important application) was developed—electronic mail. It was an immediate success and caused an explosion of growth in people-to-people traffic rather than the people-to-machine or machine-to-machine traffic that dominated usage in the first few years.

The success of the ARPANET in the 1970s led other researchers to develop similar types of computer networks to support information exchange within their own specific scientific area: HEPNet (High Energy Physics Network), CSNET (Computer Science Network), and MFENet (Magnetic Fusion Energy Network). Furthermore, corporations started to notice the success of the ARPANET and began developing proprietary networks that they planned to market to their customers: SNA (Systems Network Architecture) at the IBM Corp. and DECNet from the Digital Equipment Corporation. The 1970s were a time of rapid expansion of networks in both the academic and commercial communities.

Farsighted researchers at ARPA, in particular Robert Kahn, realized that this rapid and unplanned proliferation of independent networks would lead to incompatibilities and prevent users on different networks from communicating with each other, a situation that recalls the problems that national railway systems have sharing rail cars because of their use of different gauge track. Kahn knew that to obtain maximum benefits from this new technology, all networks would need to communicate in a standardized fashion. He developed the concept of **internetworking,** which stated that any wide-area network is free to do whatever it wants *internally*. However, at the point where two networks meet, both must use a common addressing scheme and identical protocols—that is, they must speak the same language.

This is the same concept that governs the international telephone system. Every country is free to build its own internal phone system in whatever way it wants, but all must agree to use a standardized worldwide numbering system (country code, city code), and each must agree to send and receive telephone calls outside its borders in the format standardized by the worldwide telephone regulatory agency.

Figure 7.19 is a diagram of a "network of networks." It shows four wide area networks called A, B, C, and D interconnected by a device called a **gateway** that makes the internetwork connections and provides routing between different WANs.

To allow the four WANs of Figure 7.19 to communicate, Kahn and his colleagues needed to create (1) a standardized way for a node in one WAN to identify a node located in a different WAN, and (2) a universally recognized message format for exchanging information across WAN boundaries. Kahn, along with Dr. Vinton Cerf of Stanford, began working on these problems in 1973, and together they designed the solutions that were to become the framework for the Internet. Specifically, they created both the hierarchical host naming scheme that we use today and the TCP/IP protocols that became the "common language" spoken by networks around the world. (These protocols were discussed in Sections 7.3.3 and 7.3.4.)

During the late 1970s and early 1980s, work proceeded on implementing and installing TCP/IP on not only mainframe computers but also on the PCs and desktop machines that were just starting to appear in the marketplace. It

FIGURE 7.19

A Network of Networks

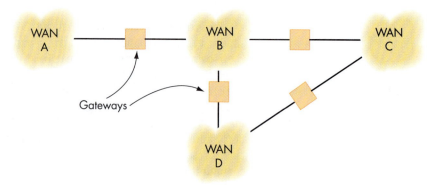

is a tribute to the power and flexibility of the TCP/IP protocols that they were able to adapt to a computing environment quite different from the one that existed when they were first created. Originally designed to work with the large mainframe computers of the 1970s, they were successfully implemented on desktop PCs connected by LANs, the computing environment of the 1980s, 1990s, and today.

By the early 1980s, TCP/IP was being used all around the world. Even networks that internally used other communication protocols implemented TCP/IP in order to exchange information with nodes outside their own community. At the same time, exciting new applications appeared that were designed to meet the growing needs of the networking community. (Many of these application protocols were introduced in Section 7.3.5.) For example, **Telnet** is a software package that allows users to log on remotely to another computer and use it as though it were their own local machine. **FTP,** an acronym for **file transfer protocol,** is a way to move files around the network quickly and easily. Along with email (still wildly popular), these and other new applications added more fuel to the superheated growth of computer networks.

With TCP/IP becoming a de facto network standard, a global addressing scheme, and a growing set of important applications, the infrastructure was in place for the creation of a truly international network. The Internet, in its modern form, had slowly begun to emerge.

However, although many of the technical problems had been solved, networking had not yet had a significant impact on the general population for one very important reason: In order to use the ARPANET, you needed a research grant from the U.S. Department of Defense (DOD)— not something that most of us have. By the early 1980s many people were using the Internet, but they were almost exclusively physicists, engineers, and computer scientists at a select set of secure military and research centers. For example, in 1982, 13 years after its creation, there were only 235 computers connected to the ARPANET.

One last step was needed, and it was taken by the National Science Foundation (NSF) in 1984. In that year the NSF initiated a project whose goal was to bring the advantages of the Internet to the *entire* academic and professional community, regardless of discipline or relationship with the DOD. NSF planned and built a national network called **NSFNet,** which used TCP/IP technology identical to the ARPANET. This new network interconnected six NSF supercomputer centers with dozens of new regional networks set up by the NSF. These new regional networks included thousands of users at places like universities, government agencies, libraries, museums, medical centers, and even high schools. Thus, by the mid-1980s this emerging "network of networks" had grown to include many new sites and, even more important, a huge group of first-time users such as students, faculty, librarians, museum staff, politicians, civil servants, and urban planners, to name just a few.

At about the same time, other countries began developing wide-area TCP/IP backbone networks like NSFNet to interconnect their own medical centers, schools, research centers, and government agencies. As these national networks were created, they were also linked into this expanding network, and the user population continued to expand. For the first time since the development of networking, the technology had begun to have an impact on the wider community. A diagram of the state of internetworking in the late 1980s is shown in Figure 7.20.

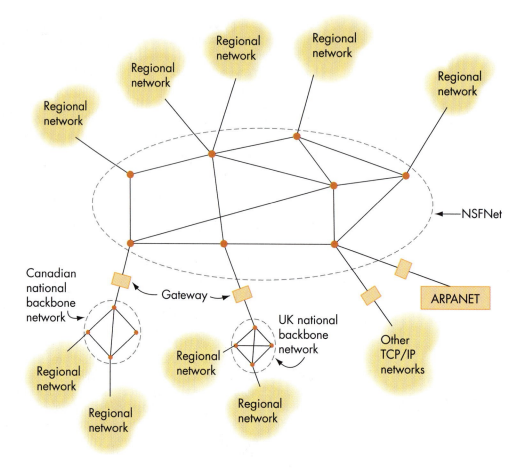

Regional network

Regional network

Regional network

Regional network

Regional network

Regional network

◄── NSFNet

Canadian national backbone network

Gateway ──►

UK national backbone network

ARPANET

Other TCP/IP networks

Regional network

Regional network

Regional network

Regional network

FIGURE 7.20

State of Networking in the Late 1980s

Some time in the late 1980s, the term ARPANET ceased to be used because, as Figure 7.20 shows, the ARPANET was now only one of many networks belonging to a much larger collection. (By 1990 it had grown to 300,000 computers on 3,000 separate networks.) People began referring to this entire collection of interconnected networks as "the Internet," though this name was not officially adopted until much later. The formal acceptance of the term **Internet** by the U.S. Government occurred on October 24, 1995.

Once people had easy access, the Internet became an immediate success and grew rapidly. By the middle of 1993, it included 1.8 million host computers, and roughly 5 to 10 million active users, and its size was doubling every year. In fact it had become so successful that the NSF decided it was time to get out of the "networking business." The goal of the National Science Foundation is to fund basic research, not to operate an ongoing commercial enterprise. In April 1995, NSFNet closed up shop. The exit of the U.S. government from the networking arena created business opportunities for new firms called **Internet service providers** that offered the Internet access once provided by the ARPANET and NSFNet.

From a humble beginning of four universities in 1969, by the middle of 2003 the Internet had grown to 171,000,000 computers located in just about

The Internet is a truly "global phenomenon" impacting the way that people work, shop, and communicate throughout the world. Consider that, while the United Nations has 191 member states, the Domain Name System (DNS) of the Internet includes entries for 239 countries, territories, and possessions—48 more than the UN. The DNS includes standardized domain names for such places as (you may want to get out your Atlas) the South Sandwich Islands (.gs), San Marino (.sm), Bouvet Island (.bv), Mayotte (.yt), Kiribati (.ki), Svalbard and Jan Mayen Islands (.sj), and even the continent of Antarctica (.aq), which includes over 100 computers in its domain. The smallest nonempty DNS domain is .pm—the St. Pierre and Miquelon Islands off the coast of Newfoundland. It includes exactly one host computer!

every country in the world. The extraordinary growth of the Internet continues to this very day. Figure 7.9 in Section 7.2.4 showed a graph of the number of host computers connected to the Internet.

The Internet has been one of the biggest success stories in moving research out of the laboratory and into the wider community. What began as the wild idea of a few dedicated researchers has grown, in only 35 years, into a global communications infrastructure moving trillions of bits of data among hundreds of millions of people. It has adapted time and time again—to changes in usage (from research and academic to commercial and entertainment), changes in hardware (from mainframes to PCs and local area networks), and changes in scale (from hundreds of nodes to hundreds of millions).

Amazing enough, however, the Internet is still undergoing massive growth and change, this time from the most important new "killer app" developed for the Internet since email—the World Wide Web.

7.5.2 *The World Wide Web*

Tim Berners-Lee, a researcher at CERN, the European High Energy Physics Laboratory in Geneva, Switzerland, first came up with the idea for a hypertext-based information distribution system in 1989. Because physics research is often done by teams of people from many different universities, he wanted to create a way for scientists throughout Europe and North America to easily and quickly exchange information such as research articles, journals, and experimental data. Although they could use existing Internet services such as FTP and email, Berners-Lee wanted to make information sharing easier and more intuitive for people not all that familiar with or comfortable with computer networks.

Beginning in 1990 he designed and built a system using the concept of **hypertext,** a collection of documents interconnected by pointers, called **links,** as shown in Figure 7.21. Most documents are meant to be read linearly from beginning to end, but users of hypertext documents (called **pages** in Web parlance) are free to navigate the collection in whatever order they want by traversing the links to move freely from page to page. Berners-Lee reasoned that the idea of hypertext matched up very well with the concept of networking and the Internet. Hypertext documents would be files stored on

FIGURE 7.21

Hypertext Documents

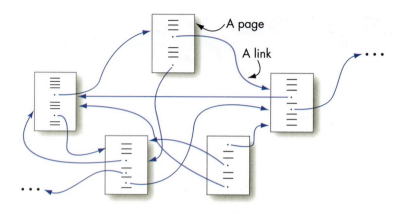

the machines of the Internet, and a link would be the name of a page along with the IP address of the machine where that page is stored. He called his hypertext link a **URL,** an acronym for *Uniform Resource Locator,* and it is the worldwide identification of a Web page located on a specific host computer on the Internet.

Berners-Lee named his new information system the **World Wide Web,** and it was completed and made available to all researchers at CERN in May 1991, the date that marks the birth of the Web. It became an instant success, and traffic on the CERN Web server increased by 1,000% in its first two years of use. In April 1993, the directors of CERN, realizing the beneficial impact that the Web could have on research throughout the world announced that, effective immediately, all Web technology developed at CERN would be freely available to everyone without fees or royalties. For many people, this important announcement really marks the emergence of the World Wide Web on a global scale.

A more powerful graphical Web browser, called Mosaic, was developed in late 1993 and made available to the general public so that they could begin to use this new service. With the appearance of Mosaic, the World Wide Web began to "take off." It was a network application that offered users exactly what they needed most—simple access to massive amounts of helpful information whenever they wanted it. Other browsers soon appeared in the marketplace, including Netscape Navigator (1994) and Microsoft Internet Explorer (1995).

In late 1995, the National Science Foundation did a study of the different types of traffic on the Internet as a percentage of all information sent. At that time the World Wide Web represented 23.9% of the total volume of Internet traffic, even though it had been in existence for only 4 years!

Since that time the Web has continued to grow exponentially, containing over 3 billion pages by early 2003. It is by far the fastest growing component of the Internet. The Web's colorful graphics and simple point and click method of accessing information has made it the Internet killer app of the 21st century. It has become the vehicle for bringing the capabilities of networking to everyone—from toddlers to senior citizens and kindergarten students to PhDs. For many people, the World Wide Web *is* the Internet.

7.6   Conclusion

Computer networking has changed enormously in the 30–35 years that it has been around. From a specialized communication system devoted to academic research, it has blossomed into a worldwide information system. What was once the esoteric domain of a few thousand scientists is now used by hundreds of millions, the vast majority of whom have no formal training in computer science. From providing access to technical databases and research journals, it has become a way for the average citizen to shop, chat, stay informed, and be entertained. There is every reason to believe that the Internet will continue to grow and evolve as much in the coming years as it has in the past.

However, the most pressing issue facing the Internet today is not technology and new applications. Those issues have been and will continue to be addressed and solved by the computer science community. The biggest concern with the Internet today is how the growth and direction of networking will be managed and controlled. In its early days, the Internet was run by a core group of specialists without a financial stake in its future, and its management was relatively simple. Currently, the Internet is managed by the *Internet Society*, the nonprofit agency first introduced in Section 7.3. Now that it is a global phenomenon that affects millions of people and generates hundreds of billions of dollars in revenue, the Internet is being pulled and tugged by many new constituencies and stakeholders, such as corporations, politicians, lawyers, advertisers, government agencies, and manufacturers. The question now is who will speak for the Internet in the future and who will help shape its destiny. As the designers of the Internet warned at the end of their paper (see footnote 4 on page 322) on the history of networking,

> If the Internet stumbles, it will not be because we lack for technology, vision, or motivation. It will be because we cannot set a direction and march collectively into the future.

7.7   Summary of Level 3

We have seen that the hardware described in Chapters 4 and 5 is, by itself, virtually unusable. Trying to work directly with the hardware components of a Von Neumann machine—processors, memory, ALU—is impossible for any but the most technically knowledgeable users. To make the system accessible, the system software must create a people-oriented *virtual environment* that is easy to use and easy to understand. In addition to ease of use, this virtual environment provides a number of other beneficial services, including resource management, security, access control, and efficient resource use. A great deal of work has been done trying to determine exactly what is an optimal virtual environment and how to create it.

Operating systems have evolved from early batch systems through multiprogramming and time-sharing to the current network and real-time operating systems. Most modern operating systems allow us to use a large collection of machines, called a computer network, almost as easily as if it were a single logical system. Future designs will incorporate multimedia interfaces and massively parallel processors, and they will encase users in a distributed system in which the user deals only with what operations need to be done, not with where or how they can be done. The future of computer systems definitely lies in the direction of more abstract and more powerful virtual environments.

Now that we have created a user-friendly virtual hardware environment in which to work, what do we want to do with it? Well, we probably want to write programs that solve important problems. In the next level of the text, we leave the domain of hardware (real and virtual) as we begin our study of the software world.

1. Show how a modem would encode the 5-bit binary sequence 11001 onto an analog carrier by

   a. Modifying its amplitude (the height of the carrier wave)

   b. Modifying its frequency (the number of waves per second)

2. A modem can also modify the *phase* of a carrier wave in order to encode binary data. Find out what the phase of a signal is and determine how it could be modified so that it could encode the same 5-bit signal 11001 used in Exercise 1.

3. Determine the total time it would take to transmit an uncompressed grayscale image (with 8 bits/pixel) from a screen with a resolution of $1,280 \times 840$ pixels using each of the following media:

   a. A 56 Kbps modem

   b. A 1.5 Mbps DSL line

   c. A 10 Mbps Ethernet link

4. a. Assume there are 1 million books in your campus library. Approximate (to the nearest order of magnitude) how many bytes of data there would be if all these books were stored online and were accessible across a computer network.

   b. How long would it take to transfer the entire collection of books if the data rate of the transmission medium were 10 Mbps, the speed of the original Ethernet? How long would it take if we had a line with a speed of 1 Gbps? (This value represents the time needed to download your entire campus library.)

5. Why is the address field needed in an Ethernet LAN protocol? Can you think of a useful situation where you might want either to omit the address field entirely or to use some "special" address value in the address field?

6. After reviewing the description of the Ethernet protocol in Section 7.3.2, how do you think this protocol would behave in a very heavily loaded network—that is, a network environment where there are lots of nodes attempting to send messages? Explain what behavior you would expect to see and why.

7. The Ethernet is a distributed LAN protocol, which means that there is no centralized control node and that the failure of a single node can never bring down the entire network. However, can you think of any advantage to the creation of a centralized LAN in which one node would be in charge of the entire network and would make all decisions about who can send a message and who must wait? Explain.

8. Agree or disagree with the following assertion and state why:

   In an Ethernet even though there are collisions, every message is guaranteed to be delivered in some maximum amount of time T.

9. a. Assume that we have a wide-area network with N nodes, where $N \geq 2$. What is the *smallest* number of point-to-point communication links such that every node in the network is able to talk to every other node? (*Note:* A network in which some nodes are unable to exchange messages with other nodes because there is no path between them is called *disconnected*.)

   b. If you are worried about having a disconnected network, what type of interconnection structure should you use when configuring your network?

10. What would happen to the store-and-forward protocol of Figure 7.8 if a packet M is repeatedly sent from node A to node B but it never correctly arrives at B? (Perhaps the link from A to B is broken.) What modifications could we make to this protocol to handle this particular situation?

11. The ARQ algorithm described in Section 7.3.2 is quite inefficient since the sending node must stop sending until it receives an explicit ACK from the receiving node. Can you design a modification to the protocol that would make it more efficient and not cause the sender to have to stop each time it sends a message? Describe your revised protocol in detail.

12. How would we *broadcast* a message using an ARQ algorithm? That is, how would we send the same message to 100 different nodes on a WAN?

13. Given the following diagram, where the numbers represent the time delays across a link:

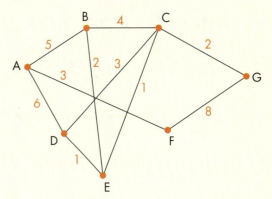

a. How many simple paths (those that do not repeat a node) are there from node A to G?

b. What is the *shortest path* from node A to node G? What is the overall delay?

c. If node E fails, would that change the shortest path? If so, what would be the new shortest path?

14. What would be some of the specific responsibilities performed by the device called a gateway (diagrammed in Figure 7.19) that is placed between two different types of networks to allow them to communicate?

15. In Section 7.3.4 we said that the transport layer turns the inherently unreliable network layer into an error-free delivery service. However, the network layer uses the services of the data link layer, which is guaranteed to correctly deliver messages on a point-to-point link. For example, assume we have the following 4-node network:

B
A   D
C

If the network layer is sending a message from A to D via B, it can be sure that a message sent by the data link layer from A to B will always correctly get to B, and a message sent from B to D will always correctly get to D. How then is it possible for the network layer to not be able to correctly deliver a message from A to D?

16. Look at the home page of the Internet Society (www.isoc.org) and read about one of the designers of the original ARPANET—Larry Roberts, Leonard Kleinrock, Vinton Cerf, Robert Kahn, John Postel, or others. Learn about the early days of networking and the contributions that these individuals made to the ultimate development of the Internet. The home page of the Internet Society has links to many other places that provide a wealth of fascinating information about networks in general and the Internet and the Web in particular.

CHALLENGE WORK

The TCP/IP protocols are the heart and soul of the Internet, and they describe the fundamental rules that govern all communications in the network. Read more about the details of the TCP/IP protocols and write a report describing their basic characteristics and giving a simple overview of the way that they work.

One of the best places to go for this information is a set of documents called **RFCs,** an acronym for **Request for Comments.** These are a series of documents produced by the Internet Engineering Task Force (IETF) that describe virtually all aspects of the Internet's behavior, including its protocols. Some contain enormously detailed technical specifications of the workings of the Internet, while others are more informational or tutorial (even humorous) in nature. A good place to start would be RFC 1180, "A TCP/IP Tutorial." A complete set of all the Internet RFCs is located at www.rfc-editor.org/rfc.html, and it can be searched using the searchable database located at that Web site.

FOR FURTHER READING

A number of texts provide good overviews of computer networking. For example, see

Kurose, J. F., and Ross, K. *Computer Networking: A Top-Down Approach Using the Internet*, 2nd Ed. Reading, MA: Addison Wesley, 2003.

Stallings, W. *Data and Computer Communications*, 6th ed. Englewood Cliffs, NJ: Prentice-Hall, 1999.

Tanenbaum, A. S. *Computer Networks*, 4th ed. Englewood Cliffs, NJ: Prentice-Hall, 2002.

In the following book, its original creator describes the creation of the World Wide Web:

Berners-Lee, T., and Fischetti, M., *Weaving the Web: The Original Design and the Ultimate Destiny of the Web*. New York: Harper Business, 2000.

This text provides excellent discussions of TCP/IP, the basis for Internet communications.

Comer, D. E. *Internetworking with TCP/IP*, 4th ed. Vol. 1, *Principles, Protocols, and Architectures*. Englewood Cliffs, NJ: Prentice-Hall, 2000.

Here are other books on various topics within the field of computer networks:

Garg, V., and Wilkes, J. E. *Wireless and Personal Communications Systems*. Piscataway, NJ: IEEE Press, 2000.

Izzo, P. *Gigabit Networking*. New York: Wiley, 2000.

The Software World

L
E
V
E
L

4

Social Issues
Chapter 15

Applications
Chapters 12, 13, 14

The Software World
Chapters 8, 9, 10, 11

The Virtual Machine
Chapters 6, 7

The Hardware World
Chapters 4, 5

The Algorithmic Foundations of Computer Science
Chapters 2, 3

LEVEL 4

In Level 4 we return to our original emphasis on algorithms as the heart of computer science. Algorithms are devised to solve problems. Applications software—computer programs—express these algorithms in the form of a programming language. It is applications software that harnesses the power of the hardware and the system software we've been talking about and brings the algorithm to life.

In Chapter 8 we see programming language ideas as implemented in one specific programming language, Java. Other examples of programming languages and different language design philosophies are introduced in Chapter 9. Chapter 10 explains how high-level programming language statements get translated into the low-level statements that can be executed in machine hardware. Yet in spite of all the power of modern hardware and software, and no matter how clever we may be in designing algorithms, problems exist that have no algorithmic solution. Chapter 11 demonstrates that the power of computing, as algorithmic problem-solving, is limited.

CHAPTER 8

Introduction to High-level Language Programming

8.1   Where Do We Stand?

As of the end of the previous chapter, we have a complete and workable computer system. We have moved up from the ungainliness of machine language programming, which the computer is designed to understand, to assembly language programming. This level of abstraction creates a virtual environment in which we can pretend that we are communicating directly with the computer even though we are using a language more suited to human communication than is binary machine language. We know about the system software needed to support this virtual environment. This includes the assembler that translates our assembly language program into machine language. It also includes the operating system that actually accepts our request to load and execute a program and coordinates and manages the other software tools needed to accomplish this task. And it includes the network technologies and protocols that extend the virtual world across our campus, our office building, and even around the world.

But we are somewhat ahead of our story. Let's go back to the "early days" of computing —say, the 1950s—when assembly language had just come into existence. As a step up from machine language, this was considered quite a satisfactory programming environment. For one thing, the people writing computer programs were for the most part very technically oriented folk. Many had backgrounds in engineering, they were familiar with the inner workings of a computer, and they were accustomed to dealing with difficult problems steeped in mathematical notation, so the tedious precision of assembly language programming did not deter them. Also, because assembly language is so closely tied to machine language, assembly language programmers could see the kinds of processor activity that the assembly language instructions would generate. By being sufficiently clever in their choice of instructions, they could often reduce this activity and shave a small amount off the execution time that their programs required. As an example, the sequence of assembly language instructions

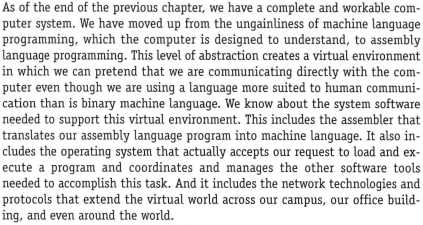

```
        LOAD    X
        ADD     ONE
        STORE   X
          .       .
          .       .
          .       .
ONE: .  DATA    1
```

could be replaced by the single instruction

INCREMENT X

This is not the sort of performance improvement obtained by changing from a sequential search algorithm to a binary search algorithm. It is a fine-tuning improvement that may save a few millionths of a second or even a few seconds if these instructions occur inside a loop that is executed many times. But remember that in this era, no one had a powerful personal computer sitting on his or her desk. Programmers were competing with one another to share the resources of a mainframe computer, and although these computers were physically large, they did not have the processing speed or memory capacity of today's personal computers. Conserving machine resources, even in tiny amounts, was important.

Over the next few decades, however, computer usage spread into more and more avenues of endeavor, permeating society to a degree that would probably not have been believed in the 1950s. "Nontechie" types needed to write programs too, and they demanded a more comfortable programming environment. This was provided through the development of high-level programming languages, which we talk about in this chapter and the next (and also through evolving operating systems and other system software, which were discussed in Chapter 6). Actually, this is a bit of a chicken and egg situation. New programmers demanded better languages, and better languages opened the door for new programmers. Each process fueled the other. Also during this period, incredible strides in technology made machines so powerful that conserving resources was generally not the issue it once was, and the overhead of execution time occasioned by the use of high-level programming languages became acceptable.

8.2 High-level Languages

Let's review some of the aspects of assembly language programming that made people look for still better alternatives. Suppose our task is to add two integers. In the assembly language of Chapter 6, the following instructions would have to be included (assume that B and C have already been assigned values):

```
        LOAD    B
        ADD     C
        STORE   A
        .       .
        .       .
        .       .
A:      .DATA   0
B:      .DATA   0
C:      .DATA   0
```

The three .DATA statements request storage for signed integers, generate the binary representation of the integer value 0 to occupy that storage initially, and ensure that the labels A, B, and C will be bound to those memory locations. The LOAD statement copies the current contents of the memory location labeled B into the ALU register R, the ADD statement adds the current contents of the memory location labeled C to what is currently in register R, and the STORE instruction copies the contents of R (which is now B + C) into the memory location labeled A.

In order to perform a simple arithmetic task, we had to manage all the data movement of the numbers to be combined as well as the resulting answer. This is a microscopic view of a task—we'd like to be able to say something like "add B and C, and call the result A," or better yet, something like "A = B + C ." But each assembly language statement corresponds to at most one machine language statement (you may recall from Chapter 6 that the pseudo-op .DATA statements do not generate any machine language statements). Therefore, individual assembly language statements, though easier to read, can be no more powerful than the underlying machine instructions. For the same reason, assembly language programs are machine-specific. An assembly language statement that runs on machine X is nothing but a slightly "humanized" machine language statement for X, and it will not execute on a machine Y that has a different instruction set. Indeed, machine Y's assembler won't know what to do with such a statement.

Finally, assembly language instructions are rather stilted. STORE A does not sound much like the sort of English we customarily speak, although STORE is certainly more expressive than its binary machine language counterpart.

To summarize, assembly language has the following disadvantages:

- The programmer must "manually" manage the movement of data items between and among memory locations (although such data items can be assigned abbreviated names).

- The programmer must take a microscopic view of a task, breaking it down into tiny subtasks at the level of what is going on in individual memory locations.

- An assembly language program is machine-specific.

- Statements are not natural-language-like (although operations are given mnemonic code words as an improvement over a string of bits).

High-level programming languages were created to overcome these deficiencies. Thus, we should have the following expectations of a program written in a high-level language:

- The programmer need not manage the details of the movement of data items within memory or pay any attention to exactly where those items are stored.

- The programmer can take a macroscopic view of tasks, thinking at a higher level of problem-solving (add B and C, and call the result A). The "primitive operations" used as building blocks in algorithm construction (see Chapter 1) can be larger.

- Programs written in a high-level language will be portable rather than machine-specific.

- Programming statements in a high-level language will be closer to standard English and will use standard mathematical notation.

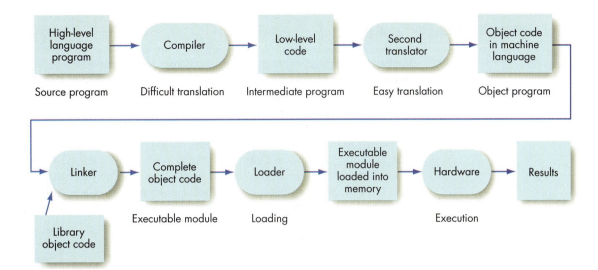

FIGURE 8.1

*Transitions of a High-level
Language Program*

High-level programming languages are often called **third-generation languages,** reflecting the progression from machine language (first generation) to assembly language (second generation) to high-level language. They are another step along the continuum shown in Figure 6.3. This also suggests what by now you have suspected: we've reached another layer of abstraction, another virtual environment designed to distance the human still further from the low-level electronic components of the machine.

There is a price to pay for our higher level of abstraction. When we moved from machine language to assembly language, we needed a piece of system software—an assembler—to translate assembly language instructions into machine language (object code). This was necessary because the computer itself—that is, the collection of electronic devices—can respond only to binary machine language instructions. Now that we have moved up another layer in the language in which we choose to communicate with the computer, we will need another translator to convert our high-level language instructions into machine language instructions. Such a piece of system software is called a **compiler.** Rather than doing the whole translation job clear down to object code, the compiler often translates high-level language instructions only into low-level code rather close to machine language (the hard part of the translation) and then turns the final (simple) translation job over to another translator.

Sometimes a group of high-level language instructions performs a task so useful (e.g., sorting or searching) that many other programs could employ this same task as part of whatever job they do. The code for this useful task can be written and then thoroughly tested to be sure it is correct. The object code for the task can then be stored in a **code library.** Another program can just "check out" a copy of this object code from the library and request that it be included along with its own object code. A piece of system software called a **linker** inserts requested object code from code libraries into the object code for the requesting program. The resulting object code is often called an **executable module.** Thus a high-level program might go through the transitions shown in Figure 8.1. Compare this with Figure 6.4.

Hundreds of high-level programming languages have been developed; a fraction of these have become viable, commercially successful languages. There are a half-dozen or so languages that could be used to illustrate some of the concepts of a high-level programming language, but we will use Java for this purpose. Other languages are discussed briefly in the next chapter.

Our intent here is not to make you an expert Java programmer—any more than our purpose in Chapter 4 was to make you an expert circuit designer. Indeed, there is much about the language that we will not even discuss. You will, however, get a sense of what programming in a high-level language is like and perhaps see why some people think it is one of the most fascinating of human endeavors.

8.3.1 *A Simple Java Program*

Figure 8.2 shows a very simple but complete Java program. Someone running this program (the "user") would see the following:

```
At 55 mph, it will take 4.0 hours
to travel 220.0 miles.
```

In order to discuss how the program works, we have rewritten it in Figure 8.3 with a number in front of each line. The numbers are there for reference purposes only and are NOT part of the program. Lines 1–3 in the program of Figure 8.3 are Java **comments.** Anything appearing on a line after the double

FIGURE 8.2

A Simple Java Program

```
//Computes and outputs travel time
//for a given speed and distance
//Written by J. Q. Programmer, 10/20/04

public class TravelPlanner
{
    public static void main(String[ ] args)
    {
        int speed;              //rate of travel
        double distance;        //miles to travel
        double time;            //time needed for this travel


        speed = 55;
        distance = 220.0;
        time = distance/speed;
        System.out.println("At " + speed + " mph, it "
            + "will take " + time + " hours ");
        System.out.println("to travel " + distance +
            " miles.");
    }
}
```

slash symbol (//) is ignored by the compiler, just as anything following the double dash (--) was treated as a comment in the assembly language programs of Chapter 6. The computer will pay no attention to comments; they are included in a program only to give information to the human readers of the code. Every high-level language has some facility for including comments, because understanding code that someone else has written (or understanding your own code after some period of time has passed) is very difficult without the additional notes and explanations that comments provide. Comments are one way to *document* a computer program to make it more understandable. The comments in lines 1–3 of Figure 8.3 give overall information about what the program does (again, just for the benefit of human readers), plus data on who wrote the program and when. These three comment lines together make up the **prologue comment** (the introductory comment that comes first) for the program. A prologue comment is always a good idea; it's almost like the headline in a newspaper, giving the big picture up front.

Line 4 and line 12 are blank lines, only there to make the program more readable. Line 5 is a **class header,** which announces that a **class** is about to be defined. The class is named *TravelPlanner,* and the curly braces at lines 6 and 19 mark the beginning and end of this class definition. All Java code (except for comments) must be either a class header or inside a class definition. The word "public" in line 5 denotes that the *TravelPlanner* class will be available for any other program that might want to make use of its capabilities.

FIGURE 8.3

The Program of Figure 8.2 (Line Numbers Added for Reference)

```
1.    //Computes and outputs travel time
2.    //for a given speed and distance
3.    //Written by J. Q. Programmer, 10/20/04
4.
5.    public class TravelPlanner
6.    {
7.       public static void main(String[] args)
8.       {
9.          int speed;              //rate of travel
10.         double distance;        //miles to travel
11.         double time;            //time needed for this
                                    //travel
12.
13.         speed = 55;
14.         distance = 220.0;
15.         time = distance/speed;
16.         System.out.println("At " +  speed + " mph, it "
                + "will take " + time + " hours ");
17.         System.out.println("to travel " + distance +
                " miles.");
18.      }
19.   }
```

We will have much more to say about classes later. For now, just think of a class as a collection of sections of code called **methods** that are able to perform various related services. In the *TravelPlanner* class, there is only one method, the **main method.** The service it performs is to compute and write out the time to travel a given distance at a given speed. Line 7,

```
public static void main(String[] args)
```

is the header for the main method. It is not necessary to understand this somewhat obscure code; just remember that every Java program must have a main method and that all main methods start out exactly this way. The curly braces at lines 8 and 18 mark the beginning and end of the main method.

Lines 9–17 are the heart of the sample program. Lines 9–11 are declarations that name and describe the items of data that will be used within the main method. Descriptive names—*speed, distance,* and *time*—have been used for these quantities as an aid in documenting their purpose in the program, and comments provide further clarification. Line 9 describes an integer quantity (type "int") called *speed*. Lines 10 and 11 declare *distance* and *time* as real number quantities (type "double"). A real number quantity is one containing a decimal point, such as 28.3, 102.0, or −17.5.

Lines 13 and 14 set the value of *speed* and *distance*. Line 15 computes the time required to travel this distance at this speed.

Finally, lines 16–17 print the two lines of output to the user's screen. The values of *speed, time,* and *distance* are inserted in appropriate places among the strings of text shown in double quotes.

8.3.2 *Running a Java Program*

As the programmer, you would type the program shown in Figure 8.2 using a text editor. When you save the file, it must have the same name as the class, with the file extension *.java*. So the file for Figure 8.2 is named

TravelPlanner.java

Running this Java program is a two-step process. First the program in the file *TravelPlanner.java* must be compiled; the result will be a file called

TravelPlanner.class

that contains low-level code called **bytecode,** which is not yet object code. The second step operates on the *TravelPlanner.class* file; it finishes the translation to object code and links, loads, and executes your program. Depending on the system on which you are working, you may have to type commands for these two steps, or you may make these steps take place by selecting appropriate menu options.

This little Java exercise was just something to look at for starters. In the rest of this chapter, we'll examine the features of the language that will enable you to write your own Java programs to carry out more sophisticated tasks.

8.4   Virtual Data Storage

One of the improvements we seek in a high-level language is freedom from having to manage data movement within memory. Although assembly language does not require us to give the actual memory address of the storage location to be used for each item, as we must in machine language, we still have to move values, one by one, back and forth between memory and the ALU as simple modifications are made. We want the computer to let us use data values by name in any sort of appropriate computation without having to think about where they are stored or what is currently in some register in the ALU. In fact, we do not even want to know that there *is* such a thing as an ALU where data are moved to be operated on; instead, we want the virtual machine to manage the details when we request that a computation be performed. A high-level language allows this, and it also allows the names for data items to be more meaningful than in assembly language.

Names in a programming language are called **identifiers.** Each language has its own specific rules for what a legal identifier can look like. In Java an identifier can be any combination of letters, digits, and the underscore symbol (_), as long as it does not begin with a digit. An additional restriction is that an identifier cannot be one of the few **keywords,** like "class," "public," "int," and so forth, that have a special meaning in Java and that you would not be likely to use anyway. The three integers *B, C,* and *A* in our assembly language program could therefore have more descriptive names, such as *subTotal, tax,* and *finalTotal.* The use of descriptive identifiers is one of the greatest aids to human understanding of a program. Identifiers can be almost arbitrarily long, so be sure to use a meaningful identifier like *finalTotal* instead of something like *A*; the improved readability is well worth the extra typing time. Java is a **case-sensitive** language, which means that uppercase letters are distinguished from lowercase letters. Thus, *FinalTotal, Finaltotal,* and *finalTotal* are three different identifiers. Most data items used in a program have either values that change as the program executes or values that are not known ahead of time but must be obtained from the computer user (or from a data file previously prepared by the user) as the program runs. These quantities are called **variables**.

We know that all data are represented internally in binary form. In Chapter 4 we noted that any one sequence of binary digits could be interpreted as a whole number, a negative number, a real number, or as a letter of the alphabet. Java asks that we give the following information about each variable in the program:

- What identifier we want to use for it
- What **data type** it represents (e.g., an integer, a real number, or a letter of the alphabet).

The data type determines how many bytes will be needed to store the variable—that is, how many memory cells are to be considered as one **memory location** referenced by one identifier and also how the string of bits in that memory location is to be interpreted. Java provides several "primitive" data types that represent a single unit of information, as shown in Figure 8.4.

A **variable declaration** consists of a data type followed by a list of one or more identifiers of that type. Our sample program used three declaration statements:

```
int speed;          //rate of travel
double distance;    //miles to travel
double time;        //time needed for this travel
```

but these could have been combined into two:

```
int speed;              //rate of travel
double distance, time;  //miles to travel and time
                        //needed for this travel
```

Where do the variable declarations go? Although the only requirement is that a variable must be declared before it can be used, all variable declarations are usually collected together at the top of the main method, as in our sample program.

FIGURE 8.4

Some of the Java Primitive Data Types

int	a positive or negative integer quantity
double	a positive or negative real number
char	a character (a single keyboard character, such as 'a')

A semicolon must appear at the end of every executable Java instruction, which means pretty much everywhere except at the end of a comment or at the end of a class header like

```
public class TravelPlanner
```

or a method header such as

```
public static void main(String[] args)
```

Java, along with every other programming language, has very specific rules of **syntax**—the correct form for each component of the language. Having a semicolon at the end of every executable statement is a Java syntax rule, as is the rule for legal identifiers. The programmer must obey all syntax rules of the language. Any violation of the syntax rules generates an error message from the compiler because the compiler does not recognize or know how to translate the offending code. In the case of a missing semicolon, the compiler cannot tell where the instruction ends. The syntax rules for a programming language are often defined by a formal grammar, much as correct English is defined by rules of grammar.

Java is a **free-format language**, which means that it does not matter where things are placed on a line. For example, we could have written

```
        int
speed;    //rate of travel
            double distance,
                time; //miles to travel
//and time needed                        for this
//travel
```

although this is clearly harder to read. The free-format characteristic explains why a semicolon is needed to mark the end of an instruction, which might be spread over several lines.

In addition to variables of a primitive data type that hold only one unit of information, we can declare a whole collection of related variables at one time. This will allow storage to be set aside as needed to contain each of the values in this collection. For example, suppose we want to record the number of "hits" on our Web site for each month of the year. The value for each month would be a single integer. We want a collection of 12 such integers, ordered in a particular way. An **array** groups together a collection of memory locations, all storing data of the same type. The following statement declares an array:

```
int[] hits = new int[12];
```

The left side of the equal sign says that *hits* is an array of integers; the right side of the equal sign actually generates (new) memory locations for 12 integer quantities. The 12 individual array elements are numbered from *hits[0]* to *hits[11]*. (Notice that a Java array counts from 0 up to 11 instead of from 1

FIGURE 8.5

A 12-Element Array Hits

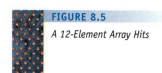

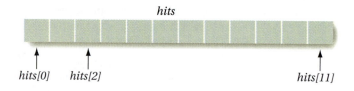

hits

hits[0]   hits[2]   hits[11]

up to 12.) Thus, we would use *hits[0]* to refer to the first entry in *hits,* which would represent the number of visits to the Web site during the first month of the year, January. Continuing this numbering scheme, *hits[2]* would refer to the number of visits during March and *hits[11]* to the number of visits during December. In this way we have used one declaration to cause 12 separate (but related) integer storage locations to be set up. Figure 8.5 shows how we can think of this array.

Here is an example of the power of a high-level language. In assembly language, we could only name individual memory locations—that is, individual items of data—but in Java we can also assign a name to an entire collection of related data items. An array thus allows us to talk about an entire table of values or the individual elements making up that table. If we were writing Java programs to implement the data cleanup algorithms of Chapter 3, we could use an array of integers to store the 10 data items.

The picture of an array in Figure 8.5 looks like a one-dimensional table of values. We can use arrays to represent two-dimensional tables also. Suppose, for example, that we wish to work with the following data, which represent two separate water meter readings at each of three distinct sites:

	Site 1	Site 2	Site 3
Final Reading	14.3	15.2	16.4
Initial Reading	13.9	14.2	12.7

Even though these six real-number values will be stored in sequential memory locations, we can think of them as displayed in a two-dimensional table with two rows and three columns. This is reflected in the following declaration:

```
double[][] waterReadings = new double[2][3];
```

We can refer to any particular member of the array by giving numbers for both its row and column location. If the water meter data above are actually stored in the array *waterReadings,* then the value of *waterReadings[1][2]* is 12.7, because this is the entry in the second row, third column (remember that Java counts up from 0). Figure 8.6 shows the virtual representation of this array in memory (that is, how our high-level virtual environment allows us to think about this array). Figure 8.7 shows its actual representation in memory, assuming the first storage location has address 1001 and that each type *double* number uses 8 bytes of storage. It will be the job of the Java

FIGURE 8.6

A Virtual 2 × 3 Table

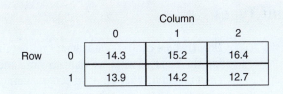

	Column 0	Column 1	Column 2
Row 0	14.3	15.2	16.4
1	13.9	14.2	12.7

FIGURE 8.7

The 2 × 3 Table Stored in Memory

14.3	15.2	16.4	13.9	14.2	12.7
Address 1001	1009	1017	1025	1033	1041

compiler to convert between these two representations. The programmer can be totally unaware that *waterReadings[1][2]* must be converted into the address for the sixth element in the one-dimensional array storage (address 1041) and may continue to think in terms of the 2 × 3 two-dimensional arrangement.

When the programmer has a mental model of a collection of data items that are related or "structured" in some way, that collection is called a **data structure.** This is a virtual arrangement; that is, the programmer thinks of these items as being arranged in some useful fashion, such as a two-dimensional table. Then the features available in the programming language must be used to implement that virtual arrangement. In the case of a two-dimensional table data structure, the implementation is easily accomplished by using a Java array.

PRACTICE PROBLEMS

1. Which of the following are legitimate Java identifiers?

   ```
   martinBradley    C3P_OH    amy3    3Right    double
   ```

2. Write a declaration for a Java program that will use one integer quantity called *number*.

3. How many memory locations will be needed to store the array *box* given the following declaration? If each integer requires 4 bytes, how many memory cells will be used?

   ```
   int[][] box = new int[4][3];
   ```

4. How would you reference the item stored in the first row and first column (upper left corner) of the array *box* declared in Problem 3?

Now that we can reserve memory for data items by the simple expedient of giving the name of what we want to store and describing its data type, we need to examine additional kinds of programming instructions (statements) that Java provides. These are the statements that will let us actually manipulate these data items and do something useful with them. The instructions in Java, or indeed in any high-level language, are designed as components for algorithmic problem-solving rather than as one to one translations of the underlying machine language instruction set of the computer. Thus, they allow the programmer to work at a higher level of abstraction. In this section we'll examine three types of high-level programming language statements. They are consistent with the pseudocode operations we described in Chapter 2 (see Figure 2.6).

One type of statement is *input/output statements*. An **input statement** collects a specific value from the user for a variable within the program. Our TravelPlanner program is particularly unrealistic because it does not collect any input; instead, it uses fixed values for speed and distance, so it can do one and only one computation. We'll fix this deficiency shortly. An **output statement** writes a message or the value of a program variable to the user's screen (or to a file on some permanent storage medium such as a disk).

A second statement type is an **assignment statement,** which assigns a value to a program variable. This sounds similar to what an input statement does, but the difference is that this value is not collected directly from the user but is computed within the program itself. Indeed, in pseudocode we called this a "computation operation."

The third type of statement we will discuss is a *control statement*. A program executes one instruction or program statement at a time. Without directions to the contrary, the instructions are executed sequentially, from first to last in the program. (In Chapter 2 we called this a straight-line algorithm.) If we imagined, beside each program statement, a little lightbulb that lights up while that statement is being executed, we would see a ripple of lights from the top to the bottom of the program. Sometimes, however, we want to interrupt this sequential progression and jump around in the program (which was accomplished by the instructions JUMP, JUMPGT, and so on, in assembly language). The pattern of lights then would not be sequential. This progression of lights would illustrate the **flow of control** in the program—that is, the path through the program that is traced by following the currently executing statement. **Control statements** direct the flow of control and can cause it to deviate from the usual sequential flow.

8.5.1   *Input Statements*

Remember that the job of an input statement is to collect from the user specific values for variables in the program. In pseudocode, to get the value for *speed* we would say something like

Get value for *speed*

It is understood, however, that when your program wants an item of data from the user, you must first print a message (a **prompt**) to the user saying what it is the program wants. Without a prompt, the user may be unaware that the program is waiting for some input; instead, it may simply seem that the program is "hung up." With this in mind, we amend our pseudocode input statement to

> Prompt user for *speed*
>
> Get value for *speed*

The Java language, surprisingly, does not provide a convenient way to collect user data entered at the keyboard. In order to make the code simpler than it would be if we used the "raw" Java capabilities, we'll use the services of a class called *Console* to take care of this process. ("Console" is another word for "keyboard.") The *Console* class is actually a separate piece of Java code that we can employ in our program without even seeing it, as long as we are aware of the services it provides and know how to use those services properly. This is in the same spirit of abstraction that led to the development of high-level languages in the first place. The *Console* class is not a standard Java class, but one written for this book.[1] Nonetheless, there is nothing particularly mysterious about it, and the *Console.java* code appears in the Appendix. Your instructor may want you to code input statements directly, using something similar to the code in the Appendix. If you do use the *Console* class, be sure the bytecode file *Console.class* (which can be found at the Web site for the lab software for this book, http://compsci.course.com/invitationlabs) is in the same directory or folder as the Java program you are running.

Using the Java *Console* class, we can handle both the prompt and the retrieval of the value in one statement:

```
speed = Console.readInt("Enter your speed in mph: ");
```

The *Console* class provides methods called *readInt, readDouble,* and *readChar* to collect input of type *int, double,* or *char,* respectively. The syntax is

```
variable1 = Console.readInt(prompt);
variable2 = Console.readDouble(prompt);
variable3 = Console.readChar(prompt);
```

The Console Class

The *Console* class is a nonstandard class designed to simplify getting input from the keyboard. The *Console.class* file can be found at the Web site for the lab software for this book:

http://compsci.course.com/invitationlabs

The *Console.java* code appears in the Appendix. **To use the *Console* class, be sure the file *Console.class* is in the same directory or folder as the Java program you are running.**

---

[1] Written by Ken Lambert, coauthor of the lab manual that accompanies this book.

where prompt is a string enclosed in double quotes (or multiple strings in quotes separated by a + sign). The variable must already have been declared, and be of the proper data type. For example, you cannot use

```
variable2 = Console.readDouble("Enter the average: ");
```

if *variable2* has been declared as type *int*. The Java compiler will give you an error message about "incompatible types." The *Console* class methods also perform some limited runtime error checking. If the user enters an alphabetic character or a number with a decimal point in response to the *readInt* method, an error message about "NumberFormatException" will be displayed and the program will terminate. A similar message will be displayed if the user enters an alphabetic character in response to the *readDouble* method. Because the *readChar* method can handle any key on the keyboard, the user can enter anything in response. Note, however, that the *readChar* method reads only one character per line, so if the user enters the string of characters "hello" in response to a *readChar* prompt, only the "h" will be collected.

Figure 8.8 shows a more useful version of our TravelPlanner program. This program can be executed repeatedly, collecting speeds and distances for different trips.

A user might have the following dialogue with this program; boldface indicates what the user types:

```
Enter your speed in mph: 58
Enter your distance in miles: 540
At 58 mph, it will take 9.310344827586206 hours
to travel 380.0 miles
```

FIGURE 8.8

The TravelPlanner Program with Input Statements

```
//Computes and outputs travel time
//for a given speed and distance
//Written by J. Q. Programmer, 10/21/04

public class TravelPlanner
{
  public static void main(String[] args)
  {
    int speed;            //rate of travel
    double distance;      //miles to travel
    double time;          //time needed for travel

    speed = Console.readInt("Enter your speed "
      + "in mph: ");
    distance = Console.readDouble("Enter your "
      + "distance in miles: ");
    time = distance/speed;
    System.out.println("At " + speed + " mph, it "
      + "will take " + time + " hours ");
    System.out.println("to travel " + distance +
      " miles.");
  }
}
```

8.5.2 *Output Statements*

A pseudocode statement for writing output in the TravelPlanner program would be something like

Print the value of *time*

But we don't want the program to simply print a number with no explanation; we want some words to make the output meaningful.

Output to the screen can be done in Java by using the following statement form:

```
System.out.println(string);
```

Here the string could be empty, as follows:

```
System.out.println();
```

This just prints a blank line, which is useful for formatting the output to make it easier to read. The string could also be a **literal string** (enclosed in double quotes); literal strings are used for the user prompt in the *Console* class input methods. Literal strings are printed out exactly as is. For example,

```
System.out.println("Here's your answer." );
```

will print

```
Here's your answer.
```

A string can also be composed of items joined by +, the **concatenation operator.**

The items can be literal strings or numbers or variables. Items that are not themselves literal strings are converted to strings for the purposes of writing them out. For example,

```
System.out.println("Give me" + 5);
```

will print the line

```
Give me5
```

on the screen. If we want a space between "me" and "5", then we can make that space part of the literal string, as in

```
System.out.println("Give me " + 5);
```

If *number* is an integer variable with current value 5, then the same output will be produced by

```
System.out.println("Give me " + number);
```

The concatenation operator is also helpful when trying to write out a long literal string; while a single Java statement can be spread over multiple lines, a line break cannot occur in the middle of a literal string. The solution is to make two smaller substrings and concatenate them, as in

```
System.out.println("Oh for a sturdy ship to sail, "
    + "and a star to steer her by.");
```

Literal strings and variables can be concatenated together in all sorts of combinations as long as the quotation marks and + signs appear in the right places. Consider again the output statements in the TravelPlanner program:

```
System.out.println("At " + speed + " mph, it "
    + "will take " + time + " hours ");
System.out.println("to travel " + distance +
    " miles.");
```

PRACTICE PROBLEMS

1. A program has computed a value for the variable *average* that represents the average high temperature in San Diego for the month of May. Write an appropriate output statement.

2. What will appear on the screen after execution of the following statement?

```
System.out.println("This is" + "goodbye" +
", Steve");
```

 ### 8.5.3 *The Assignment Statement*

As we said earlier, an assignment statement assigns a value to a program variable. This is accomplished by evaluating some expression and then writing the resulting value in the memory location referenced by the program variable. The general pseudocode operation

Set the value of "variable" to "arithmetic expression"

has as its Java equivalent

variable = expression;

The expression on the right gets evaluated, and the result is then written into the memory location named on the left. As an example, suppose that A, B, and C have all been declared as integer variables in some program. The assignment statements

```
B = 2;
C = 5;
```

would result in B taking on the value 2 and C taking on the value 5. After execution of

```
A = B + C;
```

A has the value that is the sum of the current values of B and C. Assignment is a destructive operation; whatever A's previous value was, it is now gone. Notice that this one assignment statement says to add the values of B and C and assign the result to A. Here is the one-step, higher-level-of-thinking solution to the problem we discussed early in this chapter. This one high-level statement is equivalent to the three assembly language statements we needed to do this same task (LOAD B, ADD C, STORE A). A high-level language program thus packs more power per line than an assembly language program. To put it another way, whereas a single assembly language program instruction is equivalent to a single machine language instruction, a single Java instruction is usually equivalent to many assembly language program instructions or machine language instructions.

In the assignment statement, the expression on the right is evaluated first. Only then is the value of the variable on the left changed. This means that an assignment statement like

```
A = A + 1;
```

makes sense. If A has the value 7 before this statement is executed, then the expression evaluates to

7 + 1 or 8

and 8 then becomes the new value of A. (Here it becomes obvious that the assignment instruction symbol = is not the same as the mathematical equals sign =, because $A = A + 1$ would not make sense mathematically.)

All four basic arithmetic operations can be done in Java, denoted by

+ Addition
− Subtraction
* Multiplication
/ Division

For the most part, this is standard mathematical notation rather than some-what verbose assembly language op code mnemonics such as SUBTRACT. The reason a special symbol is used for multiplication is that $\times$ would be confused with x, an identifier, $\cdot$ (a multiplication dot) doesn't appear on the keyboard, and juxtaposition (writing AB for $A*B$) would look like a single identifier named AB.

We do have to pay some attention to data types. In particular, division has one peculiarity. If at least one of the two values being divided is a real number, then division behaves as we probably expect. Thus,

7.0/2   7/2.0   7.0/2.0

all result in the value 3.5. However, if the two values being divided are both integers, the result will be an integer value. If the division doesn't "come out even," the integer value is obtained by truncating the answer to an integer quotient. Thus,

7/2

results in the value 3. Think of grade-school long division of integers:

```
      3
   2)7
      6
      1
```

Here the quotient is 3 and the remainder is 1. Java also provides an operation, with the symbol %, to obtain the integer remainder. Using this operation,

7 % 2

results in the value 1.

If the values are stored in type *int* variables, the result is the same. For example,

```
int numerator;
int denominator;
int quotient;
numerator = 7;
denominator = 2;
quotient = numerator/denominator;
System.out.println("The result of " + numerator + "/"
      + denominator + " is " + quotient);
```

will produce output of

```
The result of 7/2 is 3
```

As soon as an arithmetic operation involves one or more real numbers, any integers are converted to their real-number equivalent, and the calculations are done with real numbers.

Data types also play a role in assignment statements. Suppose the expression in an assignment statement evaluates to a real number, and your program tries to assign it to an identifier that has been declared as an integer. The Java compiler will give you an error message stating that you have incompatible types. (We mentioned that this same problem occurs if you try to use *Console.readDouble* and assign the result to an integer variable.) In fact, the error message goes on to say that you need to do an "explicit cast" to convert *double* to *int*. Java is saying that if you want to throw away the non-integer part of a decimal number by storing it in an integer, you're going to have to write code specifically to do that. However, you can assign an integer value to a type *double* variable (or input an integer value to a type *double* variable). Java does this **type casting** (changing of data type) automatically. This type cast would merely change the integer 3, for example, to its real number equivalent 3.0.

This explains why we declared *distance* to be type *double* in the Travel-Planner program. The user can enter an integer value for distance, and Java will type cast it to a real number. But if we had declared both *speed* and *distance* to be integers, then the division to compute *time* would only produce integer answers.

You should only assign an expression that has a character value to a variable that has been declared to be type *char*. Suppose that *Letter* is a variable of type *char*. Then

```
Letter = 'm';
```

would be a legitimate assignment statement, giving *Letter* the value of the character 'm'. Notice that single quotation marks are used here, as opposed to the double quotation marks used with a literal string. The assignment

```
Letter = '4';
```

would also be acceptable; note that the single quotes around the 4 mean that it is being treated as just another character on the keyboard, not as the integer 4.

Java requires that all variables have a value before they are used. It is a good idea to get into the habit of **initializing variables** as soon as they are declared, using an assignment statement. For example, you can declare and then initialize a variable by

```
int count;
count = 0;
```

but Java also allows you to combine these two statements into one:

```
int count = 0;
```

This statement is equivalent to the assembly language statement COUNT: .DATA 0 , which reserves a memory location, assigns it the identifier COUNT, and fills it with the value zero.

1. *NewNumber* and *Next* are integer variables in a Java program. Write a statement to assign the value of *NewNumber* to *Next*.

2. What will be the value of *Average* after the following statements are executed? (Note: *Total* and *Number* are type **int,** and *Average* is type **double.**)

```
Total = 277;
Number = 5;
Average = Total/Number;
```

 8.5.4   *Control Statements*

Sequential flow of control is the default mode of execution; that is, the program executes instructions sequentially from first to last. The flowchart in Figure 8.9 illustrates this situation, where S1, S2, . . . , Sk are program instructions (program statements).

As we stated in Chapter 2, no matter how complicated the task to be done, only three types of control mechanisms are needed:

1. Sequential: instructions are executed in order.
2. Conditional: the choice of which instructions to execute next depends on some condition.
3. Looping: a group of instructions may be executed many times.

Nothing need be done to achieve sequential flow of control; this is what occurs if the program does not contain any instances of the other two control structures. In the TravelPlanner program, for instance, instructions are executed sequentially, beginning with the input statements, the computation, and finally the output statement.

In this section, we'll look at the other two control mechanisms. In Chapter 2 we introduced pseudocode notation for conditional operations and looping. In Chapter 6 we saw how to write somewhat laborious assembly language code to implement conditional operations and looping. Now we'll see how Java provides instructions that carry out these control structure mechanisms directly—more evidence of the power of high-level language instructions compared to assembly language instructions. We can think in a pseudocode algorithm design mode, as we did in Chapter 2, and then translate that pseudocode almost directly into Java code.

Conditional flow of control begins with the evaluation of a **Boolean condition,** also called a **Boolean expression,** that can be either true or false. We discussed these "true/false conditions" in Chapter 2, and we also

FIGURE 8.9

Sequential Flow of Control
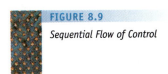

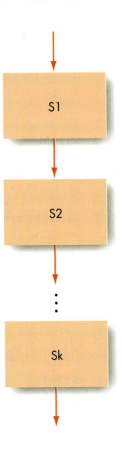

encountered Boolean expressions in Chapter 4, where they were used to design circuits. A Boolean condition often involves comparing the values of two expressions and determining whether they are equal, whether the first is greater than the second, and so on. Again assuming that A, B, and C are integer variables in a program, the following are legitimate Boolean conditions:

A == 0	(Does A currently have the value zero?)
B < (A + C)	(Is the current value of B less than the sum of the current values of A and C?)
A != B	(Does A currently have a different value than B?)

If the current values of A, B, and C are 2, 5, and 7, respectively, then the first condition is false (A does not have the value zero), the second condition is true (5 is less than 2 plus 7), and the third condition is true (A and B do not have equal values).

Comparisons need not be numeric in nature. They can also be made between variables of type *char,* where the "ordering" is the usual alphabetic ordering. If *initial* is a value of type *char* with a current value of 'D', then

```
initial == 'F'
```

is false because *initial* does not have the value 'F', and

```
initial < 'P'
```

is true because 'D' precedes 'P' in the alphabet (or, more precisely, because the binary code for 'D' is numerically less than the binary code for 'P').

Figure 8.10 shows the comparison operators available in Java. Note the use of the two equality signs to test whether two expressions have the same value. The single equality sign is used in an assignment statement, the double equality sign in a comparison.

Boolean conditions can be built up using the Boolean operators AND, OR, and NOT. Truth tables for these operators were given in Chapter 4 (Figures 4.12–4.14). The only new thing is the symbolism Java uses for these operators, shown in Figure 8.11.

A conditional statement relies on the value of a Boolean condition (true or false) to decide what programming statement to execute next. If the condition is true, one statement will be executed next, but if the condition is false, a different statement will be executed next. Control is therefore no longer in a straight-line (sequential) flow but may hop to one place or to another. Figure 8.12 illustrates the way we can think about this situation. If the condition is true, the statement S1 will be executed (and statement S2 will not); if the condition is false, the statement S2 will be executed (and statement S1 will not). In either case, the flow of control then continues on to statement S3.

The Java instruction that carries out conditional flow of control is called an **if-else** statement. It has the following form (notice that the words *if* and *else* are lower-case, and that the Boolean condition must be in parentheses):

FIGURE 8.10

Java Comparison Operators

COMPARISON	SYMBOL	EXAMPLE	EXAMPLE RESULT
the same value as	==	2 == 5	false
less than	<	2 < 5	true
less than or equal to	<=	5 <= 5	true
greater than	>	2 > 5	false
greater than or equal to	>=	2 >= 5	false
not the same value as	!=	2 != 5	true

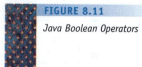

FIGURE 8.11

Java Boolean Operators

OPERATOR	SYMBOL	EXAMPLE	EXAMPLE RESULT
AND	&&	(2 < 5) && (2 > 7)	false
OR	||	(2 < 5) || (2 > 7)	true
NOT	!	!(2 == 5)	true

```
if (Boolean condition)
        S1;
else
        S2;
```

Below is a simple if-else statement, where we are again assuming that A, B, and C are integer variables:

```
if (B < (A + C))
        A = 2*A;
else
        A = 3*A;
```

Suppose that when this statement is reached, the values of A, B, and C are 2, 5, and 7, respectively. As we noted before, the condition $B < (A + C)$ is then true, so the statement

```
A = 2*A;
```

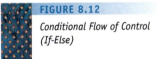

FIGURE 8.12

Conditional Flow of Control (If-Else)

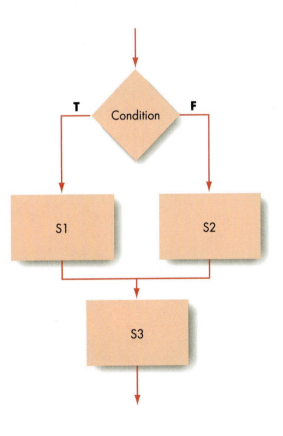

will be executed and the value of A will be changed to 4. However, suppose that when this statement is reached, the values of A, B, and C are 2, 10, and 7, respectively. Then the condition $B < (A + C)$ is false, the statement

```
A = 3*A;
```

will be executed and the value of A will be changed to 6.

A variation on the if-else statement is to allow an "empty else" case. Here we want to do something if the condition is true, but want to do nothing if the condition is false. Figure 8.13 shows how we can think about the empty else case. If the condition is true, statement S1 will be executed and after that the flow of control will continue on to statement S3, but if the condition is false, nothing happens except to move the flow of control directly on to statement S3.

This *if* variation of the if-else statement can be accomplished by omitting the word *else*. This form of the instruction therefore looks like

```
if (Boolean condition)
        S1;
```

FIGURE 8.13

If-Else with Empty Else

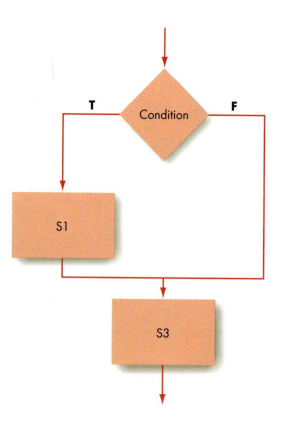

We could write

```
if (B < (A + C))
    A = 2*A;
```

This would have the effect of doubling the value of *A* if the condition is true and of doing nothing if the condition is false.

It is possible to combine statements into a group by putting them within the curly braces { and }. The group is then treated as a single statement, called a **compound statement.** A compound statement can be used anywhere a single statement is allowed. For example,

```
{
  System.out.println( "This is the first statement.");
  System.out.println( "This is the second statement.");
  System.out.println( "This is the third statement.");
}
```

would be treated as a single statement. The implication is that in Figure 8.12, S1 or S2 might be compound statements. This possibility makes the if-else statement much more powerful, and similar to the pseudocode conditional statement in Figure 2.6.

Let's expand on our TravelPlanner program and give the user of the program a choice of computing the time either as a decimal number (3.75 hours) or as hours and minutes (3 hours, 45 minutes). This situation is ideal for a conditional statement. Depending on what the user wants to do, the program should do one of two tasks.

For either task, the program still needs information about the speed and distance. The program must also collect information to indicate which task the user wishes to perform. We'll need an additional variable in the program to store this information. Let's use a variable called *choice* of type *char* to collect the user's choice of which task to perform. We'll also need two new integer variables to store the values of hours and minutes.

Figure 8.14 shows the new program. Note that all variables are now initialized as part of the declaration. The condition evaluated at the beginning of the if-else statement tests whether *choice* has the value 'D'. If so, then the condition is true and the first group of statements is executed—that is, the time is output in decimal format as we have been doing all along. If *choice* does not have the value 'D', then the condition is false. In this event the second group of statements is executed. Notice that because of the way the condition is written, if *choice* does not have the value 'D', it is assumed that the user wants to compute the time in hours and minutes, even though *choice* may have any other non-D value (including 'd') that the user may have typed in response to the prompt.

To compute hours and minutes (the "else" clause of the if-else statement), time is computed in the usual way, which results in a decimal value. The whole number part of that decimal is the number of hours needed for the trip. We can get this number by typecasting the decimal number to an integer. This is accomplished by

```
hours = (int)time;
```

FIGURE 8.14

The TravelPlanner Program with
a Conditional Statement

```
//Computes and outputs travel time
//for a given speed and distance
//Written by J. Q. Programmer, 10/22/04
public class TravelPlanner
{
  public static void main(String[] args)
  {
    int speed = 1;              //rate of travel
    double distance = 0.0;      //miles to travel
    double time = 0.0;          //time needed for travel
                               //(decimal)
    int hours = 0;              //time for travel in hours
    int minutes = 0;            //leftover time in minutes
    char choice = 'M';          //choice of output as
                               //decimal hours
                               //or hours and minutes

    speed = Console.readInt("Enter your speed in "
      + "mph: ");
    distance = Console.readDouble("Enter your "
      + "distance in miles: ");
    System.out.println("Enter your choice of format "
      + "for time ");
    choice = Console.readChar("Decimal hours (D) " +
      "or hours and minutes (M): ");
    System.out.println();
    if (choice == 'D')
    {
      time = distance/speed;
      System.out.println("At " + speed + " mph, it "
        + "will take " + time + " hours ");
      System.out.println("to travel " + distance +
        " miles.");
    }
    else
    {
      time = distance/speed;
      hours = (int)time;
      minutes = (int)((time - hours)*60);
      System.out.println("At " + speed + " mph, it "
        + "will take " + hours + " hours " + minutes +
        " minutes");
      System.out.println("to travel " + distance +
        " miles.");
    }
  }
}
```

which will drop all digits behind the decimal point and store the resulting integer value in *hours*. To find the fractional part of the hour that we dropped, we subtract *hours* from *time*. We multiply this by 60 to turn it into some number of minutes, but this is still a decimal number. We do another typecast to truncate this to an integer value for *minutes*:

```
minutes = (int)((time - hours)*60);
```

For example, if the user enters data of 50 mph and 475 miles and requests output in hours and minutes, the following table shows the computed values.

Quantity	Value
speed	50
distance	475
time = distance/speed	9.5
hours = (int)time	9
time - hours	0.5
(time - hours) *60	30.0
minutes = (int)(time - hours)*60))	30

The two statement groups in an if-else statement are identified by the enclosing curly braces, but in Figure 8.14 we also indented them to make them easier to pick out when looking at the program. Like comments, indentation is ignored by the computer but is valuable in helping people to more readily understand a program.

Now let's look at the third variation on flow of control, namely looping (iteration). Here we may want to execute the same group of statements (called the **loop body**) repeatedly. Again a Boolean condition comes into play. In the while loop of our Chapter 2 pseudocode, the loop body is executed as long as (while) some condition remains true. The condition is tested before each execution of the loop body. When the condition finally becomes false, the loop body is not executed again, usually expressed by saying that the algorithm *exits* the loop. In order to ensure that the algorithm ultimately exits the loop, the condition must be such that its truth value can be affected by what happens when the loop body is executed. Figure 8.15 shows the situation. The loop body is statement S1 (which can be a compound statement), and S1 is executed *while* the condition is true. Once the condition is false, the flow of control moves on to statement S2. If the condition is false when it is first evaluated, then the body of the loop is never executed at all.

Java uses a **while** statement to implement this type of looping. The form of the statement is

```
while (Boolean condition)
    S1;
```

As a simple example, suppose we want to write a program to add up a number of nonnegative integers that the user supplies and write out the total. We need a variable to hold the total; we'll call this variable *sum* and

FIGURE 8.15

While Loop

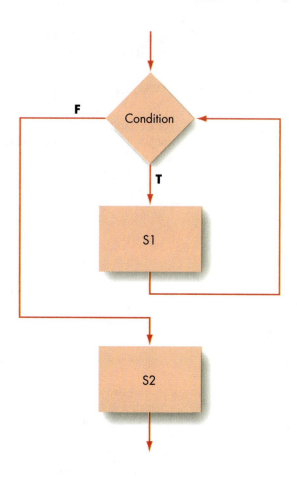

make it data type *int*. To handle the numbers to be added, we could declare some integer variables like *n1, n2, n3, . . .* , and do a series of input-and-add statements of the form

```
n1 = Console.readInt("Number 1: ");
sum = sum + n1;
n2 = Console.readInt("Number 2: ");
sum = sum + n2;
```

and so on. There are two problems with this approach. The first is that we may not know ahead of time how many numbers the user wants to add. If we declare variables *n1, n2, . . . , n25,* and the user wants to add 26 numbers, the program won't do the job. The second problem is that this approach requires too much effort. Let's suppose that we know the user wants to add 2,000 numbers. We could declare 2,000 variables, (*n1, . . . , n2000*), and we could write the above input-and-add statements 2,000 times, but it wouldn't be fun. Nor is it necessary—we should be able to use a loop mechanism to simplify the job. (We faced a similar situation in the first pass at a sequential search algorithm, Figure 2.7; our solution there was also to use iteration.)

Even if we use a loop mechanism, we will still be adding a succession of values to *sum*. Unless we are sure that the value of *sum* is zero to begin with, we cannot be sure that the answer isn't nonsense. When we declare and initialize the variable *sum,* we should set its value to zero.

Now on to the loop mechanism. First, let's note that once a number has been read in and added to *sum,* the program doesn't need to know the value of the number any longer. We can declare just one integer variable called *number,* and use it repeatedly to hold the first numerical value, then the second, and so on.

The general idea is then

```
int number = 0;
int sum = 0;


while (there are more numbers to add)
{
    number = Console.readInt("Enter next number: ");
    sum = sum + number;
}
System.out.println("The total is " + sum);
```

Now we have to figure out what the condition "there are more numbers to add" really means. Because we are adding nonnegative integers, we could ask the user to enter one extra integer that is not part of the legitimate data but is instead a signal that there *are* no more data. Such a value is called a **sentinel value.** For this problem, any negative number would be a good sentinel value. Because the numbers to be added are all nonnegative, the appearance of a negative number signals the end of the legitimate data. We don't want to process the sentinel value (because it is not a legitimate data item); we only want to use it to terminate the looping process. This might suggest the following code:

```
int number = 0;
int sum = 0;
while (number >= 0)     //but there is a problem here,
                        //see following discussion
{
    number = Console.readInt("Enter next number: ");
    sum = sum + number;
}
System.out.println("The total is " + sum);
```

Here's the problem. How can we test whether *number* is greater than or equal to 0 if we haven't read the value of *number* yet? We need to do a preliminary input for the first value of *number* outside of the loop, then test that value in the loop condition. If it is nonnegative, we want to add it to *sum* and then read the next value and test it. Whenever the value of *number* is negative (including the first value), we want to do nothing with it—that is, we want to avoid executing the loop body. The following statements will do the job; we've also added instructions to the user.

```
int number = 0;
int sum = 0;
System.out.println("Enter numbers to add; "
      + "terminate with a negative number.");
number = Console.readInt("First number: ");

while (number >= 0)
{
    sum = sum + number;
    number = Console.readInt("Next number: ");
}
System.out.println("The total is " + sum);
```

The value of *number* gets changed within the loop body by reading in a new value. The new value is tested, and if it is nonnegative, the loop body executes again, adding the data value to *sum* and reading in a new value for *number*. The loop will terminate when a negative value is read in. Remember our earlier requirement that something within the loop body must be able to affect the truth value of the condition. In this case, it is reading in a new value for *number* that has the potential to change the value of the condition from true to false. Without this requirement, the condition, once true, would remain true forever, and the loop body would be endlessly executed. This results in what is called an **infinite loop.** A program that contains an infinite loop will execute forever (or until the programmer gets tired of waiting and interrupts the program, or until the program exceeds some preset time limit).

The problem we've solved here, adding nonnegative integers until a negative sentinel value occurs, is the same one solved using assembly language in Chapter 6. The Java code above is almost identical to the pseudocode version of the algorithm shown in Figure 6.7. Due to the power of the language, the Java code embodies the algorithm directly, at a high level of thinking, whereas in assembly language this same algorithm had to be translated into the lengthy and awkward code of Figure 6.8.

We could use a while loop to process data for a number of different trips in the TravelPlanner program. During each pass through the loop, the program will compute the time for a given speed and distance. The body of the loop is therefore exactly like our previous code. All we are adding here is the framework that provides looping. To terminate the loop, we could use a sentinel value, as we did for the program above. A negative value for *speed,* for example, would not be a legitimate data value and could serve as a sentinel value. Instead of that, let's allow the user to control loop termination by having the program ask the user whether he or she wishes to continue. We'll need a variable to hold the user's response to this question. Of course, the user could answer "N" at the first query and the loop body would never execute at all—the user would just see the termination message. Figure 8.16 shows the complete program.

FIGURE 8.16

The TravelPlanner Program with Looping

```
//Computes and outputs travel time
//for a given speed and distance
//Written by J. Q. Programmer, 10/23/04
public class TravelPlanner
{
  public static void main(String[] args)
  {
    int speed = 1;              //rate of travel
    double distance = 0.0;      //miles to travel
    double time = 0.0;          //time needed for travel
                                //(decimal)
    int hours = 0;              //time for travel in hours
    int minutes = 0;            //leftover time in minutes
    char choice = 'M';          //choice of output as
                                //decimal hours
                                //or hours and minutes
    char more = 'Y';            //user's choice to do
                                //another trip
    more = Console.readChar("Do you want to plan " +
      "a trip? (Y or N): ");

    while(more == 'Y') //more trips to plan
    {
            speed = Console.readInt("Enter your speed in "
              + "mph: ");
            distance = Console.readDouble("Enter your "
              + "distance in miles: ");
            System.out.println("Enter your choice of format "
              + "for time: ");
            choice = Console.readChar("Decimal hours (D) " +
              "or hours and minutes (M): ");
            System.out.println();
            if (choice == 'D')
            {
              time = distance/speed;
              System.out.println("At " + speed + " mph, it "
                + "will take " + time + " hours ");
              System.out.println("to travel " + distance +
                " miles.");
            }
            else
            {
                time = distance/speed;
                hours = (int)time;
                minutes = (int)((time - hours)*60);
                System.out.println("At " + speed + " mph, it "
                    + "will take " + hours + " hours " + minutes
                    + " minutes");
                System.out.println("to travel " + distance +
                    " miles.");
            }
            System.out.println();
            more = Console.readChar("Do you want to plan " +
                "another trip? (Y or N): ");
    } //end of while loop
  }
}
```

PRACTICE PROBLEMS

1. What is the output from the following section of code?

```
int number1 = 15;
int number2 = 7;
if (number1 >= number2)
   System.out.println(2*number1);
else
   System.out.println(2*number2);
```

2. What is the output from the following section of code?

```
int scores = 1;
while (scores < 20)
{
   scores = scores + 2;
   System.out.println(scores);
}
```

3. What is the output from the following section of code?

```
int quotaThisMonth = 7;
int quotaLastMonth = quotaThisMonth + 1;
if ((quotaThisMonth > quotaLastMonth)  ||
   (quotaLastMonth >= 8))
{
   System.out.println("Yes");
   quotaLastMonth = quotaLastMonth + 1;
}
else
{
   System.out.println("No");
   quotaThisMonth = quotaThisMonth + 1;
}
```

4. How many times will the statement with the comment be executed in the following section of code?

```
int left = 10;
int right = 20;
while (left <= right)
{
   System.out.println(left);      //This statement
   left = left + 2;
}
```

5. Write a Java statement that outputs "Equal" if the integer values of *night* and *day* are the same, but otherwise does nothing.

▶ 8.5.5 *Another Example*

Let's briefly review the types of Java programming statements we've learned. We can do input and output—reading values from the user into memory, writing values out of memory for the user to see—using meaningful variable identifiers to reference memory locations. We can assign values to variables within the program. And we can direct the flow of control by using conditional statements or looping. While there are many other statement types available in Java, one can do just about everything using only the modest collection of statements we've described. The power lies in how these statements can be combined and nested within groups to produce ever more complex courses of action.

As a final example, suppose we write a program to assist SportsWorld, a company that installs circular swimming pools. In order to estimate their costs for swimming pool covers or for fencing to surround the pool, SportsWorld needs to know the area or circumference of a pool given its radius. A pseudocode version of the program is shown in Figure 8.17.

We should be able to translate this pseudocode fairly directly into the body of the main method. Other things we need to add in order to complete the program are

- A prologue comment to explain what the program does (optional but always recommended for program documentation)
- The class header; we'll call the class *SportsWorld*
- The main method header; remember this is always
  `public static void main(String[] args)`
- Variable declarations

Finally, the computations for circumference and area both involve the constant pi (π). We could use some numerical approximation for pi each time it occurs in the program, but the *Math* class of the standard Java library already defines the constant *PI*. We can invoke this constant value by writing

`Math.PI`

FIGURE 8.17

Pseudocode Version of SportsWorld Program

Get value for user's choice about continuing
While user wants to continue, do the following steps
    Get value for pool radius
    Get value for choice of task
    If task choice is circumference
        Compute pool circumference
        Print output
    Else (task choice is area)
        Compute pool area
        Print output
    Get value for user's choice about continuing
Stop

This notation (class name, dot, desired value or service from the class) is similar to the way we use the Console class (Console.readInt(. . .)) within our programs.

Figure 8.18 gives the complete program; the prologue comment notes the use of the *Math* class. Figure 8.19 shows what would actually appear on the screen when this program is executed with some sample data.

It is inappropriate (and messy) to output the value of the area to 14 or 15 decimal places based on a value of the radius given to one or two decimal places of accuracy. Exercise 13 at the end of this chapter tells how to format real number output to a specified number of decimal digits.

FIGURE 8.18

The SportsWorld Program

```
//This program helps SportsWorld estimate costs
//for pool covers and pool fencing by computing
//the area or circumference of a circle
//with a given radius.
//Any number of circles can be processed.
//Uses class Math for PI
//Written by J. Q. Programmer, 12/31/04
public class SportsWorld
{
  public static void main(String[] args)
  {
    double radius = 0.0;                //radius of a pool -
                                       //given
    double circumference = 0.0;        //pool circumference -
                                       //computed
    double area = 0.0;                 //pool area - computed
    char taskToDo = ' ';               //holds user choice to
                                       //compute circumference
                                       //or area
    char more = 'Y';                   //controls loop for
                                       //processing
                                       //more pools

    more = Console.readChar("Do you want to process "
      + "a pool? (Y or N): ");

    while(more == 'Y')                 //more pools to process
    {
      System.out.println();
      radius = Console.readDouble("Enter the value "
        + "of the radius of the pool: ");
      //See what user wants to compute
      System.out.println("Enter your choice of task.");
      taskToDo = Console.readChar("C to compute "
        + "circumference, A to compute area: ");
      System.out.println();

      if (taskToDo == 'C')                    //compute circumference
```

(continued)

FIGURE 8.18

(continued)

```
        {
          circumference = 2*Math.PI*radius;
          System.out.println("The circumference for a "
            + "pool of radius " + radius + " is " +
            circumference);
        }
        else                              //compute area
        {
          area = Math.PI*radius*radius;
          System.out.println("The area for a pool" +
            " of radius " + radius + " is " + area);
        }
        System.out.println();
        more = Console.readChar("Do you want to process "
          + "more pools? (Y or N): ");
      } //end of while loop

      //finish up
      System.out.println("Program will now terminate.");

  } //end of main method
}    //end of class Sports World
```

FIGURE 8.19

*A Sample Session Using the
Program of Figure 8.18*

```
Do you want to process a pool? (Y or N): Y

Enter the value of the radius of the pool: 2.7
Enter your choice of task.
C to compute circumference, A to compute area: C

The circumference for a pool of radius 2.7 is 16.964600329384883

Do you want to process more pools? (Y or N): Y

Enter the value of the radius of the pool: 2.7
Enter your choice of task.
C to compute circumference, A to compute area: A

The area for a pool of radius 2.7 is 22.902210444669592

Do you want to process more pools? (Y or N): Y

Enter the value of the radius of the pool: 14.53
Enter your choice of task.
C to compute circumference, A to compute area: C

The circumference for a pool of radius 14.53 is 91.29468251331939
Do you want to process more pools? (Y or N): N
Program will now terminate.
```

In this laboratory experience, you will execute a number of complete Java programs that have already been written. These programs make use of input, output, assignment, and control statements. You'll be asked to modify these programs to allow them to do something more or something different than before. In addition, you'll design, write, and execute a complete Java program of your own.

PRACTICE PROBLEMS

1. Write a complete Java program to read in the user's first and last initials and write them out.

2. Write a complete Java program that asks for the price of an item and the quantity purchased and writes out the total cost.

3. Write a complete Java program that asks for a number. If the number is less than 5, it is written out, but if it is greater than or equal to 5, twice that number is written out.

4. Write a complete Java program that asks the user for a positive integer *n*, and then writes out all the numbers from 1 up to and including *n*.

8.6   Meeting Expectations

At the beginning of this chapter, we gave four expectations for programs written in a high-level programming language. Now that we know the essentials of writing programs in Java, it is time to see how well this particular language allows these expectations to be met.

1. *The programmer need not manage the details of the movement of data items within memory, nor pay any attention to where specifically they are stored.* The programmer's only responsibilities are to declare all variables the program will use. This involves selecting identifiers to represent the various data items and indicating the data type of each. The identifiers can be descriptive names that meaningfully relate the data to the problem being solved. Data values are moved as necessary within memory by program instructions that simply reference these identifiers, without the programmer having any idea which specific memory locations contain which values or what value currently exists

in an ALU register. The concepts of memory address and movement between memory and the ALU, along with the effort of generating constant data values, have disappeared.

2. *The programmer can take a macroscopic view of tasks, thinking at a higher level of problem-solving.* Instead of the micromanagement level of moving data values here and there and carefully orchestrating the limited operations available at the machine language or assembly language level, the programmer can, for example, write a formula to compute the circumference of a circle given its radius. The details of how the instruction is carried out—how the data values are moved about and exactly how multiplication of real number values is done—are handled elsewhere. Compare the power of conditional and looping instructions, which are tools for algorithmic problem solving and resemble the operations with which we constructed algorithms in pseudocode, with the assembly-language instructions of LOAD, STORE, JUMP, and so on, which are tools for data and memory management.

3. *Programs written in high-level languages will be portable rather than machine-specific.* Let's consider the program developer who is writing a program for sale or distribution to many users. The program developer doesn't give the user the source code to the program, for a multitude of reasons. First, the program developer doesn't want to give away the secrets of how the program works by revealing the code to someone else, who could make a tiny modification and then sell the program himself or herself. Second, the program developer wants to protect the user from being able to change the code, render a perfectly good program into junk, and then complain to the program developer. And finally, if the program developer distributes the source code, then all users must have their own translators to get the executable module needed to run on their own machines. Therefore, for programs written in most high-level languages—but not Java—the program developer runs through the complete translation process to produce an executable module (as shown in Figure 8.1), and it is the executable module that is sold to the user, who runs it on his or her own machine.

The program developer can compile the program on any kind of machine as long as there is a compiler on that machine for the language in which the program is written. However, there must be a compiler for each (high-level language, machine-type) pair. If the program is written in C++, for example, and the program developer wants to sell his or her program to be used on a variety of computers, he or she needs to compile the same program on a PC using a C++ compiler for the PC, on a Macintosh using a C++ compiler for the Macintosh, on a Sun workstation using a C++ compiler for the Sun, and so on. Figure 8.20, where everything to the left of the vertical line is carried out on the developer's machine and the execution (right of the vertical line) is done on the user's machine, illustrates this. The program is independent of the details of each particular computer's machine language because each compiler takes care of the translation. This is the "portability" we seek from high-level language programs.

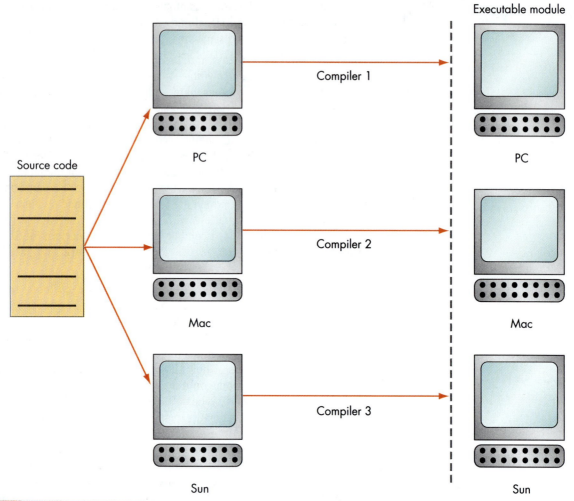

FIGURE 8.20

Each Target Machine Has a Separate Compiler

Actually, even the availability of the appropriate compiler may not guarantee that a program developed on one type of machine can be compiled on a different type of machine. Each programming language has a certain core of instructions that are considered standard. Any respectable compiler for that language must support that core. In fact, national and international standards groups such as ANSI (American National Standards Institute) and ISO (International Standards Organization), which exist to develop standards for an incredible number of things, also develop standards for programming languages. Compilers will thus be built to support "ANSI-standard language X." However, there are often useful features or types of instructions that are not considered a standard part of the language and that some compilers will support while others will not. If a program is written to take advantage of some of these extra features—often referred to as extensions, or "bells and whistles"—that are available on a particular compiler, the program may not work with a different compiler. The price for using nonstandard features is the risk of sacrificing portability.

The standardization process for any entity is necessarily a slow one because it seeks to satisfy the interests of a number of groups, such as consumers, industry, and government. If official standardization comes too late, it must bow to what may have become a de facto standard by common usage. If standardization is imposed too early, it may thwart the development of new ideas or technology.

Java was developed specifically with an eye toward being run on a variety of hardware platforms (see the "Java Is Born" box on page 343). As a result, its developers wanted to avoid the need for a separate compiler for each type of machine. Their solution was to imagine a *hypothetical* target machine called the **Java Virtual Machine (JVM).** The Java compiler translates a Java program into Java **byte-code**—very low-level code that we can think of as the language of the JVM. Bytecode is not itself the language of any real machine, but it can easily be translated into any specific machine language. The program developer only needs to do one compilation of the Java code to produce bytecode and then distributes the resulting bytecode to the various users. The Java compiler is therefore "universal."

The final translation/execution of bytecode on a particular user machine is done by software called a **Java bytecode interpreter.** Figure 8.21 shows that while the developer's task is now simpler, the work on the user's machine has increased because each user machine must have a Java bytecode interpreter. This approach is workable because the Java bytecode interpreter is a small piece of software; even your Web browser contains one (see the Which Java? box on page 379).

So Java, through its use of machine-independent bytecode, has taken another step toward achieving portability. However, Java is not immune to standardization issues. We will see in the next chapter that many of the most successful programming languages were developed by committees or by individuals at academic or research institutions. Over time, through a long process of seeking input from all interested parties, they achieved international standardization status, as discussed earlier. Java, however, is a relatively new language that was developed at a commercial computer company, and to date it has taken a different standardization path. Sun Microsystems has maintained its own "specifications" for the language and has produced several successive versions with additional features. Other companies developing Java-based software are eager to keep abreast of these changes. The Java Community Process is a set of procedures whereby such companies can submit ideas for improvements to the language. Sun has revised this process to give such expert users an earlier say in proposed specification changes.

4. *Programming statements in a high-level language will be closer to standard English, and will use standard mathematical notation.* We see in Figures 8.17 and 8.18 how closely Java resembles pseudocode. Though somewhat stilted, pseudocode is nonetheless

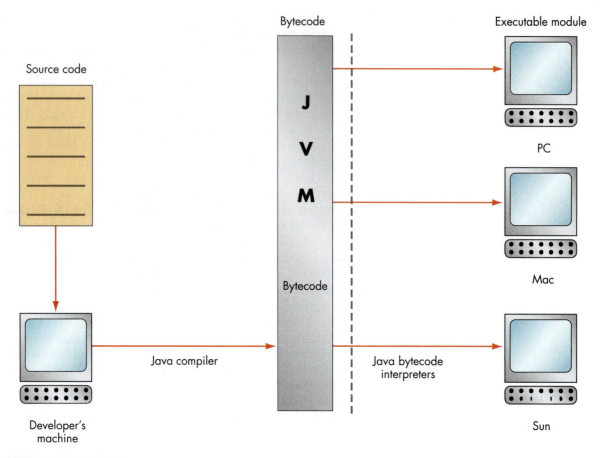

Source code

Bytecode

Executable module

J
V
M

Bytecode

Developer's machine

Java compiler

Java bytecode interpreters

PC

Mac

Sun

FIGURE 8.21

Java Compiler, Java Bytecode Interpreters

close to standard English. Java provides us with statements that give natural implementations of "while condition do something . . ." or "if condition do something . . . ." In addition, Java allows us to use standard mathematical notation such as A + B.

Java, then, seems to have been rather successful in meeting our expectations for a high-level programming language. We've used Java as an example language to illustrate one way these expectations might be satisfied, but it is far from the only language. In the next chapter, we'll look briefly at other high-level programming languages.

8.7 Managing Complexity

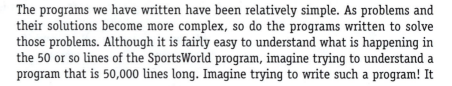

The programs we have written have been relatively simple. As problems and their solutions become more complex, so do the programs written to solve those problems. Although it is fairly easy to understand what is happening in the 50 or so lines of the SportsWorld program, imagine trying to understand a program that is 50,000 lines long. Imagine trying to write such a program! It is not possible to understand—all at once—everything that goes on in a 50,000-line program.

 ### 8.7.1 *Divide and Conquer*

Writing large programs is an exercise in managing complexity. The solution is a problem-solving approach called **divide and conquer.** Suppose a program is to be written to do a certain task; let's call it task T. Suppose we can divide this task into smaller tasks, say A, B, C, and D, such that if we could just do those four tasks in the right order, we would be able to do task T. Then our high-level understanding of the problem needs only to be concerned with *what* A, B, C, and D do and how they must work together to accomplish T. We do not, at this stage of the game, need to understand *how* tasks A, B, C, and D can be done. Figure 8.22(a), an example of a **structure chart** or **structure diagram,** represents this situation. Task T is composed in some way of sub-tasks A, B, C, and D. Later we can turn our attention to, say, subtask A, and see if it too can be reduced to smaller subtasks (Figure 8.22(b)). In this way, we continue to break the task down into smaller and smaller pieces, finally arriving at subtasks that are so simple that it is easy to write the code to carry them out. Better yet, we may find a helpful class with methods that will do these subtasks for us. By *dividing* the problem into small pieces, we can *conquer* the complexity that would be too overwhelming if we looked at the whole problem all at once.

Divide and conquer is, as we said, a problem-solving approach and not just a computer programming technique. Outlining a term paper into major and minor topics is a divide-and-conquer approach to writing the paper. Doing a Form 1040 Individual Tax Return for the Internal Revenue Service can involve subtasks of completing Schedules A, B, C, D, and so on, and then re-assembling the results. Designing a house can be broken down into subtasks of designing floor plans, wiring, plumbing, and the like. Large companies

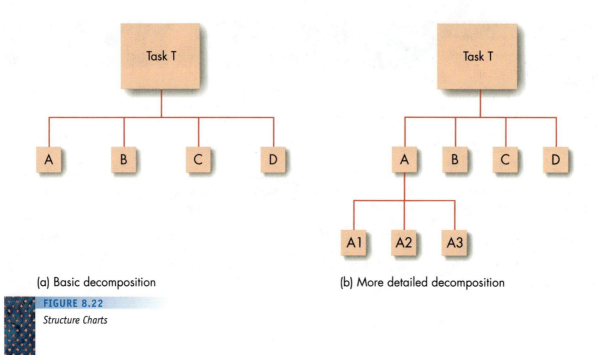

(a) Basic decomposition   (b) More detailed decomposition

FIGURE 8.22

Structure Charts

organize their management responsibilities using a divide-and-conquer approach; what we have called structure charts become, in the business world, organization charts.

How is the divide-and-conquer problem-solving approach reflected in the resulting computer program? If we thought about how to solve the problem in terms of subtasks, then the program should show that same structure; that is, part of the code should do subtask A, part should do subtask B, and so on. We divide the code into *modules* or *subprograms,* each of which does some part of the overall task. Then we empower these modules to work together to solve the original problem.

▶ 8.7.2 *Using Methods*

In Java, modules of code are called **methods.** We have already seen that a main method is required in each Java program. The SportsWorld program (Figure 8.18) has a main method, of course, and it may appear that this single method does the entire task. But the divide-and-conquer approach is already at work here. The main method does not handle the subtasks of reading various kinds of input. Instead, it calls upon methods in the *Console* class that provide those services, and we had to be sure the *Console.class* file was available when we ran the SportsWorld program. The main method does not really do all the details of writing output, either; it makes use of the *println* method. Unlike the *Console* class, *System.out* is automatically supplied with Java, which is why we didn't need to have a separate file.

Let's review what goes on in the main method of the SportsWorld program with an eye to further subdividing the task. There is a loop that does some operations as long as the user wants. What gets done? Input is obtained from the user about the radius of the circle, and input is obtained on the choice of task to be done (compute circumference or compute area). Then the circumference of the circle gets computed and written out, or the area gets computed and written out. Aside from input and output, we can identify two related subtasks: computing the area of a circle and computing the circumference of a circle. Instead of having the main method do these computations, we will create a *Circle* class (Figure 8.23) with two methods that provide these two services to the main method. A Java program can have only one main method, and that is where execution of the program begins. Figure 8.24 shows a pseudocode description of the main method using a modular approach that calls upon the methods in the *Circle* class. When the flow of control reaches the "Ask *Circle* class to compute circumference," it will transfer to the appropriate method code in the *Circle* class and execute that code. When execution of that method code is complete, flow of control will transfer back to the main method and pick up where it left off. The same thing happens for "Ask *Circle* class to compute area."

Methods are named using ordinary Java identifiers, by custom starting with a lowercase letter. We'll name the two Circle methods *doCircumference*

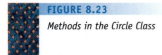

FIGURE 8.23

Methods in the Circle Class

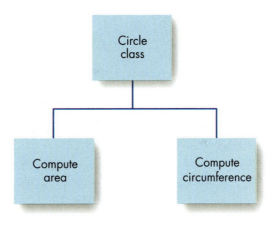

FIGURE 8.24

Pseudocode for the SportsWorld Main Method Using the Circle *Class*

Get value for user's choice about continuing
While user wants to continue, do the following steps
    Get value for pool radius
    Get value for choice of task
    If task choice is circumference
        Ask Circle class to compute circumference
        Print output
    Else (task choice is area)
        Ask Circle class to compute area
        Print output
    Get value for user's choice about continuing
Stop

and *doArea*. Because we've used meaningful identifiers, it is obvious which subtask is carried out by which method.

There are two types of methods. A **void method** carries out some task, perhaps using values it received from the main method, but does not pass any new values back to the main method. (The word *void* signifies "returning nothing.") A **nonvoid method** returns a single new value back to the main method—that is its primary job. This gives the main method information it did not have previously. This single value could be some new data value that the method has collected from the user, or it could be some new data value that the method has computed, perhaps using values it received from the main method.

The *doCircumference* and *doArea* methods compute new values (the circumference and area, respectively) and return them to the main method. So *doCircumference* and *doArea* will be nonvoid methods.

Either kind of method may need certain information from the main method in order to do its job; specifically, it may need to know the current value of certain quantities in the main method. When the main method wants a method in another class to be executed, it must "invoke" the method. It does this by giving the class name, followed by a dot, then the method name, and finally a list in parentheses of the identifiers for variables that concern that method. This is called an **argument list.** The overall form of a method invocation is thus

class-identifier.method-identifier(argument list)

The *doCircumference* and *doArea* methods each need to know the current radius value in order to carry out their computations, so when these methods are invoked, their argument lists will each contain the single variable *radius*.

The invocation of a void method is a complete Java program statement by itself (followed by the semicolon, of course), but the invocation of a nonvoid method is not. Remember that a nonvoid method returns a single value to the main method. You can think of the method invocation just as if it were a variable containing that single returned value. You cannot have the method invocation as a complete statement, just as you cannot have a single variable identifier as a complete statement. Instead, you use the method invocation as part of a statement, in the same way you use any variable identifier. For example, you can make it part of what an output statement writes out, or what an assignment statement assigns to a variable. In our circle program, when the *doCircumference* method returns the value of the circle's circumference, we would like to assign that value to the main method's *circumference* variable, so we would use the assignment statement

```
circumference = Circle.doCircumference(radius);
```

in the main method.

The *Console* class methods *readInt, readDouble,* and *readChar* are nonvoid methods that return the value entered at the keyboard. We used a similar syntax to invoke them, for example

```
variable1 = Console.readInt(prompt);
```

uses the value returned by the *readInt* method as the right side of an assignment statement.

Figure 8.25 shows the new main method. It closely follows the pseudocode of Figure 8.24. At a glance, it does not look a great deal different from our former main method. However, it is conceptually quite different; it uses a helping class (*Circle*), and the subtasks of computing the circumference and computing the area have been relegated to methods of this class. The details (in this case the formulas for computing circumference and area) are now hidden and have been replaced by method invocations. If these subtasks had required many lines of code, our new main method would indeed be shorter—and easier to understand—than before.

The main method now invokes methods of the *Circle* class. It is time to see how to write the code for these other, non-main methods.

 ### 8.7.3 *Writing Methods*

The outline for a Java method is shown in Figure 8.26. The method header has the general form

scope-indicator return-indicator identifier(parameter list)

Note that no semicolon appears at the end of a method header. Let's look at each of these parts in turn.

- *scope-indicator*. The scope indicator uses keywords to determine how and where the method can be invoked. If the scope indicator is *public static,* then any method can invoke this method by giving the name of the class, then a dot, then the method identifier and argument list. This is the syntax that the main method in Figure 8.25 uses to invoke the two methods of the *Circle* class. Similarly, the *readInt* method of the *Console* class is a public static nonvoid method, which is why we are able to invoke it using the class name, as in the statement

  ```
  number = Console.readInt("user prompt here");
  ```

- *return-indicator*. The return indicator classifies a method as void or nonvoid. If it's a void method, the return indicator is just the word *void*. If it's a nonvoid method, the return indicator is the data type of the single value the method returns.

- *identifier*. This is the name of the method and can be any legal Java identifier, although most programmers use a lowercase letter to begin the name.

- *parameter list*. The parameters in the **parameter list** correspond to the arguments in the statement that invokes this method; that is, the first parameter in the list matches the first argument given in the statement that invokes the method, the second parameter matches the second argument, and so on. It is through this correspondence between parameters and arguments that the method receives data from

FIGURE 8.25

A Modularized Version of the
SportsWorld Program

```
//This program helps SportsWorld estimate costs
//for pool covers and pool fencing by computing
//the area or circumference of a circle
//with a given radius.
//Any number of circles can be processed.
//Uses class Circle
//Written by J. Q. Programmer, 12/31/04

public class SportsWorld
{
  public static void main(String[] args)
  {
      double radius = 0.0;                //radius of a pool -
                                          //given
      double circumference = 0.0;         //pool circumference -
                                          //computed
      double area = 0.0;                  //pool area - computed
      char taskToDo = ' ';                //holds user choice to
                                          //compute circumference
                                          //or area
      char more = 'Y';                    //controls loop for
                                          //processing
                                          //more pools

      more = Console.readChar("Do you want to process "
        + "a pool? (Y or N): ");

      while(more == 'Y')                  //more pools to process
      {
        System.out.println();
        radius = Console.readDouble("Enter the value "
          + "of the radius of the pool: ");

        //See what user wants to compute
        System.out.println("Enter your choice of task.");
        taskToDo = Console.readChar("C to compute "
          + "circumference, A to compute area: ");
        System.out.println();

        if (taskToDo == 'C')              //compute circumference
        {
          circumference = Circle.doCircumference(radius);
          System.out.println("The circumference for a "
            + "pool of radius " + radius + " is " +
            circumference);
        }
        else                             //compute area
        {
          area = Circle.doArea(radius);
          System.out.println("The area for a pool" +
            " of radius " + radius + " is " + area);
        }
```

(continued)

FIGURE 8.25

(continued)

```
                    System.out.println();
                    more = Console.readChar("Do you want to process "
                      + "more pools? (Y or N): ");
                } //end of while loop

                //finish up
                System.out.println("Program will now terminate.");

            } //end of main method

    }   //end of class SportsWorld
```

FIGURE 8.26

The Outline for a Java Method

```
method header
//comment
{
    local declarations [optional]
    method body
}
```

the invoking method. The data type of each parameter must be given as part of the parameter list, and it must match the data type of the corresponding argument.

As an example, consider a method *findAverage* to compute and return the average daily rainfall over a certain number of days. The total rainfall (a real number) and the number of days (an integer) are data values the method needs to know in order to compute the daily average, and these values will be passed to the method as arguments. The value returned by the method, the daily average, will be type *double*. This method can be invoked in the main method by a statement such as

```
dailyAverage = findAverage(totalRain, numberOfDays);
```

The header for the *findAverage* method could look like

```
public static double findAverage(double total, int n)
```

Here the parameters *total* and *n* are in the correct order and have the correct data type to match up with their corresponding arguments. The argument names, *totalRain* and *numberOfDays,* are variable identifiers declared in the main method, but the parameters can have different identifiers, as they do here. Arguments and parameters correspond by virtue of their respective positions in the argument list and the parameter list, regardless of the identifiers used. Within the body of the method, it is the parameter identifiers that are used; *total* will have the value passed to it by *totalRain,* and *n* will have the value passed to it by *numberOfDays,* as follows:

```
dailyAverage = findAverage(totalRain, numberOfDays);

public static double findAverage(double total, int n)
```

Arguments in Java are **passed by value.** This means that the method can use the argument value but cannot permanently change it. What really happens is that the method receives a copy of the data value to store in a local memory location, but never knows the memory location where the original value is stored. If the method changes the value of its copy, this change has no effect when control returns to the main method.

In the Circle program, the *doCircumference* method is invoked with a single argument *radius* of type *double*. It is a nonvoid method and returns a type *double* value. Its header can be written as

```
public static double doCircumference(double radius)
```

where this time we used the same name for the parameter as for the argument.

The complete *doCircumference* method is shown in Figure 8.27. Because it is a separate method, we have added a comment right below the method header to describe specifically what this method does. A variable *circumference* is declared within the method. A variable declared within a method is known and can be used only within that method; it is said to be **local** to that method. This local variable *circumference* has nothing to do with the *circumference* variable in the main method of the *SportsWorld* class. It was natural to use the same name for each, but the program would work perfectly well if we named this local variable something entirely different.

Because *doCircumference* is a nonvoid method, it must return a single value to the main method. This is done by the **return statement,** whose syntax is

```
return expression;
```

The expression must evaluate to the data type the nonvoid method has promised to return in its header, which in the case of *doCircumference* is type *double*. All nonvoid methods must have a return statement, but void methods generally will not have a return statement.

The *doArea* method is very similar to *doCircumference*. The complete *Circle* class is given in Figure 8.28. Notice that this class has no main method. A Java program always begins execution with the main method, so the code in

FIGURE 8.27

The doCircumference *Method*

```
public static double doCircumference(double radius)
//returns circumference of a circle
{
  double circumference;
  circumference = 2*Math.PI*radius;
  return circumference;
}
```

FIGURE 8.28

The Circle Class in a Modularized Version of the SportsWorld
Program

```
//Class for circles. Computes circumference and
//area, given radius.
//Uses class Math for PI
//Written by I. M. Euclid, 2/3/04

public class Circle
{
  public static double doCircumference(double radius)
  //returns circumference of a circle
  {
    double circumference;
    circumference = 2*Math.PI*radius;
    return circumference;
  }
  public static double doArea(double radius)
  //returns area of a circle
  {
    double area;
    area = Math.PI*radius*radius;
    return area;
  }
}
```

Figure 8.28 will compile, but it cannot be executed. It is not intended as a standalone program but as a useful tool.

To run the program, each class must be in a separate file, and the file name must be the name of the class with a .java extension. So there will be a *SportsWorld.java* file and a *Circle.java* file. Each .java file is compiled into a .class file, and the .class file containing the main method is then executed. It is helpful if all these files are in the same folder or directory on your computer (along with the *Console.class* file) so that the system knows where to find them.

So there we have it—a complete modularized version of our Circle program. Because it seems to have taken a lot of effort to arrive at this second version (which, after all, does the same thing as the program in Figure 8.18), let's review what the new version does and why this effort is worthwhile. The major task is accomplished by doing a series of subtasks (computing circumference and area), and the work for these subtasks takes place within methods of a separate class. The main method doesn't need to know how these tasks are done, it only needs to invoke the appropriate method at the appropriate point. As an analogy, we may think of the president of a company calling on various assistants to carry out tasks as needed. The president does not need to know *how* a task is done, only the company division (class name) and name of the person (method name) responsible for carrying it out.

This compartmentalization is useful in many ways. It is useful when we *plan the solution* to a problem because it allows us to use a divide-and-conquer approach. We can think about the problem in terms of subtasks. This makes it easier for us to understand how to achieve a solution to a large and complex problem. We can group similar subtasks together and think of them as methods of a helping class. It is also useful when we *code the solution* to a problem. Instead of having to write every detail of the code in a monolithic main method, we can write a main method that invokes other methods of other classes as needed. We can write methods for these other classes one at a time so that the program gradually expands. Developing a large software project is a team effort, and different parts of the team can be writing different classes and methods at the same time. It is useful when we *test the program* because we can test one new method at a time as the program grows, and any errors are localized to the method being added. (The main method can be tested early by writing appropriate headers but empty bodies for the other methods.) Compartmentalization is useful when we *modify the program* because changes tend to be localized within certain subtasks, hence within certain methods in the code. And finally it is useful for anyone (including the programmer) who wants to *read* the resulting program. The overall idea of how the program works, without the details, can be gleaned from reading the main method; if and when the details become important, the appropriate code for the other methods can be consulted.

Finally, once a class has been developed and tested, it is then available for any application program to use. An application program that does quite different things than SportsWorld, but that needs the value of the area or circumference of a circle computed from the radius, can use our *Circle* class.

Figure 8.29 summarizes several terms introduced in this section.

FIGURE 8.29

Some Java Terminology

TERM	MEANING	TERM	MEANING
void method	Performs a task, but returns no value; method invocation is a complete Java statement	nonvoid method	Computes a value, must include a return statement, method invocation is used within another Java statement
argument	Variable passed to method when it is invoked	parameter	"Dummy variable" in a method that receives its value from the corresponding argument
local variable	Declared and known only within a method		
argument passed by value	Method receives a copy of the value and can make no permanent changes in the value		

LABORATORY EXPERIENCE 13

This laboratory experience builds on the previous one, again using the Java compiler. Here you will work with Java programs that use methods and some that use an array.

1. What will the output be after executing the following Java program?

```java
public class Problem1
{
  public static void main(String[] args)
  {
    int number = 10;
    int newNumber = 0;
    newNumber = Helper.doIt(number);
    System.out.println(newNumber);
  }
}
public class Helper
{
  public static int doIt(int n)
  {
    int twice = 0;
    twice = 2*n;
    return twice;
  }
}
```

2. What will the output be after executing the following Java program?

```java
public class Problem2
{
  public static void main(String[] args)
  {
    int number = 10;
    System.out.println(Helper.doIt(number));
  }
}
public class Helper
{
  public static int doIt(int n)
  {
    return 2*n;
  }
}
```

3. What will the output be after executing the following Java program?

(continued)

```
public class Problem3
{
  public static void main(String[] args)
  {
    int number = 10;
    System.out.println(Helper.doIt(number));
    System.out.println(number);
  }
}
public class Helper
{
  public static int doIt(int number)
  {
    number = 7;
    System.out.println(number);
    return 2*number;
  }
}
```

4. Suppose a nonvoid method called *tax* in a class called *Sales* gets a value *subtotal* from the main method, multiplies *subtotal* by the tax rate of 0.55, and returns the resulting tax amount. All quantities are type *double*.

   a. Write the method header.
   b. Write the method body.
   c. Write a single statement in the main method that invokes the *tax* method and writes out the resulting tax amount.

8.8   Object-Oriented Programming

 ### 8.8.1 *What Is It?*

The divide-and-conquer approach to programming that we have advocated is a "traditional" approach. The focus is on the overall task to be done: how to break it down into subtasks, and how to write algorithms for these subtasks that will be carried out by communicating modules—in the case of Java, by methods in various classes. The program can be thought of as a giant statement executor designed to carry out the major task, even though the main module may simply call upon, in turn, the various other modules that do the subtask work.

   Object-oriented programming (OOP) takes a somewhat different view. A program is considered to be a simulation of some part of the world that is the domain of interest. "Objects" populate this domain. Objects in a banking system, for example, might be savings accounts, checking accounts, and loans. Objects in a company personnel system might be employees. Objects in a medical office might be patients and doctors. Each object is an example drawn from a class of similar objects. The savings account "class" in a bank has certain properties associated with it, such as name, Social Security number, account type, and account balance. Each individual savings account at the bank is an example of (an object of) the savings account class, and each has specific values for these common properties; that is, each savings account has a specific value for the name of the account holder, a specific value for the account balance, and so forth. Each object of a class therefore has its own data values.

A class also has one or more subtasks associated with it, and all objects from that class can perform those subtasks. In carrying out a subtask, each object can be thought of as providing some service. A savings account, for example, can compute compound interest due on the balance. When an object-oriented program is executed, the program generates requests for services that go to the various objects. The objects respond by performing the requested service—that is, carrying out the subtask. Thus a program that is using the savings account class might request a particular savings account object to perform the service of computing interest due on the account balance. An object always knows its own data values and may use them in performing the requested service.

Some of this sounds familiar. We know about subtasks (methods) associated with a class. The new idea is that instead of directly asking a class to carry out a subtask, we ask an object of that class to carry out a subtask. The even bigger new idea is that such objects have data values for the class properties. Instead of storing data in variables that are available to the whole program and then passing them as arguments to subtasks, the program can simply ask an object to use its own data when it carries out a subtask.

There are three terms often associated with object-oriented programming, as illustrated in Figure 8.30. The first term is **encapsulation.** Each class has its own little program module to perform each of its subtasks. Any user of the class (which might be some other program) can request an object of that class to invoke the appropriate module and thereby perform the subtask service. The class user needs to know what services objects of the class can provide and how to request an object to perform any such service. The details of the module code belong to the class itself, and this code may be modified in any way desired, as long as the way the user interacts with the class remains unchanged. (In the savings account example, the details of the algorithm used to compute interest due belong only to the class and need not be known by any user of the class. If the bank wants to change how it computes interest, only the code for the interest module in the savings account class needs to be modified; any programs that use the services of the savings account class can remain unchanged.) Furthermore, the class properties represent data values that will exist as part of each object of the class. A class therefore consists of two components, its subtask modules and its properties, and both components are "encapsulated"—bundled—with the class.

A second term associated with object-oriented programming is **inheritance.** Once a class A of objects is defined, a class B of objects can be defined

FIGURE 8.30

Three Key Elements of OOP

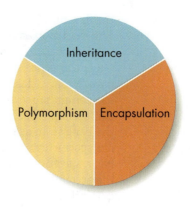

as a "subclass" of A. Every member of class B is also a member of class A; this is sometimes called an "is a" relationship. Objects in the B class will "inherit" all of the properties and be able to perform all the services of objects in A, but they may also be given some special property or ability. The benefit is that class B does not have to be built from the ground up, but rather can take advantage of the fact that class A already exists. In the banking example, a senior citizens savings account would be a subclass of the savings account class. Any senior citizens savings account object is also a savings account object, but may have special properties or be able to provide special services.

The third term is **polymorphism.** *Poly* means "many." Objects may provide services that should logically have the same name because they do roughly the same thing, but the details differ. In the banking example, both savings account objects and checking account objects should provide a "compute interest" service, but the details of how interest is computed differ in these two cases. Thus one name, the name of the service to be performed, has several meanings, depending on the class of the object providing the service. It may even be the case that more than one service with the same name exists for the same class, although there must be some way to tell which service is meant when it is invoked by an object of that class.

Let's change analogies from the banking world to something more fanciful in the sports arena and consider a football team. Every member of the team's backfield is an "object" of the "backfield" class. The quarterback is the only "object" of the "quarterback" class. Each backfield object can perform the service of carrying the ball if he or she receives the ball from the quarterback; ball-carrying is a subtask of the backfield class. The quarterback who hands the ball off to a backfield object is requesting that object to perform that subtask because it is "public knowledge" that the backfield class carries the ball and that this service is invoked by handing off the ball to a backfield object. The "program" to carry out this subtask is *encapsulated* within the backfield class in the sense that it may have evolved over the week's practice and may depend on specific knowledge of the opposing team, but at any rate, its details need not be known to other players. *Inheritance* can be illustrated by the halfback subclass within the backfield class. A halfback object can do everything a backfield object can but may also be a pass receiver. And *polymorphism* can be illustrated by the fact that the backfield may invoke a different "program" depending upon where on the field the ball is handed off. Of course our analogy is imperfect, because not all human "objects" from the same class behave in precisely the same way—fullbacks sometimes receive passes and so on.

 ### 8.8.2   *Java and OOP*

Java is very much an object-oriented programming language. In the modularized version of our SportsWorld program, we used a *Circle* class with methods that the main method in the *SportsWorld* class could invoke. The main method did not create any objects of the *Circle* class but could nevertheless invoke these methods, because each method had the word "static" in the method header. A **static method** is one that doesn't need to be invoked by an object of that class. Instead, it can be invoked by giving the class name, followed by a dot, and then the method name with an appropriate list of arguments, just as we have done with all the methods we have used so far.

Suppose we write a new *Circle* class with the thought that applications programs using this class will create objects of the class. The objects will be individual circles. A circle object will have a radius. A circle object, which will know the value of its own radius, should be able to perform the services of computing its own circumference and its own area. At this point, we have answered the two major questions about our new Circle class:

- What are the properties common to any object of this class? (In this case, there is a single property—the radius.)
- What are the services that any object of the class should be able to perform? (In this case, compute its circumference and compute its area, although as we will see shortly, we will need other services as well.)

Now we can create a truly object-oriented version of the SportsWorld program. What are the objects of interest within the scope of this problem? SportsWorld deals with circular swimming pools, but they are basically just circles. So the SportsWorld program will create a circle object. In Java terminology, objects are called **instances of a class,** the properties are called **instance variables,** and the services, as we know, are called **instance methods.**

Figure 8.31 shows the complete code for the new *Circle* class. Four instance methods are given, followed by a declaration of the single instance variable, *radius*. The first method is void, and the remaining three return values. None of the methods is static, meaning that they must be invoked by circle objects.

As before, the *SportsWorld* class will handle all of the user interaction and will make use of the *Circle* class. It will create a circle object and request that object to set the value of its radius and to find its area or find its circumference, depending on the program user's preference. The object will invoke the *Circle* methods to carry out these tasks. From Figure 8.31, we see that the

FIGURE 8.31

The New Circle *Class*

```
//Class for circle objects. A circle has a radius
//and can compute its circumference and area.
//Uses class Math for PI
//Written by Arc. I. Medes, 2/3/04

public class Circle
{
  public void setRadius(double value)
  //sets radius equal to value
  {
    radius = value;
  }

  public double getRadius()
  //returns current radius
  {
    return radius;
  }

  public double doCircumference()
  //computes and returns circumference of a circle
  {
      return 2*Math.PI*radius;
  }

  public double doArea()
  //computes and returns area of a circle
  {
    return Math.PI*radius*radius;
  }

  //instance variable
  private double radius;
}
```

setRadius method uses an assignment statement to change the value of *radius* to whatever quantity is passed to the parameter *value*. The *doCircumference* and *doArea* methods use the usual formulas for their computations, but instead of using local variables for circumference and area, we've compressed the code into a single return statement. (This has nothing to do with object-orientation; we could have done this in version 2 of the program.) The purpose of the *getRadius* method will be explained shortly.

The methods of the *Circle* class are all declared using the keyword **public.** Public methods can be used anywhere, including any other Java program (like SportsWorld) that wants to make use of this class. Think of the Circle class as handing out a business card that advertises these services: Hey, you want a circle object that can find its own area? Find its own circumference? Set the value of its own radius? I'm your class! (Class methods can also be **private,** but a private method is a sort of helping task that can be used only within the class in which it occurs.)

The single instance variable of the class (*radius*) is declared using the keyword **private.** Only methods in the *Circle* class itself can use this variable. Note that *doCircumference* and *doArea* have no parameter for the value of the radius; as methods of this class, they know the current value of *radius* at all times and it does not have to be passed to them as an argument. Because *radius* has been declared private, however, the *SportsWorld* class cannot use the value of *radius*. It will not be able to write out that value or directly change that value by some assignment statement. It can, however, request a circle object to invoke the *getRadius* method to return the current value of the radius in order to write it out. It can also request a circle object to invoke the *setRadius* method to change the value of its radius; *setRadius* does have a parameter to receive a new value for *radius*. Instance variables are generally declared private instead of public to protect the data in an object from reckless changes some application program might try to make. Changes in the values of instance variables should be performed only under the control of class objects through methods such as *setRadius*.

The new *SportsWorld* class (Figure 8.32) differs from the earlier version (Figure 8.25) in several ways. The main method must create a circle object, an instance of the *Circle* class. The following statement does this:

```
Circle SwimmingPool = new Circle();
```

The left-hand side of this statement,

```
Circle SwimmingPool
```

looks like an ordinary variable declaration such as

```
int number
```

It seems to be saying, Give me a memory location in which I will store something of type *Circle* and call it *SwimmingPool*. What we are asking for, however, is memory space to store the instance variables of the object, of which there might be many for some classes of objects. Unlike ordinary variables, Java does not give us memory locations in which to store the instance variables of an object until we specifically request "new" memory for this purpose via the right-hand side of the statement

```
new Circle()
```

After

```
Circle SwimmingPool = new Circle();
```

the object *SwimmingPool* exists, and the main method can ask *SwimmingPool* to perform the various services of which instances of the *Circle* class are capable.

The syntax to request an object to invoke a method is to give the name of the object, followed by a dot, followed by the name of the class method, followed by any arguments the method may need.

object-identifier.method-identifier(argument list)

FIGURE 8.32

The New SportsWorld *Class*

```
//This program helps SportsWorld estimate costs
//for pool covers and pool fencing by computing
//the area or circumference of a circle
//with a given radius.
//Any number of circles can be processed.
//Uses class Circle
//Written by J. Q. Programmer, 12/31/04

public class SportsWorld
{
  public static void main(String[] args)
  {
    double newRadius = 0.0;         //radius of a pool -
                                    //given
    char taskToDo = ' ';           //holds user choice to
                                    //compute
                                    //circumference or area
    char more = 'Y';               //controls loop for
                                    //processing more pools
    Circle SwimmingPool = new Circle(); //create a
                                        //circle object

    more = Console.readChar("Do you want to process "
      + "a pool? (Y or N): ");

    while(more == 'Y')                 //more pools to process
    {
      System.out.println();
      newRadius = Console.readDouble("Enter the value "
        + "of the radius of the pool: ");
      SwimmingPool.setRadius(newRadius); //give pool
                                         //this radius

      //See what user wants to compute
      System.out.println("Enter your choice of task.");
      taskToDo = Console.readChar("C to compute "
        + "circumference, A to compute area: ");
      System.out.println();

      if (taskToDo == 'C')           //compute circumference
        System.out.println("The circumference for a "
          + "pool of radius " + SwimmingPool.getRadius()
          + " is " + SwimmingPool.doCircumference() );
      else                           //compute area
        System.out.println("The area for a pool "
          + "of radius " + SwimmingPool.getRadius()
          + " is " + SwimmingPool.doArea() );
      System.out.println();

      more = Console.readChar("Do you want to process"
        + " more pools? (Y or N): ");
    }

    //finish up
    System.out.println("Program will now terminate.");
  }
}
```

The object that invokes a method is the **calling object.** Therefore the expression

```
SwimmingPool.doCircumference()
```

in the main method uses *SwimmingPool* as the calling object to invoke the *doCircumference* method of the *Circle* class. No arguments are needed because this method has no parameters, but the empty parentheses must be present.

There are no variables in the main method for the circumference and the area of the circle. The *doCircumference* and *doArea* methods are now invoked within an output statement, so these values get printed out without being stored anywhere. (This has nothing to do with object-orientation; we could have done this in version 2 of the program.) But there is also no declaration in the main method for a variable called *radius*. There is a declaration for *newRadius,* and *newRadius* receives the value entered by the user for the radius of the circle. Therefore, isn't *newRadius* serving the same purpose as *radius* did in the old program? No—this is rather subtle, so pay attention: While *newRadius* holds the number the user wants for the circle radius, it is not itself the radius of *SwimmingPool*. The radius of *SwimmingPool* is the instance variable *radius,* and only methods of the class can change the instance variables of an object of that class. The *Circle* class provides the *setRadius* method for this purpose. The main method of *SportsWorld* must ask the object *SwimmingPool* to invoke *setRadius* in order to set the value of its radius equal to the value contained in *newRadius*. The *newRadius* argument corresponds to the *value* parameter in the *setRadius* method, which then gets assigned to the instance variable *radius*.

```
SwimmingPool.setRadius(newRadius);

public void setRadius(double value)
//sets radius equal to value
{
   radius = value;
}
```

The *setRadius* method is a void method because it returns no information to the invoking method; it contains no return statement. The invocation of this method is a complete Java statement.

Finally, the output statements that print the values of the circumference and area also have *SwimmingPool* invoke the *getRadius* method to return the current *radius* value so it can be printed as part of the output. We could have used the variable *newRadius* here instead. However, *newRadius* is what we THINK has been used in the computation, whereas *radius* is what has REALLY been used.

Now that we understand the syntax, we can see that an output statement such as

```
System.out.println("Here's your output: " + answer);
```

asks the *System.out* object to invoke a *println* method using the string parameter included in the parentheses. The *System.out* object is unusual in that we do not have to explicitly create it using a "new" statement.

This completes version 3 of the SportsWorld program, a truly object-oriented version. The main method creates a circle object and repeatedly requests that object to perform (or, technically, cause to have performed) the appropriate methods of its class to set its own radius and compute its circumference and area.

8.8.3 *One More Example*

The object-oriented version of our circle program illustrates encapsulation. All data and calculations concerning circles are encapsulated in the *Circle* class. Let's look at one final example that illustrates the other two watchwords of OOP—polymorphism and inheritance.

Figure 8.33(a)–(d) shows four simple geometric shape classes. Figure 8.33(e) is the application program that uses these classes. The main method creates objects from these various classes and has those objects set their dimensions and compute their areas. Each of these five classes would be in a separate .java file of the same name as the class.

For each class, the instance variables for the class represent the properties that any object of the class possesses. A circle object has a radius property, whereas a rectangle has a width property and a height property. A square object has a side property, as one might expect, but a Square2 object doesn't seem to have any properties, or for that matter any way to compute its area. We'll talk more about the difference between the *Square* class and the *Square2* class shortly.

The output (rounded to two decimal places for simplicity) after running the program in Figure 8.33 is

```
          The area of a circle with radius 23.5 is 1734.95
The area of a rectangle with dimensions 12.4 and 18.1 is 224.44
          The area of a square with side 3 is 9
The area of a rectangle with dimensions 4.2 and 4.2 is 17.64
```

In Figure 8.33 we see polymorphism at work, because each class has its own *doArea* method. When the program executes, the class of which the calling object that is invoking the method is an instance determines the correct method to use. After all, computing the area of a circle is quite different from computing the area of a rectangle. The methods themselves are straightforward; they employ assignment statements to set the dimensions and the usual formulas to compute the area of a circle, rectangle, and square.

Square is a separate class with a *side* property and a *doArea* method. The *Square2* class, however, recognizes the fact that squares are special kinds of rectangles.

The *Square2* class is a subclass of the *Rectangle* class, as is indicated by the reference in the header of the *Square2* class that it **extends** the *Rectangle* class. The *Square2* class inherits the *width* and *height* properties from the "parent" *Rectangle* class; the "protected," rather than private, status of these properties in the *Rectangle* class indicates that they can be extended to any subclass. *Square2* also inherits the *setWidth, setHeight, getWidth, getHeight,*

FIGURE 8.33

A Java Program with Polymorphism and Inheritance

```
//Class for circles. Area can be
//computed from radius.

public class Circle
{
  public void setRadius(double value)
  //sets radius equal to value
  {
    radius = value;
  }

  public double getRadius()
  //returns current radius
  {
    return radius;
  }

  public double doArea()
  //computes and returns area of a circle
  {
    return Math.PI*radius*radius;
  }

  //instance variable
  private double radius;
}
```

(a) The *Circle* Class

```
//Class for rectangles. Area can be
//computed from length and width.

public class Rectangle
{
  public void setWidth(double value)
  //sets width equal to value
  {
    width = value;
  }

  public void setHeight(double value)
  //sets height equal to value
  {
    height = value;
  }

  public double getWidth()
  //returns width
  {
    return width;
  }
```

(continued)

FIGURE 8.33

(continued)

```
    public double getHeight()
    //returns height
    {
      return height;
    }

    public double doArea()
    //computes and returns area of a rectangle
    {
      return width*height;
    }

    //instance variables
    protected double width, height;
}
```

(b) The *Rectangle* Class

```
//Class for squares. Area can be
//computed from side.
public class Square
{
  public void setSide(double value)
  //sets side equal to value
  {
    side = value;
  }

  public double getSide()
  //returns side
  {
    return side;
  }

  public double doArea()
  //computes and returns area of a square
  {
    return side*side;
  }

  //instance variable
  private double side;
}
```

(c) The *Square* Class

```
//Square2 is derived class of Rectangle,
//uses the inherited height and width
//properties and the inherited doArea method

public class Square2 extends Rectangle
{
```

FIGURE 8.33

(continued)

```
    public void setSide(double value)
    //sets width and height equal to value
    {
      width = value;
      height = value;
    }
}
```

(d) The *Square2* Class

```
//Computes areas of geometric shapes.
//Uses classes Circle, Rectangle, Square, Square2

public class Geometry
{
  public static void main (String apps [])
  {
    Circle joe = new Circle();
    joe.setRadius(23.5);
    System.out.println("The area of a circle "
      + "with radius " + joe.getRadius()
      + " is " + joe.doArea());

    Rectangle luis = new Rectangle();
    luis.setWidth(12.4);
    luis.setHeight(18.1);
    System.out.println("The area of a rectangle "
      + "with dimensions " + luis.getWidth()
      + " and " + luis.getHeight()
      + " is " + luis.doArea());

    Square anastasia = new Square();
    anastasia.setSide(3);
    System.out.println("The area of a square "
      + "with side " + anastasia.getSide()
      + " is " + anastasia.doArea());

    Square2 tyler = new Square2();
    tyler.setSide(4.2);
    System.out.println("The area of a square "
      + "with side " + tyler.getWidth()
      + " is " + tyler.doArea());
  }
}
```

(e) The Geometry Class—Main Method

and *doArea* methods. In addition, *Square2* has its own method, *setSide,* because setting the value of the "side" makes sense for a square but not for an
arbitrary rectangle. What the user of the *Square2* class doesn't know is that
there really isn't a "side" property; the *setSide* method merely sets the inher-

FIGURE 8.34

A Hierarchy of Geometric Classes

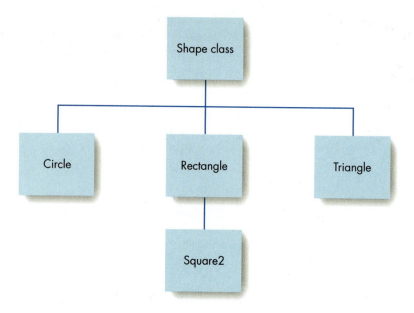

ited *width* and *height* properties to the same value. To compute the area, then, the *doArea* method inherited from the *Rectangle* class can be used, and there is no need to redefine it or even to copy the existing code. Here we see inheritance at work.

Inheritance can be carried through multiple "generations." We might re-design the program so that there is one "superclass" that is a general *Shape* class, of which *Circle* and *Rectangle* are subclasses, with *Square2* a subclass of *Rectangle* (see Figure 8.34 for a possible class hierarchy).

8.8.4   *What Have We Gained?*

Now that we have some idea of the flavor of object-oriented programming, we should ask what we gain by this approach. There are two major reasons why OOP is a popular way to program:

- Software reuse
- A more natural "world view"

SOFTWARE REUSE. Manufacturing productivity took a great leap forward when Henry Ford invented the assembly line. Automobiles could be assembled using identical parts so that each car did not have to be treated as a unique creation. Computer scientists are striving to make software development more of an assembly-line operation and less of a handcrafted, start-over-each-time process. Object-oriented programming is a step toward this goal: A useful class that has been implemented and tested is available for use in future software development. Anyone who wants to write an application program involving circles, for example, could use the already written, tried and tested *Circle* class and simply create circle objects as needed. As the "parts list" (the class library) grows, it becomes easier and easier to find a "part" that fits, and less and less time has to be devoted to writing original code. If the objects from a class don't quite fit, perhaps the class can be modified by creating a subclass; this is still less work than starting from scratch. Software reuse implies more than just rapid code generation. It also means improvements in *reliability;* these classes have already been tested, and if properly used, they will work correctly. And it means improvements in *maintainability.* Thanks to the encapsulation property of object-oriented programming, changes can be made in the details of class methods without affecting other code, although such change requires retesting the classes.

A MORE NATURAL "WORLD VIEW." The traditional view of programming is procedure-oriented, with a focus on tasks, subtasks, and algorithms. But wait—didn't we talk about subtasks in OOP? Haven't we said that computer science is all about algorithms? Does OOP abandon these ideas? Not at all. It is more a question of *when* these ideas come into play. Object-oriented programming recognizes that in the "real world," tasks are done by entities (objects). Object-oriented program design begins by identifying those objects that are important in the domain of the program because their actions contribute to the mix of activities going on in the banking enterprise, the medical office, or wherever. Then it is determined what data should be associated with each object and what subtasks the object contributes to this mix. Finally, an algorithm to carry out each subtask must be designed.

Object-oriented programming is an approach that allows the programmer to more closely model or simulate the world as we see it, rather than mimicking the sequential actions of the von Neumann machine. It provides another buffer between the real world and the machine, another level of abstraction in which the programmer can create a virtual problem solution that will ultimately be translated into electronic signals on hardware circuitry.

Finally, we should mention that a graphical user interface, with its windows, icons, buttons, and menus, is an example of object-oriented programming at work. A general button class, for example, can have properties of height, width, location on the screen, text that may appear on the button, and so forth. Each individual button object has specific values for those properties. The button class can perform certain services by responding to messages, which are generated by events (for example, the user clicking the mouse on a button triggers a "mouse-click" event). Each particular button object personalizes the code to respond to these messages in unique ways. We will not go into details of how to develop graphical user interfaces in Java, but in the next section you will see a bit of the programming mechanics that can be used to draw the graphics items that make up a visual interface.

1. What would be the output from execution of the following section of code if it were added to the main method of the Java program in Figure 8.33?

```java
Square one = new Square();
one.setSide(10);
System.out.println("The area of a square "
  + "with side " + one.getSide()
  + " is " + one.doArea());
```

2. In the *Shape* hierarchy described in this section, suppose there is a *Triangle* class that includes a *doArea* method. What two properties should any triangle object have?

8.9 Graphical Programming

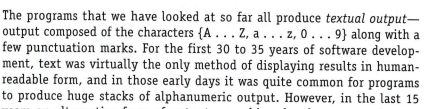

The programs that we have looked at so far all produce *textual output*—output composed of the characters {A . . . Z, a . . . z, 0 . . . 9} along with a few punctuation marks. For the first 30 to 35 years of software development, text was virtually the only method of displaying results in human-readable form, and in those early days it was quite common for programs to produce huge stacks of alphanumeric output. However, in the last 15 years an alternative form of output—*graphics*—has become much more widely used. With graphics, we are no longer limited to 100 or so printable characters; instead, programmers are free to construct whatever shapes and images they desire.

The intelligent and well-planned use of graphical output can produce some phenomenal improvements in software. We discussed this issue in Chapter 6, where we described the move away from the text-oriented operating systems of the 1970s and 1980s, such as MS-DOS and VMS, to more powerful and user-friendly graphical user interfaces (GUIs), such as Windows XP and Mac OS X. Instead of having to learn dozens of complex text-oriented commands for such things as copying, editing, deleting, moving, and printing files, GUIs can present users with simple and easy to understand visual metaphors of these operations, such as those shown in Figure 8.35.

Not only does graphics make it easier to manage the tasks of the operating system, it can help us visualize and make sense of massive amounts of output produced by programs that model complex physical, social, and mathematical systems. (We will discuss modeling and visualization further in Chapter 12.) Finally, there are many applications of computers that would simply be impossible without the ability to display output visually. Applications such as virtual reality, computer-aided design/computer-aided manufacturing (CAD/CAM), games and entertainment, medical imaging, and computer mapping would not have become anywhere near as important as they are without

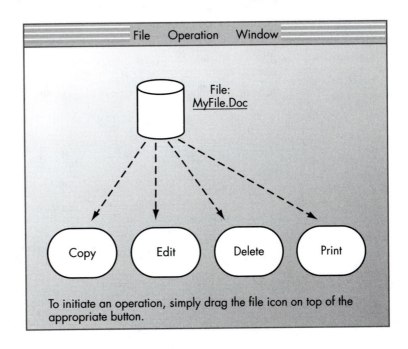

File   Operation   Window

File:
MyFile.Doc

Copy   Edit   Delete   Print

To initiate an operation, simply drag the file icon on top of the
appropriate button.

the enormous improvements that have occurred in the areas of graphics and
visualization.

So, we know that graphical programming is important. The question is,
What features must be added to a programming language like Java to produce
graphical output?

8.9.1 Graphics Hardware

Modern computer terminals use what is called a **bitmapped display,** in which
the screen is made up of thousands of individual picture elements, or **pixels,**
laid out in a two-dimensional grid. These are the same pixels used in visual
images, as discussed in Chapter 4. In fact, the display is simply one large visual image. The number of pixels on the screen varies from system to system;
typical values range from 800 × 600 up to 1560 × 1280. Naturally, the more
pixels available in a given amount of space, the sharper the visual image. Terminals with a high density of pixels are termed **high-resolution** terminals.
Again from Chapter 4, we know that a color display requires 24 bits per pixel,
with 8 bits used to represent the value of each of the three primary colors—
red, green, and blue. The memory that stores the actual screen image is called
a **frame buffer.** A high-resolution color display would need a frame buffer
with (1560 × 1280) pixels × 24 bits/pixel = 47,923,000 bits or about 6 MB
of memory for a single image. (One of the problems with graphics is that it requires many times the amount of memory needed for storing text.)

The individual pixels in the display are addressed using a two-dimensional
coordinate grid system, the pixel in the upper left-hand corner being (0, 0).

FIGURE 8.36

Pixel Numbering System in a Bitmapped Display

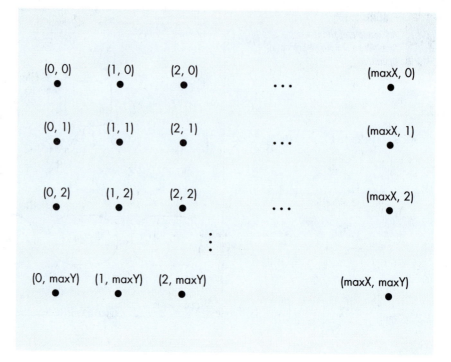

The overall pixel-numbering system is summarized in Figure 8.36. The specific values for *maxX* and *maxY* in Figure 8.36 are, as mentioned earlier, system-dependent. (Note that this coordinate system is not the usual mathematical one. Here the origin is in the upper left corner, and *y* values are measured downward.)

The terminal hardware displays on the screen the frame buffer value of every individual pixel. For example, if we have a color monitor and the frame buffer value in position (24, 47) has an RGB value of (0, 0, 0), then the hardware will set the color of the pixel located at column 24, row 47 to black, as shown in Figure 8.37 The operation diagrammed in Figure 8.37 must be repeated for all of the 500,000 to 2 million pixels on the screen. However, the setting of a pixel is not permanent; on the contrary, its color and intensity fade quickly. Therefore, each pixel must be "repainted" often enough so that our eyes do not detect any "flicker," or change in intensity. This requires the screen to be completely updated, or refreshed, 30–50 times per second. By setting various sequences of pixels to different colors, the user can have the screen display any desired shape or image. This is the fundamental way in which graphical output is achieved.

8.9.2 *Graphics Software*

To control the setting and clearing of pixels, programmers use a collection of software routines that are part of a special package called a **graphics library.** Virtually all modern programming languages, including Java, come with an extensive and powerful graphics library for creating a wide range of

FIGURE 8.37

Display of Information on the Terminal

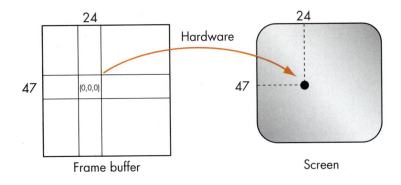

shapes and images. Typically an "industrial strength" graphics library will include dozens or hundreds of routines for everything from drawing simple geometric shapes like lines and circles, to creating and selecting colors, to more complex operations like displaying scrolling windows, pull-down menus, and buttons.

The Java library includes a package called the **Abstract Windowing Toolkit,** usually abbreviated **AWT.** This toolkit contains literally dozens of routines that allow users to create powerful interfaces. The AWT package includes routines for

- Creating the basic set of GUI components, including windows, buttons, text boxes, icons, and menus.
- Allowing the user to control the size and placement of these components.
- Allowing the user to define special objects called **listeners** that automatically activate methods when screen events, such as moving or clicking the mouse, or selecting a menu item, occur.

In 1998, Sun introduced a package of even more powerful GUI components, commonly called **Swing** components. Both the AWT package and the Swing package are huge, and their description is well beyond the scope of this text. In this discussion we will restrict our focus to a much more modest set of functions. While the set is small, the graphics routines we present will give you a good idea of what visual programming is like and will allow you to display some interesting, nontrivial images on the screen. (To access the Java graphics routines we will be discussing, you must include the statement "import java.awt.*" at the beginning of your program. This makes the classes in the Java AWT available for your program to use.)

In Java, the primary method of drawing geometric shapes is with the class called *Graphics*. Every open window contains an instance of this class called its **graphics context,** which by tradition is represented by the letter *g*. When you open a window you cannot see this "graphics context object," but it is there, and it will respond to messages (i.e., function calls) that ask it to display various shapes and patterns within the window. It carries out this drawing operation using the identical bitmapped techniques described previously.

To create a new window for our drawings (termed a **frame** in Java), we can use the following sequence of three commands:

```
Frame f = new Frame("Example 1");
f.setSize(500, 500);
f.setVisible(true);
```

The first line creates a new window called *f* containing the label "Example 1" in the title bar at the top of the window. The second line sets the size of this window at 500 pixels × 500 pixels. When setting the window size, be sure that you do not exceed the maximum value allowed on your system. Finally, the last line makes the window visible on the screen. After executing these three lines your screen should display the following:

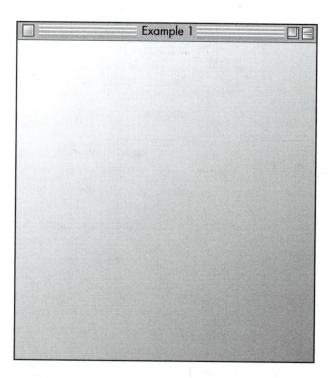

Now, to obtain the graphics context of the window *f* created above, we use the method called *getGraphics*. This method returns the graphics context *g* of the window to which the message is sent:

```
Graphics g;
g = f.getGraphics();
```

We can now send whatever drawing commands we want to *g*, and it will display the shapes that we ask for inside window *f*.

What types of messages will *g* respond to? There are literally dozens of drawing commands in the *Graphics* library that allow you to (1) draw geometric shapes (e.g., lines, rectangles, ovals, polygons); (2) set, change, and define colors; (3) fill in or shade objects; (4) create text in a range of fonts and sizes; and (5) produce a myriad of different types of graphs and charts. There are far too many routines to discuss here; instead, we introduce a few of the most important and most basic routines to give you an idea of the type of graphic operations available in Java. You will then have a chance to use these operations in Laboratory Exercise 14 as well as in the exercises at the end of this chapter.

1. *drawLine(int x1, int y1, int x2, int y2).* This draws a straight line from point (*x1, y1*) on the screen (measured in pixels) to point (*x2, y2*). Thus the operation

    ```
    g.drawLine(100, 100, 200, 200);
    ```

    would produce something like the following image:

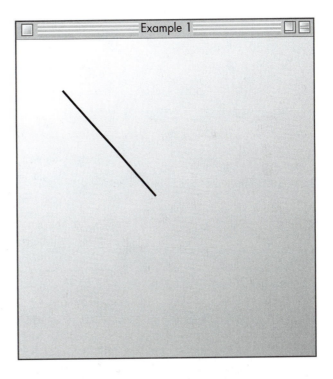

On your system, the exact location and length of the line may be slightly different because of minor differences in screen resolution. You may also need to write

```
while (true)
{
    g.drawLine(100, 100, 200, 200);
}
```

in order to hold the image on the screen.

What actually happens internally when you execute a *drawLine* command? The answer is that the terminal hardware determines (using some simple geometry and trigonometry) exactly which pixels on the screen must be "turned on" (i.e., set to the current value of the drawing color) to draw a straight line between the specified coordinates. For example, if the drawing color is black, then the command *drawLine(1, 1, 4, 4);* will cause the following four pixels in the frame buffer to be set to the RGB value (0, 0, 0).

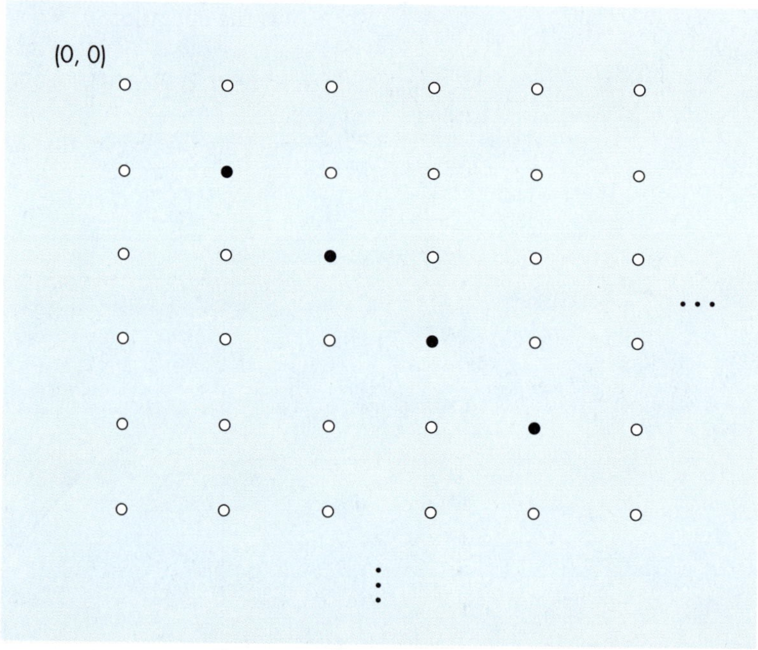

(0, 0)

Now, when the hardware draws the frame buffer on the screen, these four pixels will be colored black. Since pixels are only about 1/100th of an inch apart, our eyes will not perceive four individual black dots but an unbroken line segment.

2. *drawOval(int x, int y, int width, int height)*. This operation draws an oval that fits within a rectangle whose upper left-hand corner is located at (x, y) and whose dimensions are the specified width and height. If the width and height values are the same, you will produce a circle. Thus, the following two commands

```
g.drawOval(50, 50, 20, 100);
g.drawOval(200, 200, 30, 30);
```

will produce the following image:

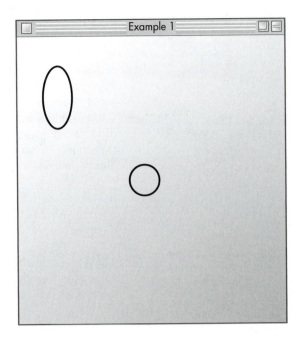

Now, using the two commands we have just introduced—*drawLine* and *drawOval*—we can produce an image of the well-known international traffic sign for No Entry:

```
g.drawOval(100, 100, 80, 80);
g.drawLine(168, 112, 112, 168);
```

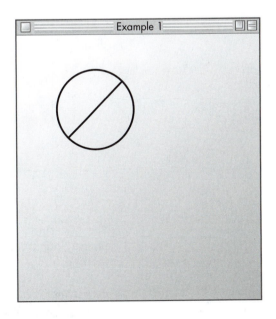

However, we also know that this No Entry sign sometimes appears in either blue or red rather than black. Java allows us to control the drawing color using the *setColor* command from the *Color* class.

3. *setColor(Color c)*. This method allows us to set our drawing color to any one of the following 12 preset colors: red, yellow, blue, orange, pink, cyan, magenta, black, white, gray, lightGray, and darkGray. (Java also lets you define totally new colors based on the intensities of their red, green, and blue components. We won't discuss that feature here.) Using this new method we can redraw our traffic sign in blue as follows:

```
g.setColor(Color.blue);
g.drawOval(100, 100, 80, 80);
g.drawLine(168, 112, 112, 168);
```

which produces the next image. Note that executing the operation *setColor* does not change the color of images already drawn, only the color of any new images subsequently placed on the screen.

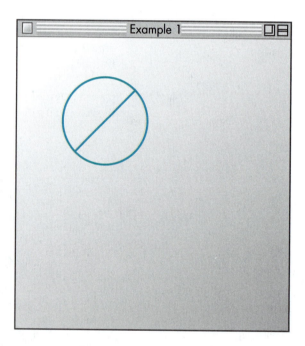

The last thing we might want to add to our traffic sign is the phrase No Entry. Java uses the method *drawString* to put text into a drawing:

4. *drawString(String str, int x, int y)*. This method writes the string *str* into the image. The lower left-hand position of the first character of

the string is placed at position (x, y). Thus, to put the desired text into the drawing, we could write the following four lines:

```
g.setColor(Color.blue);
g.drawOval(100, 100, 80, 80);
g.drawString("No Entry", 112, 145);
g.drawLine(168, 112, 112, 168);
```

which produces the desired image:

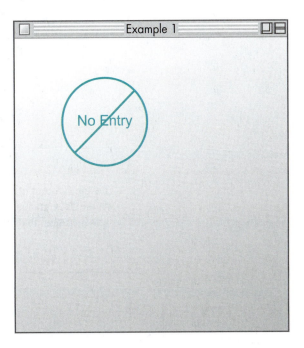

(There are a number of Java functions for controlling font size and font type, but we will not mention them here.)

There are other drawing commands to produce a variety of interesting shapes:

5. *drawRect(int x, int y, int width, int height).* This routine draws a rectangle whose upper left-hand corner is at position (*x, y*) and whose dimensions are the specified height and width.

6. *drawRoundRect(int x, int y, int width, int height, int arcWidth, int arcHeight).* This operation draws a rectangle with smoothly rounded corners. For example, the command

```
g.drawRoundRect(10, 10, 100, 100, 50, 50);
```

will produce:

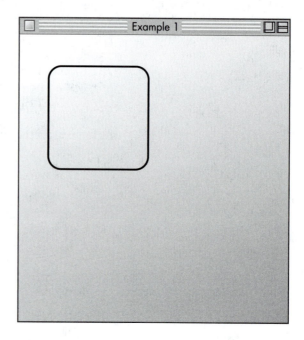

The parameters *arcWidth* and *arcHeight* set the diameter of the circles whose arcs are used to form the rounded edges of the rectangle, as shown in the next diagram.

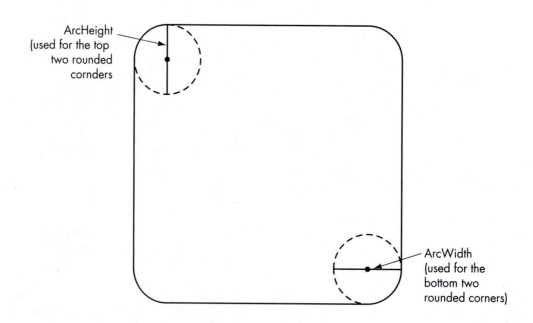

ArcHeight
(used for the top
two rounded
cornders

ArcWidth
(used for the
bottom two
rounded corners)

Sometimes we want to produce a filled shape, rather than just an outline. Java has a number of routines to draw shapes whose insides are filled using the currently declared drawing color:

7. *fillRect(int x, int y, int width, int height).*

8. *fillRoundRect(int x, int y, int width, int height, int arcWidth, int arcHeight).*

9. *fillOval(int x, int y, int height, int width).*

All three of the above commands will draw the specified shape with its insides filled with whatever color you have specified. (*Note*: if you have not specified a drawing color, then the shape will be filled with the default color, which is usually black.)

If we have defined a screen of size 300 × 300, then the following command:

```
g.fillOval(80, 80, 300, 200);
```

will produce the next image. Notice that the portions of the circle beyond the edge of the window are discarded, an operation called **clipping.** All functions in the Graphics library clip those parts of an image that lie outside its window boundaries.

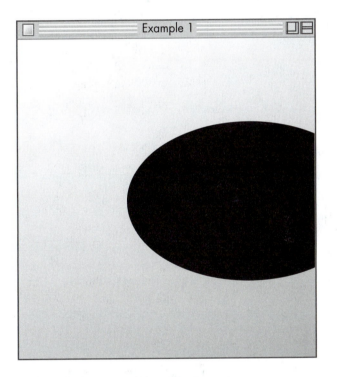

This has been only the briefest of introductions to the topic of graphics software. As mentioned earlier, the number of routines in the Java *Graphics* class or in any large-scale production graphics package is much, much larger. However, the nine operations we have introduced are sufficient to allow you to produce some interesting images and even more important, give you an appreciation for how visually oriented software is developed. You will have a chance to practice these routines in the following Practice Problem and in Laboratory Experience 14.

Write the sequence of commands to draw the following "house" on the screen:

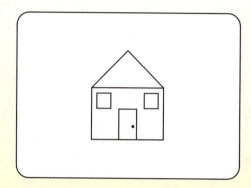

Create the house using 4 rectangles (for the base of the house, the door, and the two windows), two line segments (for the roof), and one filled circle (for the doorknob). Locate the house anywhere you want on the screen.

LABORATORY EXPERIENCE 14

The *Graphics* class and drawing routines described in this section are fully supported by all Java compilers. In this laboratory assignment you will learn more about the graphics library, and you will write some actual graphics programs that display visual images on the screen.

8.10   The Big Picture: Software Engineering

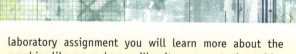

Because any Java program must ultimately be translated by a compiler, there are very stringent syntax rules about punctuation, use of keywords, and so on for each program statement. If something about a program statement cannot be understood by the compiler, then the compiler cannot translate the program; if the compiler cannot translate a program, then its instructions cannot be executed. There is no way to work around this situation. This obstacle leads beginning programming students to conclude that the major effort should be devoted to implementation—that is, restating an algorithm in computer code and ridding that code of syntax errors to the point where it finally executes.

In reality, implementation represents a relatively small part of the **software life cycle**—the overall sequence of steps needed to complete a large-scale software project. Studies have shown that on big projects (system software such as operating systems or compilers, for example, or large applications such as writing a program to manage an investment company's portfolio), the initial implementation of the program may occupy only 10–20% of the total time spent by programmers and designers. About 25–40% of their time is spent on problem specification and program design—important planning steps that must be completed prior to implementation. Another 40–65% is spent on tasks that follow implementation—reviewing, modifying, fixing, and improving the original code and writing finished documentation. Although there is no universal agreement on the exact sequence of steps in the software life cycle, Figure 8.38 summarizes one possible breakdown. We'll discuss each of these steps shortly.

The major reason why a beginning programming student may not see or appreciate the entire software development life cycle has to do with the size of the programming assignments usually solved in introductory classes. The programs are extremely and unrealistically small (like our SportsWorld program), and that single difference can create a skewed and misleading view of the software development process. It is somewhat akin to a civil engineering student building a matchstick bridge that is 5 inches long; a multitude of new problems must be addressed when that task is scaled up to a full-sized, real-life bridge.

 8.10.1 *Scaling Up*

The programs that students write in a first course may be 50 to 100 lines long. Even by the end of the course, programs are usually not longer than a few hundred lines. Real-world programs are 2, 3, or even 4 orders of magnitude larger. Operating systems or compilers contain tens or hundreds of thousands of lines. Truly large software systems, such as the NASA Space Shuttle ground control system and the data management system of the U.S. Census Bureau, may require the development of more than a million lines of code. To give you

FIGURE 8.38

Steps in the Software Development Life Cycle

1. Before implementation
   (a) Feasibility study
   (b) Problem specification
   (c) Program design
   (d) Algorithm selection or development, and analysis
2. Implementation
   (a) Coding
   (b) Debugging
3. After implementation
   (a) Testing, verification, and benchmarking
   (b) Documentation
   (c) Maintenance

an idea of how monstrously large that is, a printed listing of a one-million-line Java program would be 17,000 pages long—about the size of 50 books. The difference in complexity between a million-line software package and a 100-line homework assignment is the same as the difference between a 300-page novel and a single sentence!

Figure 8.39 categorizes software products in terms of size, the number of programmers needed for development, and the duration of the development effort. These numbers are very rough approximations, but they will give you an idea of the size of some widely used software packages. Analogous building construction projects are also listed.

Virtually all software products developed for the marketplace are neither trivial nor small, but fall instead into the Medium or Large category of Figure 8.39. The Very Large and Extremely Large categories are enormous intellectual enterprises. It would be impossible to develop correct and maintainable software systems of that size without extensive planning and design, just as it is impossible to build a 50-story skyscraper without paying a great deal of attention to project planning and project management. Both endeavors would

FIGURE 8.39

Size Categories of Software Products

Category	Typical Number of Programmers	Typical Duration	Product Size in Lines of Code	Examples	Building Analogy
Trivial	1	1–2 weeks	< 500	Student homework assignments	Small home improvement
Small	1–3	A few weeks or months	500–2,000	Student team projects, advanced course assignments	Adding on a room
Medium	2–5	A few months to 1 year	2,000–10,000	Research projects, simple production software such as assemblers, editors, recreational and educational software	Single-family house
Large	5–25	1–3 years	10,000–100,000	Most current applications—word processors, spreadsheets, operating systems for small computers, compilers	Small shopping mall
Very Large	25–100	3–5 years	100,000–1 M	Airline reservations systems, inventory control systems for multinational companies	Large office building
Extremely Large	> 100	> 5 years	> 1 M	Large-scale real-time operating systems, advanced military work, international telecommunications networks	Massive skyscraper

The Windows operating system for PCs was created by Microsoft Corporation. Development of this system (which was originally called the Interface Manager) began in 1981. Subsequently renamed Microsoft Windows, the system was not released until November 1985, after 55 person-years of effort. Since then, there have been a number of evolutions. Various versions of Windows, such as Windows 3.1 and Windows for Workgroups, followed the initial offering, each adding more features. In the mid-1990s, Microsoft developed two tracks for its operating systems. Windows 95, Windows 98, and Windows ME were intended primarily for personal or small business use. Windows NT (New Technology) and Windows 2000 were designed to provide more robust platforms with better security for heavy-duty users, multiuser systems and network support.

The Windows NT development project began with a team of 10 or 12 people and expanded to include over 200 in both technical and support staff roles. Over the 4-year development effort for the first version, which was re-leased in 1993, this translated into hundreds of person-years of labor merely to get the system out the door, to say nothing of maintenance work required to support this version and the efforts to upgrade it to new versions. The final system contains several hundred thousand lines of code. This is a Very Large project by the standard of Figure 8.39. Windows 95, released in August 1995, required about 8,000,000 lines of code, which clearly puts it into the "massive skyscraper" category (i.e., Extremely Large) of Figure 8.39.

The Windows XP operating system was released in 2001, in both a Home Edition and a Professional version to service the two markets mentioned above. Windows XP has over 45,000,000 lines of code, which even presses the envelope of our Extremely Large category.

Closer to home, the software for the laboratory component of this book contains about 20,000 lines of Java code and required 2,000 person-hours to develop. As is the case with most software development, most of this time was spent in design and testing, and a relatively small portion in actually writing code.

---

also be impossible for a single individual to carry out; a team development effort is essential in building software, just as in constructing buildings. Such projects also entail estimation of costs and budgets, personnel management, and scheduling issues, which are typical concerns for large engineering projects. In recognition of these aspects, the term **software engineering** is often applied to large-scale software development.

 ### 8.10.2   *The Software Life Cycle*

Each step in the software development life cycle, as given in Figure 8.38, has its own purpose and activities. Each should also result in a written document that reflects past decisions and guides future actions. Keep in mind that every major software project is developed as a team effort, and these documents help keep various members of the team informed and working toward a common goal. We'll outline each step.

1. *The feasibility study.* The **feasibility study** is concerned with evaluating a proposed project and comparing the costs and benefits of a computer system for the project. Even though the cost of computer hardware has dropped dramatically, computers are still not insignificant purchases. In addition to the costs of the machine itself, there may be costs for peripherals such as laser printers and telecommunications links. The costs of software (purchased or produced in-house),

equipment maintenance, and salary for developers or consultants, technical support people, and data-entry clerks must all be factored in, as well as the costs incurred in training new users on the system. The overall cost of using a computer to solve a problem can be much higher than expected, and it *can* be more than the value of the information produced. Thus the following question should be asked:

> *Is it worth it for me (or whoever the user may be) to buy a computer (or get a newer, faster system) and write or buy software to solve the problem?*

At the end of the feasibility study, a **feasibility document** expresses the resulting recommendation on whether to proceed with the planned purchase of hardware and software. The creation of this document can be a very complex process involving considerations that are the provinces of business, law, management, economics, psychology, and accounting, as well as computer science. The purpose of the feasibility study is to make users realize that a computer is simply a tool and that the first thing to determine is whether it is the right tool for the job.

2. *Problem specification.* If it is determined that the project is feasible and will benefit from a computer solution, we move on to the problem specification phase. **Problem specification** involves developing a clear, concise, and unambiguous statement of the exact problem to be solved. Because the original problem statement used in the feasibility study was no doubt written in a natural language such as English, it may be unclear, incomplete, or even internally contradictory. During the problem specification phase, the software designers and the customers (the users) must resolve each and every inconsistency, ambiguity, and gap. It is much easier and cheaper to make changes at this stage than to make changes in software months down the road. Consider how much more practical it is to change your mind when looking at the blueprints of your new home than after the foundation has been dug and the walls have started to go up. Finally, the rough initial problem statement must be transformed into a complete problem specification.

The **problem specification document** commits the final and complete problem specification to paper and serves to guide the software developers in all subsequent decisions. The specification document describes exactly how a program will behave in all circumstances—not only in the majority of cases but even under the most unusual conditions. It includes a description of the data expected to be input to the program, as well as what results should be computed and how these results are to be displayed as output. It may also include limitations on the time allotted to produce those computations or on the amount of memory the program requires.

Once agreed to by the developer and the customer, this document becomes essentially a legal contract describing what the developer promises to provide and what the customer agrees to accept. Like a contract, it usually includes a delivery schedule and a price, and it is signed by both the customer and the developer.

3. *Program design.* Now that it is clear *what* is to be done, the **program design phase** is the time to plan *how* it is to be done. In the program design phase, the appropriate objects are identified, together with their data and the subtasks they should be able to perform. This allows classes to be designed with the needed instance variables to store the data and the methods to carry out the subtasks. The larger the project, the more crucial it is to identify these cooperating classes. These smaller building blocks can be designed and created individually and then properly assembled to make a whole. Although problems that result in small programs of 50–100 lines can be thought of in one piece, problems that result in 100,000-line programs cannot.

The **program design document** must reflect the breakdown of the overall problem. The classes must be identified, along with their instance variables and subtasks. Some of this design may be documented graphically through class diagrams that give the properties and methods of each class. There must also be a complete specification of each subtask: what it is to do, what information it needs to know in order to do it, and what, if any, value it returns. This specification must be sufficiently detailed that a programmer could take the description and write, for example, a Java method with the appropriate parameters. The outline of the main method must be given, perhaps as a pseudocode description of where objects are created and which objects invoke which methods when.

The process of program design is one of the truly creative and interesting parts of the software development life cycle. It is related to coding in roughly the same way that designing an airplane is related to riveting a wing!

4. *Algorithm selection or development, and analysis.* Once the various subtasks have been identified, algorithms must be found to carry them out. For example, one subtask may be to search a list of numbers for some particular value. In Chapters 2 and 3 we encountered two different algorithms for searching—sequential search and binary search. If there is a choice of algorithms, each must be weighed to determine its suitability for this particular task and perhaps analyzed for efficiency. An algorithm may also have to be developed from scratch. This, too, is a very creative process. Documentation of this phase includes a description of the algorithms chosen or developed, perhaps in pseudocode, and the rationale for their use.

5. *Coding.* **Coding** is the process of translating the detailed class and algorithm designs into actual computer code. If the design has been carefully developed, this should be a relatively routine job. Perhaps reusable code can even be pulled from a program library, or a useful class can be employed.

Coding is the step that usually comes to mind when people think of software development. However, as we have shown, a great deal of important preparatory work must precede the actual production of code. Inexperienced programmers may think that they will save time by skipping the earlier phases and getting right to the coding. The opposite is usually true. In all but the most trivial of programs, tackling coding without first doing problem specification, program design, and algorithm selection or development will ultimately lead to more time being spent and a poorer outcome. The coding phase also results in a written document, namely the listing of the program code itself.

6. *Debugging.* **Debugging** is the process of locating and correcting program errors, and it can be a slow and expensive operation that requires as much effort as writing the program in the first place. Errors can occur because a program statement fails to follow the correct rules of syntax, which makes the statement unrecognizable by the compiler and results in an error. Though irritating, these **syntax errors** are accompanied by messages from the compiler that help to pinpoint the problem. Another class of errors, called **runtime errors,** occur only when the program is run using certain sets of data that result in some illegal operation, such as dividing by zero. The system software also provides messages to help detect the cause of runtime errors. The third, and most subtle, class of errors is **logic errors.** These are errors in the algorithm used to solve the problem. Some incorrect steps that result in wrong answers are performed, but there are no error messages to help pinpoint the problem. Indeed, the first step in debugging a logic error is to notice that the answers are wrong.

Debugging has always been one of the most frustrating, agonizing, and time-consuming steps in the programming process. Extensive time spent on debugging usually means that insufficient time was spent on carefully specifying, organizing, and structuring the solution. If the design is poorly done, the resulting program is often a structural mess, with convoluted, hard to understand logic. Devoting careful attention to the design phases can help reduce the amount of debugging that must be done.

Careful documentation of the debugging process includes noting the problems that were found and how the code was changed to solve them. This may prevent later changes from re-introducing old errors.

7. *Testing, verification, and benchmarking.* Even though a program produces correct answers for 1, 5, or even 1,000 data sets, how can we be sure that it is indeed 100% correct and will work on all data? One approach, called **empirical testing,** is to design a special set of test cases and run the program using these test data. Test data that are carefully chosen to exercise all the different logic paths through a program can help uncover errors. In a conditional statement, for example, one set of data should make the Boolean expression true, so that one block of code is executed. Another set of data should make the same Boolean expression false, so that the other block of code is executed. The quantity of the test data does not matter; what matters is that the data cover all the various cases. Having said that, though, we should note that in all but the most trivial programs it is not possible to "cover all the cases." The best that can be said is that the more thorough the testing, the higher the level of our confidence in the program's correctness.

A second approach to confirming a program's reliability is to use mathematical logic to attempt to prove that a computer program is correct. **Program verification** can be used to prove that if the input data to a program satisfy certain conditions, then, after the program has been run on these data, the output data will satisfy certain other conditions. This does not, however, give us blanket assurance that the program will absolutely behave as we wish. Furthermore, the program verification process can be difficult and time-consuming. That's why program testing is used much more than formal program verification to increase the reliability of a program.

In addition to correctness, the problem specification may have required certain performance characteristics such as the amount of time to compute the results. **Benchmarking** the program means running it on many data sets to be sure its performance falls within required limits. At the completion of testing (or verification) and benchmarking, we should have a correct and efficient program that is ready for delivery. Of course, all of the testing, verification, and benchmarking results will have been committed to paper as evidence that the program meets its specifications.

8. *Documentation.* Program documentation is all of the written material that makes a program understandable. This includes **internal documentation,** which is part of the program code itself. Good internal documentation consists of choosing meaningful names for program identifiers, using plenty of comments to explain the code, and separating the program into reasonable classes with short methods, each of which does one specific subtask. **External documentation** consists of any materials assembled to help understand the program. Although we have put this step rather late in the software development process, you will note that each preceding step produced some form of documentation.

Program documentation goes on throughout the software life cycle. The finished program documentation is written in two forms. **Technical documentation** is written so that programmers who later want to modify the program can understand the code. Such information as class descriptions, algorithm descriptions, and program listings fall in this category. **User documentation** is written to help someone run the program. Such documentation includes online tutorials or help systems that the user can bring up while the program is running and (less and less frequently) written user's manuals.

9. *Maintenance.* Programs are not static entities that, once completed, never change. Because of the time and expense involved in developing software, successful programs are used for a very long time. It is not unusual for a program to be in use 5, 10, or 15 years after it was written. In fact, the typical life cycle for a medium- to large-sized software package is 1–3 years in development and 5–15 years in the marketplace. During this long period of use, errors may be uncovered, new hardware on which the program has to run may be purchased, user needs may change, and the whims of the marketplace may fluctuate. The original program must be modified and brought out in new versions to meet these changing needs. **Program maintenance,** the process of adapting an existing software product for any of the reasons just stated, may consume as much as 65% of the total software life cycle budget. If the program has been well-planned, carefully designed, well-coded, thoroughly tested, and well-documented, then

program maintenance will be a much easier task. Indeed, it was with an eye to program maintenance (and to reducing its cost) that we stressed the importance of these earlier steps.

Maintenance should not really be viewed as a separate step in the software life cycle. Rather, it involves repetition of some or all of the steps previously described, from a feasibility study through implementation, testing, and updated documentation. Maintenance, then, reflects the fact that the software life cycle is truly a *cycle*, during which it is necessary to redo earlier phases of development as our software changes, grows, and matures.

 ### 8.10.3 *Modern Environments*

Modern software development environments have had a great impact on the software life cycle process. For one thing, most programming languages are now presented within an **Integrated Development Environment**, or IDE. The IDE lets the programmer perform a number of tasks within the shell of a single application program, rather than having to use a separate program for each task. Consider some of the system software tasks described in Section 6.2: use a *text editor* to create a program; use a *file system* to store the program; use a *language translator* to translate the program to machine language; if the program did not complete successfully, use a *debugger* to help locate the errors. A modern programming IDE provides a text editor, a file manager, a compiler, a linker and loader, and tools for debugging, all within this one piece of software. This can significantly speed up program development.

Many IDE's provide the ability to design graphical user interfaces that can be shown to the user early on in the development process. This **rapid prototyping** allows misunderstandings between the user and the programmer to be identified and corrected early in the development process.

Finally, there are software packages that track requirements from the initial specification through the design process to final code to make sure that nothing gets lost along the way. These packages may also support graphical design of the various program elements, such as classes, and facilitate their translation into code.

8.11 Conclusion

In this chapter we looked at one representative high-level programming language, Java. Of course, there is much about this language that has been left unsaid, but we have at least seen how the use of a high-level language overcomes many of the disadvantages of assembly language programming, creating a more comfortable and useful environment for the programmer. In a high-level language, the programmer need not manage the storage or movement of data values in memory. The programmer can think about the problem at a higher level of problem solving, can use program instructions that are both more powerful and more natural-language–like, and can write a program that is much more portable among various hardware platforms. We also saw how modularization, through the use of methods and parameters, allows the program to be more cleanly structured and how object orientation allows a more intuitive view of the problem solution and provides the possibility for reuse of helpful classes.

We discussed the entire software life cycle, noting that for large, real-world programs, software development must be a managed discipline. Coding is but a small part of the software development process.

As we have said, Java is not the only high-level language. Other languages have different ways to do assignments, conditional statements, and looping statements. Still other languages take quite a different approach to problem solving. In the next chapter, we look at some other languages and language approaches and also address the question of why there are so many different programming languages.

1. Write a Java declaration for one real number quantity to be called *rate*, initialized to 5.0.

2. Write a single Java statement to declare two integer quantities to be called *orderOne* and *orderTwo*, each initialized to 0.

3. A Java main method will need one character variable *choice*, one integer variable *inventory*, and one real number variable *sales*. Write the necessary declarations; initialize *choice* to the blank character and the other values to zero.

4. a. Write a Java output statement to print the value of *PI* supplied by the Math library.

   b. Constants are items of data whose value is to remain fixed throughout the program. A constant can be declared and given a value within the program, much as a variable is declared and initialized, except that a program statement cannot subsequently attempt to change the value of a constant. The statement

   ```
   public static final double PI =
   3.1416; //value of pi
   ```

   declares the constant *PI* and assigns it a value. In the declaration, "public static" roughly means that the constant *PI* will be available for use anywhere; "final" says that the value we are about to assign to *PI* is "final," that is, it is a constant value that cannot be changed; and "double" says the value we are about to assign is a real number. Write a Java declaration for a constant quantity to be called *EVAPORATION_RATE*, which is to have the value 6.15.

5. You want to write a Java program to compute the average of three quiz grades for a single student. Decide what variables your program will need and write the necessary declarations.

6. Given the declaration

   ```
   int[] list = new int[10];
   ```

   how would you refer to the eighth number in the array?

7. Write a Java declaration for a two-dimensional array *box* with 5 rows and 7 columns to hold real number values.

8. Given the declaration

   ```
   int[][] table = new int[5][3];
   ```

   how would you refer to the marked cell that follows?

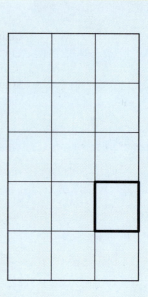

9. Can you think of a situation in which a three-dimensional table would be an appropriate data structure? Write a Java declaration to implement such a data structure.

10. Write Java statements to prompt for and collect values for the time in hours and minutes (two integer quantities).

11. An output statement may contain more than one variable identifier. Say a program computes two integer quantities *inventoryNumber* and *numberOrdered*. Write a single output statement that prints these two quantities along with appropriate text information.

12. The integer quantities *age* and *weight* currently have the values 32 and 187, respectively. Write the exact output generated by the following statement:

    ```
    System.out.println("Your age is"
    + age + "and your weight is" +
    weight + ".");
    ```

13. Output that is a real number can be formatted so that the number is rounded to a specified number of decimal places. To do this, add the following statement at the very beginning of the program

    ```
    import java.text.*;
    ```

and add the following at the beginning of the main method body:

```
DecimalFormat p = new
    DecimalFormat("0.00");
```

where the desired format for the output is given in quotes, for example, "0.00" is requesting that the output be rounded to 2 decimal digits. Output statements are then modified as follows (from the SportsWorld program):

```
System.out.println("The " +
"circumference for a pool" +
" of radius " + radius + " is "
+ p.format(circumference));
```

Write Java formatting and output statements to generate the following output, assuming that *density* is a type double variable with the value 63.78:

```
The current density is 63.8, to
within one decimal place.
```

14. What will the output be after the following sequence of statements is executed? (Assume the integer variables *a* and *b* have been declared.)

```
a = 12;
b = 20;
b = b + 1;
a = a + b;
System.out.println(2*a);
```

15. Write a Java main method that gets the length and width of a rectangle from the user and computes and writes out the area.

16. a. In the SportsWorld program of Figure 8.18, the user must respond with "C" to choose the circumference task. In a situation like this, it is polite to accept either uppercase or lowercase letters. Rewrite the condition in the program to allow this.

    b. Again in the Sports World program, rewrite the condition for continuation of the program to allow either an uppercase or a lowercase response.

17. Write a Java main method that gets a single character from the user and writes out a congratulatory message if the character is a vowel (a, e, i, o, or u), but otherwise writes out a "you lose, better luck next time" message.

18. Insert the missing line of code so that the following adds the integers from 1 to 10, inclusive.

```
value = 0;
top = 10;
score = 1;
while (score <= top)
{
   value = value + score;
   - - - -        //the missing line
}
```

19. What will the output be after the following main method is executed?

```
public static void main(String[] args)
{
   int low = 1;
   int high = 20;
   while (low < high)
   {
      System.out.println(low
         + " " + high);
      low = low + 1;
      high = high - 1;
   }
}
```

20. Write a Java main method that outputs the even integers from 2 through 30, one per line. Use a while loop.

21. In a while loop, the Boolean condition that tests for loop continuation is done at the top of the loop, before each iteration of the loop body. As a consequence, the loop body might not be executed at all. Our pseudocode language of Chapter 2 contains a do-while loop construction, in which a test for loop termination occurs at the bottom of the loop rather than at the top, so that the loop body will always execute at least once. Java has a **do-while** statement that tests for loop continuation at the bottom of the loop. The form of the statement is

    do

      S1;

    while (Boolean condition);

where, as usual, S1 can be a compound statement. Write a Java main method to add up a number of nonnegative integers that the user supplies and to write out the total. Use a negative value as a sentinel, and assume that the first value is nonnegative. Use a do-while statement.

22. Write a Java program that asks for a duration of time in hours and minutes and writes out the duration only in minutes.

23. Write a Java program that asks for the user's age in years; if the user is under 35, then quote an insurance rate of $2.23 per hundred for life insurance, otherwise quote a rate of $4.32.

24. Write a Java program that reads integer values until a 0 value is encountered, then writes out the sum of the positive values read and the sum of the negative values read.

25. Write a Java program that reads in a series of positive integers and writes out the product of all the integers that are less than 25 and the sum of all the integers that are greater than or equal to 25. Use 0 as a sentinel value.

26. a. Write a Java program that reads in 10 integer quiz grades and computes the average grade. (*Hint:* remember the peculiarity of integer division.)

    b. Write a Java program that asks the user for the number of quiz grades and computes the average grade.

27. Write a void Java method that receives two integer arguments and writes out their sum and their product.

28. Write a nonvoid Java method that receives a real number argument representing the sales amount for videos sold so far this month. The method asks the user for the number of videos rented today and returns the updated sales figure to the main method. All videos rent for $4.25.

29. Write a nonvoid Java method that receives three integer arguments and returns the maximum of the three values.

30. Write a Java *doCircumference* method for the *Rectangle* class of Figure 8.33.

31. Draw a class hierarchy diagram similar to Figure 8.34 for the following classes: *Student, Undergraduate_Student, Graduate_Student, Sophomore, Senior, PhD_Student*

32. Imagine that you are writing a program using an object-oriented programming language. Your program will be used to maintain records for a real estate office. Decide upon one class in your program and a service that objects of that class might provide.

33. Write a Java program to balance a checkbook. The main method of the *CheckbookApp* class should get the initial balance from the user, allow the user to process as many transactions as desired, and write the final balance. The *Checkbook* class should contain two public static methods to handle deposits and checks, respectively. Each method should collect and write out the amount of the transaction, and compute, write out, and return the new balance. (See Exercise 13 on how to format output to two decimal places, as is usually done with monetary values.)

34. Write a Java program to compute the cost of carpeting three rooms. *Room* objects have dimensions of width and length, and they can compute and return their area and (given the price per square unit) the cost to carpet themselves. The main method of the *RoomApp* class should create a *Room* object and use a loop to process each of three rooms: get the dimensions and carpet price, write out the individual areas and costs, add the three costs, then write out the total cost. (See Exercise 13 on how to format output to two decimal places, as is usually done with monetary values.)

35. Determine the resolution on the screen on your computer (perhaps from your instructor or the local computer center). Using this information, determine how many bytes of memory are required for the frame buffer to store

    a. A black-and-white image (1 bit per pixel)

    b. A gray-scale image (8 bits per pixel)

    c. A color image (24 bits per pixel)

36. Using the *drawLine* command described in Section 8.9.2, draw an isosceles triangle with the following configuration:

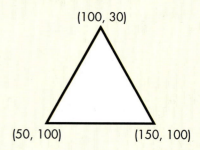

37. Discuss what problem the display hardware might encounter while attempting to execute the following operations and describe how this problem could be solved.

```
drawLine(1, 1, 4, 5);
```

38. Draw a square with sides 100 pixels in length. Then inscribe a circle of radius 50 inside the square. Position the square so its upper-left-hand corner is at position (60, 100).

39. Create the following three labeled rectangular buttons:

Have the space between the Start and Stop buttons be the same as the space between the Stop and Pause buttons.

40. Create the following image of a "teeter-totter":

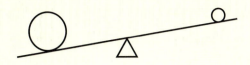

CHALLENGE WORK

1. In Chapter 7 we learned about the *routing problem* in computer networks, which consists of finding the optimal path from a source node to a destination node. Each hop along a path represents a communication channel between two nodes that will have an associated "cost"; the cost might actually be a monetary cost to use a leased line, but it could also be a cost in terms of the volume of traffic the line typically carries. In either case, the "shortest path" is the one with the lowest cost. As mentioned in Chapter 7, the Internet uses Dijkstra's shortest path algorithm to solve this problem. If node x is the source node and receives a message for node y, then x only needs to know the shortest path from itself to node y. But an alternative is to have a centralized site periodically compute the "all-pairs shortest path" from any node to any other node, and then broadcast that information to all nodes in the network. The algorithm for the all-pairs shortest path, called **Floyd's Algorithm**, is simpler to implement than Dijkstra's algorithm.

A two-dimensional array is used to represent the nodes in the network. If there are n nodes in the network, the array will be $n \times n$ in size. The entry in position i, j of the array is the length (cost) of the line from i to j. For example, the following network has five nodes, numbered 0 through 4.

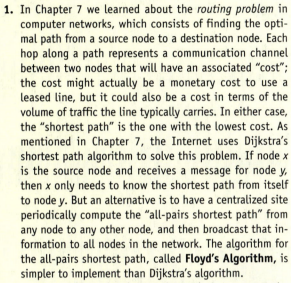

It will be represented by the 5×5 array shown here.

	0	1	2	3	4
0	0	1	4	∞	3
1	1	0	2	∞	4
2	4	2	0	1	5
3	∞	∞	1	0	3
4	3	4	5	3	0

The entry in row 1, column 4 is 4 because the length of the line between node 1 and node 4 is 4. The entry in row 0 column 3 is ∞ because there is no direct line between nodes 0 and 3. All the entries on the "main diagonal" (positions [0,0], [1,1], [2,2], [3,3], and [4,4]) are 0 because there is a 0-length link from a node to itself.

Floyd's algorithm operates on the array A of the graph. A pseudocode description of the algorithm is

set the value of k to 0
while (k <= n − 1)do
    set the value of i to 0
    while (i < = n − 1)do
        set the value of j to 0
        while (j < = n − 1)do
            if A[i, k] + A[k, j] < A[i, j]
            A[i, j] = A[i, k] + A[k, j]
        end of the j-loop
    end of the i-loop
end of the k-loop

When this algorithm terminates, the entry in position [i, j] of the array represents the length of the shortest path between nodes i and j, although this algorithm does not say what the intermediate nodes on the shortest path are.

Write a Java program to solve the all-pairs shortest path problem for a graph with five nodes. The program gets the values for each row of the array from the user, runs Floyd's algorithm, and writes out the resulting array. Use 500 for "infinity," which assumes all legitimate line lengths are less than 500.

Try your program for the graph above. From the output of your program, what is the length of the shortest path from node 2 to node 4? By looking at the graph, what are the nodes on this path?

2. Read more about software engineering and write a short paper on one or more of the following topics:
   - Black-box and white-box testing
   - CASE tools
   - Configuration management
   - Data dictionary
   - JAD (Joint Application Development) sessions
   - Quality assurance
   - Requirements tracing
   - Software metrics
   - Stubs and drivers
   - Version control
   - Waterfall model

FOR FURTHER READING

There are many textbooks on Java programming. Here are a few that are designed for beginning programmers:

Arnow, D.; Dexter, S.; and Weiss, G. *Introduction to Programming Using Java: An Object-Oriented Approach, 2nd ed.* Reading, MA: Addison-Wesley, 2004.

Bishop, J. *Java Gently: Programming Principles Explained,* 3rd ed. Reading, MA: Addison-Wesley, 2001.

Horstmann, C. *Computing Concepts with Java Essentials,* 3rd ed. New York: Wiley, 2003.

Lambert, K., and Osborne, M. *Java: A Framework for Programming and Problem Solving,* 2nd ed. Pacific Grove, CA: Brooks/Cole, 2002.

Professor Lambert is one of the coauthors of the laboratory manual that accompanies this text.

Lewis, J., and Loftus, W. *Java Software Solutions: Foundations of Program Design,* 3rd ed. Reading, MA: Addison-Wesley, 2003.

Savitch, W. *Java: An Introduction to Computer Science and Programming,* 3rd ed. Upper Saddle River, NJ: Prentice-Hall, 2004.

For really serious works on Java, the Addison-Wesley Java Series (books authored by Sun Microsystems developers) includes the following. Recall that James Gosling was the original developer of the language that came to be called Java.

Arnold, K.; Gosling, J.; and Holmes, D. *The Java Programming Language,* 3rd ed. Reading, MA: Addison-Wesley, 2000.

Other books in the Java Series are listed at http://java.sun.com/docs/books. You can download Java software and system documentation from the Web site http://java.sun.com/j2se/1.4/index.html.

The classic work on software engineering, first published in 1975, was published 20 years later in an anniversary edition because the truths it contains are still relevant today. These essays on the management of software engineering projects are relevant to most managerial situations, and they are entertaining and easy to read.

Brooks, Jr., F. P. *The Mythical Man-Month: Essays on Software Engineering,* Anniversary Edition. Reading, MA: Addison-Wesley, 1995.

CHAPTER 9

The Tower of Babel

9.1   Why Babel?

The biblical story of the Tower of Babel takes place at a time when "the whole earth had one language and few words" and all could understand one another. The people began to build a city with a mighty tower when, suddenly, all began speaking in various tongues and could no longer communicate. They became confused, abandoned the tower, and scattered "over the face of all the earth." A shared enterprise was difficult or impossible to pursue without the mutual understanding fostered by a common language, and (the message this story was intended to convey) the power of what people could do was thus forever limited. Similarly, in modern times it has been argued that if all peoples of the earth spoke a common language, the chances of war would be greatly reduced.

Although we can't address the problems of the political arena here, it might seem that having all computer programs written in the same programming language would have an appealing simplicity. In Chapter 8, we became familiar with one high-level programming language, Java. Java is a powerful general-purpose programming language, and a great many Java programs have been written to do a great many things. But as we noted in the last chapter, Java isn't the only high-level programming language. Why aren't all programs written in Java? Are there some things that can't be done using a Java program? If so, then why aren't all programs written in some other language that overcomes the deficiencies of Java?

There are multiple programming languages not so much because there are tasks that one programming language cannot do but because each programming language was designed to meet specific needs. Consequently, one language may be better suited than others for writing certain kinds of programs. The situation is somewhat analogous to the automobile market. The basic automotive needs of the country could probably be served by a single car model and a single truck model. So why do we have seemingly endless models from which to choose? The answer lies partly in competition: various automotive companies are all trying to corner a share of the market. More than that, though, the answer lies in the variety of ways we use our automobiles. Although a luxury car could be used for off-roading, it is not designed well for that use; a four-wheel-drive vehicle does the job better, more safely, and more efficiently. Although a sports car could be used to haul Little Leaguers home from the ball game, it is not designed well for that use; an SUV or minivan serves this purpose better. The diversity of tasks for which we use our automobiles has promoted a variety of automotive models, each better designed than other models to handle some range of tasks.

The same thing applies to programming languages. As an example, we *could* use Java to write programs for solving engineering problems. However, Java was not designed for engineering applications. Although Java supports the basic arithmetic operations of addition, subtraction, multiplication, and division by providing simple operators ($+$, $-$, $*$, $/$) to do these tasks, there is no operator for exponentiation—that is, raising a value to a power. Computing $2.84^{1.8}$ in a Java program, for example, can certainly be done but it requires a little effort.[1] Calculations involving exponents are performed hundreds of times in many engineering and other numerical-based applications, so why not use a language that provides an operator for exponentiation because that language was designed with such tasks in mind? We'll discuss such a language—FORTRAN—in the next section.

Similarly, suppose our program is to write out complicated sales reports with columns of figures and blocks of information strategically located on the page. Specifying the exact placement of output on the page is rather tedious in Java. Why not use a language that allows detailed output formatting because it was designed with such a purpose in mind? Again, we'll briefly discuss such a language—COBOL—in the next section.

What if we want a program to interact with a database, to manipulate graphics, or to act as a hyperlinked Web page? Any of these specialized tasks is probably best done with a specialized language designed for just that purpose.

A major reason, then, for the proliferation of programming languages is the proliferation of programming tasks to be done. Another reason is that different philosophies have developed about how people should think when they are writing programs. This has resulted in several families of programming languages that take quite different approaches from that of Java, and we'll look at some of these approaches in Section 9.4.

9.2   Procedural Languages

In this section, we briefly discuss a number of different programming languages that all follow the same "philosophy" as Java in that they are **procedural languages** (also called **imperative languages**). A program written in a procedural language consists of sequences of statements that manipulate data items; that is, they change the contents of memory cells. It is the programmer's task to devise the appropriate step by step sequence of "imperative commands"—instructions in the programming language—that when carried out by the computer will accomplish the desired task.

Procedural languages follow directly from the Von Neumann architecture of a computer described in Chapter 5, an architecture characterized by sequential fetch–decode–execute cycles. A random access memory stores and fetches values to and from memory cells. Thus it makes sense to design a language whose most fundamental operations are storing and retrieving data values. For example,

```
a = 1;      //store value 1 in location a
c = a + b; //retrieve a and b, add, store result in
            location c
```

---

1 The Java expression for $2.84^{1.8}$ is Math.pow(2.84,1.8), using the *pow* method available in the *Math* class of the standard Java library.

Even though we have seen that a high-level programming language allows the programmer to think of memory locations in abstract rather than physical terms, the programmer is still directing, via program instructions, every change in the value of a memory location.

The procedural languages we will discuss in this section differ in how the statements must be arranged on a line and in how variables can be named. They differ in the details of how a new value is assigned to a variable, in the mechanisms the language provides for directing the flow of control through conditional and looping statements, and in the statement forms that control input and output. They also differ in how programs can be broken down into modules to handle separate tasks and in how those modules share information. But once again, all are procedural languages that tell the computer in a step by step fashion how to manipulate the contents of memory locations. In a general sense, then, the languages are quite similar, just as French, Spanish, and Italian are all members of the family of romance languages. Rather than studying the syntactical differences among these programming languages, we'll concentrate on the history and "intent" of each one.

 ### 9.2.1 *FORTRAN*

The name FORTRAN derives from *FOR*mula *TRAN*slation. The very name indicates the affiliation of the language with "formulas" or engineering-type applications. Developed in the mid-1950s by a group at IBM headed by John Backus, in conjunction with some IBM computer users, the first commercial version of FORTRAN was released in 1957. This makes FORTRAN the first high-level programming language. Early computer users were often engineers who were solving problems with a heavy mathematics or computational flavor. FORTRAN has some features ideally suited to these applications, such as the exponentiation operator we mentioned earlier, the ability to carry out extended-precision arithmetic with many decimal places of accuracy, and the ability to work with the complex number system. Updated versions of FORTRAN (FORTRAN II, FORTRAN IV, FORTRAN 77, Fortran 90, and High Performance Fortran) have been introduced over the years, incorporating new data types and new statements to direct the flow of control.

Early versions of FORTRAN did not allow the use of mathematical symbols such as < to compare two quantities; the keypunches that were used to create the punched cards on which early FORTRAN programs were submitted to the computer had no such symbols. Thus the Java condition

```
number < 0
```

would have been expressed in early FORTRAN as

```
NUMBER .LT. 0
```

(FORTRAN requires variable identifiers to be uppercase.) Early versions of FORTRAN also had no while loop mechanism. The effect of a while loop was obtained by using an IF statement together with GO TO statements. The Java instructions

```
      while (number >= 0)
      {
            .
            .
            .
            number = Console.readInt("enter number");
      }
```

would have been accomplished by

```
10 IF (NUMBER .LT. 0) GO TO 20
            .
            .
            .
      READ(*,*) NUMBER
      GO TO 10
20...
```

If *NUMBER* is less than 0, the GO TO statement transfers control to statement 20. If *NUMBER* is greater than or equal to 0, something is done and then another value for *NUMBER* is obtained (READ is the equivalent of *readInt*). Control is then redirected by the second GO TO statement back to statement 10 where the new value is tested.

Directing the flow of control by GO TO statements is similar to the use of the various JUMP statements in the assembly language of Chapter 6, and it reflects the fact that FORTRAN's developers were, after all, working from assembly language. In the absence of an equivalent to the Java *while* statement, there is no choice but to use GO TO statements carefully to implement looping, as shown above. Excessive and careless use of GO TOs, however, can make a program very difficult to read. (Imagine reading a novel where in the middle of page 49 you are told to stop reading this page and to begin reading at the top of page 215. Then, when you reach page 218, you are told to stop, go back, and start reading page 125. You might wonder whether you were really following the plot.) Code filled with GO TO statements that send the flow of control all over the place can be a nightmare. Such "spaghetti code" tangled across hundreds of lines can be very difficult to unravel. Given that a GO TO statement is available, it is up to the programmer's individual discipline to avoid abusing it. The potential for such abuse prompted the well-known computer scientist E. W. Dijkstra to write a letter headed "Go To Statement Considered Harmful," which appeared in the *Communications of the ACM* (Association for Computing Machinery) in 1968. This sparked the "GO TO controversy" about the merits of programming language constructs, such as the while loop, that would remove this temptation for abuse. From our perspective 35 years later, when almost every language has a nice looping construct, this controversy seems rather quaint, but it provoked lively discussion at the time.

FORTRAN was designed to support numerical computations. This led to concise mathematical notation (aside from the early < dilemma just mentioned) and to the availability of a number of mathematical functions within the language. Another design goal was to optimize the resulting object code,

FORTRAN was first introduced over 45 years ago, in 1957. In the history of computing, this is roughly the Jurassic Age. But FORTRAN is no extinct dinosaur. Instead, it is a chameleon, changing with the times. Thanks to the ever-increasing hardware capability, FORTRAN runs on PCs while still providing the power to tackle "number-crunching" problems. However, the programmer can now use an environment with a graphical user interface to develop code, and that code can present a graphical user interface to the ultimate user of the program.

As further proof of FORTRAN's continued usefulness, evolution has taken place at the other end of the computing spectrum as well. A standard for HPF (High Performance Fortran) has been developed. This version of FORTRAN is designed to run on massively parallel processors that can bring huge amounts of computer horsepower to bear on suitable problems. Parallelism is especially useful for speeding up the kinds of calculations on large arrays that often occur in scientific and engineering problems, FORTRAN's traditional domain. Problems with real-time response requirements in the areas of signal processing and image processing are also appropriate for HPF parallelism.

FORTRAN can "talk with" many other modern programming languages, which allows mixed-language programs to be built that capture the best features of each language for the application at hand. Given these adaptations, FORTRAN, in one form or another, is likely to live on for quite some time.

PRACTICE PROBLEM

Write a FORTRAN condition to test whether the value of *ITIME* is greater than 7. Use early FORTRAN syntax.

that is, to produce object code that took as little space and executed as efficiently as possible. (Remember that when FORTRAN was developed, machine resources were scarce and precious.) In the same spirit, FORTRAN allows **external libraries** of well-written, efficient, and thoroughly tested code modules that are separately compiled and then drawn on by any program that wishes to use their capabilities. Because of FORTRAN's extensive use as a programming language over the years, a large and well-tested FORTRAN library collection exists, so in many cases programmers can use existing code instead of having to write all code from scratch. This feature is sometimes highly touted for newer languages such as Java, but FORTRAN designers got there first. FORTRAN was an extremely successful language; millions of lines of FORTRAN code are still in use, and thanks to its evolution over time, FORTRAN has remained an effective language for engineering applications.

 ### 9.2.2 *COBOL*

The name COBOL derives from *CO*mmon *B*usiness-*O*riented *L*anguage. COBOL was developed in 1959–1960 by a group headed by Grace Hopper of the U.S. Navy. FORTRAN and COBOL were the dominant high-level languages of the

1960s and 1970s. COBOL was designed to serve business needs such as managing inventories and payrolls. In such applications, summary reports are important output products. Much of the processing in the business world concerns updating "master files" with changes from "transaction files." For example, a master inventory file might contain names, manufacturers, and quantities available for various items in inventory; a transaction file would contain names and quantities of items sold out of inventory or delivered to inventory over some period of time. The master file would be updated from the transaction file on a daily or weekly basis to reflect the new quantities available, and a summary report would be printed. The user doesn't interact directly with the COBOL program; rather, the user prepares the master file (once) and the transaction file (regularly). As is consistent with this intended usage, COBOL is far more adept at handling file input than keyboard input.

In the design of COBOL, particular attention was paid to input formatting for data being read from files and to output formatting both for writing data to a file and for generating business reports with information precisely located on the page. Therefore, much of a COBOL program may be concerned with formatting, described by "PICTURE clauses" in the program.

Another design decision in developing COBOL was that programs should describe what they are doing in natural language phrases. As a result, COBOL programs are rather verbose. Instead of Java's succinct and mathematical

```
sum = a + b;
```

COBOL would say

```
ADD A TO B GIVING SUM.
```

This compromise actually sacrifices one of the goals of high-level languages that we enumerated in the previous chapter, to use standard mathematical notation, but this was a deliberate decision on the part of the COBOL language designers to allow COBOL programs to be written by people who were less "formula-oriented."

COBOL programs are highly portable across many different COBOL compilers, are quite easy to read, and are very well-suited to manipulating large data files. Because COBOL has been around for a long time, there are many existing COBOL applications programs. COBOL probably provides as much as 60% of the existing code base (between 180 billion and 200 billion lines of COBOL code), making it, even today, the most widely used language in the world.

Nonetheless, the continuing importance of COBOL as a commercial programming language had perhaps been overlooked by those outside the business world until the "Year 2000 problem" came along. The Y2K problem (K stands for *kilo,* or "thousand"), dealt with a lurking time bomb in **legacy code** (i.e., old, but still-running programs), primarily COBOL code. When these programs were written, their authors never imagined their longevity. In addition, computer memory was at a premium, so efficiency was the order of the day. Why store four digits of a date (1967, say) when two digits (67)—the "19" prefix was to be assumed—would be sufficient and would take less space? Furthermore, code was entered on punched paper cards, and no one wanted an instruction to have to be continued onto a second card because of four-digit dates instead of two. In the new millennium, "02" should mean "2002," but in these programs it would be interpreted as "1902."

Making code Y2K-compliant was technically simple: just change every date reference to four digits instead of two. It was the magnitude of the task that was staggering, since it was necessary to locate each line of code where a date entry needed to be changed. Huge sums of government and corporate money were spent to address the problem and, despite dire predictions on the potential consequences of Y2K, it proved to be a "non-event"—probably due to the massive effort made to address the problem.

So, does post-Y2K mark the death of COBOL? No—all this money was not spent on code that businesses planned to throw away. On the contrary, the majority of business transactions, billions of them per day, are still done on COBOL code that has now been updated and is likely to continue to run for the foreseeable future. A new international standard for COBOL was approved in September 2002. New applications in other languages have to integrate with these existing COBOL programs. Meanwhile, however, the pool of trained COBOL programmers is being depleted by retirements and deaths and is not being replenished by new graduates, who often have never been exposed to COBOL.

PRACTICE PROBLEM

Write Java statements that are equivalent to the COBOL statements

```
MOVE INPUT-NUMBER TO OUTPUT-NUMBER.
ADD INPUT-NUMBER TO SUM-OF-VALUES.
```

 ### 9.2.3 C/C++

C was developed in the early 1970s by Dennis Ritchie at AT&T Bell Laboratories. It was originally designed for systems programming, in particular, for writing the operating system UNIX. UNIX had been developed at Bell Labs a short time before and was originally written primarily in assembly language. Ritchie sought a high-level language in which to rewrite the operating system in order to gain all the advantages of high-level languages: ease of programming, portability, and so on.

Since that time, C has become a popular general-purpose language for two major reasons. One is the relationship between C and UNIX itself. UNIX has been implemented on many different computers, and UNIX provides many "tools" that support C programming. A second reason for C's popularity is its efficiency—that is, the speed with which its operations can be executed. This efficiency derives from the fact that C programs can make use of low-level information such as knowledge of where data are stored in memory. In this respect, C is closer to assembly language than other high-level languages are, yet it still has the powerful statements and portability to many machines that high-level languages offer. One can imagine C humming along as a high-level language but then, every once in a while when efficiency is really important,

FIGURE 9.1

User Hardware Interface and Programming Languages

(a) A high-level language shields the programmer from the hardware

Low-level C construct

(b) C can shield the programmer *or* allow direct access to hardware

slipping into a low-level, machine-dependent configuration. One of the goals of a high-level language is to provide a level of abstraction that shields the programmer from any knowledge of the actual hardware/memory cells used during program execution, as depicted in Figure 9.1(a). C provides this outlook, unless the programmer wishes to make use of the low-level constructs available in C that give him or her a direct view of the actual hardware, which Figure 9.1(b) depicts.

For example, suppose that *Number* is a variable in a C program with the value 234. The value of *Number* is stored in some specific memory location with address, say, 1000 (Figure 9.2). Then *&Number* in that same program refers to the memory address where the value of *Number* is stored, in this case, 1000. Note the distinction between the content of a memory cell and the address of that cell. *Number* refers to the value 234, but *&Number* refers to the address 1000. It is possible to write a C program statement that passes *&Number* as an argument to an output module so that the program would actually write out the memory address value (1000). The ability to print an actual memory address is not available in most other high-level languages.

C not only provides a way to see the actual memory address where a variable is stored but also gives the programmer some control over the address where information is stored. C includes a data type called **pointer**; variables of pointer type contain—instead of integers, real numbers, or characters—memory addresses. For example, the statement

```
int* intPointer;
```

declares *intPointer* as a pointer variable that will contain the address of a memory cell containing integer data. The assignment

```
intPointer = (int*) 800;
```

Identifier Address

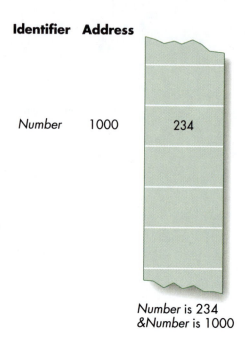

Number   1000

234

Number is 234
&Number is 1000

assigns the memory address 800 as the value of *intPointer*. Figure 9.3(a) illustrates this situation: the pointer variable *intPointer* is stored at some unknown memory address, but the content of *intPointer* is the memory address 800. The value stored at the address contained in *intPointer*, in this case stored at 800, is denoted by **intPointer*. In other words, **intPointer* is the value contained in the address to which *intPointer* points. We can find out what this value is by writing out **intPointer*. We can also assign an integer value, say 3, to be the content of memory address 800 by the statement

```
*intPointer = 3;
```

which results in Figure 9.3(b). We have controlled the content of a specific memory location, and now we know exactly what is stored in memory location 800. Similarly, if *Number* is an integer variable that has been stored somewhere in memory, then the statement

```
*intPointer = Number;
```

results in the value of *Number* being stored in memory cell 800.

This capability for low-level memory manipulation smacks of the assembly language programming of Chapter 6. It is fraught with the problems we sought to avoid by going to high-level languages in the first place; specifically, the programmer is assuming responsibility for what is stored where. For

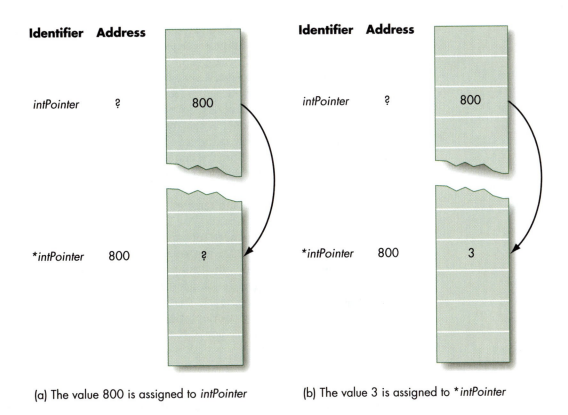

Identifier	Address	
intPointer	?	800
*intPointer	800	?

(a) The value 800 is assigned to *intPointer*

Identifier	Address	
intPointer	?	800
*intPointer	800	3

(b) The value 3 is assigned to **intPointer*

FIGURE 9.3

Storing a Value in a Specific Memory Location Using C

example, what if memory cell 800 in our example is not a memory cell allocated to this program? Perhaps something needed by another program, or even by the operating system, has been overwritten. However, the fact that it enables the programmer to reach down into the machine level is precisely why C is useful for writing system software such as operating systems, assemblers, compilers, programs that allow the computer to interact with input/output devices, and so on.

A program to interact with an I/O device is called a **device driver.** Consider, for example, the problem of writing a device driver for the mouse on a PC. The "serial port" of the computer, to which the mouse is connected, reads changes in the mouse position by changes in voltage levels. It stores the voltage levels in fixed locations in memory, as allocated by the operating system. The job of the mouse driver is to translate voltage levels to specific locations on the screen so that any application software that uses the mouse, such as a word processor, does not have to interact with low-level hardware information (abstraction again!). The mouse driver program would have to access the specific memory locations where voltage information is stored. A language like C provides such a capability.

C is the most widely used language for writing system software, again because of the versatility its design philosophy bestowed on it. It combines the power of a high-level language with the ability to circumvent that level of abstraction and work at the assembly-language-like level. But C is also used for a great deal of general-purpose computing.

The C++ language was developed in the early 1980s by Bjarne Stroustrup at AT&T Bell Laboratories (recall that C was also developed at Bell Labs a decade earlier). The C++ language is a "superset" of C. What this means is that all of the C language is part of C++, so everything that can be done in C—including changing the contents of specific memory locations—can be done in C++. But C++ adds many new features to C, making for greater sophistication and cleaner methods of performing certain tasks. The biggest extension that C++ provides over C is the ability to do object-oriented programming, which we discussed in Section 8.8.

C++ was first commercially released by AT&T in 1985. Like many of the other languages we have discussed, C++ has evolved over time. The standardization process for the language took over 10 years, in part because of this evolution. In November 1997, the combined C++ subcommittees of ANSI (American National Standards Institute) and ISO (International Standards Organization) submitted their C++ standards draft, part of a document of some 800 pages, for final ISO approval. The standards were finally approved in 1998. Standardization, object-orientation, and a strong collection of library code have helped to make C++ one of the most popular of the modern "industrial-strength" languages.

PRACTICE PROBLEMS

1. Suppose a C/C++ program uses a variable called *Rate*. Explain the distinction in the program between *Rate* and *&Rate*.

2. Suppose that *Rate* is an integer variable in a C/C++ program with the value 10 and that *intPointer* is a pointer variable for integer data. *Rate* is stored at memory address 500. After the statement

   ```
   intPointer = &Rate;
   ```

   is executed, what is the value of **intPointer*?

 ### 9.2.4 *Ada*

Probably more than any other language we have studied, Ada has a long and interesting development history. It all started in the mid-1970s when the various branches of the United States armed services set about trying to develop a common high-level programming language for use by defense contractors. They began with a process to specify the requirements that any such language would have to meet, including such characteristics as efficiency, reliability, readability, and maintainability.

The original set of requirements, first circulated for discussion in 1975, was known as "Strawman." Successively tighter and more thorough requirements bore the names "Woodenman" and "Tinman." The Tinman requirements were approved in 1976, and a large number of existing programming languages were evaluated in the light of these requirements. All were found wanting, and it became clear that a new language would have to be developed. The "Ironman" specification, issued in 1977, became the standard against which to measure a new language. A design competition was held, and the requirements were further specified in "Steelman."

The eventual language design winner was chosen in 1979, and the new language was christened Ada, after Ada Augusta Byron Lovelace, daughter of the poet Lord Byron and later the wife of Lord Lovelace. Ada was trained in mathematics and science at the wish of her mother, who sought to steer Ada away from the mental instability and moral lapses she despised in Lord Byron. Lady Ada Lovelace is regarded as the world's first programmer on the basis of her correspondence with Charles Babbage and her published notes on his work with the Analytic Engine (see the box on page 20).

An updated requirements document, less imaginatively named the Ada 9X Requirements and issued in December 1990, became the basis for the current international standard, the Ada 95 Reference Manual.

Ada, like C++, is a large language, and it was accepted not only in the defense industry, where its use was mandated by the Department of Defense, but for other technological applications and as a general-purpose language as well. Ada is known for its multiprocessing capability—the ability to allow multiple tasks to execute independently and then synchronize and communicate when directed. It is also known as a strongly object-oriented language.

The Department of Defense "Ada mandate" was terminated in 1997, but by then Ada was well-established as a programming language supporting good software engineering practice, safety, and reliability. Today Ada is still strong in the transportation industry (aircraft, helicopters, subway systems, European high-speed train control systems) and in safety monitoring systems at nuclear reactors, as well as in financial and communication systems. Its proponents tout Ada as "the language designed for building systems that really matter."

PRACTICE PROBLEM

What do you think is accomplished by the following Ada program?

```
with ada_io; use ada_io;
procedure simple is
begin
  for i in 1..10 loop
    put(i);
    put(' ');
  end loop;
  new_line;
end;
```

9.2.5   C# and .NET

In June 2000, Microsoft introduced a new language called C#. This language is a successor in spirit to C++ but it is a totally new language. Therefore, it has no backward-compatibility issues, as C++ had with C. C# is designed to make some improvements in safe usage over C++ and it shares many features with Java. As an example of safe usage, a C++ program can dynamically grab additional memory for its use during program execution; the programmer is responsible for releasing that memory when the program no longer needs it, or face the possibility of running out of memory. In C#, this process of **garbage collection**—reclaiming memory no longer needed by the program—is handled automatically.

It is impossible to discuss C# without discussing the **Microsoft .NET Framework** that supports C# and other programming languages. The .NET Framework is essentially a giant collection of tools for software development. It was designed so that traditional text-based applications, GUI applications, and web-based programs could all be built with equal ease. For example, the .NET framework provides a whole library of classes for building GUIs with menus, buttons, text boxes, and so forth. And it is the .NET framework (actually a part of the .NET framework called the **Common Language Runtime** or CLR) that handles garbage collection for a C# program, or for any other language that uses the .NET platform. All .NET programs—in whatever language—are compiled into **Microsoft Intermediate Language** (MSIL) code. Like Java bytecode, MSIL is not tied to any particular platform. The final step of compiling MSIL code into object code is done by a **Just In Time** compiler or JIT (part of the CLR) on the user's machine. So, like Java, the developer achieves portability across multiple platforms because he or she has to compile source code only once, into the MSIL.

Old Dog, New Tricks #2

BASIC (*Beginner's Allpurpose Symbolic Instruction Code*) is a programming language that was developed by John Kemeny at Dartmouth College in 1963–1964. As the name suggests, it was intended to be a general language. It was also designed to be easy to learn and use. During the 1960s, programming was a rather difficult task relegated to technical professionals or, in the academic world, to advanced undergraduate engineering, math, and physics majors. BASIC was Kemeny's attempt to design a programming language easy enough for anyone to learn, including high school and elementary school students. This effort was very successful. BASIC was the programming language supplied with most microcomputers throughout the 1980s, and as such it introduced many people, in and out of school, to simple programming ideas. Although BASIC had come a long way from its simple beginnings, it was still not viewed as a very sophisticated language.

BASIC got a new lease on life and a whole new look when Microsoft released Visual Basic in 1991. Visual Basic supplied tools to create a sophisticated GUI application by simply dragging components such as buttons and text-boxes from a Toolbox onto a form, and then writing BASIC code to allow those components to respond to events, such as the click of a button. This programming ease made Visual Basic a very popular language for rapid prototyping of Windows applications, and the number of VB programmers outstripped the total of C, C++, and Java programmers. Subsequent versions of Visual Basic produced an ever-more powerful language. Now Visual Basic.NET is a fully object-oriented language that, like the other .NET languages, can take advantage of all the built-in .NET Framework tools. Old languages that can evolve with the times need never die!

There is one notable difference between the Java approach and the .NET approach. The Java bytecode translator is an interpreter, meaning that a program is translated into object code and executed statement by statement; at the end of program execution, no object code is retained and the next time the program executes, the interpreter must repeat this task. The Just in Time compiler, on the other hand, senses when a particular module of MSIL code is being called, translates that module into object code and then executes it. At the end of program execution, the object code for that module is still there, and if the program executes again with no changes, it can be run directly without invoking the JIT compiler. This difference between interpreted and compiled code leads to more efficient program execution.

Many other programming languages are being adapted to fit into the .NET Framework—for example, FORTRAN, COBOL, C++, Visual J# (Microsoft's version of Java), and Visual Basic.NET (see the "Old Dog, New Tricks #2" box on page 446). That means applications written in any of these languages have access

PRACTICE PROBLEM

A running Visual Basic program produces the following GUI:

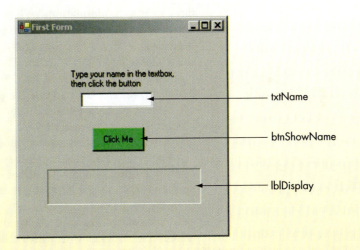

The user types a name in the text box called *txtName,* then clicks the button called *btnShowName.* This "click event" is handled by the following Visual Basic module. Explain what you think will happen as the result of executing this module.

```
Private Sub btnShowName_Click(ByVal sender As System.Object,
         ByVal e As System.EventArgs)
    lblDisplay.Text = txtName.Text
End Sub
```

to the tools provided within the .NET Framework and, because all of these languages compile to MSIL, applications can be written that mix and match modules in various languages. Thus, the choice of which language to use becomes less an issue of language capability and more a matter of personal preference and familiarity.

In April 2003, only three years after the first release of C# and .NET, C# and the CLI (Common Language Infrastructure—a significant subset of the .NET tools) were adopted as ISO standards.

You can download the .NET Framework software from Microsoft at www. microsoft.com/downloads.

9.3   Special-purpose Languages

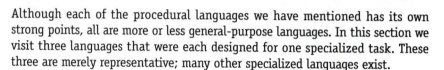

Although each of the procedural languages we have mentioned has its own strong points, all are more or less general-purpose languages. In this section we visit three languages that were each designed for one specialized task. These three are merely representative; many other specialized languages exist.

▶ 9.3.1 *SQL*

Our first specialized language is SQL, which stands for *Structured Query Language*. SQL is designed to be used with databases, which are collections of related facts and information. We'll do some work with databases in Chapter 13, but here is the general idea. A database stores data; the user of the database must be able to add new data and to retrieve data already stored. For example, the database may contain information on vendors with which a retail store does business. For each vendor, it may contain the name, address, and phone number of the vendor, the name of the product line the vendor sells, and perhaps the amount of stock purchased from that vendor during the previous business quarter. The database user should be able to add information on a new vendor and to retrieve information on a vendor already in the database.

But if this is all that a database could do, it would simply be acting as an electronic filing cabinet. Databases can also be queried—that is, the user can pose questions to the database. Queries can furnish information that is more than the sum of its parts because they combine the individual data items in various ways. For example, the vendor database could be queried to reveal the names of all vendors with whom the store has done more than $40,000 worth of business in the past quarter or all vendors from a certain zip code. Such queries might be framed in SQL as

```
SELECT NAME
FROM VENDOR
WHERE PURCHASE > 40000;

SELECT NAME
FROM VENDOR
WHERE ZIP = 95082;
```

SQL is the language used to frame database queries. SQL was originally developed by IBM. In 1986, it was adopted by the American National Standards Institute (ANSI) as the standard query language in the United States, and it has since been adopted by the International Standards Organization (ISO) as an international standard. Even database systems that provide users with simpler— even graphical—ways to frame queries are simply using a front end that eventually translates the query into an equivalent SQL statement.

 ### 9.3.2   HTML

Our second special-purpose language is HTML, which stands for *HyperText Markup Language*. This is the language used to create HTML documents that, when viewed with Web browser software, become Web pages. An HTML document consists of the text to be displayed on the Web page, together with a number of special characters called **tags** that achieve formatting, special effects, and references to other HTML documents. Tags are enclosed in angle brackets (< >) and often come in pairs. The end tag, the second tag in the pair, looks like the begin tag, the first tag in the pair, but with an additional / in front.

The overall format for an HTML document is

```
<html>
<head>
<title> stuff to go in the title bar </title>
</head>
<body>
      stuff to go on the page
</body>
</html>
```

Here we see the paired tags for the document as a whole (<html, </html>), the head (<head>, </head>), the title (<title>, </title>)—framing what will appear in the title bar of the page window—and the body (<body>, </body>)—framing what will be on the page itself.

Of course, other material needs to go between the beginning and ending "body" tags, or the page will be blank. Figure 9.4 shows an HTML document, and Figure 9.5 shows how the Web page actually looks when viewed with a Web browser. By comparing the two, you can probably understand the meaning of the tags used, as explained in Figure 9.6. In particular, the use of a single-row table helps arrange the Name prompt and the corresponding textbox in a fixed way on every browser. We have also added two attributes to the <input> tag; the "type" attribute, which here specifies a textbox, and the "name" attribute, which identifies the textbox.

Early word processors required the user to type in various codes manually to mark text for boldface, italic, and so forth. Later, more sophisticated word processors with GUI interfaces reduced these tasks to point and click. Much the same situation has come to pass with HTML code. HTML documents

FIGURE 9.4

HTML Code for a Web Page

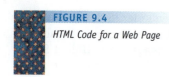

```
<html>
  <head>
    <title>First Page</title>
  </head>

<body>
  <h1>This is an H1 heading</h1>
  <p>This text is <b>BOLD </b> and this text is
      <i>italic</i></p>
  <p>Below is a bulleted list:</p>
  <ul>
    <li>First item</li>
    <li>Second item</li>
  </ul>
  <p>And here is a link to another document called
      <a href="second.htm">Second Page</a></p>

  <table>
    <tr>
      <td>Name</td>
      <td><input type = "text"  name = "Name"></td>
    </tr>
  </table>

</body>
```

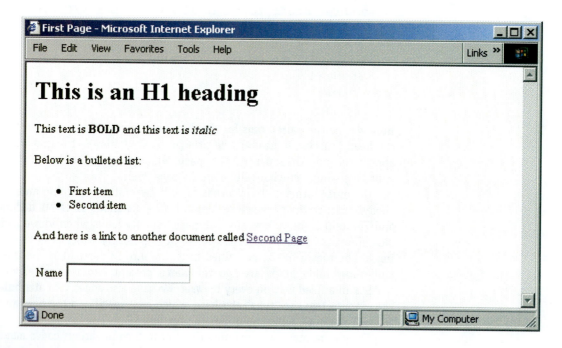

FIGURE 9.5

*Body of the Web Page
Generated by Figure 9.4*

FIGURE 9.6

Some HTML Tags

HTML TAG	PURPOSE
h1	Create H1 heading (bold with largest font size)
p	New paragraph
b	Bold
i	Italic
ul	Unordered list (bulleted list)
li	List item
a href = "..."	Provides hyperlink address
table	Table
tr	Table row
td	Table data (item in a table)

Beyond HTML

The tags in HTML are, as we have seen, specified. The tag pair <b> </b>, for example, is used to display the enclosed text as boldface. The writer of the HTML document cannot invent new tags. But **XML** (eXtensible Markup Language) is a newer markup language. It is a "metalanguage," that is, a markup language for markup languages. Using XML, the writer can create his or her own tags; an XML document is not about displaying information but about how to structure information to be displayed. An XML docu-ment usually also contains or refers to a *schema* that de-scribes the data, and the body of the XML document can then be checked against the schema to be sure that it is a well-formed document. All modern browsers support mech-anisms that translate XML documents into HTML docu-ments for display. XML allows for flexible document inter-change across the Web; for example, in May 2003, the National Library of Medicine announced a "Tagset" for journal articles to provide a single format in which journal articles that originate from many different publishers and societies can be archived.

LABORATORY EXPERIENCE 15

This laboratory experience will give you practice in HTML programming. Learning how to program in HTML will open the door for you to become a contributor to the Web in-stead of just a user. You will also learn how to use your Web browser to perform simple file transfers from special computers called FTP servers. This will enable you to ac-cess a wealth of software and data files in the public do-main.

themselves are simply text files that one can create with any text editor by typing the appropriate tags. But Web editor software makes it possible to cre-ate HTML code by, for example, highlighting text and clicking a button to in-sert the tags for making the text boldface.

 9.3.3 *JavaScript*

A scripting language is a "lightweight" language that is interpreted (trans-lated, then executed, statement by statement). Scripting language code frag-ments can be embedded in Web pages to make those pages active rather than static. JavaScript is such a language; keep in mind that JavaScript is not the same as the full-blown Java programming language we discussed in Chapter 8.

Consider the HTML page from the previous section. When this page is displayed by the Web browser, the user can indeed type his or her name into the text box, but nothing happens as a result. Suppose we want to turn this page into some sort of order form. The user downloads the page from the server machine of the online merchant, fills in the form, and submits the result. We want the information the user enters to be returned to the server. (In this case the only information is the user's name, but a real order form would require nothing more than additional text boxes.)

First, we'll add a "Submit" button at the bottom of the form using another <input> tag whose attributes create a button with the word *Submit* on it:

```
<input type = "submit" value = "Submit">
```

Next we turn the part of our page that contains the table and the Submit button into a form using the <form> </form> tags. The <form> tag needs some further attributes, as shown in Figure 9.7. The "method" attribute here is *post,* which instructs the browser to construct an HTTP POST message, indicating that data is to be passed to the server (recall the discussion of the HTTP GET message in Chapter 7, which is how the user's browser got the form page from the server in the first place). The "enctype" attribute here says that the data to be transmitted is ordinary text. The "name" attribute identifies the form, and the "action" attribute tells the browser where to send the data. Ordinarily this would be back to some active Web page on the merchant's server, but since we have no server to send to, we'll just mail the form data to ourselves. Finally, we plan to write a small JavaScript function that will execute on the client machine when the Submit button is clicked to validate that the user has indeed entered something in the Name text box; the "onSubmit" method invokes this function.

The JavaScript function ValidateName() is placed within <script></script> tags to alert the browser that these statements are to be interpreted as JavaScript commands.

```
<script language = "JavaScript">
function ValidateName()
{
  if (document.TrialForm.Name.value=="")
  {
    alert("You must enter a name");
    document.TrialForm.Name.focus();
    return false;
  }
  return true;
}
</script>
```

The ValidateName() function looks at the value of the Name object (the text box) in the form TrialForm on the current document. If it is empty (no text

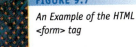
FIGURE 9.7

An Example of the HTML
<form> tag

```
<form method = "post" enctype = "text/plain"
  name = "TrialForm"
  action = "mailto:me@somewhere.edu
  onSubmit = "return ValidateName()">
```

FIGURE 9.8

JavaScript Embedded in an
HTML page

```html
<html>
<head>
<title>First Page</title>
<script language = "JavaScript">
function ValidateName()
{
  if (document.TrialForm.Name.value=="")
  {
    alert("You must enter a name");
    document.TrialForm.Name.focus();
    return false;
  }
  return true;
}
</script>
</head>

<body>
  <h1>This is an H1 heading</h1>
  <p>This text is <b>BOLD </b> and this text is
    <i>italic</i></p>
  <p>Below is a bulleted list:</p>
  <ul>
    <li>First item</li>
    <li>Second item</li>
  </ul>
  <p>And here is a link to another document called
    <a href="second.htm">Second Page</a></p>

  <form method = "POST" enctype = "text/plain"
    name = "TrialForm"
    action = " mailto:me@somewhere.edu
    onSubmit = "return ValidateName()">
    <table>
      <tr>
        <td>Name</td>
        <td><input type = "text" name = "Name"></td>
      </tr>
    <table>
    <input type = "submit" value = "Submit">
  </form>

</body>
```

data has been entered), an error message is displayed, the focus returns to the text box to encourage the user to enter data, a value of "false" is returned, and the form will not be submitted. Otherwise a value of "true" is returned and the form data is posted. Figure 9.8 shows the complete HTML page with the embedded JavaScript.

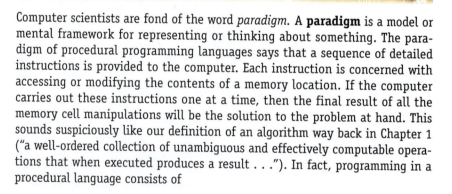

PRACTICE PROBLEMS

1. Describe the result of executing the following SQL query on the vendor database.

```
SELECT NAME
FROM VENDOR
WHERE CITY = 'CHICAGO';
```

2. Given the following HTML statement, what will the corresponding line of text on the Web page look like?

```
<p>These are the <i>times</i> that try
   <b>men's souls</b></p>
```

3. Type the HTML code of Figure 9.8 into a text editor such as Notepad. Change the email address to your own address. Save the file with a .html extension. Then double-click on the file to bring it up in your browser. What happens if you enter nothing in the text box and click the Submit button? What happens if you enter your name in the text box and click the Submit button?

9.4 Alternative Programming Paradigms

Computer scientists are fond of the word *paradigm*. A **paradigm** is a model or mental framework for representing or thinking about something. The paradigm of procedural programming languages says that a sequence of detailed instructions is provided to the computer. Each instruction is concerned with accessing or modifying the contents of a memory location. If the computer carries out these instructions one at a time, then the final result of all the memory cell manipulations will be the solution to the problem at hand. This sounds suspiciously like our definition of an algorithm way back in Chapter 1 ("a well-ordered collection of unambiguous and effectively computable operations that when executed produces a result . . ."). In fact, programming in a procedural language consists of

- Planning the algorithm
- Capturing the "unambiguous and effectively computable operations" as program instructions

In a procedural programming language, then, we must pay attention to the details of exactly how the computer is going to accomplish the desired task in a step by step fashion. In object-oriented programming, the procedural paradigm still holds, but the step by step instructions may be split into multiple small sets that are encapsulated within classes.

In this section we look at programming languages designed as alternatives to the procedural approach—languages based on other paradigms. It is as though we have studied French, Spanish, and Italian (different but related languages) and are now about to embark on a study of Arabic, Japanese, or sign language —languages totally different in form, structure, and alphabet. Alternative paradigms for programming languages include viewing a program's actions as

- A combination of various transformations upon items (functional programming)
- A series of logical deductions from known facts (logic programming)
- Multiple copies of the same subtask or multiple subtasks of the same problem being performed simultaneously by different processors (parallel programming)

We'll look briefly at each of these alternative programming paradigms, focusing on the different conceptual views rather than on the details of a language's syntax. In short, this chapter won't make you an expert programmer, or even a novice programmer, in any of these languages, but you'll have a sense of some of the different approaches to programming languages that have been developed. Both LISP, mentioned in the next section, and Prolog, discussed in Section 9.4.2, are often used in artificial intelligence work; for more information on artificial intelligence, see Chapter 14.

 ### 9.4.1 *Functional Programming*

Functional programming had its start with the design of the LISP (*LISt Processing*) programming language by John McCarthy at MIT in 1958. This makes LISP second only to FORTRAN in longevity. John Backus (who, you will recall, led the development of FORTRAN) argued for functional programming as opposed to "conventional Von Neumann languages" and introduced the language FP (for *Functional Programming*) in 1977. Other functional programming languages or dialects of LISP have been developed. We will look at examples using Scheme—a functional programming language that was derived from LISP in the late 1970s.

A **functional programming language** views every task in terms of (surprise!) functions. These are something like mathematical functions—recipes for taking an argument (or possibly several arguments) and doing something with them to compute a single value. More formally, when the arguments are given values, the function transforms those values, according to some specified rule, into a corresponding resulting value. Different values for the arguments can produce different resulting values. The doubling function $f(x) = 2x$ transforms the argument 3 into 6 because $f(3) = 2*3 = 6$, and it transforms the argument 6 into 12 because $f(6) = 2*6 = 12$. In the grand sense, we can think of a program as a function acting on input data (the arguments) and transforming them into the desired output.

In a functional programming language, certain functions, called **primitive functions** or just **primitives,** are defined as part of the language. Other functions can be defined and named by the programmer. To define the doubling function using Scheme, we could say

```
(define (double x)
    (* 2 x))
```

The keyword "define" indicates that we are defining a new function. The function name and its list of arguments follow in parentheses. The function name is *double,* and *x* is its single argument. The definition says that when this function is invoked, it is to multiply the argument value by 2. Having defined the function, we can now invoke it in a program by giving the function name, followed by a list of values for the arguments of the function. (For the *double* function, there is only one number in the list of argument values because there is only one argument.) Scheme responds immediately to a function invocation by displaying the result, so the following interaction could occur as the user invokes the *double* function with various argument values (boldface indicates what the user types).

(double 4)
8
(double 8)
16

Here's the definition of another function:

```
(define (square x)
    (* x x))
```

which says that the function named *square,* when invoked, is to multiply the single argument value by itself. Thus a dialog with Scheme could be

(square 3)
9

Functions, once defined, can be used in the definition of other functions. This can lead to nested tasks that must be performed. The function *polynomial,* defined by

```
(define (polynomial x)
    (double (square x)))
```

is the function that we would write mathematically as $g(x) = 2x^2$. Using this function, the dialog could be

```
(polynomial 3)
18
```

When the *polynomial* function is invoked with the argument 3, Scheme consults the function definition and sees that this is really

```
(double (square 3))
```

Thus, the polynomial function must invoke the *double* function, and it is to invoke that function with an argument value of (square 3). Therefore, the first thing to do is to invoke the *square* function with an argument value of 3. The result is $3^2 = 9$. This 9 gets used as the argument value for the double function, resulting in 18. The total computation is equivalent to $g(3) = 2(3)^2 = 2(9) = 18$.

Here we've defined one function (*polynomial*) in terms of another function (*double*) acting on the result of applying a third function (*square*). In functional programming languages, we can build up complex combinations of functions that use the results of applying other functions, which use the results of applying still other functions, and so on. In fact, functional programming languages are sometimes called **applicative languages** because of this property of repeatedly applying functions.

As the name LISP suggests, LISP processes lists of things and so does Scheme. The arguments to functions, then, are often lists. As a trivial case, "nothing" can be thought of as an empty list, which is called *nil*. We will use four primitive list-processing functions available in Scheme. The first function is called *list*. This function can have any number of arguments, and its action is to create a list out of those arguments. Therefore,

```
(list 3 4 5)
```

evaluates to the list 3, 4, 5, which we will write as

```
(3  4  5)
```

Two other list-processing functions are called *car* (pronounced as when it means an automobile) and *cdr* (pronounced "could-er"). (The names have historical significance from the distant past. Car stands for "Contents of Address Register," and cdr stands for "Contents of Decrement Register." These registers were part of the architecture of the IBM 704 computer on which LISP was originally implemented.) The *car* function takes a nonempty list as its argument and produces as a result the first element in that list. Therefore, a dialog with Scheme could consist of

```
(car (list 3 4 5))
3
```

The *cdr* function takes a nonempty list as its argument and produces as a result the list that remains after the first element has been removed. Therefore,

```
(cdr (list 3 4 5))
```

evaluates to the list

```
(4  5)
```

As a special case, when the *cdr* function is applied to an argument consisting of a one-element list, the empty list is produced as the result. Thus,

(cdr (list 5))

evaluates to the list *nil*. Note that the *car* function applied to a list evaluates to a list element, whereas the *cdr* function applied to a list evaluates to another, shorter list.

One final primitive list-processing function is *null?*, which has a single list as its argument and evaluates to true if the list is *nil* (empty) and to false if the list is nonempty. Armed with these primitives, we can at last write a little Scheme program (Figure 9.9) to add some nonnegative integers.

Dialog with the program in Figure 9.9 could result in

(adder (list 3 4 5))
12

Let's see how this works. Our function *adder* was defined to have one argument, symbolically denoted in the definition by *input-list*. Now we're invoking this function where the argument has the value of (*list* 3 4 5); that is to say, the function is to operate on (3 4 5). The *cond* function (short for "conditional") is acting like a Java if-else statement: it is equivalent to

```
if (null? input-list)
   total = 0;
else
   total = (car input-list) + (adder(cdr input-list));
```

The condition "null? input-list" is evaluated and found to be false because *input-list* at this point is (*list* 3 4 5). The else clause is executed, and it says to add two quantities. The first of these two quantities is (*car input-list*), which is (*car* (*list* 3 4 5)), or 3. Thus, 3 is to be added to the second quantity. The second quantity is the result of invoking the *adder* function on the argument (*cdr input-list*), which is (*cdr* (*list* 3 4 5)), or (4 5). The value, as constructed so far, is therefore

3 + (*adder* (*list* 4 5))

FIGURE 9.9

Scheme Program to Add Nonnegative Integers

```
(define (adder input-list)
  (cond ((null? input-list) 0)
     (else (+ (car input-list)
        (adder (cdr input-list))))))
```

Now the program invokes the *adder* function again, this time with an argument of (*list* 4 5) instead of (*list* 3 4 5). Once again we test whether this list is *nil* (it isn't), so we add together

(*car* (*list* 4 5)) + (*adder* (*cdr* (*list* 4 5)))

or

4 + (*adder* (*list* 5))

The *adder* function is invoked again with an argument of (*list* 5). The list still is not *nil,* so we add together

(*car* (*list* 5)) + (*adder* (*cdr* (*list* 5)))

or

5 + (*adder nil*)

A final invocation of the *adder* function, this time with the *nil* list as its argument, takes the other branch of the *cond* statement, which results in 0. Altogether, then, we've done

(*adder* (*list* 3 4 5))

or

(*adder* (3 4 5)) =
　　　3 + (*adder* (4 5)) =
　　　3 + 4 + (*adder* (5)) =
　　　3 + 4 + 5 + (*adder nil*) =
　　　3 + 4 + 5 + 0 = 12

The definition of the *adder* function involves the *adder* function again, this time acting on a shorter list. Note in our example how we had to invoke the *adder* function repeatedly—first on (3 4 5), then on (4 5), next on (5), and finally on *nil*. Something that is defined in terms of "smaller versions" of itself is said to be **recursive,** so the *adder* function is a recursive function.

Recursion is one of the features of functional languages that makes possible short and elegant solutions to many problems. Although recursion is a dominant mode of operation in functional languages, many procedural languages also support recursion, so that's not the major argument for using a functional language. Then what is the benefit of going to a functional language?

A functional language allows for clarity of thought; data values are transformed by flowing, as it were, through a stream of mathematical functions. The programmer has no concern about where intermediate values are stored, nor indeed about how a "list" could occupy many memory cells. Another layer of abstraction has been offered to the programmer—the rarefied layer of pure mathematics. Because functions are described in a mathematical way by what they do to an item of data rather than by how they modify memory cells in the process of doing it, the possibility of side effects is eliminated. A **side effect** occurs when a function, in the course of acting on its argument values to produce a result value, also changes other values that it has no business changing. Implementing a function in a procedural language, where the major mode of operation is modification of memory cells, opens the door to potential side effects.

Simplicity Is in the Eye of the Beholder

We used recursion to define the function to add a list, as follows: add the first list element to the result of adding the rest of the list elements together. The recursive way of thinking takes a bit of getting used to. For example,

- Reading a book can be defined as reading the first page followed by reading the rest of the book.
- Climbing a ladder can be defined as climbing the first rung followed by climbing the rest of the ladder.
- Eating a six-course meal can be done by eating the first course followed by eating the rest of the meal.

Having learned to program in a procedural language, some people are initially uncomfortable with the recursive style of functional languages. However, this seems to be more a matter of what one is used to rather than any inherent "difficulty factor." Many people argue for using a functional language like Scheme as a *first* programming language because of its simplicity, clarity, and elegance.

The functional language Logo was developed by Seymour Papert at MIT in 1980, specifically as an educational tool for young children, who seem to take to it readily. In Logo one can use "turtle graphics"—that is, a "turtle" can be programmed to move about on the screen, tracing lines as it travels, and thereby drawing various figures. (The original MIT turtle was an actual mechanical model of a turtle that children could direct to move about on the floor, tracing lines on a sheet of paper.) For example, the turtle can be programmed to draw a square recursively by first drawing one side and then drawing the remaining three sides of the square. Here's the Logo (recursive) version of the sequential search algorithm, as expressed by one of the authors' children: "To find the elephant in the zoo, look in the first cage, and if it's not there, then look in the rest of the zoo!" Does this seem like an easier way to think about sequential searching than the algorithm we developed in Chapter 2?

LABORATORY EXPERIENCE 16

If you have access to a LISP or Scheme interpreter, this laboratory experience will guide you through some functional programming exercises. You'll see that a higher level of problem solving is possible than in the Java exercises, where you had to write step by step instructions to manipulate data values by way of specific memory locations.

PRACTICE PROBLEMS

1. To what does each of the following evaluate?

   a. `(cdr (list 1 2 3 4))`
   b. `(car (cdr (list 4 5 6)))`

2. Define a function in Scheme that adds 3 to a number.

9.4.2 *Logic Programming*

We saw that functional programming gets away from explicitly instructing the computer about the details of each step to be performed; instead, it specifies various transformations of data and then allows combinations of transformations to be performed. **Logic programming** goes a step further in the direction of not specifying exactly how a task is to be done. In logic programming, various facts are asserted to be true, and on the basis of these facts, a logic program can infer or deduce other facts. When a **query** (a question) is posed to the program, it begins with the storehouse of facts and attempts to apply logical deductions, in as efficient a manner as possible, to answer the query. Logic programming languages are sometimes called **declarative languages** (as opposed to imperative languages) because their programs, instead of issuing commands to do certain things, make declarations or assertions that various facts are true.

A domain of interest is defined in which the declarations make sense (such as medicine, literature, or chemistry), and the queries are related to that domain. Logic programming has been used to write **expert systems**. In an expert system about a particular domain, a human "expert" in that domain contributes facts based on his or her knowledge and experience. A logic program using these facts as its declarations can then, presumably, make inferences that are close to those the human expert would make.

The best-known logic programming language is Prolog, which was developed in France at the University of Marseilles in 1972 by a group headed by A. Colmerauer. Prolog stands for *PRO*gramming in *LOG*ic; the language was originally intended as a tool for natural language processing. Interest in Prolog received a great boost when the Japanese announced their Fifth Generation Project in 1981. The goal of this effort, which later proved to be too ambitious, was to provide a knowledge-based society through the use of computers that make logical inferences and can interact with human beings in a "natural" way through both spoken and written language.

Prolog programs consist of *facts* and *rules*. A **fact** expresses a property about a single object or a relationship among several objects. As an example, let us write a Prolog program about the domain of American history. We are interested in which U.S. presidents were in office when certain events occurred and in the chronology of those presidents' terms in office. Here is a short list of facts (declarations):

```
president(lincoln, gettysburg_address).
president(lincoln, civil_war).
president(nixon, first_moon_landing).
president(jefferson, lewis_and_clark).
president(kennedy, cuban_missile_crisis).
president(fdr, world_war_II).

before(jefferson, lincoln).
before(lincoln, fdr).
before(fdr, kennedy).
before(kennedy, nixon).
```

The interpretation of these facts is fairly obvious. For example, the declaration

```
president(jefferson, lewis_and_clark).
```

asserts or declares that Jefferson was U.S. President during the Lewis and Clark expeditions. And

```
before(kennedy, nixon).
```

asserts that Kennedy was president before Nixon. (There are a number of versions of Prolog available; the version we used requires that identifiers for specific items begin with lowercase letters and have no internal blanks.)

This list of facts constitutes a Prolog program. We interact with the program by posing queries; this is the way Prolog programs are executed. For example, the user could make the following query (boldface indicates what the user types):

?-before(lincoln, fdr).

Prolog will respond

```
Yes.
```

because "before(lincoln, fdr)" is a fact in the program. After every response, Prolog will also ask

```
More?  (Y/N):
```

because there may be multiple responses to the query. If we wish to see further responses, we answer Yes. If we answer yes when there are no further responses, as in this case, Prolog will simply respond

```
No.
```

Here's some further dialog with Prolog using this same program. We won't bother to write the "More? (Y/N):" that appears after each Prolog response.

?-president(lincoln, civil_war).
```
Yes.
```
?-president(truman, world_war_II)
```
No.
```

The first query corresponds to a declaration in the program, and the second does not.

More complicated queries can be phrased. A query of the form A, B is asking Prolog whether fact A and fact B are both in the program. Thus, a query such as

?-president(lincoln, civil_war), before(lincoln, fdr)

will produce a Yes response because both facts are in the program. The interpretation is that Lincoln was president during the Civil War and that Lincoln was president before FDR.

So far, Prolog appears to be little more than some sort of retrieval system that does lookups on a table of facts. But Prolog can do much more. Variables can be used within queries, and this is what gives Prolog its power. Variables must begin with uppercase letters. The query

?-president(lincoln, X).

is asking for a match against facts in the program of the form

president(lincoln,"something")

In other words, X can stand for anything that is in the "president relation" with Lincoln. The responses are

```
X = gettysburg_address
X = civil_war
```

because both

```
president(lincoln, gettysburg_address).
president(lincoln, civil_war).
```

are facts in the program. (Remember that in order to see more than one response, we have to keep answering Yes when asked "More? (Y/N): ".)

Let's describe what it means for one president to precede another in office. It may appear that the *before* relation already takes care of this. Certainly if "before(X, Y)" is true, then President X precedes President Y. However, in our example program,

```
before(lincoln, fdr).
before(fdr, kennedy).
```

are both true, but that does not tell us that Lincoln precedes Kennedy (which is also true). Of course, we could add another *before* fact to cover this case, but that is an *ad hoc* patch. Instead, let's add further declarations to the program to define the *precede* relation. We already know that two presidents in the *before* relation should also be in a *precede* relation. Furthermore, from the example above, it would appear that if X is before Z and Z is before Y, then "precede(X, Y)" should also be true. But we can say more than that: if X is before Z and Z precedes Y, then "precede(X, Y)" should be true. This extension means that Jefferson precedes Kennedy because

	before(fdr, kennedy)
implies	precedes(fdr, kennedy)

	before(lincoln, fdr)
	precedes(fdr, kennedy)
implies	precedes(lincoln, kennedy)

and

> before(jefferson, lincoln)
> precedes(lincoln, kennedy)
> implies   precedes(jefferson, kennedy)

Using this reasoning, we have derived three new "precedes" facts that were not in the original list of facts.

Thus, we want to say that there are two ways in which X can precede Y:

precedes(X,Y) if before(X,Y)
precedes(X,Y) if before(X,Z) and precedes(Z,Y)

We can make declarations in our Prolog program that express the *precedes* relation, but this time the declarations are stated as rules rather than as facts. A Prolog **rule** is a declaration of an "if A then B" form, which means that if A is true (A is a fact), then B is also true (B is a fact). The actual Prolog declarations follow; think of the notation B :- A as meaning "if A then B."

```
precedes(X,Y)  :- before(X,Y).
precedes(X,Y)  :- before(X,Z), precedes(Z,Y).
```

The rule for *precedes* includes *precedes* as part of its definition; it is therefore a recursive rule.

Our Prolog program now consists of the facts and rules shown in Figure 9.10. Here's some further dialog, using the new program. Be sure you understand why each query receives the response or responses it does.

?-precedes(fdr, kennedy).

```
Yes.
```

?-precedes(lincoln, nixon).

```
Yes.
```

?-precedes(lincoln, X).

```
X = fdr
X = kennedy
X = nixon
```

Let's add one final declaration to the program—a declaration that says that event X occurred earlier than event Y if X took place during president R's term in office, Y took place during president S's term in office, and president R precedes president S. (Do you agree with this definition of the *earlier* relation?) Here's the rule:

```
earlier(X,Y)  :- president(R,X),
                 president(S,Y),precedes(R,S).
```

Then a final query of

?-earlier(world_war_II, X)

FIGURE 9.10

A Prolog Program

```
president(lincoln, gettysburg_address).
president(lincoln, civil_war).
president(nixon, first_moon_landing).
president(jefferson, lewis_and_clark).
president(kennedy, cuban_missile_crisis).
president(fdr, world_war_II).

before(jefferson, lincoln).
before(lincoln, fdr).
before(fdr, kennedy).
before(kennedy, nixon).

precedes(X,Y) :- before(X,Y).
precedes(X,Y) :- before(X,Z), precedes(Z,Y).
```

produces the responses

```
X = first_moon_landing
X = cuban_missile_crisis
```

In this simple example, it is easy to check that the responses to our queries are correct, and it is also not difficult to do the necessary comparisons with the program declarations to see how Prolog was able to arrive at its responses. The interesting thing to note, however, is that the program consists solely of declaratives (facts and rules), not instructions about what steps to take in order to produce the answers. The program provides the raw material, and in the logic programming paradigm, this raw material is inspected more or less out of our sight, and without our detailed instructions, to deduce the answers to a query.

Figure 9.11 illustrates the situation. The programmer builds a **knowledge base** of facts and rules about a certain domain of interest; this knowledge base constitutes the program. Interaction with the program takes place by posing queries—sometimes rather complex queries—to an **inference engine** (also called a **query interpreter**). The inference engine is a piece of software that is supplied as part of the language itself; that is, it is part of the compiler or interpreter, not something the programmer has to write. The inference engine can access the knowledge base, and it contains its own rules of deductive reasoning based on symbolic logic. For example, a Prolog inference engine processing the program in Figure 9.10 would conclude that

    precedes(fdr, kennedy)

is true from the rule of the form

    if before(X, Y) then precedes(X, Y)

together with the fact

    before(fdr, kennedy).

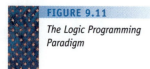

FIGURE 9.11

The Logic Programming Paradigm

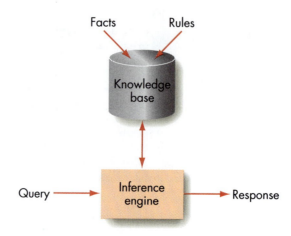

because it is a rule of deductive reasoning (known as **modus ponens**) that "if A then B" together with "A" must result in "B." The programmer need not supply this rule or instruct the inference engine when it should be applied. Thus, the inference engine can be thought of as providing still another layer of abstraction between the programmer and the machine. The programmer supplies the fundamental facts and rules about the domain but does not direct the computer's step by step processing of those facts and rules to answer a query.

This is a somewhat idealistic view of logic programming; in actuality, the idiosyncrasies of Prolog compilers mean that programmers do need to understand something about the order in which rules of logic will be applied. Yet, Prolog still gives us a good sense of the logic programming paradigm, where the intent is to concentrate on the "what" [is true] rather than on the "how" [to find it] that is the hallmark of procedural programming.

PRACTICE PROBLEMS

Using the Prolog program of Figure 9.10, what will be the result of each of the following queries?

1. ?-before(jefferson, kennedy).

2. ?-president(X, lewis_and_clark).

3. ?-precedes(jefferson, X).

FIGURE 9.12

*"Grand Challenge" Computing
Problems*

- 72-hour weather prediction
- Modeling oil reservoirs
- Chemical dynamics
- Vehicle dynamics
- Fluid turbulence
- Human genome project
- Ocean circulation model

 ### 9.4.3 *Parallel Programming*

We mentioned in Chapter 5 that the computing problems of the 21st century are pushing the boundaries of the Von Neumann model of sequential processing. Figure 9.12 lists some of the "grand challenges" identified by the government-sponsored High Performance Computing and Communications Initiative for the 1990s. For the most part, these remain challenges today. Parallel processing, in one of its several forms, seems to hold promise of providing the necessary speed to solve problems of this type, which require great computational resources.

Parallel processing is really a catch-all term for a variety of computing architectures and approaches to algorithms. Let's review the two approaches to parallel architectures discussed in Chapter 5:

SIMD (single instruction stream/multiple data stream): a single control unit broadcasts a single program instruction to multiple ALUs, each of which carries out that instruction on its own local data stored in its local memory.

MIMD (multiple instruction stream/multiple data stream): numerous interconnected processors execute their own programs on their own data, communicating results as necessary.

The algorithms with which we are familiar operate sequentially (because they were designed for Von Neumann–type execution). To reap the benefits of parallel architecture, new algorithms must be found, which may involve new ways of thinking about problem solutions. In contrast to our approach in the other sections of this chapter, we're not going to talk about a specific "parallel programming language." Instead, we will discuss some of the general approaches to parallel programming.

An example (given in Chapter 5) of SIMD processing is adding a constant value K to each element in a 6-element vector V. There would be six ALUs, each with an ID number from 1 to 6. Each ALU would have its own local or "private" data consisting of one of the six vector components; that is, the ALU with ID 1 would have a private copy of V in its local memory which would actually consist of just $V[1]$. The ALU with ID 2 would have $V[2]$ as its private copy of V. All ALUs would need access to the constant value K, which could be stored in a shared memory accessible by all. We can imagine that programming instructions for this operation in a language designed to support SIMD processing would look something like

```
V : private;  K : public
   .
   .
   .
PARALLEL [1..6]
  V = V + K;
END PARALLEL
```

Here *V* has been declared as a "private" data item that is stored in the local memory of the appropriate ALU and that differs from one ALU to the next. *K* has been declared as a "public" data item stored in shared memory and identical to each ALU. The PARALLEL instruction says that all ALUs with ID numbers 1 to 6 are to do, in lockstep, the statement V = V + K.

The MIMD example from Chapter 5 has to do with the name search task. Here the 20,000,000-entry list to be searched is partitioned into 100 separate chunks of size 200,000 and parceled out to 100 processors. All of the processors execute simultaneously—but not necessarily in instruction by instruction lockstep—the search task on their portion of the data. In a language designed to support MIMD processing, we might see something like

```
YOURLIST = LIST[1..200000] : private
NAME : public
.
.
.
PARALLEL[1..100]
   SEQSEARCH (YOURLIST, NAME, FOUND, INTERRUPT)
   IF FOUND, SEND INTERRUPT
END PARALLEL
```

Here a section of the overall list has been declared as private data (stored in the local memory of the appropriate processor), and NAME has been declared as "public" data (to be broadcast to all processors). The PARALLEL instruction says that all processors with ID numbers 1 to 100 are to initiate a sequential search for NAME on their 200,000-element portion of the list. If NAME is found, the processor is to broadcast this information to all other processors by sending an INTERRUPT signal. Each processor's sequential search algorithm is modified to halt if an INTERRUPT signal is received, because that means another processor has found NAME, and the search can be halted.

MIMD processing does not require that each processor be doing the same task. For example, an instruction like

```
PARALLEL
   PROC 1: A = 1
   PROC 2: READ(B)
   PROC 3: AVERAGE(X,Y,Z)
END PARALLEL
```

tells processor 1 to do an assignment, processor 2 to read a value, and processor 3 to execute an "average" function. These actions are to be done in parallel, but they may not be completed simultaneously because they are of different complexity. The PARALLEL statement as a whole will be completed when all of these actions are finished (see Figure 9.13).

A slightly more sophisticated level of MIMD parallel processing occurs when a divide-and-conquer approach can be used on a task. The task is successively partitioned into smaller and smaller parts and handed off to other processors, until a number of processors have a trivial case of the task to perform. They perform this task and give the results back to the processors that gave the task to them. These processors in turn do a little work and then give the results back to the processors that gave the task to them, and so on, back to the originating processor. For example, finding the largest element in a list of elements can be the task assigned to the highest-level processor, which partitions the list in two and hands each half to a processor. Each of these two processors hands off half of its list to one of two processors, and so on, creating the pyramid effect shown in Figure 9.14. At the bottom of the pyramid is a collection of processors that only have to find the largest element in a one-element or two-element list, a trivial task. They each pass their result up to their "parent" processor, which must select the larger of two numbers and pass that value up to its parent. All the way back up the pyramid, each processor has only to select the larger of two numbers. When the processor at the top of the pyramid completes this minor task, the entire major task of finding the overall largest number has been completed. Here not every processor is doing the same thing at exactly the same time, but each one (except for those at the bottom of the pyramid) must both move the data down and push results back up.

Still higher levels of parallelism involve careful identification of separate subtasks that may be executed concurrently. None of these subtasks can require any results from any of the other subtasks. For a large-scale problem—one that can make use of a large number of processors—this can be a very difficult job. It requires thorough understanding of the flow of information from one subtask to another.

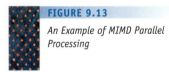

FIGURE 9.13

An Example of MIMD Parallel Processing

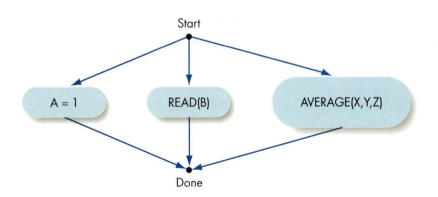

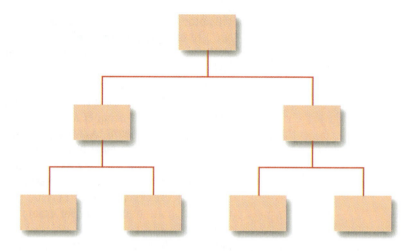

FIGURE 9.14

A Divide-and-Conquer Approach Using Multiple Processors

A final form of parallelism, a type we will discuss again in Chapter 14, is the neural network. Patterned after the human brain, **neural networks** can involve massive interconnections of many extremely simple devices. They are one of the most interesting areas of artificial intelligence today.

We expect the use of parallelism to speed up processing time because subtasks are being executed concurrently. But one potential drawback concerns the amount of communications traffic between the separate processors, both to distribute code and data and to share results. At some point, an increase in the number of processors can become more of a hindrance than a help in speeding up the overall processing time required for the task because of the increased data communication involved. This is analogous to having too many people on a committee. The work involved in keeping everyone informed slows down the real work, so it would have been more efficient to have fewer people doing the job.

One of the important aspects of work in parallel processing is the design of efficient algorithms that keep all the processors busy, cut down on the communications required, and significantly speed up execution time over that required for sequential processing.

PRACTICE PROBLEM

Explain how parallel processing could be used to evaluate the expression

$A + B + C + D$

If each addition operation takes one "time slot," what is the savings that can be achieved by using parallel processing instead of sequential processing?

We've seen that there is an entire spectrum of programming languages, each with its own features that make it more suitable for some types of applications than for others. A number of well-known languages (we looked at FORTRAN, COBOL, C, and Ada) fall into the traditional, procedural paradigm. Procedural languages can be object-oriented (Java, C++, C#, Visual Basic), leading to a different program design perspective and the promise of software reuse. Some languages (such as SQL, HTML, and JavaScript) are designed as special-purpose tools. Still others rely on combinations of function evaluations (a functional language—Scheme), logical deductions from specified facts (a logic programming language—Prolog), or a parallel programming approach. Figure 9.15 lists the languages we have discussed, along with some of the other major languages. A few words about this table are in order. It is hard to pinpoint a date for a programming language. Should it be when the language

FIGURE 9.15

Programming Languages at a Glance

NAME	DATE	TYPE
FORTRAN	1955–57	Procedural
ALGOL-60	1958–60	Procedural
COBOL	1959–60	Procedural
BASIC	1963–64	Procedural
PL/1	1964	Procedural
ALGOL-68	1968	Procedural
Pascal	1971	Procedural
C	1974	Procedural
Modula-2	1977	Procedural
Ada	1979	Procedural/Parallel
Oberon	1988	Procedural/Parallel
Smalltalk	1971–1980	Object-oriented
Flavors	1979	Object-oriented
C++	1983	Object-oriented
Eiffel	1987	Object-oriented
Visual Basic	1988	Object-oriented
Java	1995	Object-oriented
C#	2000	Object-oriented
SQL	1986	Database queries
Perl	1987	Text extraction/reporting
HTML	1994	Hypertext authoring
LISP	1958	Functional
APL	1960	Functional
Scheme	1975	Functional
FP	1977	Functional
ML	1978	Functional
Prolog	1972	Logic
Occam II	1987	Parallel
Linda	1989	Parallel
High Performance Fortran	1993	Parallel
JavaScript	1996	Scripting language
VBScript	1996	Scripting language

was developed, when it was first commercially used, or when it became standardized? It is also sometimes hard to pigeonhole a language as to paradigm. Although we've tried to make clear distinctions in this chapter, some languages combine features drawn from several approaches. Finally, someone's favorite language may have been omitted. (By all means, add it to the table.) At any rate, it is certain that the programming language world has been and continues to be a "Tower of Babel."

The trend in programming language design is to develop still higher levels of abstraction in our programming languages. This allows the human programmer to think in bigger pieces and in more novel or conceptual ways about solving the problem at hand. We would like eventually to be able to write programs that contain only the instruction "Solve the problem." Yet, we must remember that code written in any high-level programming language is still of no use to the computer trying to execute that code. No matter how abstract and powerful the language for front-end communication with the computer, the machine itself is still toiling away at the bit level. The services of an appropriate translator must be employed to take the code down into the machine language of that computer. The workings of a translator are discussed in the next chapter.

1. What do you think the output from the following section of FORTRAN code will be?

   ```
         ISUM = 0
         I = 1
   20 IF (I .GT. 4) GO TO 30
         ISUM = ISUM + I
         I = I + 1
         GO TO 20
   30 WRITE(*,*) ISUM
   ```

2. Exponentiation is expressed in FORTRAN by **; that is, 3**2 means 3^2. If *I* has the value 7 and *J* has the value 3, what is the value of the FORTRAN expression

   ```
   ((I - J)**2)/2
   ```

3. What do you think is the value of *RESULT* after execution of the following COBOL code? Assume that *INITIAL* has the value 100.

   ```
   MOVE INITIAL TO INDEX.
   ADD 1 TO INDEX.
   ADD INITIAL TO INDEX.
   ADD INITIAL TO INDEX GIVING
      RESULT.
   ```

4. What is true after the following statements in a C/C++ program have been executed?

   ```
   int* intPointer;
   intPointer = (int*) 500;
   *intPointer = 10;
   ```

5. Write a section of C/C++ code that stores in memory location 1000 the integer value currently in *SAM*.

6. The following section of Ada code conveys the services that a "teller" object can perform. What are these services?

   ```
   task type teller is
      -- Entries to do simple
      -- transactions and return status
      entry deposit ( id : cust_id;
        val : in money; stat : out
        status );
      entry withdraw( id : cust_id;
        val : in money; stat : out
        status );
      entry balance ( id : cust_id;
        val : out money; stat :
        out status );
   end teller;
   ```

7. C# writes output to the screen by having the Console object invoke a WriteLine() method, for example,

   ```
   Console.WriteLine("Hello World");
   ```
   Write the corresponding Java statement.

8. Which procedural language might be most appropriate for a program to do each of the following applications and why?

   a. Compute trajectories for a satellite launcher.

   b. Monitor an input device feeding data from an experiment to the computer.

   c. Process the day's transactions at an ATM (automated teller machine).

9. In the vendor database described in Section 9.3.1, the user wants to know all of the cities where there are vendors from whom the store bought more than $10,000 worth of stock the previous business quarter. Write an SQL query for this information.

10. Describe what you think the corresponding text on a Web page will look like if this is the HTML statement:

    ```
    <p><center> <font size = 12 color
    = "green"> How Now Brown Cow
    </center></p>
    ```

11. Suppose the Web form in Figure 9.5 had a second text box named Age to collect the user's age. Add to the JavaScript code of Figure 9.8 to check that the Age textbox contains data.

12. What will be the result of the following Scheme expression?

    ```
    (car (cdr (cdr (list 16 19 21))))
    ```

13. Write a Scheme function that returns a list consisting of the first two values in the input list but in the opposite order.

14. Consider the following Scheme function:

    ```
    (define (mystery input-list)
      (cond ((null? input-list) 0)
         (else ( + 1 (mystery (cdr
    input-list))))))
    ```
    What is the result of invoking the function as follows?

    (mystery (list 3 4 5))

    Explain what this function does in general.

15. Consider the following Scheme function:

    ```
    (define (unknown n)
      (cond ((= n 1) 1)
         (else (* n (unknown (- n 1)))))
    ```

The condition (= n 1) means "If $n = 1 \ldots$ ". What do you think will be the result of the following function invocation?

(unknown 4)

16. After the rule

```
earlier(X,Y) :- president(R,X),
   president(S,Y), precedes(R,S).
```

is added to the Prolog program of Figure 9.10, what is the result of each of the following queries?

a. **?-earlier(lewis_and_clark, civil_war).**

b. **?-earlier(world_war_II, first_moon_landing).**

c. **?-earlier(X, world_war_II).**

17. Here is the beginning of a Prolog program about a family. The facts are

```
male(eli)
male(bill)
male(joe)
female(mary)
female(betty)
female(sarah)
parent-of(eli, bill)
parent-of(mary, bill)
parent-of(bill, joe)
parent-of(bill, betty)
parent-of(bill, sarah)
```

The declaration

```
male(eli)
```

asserts that Eli is male, and

```
parent-of(eli, bill)
```

asserts that Eli is Bill's parent. Draw a "family tree" based on these facts.

18. Add to the Prolog program of Exercise 17 a rule to define "father-of".

19. Add to the Prolog program of Exercise 17 a rule to define "daughter-of".

20. a. Add to the Prolog program of Exercise 17 a rule to define "ancestor-of".

   b. After this rule is added, determine the result of the query

   ?-ancestor-of(X, sarah)

21. Suppose the symbolic arrangement of Figure 9.14 is used in a divide-and-conquer algorithm to compute the largest element in a list of eight elements. Assume that the time to partition a list in half and pass it to subprocessors is $0.003n$ µsec, where n is the size of the list to be partitioned. Assume that the time to compare two values and find the larger of the two is 1 µsec. Assume that the time to pass the larger value back to a parent processor is 0.001 µsec. Compute the time required to do this task compared with doing it on a sequential processor that uses the Find Largest algorithm of Chapter 2, which also involves a series of comparisons of two values and finding the larger of the two.

1. Visual Basic.NET (see the box on page 446) supplies a "toolbox" that makes creation of a graphical user interface a simple matter of dragging and dropping the objects you want (e.g., buttons, labels, and text boxes) onto a form object. The resulting windows-based programs operate in an **event-driven mode.** Instead of proceeding from beginning to end under the control of the program instructions, an event-driven program will start up and then sit and wait for some "event" to occur. An event is generally caused by some user action such as clicking on a button. Each of the form objects can have a code module to respond to such events.

    The following shows a simple Visual Basic.NET form that contains two text boxes, a label, and a button. The user types his or her first name and last name into the two textboxes. When the user clicks the button, the name is displayed in the label as

    Lastname, Firstname

    If you have Visual Basic.NET (available in Microsoft Visual Studio), open a new Visual Basic Windows Application. Drag objects from the Toolbox to create a form that looks like the one shown. Give each of these objects a meaningful name by changing its Name property in the Properties window. Use the Text property of each object to set what that object displays (the textboxes and label should initially be blank and the button should say "Name Writer").

    The only code required occurs in response to the button's Click event. Double-click on the button and then write a code statement that concatenates— in the correct order—the Text properties of the two text boxes, together with a comma, and assigns the result to the Text property of the label. Run your program (press the function key F5 on the keyboard) to test it. (*Hints:* Visual Basic uses & as the concatenation operator. A form object's property is referenced by giving the name of the object, followed by a dot, followed by the property name, as in lblOutput.Text.)

2. Find information on one of the Grand Challenge problems of Figure 9.12. Write a report on
    - What the problem involves
    - The benefits to be obtained from solving it
    - Why it is computationally challenging
    - Why parallel processing may be able to, or has been able to, help solve it
    - The current state of progress toward a solution

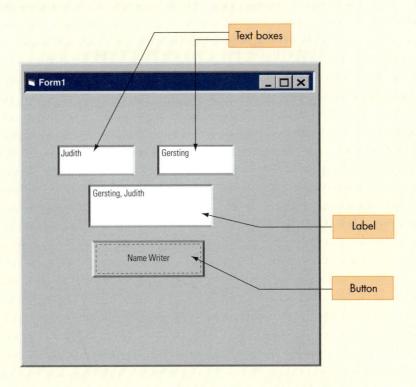

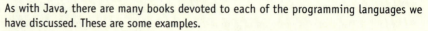
As with Java, there are many books devoted to each of the programming languages we have discussed. These are some examples.

Covington, M. A.; Nute, D.; and Vellino, A. *Prolog Programming in Depth*. Englewood Cliffs, NJ: Prentice-Hall, 1997.

Deitel, H. M., and Deitel, P. J. *C: How to Program,* 4th ed. Englewood Cliffs, NJ: Prentice-Hall, 2004.

Feldman, M., and Koffman, E. *Ada 95: Problem Solving and Program Design,* 3rd ed. Reading, MA: Addison-Wesley, 1999.

Friedman, F., and Koffman, E. *Problem Solving, Abstraction, and Design Using C++,* 4th ed. Reading, MA: Addison-Wesley, 2004.

Grillmeyer, O. *Exploring Computer Science with Scheme.* Heidelberg, Germany: Springer-Verlag, 1997.

Hanly, J. R., and Koffman, E. *Problem Solving and Program Design in C,* 4th ed. Reading, MA: Addison-Wesley, 2004.

Lambert, K.; Nance, D.; and Naps, T. *Introduction to Computer Science with C++,* 2nd ed. Pacific Grove, CA: Brooks/Cole, 2000.

   Professor Lambert is one of the coauthors of the laboratory manual and software that accompany this text.

Morrison, M. *HTML & XML for Beginners*. Redmond, WA: Microsoft Press, 2001.

Nyhoff, L., and Leestma, S. *Introduction to FORTRAN 90*. 2nd ed. Englewood Cliffs, NJ: Prentice-Hall, 1999.

Pohl, I. *C# by Dissection, The Essentials of C# Programming*. Reading, MA: Addison-Wesley, 2003.

Savitch, W. *Problem Solving with C++: The Object of Programming,* 4th ed. Reading, MA: Addison-Wesley, 2003.

Stern, N.; Stern, R.; and Ley, J.; *COBOL for the 21st Century,* 10th ed. New York: Wiley, 2003.

The following books offer more advanced discussions on the theory and issues behind programming language design and implementation.

Pratt, T. W., and Zelkowitz, M. *Programming Languages: Design and Implementation,* 4th ed. Englewood Cliffs, NJ: Prentice-Hall, 2001.

Sebesta, R. W. *Concepts of Programming Languages,* 6th ed. Reading, MA: Addison-Wesley, 2004.

CHAPTER 10

Compilers and Language Translation

The previous two chapters described a number of high-level languages that differ widely in structure and behavior. Although quite different in design, they are, however, all identical in one respect: No computer in the world can understand them. There are no "Java computers" or "C++ processors" that can execute programs directly in the high-level languages of Chapters 8 and 9. In Chapter 6 we learned that assembly language must be translated into machine language prior to execution. High-level languages must also be translated into machine language prior to execution—this time by a special piece of system software called a **compiler.** Compilers for languages like those discussed in Chapters 8 and 9 are very complex programs. They contain thousands of lines of code and require dozens of person-years to complete. Unlike the assemblers of Chapter 6, these translators are definitely not easy to design or implement.

There is a simple explanation for the vast difference in complexity between assemblers and compilers. Assembly language and machine language are related *one to one*; that is, one assembly language instruction produces exactly one machine language instruction. In this case, translation is really a replacement process in which the assembler looks up a symbolic value in a table (either the op code table or the symbol table) and replaces it by its numeric equivalent:

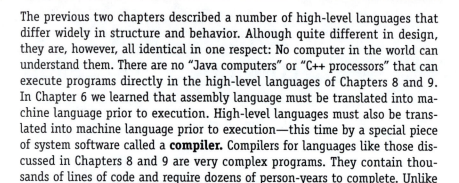

This is equivalent to translating English into Spanish by looking up each individual English word in an English/Spanish dictionary and replacing it with exactly one Spanish word:

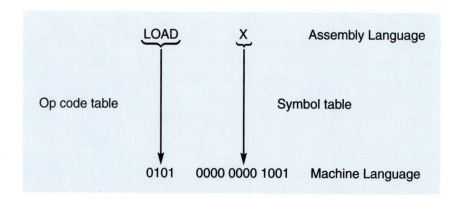

This is a book.

Este es un libro.

This is a simple way to do translation, and this approach does work for assemblers. Unfortunately, it does not work for most English sentences. Often, a single English word must be translated into a multiword Spanish phrase or vice versa. This same problem exists in the translation of high-level programming languages like Java or C++.

The relationship between a high-level language and machine language is not one to one but *one to many*. That is, one high-level language statement, such as an assignment or conditional, usually produces *many* machine language or assembly language instructions. For example,

Java		**Assembly Language**
a = b + c − d;	→	LOAD B
		ADD C
		SUBTRACT D
		STORE A

To determine which machine language instructions must be generated, a compiler cannot simply look up a name in a table. Instead, it must do a thorough linguistic analysis of the structure (syntax) and meaning (semantics) of each high-level language statement. This is far more difficult than table lookup, and writing a compiler can be a daunting task, not unlike building the operating systems discussed in Chapter 6. In fact, building a compiler for a modern high-level programming language can be one of the most difficult of system software projects.

When performing a translation, a compiler has two distinct goals. The first is **correctness.** The machine language code produced by the compiler must do exactly what the high-level language statement describes, and nothing else. For example, here is a typical Java assignment statement:

```
A = (B + C) - (D + E);
```

Assume that a compiler translates this statement into the following assembly language code:

```
-- Compute the term (B + C)
LOAD B      -- Register R holds the value of B
ADD C       -- Now it holds the result (B + C)
STORE B     -- Let's store the result temporarily in B (see comments below)
-- Next compute the term (D + E)
LOAD D      -- Register R holds the value of D
```

```
ADD E        -- Now it holds the result (D + E)
STORE D      -- Let's store the result temporarily in D (see comments below)
-- Finally, subtract the two terms and store the result in A
LOAD B       -- This loads (B + C)
SUBTRACT D   -- This is (B + C) − (D + E)
STORE A      -- Put the result in A. We are done translating the statement.
```

This translation is *wrong*. Although the code does evaluate $(B + C) − (D + E)$ and store the result into A, it does two things it should not do. The translated program destroys the original contents of the variables B and D when it does the first two STORE operations. This is *not* what the Java assignment statement is supposed to do, and this compiler has produced an incorrect translation. All of its efforts to translate this statement into machine language have been for naught.

In addition to correctness, a compiler has a second goal. The code it produces should be reasonably **efficient and concise.** Even though memory costs have come down and processors are much faster, programmers will not accept gross inefficiencies in either execution speed or size of the compiled program. They may not care whether a compiler eliminates every wasted microsecond or every unnecessary memory cell, but they do want it to produce reasonably fast and efficient machine language code. For example, to compute the sum $2x_0 + 2x_1 + 2x_2 + \ldots + 2x_{50000}$, an inexperienced programmer might write something like the following:

```
sum = 0.0;
i = 0;
while (i <= 50000)    {
        sum = sum + (2.0 * x[i]);
        i = i + 1;
}
```

This loop includes the time-consuming multiplication operation $(2.0 * x[i])$. By the rules of arithmetic, this operation can be moved outside the loop and done just once. A "smart" compiler should recognize this and translate the previous fragment as though it had been written as follows:

```
sum = 0.0;
i = 0;
while (i <= 50000)    {
        sum = sum + x[i];
        i = i + 1;
};
sum = sum * 2.0;
```

By restructuring the loop, a smart compiler saves 49,999 unnecessary multiplications.

As you can see, we have our work cut out for us in this chapter. We want to describe how to construct a compiler that can read and interpret high-level language statements, understand what they are trying to do, correctly translate their intentions into machine language without errors or unexpected side

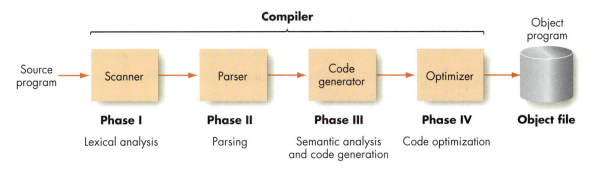

Compiler

Source program → Scanner → Parser → Code generator → Optimizer → Object program

Phase I — Lexical analysis
Phase II — Parsing
Phase III — Semantic analysis and code generation
Phase IV — Code optimization
Object file

FIGURE 10.1
General Structure of a Compiler

effects, and do all of this cleverly and efficiently. Building a compiler is a major undertaking.

The remainder of this chapter gives an overview of the steps involved in building a compiler for a procedural, Java- or C++-like language. No single chapter could investigate the subtleties and complexities of this huge subject. We can, however, give you an appreciation for some of the issues and concepts involved in designing and implementing this important piece of system software.

10.2   The Compilation Process

The general structure of a compiler is shown in Figure 10.1. However, there is a good deal of variability in the design and organization of a compiler, so this diagram should be viewed more as an idealized model than as an exact description of how all compilers are structured.

The four phases of compilation listed in Figure 10.1 are

- *Phase I: Lexical analysis.* Here is where the compiler examines the individual characters in the source program and groups them into syntactical units, called tokens, that will be analyzed in succeeding stages. This operation is analogous to grouping letters into words prior to analyzing text.

- *Phase II: Parsing.* During this stage the sequence of tokens formed by the scanner is checked to see whether it is syntactically correct according to the rules of the programming language. This phase is roughly equivalent to checking whether the words in the text form grammatically correct sentences.

- *Phase III: Semantic analysis and code generation.* If the high-level language statement is structurally correct, then the compiler analyzes its meaning and generates the proper sequence of machine language instructions to carry out these actions.

- *Phase IV: Code optimization.* During this phase the compiler takes the generated code and sees whether it can be made more efficient, either by making it run faster or having it occupy less memory.

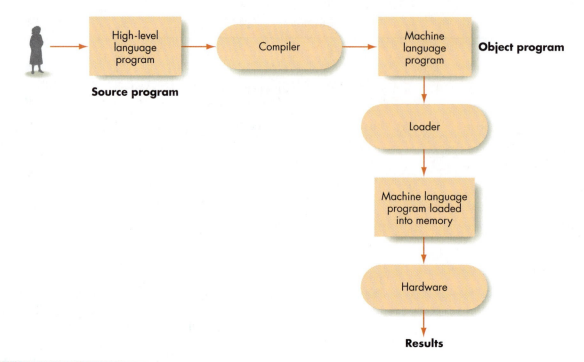

Source program

Object program

FIGURE 10.2

Overall Execution Sequence on a High-level Language Program

When these four phases are complete, we will have a correct and efficient machine language translation of the original high-level language **source program.** In the final step this machine language code, called the **object program,** is written to an **object file.** We have reached the stage labeled "Machine language program" in Figure 6.4, and the resulting object program can be handled in exactly the fashion shown in that figure. That is, it can be loaded into memory and executed by the processor to produce the desired results.

The overall sequence of operations performed on a high-level language program is summarized in Figure 10.2. The following sections take a closer look at each of the four phases of the compilation process.

 ### 10.2.1 *Phase I: Lexical Analysis*

The first step in the compilation process is **lexical analysis,** and the program that performs it is called, appropriately enough, a **lexical analyzer,** although it is more commonly termed a **scanner.** Its job is to group input characters into units called **tokens.** These are syntactical units that are treated as single, indivisible entities for the purposes of translation. For example, take a look at the following assignment statement:

```
a = b + 319 - delta;
```

Your eyes probably saw an assignment statement containing some symbols (*a, b, delta*), a number (319), and some operators (=, +, −, ;). However, your eyes and your brain actually had to do a great deal of processing to create these objects, just as they have to do a great deal of processing to create words, sentences, and paragraphs from the individual characters on this page. In the assignment statement shown above, high-level linguistic objects such as symbols and numbers do not yet exist. Initially, there are only the following 21 characters:

tab, a, blank, =, blank, b, blank, +, blank, 3, 1, 9, blank, −,
blank, d, e, l, t, a, ;

It is the task of the scanner to discard nonessential characters, such as blanks and tabs, and then group the remaining characters into high-level syntactical units such as symbols, numbers, and operators. In the example shown above, a scanner would construct the following eight tokens:

a

=

b

+

319

−

delta

;

From now on, our compiler will no longer have to deal with individual characters. Instead, it can work at the level of symbols (*a, b, delta*), numbers (319), and operators (+, −, =).

In addition to building tokens, a scanner must classify tokens as to their type—that is, is it a symbol, a number, an assignment operator? While a modern high-level language like C++ or Java may have 50 or more different token types, our simple examples will be limited to the eleven classifications listed in Figure 10.3.

The scanner assigns the classification number 1 to all legal symbols, such as *a, b,* and *delta.* Similarly, all numbers, regardless of their specific value, are assigned classification number 2. The reason why all symbols and all numbers

FIGURE 10.3

Typical Token Classifications

TOKEN TYPE	CLASSIFICATION NUMBER
symbol	1
number	2
=	3
+	4
−	5
;	6
==	7
if	8
else	9
(	10
)	11

can be grouped into a single classification is that the grammatical correctness of a statement depends only on whether a legal symbol or a legal number appears in a given location. It does not depend on exactly which symbol or which number is actually used. For example, given the following model of an assignment statement:

"symbol" = *"symbol"* + *"number"*;

it is possible to state that this assignment statement is syntactically correct, regardless of which specific "symbol" and "number" are actually used (as long as they are all legal).

Using the token types and classification values shown in Figure 10.3, it is now possible to describe exactly what a scanner must do:

The input to a scanner is a high-level language statement from the source program. Its output is a list of all the tokens contained in that statement, as well as the classification number of each token found.

Here are some examples (using the classification values shown in Figure 10.3):

Input:	$a = b + 319 - delta;$	
Output:	*Token*	*Classification*
	a	1
	=	3
	b	1
	+	4
	319	2
	−	5
	delta	1
	;	6

Input:	**if** (*a* = = *b*) *xx* = 13; **else** *xx* = 2;	
Output:	*Token*	*Classification*
	if	8
	(	10
	a	1
	= =	7
	b	1
	)	11
	xx	1
	=	3
	13	2
	;	6
	else	9

xx	1
=	3
2	2
;	6

Regardless of which programming language is being analyzed, every scanner does virtually the same set of operations: (1) it discards blanks and other nonessential characters looking for the beginning of a token; (2) when it finds the beginning, it puts characters together until (3) it detects the end of the token, at which point it classifies the token and begins looking for the next one. This algorithm works properly regardless of what the tokens look like.

We can see this process more clearly by looking at an algorithm for grouping natural language characters into words:

This is English.
Este es Espanol.
Kore wa Nihongo desu.

Even though these three sentences are in different languages, the algorithm for constructing words is identical: (1) discard blanks until you find a non-blank character; (2) group characters together until (3) you encounter either a blank or the character ".". You have now built a word. Go back to step 1 and repeat the entire sequence to locate the next word. This is essentially the same algorithm that is used to build a lexical scanner for high-level programming languages.

PRACTICE PROBLEMS

Using the token types and classification numbers given in Figure 10.3, determine the output of a scanner given the following input statements:

a. $x = x + 1;$
b. if $(a + b42 = = 0)$ $a = zz - 12;$

 ## 10.2.2 *Phase II: Parsing*

INTRODUCTION. During the parsing phase, a compiler determines whether the tokens recognized by the scanner during phase I fit together in a grammatically meaningful way. That is, it determines whether they are a syntactically legal statement of the programming language. This step is analogous to the operation of "diagramming a sentence" that is taught in elementary school. For example, to prove that the sequence of words

The man bit the dog

is a correctly formed sentence, we must show that the individual words can be grouped together structurally to form a proper English language sentence:

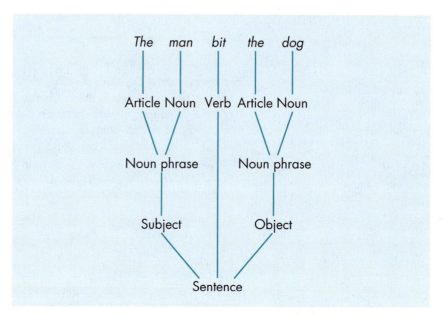

If we are unable to diagram the sentence, then it is not correctly formed. For example, when we try to analyze the sequence, "The man bit the", here is what happens:

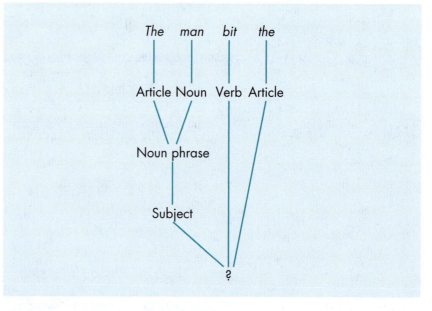

At this point in the analysis we are stuck, because there is no object for the verb "bit." We cannot diagram the sentence and must conclude that it is not properly formed.

The same thing happens with statements in a programming language, which are roughly analogous to sentences in a natural language. If a compiler is able to "diagram" a statement such as $a = b + c$, it concludes that the statement is structurally correct:

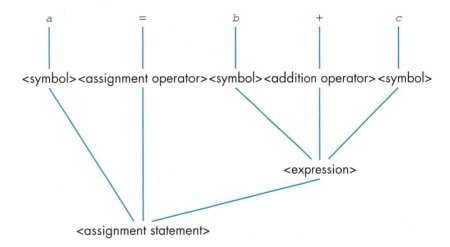

The structure shown above is called a **parse tree.** It starts from the individual tokens in the statement, *a,* =, *b,* +, and *c,* and shows how these tokens can be grouped into predefined grammatical categories such as <symbol>, <assignment operator>, and <expression> until the desired goal is reached—in this case, <assignment statement>. (We will explain shortly why we are writing the names of these grammatical categories inside the angle brackets "<" and ">".) The successful construction of a parse tree is proof that this statement is correctly formed according to the rules of the language. If a parser cannot produce such a parse tree, then the statement is not correctly formed.

In the field of compiler design, the process of diagramming a high-level language statement is called **parsing,** and it is done by a program called a parser. The output of a parser is a parse tree, if such a tree exists, or an error message if one cannot be constructed.

GRAMMARS, LANGUAGES, AND BNF. How does a parser know how to construct the parse tree? What tells it how the pieces of a language fit together? For example, in the statement shown above, you might wonder how the parser knows that the format of an assignment statement in our language is

    <symbol> = <expression>

The answer is that it does not know; we must tell it. The parser must be given a formal description of the **syntax**—the grammatical structure—of the language that it is going to analyze. The most widely used notation for representing the syntax of a programming language is called **BNF,** an acronym for **Backus-Naur Form,** named after its designers John Backus and Peter Naur.

In BNF, the syntax of a language is specified as a set of **rules,** also called **productions.** The entire collection of rules is called a **grammar.** Each individual BNF rule looks like this:

    left-hand side ::= "definition"

The **left-hand side** of a BNF rule is the name of a single grammatical category, such as <symbol>, <expression>, or <assignment statement>. The BNF operator ::= means "is defined as" and "definition," which is also called the **right-hand side,** specifies the grammatical structure of the symbol appearing on the left-hand side of the rule. The definition may contain any number of objects. For example, here is a BNF rule that defines how an <assignment statement> is formed:

<assignment statement> ::= <symbol> = <expression>

This rule says that the syntactical construct called <assignment statement> is defined as a <symbol> followed by the token = followed by the syntactical construct called <expression>. In order to have a structurally correct assignment statement, these three objects must all be present in exactly that order.

A BNF rule that gives one possible definition for the English language construct called <sentence> follows.

<sentence> ::= <subject> <verb> <object>

This rule says that a <sentence> is defined as a <subject> followed by a <verb> followed by an <object>. It is this rule that allowed us to parse "The man bit the dog".

Finally, the simple BNF rule

<addition operator> ::= +

says that the grammatical construct <addition operator> is defined as the single character +.

If a parser is analyzing a statement in a language and it sees exactly the same sequence of objects that appears on the right-hand side of a BNF rule, it is allowed to replace them with the one grammatical object on the left-hand side of that rule. For example, given our BNF rule for <assignment statement>:

<assignment statement> ::= <symbol> = <expression>

if a parser encounters the three objects <symbol>, =, and <expression> next to each other in the input, it can replace them with the object appearing on the left-hand side of the rule—in this case, <assignment statement>. In a sense, the parser is constructing one branch of the parse tree, which looks like this:

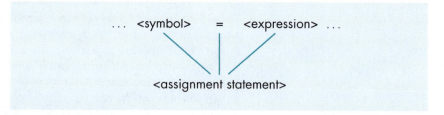

We say that the three objects, <symbol>, =, and <expression>, **produce** the grammatical category called <assignment statement>, and that is why a BNF rule is also called a **production.**

BNF rules use two different types of objects, called terminals and nonterminals, on the right-hand side of a production. **Terminals** are the actual tokens of the language recognized and returned by a scanner. The terminals of our language are the 11 tokens listed in Figure 10.3:

<symbol>	==
<number>	**if**
=	**else**
+	(
−	)
;	

The important characteristic of terminals is that they are not defined any further by other rules of the grammar. That is, there is no rule in the grammar that explains the "meaning" of such objects as <symbol>, =, +, and **if.** They are simply elements of the language, much like the words man, bit, and dog in our earlier example.

The second type of object used in a BNF rule is a **nonterminal.** A nonterminal is not an actual element of the language but an intermediate grammatical category used to help explain and organize the language. For example, in the analysis of the English sentence, "The man bit the dog," we created grammatical categories called article, noun, verb, noun phrase, subject, and object. These categories help us to understand the structure of the sentence and show that it is correctly formed, but they are not actual words of the sentence being studied.

In every grammar, there is one special nonterminal called the **goal symbol.** This is the highest-level nonterminal, and it is the nonterminal object that the parser is trying to produce as it builds the parse tree. When the parser has produced the goal symbol using all the elements of the sentence or statement, it has proved the syntactical correctness of the sentence or statement being analyzed. In our English language example, the goal symbol is <sentence>; in our assignment statement example, it is, naturally, <assignment statement>. When this nonterminal goal symbol has been produced, the parser has finished building the tree, and the statement has been successfully parsed. The collection of all statements that can be successfully parsed is called the **language** defined by a grammar.

All nonterminals are written inside angle brackets; examples include <expression> and <assignment statement>. Some terminals also are written in angle brackets when they do not represent actual characters of the language but rather groups of characters constructed by the scanner, such as <symbol> or <number>. However, it is easy to tell the difference between the two. A terminal like <symbol> is not defined by any other rule of the language. That is, there is no rule anywhere in the grammar that looks like this:

<symbol> ::= "definition of a symbol"

Terminal symbols are like the words and punctuation marks of a language, and a parser does not have to know anything more about their syntactical structure in order to analyze a sentence.

However, nonterminals are constructed by the parser from more elementary syntactical units. Therefore, nonterminals such as <expression> and <assignment statement> must be further defined by one or more rules that specify exactly how this nonterminal is constructed. For example, there must exist at least one rule in our grammar that has the nonterminal <expression> as the left-hand side. This rule tells the parser how to form expressions from other terminals and nonterminals:

<expression> ::= "definition of expression"

Similarly, there must be at least one rule that specifies the structure of an assignment statement:

<assignment statement> ::= "definition of assignment statement"

We can summarize the difference between terminals and nonterminals by saying that terminals never appear on the left-hand side of a BNF rule, whereas nonterminals must appear on the left-hand side of one or more rules.

The three symbols <, >, and ::= used as part of BNF rules are termed **metasymbols.** This means that they are symbols of one language (BNF) that are being used to describe the characteristics of another language. In addition to these three, there are two other metasymbols used in BNF definitions. The vertical bar, |, means OR, and it is used to separate two alternative definitions of a nonterminal. This could be done without the vertical bar by just writing two separate rules:

<nonterminal> ::= "definition 1"
<nonterminal> ::= "definition 2"

However, it is sometimes more convenient to use the | character and write a single rule:

<nonterminal> ::= "definition 1" | "definition 2"

For example, the rule

<arithmetic operator> ::= + | − | * | /

says that an arithmetic operator is defined as either a + or a − or a * or a /. Without the | operator, we would need to write four separate rules, which would make the grammar much larger. Here is a rule that defines the nonterminal <digit>:

<digit> ::= 0 | 1 | 2 | 3 | 4 | 5 | 6 | 7 | 8 | 9

We will see many more examples of the use of the OR operator.

The final metasymbol used in BNF definitions is the Greek character lambda, Λ, which represents the **null string**—nothing at all. It is possible that a nonterminal can be "empty," and the symbol Λ is used to indicate this. For example, the nonterminal <signed integer> can be defined as an optional sign preceding an integer value, such as +7 or −5 or 8. To define the idea of an optional sign in BNF, we could say:

<signed integer> ::= <sign> <number>
<sign> ::= + | − | Λ

which says that <sign> may be either a + or a −, or it may be omitted entirely.

1. Write a single BNF rule that defines the nonterminal <Boolean operator>. (Assume that the three possible Boolean operators are AND, OR, and NOT.)

2. Create a BNF grammar that describes all 1- or 2-character identifiers that begin with the letter *i* or *j*. The second character, if present, can be any letter or digit. What is the goal symbol of your grammar?

3. Write a BNF grammar that describes Boolean expressions of the form

   (var op var)

   where "var" can be one of the symbols *x, y,* and *z,* and "op" can be one of the three relational operators $==$, $>$, and $<$. The parentheses are part of the expression.

4. Using the grammar created in Problem 3, show the parse tree for the expression $(x > y)$.

5. Using the grammar created in Problem 3, show what happens when you try to parse the illegal expression ($x ==$).

6. Modify your grammar from Problem 3 so that the enclosing parentheses are optional. That is, Boolean expressions can be written as either (var op var) or var op var.

PARSING CONCEPTS AND TECHNIQUES. Given this brief introduction to grammars, languages, and BNF, we can now explain how a parser works. A parser receives as input the BNF description of a high-level language and a sequence of tokens recognized by the scanner. The fundamental rule of parsing follows.

If, by repeated applications of the rules of the grammar, a parser can convert the sequence of input tokens into the goal symbol, then that sequence of tokens is a syntactically valid statement of the language. If it cannot convert the input tokens into the goal symbol, then this is not a syntactically valid statement of the language.

To illustrate this idea, here is a three-rule grammar:

Number	Rule
1	<sentence> ::= <noun> <verb> .
2	<noun> ::= bees | dogs
3	<verb> ::= buzz | bite

The grammar contains five terminals, bees, dogs, buzz, bite, and the character "." and three nonterminals, <sentence>, <noun>, and <verb>. The goal symbol is <sentence>. In addition to the grammar, we also provide a sequence of tokens such as "dogs", "bite", and ".". The parser attempts to transform these tokens into the goal symbol <sentence> using the three BNF rules given above:

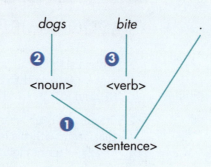

In this case the parse was successful. (The numbers in the diagram indicate which rule is being applied.) Thus, "dogs bite." is a syntactically valid sentence of the language defined by this three-rule grammar. However, the following sequence of tokens:

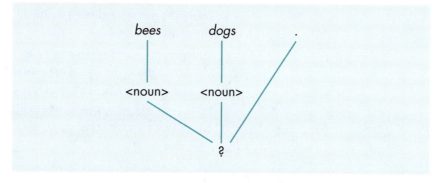

leads to a dead end. We have not yet produced the goal symbol <sentence>, but there is no rule in the grammar that can be applied to the sequence <noun> <noun> ".". That is, no sequence of terminals and nonterminals in the parse tree constructed so far matches the right-hand side of any rule. This means that "bees dogs." is not a valid sentence of this language.

Grammars for "real" high-level languages like C++ or Java are very large, containing many hundreds of productions; therefore, it is not feasible to use these grammars as examples. Even a grammar describing individual statements can be quite complex. For example, the BNF description of an assignment statement, complete with variables, constants, operators, parentheses, and procedure calls, can easily require 20 or 30 rules. Therefore, the following examples all use highly simplified "toy" languages to keep the level of detail manageable and enable us to focus on important concepts.

Our first example is a grammar for a highly simplified assignment statement in which the only operator is +, numbers are not permitted, and the only allowable variable names are x, y, and z. A first attempt at designing a grammar for this simplified assignment statement is shown in Figure 10.4.

If the input statement is x = y + z, then the parser can determine that this statement is correctly formed because it can construct a parse tree (Figure 10.5). The parse tree of Figure 10.5 is the output of the parser, and it is the information that is passed on to the next stage in the compilation process.

Building a parse tree like the one in Figure 10.5 is not as easy as it may appear. Often two or more rules of a grammar may be applied to the current

FIGURE 10.4

First Attempt at a Grammar for a Simplified Assignment Statement

NUMBER		RULE
1	<assignment statement>	::= <variable> = <expression>
2	<expression>	::= <variable> | <variable> + <variable>
3	<variable>	::= x | y | z

FIGURE 10.5

Parse Tree Produced by the Parser

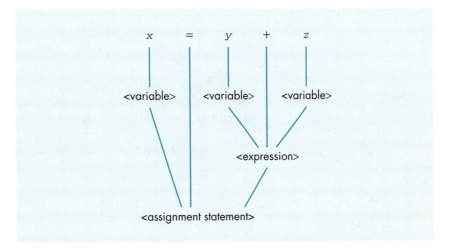

input string, and the parser is not sure which one to choose. For example, assume that our grammar includes the following two rules:

Number	Rule
1	<t1> ::= A B
2	<t2> ::= B C

and that the statement being parsed contains the three-character string . . . A B C . . . . We could apply either rule 1:

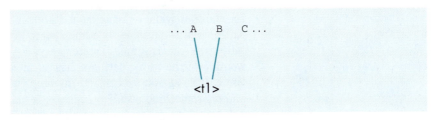

or rule 2:

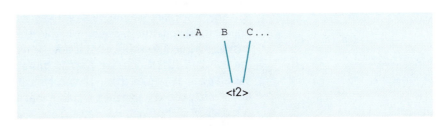

One of these choices may be correct, whereas the other may lead down a grammatical dead end, and the parser has no idea which is which.

You were probably not aware that an identical situation occurred in the example shown in Figure 10.5. Assume that the parser has reached this position in building the parse tree for the statement $x = y + z$:

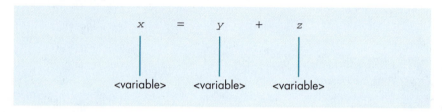

In Figure 10.5, the parser next grouped the three objects <variable>, +, and <variable> into an <expression> using rule 2. However, at this point the parser has other options. For example, it could choose to parse the nonterminal <variable> generated from the symbol y to <expression> using rule 2 and then parse the sequence <variable> = <expression> to <assignment statement> using rule 1. This produces the following parse tree:

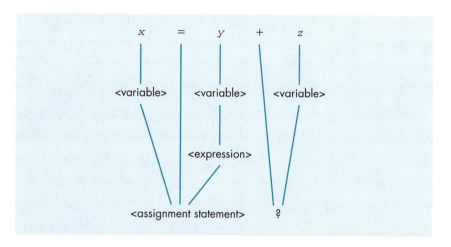

Unfortunately, this was the wrong choice. Although the parser did generate the goal symbol <assignment statement>, it did not use all of the tokens. An extra plus sign and <variable> were not used. (What it did was accidentally parse the assignment statement $x = y$ instead of $x = y + z$.) The parser went down the wrong path and has reached a point where it is unable to continue. It must now go back to the point where it made the incorrect choice and try something else. For example, it might choose to parse the nonterminal <variable> generated from z to <expression> using rule 2. Unfortunately, this is also a dead end; it produces the sequence <variable> + <expression>, which does not match the right-hand side of any rule.

The process of parsing is a complex sequence of applying rules, building grammatical constructs, seeing whether things are moving toward the correct answer (the goal symbol), and, if not, "undoing" the rule just applied and trying another. It is much like finding one's way through a maze. You try one path and if it works, fine. If not, you back up to where you made your last choice and try another, hoping that this time it will lead in the right direction.

This sounds like a haphazard and disorganized way to analyze statements, and in fact it is. However, "real" parsing algorithms don't rely on a random selection of rules, as our previous discussion may have implied. Instead, they try to be a little more clever in their choices by looking ahead to see whether the rule they plan to apply will or will not help them to reach the goal. For example, assume we have the following input sequence:

A B C

and this grammar:

<goal> ::= <term> C
<term> ::= A B | B C

We have two choices on how to parse the input string. We can either group the two characters A B to form a <term>, or we can group B C instead. A totally random choice will cause us to be wrong about half the time, but if a parser is clever and looks ahead, it can do a lot better. It is easy to see that grouping B C to produce the nonterminal <term> leads to trouble, because there is no rule telling us what to do with the sequence A <term>. We quickly come to a dead end:

However, by choosing to group the tokens A B into <term> instead of B C, the parser quickly produces a correct parse tree:

There are many well-known **look-ahead parsing algorithms** that use the ideas just described. These algorithms "look down the road" a few tokens to see what would happen if a certain choice were made. This helps keep the parse moving in the right direction, and it significantly reduces the number of false starts and dead ends. These algorithms can do very efficient parsing, even for large languages with hundreds of rules.

There is another important issue in the design of grammars. Let's assume we attempt to parse the following assignment statement:

$x = x + y + z$

using the grammar in Figure 10.4. No matter how hard we try to build a parse tree, it is just not possible:

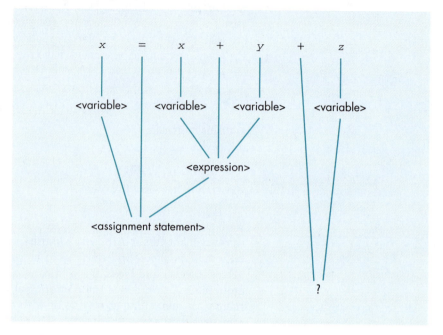

All other attempts lead to a similar fate.

The problem is that the grammar in Figure 10.4 does not correctly describe the desired language. We wanted a language that allowed expressions containing an *arbitrary number* of plus signs. However, the grammar of Figure 10.4 describes a language in which expressions may contain at most a single addition operator. More complicated expressions such as $x + y + z$ cannot be parsed, and they are erroneously excluded from our language.

One of the biggest problems in building a compiler for a programming language is designing a grammar that

- Includes every valid statement that we want to be in the language
- Excludes every invalid statement that we do not want to be in the language

In this case, a statement that should be a part of our language ($x = x + y + z$) was excluded. If this statement were contained in a program, the parser would not recognize it and would not be able to translate it into machine language. The grammar in Figure 10.4 is wrong in the sense that it does not define the language that we want.

Let's redo the grammar of Figure 10.4 so that it describes an assignment statement that allows expressions containing an arbitrary number of occurrences of the plus sign. That is, our language will include such statements as

$$x = x + y + z$$
$$x = x + y + x + y + x + z + z$$

This second attempt at a grammar is shown in Figure 10.6, on page 498.

The grammar in Figure 10.6 does recognize and accept expressions with more than one plus sign. For example, here is a parse tree for the statement x = x + y + z:

CHAPTER 10: Compilers and Language Translation

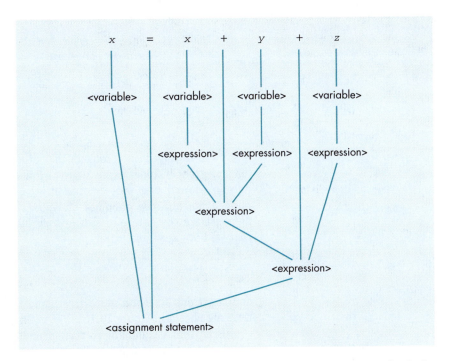

Note that rule 2 of Figure 10.6 uses the nonterminal <expression> on both the left-hand and the right-hand side of the same rule. In essence, the rule defines the nonterminal symbol <expression> in terms of itself. This is called a **recursive definition,** and its use is very common in BNF. It is recursion that allows us to describe an expression not just with one or two or three or . . . plus signs but with an *arbitrary* and *unbounded* number, as shown here.

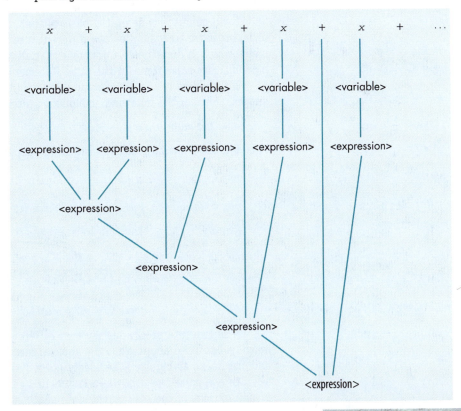

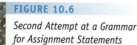

FIGURE 10.6

Second Attempt at a Grammar for Assignment Statements

RULE NUMBER	RULE
1	<assignment statement> ::= <variable> = <expression>
2	<expression> ::= <variable> | <expresssion> + <expression>
3	<variable> ::= x | y | z

We have solved one problem, that of making sure our grammar defines a language that includes expressions with multiple addition operators. Unfortunately, though one problem has disappeared, another has unexpectedly popped up, and the grammar of Figure 10.6 is still not quite correct. To demonstrate the nature of this new problem, let's take the same statement that we have been analyzing:

$$x = x + y + z$$

and construct a second parse tree using the grammar of Figure 10.6. Both trees are shown in Figure 10.7.

Using this assignment statement and the grammar in Figure 10.6, it is possible to construct *two* distinct parse trees. This may not seem to be a problem, because the construction of a parse tree has been used only to demonstrate that a statement is correctly formed. Building two parse trees would imply that the parser has demonstrated correctness in two different ways. This should be twice as good as demonstrating correctness in only one way.

However, a parse tree not only serves to demonstrate that a statement is correct; it also assigns it a specific *meaning,* or *interpretation.* The next phase of compilation will use this parse tree to understand what a statement means, and it will generate code on the basis of that meaning. The existence of two different parse trees implies two different interpretations of the same statement, which is disastrous. A grammar that allows the construction of two or more distinct parse trees for the same statement is said to be **ambiguous.**

This problem can occur in natural languages as well as programming languages. Consider the following ambiguous sentence:

I saw the man in the store with the dogs.

This sentence has two distinct meanings depending on how we choose to parse it:

Interpretation 1:   I saw the man in the *store* (with the dogs).

Meaning: The man I viewed was in a pet store that sells dogs.

Interpretation 2:   I saw the *man* in the store (with the dogs).

Meaning: The man I viewed was walking his dogs and was inside some type of store.

These two interpretations say very different things, so the sentence can leave us confused about what the speaker meant. In the areas of languages and grammars, ambiguity is decidedly not a desirable property.

The two parse trees shown in Figure 10.7 correspond to the following two interpretations of the assignment statement $x = x + y + z$.

FIGURE 10.7

Two Parse Trees for the Statement
x = x + y + z

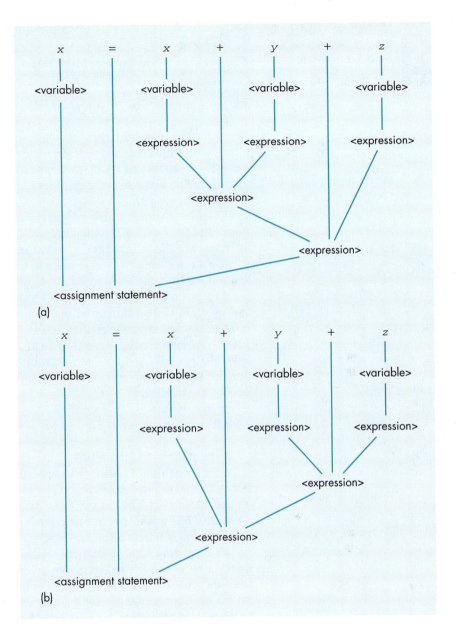

(a)

(b)

$$x = (x + y) + z \quad \text{(Do the operation } x + y \text{ first.)}$$
$$x = x + (y + z) \quad \text{(Do the operation } y + z \text{ first.)}$$

Because addition is associative—that is, $(a + b) + c = a + (b + c)$—in this case the ambiguity does not cause a serious problem. However, if the statement were changed slightly to

$$x = x - y - z$$

then these two different interpretations could lead to completely different results:

$$x = (x - y) - z \quad \text{which evaluates to } x - y - z$$
$$x = x - (y - z) \quad \text{which evaluates to } x - y + z$$

FIGURE 10.8

Third Attempt at a Grammar for Assignment Statements

RULE NUMBER	RULE
1	<assignment statement> ::= <variable> = <expression>
2	<expression> ::= <variable> | <expresssion> + <variable>
3	<variable> ::= x | y | z

We now have a situation where a statement could mean one thing using compiler C on machine M and something totally different using compiler C′ on machine M′, depending on which parse tree it happens to construct. This contradicts the spirit of machine independence, which is a basic characteristic of all high-level languages.

To solve the problem, the assignment statement grammar must be rewritten a third time so that it is no longer ambiguous. This new grammar is shown in Figure 10.8. To see that the grammar of Figure 10.8 is not ambiguous, try parsing the statement $x = x + y + z$ in the two ways shown in Figure 10.7. You will see that one of these two parse trees cannot be built.

As a second example, Figure 10.9 shows the BNF grammar for a simplified version of an **if-else** statement that allows only a single assignment statement in the two separate clauses and allows the **else** clause to be omitted. The <Boolean expression> can include at most a single use of the relational operators ==, <, and >. The nonterminal <assignment statement> is defined in the same way as in Figure 10.8. Figure 10.10 then shows the parse tree for the statement

```
if (x == y) x = z;   else x = y;
```

using the grammar of Figure 10.9.

Even though this **if-else** statement has been greatly simplified, its grammar still requires seven rules, and its parse trees are quite "bushy." Grammars for real statements, not our toy ones, can rapidly become large and complicated, and BNF grammars for programming languages like C++ and Java can contain many hundreds of productions.

We have progressed a long way from our original input file, which was simply a sequence of characters. Our compiler has produced a set of tokens and built a parse tree showing how these tokens form a grammatically correct statement. However, we are not yet finished, because we still do not have the necessary end product of compilation—the translated machine language program. That happens in the next stage.

FIGURE 10.9

*Grammar for a Simplified Version of an **if-else** Statement*

NUMBER	RULE
1	<if statement> ::= **if** (<Boolean expression>) <assignment statement> ; <else clause>
2	<Boolean expression> ::= <variable> | <variable> <relational> <variable>
3	<relational> ::= == | < | >
4	<variable> ::= x | y | z
5	<else clause> ::= **else** <assignment statement> ; | Λ
6	<assignment statement> ::= <variable> = <expression>
7	<expression> ::= <variable> | <expression> + <variable>

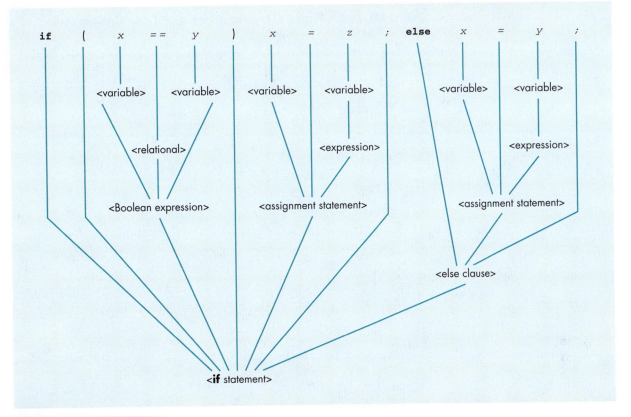

FIGURE 10.10

Parse Tree for the Statement **if**
$(x == y)$ x = z; **else** x = y;

PRACTICE PROBLEMS

1. Using the grammar of Figure 10.8, show the parse tree for the assignment statement

   x = x + y

2. Using the grammar of Figure 10.8, show the parse tree for the assignment statement

   x = x + y + z

3. Using the grammar of Figure 10.9, show the parse tree for the statement

   if (x > y) x = y;

4. Tell what language is described by the following pair of rules:

   ```
   <string> ::= <character> | <character> <string>
   <character> ::= a | b
   ```

5. Write a BNF grammar that describes strings containing any number of repetitions of the character pair AB. That is, all of the following strings are part of the language: AB ABAB ABABAB ABABABABAB . . .

Let's look back at one of the example grammars used in the previous section:

```
<sentence> ::= <noun> <verb> .
<noun> ::= dogs | bees
<verb> ::= bite | bark
```

The language defined by this grammar contains exactly four sentences:

> dogs bite.
>
> dogs bark.
>
> bees bite.
>
> bees bark.

For each of these four sentences, we can construct a parse tree showing that it is (structurally, at least) a valid sentence of the language:

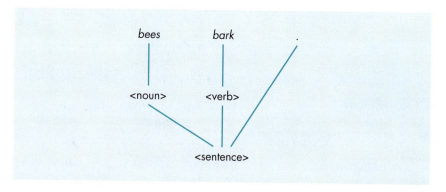

There is one problem, though. Although the sentence "bees bark." is structurally valid, it makes no sense whatsoever! During parsing, a compiler deals only with the **syntax** of a statement—that is, its grammatical structure. At that point, the only "correctness" that a compiler can determine is grammatical correctness with respect to the syntactical rules of the language. Another example of this limitation is the sentence, "The man bit the dog." This sentence was shown to be structurally correct, but in terms of meaning it is somewhat unusual! (It certainly would be news.)

This problem is dealt with during the next phase of translation. During this phase, a compiler examines the semantics of a programming language statement. It analyzes the meaning of the tokens and tries to understand the *actions* they perform. If the statement is meaningless, as "bees bark." is, then it is semantically rejected, even though it is syntactically correct. If the statement is meaningful, then the compiler translates it into machine language.

It is easy to give examples of English-language sentences that are syntactically correct but semantically meaningless:

The orange artichoke flew through the elephant.

But what are semantically meaningless statements in high-level programming languages?

One possibility is the following assignment statement:

sum = a + b;

This is obviously correct syntactically, but what if the variables *sum, a,* and *b* are declared as follows:

```
char a;
double b;
int sum;
```

What does it mean to add a character to a real number? What would possibly be the result of adding the letter *Q* to 3.1416? In most cases this operation has no meaning, and perhaps it should be rejected as semantically invalid.

To check for this semantic error, a compiler must look at the parse tree to see whether there is a branch that looks something like this:

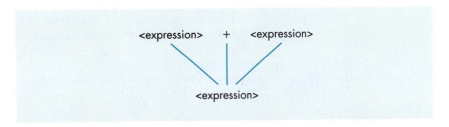

If there is such a branch, then the compiler must examine the data types of the two expressions being added to see whether they "make sense." That is, it must determine whether addition is defined for the data types of the two expressions.

The compiler does this by examining the **semantic records** associated with each nonterminal symbol in the grammar, such as <expression> and <variable>. A semantic record is a data structure that stores information about a nonterminal, such as the actual name of the object and its data type. For example, the nonterminal <variable> might have been constructed from the actual character variable named CH. This relationship would be represented by a link between the nonterminal <variable> and a semantic record containing the name CH and its data type, char. Pictorially, we would represent this link as follows:

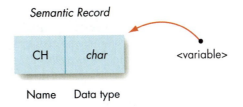

The initial semantic records in our parse tree would be built by the compiler when it saw the declarations of new objects. Additional semantic records would be constructed as the parse tree grew and new nonterminals were produced. Thus, a more realistic picture of the parse tree for the expression a + b (assuming both are declared as integers) might look like this:

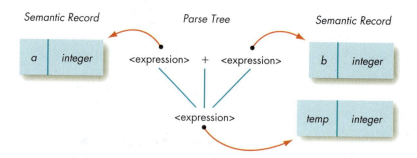

This parse tree says that we are adding two <expression>s that are integer variables named *a* and *b*. The result will be an <expression> stored in the integer variable *temp*, a name picked by the compiler. Because addition is well defined for integers, this operation makes perfectly good sense, and the compiler can generate machine language instructions to carry out this addition. If, however, the parse tree and its associated semantic records looked like this:

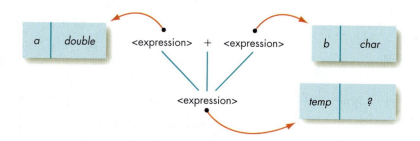

the compiler could determine that this is not a meaningful operation, because addition is not defined between a real number and a character. The compiler would reject this parse tree for semantic rather than syntactical reasons.

Thus, the first part of code generation involves a pass over the parse tree to determine whether all branches of the tree are semantically valid. If so, then the compiler can generate machine language instructions. If not, there is a semantic error, and generation of the machine language is suppressed because we do not want the processor to execute meaningless code. This step is called **semantic analysis.**

Following semantic analysis, the compiler makes a second pass over the parse tree, not to determine correctness but to produce the translated code. Each branch of the parse tree represents an action, a transformation of one or more grammatical objects into another. The compiler must determine how that transformation can be accomplished in machine language. This step is called **code generation.**

Let's work through the complete semantic analysis and code generation process using the parse tree for our old standby, the assignment statement *x = y + z*, where *x*, *y*, and *z* are all integers. The example uses the instruction set shown in Figure 6.5.

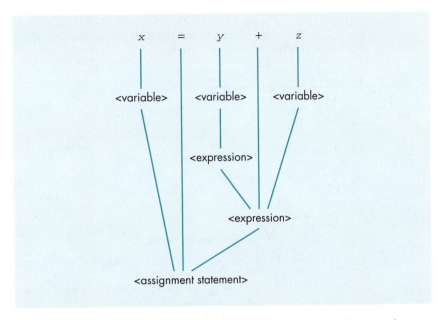

Typically, code generation begins at the productions in the tree that are nearest to the original input tokens. The compiler takes each production and, one branch at a time, translates that production into machine language operations or data generation pseudo-ops. For example, the following branch in the parse tree:

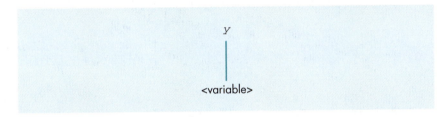

could be implemented by allocating space for the variable y using the .DATA pseudo-op

    Y: .DATA   0

In addition to generating this pseudo-op, the compiler must build the initial semantic record associated with the nonterminal <variable>. This semantic record will contain, at a minimum, the name of this <variable>, which is y, and its data type, which is integer. (The data type information comes from the **int** declaration, which is not shown.) Here is what is produced after analyzing and translating the first branch of the parse tree:

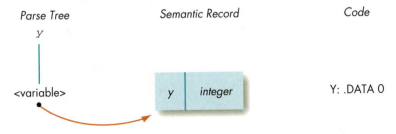

Identical operations are done for the branches of the parse tree that produce the nonterminal <variable> from the symbols x and z, leading to the following situation:

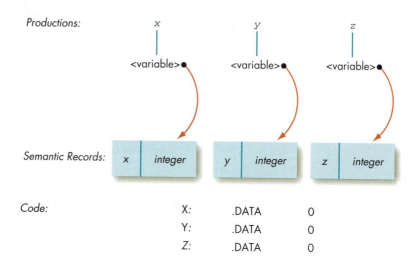

Productions:

Semantic Records:

Code:

X:	.DATA	0
Y:	.DATA	0
Z:	.DATA	0

The production that transforms the nonterminal <variable> generated from y into the nonterminal <expression>:

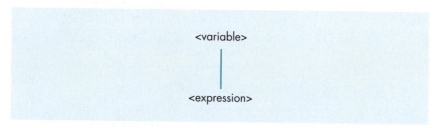

does not generate any machine language code. This branch of the tree is really just the renaming of a nonterminal to avoid the ambiguity problem discussed earlier. This demonstrates an important point: although most branches of a parse tree produce code, some do not. However, even though no code is produced, the compiler must still create a semantic record for the new nonterminal <expression>. It is identical to the one built for the nonterminal <variable>.

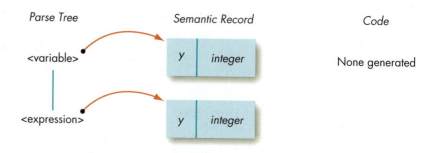

The branch of the parse tree that implements addition:

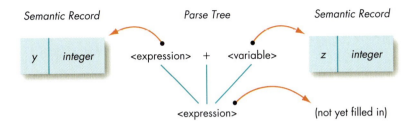

can be translated into machine language using the assembly language instruction set presented in Section 6.3.2. The compiler loads the value of <expression> into a register, adds the value of <variable>, and stores the resulting <expression> into a temporary memory location. This can be accomplished using the LOAD, ADD, and STORE operations in our instruction set. The names to use in the address field of the instructions can be determined by looking in the semantic records associated with the nonterminals <expression> and <variable> . The code generated by this branch of the parse tree is

```
LOAD    Y
ADD     Z
STORE   TEMP
```

TEMP is the name of a memory cell picked by the compiler to hold the result (Y + Z). Whenever the compiler creates one of these temporary variables, it must also remember to generate memory space for it using the DATA pseudo-op

```
TEMP:    .DATA    0
```

In addition, the compiler records the name (TEMP) and the data type (*integer*) of the result in the semantic record associated with this new nonterminal called <expression>. Here is what is produced by this branch of the parse tree:

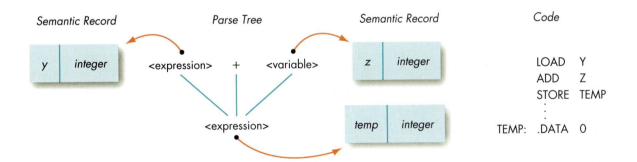

The final branch of the parse tree builds the nonterminal called <assignment statement>:

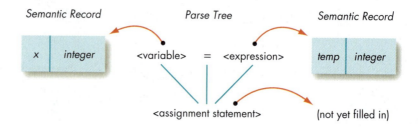

Semantic Record   Parse Tree   Semantic Record

| x | integer | <variable> = <expression> | temp | integer |

<assignment statement>   (not yet filled in)

This production is translated into machine language by loading the value of the <expression> on the right-hand side of the assignment operator, using a LOAD instruction, and storing it, via a STORE operation, into the <variable> on the left-hand side of the assignment operator. Again, the names to use in the address fields of the machine language instructions are obtained from the semantic records associated with <variable> and <expression>. The machine language code generated by this branch of the parse tree is

```
LOAD    TEMP
STORE   X
```

The compiler must also build the semantic record associated with the newly created nonterminal <assignment statement>. The name (x) and the data type (integer) of the variable on the left-hand side of the assignment operator are copied into that semantic record because the value stored in that variable is considered the value of the entire assignment statement.

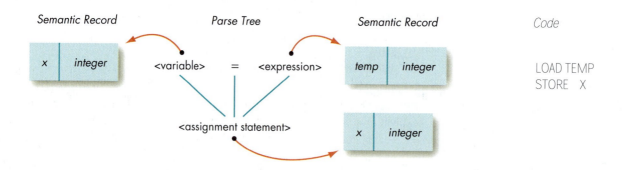

Semantic Record   Parse Tree   Semantic Record   Code

| x | integer | <variable> = <expression> | temp | integer | LOAD TEMP
STORE   X

<assignment statement> | x | integer |

Our compiler has now analyzed every branch in the parse tree, and it has produced the following translation. (We have separated the pseudo-ops and executable instructions for clarity.)

```
LOAD    Y
ADD     Z
STORE   TEMP
LOAD    TEMP
STORE   X
  .
  .
  .
```

X:	.DATA	0
Y:	.DATA	0
Z:	.DATA	0
TEMP:	.DATA	0

This is an exact translation of the assignment statement $x = y + z$. After many pages of discussion, we have achieved our original goal, the correct translation of a high-level programming language statement into machine language.

Figure 10.11 shows the code generation process for the slightly more complex assignment statement $x = x + y + z$. The branches of the parse tree are labeled and referenced by comments in the code. (The parse tree was constructed using the grammar shown in Figure 10.8.)

LABORATORY EXPERIENCE 17

In the laboratory experience for this chapter, you will see how a compiler actually translates the high-level statements you first learned in Chapter 8. You will observe as a compiler carries out each of the phases of translation de-

scribed in the preceding sections. You will see how a compiler interprets each of the three basic statement types—sequential, conditional, and iterative—and better understand how it is able to produce a correct machine language translation.

PRACTICE PROBLEM

Go through the code generation process for the simple assignment statement $x = y$. The parse tree for this statement is

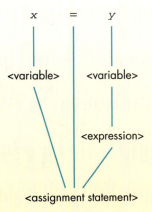

For each branch in the tree, show what semantic records are created and what code is generated.

FIGURE 10.11

Code Generation for the Assignment Statement x = x + y + z

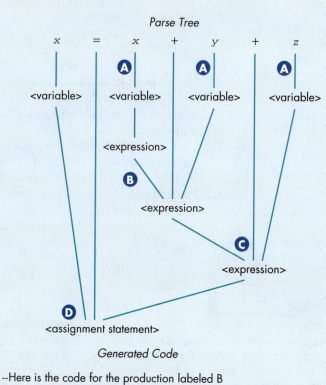

Parse Tree

Generated Code

--Here is the code for the production labeled B
    LOAD   X
    ADD   Y
    STORE   TEMP   -- Temp holds the expression (x + y)
--Here is the code for the production labeled C
    LOAD   TEMP
    ADD   Z
    STORE   TEMP2   -- Temp2 holds (x + y + z)
--Here is the code for the production labeled D
    LOAD   TEMP2
    STORE   X   -- X now holds the correct result
                     -- The remainder of the program goes here
--These next three pseudo-ops are generated by the productions labeled A
X: .DATA 0
Y: .DATA 0
Z: .DATA 0
-- The pseudo-ops for these temporary variables are generated
by productions B and C
TEMP: .DATA 0
TEMP2: .DATA 0

The code of Figure 10.11 could represent the end of the compilation process, because generating a correct machine language translation was our original goal. However, we are not quite finished. In the beginning of the chapter, we said that a compiler really has *two* goals: correctness and efficiency. The first goal has been achieved, but not necessarily the second. We have produced correct code, but not necessarily good code. Therefore, the next and final operation is **optimization,** where the compiler polishes and fine-tunes the translation so that it runs a little faster or occupies a little less memory.

10.2.4   *Phase IV: Code Optimization*

As we noted in Chapter 9, the first high-level language and compiler was FORTRAN, which appeared in 1957. (It was created by John Backus, the *B* of *BNF*.) At that time everyone programmed in assembly language because nothing else was available. Given all the shortcomings of assembly language, one would have expected programmers to flock to FORTRAN and thank their lucky stars that it was available. After all, it is certainly a lot easier to understand the statement a = b + c than the rather cryptic sequence LOAD B, ADD C, STORE A.

Surprisingly, programmers did not accept this new language very quickly. The reason had nothing to do with the power and expressiveness of FORTRAN. Everyone admitted that it was far superior to assembly language in terms of clarity and ease of use. The problem had to do with **efficiency**—the ability to write highly optimized programs that contained no wasted microseconds or unnecessary memory cells.

In 1957 (early second-generation computing), computers were still enormously expensive; they typically cost millions of dollars. Therefore, programmers cared more about avoiding wasted computing resources than simplifying their job. No one worried about the productivity of programmers earning $2.00/hour compared to optimizing the use of a multimillion-dollar computer system. In 1957 the guiding principle was "Programmers are cheap, hardware is expensive!"

When programmers used assembly language, they were working on the actual machine, not the virtual machine created by the system software (and described in Chapters 6 and 7). They were free to choose the instructions that ran most quickly or used the least amount of memory. For example, if the INCREMENT, LOAD, and STORE instructions execute in 1 μsec, whereas an ADD takes 2 μsec, then translating the assignment statement $x = x + 3$ as

INCREMENT	X	-- x +1	1 μsec
INCREMENT	X	-- x +2	1 μsec
INCREMENT	X	-- x +3	1 μsec

requires 3 μsec to execute. This code runs 25% faster than if it had been translated as

LOAD	X		1 μsec
ADD	THREE	-- x+3	2 μsec
STORE	X		1 μsec
.			
.			
.			
THREE: .DATA	3		

which takes 4 μsec to execute and requires an additional memory cell for the integer constant 3. When programmers wrote in assembly language, they were free to choose the first of these sequences rather than the second, knowing that it is faster and more compact. However, in a high-level language like FORTRAN, a programmer can only write $x = x + 3$ and hope that the compiler is "smart enough" to select the faster of the two implementations.

Because efficiency was so important to programmers of the 1950s and 1960s, these early first- and second-generation compilers spent a great deal of time doing **code optimization.** In fact Backus himself said that ". . . we did not regard language design as a difficult problem, but merely a prelude to the real problem: designing a compiler which could produce efficient programs." These compiler pioneers were quite successful in solving many of the problems of optimization, and early FORTRAN compilers produced object programs that ran nearly as fast as highly optimized assembly language code produced by topnotch programmers. After seeing these startling results, programmers of the 1950s and 1960s were eventually won over. They could gain the benefits of high-level languages—a powerful virtual environment—without loss of efficiency. The code optimization techniques developed by Backus and others were one of the most important reasons for the rapid acceptance of high-level programming languages during the early years of computer science.

However, conditions have changed dramatically since 1957. Because of dramatic reductions in hardware costs, code optimization no longer plays the central role it did 35 or 40 years ago. Programmers rarely worry about saving a few memory cells when even a tiny PC has 256 Mbytes, and 512 Mbytes to 1 Gbyte of memory is quite common. Similarly, as processor speeds increase to 300–500 MIPS (million instructions per second) for small machines and to 1,000 MIPS for bigger ones, removing a few instructions becomes much less important. For example, eliminating the execution of 1,000 unnecessary instructions saves only 0.000002 second on a 500-MIPS machine. Therefore, compilers are no longer judged solely on whether they produce highly optimized code.

At the same time that hardware costs are dropping, programmer costs are rising dramatically. A powerful high-speed graphics workstation can be purchased for as little as $2,000, but the programmers developing software for that system will earn 30 to 50 times that in annual salary. The operational phrase of the 21st century is the exact opposite of what was true in the 1950s: "Hardware is cheap, people are expensive!" The goal in compiler design today is to provide a wide array of **compiler tools** to simplify the programmer's task and increase his or her productivity. This includes such tools as **visual development environments** that use graphics and video to let the programmer see what is happening, sophisticated **on-line debuggers** to help programmers locate and correct errors, and **reusable code libraries,** which contain a large collection of pre-written program units. When a compiler is embedded within a collection of supporting routines such as debuggers, editors, and libraries, it is called an **integrated development environment.** It is these types of programmer optimizations, rather than code optimizations, that have taken center stage in language and compiler design.

This does not mean that code optimization is no longer of any importance or that programmers will tolerate any level of code inefficiency. A little bit of effort by a compiler can often pay large dividends in reduced memory space and lower running time. Thus, optimization algorithms are still part of most compilers. Let's briefly survey what they do and how they help improve the finished product.

There are two types of optimization: local optimization and global optimization. The former is relatively easy and is included as part of most compilers. The latter is much more difficult, and it is usually omitted from all but the most sophisticated and expensive production-level **optimizing compilers.**

In **local optimization,** the compiler looks at a very small block of instructions, typically from one to five. It tries to determine how it can improve the efficiency of this local code block without regard for what instructions come before or after. It is as though the compiler has placed a tiny "window" over the code, and it optimizes only the instructions inside this optimization window:

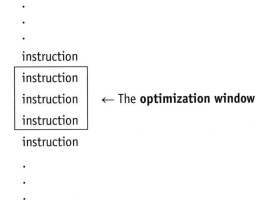

Here is a list of some possible local optimizations:

1. **Constant evaluation.** If an arithmetic expression can be fully evaluated at compile time, it should be, rather than evaluating it at execution time.

   High-level Statement: $x = 1 + 1$;

Nonoptimized code:	LOAD	ONE	*Optimized code:*	LOAD	TWO
	ADD	ONE		STORE	X
	STORE	X			

2. **Strength reduction.** The compiler replaces a slow arithmetic operation with a faster one. For example, on most computers increment is faster than addition, addition is faster than multiplication, which is faster than division. Whenever possible, the compiler replaces an operation with one that is equivalent but executes more quickly.

   High-level Statement: $x = x * 2$;   // x times 2 is equivalent to $x + x$

Nonoptimized code:	LOAD X	*Optimized code:*	LOAD	X
	MULTIPLY TWO		ADD	X
	STORE X		STORE	X

3. **Eliminating unnecessary operations.** It is possible that the compiler will produce instructions that are not incorrect, just unnecessary. For example, because of the nondestructive read principle, when a value is stored from a register into memory, its value is still in the

register, and it does not need to be reloaded. However, because the code generation phase translates each statement individually, there may be some unnecessary LOAD and STORE operations:

High-level Statement: $x = y$;

$z = x$;

Nonoptimized code: LOAD Y   -- This is $x = y$ *Optimized code:*   LOAD Y

          STORE X   STORE X

          LOAD X   -- This is $z = x$ STORE Z

          STORE Z

Looking at the code in Figure 10.11, we can see two local optimizations:

- There are unnecessary LOAD and STORE operations. For example, the first four instructions in Figure 10.11 read

```
LOAD      X
ADD       Y
STORE     TEMP
LOAD      TEMP
```

The STORE and LOAD operations on lines 3 and 4 are both unnecessary because the sum (X + Y) is still in register R.

- The code uses two memory cells called TEMP and TEMP2 to hold temporary values. Neither of these variables is needed.

Locally optimized code for the assignment statement $x = x + y + z$ is shown in Figure 10.12. It uses only 7 instructions and data generation pseudo-ops rather than the 13 of Figure 10.11, a savings of about 45%.

The second type of optimization is **global optimization,** and it is much more difficult. In global optimization the compiler looks at large segments of the program, not just small pieces, to decide how to improve performance. The compiler examines large blocks of code such as **while** loops, **if** statements, and procedures to determine how to speed up execution. This is a much harder problem, both for a compiler and for a human programmer, but

FIGURE 10.12

Optimized Code for the Assignment Statement
$x = x + y + z$

```
        LOAD     X
        ADD      Y
        ADD      Z
        STORE    X      — X now holds the correct result
          .
          .             — The remainder of the program goes here
          .
X:      .DATA    0
Y:      .DATA    0
Z:      .DATA    0
```

it can produce enormous savings in time and space. For example, earlier in the chapter we showed a loop that looked like this:

```
sum = 0.0;
i = 0;
while (i <= 50000) {
    sum = sum + (2.0 * x[i]);
    i = i + 1;
}
```

By moving the multiplication operation outside the loop, it is possible to eliminate 49,999 unnecessary and time-consuming operations. A good

"I Do Not Understand," Said the Machine

Chapter 6 showed that translating assembly language into machine language is quite easy. This chapter demonstrated that translating high-level programming languages into machine language is more difficult, but it can be done. What about the next step—the translation of natural languages such as English? If a computer could understand our own spoken languages, then we could use them, rather than the artificial languages studied in Chapters 8 and 9, to communicate.

Unfortunately, getting computers to understand and use natural language is nowhere near a reality. In fact, **natural language understanding** may be the single most difficult research problem in computer science. Success in this area may be dozens of years away, or it may never be achieved. After all, millions of years of evolution have left virtually every animal except humans without sophisticated language capabilities.

What makes natural languages so much more difficult to understand than formal languages? Why is this problem of such immense magnitude? There are far too many reasons to discuss in these brief paragraphs, but most have to do with the immense richness and complexity of natural languages. The number of rules in an English language grammar would probably number in the tens or hundreds of millions, far beyond the ability of any modern computer. Furthermore, most words in English have many meanings, and we must determine by the context what is meant. This type of sophisticated linguistic discrimination is very difficult, and a complete, unambiguous semantic analysis of English sentences is beyond the ability of computer systems.

It actually gets much worse, because meaning may be extracted from a sentence using not just context but also our own human experiences. Computers do not have human experiences, so it is enormously difficult for them to determine the full meaning of many sentences.

This is a rather pessimistic outlook. Is there any hope at all for getting computers to understand natural languages? In two special areas, the answer is a qualified yes. First, limited success can be achieved when a computer works with a very small vocabulary and grammar within a very limited problem domain. This has been demonstrated, for example, in the flying of planes by voice. The pilot speaks commands in English that are interpreted by a computer and translated into the proper actions on the airplane. In this very specialized problem domain, the computer has only to understand a few hundred words (*up, down, turn,* and so on) and some simple sentence structures. It does not have to discuss global politics or existential philosophy.

A second area where some successes have been demonstrated is using a computer to do initial "rough" translations from one natural language to another. A human would complete the translation, smoothing out choppy phrases and filling in areas where the computer was either in error or was unable to determine the correct meaning.

No matter how it is done, there is no doubt that having a computer understand natural language is a task whose solution is not on the immediate horizon. In fact, just as the use of sophisticated language distinguishes humans from animals, it may also end up being what distinguishes humans from computers.

optimizing compiler would analyze the entire loop and restructure it in the following way:

```
sum = 0.0;
i = 0;
while (i <= 50000) {
    sum = sum + x[i];
    i  =  i + 1;
};
sum = sum * 2.0;
```

Such restructuring requires the ability to look at more than a few instructions at a time. The compiler cannot look at only a small "optimization window" but must be able to examine and analyze large segments of code. It requires a compiler that can see the "big picture," not just a small scene. Seeing this big picture is difficult, and many compilers are unable to do the type of global optimizations just discussed.

There is one final comment about code optimization that is extremely important: optimization *cannot* make an inefficient algorithm efficient. As we learned in Chapter 3, the efficiency of an algorithm is an inherent characteristic of its structure. It is not something programmed in by a programmer or optimized in by a compiler. A sequential search program written by a team of world-class programmers and optimized by the best compiler available still will not run as fast as a nonoptimized binary search program written by first-year computer science students. Code optimization should not be seen as a way to create fast, efficient programs. That goal is achieved when we decide which algorithm to use to solve a problem. Optimization is more like the "frosting on the cake," whereby we take a good algorithm and make it just a little bit better.

10.3   Conclusion

This chapter has merely touched on some of the many issues involved in compiler design. Topics such as syntax, grammars, parsing, semantics, and optimization are rich and complex, each worthy of an entire book rather than one brief chapter. In addition, there are topics not even mentioned here that play an important role in compiler design:

- Development environments and support tools
- Compilers for alternative languages, such as functional, object-oriented, or parallel languages
- Language standardization
- Top-down versus bottom-up parsing algorithms
- Error detection and recovery

The key point is that, unlike building the assemblers of Chapter 6, building a compiler is hard, and compilers for languages like C++ and Java are large, complicated pieces of software. John Backus reported that the construction of the first FORTRAN compiler in 1957 required about 18 person-years of effort to design, code, and test. Even though we know much more today about how to build compilers, and numerous support tools are available to assist in this effort, it still requires a large team of programmers working months or years to build a correct and efficient compiler for a modern high-level programming language.

The previous three chapters looked at the implementation phase of software development. They focused on the languages used to write programs and the methods used to translate programs into instructions that can be executed by the hardware. However, there are limits to computing. The next chapter will show that no matter how powerful your hardware capabilities and no matter how sophisticated and expressive your programming language, there are some problems that simply cannot be solved algorithmically.

1. Identify the tokens in each of the following statements. (You do not need to classify them; just identify them.)

   a. **if** (a == b1) a = x + y;

   b. delta = epsilon + 1.23 − sqrt(zz);

   c. print(Q);

2. Assume that we are working in a programming language that allows underscores (_) to appear in variable names. When a scanner sees a character string such as AB_CD, would it be more likely to classify this string as the single five-character token AB_CD or as three separate tokens: AB, _, CD? Explain your answer.

3. In some programming languages a comment can be enclosed either in braces { } or in the symbols (* *). How do you think a scanner would group the four symbols {, }, (*, *) for purposes of classification? That is, would each symbol be given its own classification number or would some share classifications?

4. Using the token types and classification values given in Figure 10.3, show the output of a scanner when it is presented with each of the following statements:

   a. limit = begin + end

   b. a = b − 1;

   c. **if** (c == 50) x = 1; **else** y = x + 44;

   d. thenelse == error −

5. a. Write a BNF grammar that describes the structure of a nonterminal called <number>. Assume that <number> contains an optional + sign followed by exactly 2 decimal digits, the first of which cannot be a 0. Thus 23, +91, and +40 are legal, but 9, +01, and 123 are not.

   b. Using your grammar from part (a), show a parse tree for the value +90.

6. a. Write a BNF grammar that describes the structure of U.S. telephone numbers, which can be either (xxx)xxx-xxxx or xxx-xxxx, where x can be any digit from 0 to 9.

   b. Modify your grammar from part (a) so that (1) the middle digit of an area code must be either a 0 or a 1, (2) the first digit of an area code cannot be a 0 or a 1, and (3) the first digit of the seven-digit phone number cannot be a 0 or a 1.

   c. Using your grammar from either part (a) or part (b), show a parse tree for the phone number (612) 555-1212.

7. a. Write a BNF grammar for identifiers that consist of an arbitrarily long string of letters and digits, the first one of which must be a letter.

   b. Using your grammar from part (a), show a parse tree for the identifier AB5C8.

8. Assume that we represent dollar amounts in the following way:

   $number.numberCR

   The dollar sign and the dollar value must be present. The cents part (including both the decimal point and the number) and the CR (which stands for CRedit and is how businesspeople represent negative numbers) are both optional, and "number" is a variable-length sequence of one or more decimal digits. Examples of legal dollar amounts include $995, $99CR, $199.95, and $500.000CR.

   a. Write a BNF grammar for the dollar amount just described.

   b. Modify your grammar so that the cents part is no longer an arbitrarily long sequence of digits but is exactly two digits, no more and no less.

   c. Using your grammar from either part (a) or part (b), show a parse tree for $19.95CR.

9. Describe the language defined by the following grammar:

   <goal> ::= <letter> | <letter> <next>

   <next> ::= , <letter>

   <letter> ::= A

10. How does the language defined by the following grammar differ from the language defined by the grammar in Exercise 9?

    <goal> ::= <letter> | <letter> <next>

    <next> ::= , <letter> | <letter> <next>

    <letter> ::= A

11. a. Create a BNF grammar that describes simple Boolean expressions of the form

    var AND var

    var OR var

    where var is one of the symbols w, x, y, and z.

    b. Modify your grammar from part (a) so that the Boolean expressions can be of the form

    expr AND expr

    expr OR expr

    where expr is either a simple variable (w, x, y, or z) or an expression of the form

    (var == var)   (var < var)   (var > var)

    c. Modify your grammar one more time to allow a Boolean expression to have an *arbitrary* number of terms connected by either AND or OR. That is, your expressions can be of the form

    expr AND expr OR expr OR expr AND expr . . . .

12. Using the grammar of Figure 10.8, show a parse tree for the statement

$$y = x + y + y + z$$

Is your parse tree unique? If not, how many other parse trees exist for this statement? What does the existence of these different trees imply about the meaning of this assignment statement?

13. What is the language defined by the following pair of BNF rules?

        <number> ::= <digit> | <digit> <number>

        <digit> ::= 0 | 1

Where have you seen this language before?

14. Write a BNF grammar that describes an arbitrarily long string of the characters *a, b,* and *c.* The string can contain any number of occurrences of these three letters (including none) in any order. The strings "empty", a, accaa, abcabccba, and bbbbb are all valid members of this language.

15. What are the different interpretations of the English language sentence

    I bought a shirt in the new store that was too large.

16. Write a BNF grammar to describe the following hypothetical input statement:

```
input(var, var,  . . . , var);
```

The statement begins with the word "input," followed by a left parenthesis, and then one or more variables, each variable separated from the one after it by a comma. The entire statement ends with a right parenthesis and a semicolon. Variable names are arbitrarily long strings of digits and letters, the first of which must be a letter.

17. Discuss what other information, in addition to name and data type, might be kept in a semantic record. From where would this other information come?

18. How do you think a compiler would translate into machine language a branch in the parse tree that looked like the following?

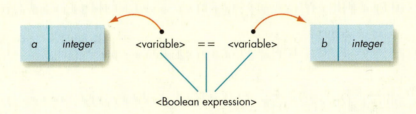

Show the code that could be generated from this production and the semantic record created for the new nonterminal symbol <Boolean expression>.

19. Referring to the parse tree in Figure 10.11, why is the production that appears to the left of the = sign in that figure, not labeled with an Ⓐ? Does this production generate any code?

20. Assume that our language specifically permits you to assign an integer value to a real variable. The compiler handles this **mixed mode** by generating code to perform data conversion from an integer to a real representation. Consider the following declarations:

```
int x;
double y;
```

The assignment statement *y = x* is legal in this language. Explain how a compiler would handle the assignment statement above. You do not have to show the exact code that would be generated. Just describe how a compiler would deal with the statement, and show at what point in the code generation process the compiler would discover that it needs to produce the data conversion instructions.

21. Explain how the concept of **algebraic identities** could be exploited during the code optimization phase of compilation. An identity is a relationship that is true for all values of the unknowns. For example,

    x + 0 = x for all values of x.

Describe other identities and explain how they could become part of the optimization phase. Would this be considered local or global optimization?

22. Assume that we wrote the following pairs of assignment statements:

   Delta = 2.9 + (a + b + c * 3) / (x − 5.7);

   Epsilon = (a + b + c * 3) + sqrt(3.1 * y);

How could a compiler optimize the execution of these two statements? Would this be considered local or global optimization?

23. If we assume that all mathematical operations take 5 nsec (5 billionths of a second) to execute, how much time did your optimization from Exercise 22 actually save? What does this value say about the importance of compiler optimizations?

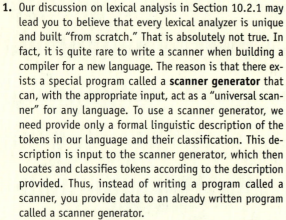

CHALLENGE WORK

1. Our discussion on lexical analysis in Section 10.2.1 may lead you to believe that every lexical analyzer is unique and built "from scratch." That is absolutely not true. In fact, it is quite rare to write a scanner when building a compiler for a new language. The reason is that there exists a special program called a **scanner generator** that can, with the appropriate input, act as a "universal scanner" for any language. To use a scanner generator, we need provide only a formal linguistic description of the tokens in our language and their classification. This description is input to the scanner generator, which then locates and classifies tokens according to the description provided. Thus, instead of writing a program called a scanner, you provide data to an already written program called a scanner generator.

   One of the most widely used scanner generators is a program called **lex,** and it has been used to build dozens of compilers, assemblers, and other linguistic interfaces. Read about scanner generators in general and lex in particular. Find out how they work and the techniques for describing the structure and classification of tokens. Then show how you would formally describe in lex the following token types:

   a. Identifiers

   b. Signed integers

   c. Signed real numbers

If your installation has lex available, enter your formal descriptions and have lex locate tokens of each of these types.

2. The techniques described in Challenge Exercise 1 also work for the parsing phase of the compilation process. That is, instead of writing a parsing program, we can provide data to an already written program that will do the job for us. A special program called a **parser generator,** also called a **compiler-compiler,** can act as a universal parser for any language that can be described using BNF notation. To use a parser generator, you simply input the productions of the grammar of your language and the sequence of tokens to be parsed. The output of the parser generator is a parse tree, if the sequence of tokens is legal according to your productions, or an error message if it is not.

   The most widely used parser generator is a program called **yacc,** an acronym for "Yet Another Compiler-Compiler." Yacc, like lex, has been used to build a great number of compilers. Read about parser generators and yacc, and write a report describing how yacc works and how you formally represent BNF productions. If you have yacc available at your installation, enter the BNF rules for <assignment statement> and let yacc parse the statement

   x = y + z;

FOR FURTHER READING

The classic book on compiling is the "Dragon Book," so called because of the dragon motif on its cover:

Aho, A.; Sethi, R.; and Ullman, J. *Compilers: Principles, Techniques, and Tools*. Reading, MA: Addison-Wesley, 1986.

There are also a large number of good reference books on languages, BNF, and compilers. Here is a sampling of these books:

Appel, A., and Palsberg, J. *Modern Compiler Implementation*. Cambridge, England: Cambridge University Press, 2002.

Fisher, C., and LeBlanc, R. *Crafting a Compiler*. Chicago, IL: Addison-Wesley, 1991.

Louden, K. *Compiler Construction: Principles and Practice*. Boston, MA: Brooks/Cole, 1997.

Pittman, T., and Peters, J. *The Art of Compiler Design*. Englewood Cliffs, NJ: Prentice-Hall, 1992.

CHAPTER 11

Models of Computation

11.1 Introduction

The central theme throughout this book has been, in one way or another, algorithmic problem-solving. We've discussed the concept of an algorithm, how to represent algorithms, the importance of their correctness and efficiency in solving problems, the hardware that executes algorithms, the various levels of abstraction in which a programmer deals with algorithms, and, finally, the system software that translates these abstractions back to the elementary hardware level. It seems as though algorithms, and problems solvable by algorithms, represent the entire scope of the computer science universe.

But we are about to bump up against the limits of that universe. *There are problems that do not have any algorithmic solution.* Be sure you understand why this is such a powerful statement. There are many problems for which no algorithmic solution has yet been found, but we might find one if we were only clever enough to discover it. Indeed, such new discoveries are being made all the time. But here we are saying that there are also problems for which no algorithmic solution exists; it does not matter how inventive we may be, how much time we spend looking, or how remarkable our hardware or software; *no algorithms will ever be found that solve these problems.*

We will prove this statement later in this chapter by actually finding such a problem. This is a rather difficult task. If we pose a candidate for such a problem, search for an algorithmic solution and fail to find one, that does not prove that one does not exist. It might only mean that the algorithm is a difficult one, and we have not yet been able to figure it out. Instead, we must show that no one can ever find such an algorithm—that one does not exist.

Algorithms, as noted in Chapter 1, are carried out by computing agents (people, robots, computers). Throughout most of this book, we've assumed that the computing agent is a real computer. Ordinarily, we would choose to execute an algorithm on the most modern, high-speed computer available, with all the bells and whistles we could possibly find. But to show that something cannot be done by *any* computer, we want the bells and whistles to get out of the way so we can concentrate on the fundamental nature of "computerness." What we need is a simple, "ideal" computer—something easy to work with yet theoretically as powerful as the real thing. We need a **model** of a computer; indeed, to consider algorithms in general, we need a model of a computing agent.

11.2   What Is a Model?

Many toys for children (and some toys for grownups) are models. Model cars, model trucks, model airplanes, and dolls (model people) are forever popular with children. Children use these toys to "play" at being grown up—at being drivers, pilots, and parents—because the toys capture the spirit of the objects they model. A model car, for example, looks like a car. The more expensive the model, the more features it has that make it look more realistic. The model is never a real car, however. Alhough it captures the essence of a car, it is (usually) smaller in scale, suppresses many of the details of a real car, and does not have the full functionality of a real car.

Models are an important way of studying many physical and social phenomena. Weather systems, climate cycles, the spread of epidemics, population demographics, and chemical molecules—all are phenomena that have been studied via modeling. (In fact, we will look at some of these applications in Chapter 12.) Like a model car, a model of such a phenomenon

1. Captures the essence—the important properties—of the real thing
2. Probably differs in scale from the real thing
3. Suppresses some of the details of the real thing
4. Lacks the full functionality of the real thing

The model might be a physical model or a pencil and paper mathematical model. For example, a physical model of a chemical molecule might use Velcro®-covered balls stuck together in a certain way to represent the molecular structure. This model illustrates certain important properties: how many atoms of each element are present and where they are located in relation to one another. It is much larger than the real molecule, does not display the details of the chemical bonding, and is certainly not a real molecule.

A simple example of a mathematical model is the equation for the distance d that a moving vehicle travels as the product of rate r and time t:

$$d = r \times t$$

Although this equation can give approximate information, it ignores the details of variations in the speed of the vehicle by assuming that the rate is a constant. Because this is not a physical model, it does not have a size as such, but there is a difference in time scale from the actual moving vehicle. A calculation that a vehicle traveling at a constant rate of 60 miles per hour for 2 hours will cover a distance of 120 miles can be done in an instant by simply plugging values into the equation.

What can be gained by studying models if they do not behave in exactly the same way as the real thing? For one thing, they can enhance our understanding of the real system being modeled. By changing some aspect within the model we can immediately see the effects of that change. These changes might be very costly, difficult, or dangerous to make in the real phenomena. The benefit is that models give us a safe and controlled environment to play with "what ifs"—what might be the effect if this or that factor in the real system were changed? The answers can be used to guide future decisions. Models can also provide environments for learning and practicing interactions with various phenomena. An aircraft flight simulator, for example, can give the trainee pilot realistic experience in a danger-free setting. Finally, not only can models give us information about existing phenomena, they can also be used as design tools. A model of the new design may reveal its capabilities and limitations with considerably less time, expense, and potential danger than building a prototype only to find that the design contains a major flaw. (We will look more closely at these applications of models in Chapter 12.)

Whether a model is used to predict the behavior of an existing system or as a test bed for a proposed design, the information it provides is only as good as the assumptions made in building the model. If the model does not incorporate the major aspects of the system being studied, if relationships are represented incorrectly, or if so much detail has been omitted as to make the model a totally inaccurate representation, then little faith can be placed in the results it produces.

PRACTICE PROBLEMS

1. Describe some situation (besides aircraft pilot training) where a simulator would be useful as a training device.

2. What factors might a model of groundwater pollution need to include? What would be the advantages of a good model? Are there potential disadvantages to using such a model?

11.3   A Model of a Computing Agent

We want to construct a model for the "computing agent" entity. If it is a good model, it will capture the fundamental properties of what it means to be a computing agent and, thus, will enable us to explore the capabilities and limitations of computation in the most general sense.

 ### 11.3.1 *Properties of a Computing Agent*

Our job in constructing a model is to abstract the important properties of the phenomenon being modeled while suppressing lower-level details. This means we must decide which features are central to a computing agent and which are relatively incidental and can be ignored. For example, a computing agent must be able to follow the instructions in an algorithm. The instructions must be presented in some form that makes sense to the computing agent, but we don't want to worry about whether the instructions are presented in English or Japanese, or words as opposed to pictures.

However the instructions are presented, the computing agent must be able to read them, listen to them, scan them, or absorb them in some way. Likewise, the computing agent must be able to take in any data pertinent to the task. When we dealt with real computers, we described this as an input task, but the ability to accept input is central to any computing agent—from a human being following instructions to a programmable VCR. The instructions and data must be stored somewhere during the period of time when the algorithm is being executed. In addition, they must be retrievable as needed, whether it be from a computer's memory, the VCR microprocessor's memory, a human being's memory, or a written sheet of paper to which the human being refers.

The computing agent must be able to take action in accordance with algorithm instructions. These instructions may take into account the present situation or state of the computing agent, as well as the particular input item being processed. In a real computer, a conditional operation may say, If condition A then do B else do C. Condition A may involve the value of some variable or variables that have already been read into memory; we may think of the contents of memory (i.e., how the various bits are set) as the present state of the computer. The VCR microprocessor may have an instruction that says, If the time is 7 P.M. and I have been programmed to record at 7 P.M., then turn on. Here the action of the VCR depends on both the input of the current time from its clock and the "state" of its programming, just as a human being carrying out the algorithm of ordering lunch from a menu reacts both to the "input" (what items are on the menu) and to his or her present state of hunger.

Finally, the computing agent is expected to produce output because we required that the outcome of an algorithm be an observable result. The computer displays results on a screen, prints them on a sheet of paper, or writes them to a file; the VCR puts signals on a magnetic tape; the human being speaks or writes.

To summarize, we shall require that any computing agent be able to do all of the following operations:

1. Accept input
2. Store information in and retrieve it from memory
3. Take actions according to algorithm instructions; the choice of what action to take may depend on the present state of the computing agent, as well as on the input item presently being processed
4. Produce output

Of course, a real computer has all of these capabilities and is an example of a computing agent, as are a human being and a programmable VCR. The VCR, however, has a very limited set of primitive operations it can perform, so it can react only to a very limited algorithm. The computer, though it has a limited set of simple primitives, is a general-purpose computing agent because, as we have seen in the previous chapters, those primitives can be combined and organized to accomplish complex tasks. The "primitive operations" available for human beings to draw on haven't been fully explored, but in many ways they seem to exceed those of a computer, and we would certainly classify a human being as a general-purpose computing agent.

In the next section, we will discuss one particular model for a computing agent. It will have the four required properties just specified, and it will represent a general-purpose computing agent able to follow the instructions of many different algorithms.

11.3.2   The Turing Machine

We think of "computing" as a modern activity—something done by electronic computers. But interest in the theoretical nature of computation far predated the advent of modern computers. By the end of the 19th century, mathematicians were interested in formalizing the nature of proof, with two goals in mind. First, a formal basis for mathematical proofs would guarantee the correctness of a proof because the proof would contain no intuitive statements, such as "It is clear that . . ." or "We can now see that . . . ." Second, a formal basis for proofs might allow for mechanical theorem-proving, where correct proofs could be generated simply by following a set of rules. In 1931, an Austrian logician named Kurt Gödel looked at formal systems to describe the ordinary arithmetic of numbers. He demonstrated that in any reasonable system, there will be true statements about arithmetic that cannot be proved using that system. This led to interest in finding a way to recognize which statements are indeed unprovable in a formal system—that is, in finding a computational procedure (what we have called an algorithm) to recognize such statements. This in turn led to an investigation of the nature of computation itself, and a number of mathematicians in the mid-1930s proposed various models of computational procedures, along with models of computing agents to carry out those procedures. We will look at the model proposed by Alan Turing.

A **Turing machine** includes a (conceptual) tape that extends infinitely in both directions. The tape is divided into cells, each of which contains one symbol. The symbols must come from a finite set of symbols called the **alphabet.** The alphabet for a given Turing machine always contains a special

Alan Turing, Brilliant Eccentric

The Turing machine was proposed as a model for a computing agent by the brilliant British mathematician Alan Turing in 1936. Turing began by thinking of how to generalize the typewriter as an "automatic device." But despite its name, the Turing machine is not a machine at all. It is a model of the pencil and paper type that captures the essential features of a computing agent.

Alan Turing (1912–1954) was a colorful individual and a brilliant thinker. Stories abound about his "absent-minded professor" demeanor, his interest in running (through the streets of London with an alarm clock flopping about, tied to his belt by a piece of twine), and his fascination with a children's radio show whose characters he would discuss daily with his mother. Convicted of homosexual acts in 1952, he chose drug treatment over prison, primarily because he feared a prison term would impede his intellectual work. There was even a Broadway play (*Breaking the Code*) written about him, years after his death by suicide.

Turing made three distinct and remarkable contributions to computer science. First, he devised what is now known as the Turing machine, using it—as we will see in this chapter—to model computation and to discover that some problems have no general computable solution. Second, during World War II, his team at the British Foreign Office built the Colossus machine, which used cryptanalysis, the science of code breaking, to break the secret code used on the German Enigma machine. The details of this work, carried on in a Victorian country mansion called Bletchley Park, were kept secret until many years later. Breaking the code allowed the British to gain access to intelligence about German submarine movements that contributed significantly toward winning the war. Third, after the war Turing investigated what it means for machines to "think." We'll discuss his early contribution to *artificial intelligence* in Chapter 14.

FIGURE 11.1

A Turing Machine Tape

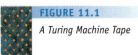

.	.	.	b	b	0	1	1	b	b	.	.	.

symbol *b* (for "blank"), usually both of the symbols 0 and 1 (zero and one), and sometimes a limited number of other symbols, let's say *X* and *Y*, used as placeholders or markers of some kind. At any point in time, only a finite number of the cells contain nonblank symbols. Figure 11.1 shows a typical tape configuration, with three nonblank cells containing the alphabet symbols 0, 1, 1, respectively.

The tape will be used to hold the input to the Turing machine. We know that input must be presented to a computing agent in a form it can understand; for a Turing machine, this means that the input must be expressed as a finite string of nonblank symbols from the alphabet. The Turing machine will write its output on the tape, again using the same alphabet of symbols. The tape will also serve as memory.

The rest of the Turing machine consists of a unit that reads one cell of the tape at a time and writes a symbol in that cell. There is a finite number *k* of "states" of the machine, labeled 1, 2, . . . , *k*, and at any moment the unit is in one of these states. A state can be thought of as a certain condition; the Turing machine may reach this condition partly on the basis of its history of events, much as your "hungry state" is a condition reached because of the meals you have skipped recently.

Figure 11.2 shows a particular Turing machine configuration. Using the tape of Figure 11.1, the machine is currently in state 1 and is reading the cell containing the symbol 0, so the 0 is what the machine is seeing as the current input symbol.

The Turing machine is designed to carry out only one type of primitive operation. Each time such an operation is done, three actions take place:

1. Write a symbol in the cell (replacing the symbol already there).

2. Go into a new state (it might be the same as the current state).

3. Move one cell left or right.

The details of the actions (what to write, what the new state is, and which direction to move) depend on the current state of the machine and on the contents of the tape cell currently being read (the input). Turing machines follow instructions that describe these details. Each instruction tells what to

FIGURE 11.2

A Turing Machine Configuration

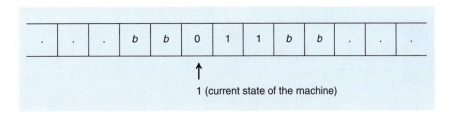

.	.	.	b	b	0	1	1	b	b	.	.	.

↑
1 (current state of the machine)

do for a specific current state and current input symbol. Each instruction therefore says something like

> if (you are in state *i*) and (you are reading symbol *j*) then
>> write symbol *k* onto the tape
>>
>> go into state *s*
>>
>> move in direction *d*

The single primitive operation the Turing machine does is to check its current state and the current input symbol being read, look for an instruction that tells what to do under these circumstances, and then carry out the three actions specified by that instruction. For example, one Turing machine instruction might say

> if (you are in state 1) and (you are reading symbol 0) then
>> write symbol 1 onto the tape
>>
>> go into state 2
>>
>> move right

If a Turing machine is in the configuration shown in Figure 11.2 (where the current state is 1 and the current input symbol is 0), then this instruction applies. After the machine executes this instruction, its next configuration will be that shown in Figure 11.3, where the previous 0 symbol has been overwritten with a 1, the state has changed to state 2, and the "read head" has moved one cell to the right on the tape.

Let's develop a shorthand notation for Turing machine instructions. There are five components:

- Current state
- Current symbol
- Next symbol
- Next state
- Direction of move

We'll give these five things in order and enclosed in parentheses.

(current state, current symbol, next symbol, next state, direction of move)

FIGURE 11.3

The Next Turing Machine Configuration after Executing One Instruction

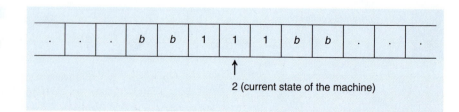

The instruction that we talked about earlier,

> if (you are in state 1) and (you are reading symbol 0) then
>> write symbol 1 onto the tape
>>
>> go into state 2
>>
>> move right

is therefore represented by the 5-tuple:

$(1,0,1,2,R)$

Similarly, the Turing machine instruction

$(2,1,1,2,L)$

stands for

> if (you are in state 2) and (you are reading symbol 1) then
>> write symbol 1 onto the tape
>>
>> go into state 2
>>
>> move left

Note that in following this instruction, the machine writes in the current cell the same symbol (1) as was already there and remains in the same state (state 2) as before.

A Turing machine can execute a whole sequence of instructions. A clock governs the action of the machine. Whenever the clock ticks, the Turing machine performs its primitive operation; that is, it looks for an instruction that applies to its current state and the symbol currently being read and then follows that instruction. Instructions may be used more than once.

There are a couple of details we've glossed over. What if there is more than one instruction that applies to the current configuration? Suppose, as in Figure 11.2, that the current state is 1, that the current symbol is 0, and that

$(1,0,1,2,R)$

$(1,0,0,3,L)$

both appear in the same collection of instructions. Then the Turing machine has a conflict between the actions to be taken. Should it write a 1, go to state 2, and move right, or should it write a 0, go to state 3, and move left? We'll avoid this ambiguity by requiring that a set of instructions for a Turing machine can never contain two different instructions of the form

$(i, j, -, -, -)$

$(i, j, -, - ,-)$

On the other hand, what if there is no instruction that applies to the current state–current symbol for the machine? In this case, we specify that the machine halts, doing nothing further.

We impose two additional conventions on the Turing machine regarding its initial configuration when the clock begins. The start-up state will always be state 1, and the machine will always be reading the leftmost nonblank cell on the tape. This ensures that the Turing machine has a fixed and definite starting point.

Now let's do a sample Turing machine computation. Suppose the instructions available to a Turing machine are

1. $(1,0,1,2,R)$
2. $(1,1,1,2,R)$
3. $(2,0,1,2,R)$
4. $(2,1,0,2,R)$
5. $(2,b,b,3,L)$

Also suppose the Turing machine's initial configuration is again that of Figure 11.2:

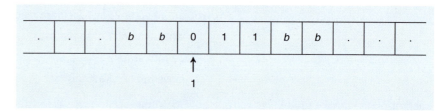

This satisfies our convention about starting in state 1 at the leftmost nonblank cell on the tape. The Turing machine looks for an appropriate instruction for its current state, 1, and its current input symbol, 0, which means it looks for an instruction of the form $(1,0,-,-,-)$. Instruction 1 applies; this was our example instruction earlier, and the resulting configuration agrees with Figure 11.3:

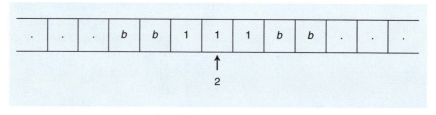

Now let's continue. At the next clock tick, with current state 2 and current symbol 1, the Turing machine looks for an instruction of the form $(2, 1, -,-,-)$. Instruction 4 applies and, after the appropriate actions are performed, the resulting configuration is

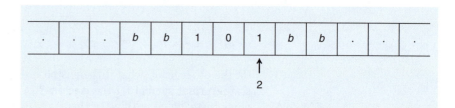

Instruction 4 applies again and results in

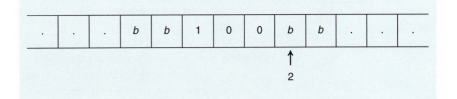

Instruction 5 now applies, leading to

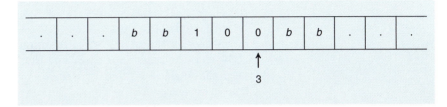

At this point the machine is in state 3 reading the symbol 0. Because there are no instructions of the form (3,0,-,-,-), the machine halts. The Turing machine computation is complete.

Although we numbered this collection of instructions for reference, we saw that the Turing machine does not necessarily execute instructions in the order of this numbering. We also saw that some instructions may not be executed at all, and some more than once. The sequence of instructions used depends on the input written on the tape.

How does the Turing machine stack up against our list of required features for a computing agent?

1. *It can accept input.* The Turing machine can read symbols on its tape.

2. *It can store information in and retrieve it from memory.* The Turing machine can write symbols on its tape and, by moving around over the tape, can go back and read those symbols at a later time, so the tape has stored that information.

3. *It can take actions according to algorithm instructions, and the choice of action to take may depend on the present state of the computing agent and on the input item presently being processed.* Certainly the Turing machine satisfies this requirement insofar as Turing machine instructions are concerned; the present state and present symbol being processed determine the appropriate instruction, and that instruction specifies the actions to be taken.

4. *It can produce output.* The Turing machine writes symbols on its tape in the course of its normal operation. If (when?) the Turing machine halts, what is written on the tape at that time can be considered output.

In the Turing machine computation that we just finished, the input was the string of symbols 011 (ignoring the surrounding blanks) and the output was the string of symbols 100. Starting with the same input tape but with a different set of instructions could result in different output. Given the benefit of hindsight, we could say that we wrote this particular set of instructions to carry out the task of transforming the string 011 into the string 100. Writing a set of Turing machine instructions to allow a Turing machine to carry out a certain task is similar to writing a computer program to allow a computer to carry out a certain task. We can call such a collection of instructions a **Turing machine program.**

Thus, it seems that a Turing machine does capture those properties we identified as essential for a computing agent, which qualifies it as a model of a computing agent. Furthermore, it represents a general computing agent in the sense that, like a real computer, it can follow many different sets of instructions (programs) and thus do many different things (unlike the one-job-only VCR). By its very simplicity of operation, it has eliminated many real-world details, such as exactly how symbols are read from or written to the tape, exactly how input data are to be encoded into a string of symbols from the alphabet in order to be written on the tape, exactly how a string of symbols on the tape is to be interpreted as meaningful output, and exactly how the machine carries out the activities of "changing state." In fact, the Turing machine is such a simple concept that we may wonder how good a model it really is. Did we eliminate too many details? We'll answer the question of how good a model the Turing machine is later in the chapter.

A Turing machine is different in scale from any real computing agent in one respect. A Turing machine can, given the appropriate instructions, move right or left to the blank portion of the tape and write a nonblank symbol. When this happens, the machine has gobbled up an extra cell to use for information storage purposes—that is, as memory. Depending on the instructions, this could happen over and over, which means that there is *no limit* to the amount of memory available to the machine. Any real computing agent has a limit on the memory available to it. In particular, a real computer, though it has a certain amount of internal memory and has access to external memory in the form of disks or tapes on which data can be stored, still has such a limit. There are only so many disks or tapes in the world available for any particular computer to use.

This difference in scale means that a Turing machine (elementary device though it may seem to be) actually has more capability in one respect than any real computer that exists or ever will exist. In this sense, we must be careful about the use of the Turing machine model and the conclusions we draw from it about "real" computing (i.e., computing on a real computer). If we find some task that a Turing machine can perform (because of its limitless memory), it *may* not be a task that a real computer could perform.

PRACTICE PROBLEMS

1. A Turing machine has the following instructions:
   (1,0,0,2,R)
   (2,1,1,2,L)
   (2,0,1,2,R)
   (1,b,1,1,L)

   For each of the following configurations of this Turing machine, draw the next configuration.

a.

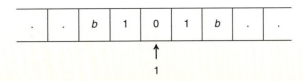

b.

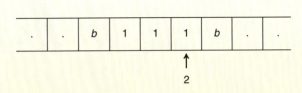

c.

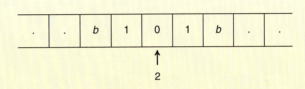

d.

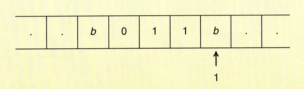

2. Consider a Turing machine that has the following two instructions

$(1,1,0,2,R)$
$(2,1,1,1,R)$

Determine its output when it is run on the following tape. (Remember that a Turing machine starts in state 1, reading the leftmost nonblank cell.)

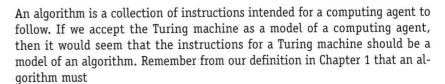

11.4 A Model of an Algorithm

An algorithm is a collection of instructions intended for a computing agent to follow. If we accept the Turing machine as a model of a computing agent, then it would seem that the instructions for a Turing machine should be a model of an algorithm. Remember from our definition in Chapter 1 that an algorithm must

1. Be a well-ordered collection

2. Consist of unambiguous and effectively computable operations

3. Halt in a finite amount of time

4. Produce a result

Let's consider an arbitrary collection of Turing machine instructions and see whether it exhibits these properties of an algorithm.

1. *Be a well-ordered collection.* The Turing machine must know which operation to carry out first and which to do next at any step. We have already specified the initial conditions for a Turing machine computation: that the Turing machine must begin in state 1, reading the leftmost nonblank cell on the tape. We have also insisted that in any collection of Turing machine instructions, there cannot be two different instructions that both begin with the same current state and current symbol. Given this requirement, there is never any confusion about which operation to do next. There is *at most* one instruction that matches the current state and current symbol of the Turing machine. If there is one instruction, the Turing machine executes the operation that instruction describes. If there is no instruction, the Turing machine halts.

2. *Consist of unambiguous and effectively computable operations.* No problem here. Recall that this property is *relative to the computing agent*; that is, operations must be understandable and doable by the computing agent. Each individual Turing machine instruction describes an operation that (to the Turing machine) is unambiguous, requiring no additional explanation, and any Turing machine is able to carry out the operation described. After all, Turing machine instructions were designed for Turing machines to be able to execute.

3. *Halt in a finite amount of time.* In order for a Turing machine to halt when executing a collection of instructions, it must reach a configuration where no appropriate instruction exists. This depends on the input given to the Turing machine—that is, the contents initially written on the tape. Consider the following set of Turing machine instructions:

   $(1,0,0,1,R)$

   $(1,b,b,1,R)$

   and suppose the tape initially contains, as its nonblank portion, the single symbol 1. The initial configuration is

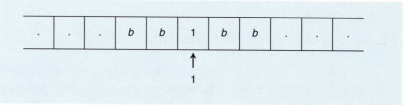

   and the machine halts immediately because there is no applicable instruction. On the other hand, suppose the same set of instructions is used with a starting tape that contains the single symbol 0. The Turing machine computation is then

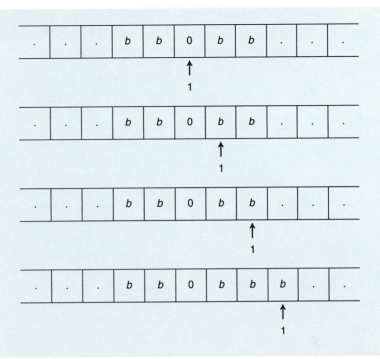

We can see that the second instruction will continue to apply indefinitely and that this Turing machine will never halt.

Typically, an algorithm is designed to carry out a certain type of task. Let us agree that *for input appropriate to that task,* the instructions must be such that the Turing machine does indeed eventually halt. If the Turing machine is run on a tape containing data that are not appropriate input for the task of interest, it need not halt.

This may seem to be a change in our definition of an algorithm, but it simply confirms that there is always a "universe of discourse" connected with the problem we are trying to solve. As an example, we can use a simple algorithm for dividing one positive integer by another using repeated subtraction until the result is negative. Thus, $7 \div 3$ can be computed using this algorithm as follows:

$$7 - 3 = 4$$
$$4 - 3 = 1$$
$$1 - 3 < 0$$

The quotient is 2 because two subtractions could be done before the result became negative. However, if we attempt to use this same approach to compute $7 \div (-3)$, we get

$$7 - (-3) = 10$$
$$10 - (-3) = 13$$
$$13 - (-3) = 16$$
$$16 - (-3) = 19$$
and so on

The process would never halt because the result would never become negative. Yet, this approach is still an algorithm *for the problem of dividing two positive numbers,* because it does produce the correct result and then halt when given input suitable for this problem.

4. *Produce a result.* We have already imposed the requirement that the Turing machine instructions must lead to a halting configuration when executed on input appropriate to the problem being solved. Whatever is written on the tape when the machine halts is the result.

A collection of Turing machine instructions that obeys these restrictions satisfies the properties required of an algorithm. Yet, it is not a "real" algorithm because it is not designed to be executed by a "real" computing agent. It is a model of an algorithm, designed to be executed by the model computing agent called a Turing machine.

Most of the time, no distinction is made between a Turing machine as a computing agent and the instructions (algorithm) it carries out, and a machine together with a set of instructions is called "a Turing machine" and is thought of as an algorithm. Thus, we say we are going to write a Turing machine to do a particular task, when we really mean that we are going to write a set of instructions—a Turing machine program, an algorithm—to do that task.

11.5 Turing Machine Examples

Because the Turing machine is such a simple device, it may seem nearly impossible to write a program for a Turing machine that carries out any interesting or significant task. In this section, we'll look at a few Turing machines that, though they do not accomplish anything earth-shaking, should convince you that Turing machines can do some rather worthwhile things.

11.5.1 *A Bit Inverter*

Let's assume that the only nonblank portion of the input tape for a particular Turing machine consists of a string of bits (0s and 1s). Our first Turing machine will move along its tape inverting all of the bits—that is, changing 0s to 1s and 1s to 0s. (Recall that our sample Turing machine computation inverted the bits in the string 011, resulting in the string 100. Do you think that machine is a bit inverter? What if the leftmost nonblank symbol on the input tape is a 1?)

The Turing machine must begin in state 1 on the leftmost nonblank cell. Whatever the current symbol that is read, the machine must invert it by printing its opposite. Machine state 1 must, therefore, be a state in which 0s are changed to 1s and 1s are changed to 0s. This is exactly what we want to happen everywhere along the tape, so the machine never needs to go to another state; it can simply move right while remaining in state 1. When we come to the final blank, we want to halt. This can be accomplished by making sure that our program does not contain any instruction of the form

$(1, b, -, -, -)$

FIGURE 11.4

State Diagram for the Bit
Inverter Machine

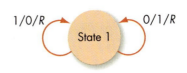

1/0/R   State 1   0/1/R

This describes the Turing machine algorithm in words, but let's represent it more precisely. In the past, we've used pseudocode to describe algorithms. Here we'll use an alternative form of representation that corresponds more closely to Turing machine instructions. A **state diagram** is a visual representation of a Turing machine algorithm, where circles represent states, and arrows represent transitions from one state to another. Along each transition arrow, we show three things: the input symbol that caused the transition, the corresponding output symbol to be printed, and the direction of move. For the bit inverter Turing machine, we have only one state and hence one circle in the state diagram shown in Figure 11.4. The arrow originating in state 1, marked 0/1/R, and returning to state 1 says that when in state 1 (the only state) reading an input symbol of 0, the machine should print the symbol 1, move right, and remain in state 1. Be sure you understand what the second arrow means.

The complete Turing machine program for the bit inverter is

1. $(1,0,1,1,R)$ Change the symbol 0 to 1.
2. $(1,1,0,1,R)$ Change the symbol 1 to 0.

(We've added a comment to each instruction to explain its purpose.) Here's a sample computation using this machine, beginning with the string 1101 on the tape:

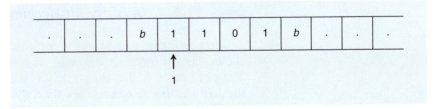

Using instruction 2,

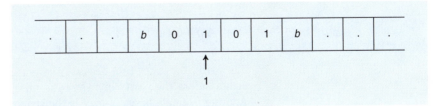

Using instruction 2 again,

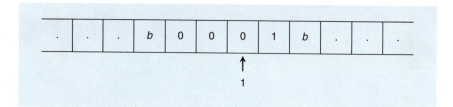

Using instruction 1,

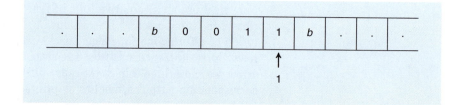

Using instruction 2,

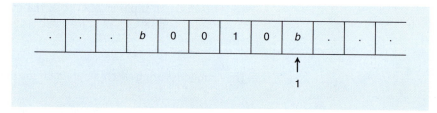

and the machine halts with the inverted string 0010 as output on the tape.

Bit inversion may seem like a trivial task, but recall that in Chapter 4 we introduced an electronic device called a NOT gate that is essentially a bit inverter and is one of the components of a real computer.

 ### 11.5.2 *A Parity Bit Machine*

An extra bit, called an **odd parity bit,** can be attached to the end of a string of bits. The odd parity bit will be set such that the number of 1s in the whole string of bits, including the parity bit, is odd. Thus, if the string preceding the parity bit has an odd number of 1s, the parity bit is set to 0 so that there is still an odd number of 1s in the whole string. If the string preceding the parity bit has an even number of 1s, the parity bit is set to 1 so that the number of 1s in the whole string is odd. As an example, the following string of bits includes as its rightmost bit an odd parity bit:

1 1 0 0 0 1 0 1 0 1

The parity bit is set to 1 because there are four 1s (an even number) in the string before the parity bit; the total number of 1s is five (an odd number). Another example of odd parity is the string

1 0 1 1 0 0

where the parity bit (the rightmost bit) is a 0 because three 1s (an odd number) appear in the preceding string. Our job here is to write a Turing machine that, given a string of bits on its input tape, attaches an odd parity bit at the right end.

We know from Chapter 4 that information in electronic form is represented as strings of bits. Parity bits are used to detect errors that occur as a result of electronic interference when transmitting such strings (see Exercise 20, Chapter 4). If a single bit (or any odd number of bits) gets changed from a 1 to 0 or from a 0 to 1, then the parity bit will be incorrect, and the error can be detected. A correct copy of the information can then be retransmitted. Again, we are devising a Turing machine for a significant real-world task.

Our Turing machine must somehow "remember" one of two conditions: whether the number of 1s so far processed is even or odd. We can use two states of the machine to represent these two conditions. Because the Turing machine begins in state 1, having read zero 1s so far (zero is an even number), we can let state 1 represent the even parity state, where an even number of 1s has been read so far. We'll let state 2 represent the odd parity state, where an odd number of 1s has been read so far.

We can read the input string from left to right. Until we get to the end of the bit string, the symbol printed should always be the same as the symbol read, because none of the bits in the input string should be changed. But every time a 1 bit is read, the parity should change, from even to odd or odd to even. In other words, the state should change from 1 to 2 or from 2 to 1. Reading a 0 bit does not affect the parity and therefore should not change the state. Thus, if we are in state 1 reading a 1, we want to go to state 2; if we are in state 1 reading a 0, we want to stay in state 1. If we are in state 2 reading a 1, we want to go to state 1; if we are in state 2 reading a 0, we want to stay in state 2.

When we come to the end of the input string (when we first read a blank cell), we write the parity bit, which will be 1 if the machine is in state 1 (the even parity state) or will be 0 if the machine is in state 2 (the odd parity state). Then we want to halt, which can be accomplished by going into state 3, for which there are no instructions. The state diagram for our parity bit machine is given in Figure 11.5.

FIGURE 11.5

State Diagram for the Parity Bit Machine

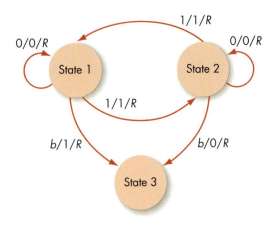

The Turing machine program is as follows:

1. (1,1,1,2,R)   Even parity state reading 1, change state.
2. (1,0,0,1,R)   Even parity state reading 0, don't change state.
3. (2,1,1,1,R)   Odd parity state reading 1, change state.
4. (2,0,0,2,R)   Odd parity state reading 0, don't change state.
5. (1,b,1,3,R)   End of string in even parity state, write 1 and go to state 3.
6. (2,b,0,3,R)   End of string in odd parity state, write 0 and go to state 3.

Let's do an example. The initial string is 101, which contains an even number of 1s. Therefore, we want to add a parity bit of 1 and have the final output be the string 1011. Since this final string contains three 1 bits, it has the correct parity. Here's the initial configuration:

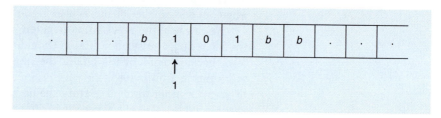

Using instruction 1,

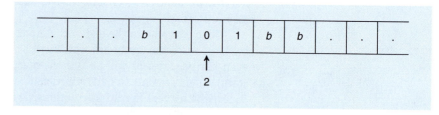

Using instruction 4,

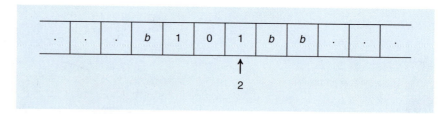

Using instruction 3,

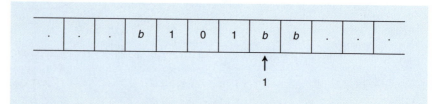

and finally using instruction 5 to write the parity bit, we get

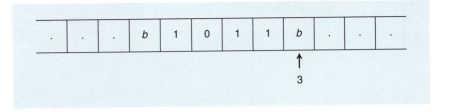

whereupon the machine halts.

11.5.3 Machines for Unary Incrementing

Turing machines can be written to accomplish arithmetic using the nonnegative numbers 0, 1, 2, and so on. Working with these numbers poses a problem we did not face with the bit inverter or the parity bit machine. In those examples, we were manipulating only bits (i.e., 0s and 1s), already part of the Turing machine alphabet of symbols. We can't put numbers like 2, 6, or 754 in cells of the Turing machine tape because these symbols are not part of the alphabet. Therefore, our first task is to find a way to encode such numbers using 0s and 1s. We could use binary representation, as a real computer does. Instead, let us agree on a simpler **unary** representation of numbers (*unary* means that we will use only *one* symbol, namely 1). In unary representation, any unsigned whole number n will be encoded by a sequence of $n + 1$ 1s. Thus,

Number	Turing Machine Representation
0	1
1	11
2	111
3	1111
.	.
.	.
.	.

(You may wonder why we don't simply use 1 to represent 1, 11 to represent 2, and so on. This scheme would mean using no 1s to represent 0, and then the machine could not distinguish a single 0 on the tape from nothing—all blanks—on the tape.)

Using this unary representation of numbers, let's write Turing machines to accomplish some basic arithmetic operations. We can write a Turing machine to add 1 to any number; such a machine is often called an **incrementer.** Using the unary representation of numbers just described, we need only stay in state 1 and travel over the string of 1s to the right-hand end. When we encounter the first blank cell, we write a 1 in it and go to state 2, which has no instructions, in order to halt. Figure 11.6 shows the state diagram.

The Turing machine for the incrementer is

1. $(1,1,1,1,R)$ Pass to the right over 1s.

2. $(1,b,1,2,R)$ Add a single 1 at the right-hand end of the string.

FIGURE 11.6

State Diagram for Incrementer

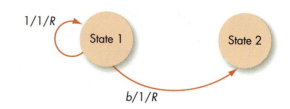

Here's a quick sample computation:

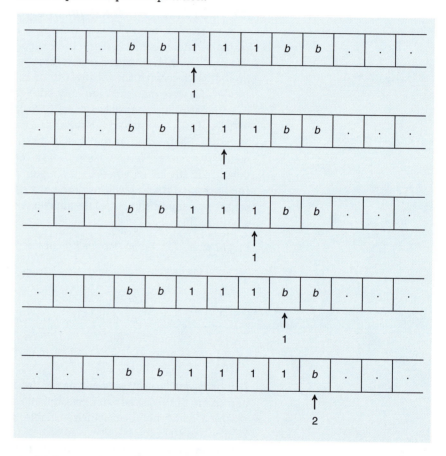

at which point the machine halts. The output on the tape is the representation of the number 3. The machine thus incremented the input, 2, to the output, 3.

Here is another algorithm to accomplish the same task. The preceding algorithm moved to the right-hand end of the string and added a 1. But the increment problem can also be solved by moving to the left-hand end of the string and adding a 1. The Turing machine program for this algorithm is

$(1,1,1,1,L)$ Pass to the left over 1s.
$(1,b,1,2,L)$ Add a single 1 at the left-hand end of the string.

If we apply this algorithm to the same input tape, the computation is

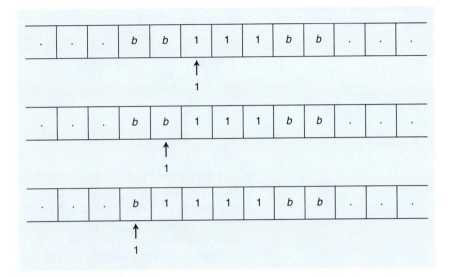

Once again, 2 has been incremented to 3. But whereas the first computation took four operations—that is, four applications of Turing machine instructions—the second computation took only two.

Let's compare these two algorithms further in terms of their time and space efficiency. We'll take the execution of a single Turing machine instruction as a unit of work, so we measure the time used by a Turing machine algorithm by the number of instructions executed. The "space" a Turing machine algorithm takes on any given input will be the number of nonblank cells on the tape that are used during the course of running the program. The input itself occupies some nonblank cells, so the interesting question is how many additional cells the algorithm uses in the course of its execution.

Suppose that the number 5 is to be incremented using algorithm 1. The initial input tape will contain six 1s (the unary representation for 5). The machine moves to the right, over all the 1s on the tape, until it encounters the first blank cell. It writes a 1 into the blank cell and then halts. An instruction is executed for each move to the right. By the time the blank cell is reached, six instruction executions have been done; actually, the first instruction has been executed six times. One final execution, this time of the second instruction, completes the task. Altogether, seven steps were required, two more than the number 5 we were incrementing. One "extra" step comes because of the unary representation, with its additional 1, and a second "extra" step is used to write over the blank cell. Therefore, it is easy to see that if the problem is to increment the number n, then $n + 2$ steps would be required using algorithm 1. Algorithm 2 does a constant number of steps (two) no matter what the size of n. Both algorithms use $n + 2$ cells on the tape: $n + 1$ for the initial input and one more for incrementing. The algorithms are equivalent in space efficiency, but algorithm 2 is more time efficient.

Looking at an input such as 5, our example here, the difference in time efficiency between the two algorithms does not seem great. Figure 11.7 shows

THE NUMBER TO BE INCREMENTED, n	NUMBER OF STEPS REQUIRED	
	ALGORITHM 1	ALGORITHM 2
10	12	2
100	102	2
1,000	1,002	2
10,000	10,002	2

the steps required by algorithms 1 and 2 for larger problems. As the input gets larger, the difference in efficiency becomes more obvious. If our hypothetical Turing machine actually existed and could do, say, one step per second, then algorithm 1 would take 2 hours, 46 minutes, and 42 seconds to increment the number 10,000. Algorithm 2 could do the same job in 2 seconds! This significant difference gives a definite edge to algorithm 2 as the preferable solution method for this problem. Using the notation of Chapter 3, algorithm 1 is a linear time $\Theta(n)$ algorithm, whereas algorithm 2 is a constant time $\Theta(1)$ algorithm.

Although we can compare two Turing machine algorithms for the same task, we can't really compare the efficiency of a Turing machine algorithm with an algorithm that will be run on a "real" computer. For one thing, the data representation is probably different (numbers aren't written in unary form). But more to the point, the basic unit of work is different. It takes many Turing machine operations to do a trivial task, because the entire concept of a Turing machine is so simplistic. Turing machines, as we saw in our few examples, work by carefully moving, changing, and keeping track of individual 0s and 1s. Given such a limited range of activities, a Turing machine must exert a lot of effort to accomplish even mildly interesting tasks. The Turing machine simply plods along, doing its little thing over and over until—eventually—the job is done.

 ### 11.5.4 *A Unary Addition Machine*

A Turing machine can be written to perform the addition of two numbers. Again using unary representation, let's agree to start with the two numbers on the tape separated by a single blank cell. When the Turing machine halts, the tape should contain the unary representation of the sum of the two numbers. The separating blank should be gone. We can think of sliding the entire first number one cell to the right on the tape if we erase the leftmost 1 and then fill in the blank with a 1. Also, both numbers are originally written on the tape using unary representation, which means that there is an extra 1 for each number. When we are finished, we want to have only one extra 1, for the unary representation of the sum. Therefore a second 1 should be removed from the tape. Our plan will be to erase the two leftmost 1s on the tape, proceed rightward to the separating blank, and replace the blank with a 1.

As an example, suppose we wish to add 2 + 3. The original tape representation (we're tired of drawing the individual cells, so we'll just show the tape contents) is

$$\ldots b\,b\,\underset{2}{\underline{1\,1\,1}}\,b\,\underset{3}{\underline{1\,1\,1\,1}}\,b\,b\ldots$$

and the final representation—somewhere on the tape—should be the unary representation for the number 5,

$$\ldots b\,b\,\underset{5}{\underline{1\,1\,1\,1\,1\,1}}\,b\,b\,b\,b\ldots$$

Our algorithm will accomplish this transformation in stages. First, we erase the leftmost 1:

$$\ldots b\,b\,b\,1\,1\,b\,1\,1\,1\,1\,b\,b\ldots$$

We then erase a second 1 from the left end (see Exercise 22 at the end of this chapter for the case when there is no "second 1"):

$$\ldots b\,b\,b\,b\,1\,b\,1\,1\,1\,1\,b\,b\ldots$$

and then move to the right and fill in the blank with a 1:

$$\ldots b\,b\,b\,b\,\underset{5}{\underline{1\,1\,1\,1\,1\,1}}\,b\ldots$$

The Turing machine begins in state 1, so we'll use that state to erase the leftmost 1 and move right, changing to state 2. The job of state 2 is to erase the second 1 and move right, changing to state 3. State 3 must move across any remaining 1s until it encounters the blank, which it changes to a 1 and then goes into a "halting state," state 4. (State 4 will be a halting state because we'll make no instructions for that state.) A state diagram (Figure 11.8) illustrates the desired transitions to next states.

Here is the Turing machine program:

1. $(1,1,b,2,R)$ Erase the leftmost 1 and move right.
2. $(2,1,b,3,R)$ Erase the second 1 and move right.
3. $(3,1,1,3,R)$ Pass over any 1s until a blank is found.
4. $(3,b,1,4,R)$ Write a 1 over the blank and halt.

Try "running" this machine on the preceding 2 + 3 problem.

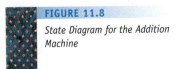

FIGURE 11.8

State Diagram for the Addition Machine

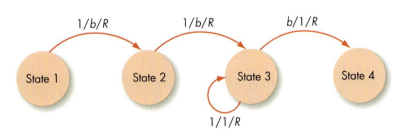

PRACTICE PROBLEMS

1. **a.** First decide what you think the output will be when the parity bit Turing machine is run on the following input:

    $...b1101b...$

    b. Now run the parity bit Turing machine on this tape and see whether you get the answer you expected from part a.

2. Set up the input and run the addition Turing machine to compute 3 + 4.

3. Write a Turing machine that, when run on the tape

    $...b1110b...$

    will produce an output tape of

    $...b11101b...$

LABORATORY EXPERIENCE 18

This laboratory experience will allow you to run simulations of Turing machines using Turing machine algorithms that we have developed in the text. You will see each Turing machine execute a sequence of its basic operations, moving along the tape, possibly modifying the input string, and then halting.

11.6 The Church–Turing Thesis

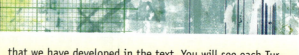

Just how good is the Turing machine as a model of the concept of an algorithm? We've already seen that any Turing machine exhibits the properties of an algorithm, and we've even produced Turing machine algorithms for a couple of important tasks. But perhaps we were judicious in our choice of tasks and happened to use those for which Turing machine instructions could be devised. We should ask whether there are other tasks that are "doable" by an algorithm but not "doable" by a Turing machine.

Of course, the answer to this question is yes. A Turing machine cannot program a VCR or shampoo hair, for example—tasks for which algorithms were given in Chapter 1. But suppose we limit the task to one for which the input and output can be represented symbolically, that is, using letters and numbers. Symbolic representation is, after all, how we traditionally record information such as names, addresses, telephone numbers, pay rates, yearly profits, temperatures, altitudes, times, Social Security numbers, grade point averages, growth rates, and so on. Taking a symbolic representation of information and manipulating it to produce a symbolic representation of other information covers a wide range of tasks, including everything done by "traditional" computing. Now let's ask a modified version of our previous question: Are there symbol manipulation tasks that are "doable" by an algorithm but not "doable" by a Turing machine?

The answer to this question is generally considered to be no, as stated by the **Church–Turing thesis,** named for Alan Turing and another famous mathematician, Alonzo Church.

> **Church–Turing Thesis:** If there exists an algorithm to do a symbol manipulation task, then there exists a Turing machine to do that task.

This is quite an extraordinary claim. It says that any symbol manipulation task that has an algorithmic solution can also be carried out by a Turing machine executing some set of Turing machine instructions. Processing the 2004 Internal Revenue Service records, for example, or directing the guidance and navigation systems on the Space Shuttle can be done (according to this

The Turing Award

The most prestigious technical award given by the Association for Computing Machinery is the annual **Turing Award,** named in honor of Alan Turing. It is sometimes called the computer science Nobel Prize, and is given to an individual selected for "contributions of lasting and major technical importance to the computer field." Some of the individuals we've mentioned in this book have been recipients of the Turing Award, which was first given in 1966:

1971: John McCarthy (Chapter 9)
1972: E. W. Dijkstra (Chapter 9)
1977: John Backus (Chapters 9 and 10)
1983: Dennis Ritchie (Chapter 9)

Other recipients of the award have made contributions in areas we have discussed or will discuss in later chapters:

1975: Allen Newell as one of the founding fathers of artificial intelligence (AI), beginning his work in this area in 1954 (Chapter 14)

1981: Edgar F. Codd for fundamental contributions to database management systems (Chapter 13)

1982: Stephen A. Cook for exploring the class of problems that in Chapter 3 we called "suspected intractable"

1986: John Hopcroft and Robert Tarjan for their work on analysis of algorithms (Chapter 3)

1990: Fernando J. Corbato for pioneering work on general-purpose, time-shared mainframe operating systems (Chapter 6)

1992: Butler Lampson for work in the 1970s and early 1980s on hardware and software that demonstrated solutions to problems of distributed computing done on personal workstations linked by a local area network (Chapter 7)

1999: Frederick P. Brooks, Jr. for landmark contributions to computer architecture, operating systems, and software engineering (Chapters 5, 6, 8)

2001: Ole-Johan Dahl and Kristen Nygaard for ideas fundamental to the emergence of object-oriented programming (Chapter 8)

2002: R. Rivest, A. Shamir, and L. Adler for seminal contributions to the theory and applications of cryptography (Chapter 13)

claim) using Turing machines. The thought of writing a Turing machine program to process IRS records is mind-boggling, but our examples may have convinced you that it is possible. Given that such a program could be written, one can hardly imagine how many centuries it would take to execute, even with a very rapid "system clock." But the Church–Turing thesis says nothing about how efficiently the task will be done, only that it *can* be done by some Turing machine.

There are really two parts to writing a Turing machine for a symbol manipulation task. One part involves encoding symbolic information as strings of 0s and 1s so that it can appear on Turing machine tapes. This is not difficult, and we know that real computers store all information, including graphical information, in binary. The other part is the heart of the challenge: Given that we get the input information encoded on a Turing machine tape, can we write the Turing machine instructions that will produce the encoded form of the correct output? Figure 11.9 illustrates the problem. The bottom arrow is the algorithmic solution to the symbol manipulation task we wish to emulate. To perform this emulation, we must first encode the symbolic input into a bit string on a Turing machine tape (upward pointing left arrow), write the Turing machine that solves the problem (top arrow), and finally, decode the resulting bit string into symbolic output (downward pointing right arrow). The Church–Turing thesis asserts that this process can always be done.

What exactly is a *thesis*? According to the dictionary, it is "a statement advanced for consideration and maintained by argument." That sounds less than convincing—hasn't the Church–Turing thesis been proved? No, and that's why it is called a thesis, not a theorem. Theorems are ideas that can be proved in a formal, mathematical way, such as "the sum of the interior angles of a triangle equals 180°." The Church–Turing thesis can never be proved, because—despite all our talk about algorithms and their properties—the definition of an algorithm is still descriptive, not mathematical. It would be like trying to "prove" that an ideal day at the beach is sunny and 85°F. We might all agree on this, but we'll never be able to "prove" it. Well, then, the Church–Turing thesis makes a remarkable claim and can never be proved! Sounds pretty suspicious—what are the arguments on its behalf? There are two.

One argument on behalf of the Church–Turing thesis is that early on, when the thesis was first put forward, whenever computer science researchers

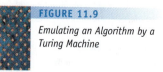

FIGURE 11.9

Emulating an Algorithm by a Turing Machine

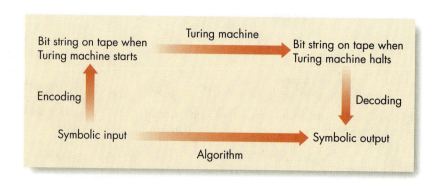

described algorithmic solutions for tasks, they also tried to find Turing machines for those tasks. They were always successful; no one was ever able to put forth an algorithm for a task for which a Turing machine was not eventually found. This does not mean that no such task exists, but it lends weight to a body of evidence in support of the thesis.

A second argument on behalf of the thesis is the fact that a number of other mathematicians attempted to find models for computing agents and algorithms. All of these were proved to be equivalent to Turing machines and Turing machine programs in the following sense: whatever could be done by these other computing agents running their algorithms could also be done by a Turing machine running a Turing machine program, and vice versa. This suggests that the Turing machine captures all of these other ideas about "algorithm."

The Church–Turing thesis is now widely accepted by computer scientists. They no longer feel it necessary to write a Turing machine when they talk about an algorithmic computation. After describing an algorithm to carry out some task, they simply say, Now let T be the Turing machine that does this task. You may make your own decision about the Church–Turing thesis, but in this book we will go along with convention and accept it as true. We are then accepting the Turing machine as an ultimate model of a computing agent and a Turing machine program as an ultimate model of an algorithm. We are saying that Turing machines define the limits of **computability**—that which can be done by symbol manipulation algorithms. What can be done by an algorithm is doable by a Turing machine, and what is not doable by a Turing machine cannot be done by an algorithm. In particular, if we find a symbol manipulation task that no Turing machine can perform (in its elementary way of moving around over a tape of 0s and 1s), then there is no algorithm for this task, and no real computer, no matter how sophisticated, will ever be able to do it either. That's why the Turing machine is so important. You can now see where this is all leading in terms of our search for a problem that has no algorithmic solution. Suppose we can find a (symbol manipulation) problem for which we can prove that no Turing machine exists to solve it. Then, because of the Church–Turing thesis, no algorithm exists to solve it either. The problem is an **uncomputable** or **unsolvable** problem.

Note again that if we pose a problem and try to construct a Turing machine to solve it but are not successful, that alone does not prove that no Turing machine exists. What we must do is actually prove that no one can ever find such a Turing machine—that it is not possible for a Turing machine to exist that solves this problem. It may appear that the introduction of Turing machines hasn't helped at all and that we are confronted by the same dilemma we faced at the beginning of this chapter. Ah, but Alan Turing, in the late 1930s, found such a problem and proved its unsolvability.

11.7 Unsolvable Problems

The problem Turing found is an ingenious one that itself involves Turing machine computations. A Turing machine that is executing an algorithm (a collection of Turing machine instructions) to solve some task must halt when begun on a tape containing input appropriate to that task. On other kinds of input, the Turing machine may not halt. It is easy enough for us to decide whether any specific configuration of a given Turing machine is a halting configuration. If a Turing machine program consists of the following four instructions:

$(1,0,1,2,R)$

$(1,1,0,2,R)$

$(2,0,0,2,R)$

$(2,b,b,2,L)$

then the configuration

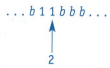

$$\dots b\,1\,1\,b\,b\,b\dots$$

is a halting configuration because there is no instruction of the form $(2,1,-,-,-)$. It is also easy to see that this configuration will arise if the Turing machine is begun on the tape

$$\dots b\,0\,1\,b\,b\,b\dots$$

Similarly, we can see that if the Turing machine is begun on the tape

$$\dots b\,1\,b\,b\,b\dots$$

then it will never halt. Instead, after the first step (clock tick), the machine will cycle forever between the two configurations

$$\dots b\,0\,b\,b\,b\dots \quad \text{and} \quad \dots b\,0\,b\,b\,b\dots$$

In a more complicated case, however, if we know the Turing machine program and we know the initial contents of the tape, then it may not be so easy to decide whether the Turing machine will eventually halt when begun on that tape. Of course, we could always simply execute the Turing machine—that is, carry out the instructions. We don't have all day to wait for the answer, so we'll set a time-out for our Turing machine system clock. Let's say we are willing to wait for 1,000 clock ticks. If we come to a halting configuration within the first 1,000 steps, then we know the answer: this Turing machine, running on this input tape, halts. But suppose we have not come to a halting configuration within the first 1,000 clock ticks. Can we say that the machine will never halt? Should we wait another 1,000 clock ticks? 10,000 clock ticks? Just running the Turing machine doesn't necessarily enable us to decide about halting.

Here is the problem we propose to investigate:

Decide, given any collection of Turing machine instructions together with any initial tape contents, whether that Turing machine will ever halt if started on that tape.

This is a clear and unambiguous problem known as the **halting problem.** Does it have a Turing machine solution? Can we find one Turing machine that will solve every instance of this problem—that is, one that will give us the answer "Yes, halts" or "No, never halts" for every (Turing machine, initial tape) pair?

This is an uncomputable problem; we will show that no Turing machine exists to solve this problem. Remember that we said it was not sufficient to look for such a machine and fail; we actually have to prove that no such machine can exist. The way to do this is to assume that such a Turing machine does exist and then show that this assumption leads to an impossible situation, so such a machine could not exist after all. This approach is called a **proof by contradiction.**

We'll assume, then, that P is a Turing machine that solves the halting problem. On the initial tape for P we will have to put a description—using the binary digits 0 and 1—of a collection T of Turing machine instructions, as well as the initial tape content t on which those instructions run. This is the encoding part of Figure 11.9. Translating Turing machine instructions into binary form is tedious but not difficult. For example, we could use unary notation for machine states and tape symbols, designate the direction in which the read unit moves by 1 for R (right) and 11 for L (left), and separate the parts of a Turing machine instruction by 0s. Let's use T^* to symbolize the binary form of the collection T of Turing machine instructions. P is then run on a tape containing both T^* and t, so the initial tape for P looks like the following, where T^* and t may occupy many cells of the tape.

$$\ldots b\, b\, T^*\, b\, t\, b\, b \ldots$$

Our assumption is that P will always give us an answer ("Yes, halts" or "No, never halts"). P's yes/no answer would be its output—what is written on the tape when P halts; therefore P itself must always halt. Again, because the output is written on P's tape, it also has to be in binary form, so let's say that a single 1 and all the rest blanks represents "yes," and a single 0 and all the rest blanks represents "no." This is the decoding part of Figure 11.9. To summarize:

When begun on a tape containing T^* and t

>*P halts with 1 on its tape exactly when T eventually halts when begun on t*

>*P halts with 0 on its tape exactly when T never halts when begun on t*

Figure 11.10 is a pictorial representation of the actions of P when started on a tape containing T^* and t.

When P halts with a single 1 on its tape, it does so because there are no instructions allowing P to proceed in its current state when reading 1. For example, P might be in state 9, and there is no instruction of the form

$$(9,1,\text{-},\text{-},\text{-})$$

for machine P. Let's imagine adding more instructions to P to create a new machine Q that behaves just like P except that when it reaches this same configuration, it moves forever to the right on the tape instead of halting. To do

FIGURE 11.10

*Hypothetical Turing Machine P
Running on T* and t*

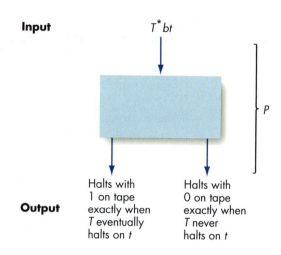

Input

T^*bt

P

Output

Halts with
1 on tape
exactly when
T eventually
halts on *t*

Halts with
0 on tape
exactly when
T never
halts on *t*

this, pick some state not in *P*, say 52, and add the following two new instructions to *P*:

$$(9,1,1,52,R)$$

$$(52,b,b,52,R)$$

Figure 11.11 represents *Q*'s behavior when started on a tape containing *T** and *t*.

Finally, we'll create a new machine *S*. This machine first makes a copy of what appears on its input tape. (This is a doable if tedious task. The machine must "pick up" a 0 or 1 by going to a particular state, move to another part of the tape, and write a 0 or 1, depending on the state. It travels back and repeats the process; however, each time it picks up a 0 or 1, it must mark the tape with some marker symbol, say *X* for 0 and *Y* for 1, so that it doesn't try to pick them up again. At the end of the copying, the markers must be changed back to 0s and 1s.) After *S* is finished with its copying job, it uses the same instructions as machine *Q*.

Now what happens when machine *S* is run on a tape that contains *S**, the binary representation of *S*'s own instructions? *S* first makes a copy of *S** and then turns the computation over to *Q*, which is now running on a tape containing *S** and *S**. Figure 11.12 shows the result; this figure follows from Figure 11.11 where *T** and *t* are both *S**. Figure 11.12 represents the behavior of *S* running on input *S**. The final outcome is either (left output)

S running on input S* never halts

> *exactly when S halts running on S*—this is a contradiction*

or (right output)

S running on input S* halts with 0 on the tape

> *exactly when S never halts running on S*—also a contradiction*

FIGURE 11.11

Hypothetical Turing Machine Q
Running on T* *and* t

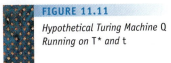

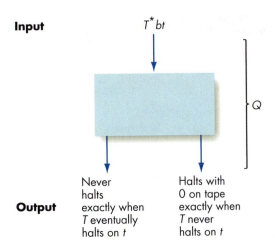

Input $T^* bt$

Q

Output
Never
halts
exactly when
T eventually
halts on *t*

Halts with
0 on tape
exactly when
T never
halts on *t*

(Perhaps you'll need to read this several times while looking at Figure 11.12 to convince yourself of what we have said.) We have backed ourselves into a real corner here, but that's good. This is exactly the impossible situation we were hoping to find.

We assumed that there was a Turing machine that could solve the halting problem, and this assumption led to an impossible situation. The assumption is therefore incorrect, and no Turing machine can exist to solve the halting problem. Therefore, no algorithm can exist to solve this problem. The halting problem is an example of an unsolvable or uncomputable problem.

FIGURE 11.12

Hypothetical Turing Machine S
Running on S*

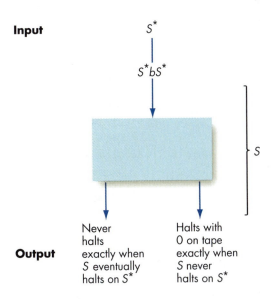

Input S^*

$S^* b S^*$

S

Output
Never
halts
exactly when
S eventually
halts on S^*

Halts with
0 on tape
exactly when
S never
halts on S^*

Unsolvable problems are not confined to problems about running programs (Java programs, C++ programs, or Turing machines).

In Chapter 10 we talked about grammars that can be described in Backus-Naur Form (BNF) and about how a compiler parses a programming language statement by applying the rules of its grammar. We noted that ambiguous grammars are not suitable for programming languages because they can allow multiple interpretations of a statement. It would be nice to have a test (an algorithm) to decide whether any BNF grammar is ambiguous. This is an unsolvable problem—no such algorithm can exist. Deciding whether any two such grammars produce the same language is also unsolvable.

One of the earliest "decision problems" was posed by the British mathematician David Hilbert in 1900. Consider quadratic equations of the form

$$ax^2 + bx + c = 0$$

where a, b, and c are integers. We can easily decide whether any one such equation has integer solutions by applying the quadratic formula to solve the equation. But consider more general polynomial equations in several unknowns, such as

$$ax^4 + by^2 + cz^6 + dw^4 + e = 0$$

where the unknowns are x, y, z, and w and the coefficients (a, b, c, d, and e) are integers. Is there an algorithm to decide whether any such equation has integer solutions? In 1970, this problem was finally shown to be unsolvable.

The halting problem seems rather abstract; perhaps we don't care whether it is unsolvable. However, real computer programs written in real programming languages to run on real computers are also symbol manipulation algorithms and, by the Church–Turing thesis, can be simulated by Turing machines. This means that the unsolvability of the halting problem has practical consequences. For example, we know that some C++ or Java programs can get stuck in infinite loops. It would be nice to have a program that you could run ahead of time on any C++ or Java program, together with its input, that would tell you, Uh-oh, if you run this program on this input, it will get into an infinite loop, or No problem, if you run this program on this input, it will eventually stop. The unsolvability of the halting problem says that this is not possible—and that such a program cannot possibly exist. Other unsolvable problems, related to the halting problem, have the following practical consequences:

- No program can be written to decide whether any given program always stops eventually, no matter what the input.

- No program can be written to decide whether any two programs are equivalent (will produce the same output for all inputs).

- No program can be written to decide whether any given program run on any given input will ever produce some specific output.

This last case means it is impossible to write a general automatic program tester—one that for any program can check whether, given input A, it produces correct output B. That is why program testing plays such an important role in the software development life cycle described in Chapter 8.

PRACTICE PROBLEMS

1. Explain how a proof by contradiction is done.

2. **a.** Write in your own words a statement of the halting problem.
   b. Write a paragraph that describes the proof of the unsolvability of the halting problem.

It is important to note, however, that these problems are unsolvable because of their generality. We are asking for *one* program that will decide something about *any* given program. It may be very easy to write a program *A* that can make a decision only about a specific program *B* by utilizing specialized properties of *B*. (*Analogy:* if I ask you to be ready to write "I love you" in English, you can do it; if I ask you to be ready to write "I love you" in any language I might later specify, you can't do it.)

LABORATORY EXPERIENCE 19

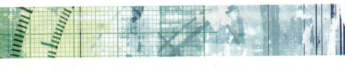

Using the same Turing machine simulator as before, you can now design and run your own Turing machine algorithms for simple problems.

11.8   Conclusion

We began this chapter by proposing that there exist unsolvable problems—problems for which no solution algorithm exists. To prove such a statement, we looked for appropriate models of "computing agent" and "algorithm" that would enable us to concentrate on the fundamental nature of computation. We discussed the nature of models in general and their importance in helping us understand real phenomena. After developing a list of properties inherent in any computing agent, we defined the Turing machine, noted that it incorporates these properties, and accepted it as a model of a computing agent. A Turing machine program incorporates the properties of an algorithm described in Chapter 1, so we accepted it as a model of an algorithm. Are these good models? Do they capture everything that is fundamental about computing and algorithms? After looking at a few Turing machines devised to do some simple tasks, we stated our position with a resounding *yes* in the form of the

Church–Turing thesis: Not only is a Turing machine program an example of an algorithm, but every symbolic manipulation algorithm can be done by a Turing machine (we believe). This leap of faith—putting total confidence in Turing machine programs as models of algorithms—allows us to define the boundaries of computability. If it can't be done by a Turing machine, then it is not computable. Thus, the real value of Turing machines as models of computability is in exposing problems that are uncomputable—problems for which no algorithmic solution exists no matter how intelligent we are or how long we keep looking. As a practical matter, recognizing uncomputable problems certainly saves time; we are less likely to devote our lives to searching for algorithms that can never be. As a philosophical matter, it is important to know that computability has its limits, beyond which lies the great abyss of the uncomputable!

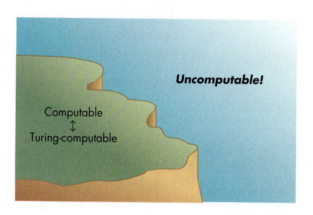

11.9 Summary of Level 4

In Level 4, "The Software World," we examined in some detail one procedural programming language as an example of a means for expressing algorithms at a high level of abstraction. Other high-level languages exist, including other procedural languages, special-purpose languages, and those that follow other philosophies, such as functional languages and logic-based languages. Because algorithms written in high-level languages ultimately run on low-level hardware, program translators must convert from one level of algorithmic expression to another. We've looked at the series of tasks that a language compiler must be able to perform in order to carry out this conversion. This final chapter of Level 4 proved that there are limits to computability—that there exist problems that can never be solved algorithmically.

With all of the hardware and software machinery in place to implement algorithmic problem solutions, we are ready to proceed to the next level—the level of applications—to see some of the ways in which computers (and algorithms) are being put to use.

Interestingly enough, the first application that we will examine in Chapter 12 relates very closely to what we have discussed in this chapter—building models. In this chapter we constructed a formal model of an algorithm in order to prove the existence of unsolvable problems. In the next chapter we will use models in a very different way. Rather than investigating the formal properties of computation, we will build simulation models that help us to solve important problems such as predicting the weather, creating new medicines, tracking our economy, and designing safe and efficient airplanes.

In this set of exercises, when writing Turing machine algorithms, include comments for each instruction or related group of instructions. The comments should convey information in terms of the algorithm the Turing machine is accomplishing. Thus, the instruction

$$(1,0,0,1,R)$$

might have a comment like Pass to the right over all the 0s, not a comment like In state 1 looking at a 0, write a 0, stay in state 1, and move right, which provides no additional information.

1. Describe what factors might be included in a model for the spread of an epidemic.

2. Say an automobile manufacturer designs a new car using a sophisticated and detailed computer simulation, but no prototype vehicles, and the automobile is later found to have a defect. Do you think the manufacturer is accountable? Is the manufacturer accountable if it builds prototypes that do not reveal the defect, but does not do a simulation?

3. Give an example of a potential use of computerized models in
   a. The pharmaceutical industry
   b. The food processing industry
   c. The insurance industry

4. Which of the following could be considered computing agents and why?
   a. A clock radio
   b. A thermostat
   c. A video camera
   d. A programmable calculator

5. Given the Turing machine instruction

$$(1,1,0,2,L)$$

and the configuration

$$...b\,1\,0\,b...$$

1

draw the next configuration.

6. Find the output for the Turing machine
   $$(1,1,1,2,R)$$
   $$(1,0,0,2,R)$$
   $$(1,b,1,2,R)$$
   $$(2,0,0,2,R)$$
   $$(2,1,0,1,R)$$

when run on the tape

$$...b\,1\,0\,0\,1\,b...$$

7. Find the output for the Turing machine
   $$(1,1,1,2,L)$$
   $$(2,b,0,3,L)$$
   $$(3,b,1,4,R)$$
   $$(4,0,1,4,R)$$

when run on the tape

$$...b\,1\,b...$$

8. Describe the behavior of the Turing machine
   $$(1,1,1,1,R)$$
   $$(1,0,0,2,L)$$
   $$(2,1,0,2,L)$$
   $$(2,b,1,3,L)$$
   $$(3,b,b,1,R)$$

when run on the tape

$$...b\,1\,0\,1\,b...$$

9. Describe the behavior of the following Turing machine on any input tape containing a binary string:
   $$(1,1,1,1,R)$$
   $$(1,0,0,1,R)$$
   $$(1,b,1,1,R)$$

10. Write a Turing machine that, when run on the tape

$$...b\,1\,1\,1\,1\,1\,b...$$

produces an output tape of

$$...b\,0\,1\,1\,1\,1\,b...$$

You should be able to accomplish this using only one instruction.

11. Say a Turing machine is supposed to change any string of 1s to a string of 0s. For example,

$$...b\,1\,1\,1\,b...$$

should become

$$...b\,0\,0\,0\,b...$$

Will the following Turing machine do the job? Why or why not?
   $$(1,1,0,2,R)$$
   $$(2,1,0,3,R)$$
   $$(3,1,0,4,R)$$

12. a. Write a Turing machine that, when run on the tape

$$...b\,1\,1\,1\,1\,1\,b...$$

produces an output tape of

   $\dots b11110b\dots$

b. Write a Turing machine that, when run on any tape containing a unary string, changes the rightmost 1 to 0 and then halts. (If your solution to part (a) was sufficiently general, you will not have to change it here.)

13. Write a Turing machine to perform a **unary decrement** (the opposite of an increment). Assume that $n > 0$.

14. Write a Turing machine to perform a unary decrement. Assume that n may be 0, in which case a single 0 should be output on the tape to signify that the operation would result in a negative number.

15. Write a Turing machine that operates on any binary string and changes it to a string of the same length with all 1s. It should, for example, change the tape

   $\dots b011010b\dots$

to

   $\dots b1111111b\dots$

However, you must write instructions that allow your Turing machine to work on *any* binary string, not just the one shown here.

16. Write a Turing machine that operates on any string of 1s and changes it to a string of alternating 1s and 0s.

17. Write a Turing machine that begins on a tape containing a single 1 and never halts but successively displays the strings

   $\dots b1b\dots$

   $\dots b010b\dots$

   $\dots b00100b\dots$

and so on.

18. Write a Turing machine that operates on the unary representation of any number and decides whether the number is 0; your machine should produce an output tape containing the unary representation of 1 if the number was 0 and the unary representation of 2 if the number was not 0.

19. A **palindrome** is a string of characters that reads the same forward and backward, such as radar or IUPUI. Write a Turing machine to decide whether any binary string is a palindrome by halting with a blank tape if the string is a palindrome and halting with a nonblank tape if the string is not a palindrome.

   Note: The world's longest single-word palindrome is the Finnish word for "lye dealer":

   Saippuakivikauppias

   Other palindromes include

   Slap a ham on Omaha pals

   Do geese see god

   A man a plan a canal Panama

20. Write a Turing machine that takes any unary string of an even number of 1s and halts with the first half of the string changed to 0s. (*Hint:* You may need to use a "marker" symbol such as X or Y to replace temporarily any input symbols you have already processed and do not want to process again; at the end, your program must "clean up" any marker symbols.)

21. Write a Turing machine that takes as input the unary representation of any two different numbers, separated by a blank, and halts with the representation of the larger of the two numbers on the tape. (*Hint:* You may need to use a "marker" symbol such as X or Y to replace temporarily any input symbols you have already processed and do not want to process again; at the end, your program must "clean up" any marker symbols.)

22. The Turing machine described in Section 11.5.4 to add two unary numbers was designed to erase the two leftmost 1s on the tape, move to the right to the blank separating the two numbers, and replace the blank with a 1. If the first of the two numbers being added is 0, then there are not two 1s before the separating blank. Does the algorithm still work in this case?

23. Draw a state diagram for a Turing machine that takes any string of 1s and changes every third 1 to a 0. Thus, for example,

   $\dots b1111111b\dots$

would become

   $\dots b110110b\dots$

24. Draw a state diagram for a Turing machine that increments a binary number. Thus, if the binary representation of 4 is initially on the tape,

   $\dots b100\dots$

then the output should be the binary representation of 5,

   $\dots b101\dots$

or if the initial tape contains the binary representation of 7,

   $\dots b111b\dots$

then the output should be the binary representation of 8,

   $\dots b1000b\dots$

25. Analyze the time and space efficiency of the following Turing machine operating on a unary string of length n.

   $(1,1,1,1,R)$

   $(1,b,b,2,L)$

   $(2,1,0,2,L)$

   $(2,b,b,3,R)$

   $(3,0,1,3,R)$

26. Suppose we already have Turing machine instructions to copy a unary string; we also know how to add two unary numbers. Describe (in words only) the design of a Turing machine to multiply two unary numbers.

27. Two other Turing machine unary addition algorithms follow.

   1. Fill in the separating blank with a 1, go to the far right end and erase two 1s

   2. Erase a 1 on the left end, fill in the separating blank with a 1, erase a 1 on the right end

   a. Do both of these algorithms work correctly?

   b. Write the Turing machine for each of these algorithms.

   c. Informally, which of the three addition algorithms (the one given in the chapter and these two) seems most time efficient?

   d. Suppose that the numbers to be added are n and m. The original tape contains the unary representation of n, followed by a blank, followed by the unary representation of m. Write exact expressions in terms of n, m, or both for the time efficiency of each of the three algorithms. Does this confirm your answer from part (c)?

   e. Again assuming that the numbers to be added are n and m, write an exact expression for the space efficiency of each of the three algorithms.

28. Your boss gives you a computer program and a set of input data and asks you to determine whether the program will get into an infinite loop running on these data. You report that you cannot do this job, citing the Church–Turing thesis. Should your boss fire you? Explain.

29. What is the significance of the unsolvability of the halting problem?

30. The **uniform halting problem** is to decide, given any collection of Turing machine instructions, whether that Turing machine will halt for every input tape. This is an unsolvable problem. Which of the three practical consequences of unsolvability problems described in Section 11.7 (page 551) follows from the uniform halting problem?

31. The **10-step halting problem** is to decide, given any collection of Turing machine instructions, together with any initial tape contents, whether that Turing machine will halt within 10 steps when started on that tape. Explain why the 10-step halting problem is computable.

CHALLENGE WORK

1. Several alternative definitions of Turing machines exist, all of which produce machines that are equivalent in computational ability to the Turing machine as defined in this chapter. One of these alternative definitions is the **multitrack Turing machine.** In a multitrack Turing machine, there are multiple tapes. The machine reads a cell from each of the tapes and, on the basis of what it reads, it writes a symbol on each tape, changes state, and moves left or right. Figure 11.13 shows a two-track Turing machine currently in state 1 reading a 1 on the first tape and a 0 on the second tape.

An instruction for this Turing machine would have the following form:

   (current state, current first tape symbol, next first tape symbol, current second tape symbol, next second tape symbol, next state, direction of move)

An instruction of the form $(1,1,0,0,0,2,R)$ applied to the machine configuration of Figure 11.13 would result in the configuration shown in Figure 11.14.

FIGURE 11.13

A Two-Track Turing Machine

.	.	.	b	b	1	1	1	b	b	.	.	.
.	.	.	b	b	0	1	1	0	b	.	.	.

       ↑
       1

FIGURE 11.14

*New Configuration for the
Two-Track Machine*

.	.	.	b	b	0	1	1	b	b	.	.	.
.	.	.	b	b	0	1	1	b	b	.	.	.

↑
2

As in the original Turing machine definition, some conventions apply. Each tape can contain only a finite number of nonblank symbols, and the leftmost nonblank symbols must initially "line up" on the two tapes. The read head begins in this leftmost nonblank position in state 1. At any time, if no instruction applies to the current machine configuration, the machine halts.

a. Design a two-track Turing machine that compares two binary strings and decides whether they are equal. If the strings are equal, the machine halts in some fixed state; if they are not equal, the machine halts in some other fixed state.

b. Solve this same problem using the regular Turing machine from this chapter.

c. Prove the following statement: Any computation that can be carried out using a regular Turing machine can be done using a two-track Turing machine.

d. On the basis of parts (a) and (b), make an argument for the following statement: Any computation that can be carried out using a two-track Turing machine can be done using a regular Turing machine.

2. Read some biographical information on Alan Turing and write a report on his life, concentrating particularly on his contributions in computability theory, cryptography, and artificial intelligence.

FOR FURTHER READING

A classic explanation of Gödel's work on the limitations of formal systems describing arithmetic can be found in

Nagel, E., and Newman, J. R. "Gödel's Proof," *Scientific American* (June 1956).

The foundational textbook in the area of models for various sorts of computation tasks, including Turing machines, is

Hopcroft, J. E., and Ullman, J. D. *Introduction to Automata Theory, Languages, and Computation.* Reading, MA: Addison-Wesley, 1979.

whereas the updated version is

Hopcroft, J. E.; Motwani, R.; and Ullman, J. D. *Introduction to Automata Theory, Languages, and Computation,* 2nd ed. Reading, MA: Addison-Wesley, 2001.

Other books that cover much the same ground, but perhaps in less detail, include

Linz, P. *An Introduction to Formal Languages and Automata,* 3rd ed. Sudbury, MA: Jones and Bartlett, 2000.

Sipser, M. *Introduction to the Theory of Computation.* Boston, MA: Brooks/Cole, 1997.

For a stimulating experience in "thinking about thinking," try the Pulitzer Prize–winning book

Hofstadter, D. R. *Gödel, Escher, Bach: An Eternal Golden Braid.* New York: Basic Books, 1979.

LEVEL 5

Applications

Social Issues
Chapter 15

Applications
Chapters 12, 13, 14

The Software World
Chapters 8, 9, 10, 11

The Virtual Machine
Chapters 6, 7

The Hardware World
Chapters 4, 5

The Algorithmic Foundations of Computer Science
Chapters 2, 3

LEVEL 5

Level 4 focused on programming languages and software development. In this section, entitled *Applications,* we answer the question, What kind of programs do we want to write? Now that we have introduced the hardware (Level 2) and software (Levels 3, 4) tools required to implement algorithms, we need to take a look at the types of problems we wish to address using these tools.

Of course, there are far too many applications to survey them all; indeed, there is hardly an area of society that has not been significantly influenced and changed by the rapid growth of information technology. Therefore, instead of trying to briefly survey a large number of applications, we will, instead, examine a few important applications in depth. These applications will serve as examples of the enormous effect that computing is having on our work and on our lives.

CHAPTER 12

Simulation and Modeling

12.1   Introduction

The computational devices of the 19th and early 20th centuries were used to solve important mathematical and scientific problems of the day. We saw this in the historical review of computing in Chapter 1: Charles Babbage's Difference Engine evaluated polynomial functions; Herman Hollerith's punched card machines carried out a statistical analysis of the 1890 census; ENIAC computed artillery ballistic tables; and Alan Turing's Colossus cranked away at Bletchly Park breaking the "unbreakable" German Enigma code. The users of these early computing devices were primarily mathematicians, physicists, and engineers.

Computing today has expanded far beyond the domains of the physical and mathematical sciences. There is hardly a field of study or aspect of our society—from art to zoology, business to entertainment—that has not been profoundly changed by information technology. Today we use computers in many "nonscientific" ways, such as playing games, surfing the Web, listening to music, and sending email.

However, the physical, mathematical, engineering, and economic sciences are still some of the largest users of computing and information technology. In this chapter we investigate in depth what is probably the single most important scientific use of computing—simulation and modeling. This application is having a major impact on a number of quantitative fields, including chemistry, biology, medicine, meteorology, ecology, geography, and economics.

12.2   Computational Modeling

 ### 12.2.1   *Introduction to Systems and Models*

In the **scientific method,** we observe the behavior of a system and formulate a hypothesis that tries to explain its behavior. We then design and carry out experiments to either prove or disprove the validity of that hypothesis. This is the fundamental way that new scientific knowledge and understanding is achieved.

Scientists often work with a model of a system rather than experimenting on the "real thing." A **model,** as first defined in Section 11.2, is an abstraction of the system being studied that we claim behaves much like the original. If that claim is true, then we can experiment on the model and use these results to understand the behavior of the actual system. For example, physical models (small-scale replicas) have been in use for many years, and we are all familiar with the idea of building a model airplane and testing it in a wind tunnel in order to understand how the full size aircraft would behave.

In this chapter we are not interested in physical models but in **computational models,** also called **simulation models.** In a computer simulation, a physical system is modeled as a set of mathematical equations and/or algorithmic procedures that capture the fundamental characteristics and behavior of a system. This model is then translated into one of the high-level languages of Chapters 8 and 9 and executed on the Von Neumann computer described in Chapters 4 and 5.

Why construct a simulation model? Why not study either the system itself or a physical replica of the system? There are many reasons:

- *Existence.* The system may not exist; therefore, it is not possible to experiment directly on the actual system.
- *Physical realization.* The system is not constructed from entities that can be represented by physical objects. For example, it may be a social system (e.g., welfare policies, labor practices) that can be simulated only on a computer.
- *Safety.* It may be dangerous to experiment on the actual system or a physical replica. For example, you would not want to build a nuclear reactor using a new and unproven technology.
- *Speed of construction.* It may take too much time to construct a physical model. Sometimes it is faster to design and build a computer simulation.
- *Time scale.* Some physical systems change too slowly or too quickly. For example, an elementary particle in a high-speed accelerator may decompose in 10^{-15} seconds. At the other end of the time scale, some ecosystems take thousands of years to react to a modification. A simulation can easily model fractions of a second or billions of years, since time is simply a parameter in an equation.
- *Ethical behavior.* Some physical models have serious moral and ethical consequences, perhaps the best known being the use of animals for medical research. In this case, a computational model could eliminate a great deal of suffering.
- *Ease of modification.* If we were not happy with our original design, we would need to construct a brand new physical model. In a simulation, we only need to change some numerical parameters and rerun the model.

This last advantage—ease of modification—makes computational modeling a particularly attractive tool for designing totally new systems. We initialize the system, observe its response, and if we are not satisfied, modify the parameters and run the model again. We repeat this process over and over, always trying to improve performance. Only when we think that we have created the best design possible would we actually build it. This "interactive" approach to design, sometimes called **computational steering,** is usually infeasible using physical models, as it would take too much time.

This interactive design methodology is diagrammed in Figure 12.1.

FIGURE 12.1

*Using a Simulation in an Inter-
active Design Environment*

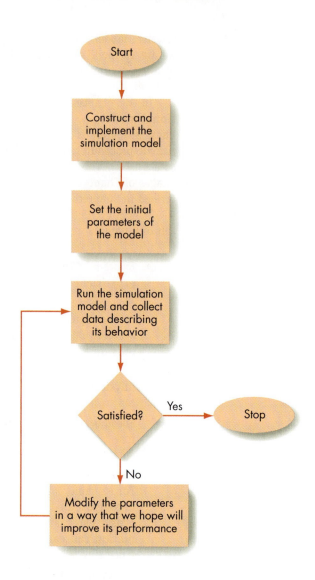

So, for all the reasons cited previously, computational models are an excellent way both to design new systems and study and improve the behavior of existing systems. Virtually every branch of science and engineering makes use of these types of models, and it is not unusual today to see chemists, biologists, physicists, ecologists, and physicians conducting research at their computer screens rather than in the laboratory.

Computational models often use advanced mathematical techniques far beyond the scope of this text (and solving them often requires the large-scale parallel computers mentioned in Chapter 5). Therefore, in the upcoming pages we often rely on rather simple examples, far simpler than the models you will encounter in the real world. However, even these simple examples will illustrate the enormous power and capabilities of computational modeling.

12.2.2 *Computational Models, Accuracy, and Errors*

Legend says that in the late 16th century the famed scientist Galileo Galilei dropped two balls from the top of the Tower of Pisa—a massive iron cannonball and a lighter wooden one—to disprove the Aristotelian Theory, which predicted that heavy objects would fall faster than light ones. When Galileo dropped the two balls they hit the ground at the same time, exactly as he had hypothesized. Whether or not this event actually took place (and there is considerable debate), it is an excellent example of scientific experimentation using a physical system, in this case two balls of different weight, a high platform, and the earth below.

Today, we do not need to climb the Tower of Pisa because there is a well-known mathematical model that describes the behavior of a falling mass acted upon only by the force of gravity:

$$d = v_{init}\, t + 1/2\; gt^2$$

This equation says that if a mass in free fall has an initial velocity v_{init} meters/sec at time 0, then at time t it will have fallen a distance of d meters. (Notice that the object's mass is not part of the equation. This is exactly what Galileo was trying to demonstrate.) The factor g is the acceleration due to gravity, which is assumed to be 9.8 meters/sec^2 everywhere along the earth's surface.

Using this model, we can reproduce aspects of Galileo's 16th century experiment without having to travel to Italy. For example, we can determine the time when the two balls Galileo dropped from the 54-meter high Tower of Pisa would have hit the ground, assuming that their initial velocity was 0.0:

$$54 = (0 * t) + 1/2 * 9.8 * t^2$$
$$t^2 = 11.02$$
$$t = 3.32 \text{ seconds}$$

This simple example shows the beauty and simplicity of computational models. Such models can provide quick answers to questions without the cumbersome setup often required of physical experiments. This model is also easy to modify. For example, if we want to know how long it would take those same two balls to hit the ground when dropped from a height of 150 meters, rather than 54, we reset d to 150 and solve the same equation:

$$150 = (0 * t) + 1/2 * 9.8 * t^2$$
$$t^2 = 30.6$$
$$t = 5.53 \text{ seconds}$$

Using physical models, Galileo would have had to scour the 16th century world to locate a 150-meter high tower. (A mathematical model is also much safer since no one ever fell off the top of an equation!)

Unfortunately, modeling is not quite as simple as we have just described, and there are a number of issues that must be addressed and solved to make this technique workable.

The first issue is achieving the proper balance between **accuracy** and **complexity.** Our model must be an accurate representation of the physical system, but at the same time, it must be simple enough to implement as a program and solve on a computer in a reasonable amount of time. Often this balance is not easy to achieve, as most real-world systems are acted upon by a large number of factors. We need to decide which of those factors are important enough to be included in our model and which can safely be omitted.

For example, the model of a falling body given earlier is inaccurate since it does not account for the effects of air resistance. (It is only an appropriate model if the object is falling in a vacuum.) While the effect of air resistance on a cannonball may not be too great, imagine dropping a feather! The model would produce inaccurate results, and our conclusions about how the system behaves would be totally wrong. It is obvious that we need to incorporate the effects of air resistance into our model if we have any hope of producing worthwhile and useful results.[1]

Our model also assumes that the Earth is a perfect sphere and that the acceleration due to gravity is the same everywhere along its surface. That assumption is not quite true. The earth is a "slightly squashed" sphere with a radius of 6,378 km at the equator and 6,357 km at the poles. This means that the acceleration due to gravity is a tiny bit greater at the North and South Poles than at the equator, since we are 21 km closer to the center of the Earth. Is this something for which we should account? Is this important when constructing a model of a freely falling body? In this case probably not, since the miniscule error resulting from this approximation will almost certainly not affect the conclusions that we would reach.

This is how computational models are built. We include the truly important factors that act upon our system so that our model is an accurate representation but omit the unimportant factors that only make the model harder to build, understand, and solve. As you might imagine, identifying these factors and distinguishing the important from the unimportant can be a daunting task.

Another problem encountered when building simulations is that we may not know, in a mathematical sense, exactly how to describe certain types of systems and behaviors. The gravitational model given earlier is an example of a **continuous model.** In a continuous model, we write out a set of explicit mathematical equations that describe the behavior of a system as a continuous function of time t. These equations are then solved on a computer system to produce the desired results. Unfortunately, there are many systems that cannot be modeled using precise mathematical equations because researchers have not discovered exactly what those equations should be. Simply put, science is not yet sufficiently knowledgeable about how some systems function to characterize their behavior using explicit mathematical formulae.

In some cases what makes these systems difficult to model is that they contain **stochastic components.** This means that there are parts of the system that display **random** behavior, much like the throw of the dice or the drawing of a card. In these cases, we cannot say with certainty what will happen to our system since it is the very essence of randomness that we can never know what specific event will occur next. An example of this would be

---

1 The resistance of the air, called drag, is given by the equation $D = KrV^2A/2.0$, where K is the coefficient of drag, r is the air density, V is the velocity of the object, and A is the reference area of the object. Now you can begin to see why computational models can quickly become so complex.

a model of a business in which customers walk into the store at random times that we cannot control. In these cases we need to build models that use **statistical approximations** rather than precise and exact equations. We will present one such example in the following section.

In summary, computational modeling is a powerful but complex technique for designing and studying systems. Building a good model can be a difficult task that requires us to capture, in computational form, all the important factors that influence the behavior of a system. If we are able to successfully build such a model, then we have at our disposal a powerful tool for studying the behavior of that system. This is how a good deal of quantitative research is being done today. Simulation is also an interesting area of study within computer science itself. Researchers in this field create new techniques, both algorithms and special-purpose languages, that allow users to design and implement computer models more quickly and easily.

 ### 12.2.3 *An Example of Model Building*

As we mentioned at the end of the previous section, there are many ways to build a model but most of them require mathematical techniques far beyond the scope of this text. In this section we will construct a model using a method that is relatively easy to understand and that does not require a lot of complex mathematics. It is called **discrete event simulation,** and it is one of the most popular and widely used techniques for building computer models.

In a discrete event simulation, we do not model time as continuous, like the falling body model in the last section, but as **discrete.** That is, we model the behavior of a system only at an explicit and finite set of times. The moments we model are those times when an event takes place, an **event** being any activity that changes the state of our system. For example, if we were modeling a department store, an event might be a new customer entering the store or a customer purchasing an item.

When we process an event, we change the state of the simulated system in the same way that the actual system would change if this event had occurred in real life. In the case of a department store, this might mean that when a customer arrives we add one to the number of customers currently in the store or, if a customer buys an item, we decrease the number of these items on the shelf. Furthermore, the processing of one event can cause new events to occur sometime in the future. For example, a customer coming into a store will create a later event related to that customer leaving the store. When we are finished processing one event we move on to the next, skipping over those times when nothing is happening.

Figure 12.2(a) shows system S and three events scheduled to occur within system S: event E_1 at time 9:00, event E_2 at time 9:04, and event E_3 at time 9:10.

Since E_1 is the event currently being processed, the variable *current time,* which functions like a "simulation clock," has the value 9:00. Let's assume that E_1 causes a new event, E_4, to be created and scheduled for time 9:17. We add this new event to the list of all scheduled events. When we are finished processing event E_1, we remove it from the list and determine the next event scheduled to occur in system S, in this case E_2. We move *current time* ahead to 9:04, skipping the period 9:01–9:03, since nothing of interest is happening, and begin processing E_2. At this point the list of events scheduled for system S is shown in Figure 12.2(b).

FIGURE 12.2

Example of Simulated Events

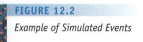

SCHEDULED EVENTS FOR SYSTEM S

System S:	E_1	E_2	E_3
	9:00	9:04	9:10

↑

current time

(a) *The List of Scheduled Events at Time t = 9:00*

SCHEDULED EVENTS FOR SYSTEM S

System S:	E_2	E_3	E_4
	9:04	9:10	9:17

↑

current time

(b) *The List of Scheduled Events at Time t = 9:04*

We repeat this same sequence—process an event, remove it from the list, add newly created events to the list, move on to the next event—as long as desired. The variable *current time* keeps advancing as we process the events in strict time order. Typically the simulation is terminated when this value reaches some upper bound. For example, in a department store we might choose to run the model until closing time. When the simulation has completed, the program displays a set of results that characterize the system's behavior and allows the user to examine these results at their leisure.

Let's apply this modeling technique to an actual problem. Assume that you are the owner of a new take-out restaurant, McBurgers, currently under construction. You want to determine the proper number of checkout stations needed in your new store. This is an important decision since, if there are too few, the lines will get long and customers will leave. If there are too many, you will waste money paying for unnecessary construction costs, equipment, and personnel. Since you took a computer science class in school, you decide to build a model of your new restaurant and use this model to determine the optimal number of servers.

The system being simulated is shown in Figure 12.3. Customers enter the restaurant and wait in a single line for service. If any of the *N* servers is available, where *N* is an input value provided by the user, the first customer in line goes to that station, places an order, waits until the order is processed, pays, and departs. During that time the server is busy and cannot help anyone else. When the server is finished with a customer, he or she can immediately begin serving the next one, if someone is in line. If no one is waiting, then the server waits until a new customer arrives.

The first thing we must do is identify the events that can change our system and that need to be included in the model. In this example there are two: a new customer arriving and an existing customer departing after receiving food and paying. An arrival changes the system because either the waiting line will grow longer or an idle cashier will become busy. A departure changes the system because the cashier serving that customer either begins serving a new customer or becomes idle because no one is in line.

For each of these two events we must develop an algorithm that describes exactly what happens to our system when this event occurs. Figure 12.4 shows the algorithm for the new customer arrival event.

FIGURE 12.3

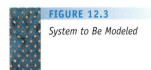

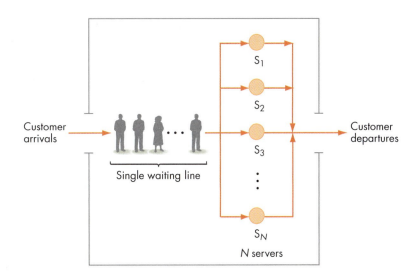

Let's look at this algorithm in more detail. When a new customer arrives, we record the time that he or she first entered the restaurant. The arrival time of each new customer is stored in a separate variable until that customer is served and departs. As we mentioned earlier, when the simulation is finished, we want to display a set of results that allow a user to determine how well the system performed. The total time a customer spent in the restaurant (waiting time + service time) is a good example of this type of result. If this value is large, we are not doing a good job serving customers, and we need to increase the number of servers so that customers don't wait so long. A large part of any simulation model is not directly involved in modeling a system but in collecting data about the system so that we can understand and analyze its performance.

The next thing in our New Customer Arrival algorithm is to determine if there is an idle server. If not, the customer goes to the end of the waiting line (no special treatment here at McBurgers), and the length of the waiting line

FIGURE 12.4

Algorithm for New Customer Arrival

New Customer Arrival
    Record the time that this customer entered the restaurant
    Check if any one of the N servers S_1, S_2, ... , S_N is currently idle
    If everyone is busy then
        Put this customer at the end of the waiting line
        Increase the length of the waiting line by 1
    Else (server S_i is idle)
        Mark that server S_i is now busy
        Determine how long it will take to serve this customer, call
            that value T_{serve}
        Schedule a customer departure event for (*current time* + T_{serve})
        Increase the total time that server S_i has worked by T_{serve}
End of New Customer Arrival

is increased by 1. If there is an idle server then the customer does not get into line but, instead, goes directly to that server who is then marked as busy. (*Note:* if more than one server is free, the customer can go to any one since our model assumes that all servers are identical.)

Now we must determine how much time will be required to service this customer. This is a good example of what we had termed a **stochastic, or random, component** of a simulation model. Exactly what a customer will order and how much time it will take to fill that order are random quantities whose value can never be known in advance with certainty. However, even though it behaves randomly, it is possible that this value, called T_{serve} in Figure 12.4, follows a pattern called a **statistical distribution.** If we knew this pattern, then the computer could generate a sequence of random numbers that follow this pattern, and this sequence would accurately model the time it takes to serve customers in real life.

How can we discover this pattern? One way is to know something about the statistical distribution of quantities that behave in a similar way. For example, if we knew something about the distribution of service times for customers in a bank or a grocery store, then this information might be able to help us understand the pattern of service times at our hamburger stand. Another way is to observe and collect data from an actual system similar to ours. For example, we could go to other take-out restaurants and measure exactly how long it takes them to service their customers. If these restaurants were similar to ours, then the McBurgers owner might be able to discover from this data the statistical distribution of the variable T_{serve}.

There are other ways to learn about and work with statistical distributions, but we will leave this topic to future courses in statistics. In this example we will simply assume that the statistical distribution for the customer service time, T_{serve}, has been discovered and is specified by the graph in Figure 12.5.

The graph in Figure 12.5 says that 5% of the time a customer is served in less than 1 minute; 15% of the time it takes 1–2 minutes; 40% of the time it takes 2–3 minutes; 30% of the time it takes 3–4 minutes; and finally, 10% of the time it takes 4–5 minutes. It never requires more than 5 minutes to serve a customer. We can model this distribution using the algorithm shown in Figure 12.6.

First, we generate a random integer v that takes on one of the values 1, 2, 3, . . . , 100 with equal likelihood. This is called a **uniform random**

FIGURE 12.5

Statistical Distribution of Customer Service Time

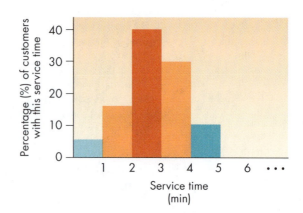

Generate a uniform random integer value v between 1 and 100
If v is in the range 1–5, then
    Set T_{serve} to a uniform random number between 0.0 and 1.0
Else if v is in the range 6–20, then
    Set T_{serve} to a uniform random number between 1.0 and 2.0
Else if v is in the range 21–60, then
    Set T_{serve} to a uniform random number between 2.0 and 3.0
Else if v is in the range 61–90, then
    Set T_{serve} to a uniform random number between 3.0 and 4.0
Else
    Set T_{serve} to a uniform random number between 4.0 and 5.0

number. We now ask if v is between 1 and 5. Since there are five numbers in this range, and there were 100 numbers that could originally have been generated, the answer to this question will be yes 5% of the time. This is the same percent of time that customers spend from 0 to 1 minute being served. Therefore, we generate another uniform random value, this time a real number between 0.0 and 1.0, which is the value of T_{serve}, the customer service time.

If the original random value v is not between 1 and 5, we ask if it is between 6 and 20. There are 15 integers in this range, so the answer to this question will be yes 15% of the time, exactly the fraction of time that customers spend 1–2 minutes being served. So, if the answer is yes we generate a T_{serve} value that is in the range 1.0 to 2.0. This process is repeated for all possible values of service time.

Once the value of T_{serve} has been generated, we then use this value to determine exactly when this customer leaves the store (*current time* $+ T_{serve}$) as well as to update the total amount of time the server has spent serving customers. This last computation will allow us to determine the percentage of time during the day that each server was busy.

The value assigned to T_{serve} using the algorithm of Figure 12.6 exactly matches the statistical distribution shown in Figure 12.5. If this graph is an accurate representation of customer service time, then our model will be an accurate depiction of what happens in the real world. However, if the graph of Figure 12.5 is not an accurate representation of the customer service time, then this model is incorrect and will produce wrong answers. This is a good example of the well-known computer science dictum **"garbage in-garbage out."** The results you get out of a simulation model are only as good as the data and the assumptions put into the model.

We now can specify how to handle the second type of event contained in our model, which is customer departures. The algorithm to handle a customer leaving the restaurant is given in Figure 12.7.

When a customer is ready to leave, we determine the total time this customer spent in the restaurant. The variable *current time* represents the time now, which is the time of this customer's departure. We recorded the time this customer first arrived on line 2 of Figure 12.4, and we can retrieve the contents of the variable storing that information. The difference between these two numbers is the total time this customer spent in the restaurant. We will use this result, averaged over all the customers, to determine if we are providing an adequate level of service.

FIGURE 12.7

Algorithm for Customer Departure Event

Customer Departure from Server S_i
    Determine the total time that this customer spent in the restaurant
    If there is someone in line then
        Take the next customer out of line and decrease the waiting line size by one
        Determine how long this new customer will take to be served,
        call that value T_{serve}
        Schedule a customer departure event for (current time + T_{serve})
        Increase the total time that server S_i has worked by T_{serve}
    Else
        Mark this server as idle
End Customer Departure

If there is another customer in line, the server begins serving that customer in exactly the same way as described earlier. If no one is waiting, then the server is idle and has nothing to do until a new customer arrives. (We don't want this to happen too often as we will be paying the salary of someone with little to do.)

We have now described the two main events that change our system: someone arriving and someone leaving the restaurant. The only thing left is to initialize our parameters and get the model started. To initialize the model we must do the following four things:

- Set the current time to 0.0 (we begin our simulation at time 0)
- Set the waiting line size to 0 (no one is in line when the doors open)
- Get a value for *N*, the number of servers, and make them all idle
- Determine the total number of customers to be served and exactly when they will arrive

The last value—customer arrival times—are like the service times discussed earlier in that they are stochastic, or random, values that cannot be known with certainty. We cannot possibly know exactly when the next customer will walk in the door. However, if we know the statistical distribution of the time interval between the arrival of any two customers, then we can generate a set of random intervals, called $T_{interval}$, that will allow us to accurately model our customer arrivals.

Assume we have a graph like Figure 12.5 that specifies the statistical distribution of the time interval that elapses between the arrivals of two successive customers. (That is, it might say something like 10% of the time two customers arrive within 0–15 seconds of each other; 20% of the time they arrive within 15–30 seconds; etc.) We schedule our first customer to arrive at time 0,0, just as the doors open. We then use an algorithm like the one in Figure 12.6 to generate a random value that matches the distribution of interarrival times. Call this value $T_{interval}$. This represents the amount of time that will elapse until the next customer arrives. Since the first customer arrived at time 0.0, we schedule the next one to arrive at $(0.0 + T_{interval}) = T_{interval}$. We repeat this for as many customers as desired, scheduling each one to arrive at $T_{interval}$ time units after the previous one. Our sequence of customer arrivals will look something like this:

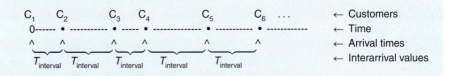

C_1 C_2 C_3 C_4 C_5 C_6 ... ← Customers
0------ • ------------ • ----- • ------------- • ------------ • ------------ ← Time
← Arrival times
← Interarrival values
$T_{interval}$ $T_{interval}$ $T_{interval}$ $T_{interval}$ $T_{interval}$

The main program to run our McBurgers simulation model is given in Figure 12.8. It allows the user to provide two inputs: M, the number of customers they want to model, and N, the number of servers. Each one of the M customer arrivals is handled by the arrival algorithm of Figure 12.4. Each arrival event will generate a customer departure event that is handled by the departure algorithm of Figure 12.7. This simulation does not terminate at a specific point in time but, instead, when there are no more events to be processed—that is, every customer who was scheduled to arrive has been served and has departed.

The last issue that we must address is how to implement the second to last line of Figure 12.8, the one that reads, "Print out a set of data that describes the behavior of our system." Looking back at Figure 12.1, we see that one of the responsibilities of a simulation is to "collect data describing its behavior." Our model must collect data that accurately measures the performance of our McBurgers restaurant so that we can configure it in a profitable manner *before* it is built. Therefore, we need to determine what data are required to meet this need. Often this cannot be done by the person building the model as that person may not know anything at all about this application area. Instead, it is the *user* of a model who determines what important data should be displayed. In our case, the user is the restaurant owner.

Let's assume that we have talked to the owner and determined that the information he or she most needs to know is the following:

- The average time that a customer spends in the restaurant, including both waiting in line and getting served

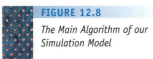

FIGURE 12.8

The Main Algorithm of our Simulation Model

Main Part of the Simulation Model
    Set *current time* to 0
    Set the waiting line size to 0
    Get an input value for N, the number of servers
    Set all N servers, S_1, S_2, ... , S_N to idle
    Get an input value for M, the total number of customers
    Schedule M customer arrivals and put them on the list of events
        Each arrival occurs $T_{interval}$ time units after the previous one
    While there is still a scheduled event on the list do
        Get the next event on the list
        Move *current time* to the time of this event
        If this is a customer arrival event
            Execute the arrival algorithm of Figure 12.4
        Else
            Execute the departure algorithm of Figure 12.7
        Remove this event from the list of all scheduled events
    End of the loop
    Print out a set of data that describes the behavior of our system
    Stop

- The maximum length of the waiting line
- The percentage of time that servers are busy serving customers

From this data the owner should be able to determine whether or not the system is functioning well. For example, if our model determines that a server was busy only 10% of the time (about 48 minutes in an 8-hour workday), we could probably reduce the number of servers without impacting service, saving a good deal in salary costs. On the other hand, if the average time that a customer spends in the restaurant is 1 hour or there are times when there are 100 people in line, then we had better increase the number of servers if we want to avoid bankruptcy (or riots)!

This model will likely be used in the interactive design approach first diagrammed in Figure 12.1. Our owner will enter his or her best estimate for the arrival time and service time distributions and then select a value for N, the number of servers. The computer will run the simulation, processing all M customers, and then print out the results, perhaps something like the following:

Servers	Average Waiting Time (min)	Maximum Line Length	Server Busy Percentage (%)
2	63.3	35	100.0

With only two servers, our customers waited on average more than one hour to be served, there were dozens of people in line, and both servers were busy every second of the day—not very good performance! The owner would certainly try to improve on this performance, perhaps by having 6 servers, rather than just 2. He or she resets the parameter N to 6 and reruns the model, which now produces the following:

Servers	Average Waiting Time (min)	Maximum Line Length	Server Busy Percentage (%)
6	2.75	1	43

Now the owner may have erred too far in the other direction. Our customers are being well served, waiting only a couple of minutes, and the line is tiny, never having more than a single person. However, our six servers are busy only 43% of the time—meaning they are idle about 4.5 hours during an 8-hour workday. Could we provide the same high quality of service to our customers with fewer servers? To answer this question, the owner might try rerunning the model with $N = 3$, 4, or 5, a compromise value between these two extremes. This is how a simulation model is used—run it, examine the results, and use these results to reconfigure the system so its performance is enhanced.

This completes the development of our McBurgers simulation, but not the end of its usefulness. In the next laboratory experience you are going to "play" with this model yourself. The laboratory will allow you to select a range of different values for the customer arrival and service times. You then take on the role of the McBurger's owner and determine the optimal number of servers to use for the selected configuration. Working with a simulation in an interactive design environment will demonstrate the enormous power and capabilities of computational models.

The restaurant modeled in this section is about as simple a system as we could present, yet it still took almost 8 pages to describe in detail. A computational model of a suspension bridge, "El Nino" Pacific Ocean currents, the human heart, or a strand of DNA would certainly be much more complex than the simulation of a hamburger joint! Real world models are mathematically intricate, highly detailed, and difficult to build. However, if we are able to build such a model or if we have access to such a model, then we have a powerful tool that can significantly enhance our ability to do high-quality research and design.

LABORATORY EXPERIENCE 20

You are going to work with the simulation model of a McBurgers restaurant that is similar to the one presented in this section. You will play the role of the restaurant owner who is trying to determine the correct number of servers for a specific pattern of customer arrivals and service times. You will configure your restaurant, run the model, see how well you serviced your customers, and then reconfigure the restaurant to try to improve upon its performance and its profit. Your goal is to achieve optimal behavior of this system.

12.3   Running the Model and Visualizing Results

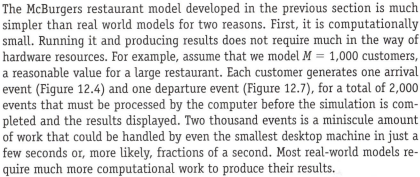

The McBurgers restaurant model developed in the previous section is much simpler than real world models for two reasons. First, it is computationally small. Running it and producing results does not require much in the way of hardware resources. For example, assume that we model $M = 1,000$ customers, a reasonable value for a large restaurant. Each customer generates one arrival event (Figure 12.4) and one departure event (Figure 12.7), for a total of 2,000 events that must be processed by the computer before the simulation is completed and the results displayed. Two thousand events is a miniscule amount of work that could be handled by even the smallest desktop machine in just a few seconds or, more likely, fractions of a second. Most real-world models require much more computational work to produce their results.

For example, the U.S. Department of Energy's National Energy Research Scientific Computing Center (NERSC) at Lawrence Berkeley National Laboratory has developed a powerful new climate system model. Using this model, simulating one year of global climatic change requires about 10^{17} computations—one hundred thousand trillion operations. A single Von Neumann machine could not handle this almost unimaginably large amount of work. A typical desktop computer executes roughly one billion instructions per second—1,000 MIPS. At this rate, completing one year of simulated time in the model would require three years of real time—we would not get our results until the actual time period being simulated had passed!

Instead, massive models like this one can be executed only on the large-scale parallel machines described in Chapter 5. In the case of the NERSC climate model, it was executed on a massively parallel IBM-SP supercomputer containing 6,080 processors and, with a peak computation rate of 6 teraflops, 6 trillion operations per second. At this rate, one year of climatic change can be modeled in about 5 hours.

These numbers are much more typical of the amount of work required by real-world simulations. It is not unusual for a model to perform 10^{15}, 10^{16}, 10^{17}, or more computations to produce a single result—amounts far beyond the capabilities of individual machines. The increasing interest in building and using computational models is one of the main reasons behind the development of larger and more powerful supercomputers.

The second reason why the McBurgers model in Section 12.2.3 is so unrealistic is that it produced only a tiny amount of output. After each run was completed the model generated only a few lines of output, such as those shown in the previous section:

Servers	Average Waiting Time (min)	Maximum Line Length	Server Busy Percentage (%)
6	2.75	1	43

Since the number of servers in a restaurant ranges from one up to about a dozen or so, the total volume of output this model would ever produce is 20–40 lines, less than a single page. With such a small amount of output, our model can display its results using a simple text format, like the preceding lines shown. A user will have no difficulty reading and interpreting this output.

Unfortunately, most simulations do not produce a few dozen lines of output but rather tens or hundreds of thousands of lines, perhaps even millions. For example, assume the NERSC climate model described earlier displayed the temperature, humidity, barometric pressure, wind velocity, and wind direction at 50-mile intervals over the surface of the earth for every simulated day the model is run. After one year of simulated time, it will have produced roughly 500 million data values—about 10 million pages of output! If these values were displayed as text, it would overwhelm its users, who wouldn't have a clue about how to deal with this mountain of paper.

Text, when it appears in such large amounts, does not lend itself to easy interpretation or understanding. The field of **scientific visualization** is concerned with the issue of how to visualize data in a way that highlights its important characteristics and simplifies its interpretation. This is an enormously important part of computational modeling, because without it we would be able to construct models and execute them, but we would not be able to interpret their results in a meaningful way.

The term *scientific visualization* is often treated as synonymous with the related term **computer graphics,** but there is an important difference. The field of computer graphics is concerned with the technical issues involved in information display. That is, it deals with the actual rendering of an image—light sources, shadows, hidden lines and surfaces, shading, contours, and perspective. Scientific visualization, on the other hand, is concerned with how to visually display a data set in a way that is most helpful to users and that maximizes its comprehension. It is concerned with issues such as **data extraction,** namely, determining which data values are important and should be part of the visual display and which ones can be omitted, and **data manipulation,** which consists of looking for ways to convert the data to other forms or to different units that will make the display easier to understand and interpret. Once we have decided exactly how we wish to display the data, then a scientific visualization package will typically use a computer graphics package to render an image on the screen or the printer.

For example, assume we have built a computer model of the ocean tides at some point along the coast. Our model will predict the height of the tide every 30 seconds in a 24-hour day, based on such factors as the lunar phase, wind speed, and wind direction. If this information were printed simply as text, it might look something like the following:

Time	Height (feet)
12:00:00 A.M.	43.78
12:00:30 A.M.	43.81
12:01:00 A.M.	43.84
12:01:30 A.M.	43.88
12:02:00 A.M.	43.92
12:02:30 A.M.	43.97
.	.
.	.
.	.
11:57:00 P.M.	45.08
11:57:30 P.M.	45.04
11:58:00 P.M.	45.01
11:58:30 P.M.	44.99
11:59:00 P.M.	44.97
11:59:30 P.M.	44.95

There are 2,880 lines of output, which at 60 lines per page would produce almost 50 printed pages. Trying to extract understanding or locate significant features from these long columns of numbers would certainly be a formidable, not to mention boring, task.

What if, instead, we displayed these two columns of values as a two-dimensional graph of time versus height. The output could also include a horizontal line showing the average water height during this 24-hour period. This latter value is not part of the original output but can easily be computed from these values and included in the output—an example of a data manipulation carried out to enhance data interpretation. Now the output of our model might look something like the graph in Figure 12.9.

FIGURE 12.9

Using a Two-Dimensional Graph to Display Output

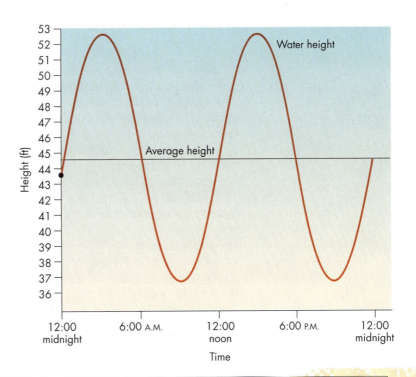

Using the graph in Figure 12.9, it is a lot quicker and easier to identify the interesting features of the model's output. For example,

- There appear to be two high tides and two low tides during this 24-hour time period.
- The high tide is about 8 feet above the average water level, while the low tide is about 8 feet below the average water level.

While it is possible to discover the same features from a textual representation of the output, it would probably take much more time. Interpreting the graph of Figure 12.9 is a great deal easier than working directly with raw numerical data. The use of visualizations becomes even more important as the amount of output increases and grows more complex. For example, what if in addition to the tidal height our model also predicted the water temperature and displayed its value every 30 seconds. Now the raw data produced by the model might look like this:

Time	Height (feet)	Temperature (°C)
12:00:00 A.M.	43.78	15.03
12:00:30 A.M.	43.81	15.02
12:01:00 A.M.	43.84	15.01
12:01:30 A.M.	43.88	14.99
12:02:00 A.M.	43.92	14.97
12:02:30 A.M.	43.97	14.94
.	.	.
.	.	.
.	.	.
11:57:00 P.M.	45.08	14.95
11:57:30 P.M.	45.04	14.98
11:58:00 P.M.	45.01	15.00
11:58:30 P.M.	44.99	15.01
11:59:00 P.M.	44.97	15.03
11:59:30 P.M.	44.95	15.05

Now there are almost 6,000 numbers, and our task has become even more difficult as we try to understand the behavior of the *two* variables, height and temperature. Working directly with the raw data generated by the model is cumbersome. However, if the value of both variables were presented on a single graph, as shown in Figure 12.10, this interpretation would be much easier.

Looking at Figure 12.10, we can quickly observe that temperature seems to move in exactly the opposite direction as the tide, but delayed by a few minutes. That is, water temperature reaches its minimum value shortly after the tidal height has reached its maximum value, and vice versa. This is exactly the type of information that could be of help to a researcher. Without the graphical visualization in Figure 12.10, we may have overlooked this important feature.

The graphs in Figures 12.9 and 12.10 were both two-dimensional, but many real-world models are used to study the behavior of three-dimensional objects, for example, an airplane wing, a gas cloud, or the surface of the Earth. The results produced by these models will also be three-dimensional, such as the spatial coordinates of a point on that airplane wing or on a gas molecule. Therefore, it is common for the output of a computational model to

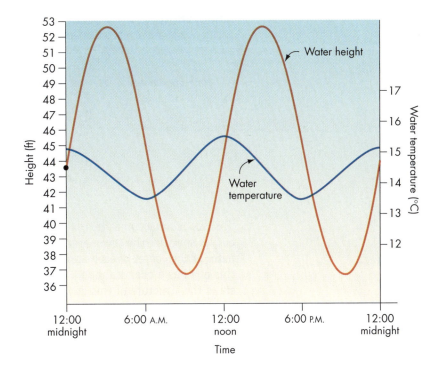

be displayed as a three-dimensional image rather than the two-dimensional graphs shown earlier. For example, Figure 12.11 shows a computer model of a portion of the Earth's surface. Using this 3-dimensional image, it is easy to locate important topographical features, such as mountains, valleys, and rivers. This type of output would be extremely useful when dealing with environmental issues such as planning the location of roads and bridges.

As a second example, suppose that medical researchers were using a simulation model to study the behavior of the chemical compound methyl

FIGURE 12.11

Three-Dimensional Image of a Region of the Earth's Surface

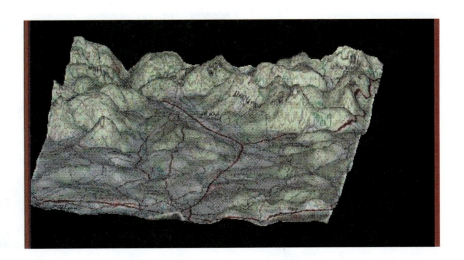

nitrite, CH_3NO_2, a potential carcinogen found in our air and drinking water. Assume that their molecular model produced the following textual output:

Molecule Number	Element	Location x	y	z	Bonded To
1	O	1.7	1.0	0.0	3, 4
2	O	3.0	0.0	0,0	3
3	N	2.6	0.3	1.0	1, 2
4	C	0.0	0.0	0.0	1, 5, 6, 7
5	H	−0.5	0.5	0.5	4
6	H	0.5	0.5	0.5	4
7	H	−0.5	−0.5	0.5	4

This is an accurate textual description of a methyl nitrite molecule. The output specifies the seven atoms in the molecule, the spatial (x, y, z) coordinates of the center of each atom, and the identity of all other atoms to which this one has a chemical bond. This is all the information required to understand the structure of this molecule. However, even though this is all that is theoretically needed, most of us would find it hard to form a mental image of what this molecule actually looks like using this table.

What if, instead, our model took this textual description of methyl nitrite and used it to create and display the three-dimensional image of Figure 12.12?

It is certainly a lot easier to work with the visualization in Figure 12.12 than with the numerical description given previously. For example, if the simulation model changed the shape or structure of this molecule, say by modeling a chemical reaction or stretching a chemical bond, we would be able to observe this change occurring on our computer screen, significantly increasing our understanding of exactly what is happening.

The image in Figure 12.12 makes use of two other features found in many visualizations—color and scale. These characteristics allow us to display information in a way that makes the image more understandable by someone looking at the diagram. In this example color was used to represent the element type—red for hydrogen, purple for carbon, yellow for oxygen, and blue for nitrogen. The relative size of each sphere was used to represent the relative size of each of the atoms.

FIGURE 12.12

Three-Dimensional Model of a Methyl Nitrite Molecule

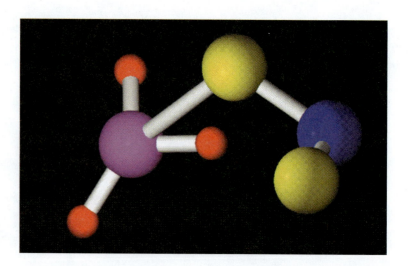

The clever use of visual enhancements such as color and size can make an enormous difference in how easy or hard it is to interpret the output of a computer model. For example, the image displayed in Figure 12.13 was generated by a simulation of the dispersion of a toxic gas cloud in the downtown area of a major city. Based on wind speed and direction, the location of buildings, and the molecular structure of the gas, this model determines the gas concentration throughout the downtown area at discrete points in time. (Figure 12.13 shows one of these time points.)

In this example color was used to indicate the concentration of toxic gas in the atmosphere. Blue and green represent the lowest two levels of concentrations, yellow represents a moderate level, while orange and red represent the highest and most deadly concentrations of gas. Using images like Figure 12.13, an emergency crew, knowing the current wind speed and direction, could quickly determine where to direct their rescue efforts in the event of a gas leak. If, instead of these color-coded, three-dimensional images, the crew was given only page after page of numerical values, it would take much longer to extract this vital information. Here is an example where enhancing comprehension is not just for convenience but for saving lives!

Finally, we mention one of the most powerful and useful forms of visualization—**image animation.** In many models, time (whether continuous or discrete) is one of the key variables, and we want to observe how the model's output changes over time. This could be the case, for example, with the gas dispersion model discussed in the previous paragraphs. The image in Figure 12.13 is a picture of a gas cloud at one discrete instant in time. While that may be of some value, what might be of even greater interest is how the cloud moves and disperses as a function of time. Some questions we could answer using this time-varying model are How long does it take for the highest levels of gas (red and orange) to dissipate completely? and What is the maximum distance from the original site of the leak where the highest levels of gas were found?

To answer these and similar questions we need to generate not one image like Figure 12.13, but many, with each image showing the state of the system

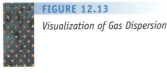

FIGURE 12.13

Visualization of Gas Dispersion

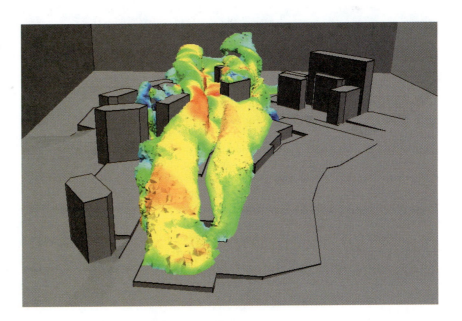

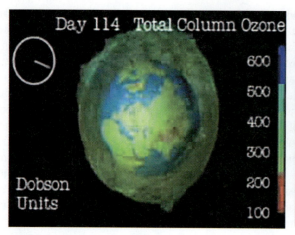

(a) On Day 114

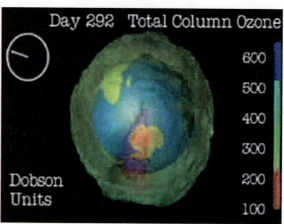

(b) On Day 292

FIGURE 12.14

Use of Animation to Model Ozone Layers in the Atmosphere

at a slightly later point in time. If we were to generate a sufficient number of these images, then we could display them rapidly in sequence, producing a visual animation of the model's output.

Obviously we cannot show an animation in this book, but Figure 12.14 shows two images (out of 365) from a program that models the total amount of ozone present in the Earth's atmosphere over a one-year period. The model computes the ozone levels for each day of the year and displays the results graphically, with green and blue representing acceptable ozone levels and red representing a dangerously low level. These 365 images can be displayed in sequence to produce a "movie" showing how the ozone level changes throughout the year.

The Mother of all Computations!

Climatic changes occur slowly, often taking hundreds or thousands of years to complete. For example, the "ice ages" were periods when large areas of the Earth's surface were covered by glaciers. These individual ice ages were separated by intervals of thousands of years during which the Earth became warmer and the glaciers receded. To study global climate change, a researcher cannot look at data for only a few years. Instead, he or she must examine changes taking place over long periods of time.

To provide this type of data, scientists at the National Center for Atmospheric Research (NCAR) used the NERSC global climate model described earlier to carry out a 1,000-year simulation of climatic changes on the surface of the Earth. NCAR used a 6,000+ processor IBM-SP super-computer and started it running in late January 2002. This massive machine worked on the problem 24 hours a day, 7 days a week, modeling decade after decade, century after century of changes to the Earth's climate. Finally, on September 4, 2002, it announced that it had finished its task. It had taken more than 200 days of uninterrupted computing and the execution of about a hundred billion billion (10^{20}) computations on a multimillion-dollar machine to obtain the results!

Data from this simulation are being made available to the research community to further the study of changes to our climate and investigate such weather-related phenomena as global warming and "El Nino" ocean currents.

The amount of output needed to produce these 365 images was probably in the hundreds of millions of data values, perhaps more. If this enormous volume of data were displayed as text, a user would be totally overwhelmed, and the truly important characteristics of the data would be buried deep within this mass of numbers, much like the proverbial "needle in a haystack." However, using the visualization techniques highlighted in this section—three-dimensional graphics, color, scale, and animation—the key features of the data, such as the presence of a significant ozone hole (the red area) over the Antarctic on day 292, can be quickly and easily located.

This is precisely the reason for the existence of these scientific visualization techniques. It is not merely a desire to produce "pretty pictures," although, admittedly, many of the images are artistically interesting. Instead, the goal is to take a massive data set and present it in a way that is more informative and more understandable for the user of that data. For without this understanding, there would be no reason to build computational models in the first place.

12.4   Conclusion

This concludes our all too brief look at the topic of simulation and modeling. It is a fascinating and highly complex subject and one that will become even more important in the coming years as computers increase in power and researchers gain experience in designing and building computational models.

Constructing models of complex systems requires a deep understanding of both mathematics and statistics so, as we have mentioned a number of times, they can be rather difficult to build. However, even if you are not directly involved in building models, you may *use* these types of models in your research, development, or design work. Simulation is impacting many fields of study. For example, in this chapter we looked at models drawn from physics (the falling body equations), economics (the McBurgers simulation), chemistry (the molecular model of methyl nitrite), cartography (a map of the Earth's surface), meteorology (tides, climatic changes), and ecology (toxic gas dispersion). We could just as easily have selected our examples from medicine, geology, biology, geography, or pharmacology. For those who work in just about any scientific or quantitative fields like these, computational modeling is rapidly becoming one of the most important tools available to the researcher.

Even though simulation is an important application of computers, you are probably more familiar with the many uses of computers in the commercial sector—things like ATM machines, paying bills online, remotely accessing corporate databases, and buying and selling products on the Web. These commercial applications, often grouped together under the generic term *electronic commerce,* or *e-commerce,* will be discussed at length in the next chapter.

1. You are probably familiar with the idea of a two-dimensional spreadsheet, like the ones created in Microsoft Excel. Would you call this type of spreadsheet a "computational model"? State why or why not, and justify your answer.

2. Look up the definition of the terms *computer aided design* (abbreviated CAD) and *computer aided manufacturing* (CAM). Find out what they mean, how they are used, and how they relate to the ideas presented in this chapter.

3. Rather than using a general-purpose programming language like the one discussed in Chapter 8, models are often constructed using special-purpose **simulation languages** designed specifically for this application. (These languages fall into the category of "special purpose languages" mentioned in Chapter 9.) Examples of simulation languages include

   - SIMULA
   - GPSS (General Purpose System Simulation)
   - Simscript

   Read about one of these languages and discuss what features it includes that makes it well-suited for implementing simulation models.

4. In Section 12.2.2 we specified two inaccuracies in the equation describing a body falling under the influence of gravity: the problems of air resistance and the fact that the Earth is not a perfect sphere. Are there additional inaccuracies contained in this mathematical model? Do you think that these other factors should be included in our falling body model? Explain why you believe they do or do not need to be included.

5. In this chapter we described a way to model a statistical distribution by using random numbers generated by a computer. How do you think it is possible for a computer to generate a truly random number that successfully passes all tests for randomness? Read about random number generators and discuss the algorithms that they use.

6. In Section 12.2.3 we specified the statistical distribution for the service time of customers in our McBurgers restaurant: 5% were serviced in less than 1 minute and so forth. Do you think this is an accurate distribution of service times in real-world take-out restaurants? Why or why not? If this distribution is not an accurate portrayal of the customer service time, what are the implications of this inaccuracy on our model?

7. Describe in detail how the customer arrival and departure event algorithms (Figures 12.4, 12.7) and the main algorithm (Figure 12.9) of our McBurgers simulation would change if we changed the system in each of the following three ways:

   a. Instead of a single waiting line, we have *N* waiting lines, one for each of the *N* servers in the restaurant. That is, our model now behaves as shown:

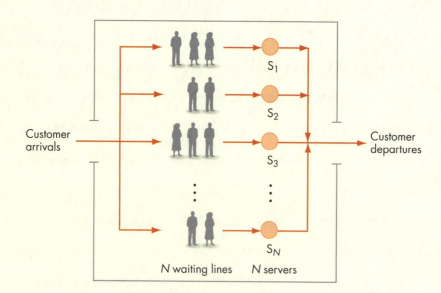

b. The waiting line has a maximum length of MAX. If the length of the waiting line is currently less than MAX, then the customer gets into line in exactly the same way as in the current model. However, if the waiting line has a length equal to MAX, then the customer must leave the store without being served.

c. Each customer is assigned a priority when they first enter the store (a value from 1 to 10), and if there is no server currently available, then they get into the waiting line in priority order. That is, a customer gets into line ahead of all people with lower priority and behind everyone with an equal or higher priority.

8. Assume that you want to model a bus system in which passengers purchase tickets and travel from city A to one of four other cities, either B, C, D, or E. An important part of the model is determining to which city a specific passenger is traveling, a random variable. How might you go about creating a statistical distribution that accurately specifies to which of these four cities a passenger will buy a ticket and travel?

9. a. Assume our model requires 10^{14} computations to simulate one hour of activity. We run the program on a desktop computer with a computation speed of 800 MIPS. How long will it take to simulate one day of activity in the model?

b. How fast a computer (in terms of MIPS) would we need to use if we want to complete the simulation of one day in 5 minutes of computing time?

10. We discussed the use of color and scale to enhance and highlight aspects of a data set being studied. In addition to these two features, suggest other ways to visually enhance the output of a model that will help to clarify its interpretation.

11. In this chapter we focused our discussions primarily on the uses of modeling in the physical sciences, life sciences, economics, and engineering. However, the use of models is certainly not limited to these areas. Read about how simulation models are currently being used to conduct research in the social sciences and humanities, such as the fields of anthropology, sociology, and political science. Write a report describing the uses of computational modeling in one of these fields.

12. Read about how simulation models are being used in your own specific field of study and write a report on exactly what these models do and what type of research is being done using these models.

CHALLENGE WORK

In this challenge problem you are going to build a computational model, much like the McBurgers simulation of Section 12.2.3. To do this, follow the same design steps that were used in this example, namely:

- Specify the events that can change the state of your system.
- For each event, specify an algorithm that shows how the system changes when this type of event occurs.
- Specify the main algorithm that will initialize your system, get the simulation started, and run the simulation until it has completed.

You do not need to specify your solution in a high-level programming language (unless you want to). Instead, you can write out your algorithms using the pseudocode presented in Chapter 2 and shown in Figure 2.6.

The system that you are going to model is a small airport with a single runway that handles both takeoffs and landings. This system is diagrammed as follows:

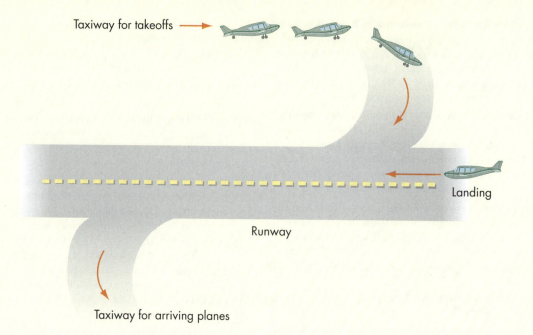

Taxiway for takeoffs

Landing

Runway

Taxiway for arriving planes

All planes take off and land from right to left. In this model departures are created, and these newly created flights taxi to the beginning of the runway, take off, and leave the system. Arrivals are created, and these new flights land, taxi off the far end of the runway, and leave the system. Only one plane at a time can use the runway, and because planes currently in the air may be low on fuel, arriving flights have priority to use the runway over departing flights. That is, if a flight is ready to depart and another flight is ready to land, the landing flight is the one that gets to use the runway, while the departing flight must wait in line.

The purpose of this model is to determine, for a given rate of flight arrivals and departures, how long a plane must wait to take off or land and the maximum number of planes in the arrival and departure lines. This type of information would be of great help to a transportation engineer trying to decide whether or not a second runway will be needed in the future as the airline traffic increases.

FOR FURTHER READING

An excellent introduction to the use of simulation and modeling in business and commercial applications is

Evans, J. R., and Olson, D. *Introduction to Simulation and Risk Analysis,* 2nd ed. Englewood Cliffs, NJ: Prentice-Hall, 2003.

An excellent introduction to simulation for a wide range of environments can be found in

Gould, H.; Tobochnik, J.; and Beresford, J. *An Introduction to Computer Simulation Methods,* 2nd ed. New York: Pearson Education, 1996.

CHAPTER 13

Electronic Commerce and Information Security

13.1   Introduction

As we mentioned in Chapter 7, the Internet has been around for quite a while (since 1969), but it has been the appearance of the World Wide Web that has had the greatest impact on our everyday lives. Increasingly, the Web is becoming our primary source of information about a variety of topics as well as a purveyor of goods and services from businesses on the other end of the wire.

If you own just about any type of business, you almost have to have a Web presence these days. For example,

- Your business provides a service, such as landscaping, that does not sell products directly to retail customers. But you still use the Web for advertising—getting your name in front of the public, disseminating information on the services you provide, and convincing people to contact you or visit your place of business because you have superior services, knowledge, capabilities, and price.

- Your business provides a service where followup information is important. For example, you are a shipping company, and you use your Web site to allow customers to track their shipments.

- Your business provides a service where customers can engage in online transactions that are not retail sales. For example, you are a bank that provides the ability for customers to see their current account balances and transfer money between accounts.

- Your company is a wholesale business that sells products or materials to other companies rather than to the general public. You maintain a **B2B (business-to-business)** Web presence in order to streamline transactions between you as the seller and other businesses as buyers. Your goal is not only to advertise and attract new business customers but also to cut down transaction costs. Note that the sales figures given in the box "Shopping on the Web" do not include these wholesale B2B transactions.

- Your company is a retail business, and you maintain a **B2C (business to consumer)** Web site. You again do this to advertise your products and to allow online purchasing by the general public.

In this chapter we'll talk mostly about the last scenario given—selling retail products to the general public. This is how most consumers will interact with and experience the Web's commercial capabilities.

The Census Bureau of the U.S. Department of Commerce estimated e-commerce retail sales in the United States for the first quarter of 2003 to be $11.921 billion, an increase of almost 26% from the first quarter of 2002, and more than double its value in the first quarter of 2000.

quarter of 2003 was $772.2 billion. Therefore, in the first quarter, 2003, e-commerce sales accounted for only 1.5% of total U.S. retail sales, also an increase over the 2000 figure for the same period.

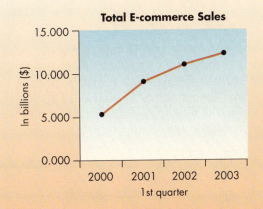

Total E-commerce Sales

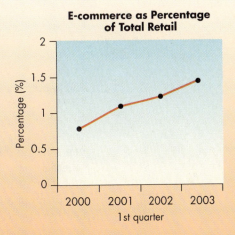

E-commerce as Percentage of Total Retail

But to keep these numbers in perspective, the estimate for total retail sales in the United States for the first

Clearly there has been significant growth in the e-commerce retail sector, but, just as clearly, there is room for much more.

Assume that you run a retail rug business—let's call it "Rugs-For-You"—out of a traditional store, that is, a store with a physical building, display windows, aisles with merchandise, and salespersons. You have decided to expand your retail business into the **e-commerce world,** where financial transactions are conducted by electronic means. During the early stages of online commerce (the early and mid-1990s) this might have meant that a customer would fill out an order via the Web and submit it. The online order would be printed out by the business at the other end, and this paper document would then be processed much like any "traditional" purchase, including rekeying the order data for both the shipping and billing departments. The Web was used to allow the customer to initiate an order, but it had little or no impact in filling the order, transferring funds, or restocking inventory.

This early approach to online commerce was cumbersome, inefficient, and error-prone. Today most businesses are moving away from this restricted model of online commerce to a total **e-business** concept where orders are processed, credit is verified, transactions are completed, debits are issued, shipping is alerted, and inventory is reduced, all electronically—at least in theory.

Let's say that this is the e-business model that you would like to implement. You decide to establish a Web presence for your business, Rugs-For-You, where customers can come, view area rugs for sale, ask questions, make a selection, purchase their rug, and have it delivered to them, all in a quick, easy, and secure electronic environment.

In the next section we'll look at some of the many considerations such a decision involves. Some of these are technical; some are purely business; many are a combination of the two. Then we'll look more closely at two of the most important technical issues arising in the e-commerce world: databases and security.

13.2   E-commerce

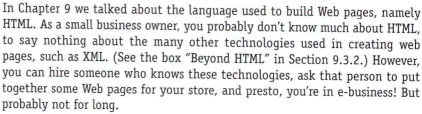

In Chapter 9 we talked about the language used to build Web pages, namely HTML. As a small business owner, you probably don't know much about HTML, to say nothing about the many other technologies used in creating web pages, such as XML. (See the box "Beyond HTML" in Section 9.3.2.) However, you can hire someone who knows these technologies, ask that person to put together some Web pages for your store, and presto, you're in e-business! But probably not for long.

Opening an online store requires at least as much planning as building another physical store location, in fact, probably more because it is a different medium in which to do business. Just because it's possible to build Web pages in a virtual environment more quickly and cheaply than constructing a building doesn't mean you should charge ahead without the proper level of planning and forethought.

 ### 13.2.1   *The Vision Thing*

The first thing you need to ask is, What is your vision for this new part of your overall commercial enterprise? Put another way, What is the business problem you are trying to solve? Do you want to

- Broaden your customer base?
- Recapture customers you are losing to competitors with online stores?
- Better serve your existing customer base?
- Better integrate departments/functions within your existing business so that the shipping department and the accounting department, for example, work off the same order form?

Any of these might be legitimate reasons for moving into e-commerce, but have you considered the risks involved with this decision?

- Will you just move your in-store customers online and achieve a zero-sum gain?
- When you expose yourself to online competition, will you have something to offer that is unique?

- Does your existing customer base need or want anything that you don't or can't provide for them in your traditional business environment? What part of your existing customer base will never shop online?

- Are the employees in your shipping and accounting departments in agreement with this idea, or do they feel threatened by change?

And we haven't even mentioned the costs involved with this decision:

- Do you have all the necessary hardware (computers), software, and infrastructure (network connectivity) to host a business Web site? If not, what will it cost you to acquire or lease them?

- Do you have the personnel and skills you need to build and maintain a Web site? If not, what will it cost to acquire new personnel or retrain existing personnel?

- Do you have the legal expertise onboard to manage issues such as (1) protecting your intellectual property; (2) navigating regulations, tariffs, and taxes in the many geographic regions where you will now be doing business (including perhaps overseas); and (3) legally handling customer data collected online? If not, what will it cost you to acquire this expertise?

- Do you know the potential costs of diverting resources away from your existing traditional business?

Let's assume that you and your company officers have assessed the objectives, the risks, and the costs, and you feel that overall your bottom line will improve by going online. What should happen next?

 ### 13.2.2 *Decisions, Decisions*

Once you decide to move into the e-commerce arena, there are still many questions to be answered and decisions to be made. The first major decision concerns the choice between **in-house development** and **outsourcing**; in fact, this is not a single decision but a whole host of decisions.

Let's talk first about the personnel issues. Are you going to use your existing staff to develop this e-business, either because they already have the necessary skills or because they will be retrained? Will you hire new personnel with the needed skills? Will you hire consultants who bring lots of expertise and will work with your people to get things up and running quickly? Or, alternately, will you turn the entire job over to an **ASP (application service provider)** who, for a fee, will design your Web site and manage it on an ongoing basis? The answers to these questions depend, of course, on the skills of your existing staff, how quickly you want your site to be up and running, the costs involved, and how much control you are willing to relinquish. Whoever is chosen to develop your Web site, it is important that business information about your company is made available and is used to inform all decisions along the way. In the end, your Web site should capture the "image" and provide the customer services of *your* company, not the company someone else may have in mind.

Similar questions follow regarding the hardware and software. You will need at least one Web server machine to host your Web site. You may need additional computers to store your customer database information, to support program development, and to supply the appropriate network connections and security. Do you have these machines? Will you buy them? Will you lease space on someone else's commercial Web server? You will also need a good deal of new software, such as programs to process the customer orders that you hope will come pouring in, to interact with your accounting, shipping, and inventory control software, and to manage and store customer information. Will you use inexpensive off-the-shelf software or more expensive packages that you can customize for your business needs? Will you use commercial software or **open source software?** (See "The Open Source Movement" box in Chapter 6, page 270.) Will your company develop its own proprietary software that is owned by the company and can be modified whenever your business needs change? Of course, if you decide to turn everything over to an ASP, you will have little or no control over these hardware and software decisions.

 ### 13.2.3 *Anatomy of a Transaction*

What draws a customer to online shopping? The number one attraction is probably convenience. Your online store is "open" 24 hours a day. People can shop from the comfort of their home, save time, and avoid the hassles of traffic. It is also easy to comparison shop merely by hopping from one Web site to another. But this also means that your competition is just a click away. Your goals are to

- Draw potential customers to your site
- Keep them there
- Set up optimum conditions for them to complete a purchase

Figure 13.1 illustrates the major components of an online purchase, which we have broken down into nine steps. Next, we'll elaborate on these steps, with an eye to the three goals mentioned above.

STEP 1: GETTING THERE How can you get customers to your Web site? Technically, once the customer knows the URL (uniform resource locator), the process works exactly as described in Chapter 7. The customer hooks up to the Internet through his or her ISP (internet service provider) and puts the URL into his or her Web browser. The browser works with the DNS (domain name system) to find the unique IP (internet protocol) address for this URL. Using this address, the TCP (transport control protocol) routes a connection through the Internet from the customer's machine to the appropriate server. The browser uses this connection to send an HTTP GET message for the desired Web page, which is then transmitted from the Web server back to the browser and painted on the user's screen, at which time the TCP/IP connection is broken.

But how does your potential customer learn your URL in the first place? There are many possibilities:

- *Conventional advertising.* You post your homepage URL on flyers, in print and TV advertisements, on letterhead, and on any other traditional promotional materials you may produce.

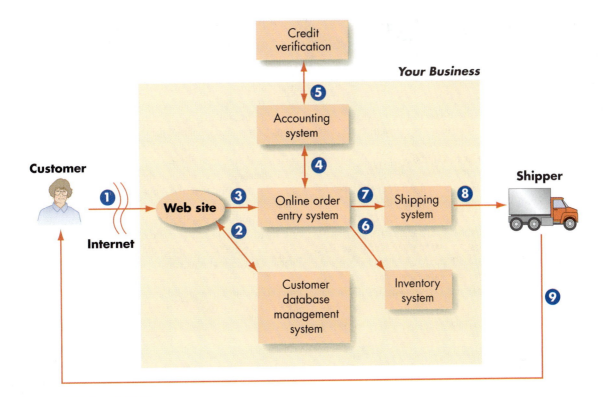

FIGURE 13.1

A Typical Online Transaction in Nine Steps

- *Obvious domain name.* You want your **domain name** (your homepage URL) to relate so closely to your business name that potential customers can easily guess it even if they don't have it written down in front of them. Who wouldn't try www.mcdonalds.com to reach this well known fast-food giant? Of course, Rugs-For-You might not be quite that well known. Domain names are registered by companies that are accredited for this purpose by **ICANN (Internet Corporation for Assigned Names and Numbers)**, a nonprofit corporation that took over the task of domain name management from the U.S. government in 1998. When a domain name is registered, it becomes part of the DNS so that Web users can find your IP address and get to your site. A list of accredited registrars can be obtained from www.internic.com, an information Web site maintained by ICANN. There you can also search to find whether a particular domain name has already been registered. In addition to registering your "real" domain name (rugs-for-you.com), you would be wise to register obvious spelling variants (rugs-for-u.com, rugs-4-u.com, etc.) if they are available so that all roads will lead to your Web site.

- *Search engine.* Your potential customer may use an Internet search engine to search for Web sites about products that you sell, and your company's Web site may turn up in the list returned as a result of this search. You can also pay for a "sponsored link" so that a search on

Cybersquatting is the name given to the practice of registering a domain name that uses the name or trademark of an existing business with the intent to sell the name to that business at a profit or to capitalize on that name for some other purpose. A 1999 federal law called the Anti-Cybersquatting Consumer Protection Act (ACPA) made cybersquatting illegal. A trademark owner claiming to be a victim of cybersquatting can file a suit under the ACPA. In order to have its claim upheld, a trademark owner must prove that it was the first to use the name or trademark for commercial purposes, that the name or trademark was distinctive at the time the domain name was first registered, that the domain name is the same as or sufficiently similar to the trademark as to cause confusion, and that the domain name registrant had a bad faith intent to profit from the trademark. A trademark owner who wins a suit can obtain the rights to the domain name and perhaps be awarded monetary damages.

ICANN also arbitrates cybersquatting disputes, with essentially the same criteria, but does not award any monetary damages. International disputes may be brought before the World Intellectual Property Organization, a United Nations agency. In 2000, AT&T won its case before WIPO against WorldclassMedia.com of Austria over the domain name attmexico.com, and Microsoft won its case against Global Net 2000, Inc., of Tehran, Iran, over the domain name microsoftnetwork.com.

Abstracts of legal claims filed over cybersquatting disputes can be found from a link at www.perkinscoie.com/casedigest/default.cfm.

appropriate keywords will bring up links to your Web site in an obvious spot on the search engine's page or near the top of the list of search results.

- *Portal.* A **portal** is an entry point Web page with links to other Web pages on some topic. It can be thought of as a starting point to learn about a particular subject, and it typically contains lots of helpful pointers to useful information on that subject. For example, www.floorbiz.com is a portal with links to retail stores selling rugs, carpet, tile, adhesives, padding, cleaning equipment, and so forth. This site also features links about flooring materials and manufacturers, links to news articles and press releases, upcoming conventions, and employment opportunities connected with the flooring industry, as well as forums for bulletin board postings, links to tips (e.g., how to maintain hardwood floors), leads for contractors to bid on floor installation jobs, and an opportunity to register to receive email. You would certainly want to have a link to Rugs-For-You from this portal page, and you may even be willing to purchase a **banner ad** (a graphical ad, often with animation, placed in a prominent position on a Web page) so that anyone who goes to this portal sees the rugs-for-you.com link right away.

STEP 2: DO I KNOW YOU? Regular customers at your traditional store are treated with special care. You may mail them promotional offers that you feel will be of interest to them, and the salespeople know them when they walk into the store and greet them by name. You pay particular attention to their needs for, after all, return customers are the basis of your business. How will your online store provide this type of personalized attention?

Some sites ask the user to register and then log-in when they revisit the site. They consult the database of registered customers and recall pertinent information—for example, how the customer browsed the site previously, what pages the customer visited, where the customer lingered, what the customer bought, as well as more mundane information like name and address. What the return customer sees is tailored to reflect this information.

Other sites that do not require a customer log-in still greet the customer with "Welcome, John" or the like and arrange a Web page with items suspiciously tied to John's apparent interests as based on his last purchase. This type of Web site personalization can be accomplished by means of "cookies." A **cookie** is a small text file that the Web server sends to the user's browser and that gets stored on the user's hard drive. It contains personal information about the user, such as name, address, time of visit, and what was looked at or bought. On the customer's next visit to that same site, the browser will send the cookie back to the server (along with the page request) so the server can create a customized page just for this shopper. This does more than merely create a friendly, personalized atmosphere. It also allows the server to record information for later use. For example, cookies enable a customer to put items into his or her online shopping basket and return at a later time to find them still there.

Transmission of Web pages between a client and server is **stateless;** that is, no information about this exchange is permanently retained by the server. Indeed, recall that the TCP/IP connection between the browser and Web server is (usually) broken once a Web page has been sent back to the browser. A totally new connection has to be established to access a different page or to return later to that same page. Without cookies, there would be no association between the customer visiting one page and the same customer visiting another page, or between the same customer visiting the same page at different times. It's possible to configure a Web browser so as not to accept cookies, but cookies cannot execute on the client machine and are harmless. They just take up a little space.

You can provide incentives and benefits for return customers—product support for items already purchased, special promotions ("John, would you like some stain guard for that new rug you just bought? Click here for our special offer!"), free shipping, a clearly stated return policy (including the ability to return items to your traditional "bricks-and-mortar" store if more convenient), and a chance to register complaints or ask questions online (to which you should pay attention and respond). And certainly you should provide a toll-free number where your customers can speak with a real, live person, although you don't want to make the number too obvious on your site because you are looking for your online business to free up staff, not burden them.

Online customers, both new and returning, can leave your site in the blink of an eye or, more properly, the click of a mouse button. Your Web site must invite them in, entice them to stay, and make their path toward purchase so convenient that there is no reason not to buy from you. This is what makes designing a Web page so much more than just an HTML programming assignment! We'll talk more about Web page features in Section 13.2.4, but for now let's assume that a customer has successfully navigated your Web site, selected an item to purchase, and is ready for Step 3.

STEP 3: COMMITTING TO AN ONLINE PURCHASE Customers are understandably hesitant to commit sensitive information such as their credit card number, or even their name and address, over the Web. Your site must provide security for transmitting this information and that security comes in two pieces: encryption and authentication. **Encryption** encodes the data to be transmitted into a scrambled form using a scheme agreed upon between the sender and the receiver. This scheme is usually based upon the existence of one or more secret keys known only to the sender and the receiver. The sender encodes the data using the encryption key so that it will be meaningless to anyone who intercepts it as it is transmitted in encoded form. The receiver decodes the data back to its original form using the decryption key. We will look more closely at encryption schemes in Section 13.4.

Encryption provides for the secure transmission of data, but this is of little use if you are not sending the data to the correct party. **Authentication** is the process of verifying the identify of the receiver of your message.

The standard method for achieving security on the Web is **SSL** (**secure sockets layer**). This is a series of protocols that allow a client (the Web Browser) and a Web server to agree on the encryption methods to be used, exchange the necessary security keys, and authenticate the identity of each party to the other. For example, the server can pass a **certificate of authentication** to the browser certifying that the keys being passed from the server are associated with the correct organization. The certificate is issued by a trusted third party certificate authority, such as VeriSign (www.verisign.com), and the browser checks with the certificate authority to be sure the certificate is still valid.

Using VeriSign SSL software also allows you to post a "secure site seal" on your Web site that human users can click on to verify that they are at the correct site. After all, they didn't walk into your physical place of business so how do they know where they really are? The URL is www.rugs-for-you.com, and there are lots of pictures of rugs, but maybe it is simply a scam where the customer will send money but receive nothing in return. **Spoofing** is the practice of impersonating a legitimate site for the purposes of stealing money or stealing identity by collecting confidential information such as credit card numbers, names, and addresses. Clicking on your VeriSign seal might bring up a window with the information shown in part in Figure 13.2.

Customers about to transmit sensitive information to your Web site will be alerted by a message saying they are being transferred to a secure site. The corresponding Web page will have the protocol heading **https,** rather than the simpler http, with the extra *s* signifying a site under the protection of SSL. Customers may also see a little lock graphic on the Web page to indicate security. When they leave the site, they will again receive a message saying they are leaving a secure site.

STEPS 4 AND 5: PAYMENT PROCESSING

Let's assume that your customers will pay with a credit card, the most common online option. The online order form communicates with your accounting system (step 4), which might verify the customer's credit and process this transaction with the credit company (step 5) on the fly, that is, while the customer waits. This way the customer can be alerted if there is some error and given another chance to enter correct information. In addition, you do not have to store the customer credit card number in your database, which reduces your security risk.

Another option is to collect information on the customer's order, including an email address (step 4), close the order process, and then evaluate the customer's credit and complete the transaction offline (step 5). Once the

FIGURE 13.2

Secure Site Assurance

WWW.RUGS-FOR-YOU.COM is a VeriSign Secure Site

Security remains the primary concern of online consumers. The VeriSign Secure Site Program allows you to learn more about Web sites you visit before you submit any confidential information. Please verify that the information below is consistent with the site you are visiting.

Name: WWW.RUGS-FOR-YOU.COM   Status: Valid

Validity Period: 14-May-03–25-May-06

Server ID Information:

> Country = U.S.
> State = Ohio
> Locality = Cleveland
> Organization = Rugs-For-You, Inc.
> Common Name = www.rugs-for-you.com

If the information is correct, you may submit sensitive data (e.g., credit card numbers) to this site with the assurance that

> This site has a VeriSign Secure Server ID.

All information sent to this site, if in an SSL session, is encrypted, protecting against disclosure to third parties.

transaction is completed, an email confirmation is sent to the customer. For this option you must maintain customer credit card information.

STEPS 6–9: ORDER FULFILLMENT Your customer's credit has been approved. Your order entry system has to alert your inventory system to decrement the items in stock by whatever the user has purchased (step 6) and must also contact your shipping system to arrange for shipping (step 7). The shipping system works with your shipping company of choice (step 8) to pick up and deliver the purchase to the satisfied customer (step 9).

 ### 13.2.4 *Designing Your Web Site*

Your Web site must be designed with your customers in mind. It has to be fresh and up to date, ever changing, and always have the latest product information. Department stores don't keep the same displays in their windows for months or years on end and neither should you. One of your earliest decisions will be your Web site **taxonomy**—how information will be classified and organized so customers can easily find what they want. At rugs-for-you.com, you could choose to organize your site by rug manufacturer, color, size, material, or the type of room in which the rug will typically go. There are many options, and you must keep in mind how your customers usually shop for their rugs.

Your customers should always know where they are on your Web site. As we mentioned in Chapter 7, hypertext allows a user to move easily from page to page by simply clicking a link. However, after a few clicks it is easy to become totally lost and not know where you are or how to get back. A **site map** or a **navigation bar** should provide a high-level overview of your site architecture, plus make it easy to navigate (i.e., move from page to page) through the site. A good rule of thumb is that the customer should be able to get from any page in your Web site to any other page in four clicks or fewer. And while you want to encourage browsing, just as you do in your physical store, you also want customers to be able to find what they are looking for quickly, so your Web pages should include the ability to search the site.

You will need electronic "shopping carts" and order checkout forms. Keep in mind that customers want to feel in control (especially of their money!). Be sure that as customers step through the ordering process they are always informed about the current order—items being ordered, quantity, price, and so on—and about what will happen with the next button click. It is also important that the customer is always either given the option to go back and change something or told clearly that, following the next click, the order will be finalized and no further changes will be possible.

Give the customer shipping options so that he or she can make the best tradeoff between cost and speed of delivery. Send email to confirm the order and do a followup email when the order is actually shipped.

Display your privacy policy on the Web page. Tell your customers what personal information you will collect, why this information is needed, how you will use it, whether you will share it and who you might share it with, and how you will store and safeguard it. Also, understand what information you can legally collect, based on the regulations of the state or country of your target users.

You may also want to offer extras to your customers. Put up a **FAQ (frequently asked questions)** page or a bulletin board for discussion groups. You can ask customers if they wish to subscribe to an email newsletter to alert them to the latest products (no spam, please) with the option to unsubscribe at any time. Give your customers a "suggestion box." Allow them to track their shipment through an order number. Post news and press releases about your business or products. And again, configure your site in a personalized way for return customers. All of these measures can help improve your customer satisfaction, build customer relationships, and bring people back to your Web site time and time again. The suggestions and ideas listed above will be part of your online **CRM (customer relationship management)** strategy.

At the same time that you want to cram all this content into your Web pages, your site must adhere to good design principles. It must look professional and uncluttered. Avoid glaring colors, flashing images, and annoying pop-up windows, although there could be a *judicious* use of animation or changing, tasteful images. Make good use of white space—it can draw attention to the items you want emphasized. All of your pages should have a consistent "look and feel" and a consistent set of navigation tools; this could be accomplished by designing a master template page from which all pages are derived. Be sure your company logo and/or slogan are part of this master template.

On the technical side, your Web pages should be designed knowing that they will be displayed on many different machines with different operating systems and browsers (e.g., Netscape Navigator, Internet Explorer, Mozilla). Not all browsers render every HTML element in exactly the same way. Users may run monitors at different screen resolutions and have widely varying communication speeds, from tens of thousands to tens of millions of bits per second. (See the discussion on Communication Links in Section 7.2.1.). Your Web design will need to use only those features that you know will work satisfactorily on virtually every machine and browser that your customers are likely to use. Offer features such as text-only options for users with slow connections. Adhere to ADA (American Disabilities Act) requirements, such as providing text equivalents for all nontext items (images, video, or audio). Text can be run through a speech synthesizer or converted to braille for the visually impaired and can be read by the hearing-impaired in place of audio files.

As you can see from our brief discussion, designing Web pages, or at least a successful set of commercial Web pages, is a difficult and complex task. It involves not only computer science skills (e.g., HTML, XML, HTTP, TCP/IP), but a knowledge of such fields as art, graphics design, business, management, and consumer psychology to name but a few. It is easy to create just any Web page, but it is devilishly difficult to create a really good one.

 ### 13.2.5 *Behind the Scenes*

Your business maintains a number of other computer applications in addition to your online order entry system. From Figure 13.1, we see that there are accounting, inventory control, and shipping systems as well as a customer database, and that's just to deal with customers. You also have systems that deal with your suppliers to manage orders, shipments, billing, and payments. Finally, you have personnel systems to deal with your employees—payroll, insurance, Social Security. Some of these systems may be brand new and just installed (like your new Web site), while others may be "legacy" code that has been around for literally dozens of years.

Obviously, these systems are not all independent of one another, and some must collaborate quite closely. For example, your inventory control system must communicate with the supplier order system whenever you run low on an item and must restock it. Your accounting system needs to inform the customer database when a payment has been made. However, these systems may have been developed by different vendors (some functions may even be done by hand) and may run on different machines using totally different protocols and formats from your new Web site. Because of this, once the Web site is up and running you may need to invest in **middleware**—software that allows separate, existing programs to communicate and work together seamlessly. These middleware packages would do such things as translate between incompatible data representations, file formats, and network protocols to allow otherwise incompatible systems to exchange information. This would allow your new e-commerce application to access and/or transmit important business data to all other parts of your company

Finally, as soon as you have your enterprise humming along smoothly as an e-commerce site, you will need an effective **disaster recovery strategy.** What are your plans for backing up critical data? What is your plan to keep your online business open even when your server fails? What will you do if a hacker breaks into your Web site and steals customer information? Without a plan, you are never more than one electrical storm, one malicious user, or one disk failure away from catastrophe.

By now you may have surmised that you need a lot of help to put together your successful e-business. You need network help, programming help, graphics design help, and legal advice, as well as input from those who know your business well.

One happy thought is that your e-business might grow to be so successful that you have to scale up beyond your expectations. Amazon.com has been one of the most successful e-businesses, and has expanded beyond its original bookselling role to include sales of toys, clothing, electronics, kitchen goods and housewares, and home and garden items.

In June 2003, *Harry Potter and the Order of the Phoenix*, the fifth book in the very popular Harry Potter series by author J. K. Rowling, went on sale at midnight on a Saturday. By Sunday night, Amazon.com was sold out, with over 1.3 million books ordered and shipped worldwide. Imagine the demand this created on the online servers, the back-office applications, and the shippers!

PRACTICE PROBLEM

1. Try to locate a portal page for at least one of the following topics: healthcare, environmental issues, basketball, higher education, and/or the steel industry.

13.3   Databases

The management and organization of data have always been important problems. It is likely that a strong impetus for the development of written language was the need to record commercial transactions ("On this day Procrastinus traded Consensius 4 sheep for 7 barrels of olive oil"). From there it is only a short step to recording inventories ("Procrastinus has 27 sheep"), wages paid, profits gained, and so on. As the volume of data grows, it becomes more difficult to keep track of all the facts, harder to extract useful information from a large collection of facts, and more difficult to relate one fact to another. With the 1890 U.S. census (Chapter 1), Herman Hollerith demonstrated the advantages that can accrue from mechanizing the storage and processing of large amounts of data.

We talked about the online customer database as part of your expansion into e-commerce, but databases are probably a key part of your business whether you have an online presence or not. You have a set of data to maintain about your employees (names, addresses, pay rates, Social Security numbers, etc.), another set of data to maintain about your suppliers (names, addresses, products, orders, etc.), and yet another set of data to maintain about your business itself (sales, expenses, taxes, etc.). Previously, such items of data were recorded by hand, but they are now maintained in electronic databases. The important thing about an electronic database is that it is more than a storehouse of individual data items; these items can easily be extracted, sorted, and even manipulated to reveal new information. To see how this works, let's examine the structure of a file containing data.

13.3.1 *Data Organization*

As we learned in Chapters 4 and 5, the most basic unit of data is a single **bit,** a value of 0 or 1. A single bit rarely conveys any meaningful information. Bits are combined into groups of eight called **bytes**; each byte can store the binary representation of a single character or of a small integer number. A byte is a single unit of addressable memory. A single byte is often too small to store meaningful information, so a group of bytes is used to represent a string of characters—say, the name of an employee in a company or a larger numerical value. Such a group of bytes is called a **field.** A collection of related fields—say, all the information about a single employee—is called a **record,** a term inherited from the pencil and paper concept of "keeping records." Related records—say, the records of all the employees in a single company—are kept in a **data file.** (*File* is another term inherited from the familiar *filing cabinet.*) And finally, related files make up a **database.** Thus,

> Bits combine to form bytes.
>
> Bytes combine to form fields.
>
> Fields combine to form records.
>
> Records combine to form files.
>
> Files combine to form databases.

Figure 13.3 shows this hierarchical organization of data elements. (This figure was drawn to look neat, but files in a database are almost never all the same size or "shape.")

Bits and bytes are too fine a level of detail for what we will discuss in this section. Also, for the moment, let's simplify the situation to the case where the database consists of only a single file. Figure 13.4 illustrates a single file made up of five records (the rows), each record composed of three fields (the columns).

Figure 13.4 looks somewhat like the array data structure described in Chapter 8. In an array, however, each array entry must be of the same data type, so that a given array could store only character data or only integer data. The various fields in a record can hold different types of data. One field

FIGURE 13.3

Data Organization Hierarchy

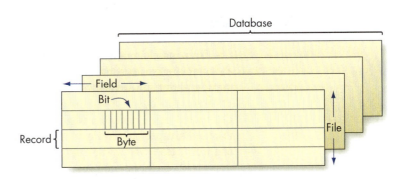

FIGURE 13.4

Records and Fields in a Single File

	Field 1	Field 2	Field 3
Record 1			
Record 2			
Record 3			
Record 4			
Record 5			

FIGURE 13.5

One Record in the Rugs-For-You Employees File

ID	LastName	FirstName	Birthdate	PayRate	HoursWorked
149	Takasano	Frederick	5/23/1966	$12.35	250

in each record might hold character strings; another field in each record might hold integer data.

Each record in a file contains information about an item in the "universe of discourse" that the file describes. In our example, we will assume that the "universe of discourse" is the set of employees at Rugs-For-You and that each record corresponds to a single employee. An individual employee record, with six different fields, is shown in Figure 13.5. Here it is clear that the *LastName* and *FirstName* fields hold character strings. The type of data being stored in the *ID* field is not clear to us as humans from looking at the record; it could be numeric data, but because it is unlikely to be involved in computations, it could also be character string data. The data type must be specified when the file is created.

 ### 13.3.2 *Database Management Systems*

A **database management system (DBMS)** manages the files in a database. We know that such files actually consist of collections of individual records. However, Edgar F. Codd (mentioned in Chapter 11 as a Turing Award winner for his work in database management systems) proposed the conceptual model of a file as simply a two-dimensional table. In this **relational database model,** the *Employees* file at Rugs-For-You would be represented by the *Employees* table of Figure 13.6.

With the change from actual records in a file to a conceptual table representing data comes some changes in terminology. The table represents information about an **entity,** a fundamental distinguishable component in the Rugs-For-You business—namely its employees. A row of the table contains data about one instance of this entity—that is, one employee—and the row is called a **tuple** (in Figure 13.6, each row is a 6-tuple, containing six pieces of information). How the tuples (rows) are ordered within the table is not important. Each category of information (*ID, FirstName,* and so on, in our

FIGURE 13.6

Employees *Table for Rugs-For-You*

EMPLOYEES

ID	LASTNAME	FIRSTNAME	BIRTHDATE	PAYRATE	HOURSWORKED
116	Kay	Janet	3/29/1956	$16.60	94
123	Perreira	Francine	8/15/1987	$ 8.50	185
149	Takasano	Frederick	5/23/1966	$12.35	250
171	Kay	John	11/17/1954	$17.80	245
165	Honou	Morris	6/9/1988	$ 6.70	53

example) is called an **attribute.** The heading above each column identifies an attribute. The table thus consists of tuples of attribute values. (In other words, in the relational model, files are thought of as tables, records as tuples, and fields as attributes.) A **primary key** is an attribute or combination of attributes that uniquely identifies a tuple. In our example, we are assuming that *ID* is a primary key; *ID* is underlined in the heading in Figure 13.6 to indicate that it is the primary key for this table. The Social Security number is often used as a primary key to uniquely identify tuples that involve people. Obviously, neither LastName nor FirstName could serve as a primary key—there are lots of people with the last name Smith and many people with a first name of Michael or Judith.

The computer's operating system functions as a basic file manager. As we learned in Chapter 6, the operating system contains commands to list all of the files on the hard drive, to copy or delete a file, to rename a file, and so forth. But a database management system, unlike a simple file manager, works at the level of individual fields in the individual records of the file; in more appropriate terminology, we should say that it works at the level of individual attribute values of individual tuples in the relation table. Given the *Employees* table of Figure 13.6, a database management system could be given the following instruction:

```
SELECT ID, LastName, FirstName, Birthdate, PayRate,
  HoursWorked
FROM Employees
WHERE ID = 123;
```

This command asks the system to retrieve all the information about the employee with ID 123. Because *ID* is the primary key, there can only be one such employee, and this is a relatively easy task. But the following request to locate all the information about an employee with a given last name,

```
SELECT ID, LastName, FirstName, Birthdate, PayRate,
  HoursWorked
FROM Employees
WHERE LastName = 'Perreira';
```

is done just as easily even though the *LastName* attribute may not uniquely identify the tuple. If multiple employees in the table have the same name, all of the relevant entries would be returned.

If only some of the attributes are wanted, an instruction such as

```
SELECT LastName, PayRate
FROM Employees
WHERE LastName = 'Perreira';
```

produces just the last name and pay rate for the employee(s) with the given name.

Database management systems usually require the use of specialized **query languages** to enable the user or another application program to **query** (ask questions of) the database in order to retrieve information. The three preceding SELECT examples are written in a language called **SQL,** *Structured Query Language.* We briefly discussed SQL in Chapter 9.

To appreciate the power of SQL, consider the following simple SQL queries for more complicated tasks:

```
SELECT *
FROM Employees
ORDER BY ID;
```

This query says to retrieve all of the attribute values (the asterisk is shorthand for listing all attributes) for all the tuples (because there is no further qualification) in the *Employees* table sorted in order by *ID.* Thus, we have effectively sorted the tuples in the relational table using a single command. This is a significant gain in productivity over the step by step process of comparing items and moving them around that was required when we wrote a sorting algorithm in Chapter 3. (Of course, what has happened internally is that SQL has invoked its own sorting algorithm. However, the user is shielded from the details of this algorithm and is allowed to work at a more abstract level.) The query

```
SELECT *
FROM Employees
WHERE PayRate > 15.00;
```

gets all the tuples for employees above a certain pay rate. Here we've effectively done a search of all the tuples on a particular attribute, again without having to specify all of the details, as we had to do when writing the sequential search or binary search algorithms of Chapter 3.

Managing a relational table involves more than just making queries about the existing table. One must be able to add new tuples to the table (which is how the existing tuples got into the table in the first place), delete tuples from a table, or change information in an existing tuple. These tasks are easily handled by the INSERT, DELETE, and UPDATE commands available in SQL.

In order to explore further the power of a DBMS, let's expand our Rugs-For-You database to include a second relational table. The *InsurancePolicies* table shown in Figure 13.7 gives information on the insurance plan type and the date of issue of the policy for an employee with a given ID.

In the *InsurancePolicies* table, there is a **composite primary key** in that both *EmployeeID* and *PlanType* are needed to identify a tuple uniquely,

FIGURE 13.7

InsurancePolicies *Table for Rugs-For-You*

INSURANCEPOLICIES		
EMPLOYEEID	PLANTYPE	DATEISSUED
171	B2	10/18/1974
171	C1	6/21/1982
149	B2	8/16/1990
149	A1	5/23/1995
149	C2	12/18/1999

because a given employee may have more than one insurance plan (e.g., both health and disability insurance plans). It is also true that an employee may have no plan; in Figure 13.7, there is no tuple with ID 116, although there is an employee with ID 116. Each value of *EmployeeID* in the *InsurancePolicies* table exists as an *ID* value in a tuple of the *Employees* table, where it is a primary key. Because of this, the *EmployeeID* attribute of the *InsurancePolicies* table is called a **foreign key** into the *Employees* table. This foreign key establishes the relationship that employees may have insurance plans.

The database management system can relate information between various tables through these key values—in our example, the linkage between the foreign key *EmployeeID* in the *InsurancePolicies* table and the primary key *ID* in the *Employees* table. Thus, the following query will give us information about Frederick Takasano's insurance plan even though Frederick Takasano's name is not in the *InsurancePolicies* table:

```
SELECT LastName, FirstName, PlanType
FROM Employees, InsurancePolicies
WHERE LastName = 'Takasano'
AND FirstName = 'Frederick'
AND ID = EmployeeID;
```

The query is an instruction to retrieve the *LastName* and *FirstName* attributes from the *Employees* table and the *PlanType* attribute from the *InsurancePolicies* table by looking for the tuple with *LastName* attribute value "Takasano" and *FirstName* attribute value "Frederick" in the *Employees* table and then finding the tuple(s) with the matching *EmployeeID* value in the *InsurancePolicies* table. (Here is the Boolean AND operation we encountered in Chapter 4 in our discussion on Boolean logic.) It is the last term in the WHERE clause of the query (the last line) that causes the two tables to be joined together by the match between primary key and foreign key. The result of the query will be

```
Takasano Frederick B2
Takasano Frederick A1
Takasano Frederick C2
```

The correspondence between primary keys and foreign keys is what establishes the relationships among various entities in a database. The SQL command to create a table requires specification of the various attributes by name and data type, identification of the primary key, identification of any foreign keys, and identification of the tables into which these are foreign keys. This information is pertinent to building the actual file that stores the data in the tuples.

We've now done a fairly complex query involving two different tables. It is easy to see how these ideas can be expanded to multiple tables, linked together by relationships represented by foreign keys and their corresponding primary keys. Figure 13.8 shows an expansion of the Rugs-For-You database to include a table called *InsurancePlans* that contains, for each type of insurance plan, a description of its coverage and its monthly cost. *PlanType* is the primary key for this table. This makes *PlanType* in the *InsurancePolicies* table a foreign key into the *InsurancePlans* table, as shown in Figure 13.8. This linkage would allow us to write a query to find, for example, the monthly cost of Mr. Takasano's insurance (see Practice Problem 2 at the end of this section).

Using multiple tables in a single database reduces the amount of redundant information that must be stored. For example, a stand-alone insurance file for Rugs-For-You employees would probably have to include employee names as well as IDs. It also minimizes the amount of work required to maintain consistency in the data (if Francine Perreira gets married and changes her name, the name change need only be entered in one place). But most important of all, the database gives the user, or the user's application software, the ability to combine and manipulate data easily in ways that would be very difficult if the data were kept in separate and unrelated files.

As we have seen by looking at some queries, SQL is a very high-level language where a single instruction is quite powerful. In terms of the language classifications of Chapter 9, it is also a nonprocedural language. An SQL

FIGURE 13.8

Three Entities in the Rugs-For-You Database

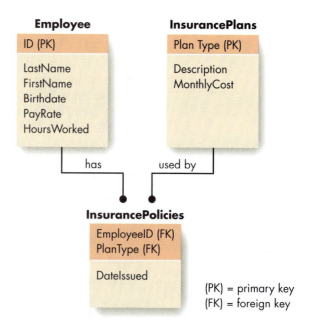

"program" merely asks for something to be done (sort all tuples in some order, search all tuples to match some condition) but does not have to issue the specific sequence of instructions on *how* it is to be done.

13.3.3 *Other Considerations*

Performance issues definitely affect the user's satisfaction with a database management system; a slow response to a query is at best annoying and at worst unacceptable. Large files are maintained on disk in secondary storage rather than being brought in total into main memory. Accessing a record in the file involves at least one disk input/output (I/O) operation, which is a much slower process than accessing information stored in main memory, sometimes as much as three or four orders of magnitude slower.

In Chapter 5 we talked about the three components that contribute to reading an individual disk sector into memory or writing from memory to a disk sector: seek time (time to position the read/write head over the correct track on the disk), latency (time for the correct sector to rotate under the read/write head), and transfer time (time to read from or write to the entire sector). Organizing the way that records are stored on the disk can help to minimize the time to access a particular record by reducing the number of disk I/O operations that must be done before finding the sector containing the desired record. For example, assume that we have a database that occupies 30 sectors on our disk and there are 15 sectors per track. It would make the most sense to store the information on surface 0, track 0, sectors 0–14 and on surface 1, track 0, sectors 0–14. By using the same track on different surfaces, the head will not have to move to a different track to obtain the data, and the seek time will always be 0.

Also, creating additional records to be stored along with the file, while using up extra storage, can significantly reduce access time. The idea here is much like that of a library catalog system. The user who wants to "access" a book first consults a smaller structure that is organized in a useful way (alphabetically) and that then directs the user to the point in the library where the desired book can be found. The smaller structure stored with the file may even be organized in a tree-like manner that is a generalization of the tree structure we used in Chapter 3 to visualize the binary search. Following the branches of the tree can quickly lead to information about the location in the file of the record with a particular primary key value. A good DBMS will incorporate the services of a sophisticated file manager to organize the disk files in an optimal way in order to minimize access time to the records.

Distributed databases allow the physical data to reside at separate and independent locations that are electronically networked together. The user at site A makes a database query that needs access to data physically stored at site B. The database management system and the underlying network will make the necessary links and connections to get the data from where it is currently stored to the node where it is needed. To the user, it appears that this is a single database on his or her own machine, except perhaps for increased access time when data have to travel across a network.

If a database management system can easily make connections between different files of data, and even data stored at different locations, how difficult would it be to electronically link information in the IRS database with information in the FBI database, the Social Security database, credit card databases, banking databases, and so on? Obviously, this would not be difficult using the technology that we have described in this chapter. Building these types of massive, integrated government databases does not raise technical issues so much as legal, political, social, and ethical ones. Remember that even the online customers of Rugs-For-You wanted assurances as to how their personal information would be used. In general, issues of personal privacy and public safety are magnified enormously by the capabilities of networked databases. We'll discuss approaches to these and other ethical issues in Chapter 15.

LABORATORY EXPERIENCE 21

If you have a commercial database package available to use, you can work through the exercises in this laboratory experience. You will write SQL queries similar to the ones discussed in this section and will also learn how to use SQL to carry out some computations.

PRACTICE PROBLEMS

1. Using the *Employees* table of Figure 13.6, what will be the result of the following SQL query?

   ```
   SELECT ID, PayRate
   FROM Employees
   WHERE LastName = 'Takasano';
   ```

2. Complete the following SQL query to find the monthly cost of Frederick Takasano's insurance; because *PlanType* is an attribute of both *InsurancePolicies* and *InsurancePlans*, we have to include the table name as well.

   ```
   SELECT LastName, FirstName, _____
   FROM Employees, InsurancePlans, InsurancePolicies
   WHERE LastName = _____
   AND ID = EmployeeID
   AND InsurancePolicies.PlanType = _____;
   ```

3. Using the *InsurancePolicies* table of Figure 13.7, write an SQL query to find all the employee IDs for employees who have insurance plan type B2.

Information security means protecting data, whether this is data stored on your computer's hard disk or data being transmitted across a network. There are many different levels at which security can be breached, and therefore many different types of precautions to be taken. We'll outline just a few here.

In the early days of computing when big mainframes were the only option, physical security was enforced via the locked rooms housing these machines. Only authorized persons had access. Now that there is a machine on virtually every desktop, that kind of physical security is harder to obtain, but you can take some obvious steps: Don't leave your laptop lying around; never leave your workstation running when you are not in the room; and do not share your password with anyone or, worse yet, leave it on a sticky note attached to your monitor.

The operating system uses the log-on password as an authentication device. It identifies a particular user. Hackers breaking into a computer system look for a file of passwords as the "Open, Sesame" for all locked doors. Once on the system, the authenticated user (remember this simply means a person with knowledge of the password!) has certain file accesses and privileges that the operating system enforces. One user may not be able to access a file at all while another user, with a different set of privileges, can do anything at all with that file, including modifying or deleting it. In Chapter 6 we discussed "system security and protection" as one of the functions an operating system has to perform, and Figure 6.17 shows an authorization list of which users have what privileges with the file of grades for a particular student.

Earlier in this chapter we mentioned SSL as the method to provide security for sensitive data traveling across the Web between the client machine and the server. Part of the SSL protocol involves passing a certificate of authentication issued by a third party certificate authority from the server to the browser.

If, despite these precautions, files on a computer hard disk or packets passing along a network connection are illegally accessed and fall into the wrong hands, we can still protect their contents through encryption. The operating system might encrypt the system files that contain the passwords and authorization lists so that, without the key to decrypt them, they would be of little use to anyone who stole them. The user might encrypt application files (such as the customer database) stored on the computer's hard disk. And, as we discussed in Section 13.2.3, personal information sent across the Web in an online order will be encrypted.

The two main thrusts of information security are, therefore, **authentication** (don't let the bad guys get the stuff) and **encryption** (make the stuff meaningless if they do get it). We'll spend the rest of this section discussing encryption. The same techniques apply to data sent or data stored.

13.4.1 *Encryption Overview*

Cryptography is the science of "secret writing." A message (**plaintext**) is encoded (encrypted) before it is sent, for the purpose of keeping its content secret if it is intercepted by the wrong parties. The encrypted message is called **ciphertext.** The ciphertext is decoded (decrypted) back to plaintext when it is received in order to retrieve the original information. **Encryption** and **decryption** date back thousands of years. The most famous instances of cryptography occur in military history, beginning with Julius Caesar of the Roman Empire, who developed the Caesar cipher, and certainly including the German Enigma code cracked by the Allies during World War II. Transmitting information securely has taken a modern turn with electronic commerce on the Internet and concerns over protection of consumer credit card numbers and other personal data.

Encryption and decryption are inverse operations because decryption must "undo" the encryption and reproduce the original text. There are many encryption/decryption algorithms, and of course both the sender and receiver must use the same system. A **symmetric encryption algorithm** requires the use of a secret key known to both the sender and receiver. The sender encrypts the plaintext using the key; the receiver, knowing the key, is easily able to reverse the process and decrypt the message. One of the difficulties with a symmetric encryption algorithm is how to securely transmit the secret key so that both the sender and the receiver know what it is; in fact, this approach seems to simply move the security problem to a slightly different level, from transmitting a message to transmitting a key. In an **asymmetric encryption algorithm,** also called a **public key encryption algorithm,** the key for encryption and the key for decryption are quite different, although related. Person A can make an encryption key public and anyone can encrypt a message using the public key and send it to A. Only A has the decryption key, however, so only A can decrypt the message. This approach avoids the difficulty of secret key transmission, but it introduces a new problem: the relationship between the decryption key and the encryption key must be sufficiently complex that it is not possible to derive the decryption key from the public encryption key.

 13.4.2 *Simple Encryption Algorithms*

CAESAR CIPHER A **Caesar cipher,** also called a **shift cipher,** involves shifting each character in the message to another character some fixed distance farther along in the alphabet. Specifically, let *s* be some integer between 1 and 25 that represents the amount of shift. Each letter in the message is encoded as the letter that is *s* units farther along in the alphabet, with the last *s* letters of the alphabet shifted in a cycle to the first *s* letters. For example, if *s* = 3, then *A* is encoded as *D*, *B* is encoded as *E*, *X* is encoded as *A*, and *Z* is encoded as *C*. The integer *s* is the secret key. Decoding a message, given knowledge of *s*, simply means reversing the shift. For example, if *s* = 3, then the code word DUPB is decoded as ARMY.

The Caesar cipher is an example of a **stream cipher;** that is, it encodes one character at a time. This makes it easy to encode just by scanning the plaintext and doing the appropriate substitution at each character. On the other hand, there are only 25 possible keys, so a ciphertext message could be decoded by brute force, that is, by simply trying all possible keys.

In addition, the Caesar cipher is a **substitution cipher,** where a single letter of plaintext generates a single letter of ciphertext. We can replace the simple shift mechanism of the Caesar cipher with a more complex substitution mechanism, for example,

(Can you guess the substitution algorithm being used?) However in any simple substitution cipher, the structure of the plaintext is maintained in the ciphertext—letter frequency, occurrence of double letters, frequently occurring letter combinations, and so forth. With a sufficiently long message, an experienced **cryptanalyst** (code-breaker) can use these clues to recover the plaintext.

BLOCK CIPHER In a **block cipher,** a group or block of plaintext letters gets encoded into a block of ciphertext, but not by substituting one at a time for each character. Each plaintext character in the block contributes to more than one ciphertext character and one ciphertext character has been created as a result of more than one plaintext letter. It is as if each plaintext character in a block gets chopped into little pieces and these pieces are scattered among the ciphertext characters in the corresponding block. This diffusion tends to destroy the structure of the plaintext and make decryption more difficult.

As a simple example, we'll use a block size of 2 and an encoding key that is a 2 × 2 arrangement of numbers called a **matrix.** Here A and B,

$$A = \begin{bmatrix} 1 & 2 \\ 3 & 4 \end{bmatrix} \qquad B = \begin{bmatrix} 5 & 1 \\ 2 & 1 \end{bmatrix}$$

are matrices. We can define an operation of matrix multiplication. The product $A \times B$ will also be a 2 × 2 matrix, where the element in row i, column j of $A \times B$ is obtained by multiplying each element in row i of A by its corresponding element in column j of B and adding the results. So to obtain the element in row 1, column 1 of the result, we multiply the row 1 elements of A by the corresponding column 1 elements of B and add the results:

$$\begin{bmatrix} 1 & 2 \\ 3 & 4 \end{bmatrix} \times \begin{bmatrix} 5 & 1 \\ 2 & 1 \end{bmatrix} = \begin{bmatrix} 9 & \\ & \end{bmatrix}$$

$$1 \times 5 + 2 \times 2 = 5 + 4 = 9$$

To obtain the element in row 1, column 2 of the result, we multiply the row 1 elements of A by the corresponding column 2 elements of B and add the results:

$$\begin{bmatrix} 1 & 2 \\ 3 & 4 \end{bmatrix} \times \begin{bmatrix} 5 & 1 \\ 2 & 1 \end{bmatrix} = \begin{bmatrix} 9 & 3 \\ & \end{bmatrix}$$

The completed product $A \times B$ is $\begin{bmatrix} 9 & 3 \\ 23 & 7 \end{bmatrix}$.

However, for encryption purposes, we are going to modify this definition. When we add up the terms for each element, whenever we exceed 25, we will start over again counting from 0. In this scheme, 26 → 0, 27 → 1, 28 → 2,

..., 52 → 0, and so on. Not every 2 × 2 matrix can serve as an encryption key; we need an **invertible matrix.** This is a matrix M for which there is another matrix M' such that

$$M' \times M = \begin{bmatrix} 1 & 0 \\ 0 & 1 \end{bmatrix}$$

For example, $M = \begin{bmatrix} 3 & 5 \\ 2 & 3 \end{bmatrix}$ is invertible because for $M' = \begin{bmatrix} 23 & 5 \\ 2 & 23 \end{bmatrix}$,

$$M' \times M = \begin{bmatrix} 23 & 5 \\ 2 & 23 \end{bmatrix} \times \begin{bmatrix} 3 & 5 \\ 2 & 3 \end{bmatrix} = \begin{bmatrix} 79 & 130 \\ 52 & 79 \end{bmatrix}$$

$$\rightarrow \begin{bmatrix} 1 & 0 \\ 0 & 1 \end{bmatrix}$$

This property is what allows M' to reverse the effect of M. Also part of our encryption algorithm is a simple substitution S that maps letters into numbers; we'll let S be really simple here: $S(A) = 1$, $S(B) = 2$, ..., $S(Z) = 26$. Obviously S is reversible, and we'll call the reverse mapping S': $S'(1) = A$, $S'(2) = B$, ..., $S'(26) = Z$.

To encode our message, we break it up into 2-character blocks. Suppose the first two characters form the block $(D \quad E)$. We apply the S mapping to this block to get $(4 \quad 5)$. Now we multiply $(4 \quad 5) \times M$ by treating $(4 \quad 5)$ as the row of some matrix (and remember to wrap around if the result exceeds 25):

$$(4 \quad 5) \times \begin{bmatrix} 3 & 5 \\ 2 & 3 \end{bmatrix} = (4*3 + 5*2 \quad 4*5 + 5*3) = (22 \quad 35) \rightarrow (22 \quad 9)$$

Finally, apply the S' mapping to get from digits back to characters: $S'(22 \quad 9) = (V \quad I)$. This completes the encoding, and $(V \quad I)$ is the ciphertext for the message block $(D \quad E)$. Notice that the digit 4 (i.e., the plaintext letter D) contributed to both the 22 (V) and the 9 (I), as did the digit 5 (i.e., the plaintext letter E). This **diffusion** (scattering) of the plaintext within the ciphertext is the advantage of a block cipher.

For decoding, we reverse the above steps. Starting with the ciphertext $(V \quad I)$, we first apply S to get $(22 \quad 9)$. We then multiply $(22 \quad 9)$ by M', the inverse of the encoding key (remembering to wrap around if the result exceeds 25):

$$(22 \quad 9) \times \begin{bmatrix} 23 & 5 \\ 2 & 23 \end{bmatrix} = (22*23 + 9*2 \quad 22*5 + 9*23) =$$

$$(524 \quad 317) \rightarrow (4 \quad 5)$$

Finally we apply S' to get back—voila!—the plaintext $(D \quad E)$.

Figure 13.9 summarizes the steps. Again, the matrix M is the secret encryption key, from which the decryption key M' can be derived.

FIGURE 13.9

*Steps in Encoding and Decoding
for a Block Cipher*

Encoding
1. Apply S mapping to plaintext block.
2. Multiply result times M, applying wraparound.
3. Apply S' to the result.
Decoding
1. Apply S to ciphertext block.
2. Multiply result times M', applying wraparound.
3. Apply S' to the result.

PRACTICE PROBLEMS

1. Using a Caesar cipher with $s = 5$, encrypt the message NOW IS THE HOUR.

2. A messenger tells you that the secret key for today for the Caesar cipher is $s = 26$. Should you trust the messenger? Why or why not?

LABORATORY EXPERIENCE 22

In this laboratory experience, you will encrypt and decrypt messages using a block cipher of block size 2. The encryption key will again be a matrix, but the encryption algorithm is quite different from that of the block cipher discussed in this section.

 ### 13.4.3 *DES*

Both of the previous algorithms are too simplistic to provide the level of security we want for Internet transactions. **DES (Data Encryption Standard)** is an encryption algorithm developed by IBM in the 1970s for the U.S. National Bureau of Standards (now called the U.S. National Institute of Standards and Technology, NIST), and is certified as an international standard by the International Standards Organization (the same organization that certifies standards for programming languages, as we discussed in Chapter 8). While one might expect this internationally standard algorithm to rest upon some extremely complex and obscure operations, the DES algorithm actually uses very simple operations—but it does many of them.

DES was designed to protect electronic information, so we may assume that the plaintext is a binary string of 0s and 1s, just as it would be stored in a computer. As we learned in Chapter 4, this means that ordinary text has already undergone an encoding using ASCII or Unicode to convert characters to bit strings. This encoding, however, was not for the purposes of secrecy, and has nothing to do with the cryptographic encoding we are talking about in this chapter.

DES is a block cipher and the blocks are 64 bits long, meaning that 64 plaintext bits at a time are processed into 64 ciphertext bits. The key is a 64 bit binary key, although only 56 bits are actually used.

The algorithm begins by sending the plaintext 64-bit string through an initial **permutation** (rearrangement). The algorithm then cycles through 16 "rounds." Each round i performs the following steps:

1. The incoming 64 bit block is split into a left half L_i and a right half R_i. The right half R_i gets passed through unchanged to become the left half of the next round, L_{i+1}.

2. In addition, the 32 bits in the right half get permuted according to a fixed formula and then expanded to 48 bits by duplicating some of the bits. Meanwhile, the 56-bit key is also permuted (the result will be passed on as the key to the next round) and then reduced to 48 bits by omitting some of the bits. These two 48-bit strings are matched bit by bit using an XOR (exclusive OR) gate for each bit. Figure 13.10 shows the standard symbol for an XOR gate, along with its truth table.

3. The resulting 48-bit string undergoes a substitution and reduction to emerge as a 32-bit string. This string is permuted one more time, and the resulting 32-bit string is matched bit by bit, using XOR gates, with the left half L_i of the input. The result is passed to the next round as the new right half R_{i+1}.

After all 16 rounds have been completed, the final left and right half is recombined into a 64-bit string that is permuted one more time, and the resulting 64-bit string is the ciphertext. Figure 13.11 outlines the steps involved in the DES algorithm.

Two important points are noteworthy about the DES algorithm. One is that every substitution, reduction, expansion, and permutation is determined by a well-known set of tables. So given the same plaintext and the same key, everyone using DES would end up with the same ciphertext. The "secret" part

FIGURE 13.10

The XOR Gate

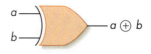

$a \oplus b$

a	b	a ⊕ b
0	0	0
0	1	1
1	0	1
1	1	0

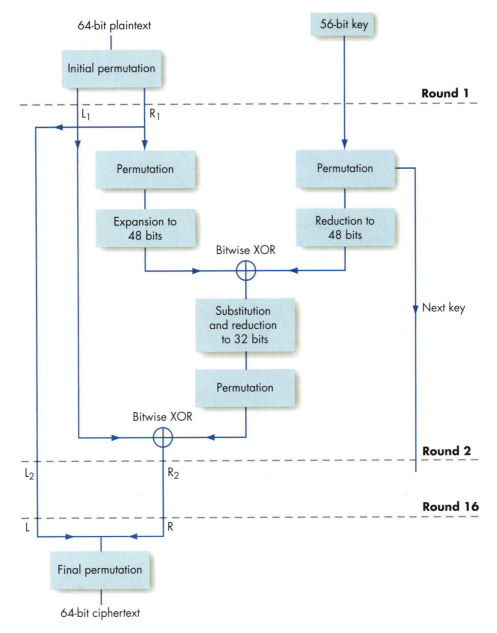

64-bit plaintext

Initial permutation

56-bit key

Round 1

L₁   R₁

Permutation

Permutation

Expansion to 48 bits

Reduction to 48 bits

Bitwise XOR

⊕

Next key

Substitution and reduction to 32 bits

Permutation

Bitwise XOR

⊕

Round 2

L₂   R₂

Round 16

L   R

Final permutation

64-bit ciphertext

FIGURE 13.11

The DES Encryption Algorithm

is the initial key. The second point is that the same algorithm serves as the decryption algorithm—just start with the ciphertext and apply the sequence of keys in reverse order, that is, the round 16 key first and the original secret key last.

With increased computing power in the hands of those trying to break a code, a 56-bit key does not seem as formidable as when DES was first introduced. It might even be feasible to try all 2^{56} (72,057,594,037,927,936) possible keys. **Triple DES** improves the security of DES; it requires two 56-bit

In 1997, the Electronic Frontier Foundation, a nonprofit civil-liberties organization, began to build the DES Cracker, a PC connected to a large array of custom chips. The entire configuration cost under $250,000 to build. This machine was intended to apply brute-force techniques (trying all possible 56-bit keys) to crack ciphertext encoded using DES. In 1998, the machine was used to respond to a challenge in the form of a ciphertext message posed by RSA Laboratories, the research component of RSA Security, a leading electronic security company. The DES Cracker could test 88 billion keys per second, and it found the correct 56-bit key in less than three days.

This result also had political and economic overtones because the U.S. government had strict controls on the export of cryptographic software, most of which was limited to encryption algorithms using a 40-bit key or less. This hampered major software vendors from overseas sales of products with strong encryption. The government also pressured industry within the United States to limit the use of cryptography to DES, claiming that DES codes were highly secure and nearly impossible to crack, a claim clearly refuted by this challenge. The designer of the DES Cracker machine noted that searching for a 40-bit key (the export limit at the time) using the DES Cracker would take 3–12 seconds.

Some people suspected that the government wanted to keep weak encoding in use in order to be able to access information, perhaps infringing on personal privacy. The U.S. export policy was made less restrictive in 1998, although not as a result of the DES Cracker. In Chapter 15, we'll examine the ethical issues raised in a specific instance of government regulation of encryption.

keys (which can be thought of as a 112-bit key length), and runs the DES algorithm three times: Encode using key 1, decode the result using key 2, encode the result using key 1 again.

Concerns about the eventual breakdown of DES in the face of ever-increasing computing power prompted NIST in 1997 to request proposals for a successor encryption scheme. The result was **AES** (**Advanced Encryption Standard**), which was adopted for use by the U.S. government in 2001. Like DES, AES also uses successive rounds of computations that mix up the data and the key. The key length can be 128, 192, or even 256 bits, and the algorithm appears to be very efficient.

13.4.4 Public-Key Systems

The encryption algorithms we have discussed so far have all been symmetric encryption algorithms, requiring that both the sender and receiver have knowledge of the key. Our final algorithm is an asymmetric, or public key, encryption algorithm. Remember that the main difficulty with a symmetric algorithm is how to securely transmit the secret key. In a public key system, the encryption key for messages to go to a particular receiver is broadcast to everyone, but the decryption key cannot be derived from it and is known only by the receiver.

The most common public key encryption algorithm is **RSA,** named for its developers, Ron Rivest, Adi Shamir, and Len Adleman at MIT (founders of RSA Security—see the box "Cracking DES"—and winners of the 2002 ACM Turing Award). This algorithm, developed in 1977, is based on results from the field of mathematics known as **number theory.**

A **prime number** is an integer greater than 1 that can only be written as the product of itself and 1. For example, 2, 3, 5, 7, 11, . . . are prime numbers;

you can only write 7, for example, as 7 = 1*7, the product of 1 and 7. The numbers 4, 6, 8, 10, and 12, for example, are not prime because they can be factored in a nontrivial way:

```
 4 = 2*2
 6 = 2*3
 8 = 2*2*2,
10 = 2*5
12 = 2*2*3
```

The result from number theory is that any positive integer is either a prime number or it can be written in a unique way as a product of prime factors. For example, 12 = 2*2*3 is the product of three prime factors. The success of RSA encryption depends on the fact that if n is a large number, it is extremely difficult to find the prime factors for n. So while information encrypted using RSA is technically not secure, it is in practice secure because of the large amount of computation necessary to find the prime factors of the encoding key.

Here's how RSA works. Two large prime numbers p and q are chosen at random and their product $n = p*q$ is computed. The product $m = (p - 1)*(q - 1)$ is also computed. Next, a large random number e is chosen in such a way that e and m have no common factors other than 1. This step guarantees the existence of a unique integer d between 0 and m, such that when we compute $e*d$ using the same sort of wraparound arithmetic we used in the block encoding scheme—that is, whenever we reach m, we start over again counting from 0—the result is 1. There are computationally efficient ways to produce p, q, e, and d. Let's stop at this point for a small example.

Suppose we pick $p = 3$ and $q = 7$. Then,

1. $n = p*q = 3*7 = 21$
2. $m = (p - 1)*(q - 1) = 2*6 = 12$
3. Choose $e = 5$ ($e = 5$ and $m = 12$ have no common factors)
4. Then $d = 5$ because $e*d = 5*5 = 25 = 2*12 + 1$, so when we compute $e*d$ using wraparound arithmetic with respect to 12, we get 1.

Now the number pair (n, e) becomes the public encryption key and d is the decryption key. Let's suppose that the plaintext message has been converted into an integer P, using some sort of mapping from characters to numbers. The encryption process is to compute P^e using wraparound arithmetic with respect to n (when you reach n, make that 0). Continuing with our small example, suppose $P = 3$. Then the ciphertext is computed as

5. $3^5 = 243 = 11*21 + 12 \rightarrow 12$

(Note that the sender uses both parts of the public key, e and n, to compute the ciphertext.) The receiver decodes the ciphertext C by computing C^d using wraparound arithmetic with respect to n. In our example,

6. $12^5 = 248832 = = 11849*21 + 3 \rightarrow 3$

Of course, our example has a major problem in that d is the same as e. Obviously, in a real case, you want e and d to be different. The whole point is that even though n and e are known, the attacker must determine d, which involves

FIGURE 13.12

An SSL Session

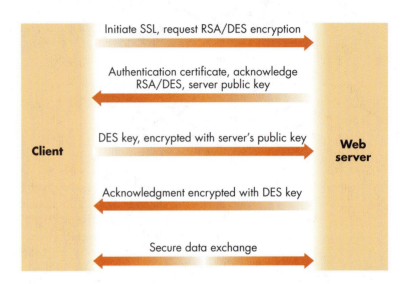

Initiate SSL, request RSA/DES encryption

Authentication certificate, acknowledge
RSA/DES, server public key

Client

DES key, encrypted with server's public key

**Web
server**

Acknowledgment encrypted with DES key

Secure data exchange

finding the prime factors p and q of n. There is no known computationally efficient algorithm for this task.

One of the problems with the RSA algorithm is the computational overload for encryption/decryption. What often happens is that RSA is used in the initial stage of communication between client and server; for example, in response to a client request, the server may send the client its public key along with an authentication certificate. The client, using RSA and the public key of the server, encodes a short message containing the keys for a symmetric encryption algorithm. Because only keys are being encrypted, the message is short and the encryption can be done quickly. The server receives and decodes this message and responds to the client with a message encoded using the symmetric key. The client and server have now established a secure exchange of keys and can complete the transaction using, for example, DES. As we noted earlier, these authentication and key exchange steps are part of the Secure Socket Layer protocols supported by all Web browsers. Figure 13.12 illustrates this process.

13.5 Conclusion

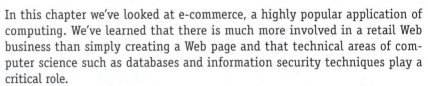

In this chapter we've looked at e-commerce, a highly popular application of computing. We've learned that there is much more involved in a retail Web business than simply creating a Web page and that technical areas of computer science such as databases and information security techniques play a critical role.

In the next chapter we will look at another application of computer science, one that has long captured the public's attention through its association with science fiction literature and movies—artificial intelligence.

1. Find an example of what you consider an excellent retail Web site. Comment on
   a. The use of color and whitespace
   b. The ease of navigation
   c. The taxonomy
   d. Whether the site displays its privacy policy
   e. Whether the site displays a security assurance
   f. Your experience walking through the online purchase process (of course, cancel before you commit to the final purchase!) and whether it seems as if the customer is in control and informed at each step

2. Find an example of what you would consider to be a poor retail Web site. Use the same list as for Exercise 1 and note the differences you find.

3. Depending on your Web browser, you may be able to locate a folder on your machine called "Cookies," or a single file "cookies.txt." Look through the folder or open the cookies.txt file. List references to three Web sites you have visited.

4. Using the *Employees* table of Figure 13.6, what will be the result of the following SQL query?

   ```
   SELECT * FROM Employees
   WHERE HoursWorked < 100;
   ```

5. Write an SQL query that retrieves first and last names and pay rate, ordered by *PayRate,* from the *Employees* table of Figure 13.6.

6. Using the *Employees* table of Figure 13.6 and the *InsurancePolicies* table of Figure 13.7, what will be the result of the following SQL query? (The # marks allow the date to be treated numerically.)

   ```
   SELECT ID, PlanType
   FROM Employees, InsurancePolicies
   WHERE Birthdate > #1/01/1960#
   AND ID = EmployeeID;
   ```

7. Using the *Employees* table of Figure 13.6 and the *InsurancePolicies* table of Figure 13.7, write an SQL query that retrieves first and last names, hours worked, and insurance plan types for all employees who have worked fewer than 100 hours.

8. Figure 13.8 describes the attributes in an *InsurancePlans* table. Write some possible tuples for this table.

9. Assuming the existence of an *InsurancePlans* table as described in Figure 13.8, write an SQL query that retrieves the employee first and last name, insurance plan type, and monthly cost for John Kay's insurance.

10. Using a Caesar cipher with $s = 5$, decode the received message RTAJ TZY FY IFBS.

11. The centurian who was supposed to inform you of s was killed en route, but you have received the message MXX SMGX UE PUHUPQP in a Caesar cipher. Find the value of s and decode the message.

12. You receive a message that was encoded using a block encoding scheme with the encoding matrix $M = \begin{bmatrix} 3 & 2 \\ 7 & 5 \end{bmatrix}$.

    a. Verify by computing $M' \times M$ that $M' = \begin{bmatrix} 5 & 24 \\ 19 & 3 \end{bmatrix}$.
    (Remember to wrap around if a value is greater than 25.)
    b. Decode the ciphertext message MXOSHI.

13. The DES algorithm combines two bit strings by applying the XOR operator on each pair of corresponding bits. Compute the 6-bit string that results from $100111 \oplus 110101$.

14. Using the RSA encryption algorithm, pick $p = 11$ and $q = 7$. Find a set of encryption/decryption keys e and d.

15. Using the RSA encryption algorithm, let $p = 3$ and $q = 5$. Then $n = 15$ and $m = 8$. Let $e = 11$.
    a. Compute d.
    b. Find the code for 3.
    c. Decode your answer to part (b) to retrieve the 3.

CHALLENGE WORK

1. Implement the Caesar cipher algorithm in a high-level programming language such as C++ or Java.
   a. Write a main function (method) that collects a message from the user and writes it out again. Assume for simplicity that the message consists of a single word no more than 10 characters in length and that only the 26 uppercase letters of the alphabet are used. Use an array of 10 elements of type **char** to store the

message. Ask the user to enter no more than 10 characters, one per line, and to terminate the message by entering some special character such as "%." Use a variable to keep track of the number of array elements actually used (which could be fewer than 10 if the message word is short) so that you do not write out meaningless characters stored at the end of the array.

b. Because you will be writing out the contents of the message array several times, write a helper function (method) *WriteMessage* to do this task. Now rewrite your main function so that it uses *WriteMessage* to write out the message array.

c. Write a function (method) to modify the array to represent the encoded form of the message using a Caesar cipher. Have the main function ask for the shift amount. Pass this information, along with the message array and the number of array elements actually used, to the encoding function. To get from one character to the character *s* units along in the alphabet, you can simply add *s* to the original character. This will work for everything except the end of the alphabet; here you will have to be a bit more clever to cycle back to the beginning of the alphabet once the shift is applied. You may have to apply an explicit

typecast to turn the result back into an integer to store in the array. Have the main function invoke the encoding function and then invoke *WriteMessage* to write out the encoded form of the message.

d. Write a function (method) to modify the array containing the encoded message back to its original form. This function will also need the number of array elements used and the value of the shift amount as arguments, as well as the array itself. The body of the function should accomplish the reverse of the encoding function. Have the main function invoke the decoding function and then write out the decoded form of the message, which should agree with the original message.

e. Be sure to test your program with different values for *s* and different word lengths.

2. Make a list of all the databases (county, state, federal, school, credit card, bank, and so forth) that you think currently contain information about you. Investigate what laws or restrictions, if any, exist to protect your privacy. Then write a short paper on what additional legislation at the county, state, or federal level you believe is needed to protect consumer privacy, or write a newspaper editorial explaining why no further laws need to be passed.

FOR FURTHER READING

The following books address various aspects of e-commerce:

Carter, J. A. *Developing E-Commerce Systems*. Englewood Cliffs, NJ: Prentice-Hall, 2002.

Laudon, K. C., and Traver, C. G. *E-Commerce: Business, Technology, Society*, 2nd ed. Reading, MA: Addison-Wesley, 2004.

Urban, G., *Digital Marketing Strategy: Text and Cases*. Englewood Cliffs, NJ: Prentice-Hall, 2004.

Web development for a business environment is addressed in

Frost, R., and Strauss, J. *Building Effective Web Sites*. Englewood Cliffs, NJ: Prentice-Hall, 2002.

The following reference gives a complete grounding in the theory of databases:

Date, C. J. *An Introduction to Database Systems*, 8th ed. Reading, MA: Addison-Wesley, 2004.

For a look at the use of databases with Internet applications:

Riccardi, G. *Database Management: With Website Development Applications*. Reading, MA: Addison-Wesley, 2003.

Much of the field of cryptography is based on highly technical mathematics, but the following book gives a managerial-level view of cryptography intended for e-commerce transactions:

Graff, J. *Cryptography and E-Commerce: A Wiley Tech Brief*. Hoboken, NJ: Wiley, 2000.

Finally, a really remarkable website, http://digitalenterprise.org, presents an entire online course called "Managing the Digital Enterprise," maintained by Professor Michael Rappa of North Carolina State University.

CHAPTER 14

Artificial Intelligence

14.1   Introduction

Artificial intelligence (AI) is the part of computer science that explores techniques for incorporating aspects of intelligence into computer systems. This definition, however, raises more questions than it answers. What really is "intelligence"? And whatever it is, is it a uniquely human attribute? If a computer system appears to exhibit behavior that we might characterize as demonstrating intelligence, does that make it truly intelligent? And what sorts of behaviors do demonstrate intelligence?

Alan Turing, whose investigations into the fundamental nature of computation led to the Turing machine (Chapter 11), was also interested in artificial intelligence. In 1950, before the term *artificial intelligence* was coined, he proposed a test for intelligent behavior of machines. The **Turing test** allows a human to interrogate two entities, both hidden from the interrogator (Figure 14.1). One entity is a human and the other a machine (a computer). The interrogator can ask the entities questions and can receive their responses. The

FIGURE 14.1

The Turing Test

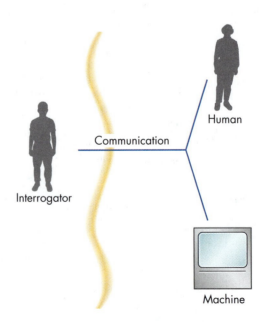

Human

Communication

Interrogator

Machine

The Loebner Prize Competition has been held annually since 1991. This competition is essentially a Turing test. Dr. Hugh Loebner, a sociologist and inventor, has posted a $100,000 grand prize and a gold medal for the first computer program whose responses are indistinguishable from a human's. While the grand prize remains unclaimed, a prize of $2,000 and a bronze medal is awarded each year to the computer program judged to be "most human" in that year's competition. For details, see www.loebner.net/Prizef/loebner-prize.html.

One of the most famous early AI experiments occurred in the laboratory of Professor Joseph Weizenbaum at MIT in 1966. A program named ELIZA conversed with people in the fashion of a psychotherapist, picking up on key words and echoing them back in a sentence. This was quite mechanical and there was no understanding involved. For example, an ELIZA conversation might go something like this:

Human: I am not feeling well today.
Computer: I AM SORRY TO HEAR THAT YOU ARE NOT FEELING WELL.
Human: I had a fight with my wife.
Computer: TELL ME ABOUT YOUR WIFE.
Human: My house ate my zebra.
Computer: TELL ME ABOUT YOUR ZEBRA.

Weizenbaum was horrified at the ease with which people who interacted with ELIZA became convinced that they were talking with a real person. Today, there are many "chatterbot" programs available on the Web; for a list go to http://directory.google.com/Top/Computers/Artificial_Intelligence/Natural_Language/Chatterbots

communication is carried on in some form that does not by itself give away which entity is the computer; for example, the interrogator's questions could be typed on a keyboard and the responses printed out. If, as a result of this questioning, the interrogator is unable to determine which entity is the human and which the computer, then the computer has exhibited sufficiently human intelligence to pass the Turing test. This test does not explore the nature of human intelligence in some deep philosophical way; it merely says that if a machine exhibits behavior indistinguishable from that of a human, then what's the difference? Carrying this to extremes, one is led to science fiction scenarios in which aliens cannot be distinguished from human beings. Do we really know *for sure* that the other people we interact with daily are human beings, or do they only act like humans?

In Chapter 12 we discussed models of physical phenomena (objects falling under the force of gravity, customers in a store). We can think of artificial intelligence as constructing computer models of human intelligence. Just as we learned in Chapter 12 that a model cannot capture all aspects of the system it represents, so artificial intelligence cannot capture all aspects of "intelligence." Contrary to the science fiction visions of thinking computers controlling the world, the advances in artificial intelligence have been more modest. Nonetheless, artificial intelligence has produced practical results in natural language understanding, robotics, game playing, problem-solving, machine learning, expert systems, pattern recognition, and other areas. And conversely, attempts to model intelligence within a computer have in turn made contributions to **cognitive science,** the study of how we as humans think and learn.

In order to understand better what artificial intelligence is all about, let's consider a division of task types. Humans can perform a great variety of tasks, but we'll divide them into three categories, representative but by no means exhaustive:

- *Computational tasks*
  - Adding columns of numbers
  - Sorting a list of numbers into numerical order
  - Searching for a given name in a list of names
  - Managing a payroll
  - Calculating trajectory adjustments for the Space Shuttle

- *Recognition tasks*
  - Recognizing your best friend
  - Understanding the spoken word
  - Finding the tennis ball in the grass in your backyard

- *Reasoning tasks*
  - Planning what to wear today
  - Deciding on the strategic direction a company should follow for the next 5 years
  - Running the triage center in a hospital emergency room after an earthquake

Humans can perform computational tasks. These are tasks for which algorithmic solutions exist (we devised algorithms for sorting and searching in the early chapters of this book). As humans, we can, in principle at least, follow the step by step instructions. Computational tasks are also tasks for which accurate answers must be found—sometimes very quickly—and that's where we as humans fall down. We make mistakes, we get bored, and we aren't very speedy. Computers are better (faster and more accurate) at performing computational tasks, provided they are given programs that correctly embody the algorithms. Throughout most of this book, with its emphasis on algorithms, we've been talking about procedures to solve computational tasks, how to write those procedures, how to get the computer to execute them, and so on.

Humans are better at recognition tasks. We should perhaps expand the name of this task type to sensory/recognition/motor-skills tasks, because we receive information through our senses (primarily seeing and hearing), we recognize or "make sense of" the information we receive, and we often respond to the information with some sort of physical response that involves controlled movement. Although we wait until the second grade to learn how to add, an infant a few weeks old, on seeing its mother's face, recognizes that face and smiles; soon that infant will understand the spoken word. You spot the tennis ball in the yard even though it is green and nestled in among other green things (grass, dandelions). You register whether the tennis ball is close or farther away, and you manipulate your legs and feet to propel you in the right direction.

How do we as humans do these things? Traditional step by step procedural algorithms don't seem to apply, or if they do, we don't know what those algorithms are. Rather, it seems that we as humans succeed at these tasks by processing a huge amount of data and then matching the results against an even larger storehouse of data based on our past experiences. Consider the task of recognizing your best friend. You have, in effect, been shown a number of "pictures" of your friend's face that seem to be "burned into" your memory, along with pictures of the faces of everyone else you know well. When you see your friend, you sort through your mental picture file until you come to a match. It is a bit more complicated than that, however, because if you encounter your friend's sister, you may know who it is even though you have never met her before. You find, not an exact match to one of the images in your mental picture file, but a close approximation. Approximation, unlike the exactness required in computational tasks, is good enough. These complex recognition tasks that we as humans find so easy are difficult for computers to perform.

When humans perform reasoning tasks, they are also using a large storehouse of experience. This experience involves not just images but also cause and effect situations. You know that you should wear a coat when it's going to be cold because you've experienced being uncomfortable when the weather is cold and you haven't worn a coat. You may reason as follows:

1. I don't want to be uncomfortable.
2. If the weather is cold and I don't wear a coat, then I will be uncomfortable.
3. The weather will be cold.

Conclusion: I will wear a coat.

This could be considered "mere" commonsense reasoning, but getting a computer to mimic "mere" common sense, to say nothing of higher-order conceptual, planning, or reasoning tasks, is extremely challenging. There may be no "right" answer to such tasks, and the way humans arrive at their respective answers sometimes seems ambiguous or based at least in part on "intuition," which may be just another name for knowledge or reasoning that we don't yet understand.

Figure 14.2 summarizes what we've outlined as the relative capabilities of humans and computers in these three types of tasks. Again, where computers fall below humans is where procedural algorithms either don't work or aren't known, and there seems to be a high level of complexity and perhaps approximation or ambiguity. Artificial intelligence seeks ways to improve the computer's capabilities in recognition and reasoning tasks, and we'll look at artificial intelligence approaches in these two areas in the rest of this chapter. As mentioned earlier, however, both types of tasks seem to require a storehouse of information—images, past experiences, and the like—for which we'll use the general term *knowledge*. Therefore, we'll first look at various approaches to representing knowledge.

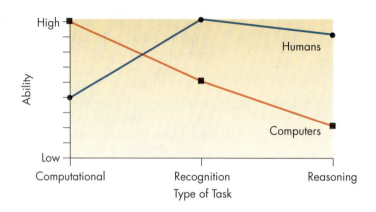

FIGURE 14.2

Human and Computer Capabilities

14.3 Knowledge Representation

We can consider **knowledge** about some topic as a body of facts or truths. In order for the computer to make use of that knowledge, there must be some representational form in which the knowledge is stored within the computer. (At the lowest level, of course, only 0s and 1s are stored within the computer, but strings of 0s and 1s are organized and interpreted at a higher level of abstraction—as integers or characters, for example.) For computational tasks, the relevant knowledge is often isolated numeric or textual items. This is the usual data that we've manipulated with procedural programs. What about more complex knowledge?

There are many workable representation schemes; let's consider four possibilities.

1. *Natural language.* A paragraph or a page of text that contains all the knowledge we are trying to capture is written in English, French, Spanish, or some other natural language. Here is an example:

   > *Spot is a brown dog and, like any dog, has four legs and a tail. Also like any dog, Spot is a mammal, which means Spot is warm-blooded.*

   Note that although this representational form is text, it is text in a different sense from the character strings that are used in computational tasks. Here it is not simply the strings of characters that are important but also the meaning that those strings of characters convey. When reading a natural language paragraph, we use our understanding of the richness of the language's vocabulary to extract the meaning. Some researchers believe that the words we read or hear do not actually communicate meaning, but merely act as "triggers" to meanings stored in our brains.

2. *Formal language.* A formal language sacrifices richness of expression for precision of expression. Attributes and cause and effect relationships are more explicitly stated. A formal language version of the foregoing natural language paragraph might look like this:

Spot is a dog.

Spot is brown.

Every dog has four legs.

Every dog has a tail.

Every dog is a mammal.

Every mammal is warm-blooded.

The term *language* was used in Chapter 10 to mean the set of statements derivable by using the rules of a grammar. But here the term **formal language** means the language of formal logic, usually expressed more symbolically than we have done in our example. In the usual notation of formal logic, we might use *dog(x)* to symbolize that the symbolic entity *x* has the attribute of being a dog and *brown(x)* to mean that *x* has the attribute of being brown. Similarly *four-legged(x)*, *tail(x)*, *mammal(x)*, and *warm-blooded(x)* could symbolize that *x* has these various attributes. The specific entity Spot could be represented by *S*. Then *dog(S)* would mean that Spot has the attribute of being a dog. Cause and effect relationships are translated into "if-then" statements. Thus, "Every dog has four legs" is equivalent to "For every *x*, if *x* is a dog, then *x* has four legs." An arrow symbolizes cause and effect (if-then); "If *x* is a dog, then *x* has four legs" would be written symbolically as

$$dog(x) \rightarrow four\text{-}legged(x)$$

To show that every *x* that has the dog property also has the four-legged property, we would use a *universal quantifier*, $(\forall x)$, which means "for every *x*." Therefore,

$$(\forall x)(dog(x) \rightarrow four\text{-}legged(x))$$

means "For every *x*, if *x* is a dog, then *x* has four legs" or "Every dog has four legs." Symbolically, the preceding six formal language statements become

Natural Language Statement	Symbolic Representation
Spot is a dog.	$dog(S)$
Spot is brown.	$brown(S)$
Every dog has four legs.	$(\forall x)(dog(x) \rightarrow four\text{-}legged(x))$
Every dog has a tail.	$(\forall x)(dog(x) \rightarrow tail(x))$
Every dog is a mammal.	$(\forall x)(dog(x) \rightarrow mammal(x))$
Every mammal is warm-blooded.	$(\forall x)(mammal(x) \rightarrow warm\text{-}blooded(x))$

The use of formal languages represents one of the major approaches to building artificial intelligence systems. Intelligent behavior is achieved by using symbols to represent knowledge and by manipulating these symbols according to well-defined rules. We'll see an example of this when we discuss expert systems later in this chapter.

3. *Pictorial.* Information can be stored in pictorial form as an image—a grid of pixels that have attributes of shading and color. Using this

representation we might have a picture of Spot, showing that he is brown and has four legs and a tail. We might have some additional labeling that says something like, This is Spot, the dog. This visual representation might contain additional knowledge about Spot's appearance that is not embodied in the natural language paragraph or the formal language statements, but it would also fail to capture the knowledge that Spot is a mammal and that mammals are warm-blooded. It also wouldn't tell us that all dogs have four legs and a tail. (After all, a photo of a three-legged dog does not tell us that all dogs have three legs.)

4. *Graphical.* Here we are using the term *graphical* not in the sense of "visual" (we have already talked about pictorial representation) but in the mathematical sense of a graph with nodes and connecting arcs. Figure 14.3 is such a graph, also called a **semantic net,** for our dog example. In the terminology of object orientation that we used in Chapter 8, the rectangular nodes represent classes or objects, the oval nodes represent properties, and the arcs represent relationships. The "is a" relationship represents a subclass of a class that will inherit properties from the parent class; "dog" is a subclass of "mammal," and any dog object inherits all the properties of mammals in general, such as being warm-blooded. Objects from the dog class may also have properties of their own. The "instance" relationship shows that something is an object of a class; Spot is a particular object from the dog class and may have a unique property not necessarily shared by all dogs.

Any knowledge representation scheme that we select must have the following four characteristics:

1. *Adequacy.* The representation method must be adequate to capture all of the relevant knowledge. Because of its rich expressive powers, a natural language representation will surely capture a lot of knowledge. However, it may be difficult to extract exactly what that knowledge is. One may have to wade through a lot of unnecessary verbiage, and one must also understand the nuances of meaning within the natural language. A formal language representation has the advantage of extracting the essentials.

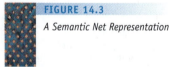

FIGURE 14.3

A Semantic Net Representation

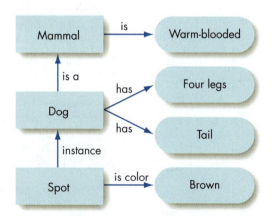

2. *Efficiency*. We want the representational form to be minimalist. This means avoiding redundant information wherever possible. It also means allowing some knowledge that is not explicitly represented to be inferred from the knowledge that is explicitly represented. In the preceding example, it is easy to infer from the natural language, the formal language, or the semantic net that because Spot is a dog, he has four legs and a tail and also is a mammal and therefore warm-blooded. This knowledge, as we have said, is not captured in the pictorial format. On the other hand, it would take a much longer natural language paragraph to describe all the additional knowledge about Spot that is captured in the picture.

3. *Extendability*. It should be relatively easy to extend the representation to include new knowledge. For example, the semantic net can easily be extended to tack on another "dog" instance. It would also be easy to capture the fact that dogs have two eyes or that mammals do not lay eggs; these properties can simply be plugged in as new ovals connected into the network.

4. *Appropriateness*. The representation scheme used should be appropriate for the knowledge domain being represented. For example, a pictorial representation scheme would appear to be the most appropriate way to represent the knowledge base for a problem dealing with recognition of visual images. We saw before that a pictorial representation is probably not appropriate for the kind of knowledge about Spot that is difficult to display visually. The level of granularity needed for the intended application might also influence the appropriateness of a particular scheme. Is a given pictorial representation sufficient, or do we need the knowledge behind the image that would allow us to "zoom in" and expose more detail in a particular section? The choice of representational form for knowledge therefore depends on the knowledge to be captured and on the type of task for which the knowledge is to be used.

PRACTICE PROBLEM

Write a natural language paragraph that describes the concept of a hamburger. Now draw a semantic net that incorporates the same knowledge as your natural language description. Which one was easier for you to produce?

14.4 Recognition Tasks

If artificial intelligence aims to make computers "think" like humans, then it is natural to investigate and perhaps attempt to mimic the way the human brain functions. It is estimated that the human brain contains about 10^{12} neurons (that's 1 trillion, or 1,000,000,000,000). Each **neuron** is a cell capable of receiving stimuli, in the form of electrochemical signals, from other neurons through its many **dendrites** (Figure 14.4). In turn, it can send stimuli to other neurons through its single **axon.** The axon of a neuron does not directly connect with the dendrites of other neurons; rather, it sends signals over small gaps called **synapses.** Some of the synapses appear to send the neuron activating stimuli, whereas others seem to send inhibiting stimuli. A single neuron collects all the stimuli passing through all the synapses around its dendrites. The neuron sums the activating (positive) and inhibiting (negative) stimuli it receives and compares the result with an internal "threshold" value. If the sum equals or exceeds the threshold value, then the neuron "fires," sending its own signal down its axon to affect other neurons.

Each neuron can be thought of as an extremely simple computational device with a single on/off output. The power of the human brain lies in the vast number of neurons, the many interconnections between them, and the activating/inhibiting nature of those connections. To borrow a term from computer science, the human brain uses a **connectionist architecture,** characterized by a large number of simple "processors" with multiple interconnections. This contrasts quite noticeably with the Von Neumann architecture discussed in Chapter 5 and used by virtually all computers today. In that model there are a small number (maybe only one) of very powerful processors with a limited number of interconnections between them.

In some areas of the brain, an individual neuron may collect signals from as many as 100,000 other neurons and send signals to an equally large number of other neurons. This extensive parallelism is evidently required because of the relatively slow time frame within which a neuron fires. In the human brain, neurons operate on a time scale of milliseconds (thousandths of a second), as opposed to the nanoseconds (billionths of a second) in which computer operations are measured, a difference of 6 orders of magnitude. In a human processing task that takes about 1/10 second (recognition of your friend's face), the number of steps that could be executed by a single neuron would be on the order of 100. To carry out the complexity of a recognition

FIGURE 14.4

A Neuron

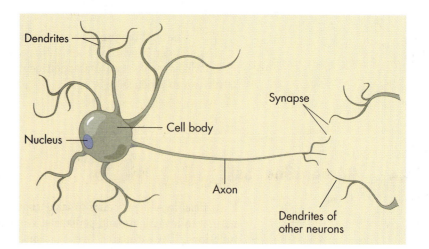

task, then, requires the parallel activities of a large number of neurons executing cooperatively within this short time frame. In addition, massive parallelism supplies redundancy so that information is not stored only in one place but is shared within the network of neurons. Thus, the deterioration of a limited number of single neurons (a process that happens constantly as biological cells wear out) does not cause a failure of the information processing capabilities of the network.

Artificial intelligence systems for recognition tasks have used this connectionist approach. **Artificial neural networks,** usually just called **neural networks,** can be created by simulating individual neurons in hardware and connecting them in a massively parallel network of simple devices that act somewhat like biological neurons. (Recall our discussion in Chapter 5 of parallel processing and non–Von Neumann architectures.) Alternatively, the effect of a neural network may be simulated in software on an ordinary sequential-processing computer. In either case, each neuron has a threshold value, and its incoming lines carry weights that represent stimuli. The neuron fires when the sum of the incoming weights equals or exceeds its threshold value. The input lines are activated as a result of the firing of other neurons. A single neuron could be represented as shown in Figure 14.5.

The neuron in Figure 14.5 has a threshold value of 3, and it has three input lines with weights of 2, −1, and 2, respectively. If all three input lines are activated, the sum of the incoming signals is 2 + (−1) + 2 = 3 and the neuron will fire. It will also fire if only lines 1 and 3 are activated, because the sum of the incoming signals is then 2 + 2 = 4 > 3. Any other combination of activated input lines will not carry sufficient stimulation to fire the neuron. (Real, biological neurons fire with intensities that vary through a continuous range but, as usual, our simplified computer representation of such analog values uses a set of discrete values.)

Figure 14.6 presents a general picture of a neural net with an input layer and an output layer of neurons. An input value x_i is presented to neuron N_j in the input layer via a line with signal strength $x_i * w_{ij}$. The values of x_i are usually binary (0 or 1), so that this line carries a signal of either 0 when x_i is 0, or the weight w_{ij} when x_i is 1. The weights to the input neurons, as well as the weights from the input layer to the output layer, could be positive, negative, or zero.

Figure 14.7 shows a simple example of a neural network, where we have eliminated connections of weight 0. Here x_1 and x_2 have binary values of 0 or 1. If x_1 or x_2 or both have the value 1, then a signal of 1 is passed to one or both of the neurons in the input layer, causing one or both of them to fire, which causes the single neuron in the output layer to fire and produce an output of 1. If both x_1 and x_2 have the value 0, then neither neuron in the

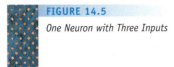

FIGURE 14.5

One Neuron with Three Inputs

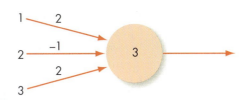

FIGURE 14.6

Neural Network Model

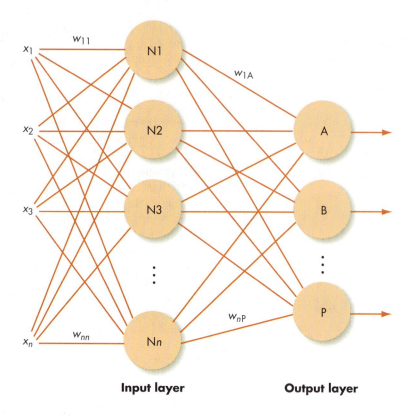

Input layer   Output layer

FIGURE 14.7

A Simple Neural Network—
OR Gate

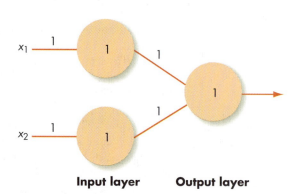

Input layer   Output layer

input layer fires, the single neuron in the output layer does not fire, and the network output is 0. From this behavior of this neural network, we see that the network is acting like an OR gate.

It turns out to be impossible to build such a network to represent the Boolean operation called exclusive OR, or XOR, whose truth table is shown in Figure 14.8. Here the output is true (1) when one or the other input is true, but not when both are true. In Figure 14.9, no matter what values we give for the weights and thresholds, it is not possible to generate this behavior. If exactly one input signal of 1 is enough to fire the output neuron, which is the desired behavior, then two input signals of 1 can only increase the tendency for the output neuron to fire. To represent the XOR operation requires a "hidden layer" of neurons between the input and output layers. Neural networks with a hidden layer of neurons are useful for recognition tasks, where we desire a certain pattern of output signals for a certain pattern of input signals. The XOR network, for example, would recognize when its two binary inputs do not agree.

Conventional computer processing can be said to work on a knowledge base where the information is stored as data in specific memory cells that can be accessed by the program as needed. In a neural network, both the knowledge representation and also the "programming" are stored in the network itself as the weights of the connections and the thresholds of the neurons. If you want to build a neural network to perform in a certain way, how do you determine these values? In a simple network, trial and error could produce a solution, but such is not the case for a network with thousands of neurons. Fortunately, the right answer doesn't have to be found the first time. Remember that neural networks are modeled on the human brain; you learned to recognize your best friend through repeated "learning experiences" that modified your knowledge base until you came to associate certain features or characteristics with that individual.

Similarly, a neural network can learn from experience by modifying the weights on its connections (even making some connections "disappear" by assigning them 0 weights). A network can be given an initial set of weights and thresholds that is simply a first guess. The network is then presented with **training data,** for which the correct outputs are known. The actual output from the network is compared to the correct output for one set of input

FIGURE 14.8

The Truth Table for XOR

INPUTS		OUTPUT
x_1	x_2	
0	0	0
1	0	1
0	1	1
1	1	0

FIGURE 14.9

An Attempt at an XOR Network

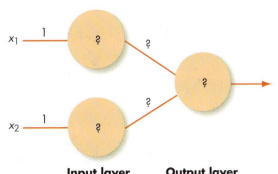

Input layer   Output layer

values from the training data. For those output neurons that produce correct values, their threshold values and the weights on their inputs will not be changed. Output neurons that produce erroneous values can err in one of two ways. If an output neuron fires when it is not supposed to, then the positive (excitatory) input values coming into it are adjusted downward, and the negative (inhibitory) weights coming into it are adjusted upward. If it fails to fire when it is supposed to, the opposite adjustment is made. But before these adjustments take place, information on the errors is passed back from each erroneous output neuron to the neurons in the hidden layer that are connected to it. Each hidden-layer neuron adds these error counts to derive an estimate of its own error. This estimate is used to calculate the adjustments to be made on the weights of the connections coming to it from the input-layer neurons. Finally, the weights are all adjusted, and then the process is repeated for the next set of input values from the training data.

This **back propagation algorithm,** so named for the error estimates that are passed back from the output layer, eventually causes the network to settle into a stable state where it can correctly respond, to any desired degree of accuracy, to all inputs in the training set. In effect, the successive changes in weights have reinforced good behavior and discouraged bad behavior (much as we train our pets) until the paths for good behavior are imprinted on the connections (as in Fido's brain). The network has "learned" what its connection weights should be, and its ability to recognize the training data is embedded somehow in the collective values of these weights. At the end of its training, the neural network is ready to go to work on new recognition problems that are similar to, but not the same as, the training data and for which the answers are unknown.

Neural networks have found their way into dozens of real-world applications. A few of these are handwriting recognition, speech recognition, recognizing patterns indicative of credit card fraud, recognizing bad credit risks for

Read Me a Story

NETtalk, developed in 1986, was a neural network designed to produce synthesized speech from written English text. The input layer consisted of 7 groups of 29 neurons each. The 7 groups represented a "sliding window" of 7 characters from the text because pronunciation of a single letter depends on the context of the letters surrounding it; the 29 neurons per character represented the 26 letters of the alphabet plus 3 for blanks and punctuation. The output layer neurons represented the 21 basic units of human sound plus 5 levels of stress (volume). Altogether there were 309 neurons and 18,629 connections in the NETtalk neural network. The system was trained to 98% accuracy on 1,000 English words. When further tested on 80,000 words, it was 80% accurate with no further training.

Like humans, NETtalk seemed able to correctly pronounce new words better the more words it already knew. And a damaged network (a trained network which then had some of its weights altered) was able to relearn quickly. Systems such as NETtalk are useful, not only for their basic functionality, but for what they may reveal about how humans store information and perform recognition tasks This may lead to medical advances in the treatment of brain injury, Alzheimer's disease, and other illnesses that rob humans of memory and recognition capability.

Modern TTS (Text To Speech) technology is incorporated in applications for email and fax reading over phone lines, on-board navigation aids, online spoken help systems, and in tools for learning language and for the visually impaired.

loans, predicting the odds of susceptibility to cancer, limited visual recognition systems, segmenting magnetic resonance images in medicine, adapting mirror shapes for astronomical observations, and discovering the best routing algorithm in a large communications network (a problem we mentioned in Chapter 7). With the ever-lower cost of massively parallel networks, it appears that neural networks will continue to find new applications.

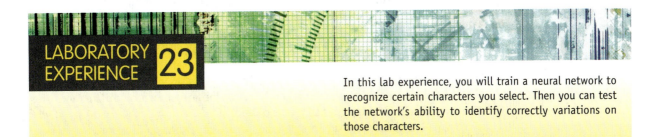

LABORATORY EXPERIENCE 23

In this lab experience, you will train a neural network to recognize certain characters you select. Then you can test the network's ability to identify correctly variations on those characters.

PRACTICE PROBLEM

If input line 1 is stimulated in the following neural network (and line 2 is not stimulated), will the output line fire? Explain.

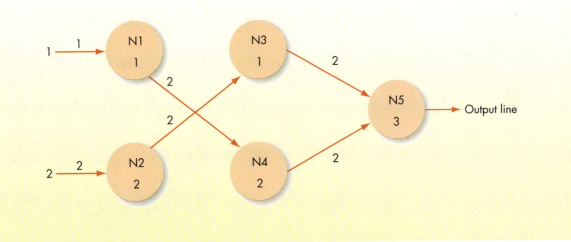

14.5 Reasoning Tasks

We noted that one of the characteristics of human reasoning seems to be the ability to draw on a large body of facts and past experience to come to a conclusion. In this section we look at several ways in which artificial intelligence specialists try to get computers to emulate this characteristic.

14.5.1 Intelligent Searching

Earlier in this book, we investigated two algorithms for searching—sequential search and binary search. These search algorithms look for a perfect match between a specific target value and an item in a list. The amount of work involved is $\Theta(n)$ for sequential search and $\Theta(\lg n)$ for binary search.

A **decision tree** for a search algorithm illustrates the possible next choices of items to search if the current item is not the target. In a sequential search, there is only one item to try next: the next item in the list. The decision tree for sequential search is linear, as shown in Figure 14.10. A decision tree for a binary search, such as the one shown in Figure 14.11, reflects the fact that if the current item is not the target, there are only two next choices: the midpoint of the sublist before this node or the midpoint of the sublist after this node. Furthermore, the binary search algorithm specifies which of the two nodes to try next.

The classical search problem benefits from two simplifications:

1. The search domain (the set of items being searched) is a linear list. At each point in the search, if the target is not found, the choice of where to look next is highly constrained.

FIGURE 14.10

Decision Tree for Sequential Search

FIGURE 14.11

Decision Tree for Binary Search

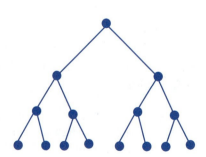

2. We seek a perfect match, so the comparison of the target against the list item results in a binary decision—either they match or they do not.

Suppose, however, that condition 1 does not hold; the search domain is such that after any one node has been searched, there are a huge number of next choices to try, and there is no algorithm to dictate the next choice. Figure 14.12 attempts to convey this idea. In the terminology of artificial intelligence, such a figure is called a **state-space graph,** and we seek to perform a **state-space search** to find a **solution path** through the graph. The idea is that each node of the graph represents a "state" of our problem, and we have some "goal state" or states in mind. For example, in a game of tic-tac-toe, our initial state is the empty game grid, and our goal state is a winning configuration. A solution path takes us from the initial state to a winning configuration, and the graph nodes along the way represent the intermediate configurations. In addition to finding a winning sequence of moves for a board game (tic-tac-toe, checkers, chess, and so forth), many other types of problems, such as finding the shortest path through a network or finding the most successful investment strategy in the stock market, fall into the state-space search category. In some of these problems, condition 2 of the classical search problem—that of seeking an exact match with a specified target value—is not present either. We simply want to acquire as many characteristics of the desired goal as possible, and we need some measure of when we are "close enough."

A brute force approach for a solution path traces all branches of the state-space graph so that all possible choices are tested and no test cases are repeated. This becomes a massive bookkeeping task because the number of branches grows exponentially. Given that time and computing resources are limited, an intelligent search needs to be employed. An intelligent search narrows the number of branches that must be tried and thereby puts a cap on the otherwise exponential growth of the problem. Intelligent searching involves applying some **heuristic** (which means, roughly, an "educated guess") to evaluate the differences between the present state and the goal state and to move us to a new state that minimizes those differences—namely, the state that maximizes our progress toward the goal state.

An intelligent chess-playing strategy, for example, is one that makes an appropriate first move and that, at each step, makes a move more likely than others to lead to a winning board configuration. Even a grand master of chess cannot pursue the brute force approach of mentally trying out all the possible next moves, all the possible moves following from each of those moves, and so on, for very many steps. (In Section 1.2 we showed that using a brute force approach, a computer would require a billion billion billion years to

FIGURE 14.12

A State-Space Graph with Exponential Growth

In May 1997, international attention was focused on a historic chess match between world champion Garry Kasparov and the IBM chess-playing computer known as Deep Blue. Kasparov and Deep Blue played neck and neck, but in the final game Kasparov lost the match by falling for a well-known trap. Kasparov's error, which was considered a major blunder for a player of his ability, probably reflected his weariness and the emotional strain of competing against an unexpectedly strong, utterly impassive foe. These human frailties, of course, were not shared by Deep Blue.

Although some hailed the victory of Deep Blue as a triumph of machine over human being, it is worthwhile to look at the differences between how the human (Kasparov, of Russian birth, was 34 years old at the time) and the machine (Deep Blue was based on the IBM RS/6000 massively parallel computer system) played chess.

Both Kasparov and Deep Blue relied on the respective strengths of their "species," Kasparov utilizing recognition and reasoning, and Deep Blue churning out its high-speed

Kasparov	Deep Blue
Could evaluate up to 3 chess positions per second, or 540 in the 3 minutes allowed between moves	Could evaluate up to 200,000,000 chess positions per second, or 50 billion in 3 minutes
Selected which few positions to evaluate on the basis of recognition of successful strategies or tactical approaches	Evaluated a large number of random positions to determine the optimal move
Used his brain, including experience and intuition	Used its 512 communicating processors, which act algorithmically following their C programming
Could assess his opponent's weaknesses and dynamically adjust his playing strategy	Could be modified by its development team between games to change its approach
Was subject to human emotions and weaknesses	Did not tire or have emotional responses to alter its play
Was cognizant of being Garry Kasparov playing a world-class chess tournament against a machine	Was unaware of its own existence, the identity of its competitor, or the relative importance of the game

Gary Kasparov vs Big Blue © Laurence Kesterson/CORBIS Sygma

computations (see Figure 14.2). But the biggest difference is the last one shown in the accompanying table; Deep Blue had no idea what it accomplished by winning this chess match, whereas Kasparov immediately issued a challenge for a rematch.

The "Man vs. Machine" rematch that Kasparov sought was held in New York early in 2003, but not with Deep Blue, which IBM had retired. Instead, Kasparov played the 2001 and 2002 Computer Chess World Champion program Deep Junior. Deep Junior is a commercial chess program developed by two Israelis, Amir Ban and Shay Bushinsky. For this tournament, Deep Junior ran on a multiprocessor PC. On such a machine, Deep Junior can evaluate up to 3 million moves a second, far fewer than Deep Blue. The details of Deep Junior's algorithms are not known, but it is known to engage in riskier, more human-like play than previous computer programs, including Deep Blue. The final game ended in a draw, resulting in a 3-3 tie for the match. Kasparov later said that his top priority in Game 6 had been "not to lose."

The lesson to be learned from the human-computer chess competition that has been going on for 45 years is that chess playing—originally thought to be the epitome of "machine intelligence"—is actually easier to program into a machine than the many things that every human can easily accomplish (e.g., pattern recognition, intelligent search, higher-order reasoning). In fact, some artificial intelligence researchers feel that it is the last of the "easy" hard problems.

make its first move!) Intelligent searching is required. There must be a deep storehouse of experience that can be "consulted" on the basis of the overall present configuration of the board—experience that suggests the best course of action for this configuration. A grandmaster-level player may need a mental database of around 50,000 of these board configurations, each with its associated information about the best next move.

Building a machine that could beat a human at chess was long thought to be a supreme test to demonstrate artificial intelligence—machines that "think." Successfully playing chess, it was believed, would surely epitomize logical reasoning, true "intelligence." Chess is difficult for humans. Yet, the rules for chess are straightforward; it is simply the size of the state-space that is overwhelming. As artificial intelligence researchers delved deeper into supposedly "simpler" problems such as visual recognition—things we humans do easily—it became clear that these were the harder challenges for machines. Nonetheless, the contest of human being versus machine at the chessboard is irresistibly fascinating.

 ### 14.5.2 *Swarm Intelligence*

Recall that the connectionist architecture—neural networks—draws its inspiration from nature, namely, the human brain. Another approach to achieving a desired end also draws its inspiration from nature. Swarm intelligence models the behavior of, say, a colony of ants. Each ant is an unsophisticated creature with limited capabilities, yet acting as a collective, a colony of ants can accomplish remarkable tasks. They can find the shortest route from a nest to a food source, carry large items, emigrate as a colony from one location to another, and form bridges. An ant "communicates" with other ants by laying down a scent trail, called a pheromone trail; other ants follow this scent trail and reinforce its strength by laying down their own pheromones. Given a choice, ants have a higher probability of following the strongest pheromone trail. Hence, the ant that took the shortest path to food and returned to tell about it lays down a trail that other ants will follow and reinforce faster than the trail laid down by an ant that took a longer path. Because pheromone trails evaporate quickly, the collective intelligence of the colony is constantly updated to respond to current conditions of its environment.

The **swarm intelligence model** captures this behavior by using simple agents (analogous to the ants in our example) that operate independently, can sense certain aspects of their environment, and can change their environment. Research is underway to use such simple agents in telecommunications networks to avoid the complexity of a centralized control system to compute and distribute routing tables within a network. Vehicle routing, job scheduling, and sensing of biological or chemical contaminants are other applications in which researchers are applying swarm intelligence. The "ants," if you will, may even "genetically evolve" and acquire additional capabilities over time.

 ### 14.5.3 *Intelligent Agents*

The intelligence in swarm intelligence rests in the colony as a whole, which seems to acquire "knowledge" that is greater than the sum of its parts. At the opposite end of the spectrum are **intelligent agents.** An intelligent agent is a form of software technology that is designed to interact collaboratively with a user somewhat in the mode of a personal assistant. Imagine that you have hired your own (human) personal assistant. In the beginning, you will have to tell your assistant what to do and how you would like it done. Over time, however, your assistant comes to know more about you and soon can anticipate what tasks need to be done and how to perform them, what items to bring to your attention, and so forth. Your assistant becomes more valuable as he or she becomes more self-directed, always acting with your best interests in mind. You, in turn, put more and more trust in your assistant.

Like the human personal assistant, an intelligent agent will soon not merely wait for user commands but will initiate communication, take action, and perform tasks on its own on the basis of its increasing knowledge of your needs and preferences. Here are some examples that exist today:

- Desktop office software may come with the services of an assistant that is sometimes called a **wizard.** This little animated object attempts to display appropriate help messages as you work by assessing the context of the task you are trying to perform. Suppose you are using a word processor to create a document, and you decide to insert a table. If your assistant is active as you begin to insert a table, it may automatically provide you with a "tip" on how to use some feature of the software to make this task easier. Or, again while creating a table, you can click on the assistant image, and it will provide you with a choice of help topics related to working with tables. Finally, you can ask the assistant a specific query, and it will search its database and display a choice of relevant help topics. Here the assistant doesn't learn more about you as you work, but it is aware of the task you are trying to perform.

- A personalized Web search engine allows you to profile items of interest to you and then automatically delivers appropriate information from the Web. For example, you may request updated weather conditions for your geographic area, along with news items related to sports and European trade. At periodic time intervals, this **push technology** downloads your updated, personalized information to your screen to be displayed whenever no other task is active.

- A more intelligent version of this personalized Web searcher enables you to "vote" on each article it sends you and then dynamically adjusts what it sends in the future as it learns about your preferences.

- An even more intelligent search agent not only narrows down choices from topics you have chosen but can suggest new, related topics for you to explore. This is accomplished by having your agent run around the Web and communicate with similar agents, even when you are not online. If your agent knows of your interest in French cuisine, for example, it will communicate with other agents to find those that represent users with the same interest. It may learn from these agents that many of their users are also interested in Cajun cooking. Your agent will then judge whether these suggestions are coming from agents whose recommendations on the whole have been well received by you in the past. If so, it will ask whether you also want information about Cajun cooking. If you do not agree to this proposal, your agent will note what agents made that suggestion and, on the next pass, will give less consideration to their ideas. The more agents that participate, the more accurate each one becomes at "understanding" the interests of its user.

- An online catalog sales company uses an agent that monitors incoming orders and makes suggestions. For example, a customer who orders a camera may be presented with a list of related accessories for sale, such as tripods and lens filters.

- A manufacturing plant uses an intelligent agent to negotiate with suppliers on the price and scheduling of parts delivery in order to maximize efficiency of production.

Intelligent agent technology has been an area of interest in artificial intelligence for many years. However, intelligent agents will need to display significantly greater learning capabilities and "common sense" before most users will trust them to make autonomous decisions regarding the allocation of time and money. Until then, they will be relegated to presenting suggestions to their human users. However, when a sufficient level of trust in intelligent agent technology has been achieved, and when human users are willing to allow their software to make independent decisions, we will begin to see such exciting new applications as

- *Financial agents* that negotiate with one another over the Web for the sale and purchase of goods and services, using price/cost parameters set by the sellers and buyers.

- *Travel and tourism agents* (electronic, not human) that book airline flights, rent automobiles, and make hotel reservations for you on the basis of your destination, schedule, price range, and preferences.

- *Office manager agents* that screen incoming telephone calls and email, putting meetings on their users' schedules, and drafting replies.

 ### 14.5.4 *Expert Systems*

Although intelligent agents incorporate a body of knowledge to "filter" their choices and thereby appear to capture certain aspects of human reasoning, they still perform relatively limited tasks. Consider the more unstructured scenario of managing the triage center in a busy hospital emergency room. The person in charge draws on (1) past experience and training to recognize various medical conditions (which may involve many recognition subtasks), (2) understanding of those conditions and their probable consequences, and (3) knowledge about the hospital's capabilities and resources in general and at the moment. From this knowledge base, a chain of reasoning is followed that leads, for example, to a decision to treat patient A immediately in a particular fashion and to let patient B wait. We consider this to be evidence of quite general "logical reasoning" in humans.

Artificial intelligence simulates this kind of reasoning through the use of **rule-based systems,** which are also called **expert systems** or **knowledge-based systems.** (The latter term is a bit confusing, because all "intelligent activity" rests on some base of knowledge.) A rule-based system attempts to mimic the human ability to engage pertinent facts and string them together in a logical fashion to reach some conclusion. A rule-based system must therefore contain these two components:

- A knowledge base: a set of facts about the subject matter
- An inference engine: a mechanism for selecting the relevant facts and for reasoning from them in a logical way

Note that the knowledge base contains facts about a *specific* subject domain in order to narrow the scope to some manageable size.

The facts in the knowledge base consist of certain simple assertions. For example, let's say that the domain of inquiry is U.S. presidents. Three simple assertions are

1. Lincoln was president during the Civil War.
2. Kennedy was president before Nixon.
3. FDR was president before Kennedy.

Another type of fact is a *rule,* a statement of the form *if . . . then . . .* , which says that whenever the clause following "if" is true, so is the clause following "then." For example, here are two rules that, taken together, define what it means for one president to precede another in office. In these rules, X, Y, and Z are variables.

I. If X was president before Y, then X precedes Y.
II. If X was president before Z and Z precedes Y, then X precedes Y.

Here we are using a formal language to represent the knowledge base.

What conclusions can be reached from this collection of three assertions and two rules? Assertion 2 says that Kennedy was president before Nixon. This matches the "if" clause of rule I, where X is Kennedy and Y is Nixon. From this, the "then" clause of rule I yields a new assertion, that Kennedy precedes Nixon, which we'll call assertion 4. Now assertion 3 says that FDR was president before Kennedy, and assertion 4 says that Kennedy precedes Nixon. This matches the "if" clause of rule II, where X is FDR, Z is Kennedy, and Y is Nixon. From this, the "then" clause of rule II yields a new assertion, that FDR precedes Nixon, which we'll call assertion 5. Hence,

4. Kennedy precedes Nixon.
5. FDR precedes Nixon.

are two new conclusions or assertions. These assertions were previously unknown and were obtained from what was known through a process of logical reasoning. The knowledge base has been extended. We could also say that the system has *learned* two new pieces of knowledge.

If this example sounds familiar, it is because this is part of the example we used in Chapter 9 to illustrate the logic programming language Prolog. Prolog provides one means of implementing an inference engine for a rule-based system.

The inference engine is basically using the following pattern of reasoning:

Given that the rule

If A then B

and the fact

$$A$$

are both in the knowledge base, then the fact

$$B$$

can be inferred or concluded.

This reasoning process, as we noted in Chapter 9, goes by the Latin name of **modus ponens,** which means "method of assertion." It gives us a method for making new assertions. We humans use this deductive reasoning process all the time. However, it is also suitable for computerization because it is basically a matching algorithm that can be implemented by brute force trial and error. Systems like Prolog, however, apply some additional guidelines in their search for matches in order to speed up the process; that is, they employ a form of intelligent searching.

Inference engines for rule-based systems can proceed in several ways. **Forward chaining** begins with assertions and tries to match those assertions to the "if" clauses of rules, thereby generating new assertions. These may in turn be matched with "if" clauses, generating still more assertions. This is the process we used in our example. **Backward chaining** begins with a proposed conclusion and tries to match it with the "then" clauses of rules. It then looks at the corresponding "if" clauses and tries to match those with assertions, or with the "then" clauses of other rules. This process continues until all "if" clauses that arise have been successfully matched with assertions, in which case the proposed conclusion is justified, or until no match is possible, in which case the proposed conclusion is rejected. Backward chaining in our example would have said, Here's a hypothesis: FDR precedes Nixon, and the system would have worked backwards to justify this hypothesis.

In addition to the knowledge base and the inference engine, most rule-based systems also have an **explanation facility.** This allows the user to see the assertions and rules used in arriving at a conclusion, as a sort of check on the path of reasoning or for the user's own enlightenment.

Of course, a rule-based system about some particular domain is only as good as the assertions and rules that make up the knowledge base. The builder of such a system acquires the information for the knowledge base by consulting "experts" in the domain and mining their expertise. This process, called **knowledge engineering,** requires a great deal of interaction with the human expert, much of it in the domain environment. If the domain expert is the manager of a chemical processing plant, for example, a decision to "turn down valve A whenever the temperature in pipe P exceeds 235°F and valves B and C are both closed" may be such an ingrained behavior that the expert won't remember it as part of a question and answer session on "what you do on your job." It only emerges by on-site observation. For the hospital example, one might need to follow people around in the emergency room, observe their decisions, and later question them on why those decisions were made. It is also possible to incorporate probabilities to model the thinking process, for example, If the patient has fever and stomach pains, the probability of appendicitis is 73% and the probability of gall bladder problems is 27%, therefore I first check A and then B.

Rule-based systems have been implemented in many domains, including specific forms of medical diagnosis, computer chip design, monitoring of manufacturing processes, financial planning, purchasing decisions for retail stores, automotive troubleshooting, and diagnosis of failures in electronic systems. They will no doubt be even more commonplace in the future.

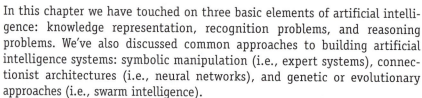

1. Given the assertion "Frank is bald" and the rule "If X is bald, then X is tall," what conclusion can be inferred? If Frank were known to be tall, would that necessarily imply that he was bald?

2. Given the assertion "Frank is not bald" and the rule "If X is bald, then X is tall," what conclusion can be inferred?

14.6   Conclusion

In this chapter we have touched on three basic elements of artificial intelligence: knowledge representation, recognition problems, and reasoning problems. We've also discussed common approaches to building artificial intelligence systems: symbolic manipulation (i.e., expert systems), connectionist architectures (i.e., neural networks), and genetic or evolutionary approaches (i.e., swarm intelligence).

We have mentioned only some of the many application areas of AI. Others include speech recognition, natural language translation, image analysis, target recognition, robotics, and game playing. Today we can use speech recognition systems to control our telephones, appliances, and computers by talking to them, use a tablet PC with handwriting recognition software, and instruct a robotic system to handle routine household chores.

14.7   Summary of Level 5

At the beginning of Level 5, we noted that we would be able to give only a sampling of the important applications of computers. After looking at simulation and modeling, new business applications, and artificial intelligence, we hope your appetite has been whetted to learn more about application areas that interest you.

There is, however, one more level to our story. With all the capabilities that exist today and will be developed tomorrow, what is the larger picture of computer technology within society? What are the ethical, legal, and social consequences of these capabilities? What should we welcome? What should we monitor or regulate? Is there anything we should prohibit? Are there any tools that can help us clarify thorny ethical decisions? Level 6 raises some of these questions in more detail, though of course, it provides no definitive answers. Each individual, armed with adequate knowledge, must hammer out his or her own position on many of these complex social issues. This is one of the responsibilities that comes with our unprecedented opportunity to enjoy the benefits of computer technology.

1. Suppose that in a formal logic, *green*(*x*) means that *x* has the attribute of being green, *frog*(*x*) means that *x* has the attribute of being a bullfrog, and *J* stands for the specific entity Jeremiah. Translate the following formal statements into English:

   a. *frog*(*J*)

   b. $(\forall x)(frog(x) \longrightarrow green(x))$

2. Draw a semantic net that incorporates the knowledge contained in the following paragraph:

   > If I had to describe what distinguishes a table from other pieces of furniture, I guess I would say it has to have four legs and a flat top. The legs, of course, hold up the top. Nancy's table is made of maple, but mine is bigger and is walnut.

3. a. Use an English-like formal language to represent the knowledge explicitly contained in the following semantic net:

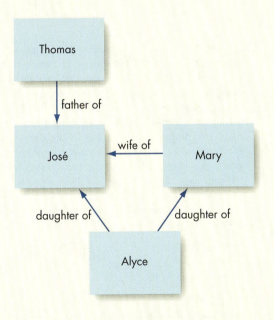

   b. Add to your list from part (a) the knowledge that can be inferred from the semantic net.

4. In the following neural network, which event or events will cause node N3 to fire?

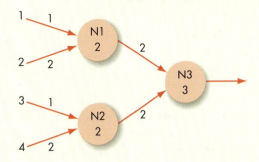

5. Assign weights and threshold values in the following neural network so that the output neuron will fire only when x_1 and x_3 have the value 1 and x_2 has the value 0. Remember that weights can be negative.

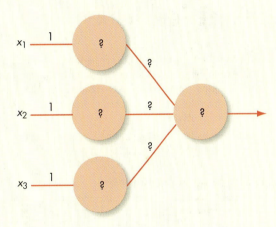

6. Try to find some literature or product information on a **PDA** (**personal data assistant**) device or tablet PC that allows pen-based handwritten entries. What sort of scheme does this system use for handwriting recognition? Does the system use a neural network? Does it require initial training on the user's handwriting?

7. You are a knowledge engineer and have been assigned the task of developing a knowledge base for an expert system to advise on mortgage loan applications. What are some sample questions you would ask the loan manager at a bank?

8. We described both forward chaining and backward chaining as techniques used by inference engines in rule-based systems. In Section 10.2.2 we described how a parser might analyze a programming statement to produce a parse tree. Does the method described in Chapter

10 correspond more closely to forward chaining or to backward chaining? Explain.

9. A rule-based system for writing the screenplays for mystery movies contains the following assertions and rules:

> The hero is a spy.
>
> The heroine is an interpreter.
>
> If the hero is a spy, then one scene should take place in Berlin and one in Paris.
>
> If the heroine is an interpreter, then the heroine must speak English.
>
> If the heroine is an interpreter, then the heroine must speak Russian.
>
> If one scene should take place in Berlin, then there can be no car chase.
>
> If there can be no car chase, then there can be no crash scene.

> If one scene should take place in Berlin, then the hero is European.
>
> If one scene should take place in Paris, then the hero must speak French.
>
> Can the following assertion be inferred? Explain.
>
> The hero must speak French and there can be no crash scene.

10. In Exercise 9, is it possible to add the following assertion to the knowledge base? Why or why not?

> The hero is American.

11. If you studied Prolog in Chapter 9 and have a Prolog interpreter available, try implementing the rule-based system of Exercise 9 in Prolog.

CHALLENGE WORK

1. A neural network is to be built that behaves according to the table in Figure 14.13, which represents the Boolean AND operation. Input to the network consists of two binary signals; the single output line fires exactly when both input signals are 1.

a. Find values for the weights and the threshold of the output neuron in Figure 14.14 that will cause the network to behave properly.

b. Because this is a relatively simple problem, it is easy to guess and come up with a combination of weights and threshold values that works. The solution is not unique; there are many combinations that will produce the desired result. In a large network with many connections, it is impossible to find a solution by guessing. Instead, the network learns to find its own solution as it is repeatedly exercised on a set of training data. For networks with hidden layers, the back propagation algorithm can be used for training. For a general class of networks of the form shown in Figure 14.15, an easier training algorithm exists, which will be described here. Note that in Figure 14.15, the input signals are binary, and all neurons are assumed to have the same threshold value Θ. The table in Figure 14.16 sets up the notation needed to describe the algorithm.

Initially, the network is given arbitrary values between 0 and 1 for the weights $w_1, w_2, \ldots$, and the threshold value Θ. A set of input values $x_1, x_2, \ldots$ from the training data is then applied to the network. Because we are working with training data, the cor-

rect result t for this set of input values is known. The actual result from the network, y, is computed and compared to t. The difference between the two values is used to compute the next round of values for the weights and the threshold value, which are then tested on another set of values from the training data. This process is repeated until the weights and threshold value have settled into a combination for which the network behaves correctly on all of the training sets. The network is fully trained at this point.

Each new weight w_i' is computed from the previous weight by the formula

$$w_i' = w_i + \alpha(t - y)x_i \qquad \text{(A)}$$

and the new threshold value Θ' is computed from the previous value by the formula

$$\Theta' = \alpha(t - y) \qquad \text{(B)}$$

There are three cases to consider:

i. If the network behaved correctly for the current set of data—that is, if the computed output y equals the desired output t—then the quantity $\alpha(t - y)$ has the value 0, so when we use formulas (A) and (B), the new weights and threshold value will equal the old ones. The algorithm makes no adjustments for behavior that is already correct.

ii. If the output y is 0 when the target output t is 1, then the quantity $\alpha(t - y)$ has the value α, a small positive value. Each weight corresponding to an input x_i that was active in this computation

FIGURE 14.13

The AND Truth Table

INPUTS		OUTPUT
x_1	x_2	
0	0	0
1	0	0
0	1	0
1	1	1

FIGURE 14.14

A Skeleton for the AND Network

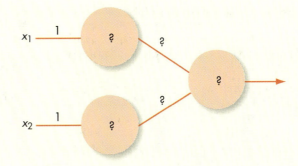

FIGURE 14.15

A General Network for a Training Algorithm

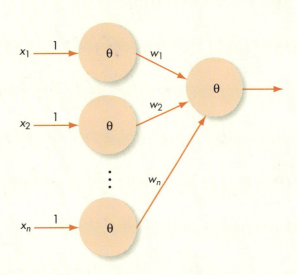

FIGURE 14.16

Notation for the Training Algorithm

SYMBOL	MEANING
$x_1, x_2, \ldots$	Binary input values from the training set
y	The binary output value from the network
t	The target binary output value from the network for this set of input values
α	The "learning rate" for the network; a small positive value that controls how rapidly the weights change during training
$w_1, w_2, \ldots$	The current set of weights
θ	The current threshold value
$w_1', w_2', \ldots$	The next set of weights
θ'	The next threshold value

(i.e., had the value 1) gets increased slightly by formula (A). This is because the output neuron didn't fire when we wanted it to, so we stimulate it with more weight coming into it. At the same time, we lower the threshold value by formula (B), again so as to stimulate the output neuron to fire.

iii. If the output y is 1 when the target output t is 0, then the quantity $\alpha(t - y)$ has the value $-\alpha$, a small negative value. Each weight corresponding to an input x_i that was active (i.e., had the value 1) gets decreased slightly by formula (A). This is because the output neuron fired when we didn't want it to, so we dampen it with less weight coming into it. At the same time, we raise the threshold value by formula (B), again so as to discourage the output neuron from firing.

We will use the training algorithm to train an AND network. The training set will be the four pairs of binary values shown in the table of Figure 14.13. (Here the training set is the entire set of possible input values; in most cases, a neural network is trained on some input values for which the answers are known and then is used to solve other input cases for which the answers are unknown.) For starting values, we choose (arbitrarily) $w_1 =$ 0.6, $w_2 = 0.1$, $\Theta = 0.5$, and $\alpha = 0.2$. The value of α stays fixed and should be chosen to be relatively small; otherwise, the corrections are too big and the values don't have a chance to settle into a solution. The initial picture of the network is therefore that of Figure 14.17. Note that with these choices we did not stumble on a solution because input values of $x_1 = 1$ and $x_2 = 0$ do not produce the correct result.

The following table shows the first three training sessions. The current network behaves correctly for the first two cases ($x_1 = 0$ and $x_2 = 0$; $x_1 = 0$ and $x_2 = 1$), so no changes are made. For the third case ($x_1 = 1$ and $x_2 = 0$), an adjustment takes place in the weights and in the threshold value.

After these changes, the new network configuration is that shown in Figure 14.18.

Continue the table from this point, cycling through the four sets of input pairs until the network produces correct answers for all four cases.

2. Pick one of the technologies discussed in this chapter (neural networks, swarm intelligence, intelligent agents, or expert systems) and write a report on how it has been applied to a real-world product or problem.

w_1	w_2	Θ	x_1	x_2	y	t	$\alpha\,(t-y)$	w_1'	w_2'	Θ'
0.6	0.1	0.5	0	0	0	0	0	0.6	0.1	0.5
0.6	0.1	0.5	0	1	0	0	0	0.6	0.1	0.5
0.6	0.1	0.5	1	0	1	0	−0.2	0.4	0.1	0.7

FIGURE 14.17

Initial Configuration of Network to Be Trained

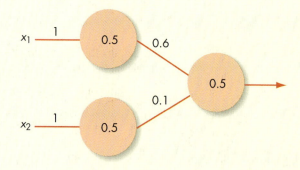

FIGURE 14.18

*Configuration of the Network
After One Adjustment*

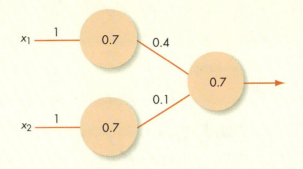

FOR FURTHER READING

For a general overview of artificial intelligence, try the following textbooks:

Luger, G. *Artificial Intelligence: Structures and Strategies for Complex Problem Solving,* 4th ed. Reading, MA: Addison-Wesley, 2002.

Negnevitsky, M. *Artificial Intelligence: A Guide to Intelligent Systems.* Reading, MA: Addison-Wesley, 2002.

Russell, S., and Norvig, P. *Artificial Intelligence: A Modern Approach,* 2nd ed. Englewood Cliffs, NJ: Prentice-Hall, 2003.

The following books provide more specialized information:

Ferber, J. *Multi-Agent Systems: An Introduction to Distributed Artificial Intelligence.* Reading, MA: Addison-Wesley, 1999.

Haykin, S. *Neural Networks: A Comprehensive Foundation,* 2nd ed. Englewood Cliffs, NJ: Prentice-Hall, 1999.

The original paper on NETtalk was

Sejnowski, T., and Rosenberg, C. "Parallel Networks That Learn to Pronounce English Text," *Complex Systems,* vol. 1, no. 1 (1987), pp. 145–168.

The following fascinating study of the chess-playing computer HAL of the film *2001, A Space Odyssey* reveals which of HAL's capabilities had been achieved and which were still beyond the grasp of artificial intelligence at the time of its publication.

Stork, D. G., ed. *HAL's Legacy: 2001's Computer as Dream and Reality.* Cambridge, MA: MIT Press, 1997.

Commentaries on the chess match between Kasparov and Deep Blue can be found in

Seirawan, Y., Simon, H., and Muakata, T. Viewpoint. *Communications of the ACM* (August 1997), pp. 21–25.

Hamilton, S., and Garber, L. Deep Blue's Hardware-Software Synergy. *IEEE Computer* (October 1997), pp. 29–35.

An interesting Web site on intelligent agents is http://agents.umbc.edu.

L
E
V
E
L

6

Social Issues in Computing

Social Issues
Chapter 15

Applications
Chapters 12, 13, 14

The Software World
Chapters 8, 9, 10, 11

The Virtual Machine
Chapters 6, 7

The Hardware World
Chapters 4, 5

The Algorithmic Foundations of Computer Science
Chapters 2, 3

LEVEL 6

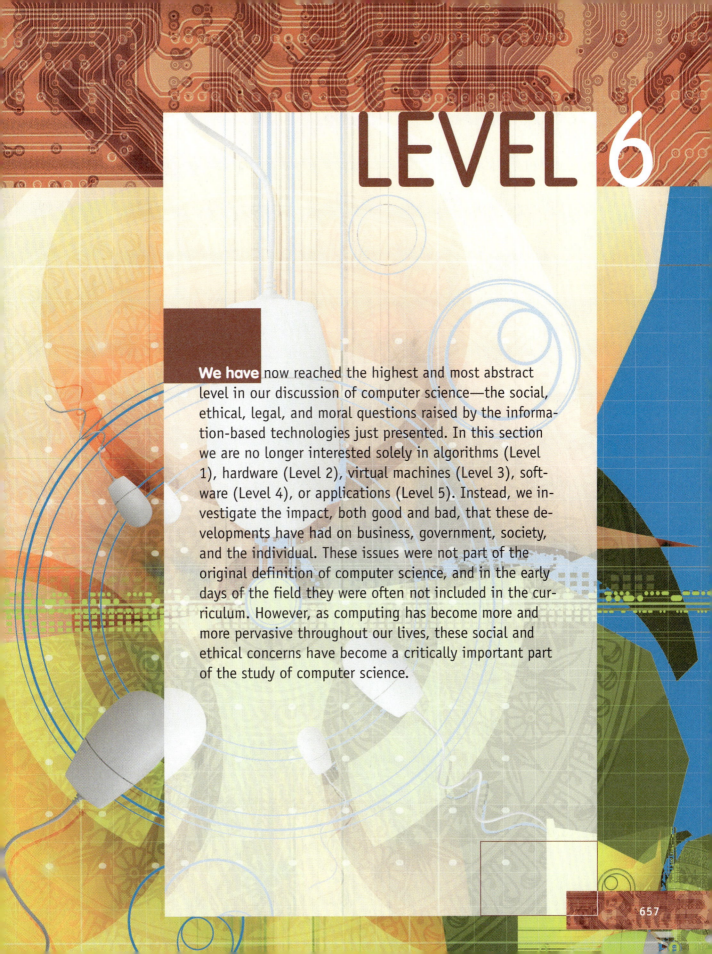

We have now reached the highest and most abstract level in our discussion of computer science—the social, ethical, legal, and moral questions raised by the information-based technologies just presented. In this section we are no longer interested solely in algorithms (Level 1), hardware (Level 2), virtual machines (Level 3), software (Level 4), or applications (Level 5). Instead, we investigate the impact, both good and bad, that these developments have had on business, government, society, and the individual. These issues were not part of the original definition of computer science, and in the early days of the field they were often not included in the curriculum. However, as computing has become more and more pervasive throughout our lives, these social and ethical concerns have become a critically important part of the study of computer science.

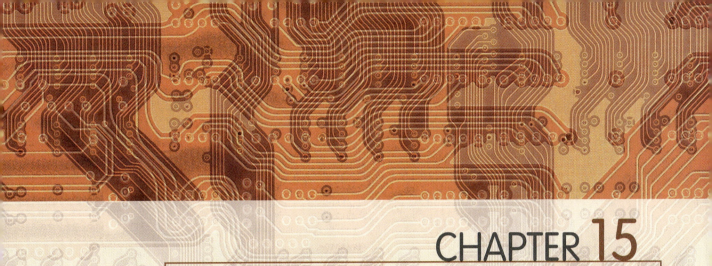

CHAPTER 15

Making Decisions about Computers, Information, and Society

15.1   Introduction

Most of this book has focused on the technical details of computing. For example, you have read about the mathematics of algorithmic efficiency (Chapter 3), the hardware implementation of computer systems (Chapters 4 and 5), building computer networks (Chapter 7), and software development (Chapters 8 and 9). However, in this chapter we focus on the *human* issues lurking behind these technical details. We can't give you a comprehensive list of such issues; such a list would already be way too long, and it is growing daily. Instead, we introduce skills that will help you to think and reason carefully when making personal decisions about computing. The chapter will also discuss important societal issues related to information technology and point you toward resources to help you explore these issues in greater detail. Making critical decisions about computing technology is unavoidable. Increasingly, our society is being driven by the access to and the control of information. As citizens of our communities, our country, and the world, we want our decisions to be well-informed and well-reasoned.

When humans make decisions about things they value, there are conflicts and trade-offs. The scholarly field of ethics has a long history of studying how to identify and resolve such conflicts, and we will be borrowing from several classical theories of applied ethics. In this chapter we present a number of case studies built around complex ethical issues related to computing and information. For each case study, we present the issues as well as arguments used to support and oppose certain positions. We then describe methods that allow us to understand and evaluate these arguments in terms of their ethical implications. When you finish this chapter you will have an increased appreciation for the complexities of human/computer interactions as well as an enhanced set of skills for thinking and reasoning about these interactions.

15.2   Case Studies

 ### 15.2.1   *Case 1: The Story of MP3—*
Compression Codes, Musicians, and Money

In 1987 some scientists in Germany started working on an algorithm to compress digital files that store recorded music on CDs. Using a complex model of how humans perceive sound, the Fraunhofer Institute in Erlangen, Germany, devised a method with the rather ungainly title of Moving Picture Experts Group, Audio Layer III. This algorithm (or protocol) quickly got the nickname "MP3."

We first introduced MP3 in our discussion of the binary representation of sound in Section 4.2.2. In that section we showed how the digital representation of audio information can produce massive and unwieldy data files. To reduce these files to a more manageable size, we must compress them using a compression algorithm such as MP3. The MP3 protocol allows various levels of compression. The more you compress the music data, the more sound quality you lose. A compression ratio of 12 to 1 has become popular, with the resulting sound quality almost comparable to a music CD purchased at a store.

In 1989, the Fraunhofer Institute patented MP3 in Germany, and a few years later MP3 became an international standard. It might simply have become another technical detail known to only a few engineers had it not been for the World Wide Web and an army of young people enthusiastic about recorded music.

In 1997, Tomislav Uzelac, a software developer at Advanced Multimedia Products, created what is regarded as the first commercially viable MP3 playback program. Two students from the University of Utah, Justin Frankel and Dmitry Boldyrev, used Uzelac's player to develop a user-friendly Windows application called WinAmp that played MP3 music. WinAmp was offered for free on the Internet in 1998. Suddenly MP3 became *very* well-known.

Prior to the release of WinAmp, there had been some sharing of digital music from copyrighted CDs. However, uncompressed sound files produced from traditional CDs were massive and transferring these files using a 56 Kb modem (the most widely used communication link on the Internet in the late 1990s) was slow and clumsy. But since MP3 sound files were so much smaller, and because Internet connections were getting faster and faster (especially in university computer labs), the sharing of MP3 music files became increasingly popular, and the people who make and sell music CDs became increasingly nervous.

In the spring of 1999, the situation became even more interesting. Two Northeastern University students, Shawn Fanning and Sean Parker, created a file-sharing system that spread quickly over the Internet. The users of the system were mostly other university students, who had ready access to fast Internet connections and who were very interested in obtaining music files that other students were willing to share. Fanning and Parker called their system "Napster," and it became so popular that several universities noticed that their campus networks were slowing to a crawl because of all the MP3 downloads being done by students.

The Napster system is a fine example of how technical details about computing systems can have significant social effects. The Napster software sets up what's called **peer-to-peer file sharing.** As diagrammed in Figure 15.1, this means that Napster's software electronically "introduces" two users who are distant from Napster and from each other. (This approach is quite different from the client/server model described in Section 7.4. In that approach the two users are the ones that directly exchange files.) Once Napster has helped these users find each other electronically, the file sharing goes on between the users, *not* through Napster. Although that sounds like a low-level and unimportant technical detail, this distinction turned out to be significant in the many court battles to follow.

These court battles came quickly. On December 7, 1999, an organization of recording companies filed suit against Napster in U.S. District Court on grounds of copyright infringement. During the highly publicized arguments that followed, the recording companies insisted that Napster was a conspiracy to encourage mass infringement of U.S. copyright law. By most accounts, the majority of MP3 music that Napster users "shared" was copyrighted, and most

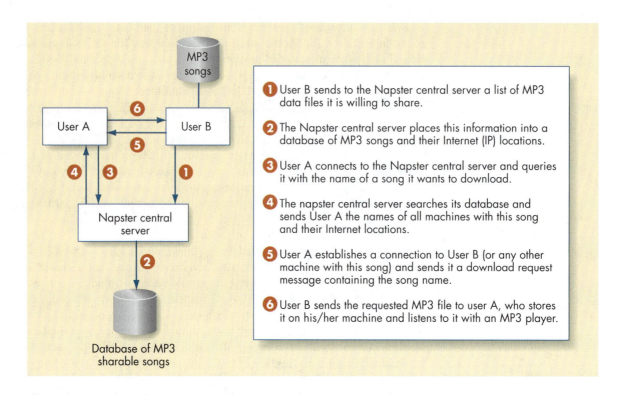

1. User B sends to the Napster central server a list of MP3 data files it is willing to share.

2. The Napster central server places this information into a database of MP3 songs and their Internet (IP) locations.

3. User A connects to the Napster central server and queries it with the name of a song it wants to download.

4. The napster central server searches its database and sends User A the names of all machines with this song and their Internet locations.

5. User A establishes a connection to User B (or any other machine with this song) and sends it a download request message containing the song name.

6. User B sends the requested MP3 file to user A, who stores it on his/her machine and listens to it with an MP3 player.

FIGURE 15.1

Peer-to-Peer File Sharing Created by Napster

of the copyright holders objected to the copying of this music without royalty payments. Some artists wanted their music copied, but they were said to be in the minority.

Its supporters argued that the Napster system was merely acting as a common carrier, much like a telephone company. They claimed that they were simply providing information on songs and their location and did not participate in the actual exchange of copyrighted information. They argued that they could not be held responsible for what peers (Users A and B) did with that information in the peer-to-peer file sharing system depicted in Figure 15.1. In addition, Napster contended that peer-to-peer copying was very similar to a user making a backup copy of a file. They pointed out that copyright law allows a person who has purchased a recording in one format to transfer it to a different format as long as it is for personal use and is not resold. Napster claimed that both peers in each swap were transferring the file without any payment to each other or to Napster, and therefore the copying should be considered "fair use."

Eventually, Napster lost the case and subsequent appeals, and as of this writing it is bankrupt and shut down.[1] However, as Napster faded, new peer-to-peer file-sharing systems, such as Kazaa, sprang up on the Web, and MP3 music continues to flow across the Internet, much to the chagrin of recording companies. The MP3 file-swapping saga will no doubt continue for years, both on the Internet and in the courts. But for the rest of our discussion of MP3, we'll concentrate on a question that isn't exactly a legal question and isn't exactly a computer science question: Is it ethically right to swap copyrighted MP3 files?

---

1 Napster was bought in bankruptcy auction; in October, 2003, a new legal Napster began business as a songs-for-sale Web site.

ASKING ETHICAL QUESTIONS A legal question we take to a judge. A technical question we take to a scientist or an engineer. But who can help us with an ethical question? An ethicist studies these questions, and in this section we'll look to ethicists for guidance about getting an answer to an ethical question.

We'll define **ethics** as the study of how to decide if something is morally right or wrong. A fundamental question in ethics is what criteria to use when "measuring" the rightness or wrongness of a particular act. Over the centuries ethicists have championed different criteria and developed schools of thought about how to label an act as good or bad, better or worse. One of the most influential schools is called **consequentialism.** As the name implies, a consequentialist focuses on the consequences of an act to determine if the act is good or bad. If the consequences are on the whole good, then the act is good. If the consequences are mostly bad, then the act is bad. However, in focusing on the goodness of an act, we have to ask, Good for whom? For instance, in our MP3 example the copying is certainly good for people who get free music. But just as clearly, the music copyright holders are convinced that MP3 copying is bad.

The most well-known consequentialists are the **utilitarians.** Utilitarians answer the question Good for whom? with a hearty, Good for everyone! Imagine a cosmic calculator that is capable of adding up human happiness. The utilitarian theory says that a moment before an act takes place, the cosmic calculator adds up all human happiness and puts a happiness number into the variable HAPPINESS_BEFORE. Then the act occurs. We wait awhile, long enough for the consequences of the act to become visible; then we use our cosmic calculator again and put a second happiness total into the variable HAPPINESS_AFTER. According to a utilitarian, the act in question is "good" if

$$\text{HAPPINESS\_AFTER} > \text{HAPPINESS\_BEFORE}.$$

If

$$\text{HAPPINESS\_AFTER} < \text{HAPPINESS\_BEFORE},$$

then the act is said to be "bad." (Just to satisfy the law of trichotomy, if HAPPINESS_AFTER = HAPPINESS_BEFORE, a careful utilitarian would declare the act to be ethically neutral.

Of course, there is no cosmic calculator, and quantifying happiness is no easy trick. Clearly, there are subjective judgments required to use the utilitarians' criterion. But the idea that consequences count and the idea that all people have to be taken into account to make a proper ethical judgment both seem like good ideas. So let's try out two short utilitarian arguments to explore whether or not mass copying of MP3 music files is right. First, we'll build a utilitarian argument that says such copying is OK, and then we'll build a second utilitarian argument that says such copying is not OK.

UTILITARIAN ARGUMENT #1: MP3 COPYING IS OK First of all, there are many more music listeners than there are music publishers. Music listeners are very pleased to get convenient, virtually free access to this music. Furthermore, music publishers should be pleased to get so much free publicity for their product. When radio stations play music, it's free to listeners, and many listeners go out and buy music that they've heard on the radio. The same thing happens to listeners who download MP3 files. That makes perfect sense, since the music on a CD provides slightly better sound quality than MP3 music. There is market research that shows that MP3 downloading has increased the sale of music CDs. So everyone should be happier because of MP3 file sharing.

UTILITARIAN ARGUMENT #2: MP3 COPYING IS NOT OK Although some early research suggested that MP3 file copying may have initially encouraged CD buying, more recent research shows that music CDs sales are declining rapidly. That's the real, long-term effect of widespread copying of copyrighted materials. If the people who publish music can't make a fair profit, then less and less music will be published. Eventually, both music listeners and music publishers (including the people who make the music) will lose. In addition, copyright protection is the law. This widespread criminal activity will result in a widespread disrespect for the law in general, and that is a very dangerous consequence.

Hmmm. We have used an ethicist's idea, a utilitarian argument, to try to clarify the MP3 question. But instead of getting a clear answer to our question, you may be thinking we've only managed to make things more confusing. Both sides of this issue seem to have some reasonable points. How are we to decide between them?

Let's admit something up front: deciding right and wrong is not always an easy call. If you want to do a binary search on a sorted array, there is a "plug-and-chug" algorithm that does the job quite nicely. Unfortunately, there isn't an all-purpose "ethics algorithm" that is guaranteed to provide a definitive answer to every ethical question. Still, we do have to make decisions about these issues, and we want to make those decisions on reasonable grounds, not just on a whim or instinct.

Ethicists depend on what is called a **dialectic** to try to get better and better ethical decisions. In a dialectic, we move back and forth between different viewpoints, criticizing each and trying to learn from each. In a debate, one side is trying to win by undermining the opposition and building up the arguments for its position. Ideally, in a dialectic the ultimate goal is for both sides to "win" by moving closer to the truth from two different perspectives. It's perfectly OK for people engaged in a dialectic to change their minds; in fact, that's the point. By systematically reasoning about the issue, the back and forth of argument can bring all parties to a more well-reasoned and justified decision. There's never a guarantee that the two sides in a dialectic will arrive at identical positions (although that is possible). More often, the participants end the dialectic still disagreeing, but hopefully with a better understanding of the reasons why there are still disagreements.

In the spirit of a dialectic, let's examine the strengths and weaknesses of the two utilitarian arguments above on the issue of MP3. Both arguments cite evidence about the sales of CDs to bolster their position: people for MP3 copying claim that it increases the sales of music CDs; people against the copying claim that it decreases the sales of music CDs. This is an example of a difference in fact, not just a difference of opinion. If the effect of MP3 copying is, in fact, to increase CD sales, then the "copying is OK" people have a strong argument; if the effect is instead to decrease sales, then the "copying is not OK" people have a strong argument. When the dialectic uncovers an empirical question at the heart of a disagreement, the smart move is to check the facts.

According to recently published statistics, music CD sales are down significantly (www.beaufortgazette.com/24hour/entertainment/story/700530p-5180204c.html). In the early days of Napster, CD sales were climbing; but as more and more files were downloaded for free and as more and more MP3 hardware was sold, CD sales have gone down. So it seems that, on this point, the MP3 opponents have a stronger argument. It often happens that consequences take awhile to become visible, and that seems to be the case here.

Next, let's examine the other main point in support of MP3 copying: the happiness of legions of listeners at getting free music. The opponents of the copying again make an argument about short-term and long-term effects of copying: in the short run, listeners might get tremendous benefits, but in the long run there may be far less music available for copying since artists and publishers will have far less incentive to create and disseminate music. This seems to make a certain amount of economic sense.

A third point raised by opponents of MP3 copying is the issue of illegality. The claim is that widespread disregard of copyright protections will have as a consequence widespread disrespect of the law. This claim is harder to demonstrate empirically than the CD sales claim, so we're probably not going to be able to settle this with statistics. But MP3 advocates don't often claim that breaking the law will have particularly salutary effects, and we don't see many legitimate claims for anarchy.

The dialectic so far seems to favor banning MP3 copying, but there are a few interesting counter-arguments. For example, some musicians (particularly relatively unknown ones) are great enthusiasts of MP3. These musicians have not yet been able to get recording contracts, so they use MP3 Internet file copying as a way to distribute and publicize their music. For them, MP3 copying has positive consequences for both listeners and music makers. Advocates of MP3 copying also point out that only a small percentage of the money spent on CDs goes to the artists. The rest of the money goes to the people who market the music. Some artists (including a few bands who have not achieved commercial success) have decided to happily give away their music on the Internet and make their money via live concerts. They are content to benefit from reduced but nonzero sales of their CDs for people who still like that medium.

Seen from this perspective, MP3 copying is merely the first wave of a new way of thinking about making and sharing music. This new way will favor music listeners and music makers who like to perform live. The new way will deemphasize the need for large publishing companies. Some people think that these are good directions to go, although, quite obviously, most music company executives don't agree.

Notice something technically interesting about the MP3 debate. If you buy a light bulb, you are mostly paying for the materials and the manufacture of the bulb. When you buy a CD, very little of the cost has to do with the materials and manufacture of the disk; that costs only pennies per disk. You mostly pay for the *information* encoded on the disk, not the physical disk itself. That's why MP3 copying is so dangerous for music publishers—the information on the Internet bypasses the physical intermediary, and it was always the transfer of a physical form during which publishers made their money.

An ethical dialectic rarely has a clean stopping point. We can almost always make better and better arguments, and there are often strong points remaining on different sides of an argument. As an example of arguments we glossed over above, we haven't discussed the fact that much of the MP3 music copying takes place using university and corporate computers (which tend to have better Internet connections than home computers), and that such equipment usually isn't supposed to be used for such purposes. In order to move on in this chapter, we'll leave that and other issues for you, our readers, to pursue on your own. We will make some closing remarks on MP3 copying, but we don't think this is a final word on the issue, and we certainly don't want you to think so either.

The consequences of widespread disregard of the law seem troubling and a strong argument against illegally copying copyrighted music. If the U.S. decides as a country that we are better off without copyrighted music, then the law should be changed. Until then, it seems unethical to encourage breaking the law that currently protects copyrighted music. For those musicians and listeners who are excited about free music on the Internet, the current laws don't have to stand in the way completely. The revolution in music distribution can be accomplished without the artists who insist on CD sales. Music lovers can simply avoid those artists completely. If the new system works and the old system dies, then artists who now insist on selling copyrighted CDs will either get onboard or stop making music. Either way, listeners who copy only MP3 music that isn't copyrighted won't have to jeopardize their integrity or risk the legal actions of angry music publishers.

Some music distributors are experimenting with new ways to sell online music, attempting to avoid the ethical and legal problems we've seen in the current situation. For example, Apple Computer's new music distribution system is called the Itunes Music Store and coordinates with the IPod, Apple's music player (www.pcworld.com/news/article/0,aid,111168,00.asp). Itunes and similar systems by other companies let users download songs for a relatively small fee after previewing the song online. The hope is that music consumers will opt for legal copying if the system is convenient and reasonably priced. If such systems succeed, both consumers and producers of music will benefit from transactions that have far fewer ethical problems.

PRACTICE PROBLEMS

1. Talk to someone you know about copying MP3 files using the Internet. Ask them to show you how they do it. Does the software they use differentiate between music that is copyrighted and music that isn't copyrighted? Ask the person showing you how to copy the files if they've ever thought about the ethical implications.

2. Not every decision is an ethical one. For example, we usually don't think of choosing an ice cream flavor as being "good" or "bad." Write down 10 choices you have made in the past week. Then go back over the list and label each as ethical or not ethical. (Note: "not ethical" is different from "unethical.") After you've labeled all 10 choices, see if you can convince yourself to change your mind about one of the choices you labeled "not ethical."

3. In order to effectively build a utilitarian argument, we need to think of all the people who are affected by a decision. We call these people "stakeholders" in the decision. Chose one of the "ethical" choices you listed in Problem 2. Now write down all the people or groups of people who are potentially affected, directly or indirectly, by your decision. Finally, list what each stakeholder may gain or lose from your decision.

15.2.2 *Case 2: PGP: The U.S. Government vs. Phil Zimmermann*

In Chapter 13 on e-commerce, we discussed the concepts of encryption and cryptography. Not surprisingly, the "secret codes" used in computing and on-line business can raise interesting ethical questions. A particularly controversial case involves the encryption code called "PGP."

In 1991, a software engineer named Phillip Zimmermann developed an encryption algorithm that he humorously called "Pretty Good Privacy," nick-named PGP. Zimmermann was concerned about bills introduced in the U.S. Congress that would allow the government to restrict the use of encryption for keeping electronic communications private. To combat this restriction, he made PGP freely available to anyone who wanted it, and the program was soon available from multiple sources on the Internet.

In response, the U.S. Government started a criminal investigation against Zimmermann. Their claim was that by releasing this algorithm to the world, Zimmermann was unleashing a powerful technology that would allow criminals and terrorists to avoid detection by law enforcement agencies. In the hope of improving public safety, the government had for years banned the export and publication of cryptographic products and information. Zimmermann countered that this was primarily a matter of free speech. Just because some people might misuse the technology for evil purposes shouldn't mean everyone should be denied the benefits of enhanced online privacy.

After years of litigation and threats by the government, the investigations of Zimmermann and others who supported him were closed in 1996. Some people interpret this as a victory for free speech and individual privacy; others interpret it as merely an admission that the Internet distribution of PGP had already taken place and that trying to squeeze the "toothpaste back into the tube" was hopeless. Either way, Zimmermann was out from under a cloud. Technically, PGP is still illegal to export to other countries, but it is available globally via the Internet. (For an interesting history of PGP take a look at www.cypherspace.org/~adam/timeline/.)

The saga of PGP has fascinating legal aspects, but we'll focus here on ethical issues, not legal ones. Was it right for Zimmerman to distribute his encryption program, or was the government right to try to prohibit its distribution? We used utilitarian arguments to explore ethical questions about MP3 copying. In this case study we will use a different kind of argument, analogies, to explore questions about PGP.

Analogies are commonplace, and that's one of the reasons they can be a useful way to think about ethical concerns. Most people are familiar and comfortable with the idea of explaining something less well known by comparing it to something better known. "It tastes a little like chicken, but drier" is a pedestrian example. But when we apply analogies to ethics, we need to be more careful about the analogies that we choose.

The power of an analogy is that it can transfer our understandings and intuitions about something well-known to a situation or entity that is less well-known. The tricky part is that sometimes that transfer is ethically appropriate, and sometimes it isn't. In a dialectic argument that uses analogies, there may be competing analogies presented; one analogy supports a particular view of the situation being discussed and the other analogy supports an opposing view of the exact same situation. In a productive dialectic using analogies, the participants in the discussion explore the strengths and weaknesses of each argument.

In any analogy between two "things," there are both similarities and differences. For example, someone might say "swimming is like riding a bike—once you learn it, you never forget." Clearly, swimming is not *exactly* like riding a bike. (Just try swimming on a driveway or riding a bike in a lake.) The point of this analogy is clear: the person making the analogy thinks that the similarity (you don't forget it once it has been learned) is most important to the current conversation.

In order to explore both the PGP controversy and ethical reasoning using analogies, we will examine two analogies that have been used in public debates about PGP. The first comes from Phillip Zimmermann, the author of PGP, and the second is an argument used by law enforcement to argue against the private, unrestricted use of encryption. Just to make this analysis a little easier, we're going to narrow our discussion to the use of the PGP algorithm for email security, even though PGP could also be used for many other types of communications, including digital phone calls.

ANALOGY #1: EMAIL IS LIKE A PRIVATE CONVERSATION

> If you and I decide to go for a walk in the woods and just talk, no one in his right mind believes that we should be forced by the government to carry microphones along to record our conversation so that they can listen to it. Before all this technology came in, every conversation was private.   —Phil Zimmermann in *Life on the Internet: Cyber Secrets* (PBS, 1996).

ANALOGY #2: EMAIL IS LIKE PHONE CONVERSATIONS
Criminals and terrorists increasingly use email for their communication. Analog phone conversations can, with a court order, be intercepted via a wiretap, and that can be effective in fighting criminal conspiracies. A court order to look at emails is futile if the emails are encrypted and unintelligible to the law enforcement community. Unless something is done to limit the power of encryption technologies, criminals and terrorists will be harder to stop because a valuable tool for law enforcement won't be available.

Both these analogies have a certain intuitive appeal. It doesn't seem sensible to require all conversations to be recorded; it doesn't seem sensible to allow criminals to avoid law enforcement. Good analogies often have a strong intuitive appeal, but we should look deeper than an initial reaction when using analogies in an ethical analysis. It's smart to think methodically about both the similarities and the differences in each analogy.

SOME SIMILARITIES AND DIFFERENCES IN ANALOGY #1
Private physical conversations are the same as emails in that people want to communicate with each other. Also, both types of communication are meant to include a limited number of people. In both types, however, the presumed audience may be larger than intended: in a voice conversation, people may be eavesdropping either by being physically close but unnoticed by the speakers, via a hidden microphone or by a distant parabolic listening device. In an email exchange, the email may be intercepted at any number of places along the electronic path between sender and receivers. Major differences between private conversations and emails derive from the medium of information exchange. A private conversa-

tion is high-bandwidth, including auditory, visual, and other sensory information; emails are much more restricted, often involving only text. Conversation happens in real time, with participants together in time and space; emails are asynchronous, and participants can be distant in time and space. Conversations are commonplace and an ancient form of communication; emails are relatively recent. Private physical conversations require only humans in close proximity; emails require extensive technologies and infrastructure. Private physical conversations are presumed to be free, although sometimes people are paid to talk (for example, consultants and therapists). Having email capability costs money, but once you have the capability, the cost does not increase in proportion to the number of emails you send or receive.

SOME SIMILARITIES AND DIFFERENCES IN ANALOGY #2 As in the first analogy, both phone calls and emails are a means of communicating. Both phone calls and emails have an intended audience, and in both types there may be someone unknown "listening in." Phone calls typically include more information than emails, since a phone conversation includes voices and emails are often limited to text. Both phone calls and emails are done at a physical distance. Phone calls are meant to be in real time (excluding answering machine messages), but emails are asynchronous. Both phone calls and emails require extensive technology support, and the information in both passes through circuits and routing systems that are controlled by others. Phones have been available for a longer time than emails. Phone calls and emails are paid for differently: using the phone more usually means you pay more, whereas using email more typically does not cost more.

ANALYZING THE ETHICAL SIGNIFICANCE OF THE SIMILARITIES AND DIFFERENCES The similarities and differences discussed so far are pretty straightforward, and with some additional thought we could probably list many more. But instead of making a longer list, we'll look more closely at the items we've already generated. In order to make progress in our ethical analysis, we need to examine which of these similarities and which of these differences are most relevant to our ethical question.

The three methods of communication—face to face conversation, phone calls, and email—all differ in the amount of information exchanged. (Engineers call this "communication bandwidth," and measure it in the number of bits communicated per second.) That difference surely is significant for the participants' shared experience. The different modes of communication involved also determine, to a large extent, how difficult it is for the government to gain access to the information. However, the technical issue of bandwidth and the practical issue of convenience of interception don't seem to be central to our *ethical* question. Either the government should be allowed to eavesdrop or not, no matter what the mode of communication. So we'll now ignore the modes and concentrate on other aspects of the analogies.

Private voice conversations are ancient, phone calls are more recent, and emails more recent still. This may be relevant ethically because societies have had more time to make decisions about private conversations. Focusing on our own society, private conversations are, as the default, free from government intrusion. This is not an absolute right—court orders can be obtained by law enforcement to use technology that invades private physical conversations. But these are the exceptions that prove the rule. Unless law enforcement can demonstrate probable cause, they are not supposed to take extraordinary measures to listen in on private physical conversations. The same is true for phone calls; a court order is required for an exception to the rule of not "listening in." Thus, if emails are subject to routine screening by law enforcement without a court order (and many people believe that this is currently done), then information in emails is far less protected than information in phone calls and private conversations. This difference seems directly relevant to our ethical question.

PGP allows email users to return to the default of privacy. If the encryption works (and most experts think it works pretty well), then it will be impractical, if not impossible, for law enforcement to routinely eavesdrop on emails encrypted with PGP. Without PGP, emails afford less privacy than a phone call or physical conversation; but with PGP, emails afford *more* privacy than a phone call or physical conversation, since it is more difficult for law enforcement to break the PGP code than it is to eavesdrop on a physical conversation or to tap an analog phone line.

Now that we understand some similarities and differences in the modes of communication, and we recognize important technical details that distinguish the three modes, we may be better able to understand the ethical issues behind the PGP debate. Most of us think catching criminals and stopping terrorists are two good things. Most of us think having personal privacy is a good thing. A decision about PGP affects both our security and our privacy. At least from what we've considered to this point, we can't seem to improve *both* with our decision about PGP; if that's true, we have to choose between them, at least in this case.

In order to make progress on the PGP question, we'll use the utilitarian perspective introduced earlier in this chapter. What would be the consequences of enforcing a ban on PGP, and what would be the consequences of allowing people to use PGP? We've already agreed that allowing the use of PGP will facilitate privacy and incur security risks. What will banning PGP do? Clearly, banning PGP would reduce privacy. In addition, we'd expect that most people would avoid something that is likely to get them in trouble with the law, and corporations would certainly avoid promoting illegal software (corporations are more vulnerable legal targets when it comes to software use). In this case email will become like postcards—everyone will know that there isn't much privacy in email. In fact, many people treat email in exactly that way today.

However, banning PGP is a complicated undertaking. Would the government ban its use or its dissemination? Banning dissemination on the Web is difficult, since the Web is global and most laws are limited to physical borders. PGP is, in its most fundamental form, just an idea. Would the government ban people from having the idea? Would it be illegal to express the idea on, for example, a piece of paper? (Opponents of government restrictions on PGP have taken to wearing T-shirts with the PGP algorithm printed on the front.) The United States has a tradition of free speech and free thought that seems incompatible with banning ideas, and the prohibition against PGP appears to run counter to that tradition. Free speech is not an absolute right; you aren't supposed to yell "Fire!" in a crowded theatre unless there really is a fire. But the drama of this example demonstrates that limits to free speech are not to be taken lightly. We've discovered an ethically significant difference between physical conversations, analog phone communications, and email: only in the case of email has the government proposed restrictions on an *idea*. This does not necessarily decide the issue, but it is certainly an important cost if the ban is enforced, and that cost should be taken into account when weighing whether or not to try to enforce a ban on PGP.

Although the U.S. government still has some regulations against export-

PRACTICE PROBLEMS

1. An important skill in using analogies is noticing both similarities and differences. This skill can be practiced. Think of a book and a Web site that contain essentially the same information. How are they alike? How are they different? Make a list of similarities and differences, at least 10 of each. Don't ignore the obvious, but don't limit yourself to the obvious either.

2. Imagine that your public library decides to go completely digital. The library now has a policy to phase out books and replace them with Web sites, CDs, and public access computers in the library. Using the list you made in Problem 1, make another list of the people who would gain from this decision and a list of the people who would lose. Build a utilitarian argument either for or against the decision.

3. Some people think that the content of Internet sites should be regulated just as the content of radio and TV broadcasts are regulated, for example with rules regarding obscenity and the amount of advertising. Other people think that the content of Internet sites, like private phone conversations, should not be regulated. Is the analogy between Internet sites and radio and TV broadcasts more appropriate, or is the analogy between Internet sites and telephone conversations more appropriate? Justify your position.

The Cyborg

On Monday, 24 August 1998, at 4:00 P.M., Professor Kevin Warwick underwent an operation to surgically implant a silicon chip transponder in his forearm. Dr. George Boulous carried out the operation at Tilehurst Surgery in Reading, Berkshire, using only a local anesthetic. This experiment allowed a computer to monitor Professor Warwick as he moved through halls and offices of the Department of Cybernetics at the University of Reading, using a unique identifying signal emitted by the implanted chip. He could operate doors, lights, heaters and other computers without lifting a finger (www.rdg.ac.uk/KevinWarwick/html/project_cyborg_1_0.html).

Kevin Warwick is physically intertwined with the computer in his left arm, officially becoming a "cyborg," a human being with bodily functions aided or controlled by technological devices (http://whatis.techtarget.com/definition/0,,sid9_gci296606,00.html). Based on his initial experiences as a cyborg, Professor Warwick extended his personal man/machine interface in March of 2002, when a one hundred electrode array was surgically implanted into the median nerve fibers of his left arm (www.rdg.ac.uk/KevinWarwick/html/project_cyborg_2_0.html).

Most of us do not yet have electronics embedded in our bodies, although some of us do (think about cardiac pacemakers, for example). But almost everyone reading this book is surrounded by computers. In everything from watches to washing machines, televisions to tractors, from PCs to SUVs, computers make things work. Some computers are obvious—desktops, laptops, and personal digital assistants at work and at home—but most computers are embedded inside other machines. Both kinds of computers increasingly matter to our health and happiness.

Some people, like Professor Warwick, enthusiastically embrace computing. Some people have serious qualms about how much computers are changing our lives. (Ted Kaczinsky, the "Unabomber," was an extreme case of someone who objected to this trend.) In this chapter we invite you to make your own judgments about the good and bad of information, technology, and society.

ing PGP, there is currently no active effort to ban PGP domestically. And our ethical analysis above suggests that avoiding the costs of a PGP ban is a defensible position. At least in this case, the increased security of such a ban would be bought at a very high price, a price made clearer by the use of analogies and a utilitarian analysis.

 ### 15.2.3   *Case 3: Hackers: Public Enemies or Gadflies?*

During the middle ages, a "hacker" was someone who made hoes. In the 17th century, a hacker was a "lusty laborer" who enthusiastically wielded a hoe [V. Gehring, Do hackers provide a public service? *Philosophy & Public Policy Quarterly,* vol. 22, no. 3 (Summer 2002), pp. 21–27]. But hacker has quite a different meaning today, far removed from its agricultural roots (see the box entitled "Hackers" on page 266, Chapter 6).

The term *hacker* is used in several different ways, but a common definition of a hacker is someone who breaks into computer systems, launches Internet worms and viruses, or perpetrates other dubious computer-related vandalism. Still, some people think at least some of the activities lumped under "hacking" constitute a public service, and several computer hackers have written books and articles about the ethics of computer hacking. In this section we'll explore whether there is an ethical case to be made in support of computer hackers. In order to focus our discussion, we'll concentrate on a single type of hacking: gaining unauthorized access to someone else's computer system. (This is sometimes referred to as "cracking," to distinguish it from the more general and ambiguous term *hacking*.) This could be as simple as using a coworker's laptop while he or she is at lunch or as elaborate as using an Internet connection to crack several levels of security and gain entry into a sensitive government database.

ANALOGY: BREAKING INTO A COMPUTER IS LIKE BREAKING INTO SOMEONE'S HOUSE
Imagine that a burglar picks the lock on your back door, wanders around picking up valuables and then escapes into the night undetected until morning. When you find out you've been robbed, you feel outrage and fear. If computer hacking is ethically linked to burglary, then we will have an instinctive revulsion toward both.

Clearly there are similarities between burglars and hackers; in both cases the intruders are there without our permission and (at least in most cases) without us being aware of their presence. In most homes and with most computers, the owners take some precautions to discourage unwanted visitors, precautions that must be overcome by the intruder. There are laws against both forms of intrusion, although the laws against physical break-ins are clearer and easier to enforce.

There are also differences between the intrusions. A burglar is likely to take something from your house, and that removal will deprive you of an item you used to own. A hacker may look at things, and even copy things from your computer, but the hacker is less likely to remove or destroy things from your system. The taking a hacker does involves intellectual property and privacy, and that is different from physical taking.

When someone breaks into a house, there is a palpable threat of violence. When a burglar is detected, things may turn nasty. This physical threat is not present in a computer break-in, although the information that's stolen may be personal and could lead to future physical threats. The physical degree of separation of a virtual break-in seems to be an ethically relevant distinction.

The analogy between a house break-in and a computer break-in helps us to clarify differences and similarities, both of which seem important in this case. Next we'll look at a pair of utilitarian arguments to extend the dialectic.

UTILITARIAN ARGUMENT: COSTS AND BENEFITS OF HACKING What is gained and lost when a computer is hacked? First, whoever owns the hacked computer loses some control over the information in that computer, and the hacker gains access to that information. Second, as a consequence of the break-in, there may be intentional or unintentional deletions or corruptions of data on the computer. These changes may be largely benign or may subsequently cause significant harm. Neither the hacker nor the person hacked can know with certainty the eventual consequences of these changes.

When computer system owners or system administrators discover that a system has been hacked, they often increase system security to reduce the probability of another successful intrusion. Some hackers claim that they provide a public service by alerting people to security holes in their systems. As long as the hacker doesn't hurt anything while "inside" the system, and especially if the hacker makes the intrusion obvious, then they would argue that the consequence of the hacking is improved security against malicious hackers. An alternative consequential argument says that increased security wouldn't be necessary if hackers weren't such a threat.

The discussion above illustrates two challenges when using a utilitarian argument in a dialectic about hacking:

1. It is sometimes hard to predict consequences with any accuracy.
2. There seems to be a distinction between "good hackers" (who don't want to hurt anything when they break in) and "bad hackers" (who do want to do damage or steal things).

These kinds of challenges arise in other discussions, and some people think they are difficult to overcome using a utilitarian argument. Let's try a different kind of ethical argument, a *deontological argument,* to try to meet these challenges in a different way.

DEONTOLOGICAL ARGUMENT: HACKING WITH A GOLDEN HEART Utilitarian and other consequentialist arguments focus on the consequences of an act to determine if the act is ethical. Deontological arguments focus on the inherent nature of the act instead. A deontologist focuses more on the intent of an act and how that act either is or isn't a defensible, responsible act.

The word *deontology* is from the Greek and means "the science of duty." Perhaps the most famous deontologist was the German philosopher Immanuel Kant (1724–1804). Kant wrestled eloquently (and at great length) about what duties we humans have to each other. He came up with "categorical imperatives" that characterized these duties. His second categorical imperative goes something like this:

Never treat a fellow human merely as a means to an end.

To boil that down to a bumper sticker slogan, we might say, "Every human being deserves respect."

Let's try out a deontological perspective on our question about hacking. Is the act of hacking into another person's computer system inherently unethical? If we take some hackers at their word, their intent is not to harm. They characterize themselves as insatiably curious about how computers and networks work, and they characterize hacking as an intellectually satisfying activity related to that curiosity. They claim to want to help people discover security holes to protect against malevolent hackers.

To move forward in our dialectic, let's stipulate that hackers who explicitly want to destroy and corrupt data are doing something unethical by any of the three arguments we've seen so far in this section (analogy, utilitarian, deontological). For the rest of this section we'll concentrate on hackers who claim a benign if not benevolent intent to their computer break-ins. That seems to require a bit more exploration.

First, we will assume that "good hackers" are telling the truth when they claim to mean no harm. (If some good hackers are lying about that, we'll reclassify them as "bad hackers" and focus on those hackers who are telling the truth.) Next, we'll explore how hackers describe the "goodness" of what they do. According to the Web site, http://info.astrian.net/jargon/terms/h/hacker_ethic.html, the "hacker ethic" makes two claims:

1. Information-sharing is a powerful positive good, and it is the ethical duty of hackers to facilitate access to information and computing resources wherever possible.

2. System cracking for fun and exploration is ethically OK as long as the cracker commits no theft, vandalism, or breach of confidentiality.

We'll examine each of these ethical claims. (For a more detailed discussion, see *Computer Ethics,* 3rd ed., by Deborah Johnson, which is listed in the "For Further Reading" section at the end of this chapter.) In claim 1, the idea of sharing information sounds pretty good at first glance. But it seems a bit less noble when we remember that much of the information that hackers share isn't *their* information, it's someone else's! It's one thing to share open source computer code (like Linux) or the works of Shakespeare on the Web. It's quite another thing to share material whose copyright is legally still in force (like Metallica's latest CD), or to share someone else's credit card number. Unless hackers consciously make these kinds of distinctions (and many hackers do not), then the duty to respect other people (and their intellectual property) isn't being followed.

The second claim has a similar weakness. Although a hacker might avoid inflicting a consequential harm (no theft or vandalism), you can't hack a system without breaking through the owner's security, and that act on its own breaches a duty to respect certain boundaries between people. To use an analogy to bolster the deontological argument, consider someone who breaks into your house but doesn't harm or steal anything. Just knowing that someone entered and occupied your physical home can make you feel uncomfortable and unsafe. Many of us feel the same way about our computer "homes." Computer security exists because we don't like trespassers, and hacking violates our boundaries.

Hackers might argue that our expectation of electronic privacy is the problem, not their violation of that expectation. What's missing from the hacker argument is why their ideas about information ("all information should be free") should take priority over the majority view ("some information should be private"). Ethically, there's no problem with thinking and arguing that all information should be free; there is a big problem with acting on that belief in contradiction of law and custom.

The arguments above won't convince most hackers, and you too might have some questions that remain about this issue. For example, open source efforts such as GNU, Linux, and Apache provide useful software for little or no money to many computer users. It can certainly be argued that such software is a positive good, and in this case "free" information (in the form of source code that is shared without charge) seems to support some of the hacker ideas. Also, some people deeply concerned about the increasing amount of personal information in corporate computers have suggested that hackers are a defense against the concentration of informational power. Again, some resistance to this centralization of power may sound like a positive thing. But the existence of positive good is not a slam-dunk ethical argument. Acts have both good and bad consequences, and utilitarians remind us that we have to weigh these consequences and think of them globally. Deontologists encourage us to remember that acts can be inherently good or bad outside the consequences. At the very least, the preceding brief analysis raises serious questions about the claims of the hacker ethic. In the Practice Problems that follow, you're invited to continue the dialectic about this ongoing controversy.

PRACTICE PROBLEMS

1. There are times when we want someone to break into our house. For example, if my house is on fire, I probably won't object if firefighters use an ax on the front door. Can you think of other such situations? Try to make an argument based on an analogy between firefighters and hackers that supports the hacker ethic. Do you find this analogy convincing? Why or why not?

2. Sometimes we are invited to look into windows and to enter privately owned property. For example, stores spend money to make attractive windows to draw us in. What are some ethically significant differences between a store inviting us in and a computer being hacked? Focus on the issue of intent as you consider this question.

3. Some Internet chat rooms allow and even encourage people to remain anonymous. As people type to each other in real time, the people chatting are identified by fictitious "handles." Is this a good idea? Think of two reasons why such Internet anonymity may be a good thing and two reasons why it may be a bad thing. Here is an analogy you might consider: a phone solicitor and children at Halloween.

15.2.4 *Thinking Straight about Technology and Ethics*

So far in this chapter we've looked at three different cases using three different techniques: reasoning by analogy, utilitarian analysis, and deontological analysis. In this section we'll suggest a "paramedic method" for computer ethics, and we'll invite you to practice that method on another case.

PARAMEDIC ETHICS FOR TECHNOLOGY When you get sick, you often need medical help in a hurry. Paramedics aren't necessarily medical doctors, but they know quite a bit about how to help people, and they know who to ask when they aren't certain about a particularly puzzling case. We don't expect you to become a research ethicist by reading this chapter, but we hope you have started to gain some new skills: recognizing ethical questions regarding computing and reasoning carefully about answers to those questions. When you recognize an ethical problem, we think there are several important questions you should ask yourself:

1. Who are the stakeholders in this situation?
2. What does each stakeholder have to gain or lose? (This is the utilitarian step.)
3. What duties and responsibilities in this situation are important to the stakeholders? (This is the deontological step.)
4. Can you think of an analogous situation that doesn't involve computing? If so, does that analogous situation clarify the situation that does involve computing? (Here we reason by analogy.)
5. Either make a decision or revisit the steps.

Before we illustrate how to apply these questions to a particular case, we need to announce a disclaimer. Unlike the formal algorithms studied earlier in this book, this "paramedic method" is not a step by step solution method, guaranteed to produce a result and halt. Instead, it is an outline of ideas that can help guide you into a productive dialectic. That dialectic may be in your own head or with others interested in the case. Either way, you want to think carefully and move toward a better understanding of the problem and toward better ethical solutions.

 15.2.5 *Case 4: Genetic Information and Medical Research*

Many people believe that the Industrial Age is over and we are now living in the Information Age. In the last few years, human genetic information has taken center stage in scientific exploration. Computers are an integral part of this research and of the growing commerce connected to the human genome. Since this "new" information is contained in the cells of our bodies, the computerization of this information is simultaneously personal and mysterious. In our final case study we will explore a fictional case involving genetic information. We'll use the paramedic method outlined in the previous section to examine this case from several different perspectives.

Imagine that you are at your family doctor for a routine checkup. The doctor asks you to participate in a study of genetic diversity and disease by donating some skin cells for the study. The doctor informs you that your skin cells will be identified only by a randomly assigned number and your zip code. Should you donate your cells?

STEP 1. IDENTIFY STAKEHOLDERS According to our paramedic method, the first question to ask is, Who are the stakeholders? Clearly the doctor and you are two stakeholders. But are these the only ones you should consider? Probably not. Unless the doctor is doing this study on her own (unlikely), there is someone else involved in this research. When you inquire, the doctor tells you that a pharmaceutical company is sponsoring the research and that they hope to use the information gathered from around the country to identify genetic links to several diseases, some of them fatal. Now you've identified three more stakeholders: the pharmaceutical company (let's call the company PHARM CO), skin cell donors all over the country, and people who have or will have these genetic diseases.

STEP 2. WHAT IS AT STAKE? There may be more stakeholders, but this list seems long enough for now. We move to the next step in the paramedic method, and we ask what each stakeholder might gain or lose from our decision. If we say yes and donate our skin cells, then we will undergo some sort of procedure and lose a few cells; our doctor will participate more fully in the study; PHARM CO will get a larger database and may be able to develop new drugs; if the drugs are successful, then people with diseases may have new therapies. If we say no to the donation, then our doctor, PHARM CO, and patients will have a slightly smaller chance of success with the research.

Just thinking about these possible costs and benefits might lead to a few more questions. First of all, is the procedure for donating the cells dangerous? Your doctor assures you that the procedure is harmless and requires just a moment to scrape a tongue depressor lightly against your arm.

Probably, you also would have questions about how your genetic information is going to be stored and processed. (Since you've almost finished this book, you have quite a bit of sophistication about computerized information!) A logical way to store this information would be to assign a randomly generated number for each donor in the study, perhaps linked to information your doctor already has. We might envision information like the following table, which includes the use of your Social Security number (SSN):

RANDOM NUMBER	SSN	NAME	ZIP CODE	GENDER	DOCTOR
10568322	532 12 3456	Joe Smith	45321	M	Goodgene
952990981	532 11 9503	Sue Jones	45321	F	Goodgene
.					
.					
.					

The doctor has assured you that only the random number (from the first column) and the zip code (from the fourth column) will be associated with your genetic sample and the information derived from it. If we believe that the doctor will in good faith send only that information to PHARM CO, should you be confident that your privacy is assured? The answer is probably not. If a table such as the one just shown exists, then PHARM CO could potentially link the information they receive from your doctor back to you by gaining access to that table. At the very least, PHARM CO could likely find out the names and addresses of all the people who donated cells from a particular zip code, and there may not be many from your particular zip code. Furthermore, computerized files like our table have a habit of hanging around, in one form or another, for a long time unless they are explicitly and carefully deleted. Unless your doctor has been scrupulous about data deletion (including cleaning up any backups and the like), PHARM CO may indeed be able to track down your personal information if it becomes important for them to do so.

You've also read in Chapter 7 some technical details about networks and communication over those networks. You know that information on the Internet can be intercepted at various points. Will your genetic information and/or the table described above be sent electronically to PHARM CO or anyone else? If so, will it be encrypted using the algorithms described in Chapter 13? Will access to the information be password protected?

A final question involves finances. Presumably, PHARM CO plans to make a profit from these drugs. Is anyone getting paid for this research? Let's assume that the doctor is getting paid a nominal fee for collecting the samples, say $5 for each patient who donates cells. PHARM CO is paying for all the collection kits and for all the analysis. Because PHARM CO is paying for the research, the information collected and any information developed will belong to PHARM CO.

STEP 3. IDENTIFY DUTIES AND RESPONSIBILITIES Now that we have a clearer picture of possible costs and benefits, we'll move to the third step of the paramedic method: analyzing duties and responsibilities. Your doctor has a primary responsibility to you, her patient. You have a duty to pay your bills promptly and to follow instructions that the doctor prescribes. PHARM CO is responsible for developing safe and useful drugs, and in return its customers pay for those drugs. In this research effort, PHARM CO is hoping that doctors will enlist volunteer patient donors, and in return PHARM CO is promising doctors a small fee for each patient who volunteers. Both your doctor and PHARM CO have promised to protect donors' privacy and are obligated to make a good faith effort to fulfill that promise.

Most of the responsibilities we've discussed so far are fairly straightforward and uncontroversial. There are other possible responsibilities that are less obvious and more controversial. We've already discussed intellectual property, the value of information, in the preceding MP3 case. Analogous to the music in that case study, this example also involves valuable information. What if your genetic information includes an important clue to the treatment of cancer or some other fatal disease? If PHARM CO develops an effective drug based on your genetic information, they stand to make billions of dollars. Should you get a royalty on the information in your genes? Does PHARM CO have a duty to share your genetic information and the information from others, or does their initial funding of this research give them proprietary control of that information?

Your doctor told you that only a random number and a zip code would identify your donated skin cells. This coding procedure seems to afford you some confidentiality, and that's a good thing. But you might also want to know why the zip code is required at all. Is geographic location part of the research, or is the zip code important for subsequent marketing of drugs? Is this study being done all over the world, only in the United States, or only in select zip codes in the United States? If it turns out your genetic information is particularly valuable, can the doctor give you assurances that your privacy will not be invaded? As we've seen previously, maintaining strict confidentiality would require a sophisticated protocol to make sure information could not be linked back to you and to protect information stored on computers and communicated over a network. Since both PHARM CO and your doctor want you to volunteer for this process, we expect that they have a duty to disclose these kinds of details before asking for your genetic information.

Another question is whether you have a duty to try to help cure disease in this case. If there is a chance for you to advance medicine by a simple donation process, is there an obligation for you to donate? In a situation like this, is altruism required?

STEP 4. THINK OF ANALOGIES As we move through the paramedic method, the seemingly simple request for a few skin cells has taken on added depth and complexity. Ethical analysis often reveals a broader perspective than our first thoughts about a situation. Now let's move on to our final step in the paramedic method, reasoning by analogy. An important aspect of this case is the promise of confidentiality to donors. Another aspect of the case that emerged during the first steps is that two of the stakeholders are potentially gaining money, PHARM CO and the doctors. The other two stakeholders, you and patients who potentially will want the drugs developed, are not getting money now and may be paying later. In order to explore both the confidentiality and the financial aspects of donors and users of donations, we'll explore blood donations.

The Red Cross solicits blood donations. The Red Cross is concerned about the quality of the blood that they distribute. Therefore, when you give a blood donation, the blood is tested for certain diseases. If your donated blood turns out to be unusable, then your name is entered into a "deferred donor database" and you are prevented from giving blood. Clearly, the Red Cross cannot offer you complete confidentiality about your blood and any diseases it discovers in your donation. However, the Red Cross is sensitive to the issue of confidentiality. On the web site www.givelife2.org/donor/faq.asp#5, the following appears on a FAQ (frequently asked questions) list:

> **Are the health history questions and my test results confidential?** Yes. The health history will be conducted by a trained professional in an individual booth arranged to preserve confidentiality. Your answers will be kept confidential, except where required by law. If your blood tests positive to any of the administered standard tests, you will receive confidential notification. The Red Cross maintains strict confidentiality of all blood donor records.

The Red Cross is a not-for-profit organization, but they incur processing costs associated with collecting, testing, and distributing blood. To recover these processing costs, the Red Cross charges a reimbursement fee to hospitals that use the donated blood. The hospitals also incur operating costs, which appear on your hospital bill. One of the reasons that the Red Cross prefers volunteer donors is that they've found that people who donate blood for altruistic reasons are the safest blood donors. Blood donation and skin cell donation (as proposed by your doctor) are similar in that the donors are volunteers, but the collectors and eventual users of the donated materials are paid. In both cases, it is something from donors' bodies that is being collected. And in both cases, the donors are asked to volunteer for altruistic reasons.

There are differences between the two situations. In the case of blood donation, the blood itself is the item of value, and both donor and collector are clear about what will happen with the blood. In the case of the skin cells, it is the genetic information in the cells that is of value, not the cells themselves. Also, PHARM CO is looking for something it may or may not find in your cells. If it finds valuable information, PHARM CO stands to make a profit; if it doesn't find valuable information, it may take a loss on the project. The Red Cross and hospitals presumably won't make large profits on your blood, although they do charge for its use.

Let's examine another analogy: companies that solicit money for a charity. In this case, a for-profit company solicits donations from volunteers. Again, confidentiality is an issue. On the one hand, we expect that a charity will keep records that we can use to confirm our donation if the IRS audits our tax returns; on the other hand, there are many reasons why we might not want our history of donations to become public information.

On the issue of finances, a for-profit solicitation company takes a certain percentage of donations to pay for its costs in soliciting and processing the donations and then passes on the rest of the money to the charity. This process becomes ethically objectionable when the percentage of money that goes to the solicitor becomes comparatively large. If the soliciting company pockets 80% of the donations it collects and passes along only 20% to the charity, donors feel cheated. If the soliciting organization keeps only 2% of the donations and passes along 98% to the charity, most people would not object.

The charity solicitation scenario is similar to the skin cell donation in that volunteers are asked to donate by someone who has a financial interest in that donation. In both situations, the donors are asked to make the donation for altruistic reasons. In both cases, the amount of money given to the person in the middle (the solicitor or the doctor) seems ethically relevant, as does the control of information about donors. In all of the cases we've examined, this donor information is almost certainly in the form of computer files and therefore easy to store and distribute.

The scenarios are different in that the donation requested for charity is monetary, not physical. In the charity solicitation, only the solicitor is for-profit. In the skin cell donation, both the doctor and PHARM CO are for-profit entities, although the doctor is making just a little money and PHARM CO is both spending and hoping to make much larger sums.

STEP 5. MAKE A DECISION OR LOOP THROUGH THE METHOD AGAIN

You've moved through the first four steps of the paramedic method and now, hopefully, you've developed a better understanding of the situation. If you have to make a decision right away (the doctor is waiting!), you can do so with a more reasoned response than before. But perhaps you have the luxury of thinking it over some more ("Doc, let me get back to you about the skin cell donation, OK?"). You might want time to ask a few more questions of the doctor or PHARM CO. You also might want to think about it more carefully on your own. In cases where the decision was potentially more critical to you or someone important to you, you might want to seek out help in making your decision. If you have the time, you could revisit earlier steps in the paramedic method.

Just to give this section some closure, let's imagine that the doctor wants you to decide about the donation while you're there at the office. ("The study is only going on for a few more days, and we wouldn't want you to have to come in again for such a trivial procedure.") We think that the analysis above would give you sufficient reasons to decline the invitation unless the doctor could give you more assurance about how PHARM CO was going to store and use your genetic information. On the one hand, helping find cures to serious diseases seems like a good thing, and the donation procedure sounds harmless. On the other hand, you haven't been given much assurance about how your genetic privacy will be maintained, and the financial interests of the other stakeholders may give you pause.

A thoughtful reader may or may not agree with that conclusion, but we hope any reader recognizes that this seemingly straightforward request has some surprisingly complex issues attached to it.

15.3 What We Covered and What We Did Not

We don't want to leave this chapter without warning you that we've only scratched the surface of some of the issues involving technology and society. In the chapter exercises we'll invite you to look at some of the many controversies in this developing area of applied ethics. And although we've discussed how to apply utilitarian ideas, deontological ideas, and analogies to computer ethics, we haven't even mentioned Rawlsian negotiation, virtue ethics, or any other number of ethical techniques. Please examine the Further Readings section if we've piqued your interest.

You may think that the paramedic method is too involved for your decisions, and just trying to remember how to spell *deontological* gives you a headache. But we hope you'll at least remember that technical decisions involve human values, whether we recognize it or not. And when you have to decide if something having to do with technology is right or wrong, we hope you remember to think carefully about consequences and duties. Computers give us tremendous power. Let's hope we learn to use the power well. Happy computing!

15.4 Summary of Level 6

In this last and highest level of abstraction in our study of computer science, we have looked at several case studies involving computer technology and have seen how even seemingly straightforward situations, when examined closely, reveal multiple facets of ethical implications. But more than the particular cases involved, this level has provided some tools for coping with ethical decision-making.

Because of the increasing capabilities of computers and their increasingly pervasive presence in our private and public lives, the path ahead will be filled with instances where there are ethical consequences to the use of computers, information, and technology. As private citizens and as members of society, we cannot avoid decisions on such issues, because in many instances doing nothing is a decision with ethical consequences. Finally, ethical decision-making seems to be a purely human responsibility, not one that our computers can help us with.

1. Here are some issues that you may have noticed in the news, each of which involves the intertwining of technology and human values:

> Personal privacy when surfing the web
>
> Software quality issues: how good is good enough?
>
> Licensing of software engineers
>
> The digital divide: the haves and have-nots of information
>
> U.S. Supreme Court ruling on virtual kiddie porn
>
> U.S. Supreme Court ruling on filters in public library Internet use
>
> Tracking terrorist Web sites
>
> Censoring information about bombs on the web
>
> The Clipper Chip: FBI wants encryption keys
>
> Loss of jobs due to technology
>
> Virtual reality as recreation
>
> Computer simulations in the courtroom
>
> Email spam and legislation to stop it
>
> Online education and cheating
>
> Surveillance cameras in public areas
>
> Face recognition used to scan for terrorists at the Super Bowl
>
> FBI databases of criminals
>
> Web sites with convicted pedophiles' addresses
>
> E-commerce replacing face to face businesses
>
> Stolen credit card numbers posted on the Internet
>
> Sales taxes on Internet sales
>
> Computing for the disabled
>
> Open source software versus commercial software
>
> Using pictures found on the Web to create electronic art
>
> Term papers for sale on the Internet
>
> States selling information compiled from drivers' licenses
>
> Database matching to find deadbeat parents
>
> Internet casino gambling
>
> Workplace monitoring using computers
>
> Smart bombs
>
> Artificial intelligence devices for medical diagnosis
>
> DNA evidence in capital cases

a. *Practice creating analogies.* Pick three topics from the list shown, or make up some topics of your own that involve technology and humans. For each topic, think of an analogous situation that does *not* involve computing. For example, if I picked "online education and cheating," an obvious analogy would be to consider face to face education and cheating. If I picked "personal privacy when surfing the web," an analogy might be "personal privacy when checking out library books." When you've picked your three topics and your analogy for each, make a short list of how each analogy is like the topic and how the analogy is different from the topic.

b. *Practice finding stakeholders.* Pick your favorite topic from among the three topics you chose in part (a). For that topic, make a new list of all the significant stakeholders in the topic. (*Hint:* remember that a stakeholder can be an individual, a group of individuals, a corporation, or any other entities you think are important in your topic.) For each stakeholder, list what the stakeholder most values in this situation.

   It may help you to frame a specific question or propose a particular action related to the topic. For example, if your topic is "online education and cheating," you might propose the action, "online education should be suspended until online cheating can be better controlled" or "online education should include automated cheating detection." This narrowing of the topic sometimes simplifies the task of imagining what people value with respect to this issue.

c. *Practice identifying costs and benefits.* For each stakeholder you identified in part (b), list the possible costs and benefits in the situation you chose. In many cases, these will be *potential* costs and benefits, things that might or might not happen. Sometimes the words "vulnerability" and "opportunity" can be more accurate than "cost" and "benefit" because of uncertainties in the situation.

d. *Practice looking for duties and responsibilities.* In the previous two parts, you identified some stakeholders. I'll use the letter N to stand for the number of stakeholders you identified. Next, make a two-dimensional table that has $N \times N$ cells. At the top of the table, label each column with one of your stakeholders. At the left of the table, copy the list of stakeholders, one for each row. If my stakeholders were {Fred, Ethel, Lucy}, then the table would look like this:

	Fred	Ethel	Lucy
Fred			Things that Fred owes Lucy
Ethel		Things that Ethel owes Ethel	
Lucy	Things that Lucy owes Fred		

Inside each cell, list any duties or responsibilities that the stakeholder on the left owes the stakeholder above. For example, I've marked three of the cells in the table shown. Don't neglect the cells that describe duties people have to themselves.

2. *Pull it all together.* In Exercise 1, you looked at one topic in some detail. In this exercise, write a short paragraph about what you think is the right thing to do in the situation you selected. Justify your decision on the basis of the analogy you developed, the costs and benefits you listed, and the duties in your table. After you've devised the best argument you can to show that you're right, write out a short description of what you think is the best argument *against* your decision.

FOR FURTHER READING

Books

Here are three textbooks that focus on the kinds of social and ethical issues we've explored in this chapter:

Basse, S. *A Gift of Fire: Social, Legal, and Ethical Issues in Computing.* Englewood Cliffs, NJ: Prentice-Hall, 1997.

Johnson, D. *Computer Ethics,* 3rd ed. Upper Saddle River, NJ: Prentice-Hall, 2001.

Woodbury, M. *Computer & Information Ethics.* Champaign, IL: Stipes, 2002.

The late Ann Wells Branscomb wrote an influential book about privacy and personal information:

Branscomb, A. W. *Who Owns Information? From Privacy to Public Access.* New York: Basic Books, 1994.

Richard Epstein writes clever fiction about the intersection of human values and technological advances. His most famous piece so far is about a "killer robot":

Epstein, R. *The Case of the Killer Robot.* New York: Wiley, 1996.

The following are collections of articles about social issues in computing:

Johnson, D. G., and Nissenbaum, H., eds. *Computers, Ethics & Social Values.* Englewood Cliffs, NJ: Prentice-Hall, 1995.

Kling, R., ed. *Computerization and Controversy: Value Conflicts and Social Choices,* 2nd ed., San Diego, CA: Academic Press, 1996.

Schellenberg, K., ed. *Computers in Society,* 10th ed. Guilford, CT: McGraw-Hill/Dushkin, 2003.

Spinello, R., and Tavani, H., eds. *Readings in CyberEthics,* Sudbury, MA: Jones and Bartlett, 2001.

Web Sites

Herman Tavani maintains an extensive online bibliography for "Computing, Ethics, and Social Responsibility." Find it at http://cyberethics.cbi.msstate.edu/biblio.

Chuck Huff has several well-documented computer ethics cases online at http://www.computingcases.org.

J.A.N. Lee at Virginia Tech's Department of Computer Science has a large collection of online materials about computer ethics at http://courses.cs.vt.edu/professionalism.

Edward F. Gehringer has a clever interface on his site about "Ethics in Computing" at http://courses.ncsu.edu/classes-a/computer_ethics.

For an international view of computer ethics, see http://icie.zkm.de.

Robert Barger maintains a set of computer ethics cases at http://www.nd.edu/~rbarger/cases.html.

Terry Bynum has a large collection of materials at the Research Center on Computing and Society at Southern Connecticut State University: http://www.southernct.edu/organizations/rccs.

Kevin Bowyer's "Ethics and Computing" site has teaching materials sponsored by the National Science Foundation (NSF) at http://www.cse.nd.edu/%7Ekwb/nsf-ufe.

The DOLCE site is also NSF-sponsored: http://csethics.uis.edu/dolce.

The Online Ethics Center for Engineering and Science was founded by Caroline Whitbeck at Case Western Reserve University: http://onlineethics.org.

Don Gotterbarn at East Tennessee State University heads up the Software Engineering Ethics Research Institute: http://seeri.etsu.edu/default.htm.

Organizations

In addition to the organizations associated with the Web sites above, we take special note of two professional organizations:

ACM SIGCAS: Special Interest Group on Computers and Society: http://www.acm.org/sigcas.

SSIT: The IEEE Society on Social Implications of Technology: http://radburn.rutgers.edu/andrews/projects/ssit/default.htm.

The *Console* class is used in Chapter 8 for keyboard input to Java programs. This appendix contains the *Console.java* code. The *Console.class* file is available for download on the Web site for the lab software for this book:

http://compsci.course.com/invitationlabs

```java
import java.io.*;
public class Console{
    public static void pause (){
        System.out.print ("\nHit Enter to continue: ");
        try {
            InputStreamReader reader = new
                InputStreamReader (System.in);
            BufferedReader buffer = new BufferedReader
                (reader);
            buffer.readLine();
        }
        catch (Exception e) {
            System.exit(0);
        }
    }

    public static int readInt(String prompt) {
        int value = 0;
        System.out.print (prompt);
        try {
            InputStreamReader reader = new
                InputStreamReader (System.in);
            BufferedReader buffer = new BufferedReader
                (reader);
            String s = buffer.readLine();
            value = Integer.parseInt(s);
        }
        catch (Exception e){
            System.out.println(e.toString());
            Console.pause();
            System.exit(0);
        }
        return value;
    }
    public static double readDouble(String prompt){
        double value = 0;
        System.out.print (prompt);
        try {
```

```java
            InputStreamReader reader = new
                InputStreamReader (System.in);
            BufferedReader buffer = new BufferedReader
                (reader);
            String s = buffer.readLine();
            value = (Double.valueOf(s)).doubleValue();
        }
        catch (Exception e){
            System.out.println(e.toString());
            Console.pause();
            System.exit(0);
        }
        return value;
    }
    public static char readChar(String prompt){
        char value = ' ';
        System.out.print (prompt);
        try {
            InputStreamReader reader = new
                InputStreamReader (System.in);
            BufferedReader buffer = new BufferedReader
                (reader);
            String s = buffer.readLine();
            if (s.length() == 0)
                throw new Exception("No character"
                    "entered");
            value = s.charAt(0);
        }
        catch (Exception e){
            System.out.println(e.toString());
            Console.pause();
            System.exit(0);
        }
        return value;
    }
    public static String readString(String prompt){
        String value = "";
        System.out.print (prompt);
        try {
            InputStreamReader reader = new
                InputStreamReader (System.in);
            BufferedReader buffer = new BufferedReader
                (reader);
            value = buffer.readLine();
        }
        catch (Exception e){
            System.out.println(e.toString());
            Console.pause();
            System.exit(0);
        }
        return value;
    }
}
```

ANSWERS TO PRACTICE PROBLEMS

CHAPTER 2

Section 2.2.2

1.

Step	Operation
1	Get values for x, y, and z
2	Set the value of *average* to $(x + y + z)/3$
3	Print out the value of *average*
4	Stop

2.

Step	Operation
1	Get a value for r, the radius of the circle
2	Set the value of *circumference* to $2 * \pi * r$
3	Set the value of *area* to $\pi * r^2$
4	Print out the values of *circumference* and *area*
5	Stop

3.

Step	Operation
1	Get values for *amount*, the amount of electricity used, and for *cost*, the cost per kilowatt-hour
2	Set the value of *subtotal* to *amount* * *cost*
3	Set the value of *tax* to 0.08 * *subtotal*
4	Set the value of *total* to *subtotal* + *tax*
5	Print out the value of *total*
6	Stop

4.

Step	Operation
1	Get values for *balance*, the current credit card balance, for *purchases*, the total dollar amount of new purchases, and for *payment*, the total dollar amount of all payments
2	Set the value of *unpaid* to *balance* + *purchases* − *payment*
3	Set the value of *interest* to *unpaid* * 0.12
4	Set the value of *newbalance* to *unpaid* + *interest*
5	Print out the value of *newbalance*
6	Stop

Section 2.2.3

1.
```
If x ≥ 0 then
    Set the value of y to 1
Else
    Set the value of y to 2
```

2.
```
Get values for x, y, and z
If x > 0 then
    Set the value of average to ( x + y + z )/3
    Print out the value of average
Else
    Print out the message 'Bad Data'
Stop
```

3. Get values for *balance, purchases, payment*
Set the value of *unpaid* to *balance* + *purchases* − *payment*
If *unpaid* < 100 then
    Set the value of *interest* to *unpaid* ∗ 0.08
Else
    If *unpaid* ≤ 500 then
        Set the value of *interest* to *unpaid* ∗ 0.12
    Else
        Set the value of *interest* to *unpaid* ∗ 0.16
Set the value of *newbalance* to *unpaid* + *interest*
Print out the value of *newbalance*
Stop

4. Get a value for x
While $x \neq 999$
    Set the value of a to x^2
    Set the value of b to $\sin(x)$
    Set the value of c to $1/x$
    Print out the values of a, b, and c
    Get a value for x
End of the loop
Stop

Section 2.3.2

1. You must change the operation on line 7 from a greater than (>) to a less than (<). That line will now read as follows:

    If Ai < *largest so far* then . . .

That is the only required change. However, to avoid confusion about what the algorithm is doing, you probably should also change the name of the variable *largest so far* to something like *smallest so far* on lines 3, 7, 8, and 12. Otherwise, a casual reading of the algorithm might lead someone to think incorrectly that it is still an algorithm to find the largest value rather than the smallest.

2. If $n = 0$ (the list is empty) then there are no values for $A_1, A_2, \ldots, A_n$. In particular, setting the value of *largest so far* to A_1 gives a meaningless value to *largest so far*. The while loop will not execute at all because i has the value 2 and n has the value 0, so the condition $i <= n$ is false. The algorithm will print out nonsense values for *largest so far* and *location*.

    The algorithm can be fixed by putting a conditional statement after line 1. If $n = 0$, the algorithm should print a message that says the list is empty. The "else" case will be the rest of the current algorithm.

Section 2.3.3

1.

a. NAME = Adams

i	Operation	Found
1	Compare Adams to N_1, Smith. No match	No
2	Compare Adams to N_2, Jones. No match	No
3	Compare Adams to N_3, Adams. Match	Yes

Output = 921−5281

b. NAME = Schneider

i	Operation	Found
1	Compare Schneider to N_1, Smith. No match	No
2	Compare Schneider to N_2, Jones. No match	No
3	Compare Schneider to N_3, Adams. No match	No
4	Compare Schneider to N_4, Doe. No match	No

Output = Sorry, but the name is not in the directory.

2. $n = 7$, $A = 22, 18, 23, 17, 25, 30, 2$

Largest So Far	Location	i	Operation
22	1	2	Compare A_2 and *largest so far*. Is $18 > 22$? No
22	1	3	Compare A_3 and *largest so far*. Is $23 > 22$? Yes, so reset values
23	3	4	Compare A_4 and *largest so far*. Is $17 > 23$? No
23	3	5	Compare A_5 and *largest so far*. Is $25 > 23$? Yes, so reset values
25	5	6	Compare A_6 and *largest so far*. Is $30 > 25$? Yes, so reset values
30	6	7	Compare A_7 and *largest so far*. Is $2 > 30$? No

Output: Largest $= 30$. Location $= 6$.

3. Pattern = an $m = 2$. The pattern has 2 characters.
Text = A man and a woman $n = 17$. The text has 17 characters.

k	i	Mismatch	Operation
1	1	No	Compare P_1, the "a", to T_1, the "A". No match.
		Yes	End of the check for a match at position 1 of the text.
2	1	No	Compare P_1, the "a", to T_2, the blank. No match.
		Yes	End of the check for a match at position 2 of the text.
3	1	No	Compare P_1, the "a", to T_3, the "m". No match.
		Yes	End of the check for a match at position 3 of the text.
4	1	No	Compare P_1, the "a", to T_4, the "a". Match.
4	2	No	Compare P_2, the "n", to T_5, the "n". Match.
4	3	No	i (3) is greater than m (2), so we exit the loop.

Output: There is a match at position 4

In a similar way, the program will produce the following two additional lines of output:

There is a match at position 7
There is a match at position 16

4. If $m > n$, then $n - m + 1 \leq 0$. Because the value of k is set to 1 right before the outer while loop, the condition $k \leq (n - m + 1)$ is false, the loop is not executed, and the algorithm terminates with no output.

CHAPTER 3
Section 3.2

The numbers from 1 to n, where n is even, can be grouped into $n/2$ pairs of the form

$$1 + n = n + 1$$
$$2 + (n - 1) = n + 1$$
$$\cdots$$
$$n/2 + (n/2 + 1) = n + 1$$

giving a sum of $(n/2)(n + 1)$. This formula gives the correct sum for all cases shown, whether n is even or odd.

Section 3.3.2

n	Best Case	Worst Case	Average Case
10	1	10	5
50	1	50	25
100	1	100	50
1000	1	1000	500
10,000	1	10,000	5,000
100,000	1	100,000	50,000

Section 3.3.3

a. 4, 8, 2, 6
4, 6, 2, 8
4, 2, 6, 8
2, 4, 6, 8

b. 12, 3, 6, 8, 2, 5, 7
7, 3, 6, 8, 2, 5, 12
7, 3, 6, 5, 2, 8, 12
2, 3, 6, 5, 7, 8, 12
2, 3, 5, 6, 7, 8, 12

c. D, B, G, F, A, C, E
D, B, E, F, A, C, G
D, B, E, C, A, F, G
D, B, A, C, E, F, G
C, B, A, D, E, F, G
A, B, C, D, E, F, G

Section 3.3.4

The basic shape of the curve as n gets large is still n^2 because as n gets large, the n^2 term dominates the other two terms.

Section 3.4.1

1. $legit = 3$

2	4	1	1

2.

2	0	4	1

2	4	1

3. $legit = 3$

2	1	4	1

4. For example,

1	2	0	9.5

Section 3.4.2

Devi, Nathan, Grant

Section 3.4.3

Pattern = AAAB; Text = AAAAAAAAA; $m = 4$; $n = 9$; $m \times n = 36$; the exact number of comparisons is $4 \times 6 = 24$.

Section 3.5

1. 38 paths

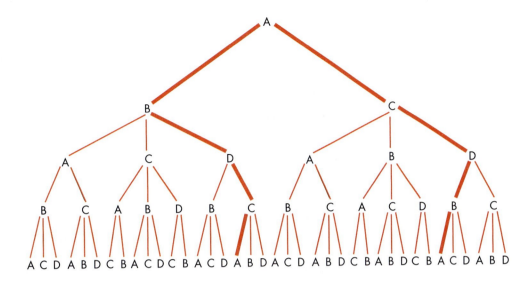

A C D A B D C B A C D C B A C D A B D A C D A B D C B A B D C B A C D A B D

2.

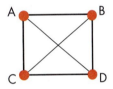

CHAPTER 4
Section 4.2.1

1. a. 10101000 $= (1 \times 2^3) + (1 \times 2^5) + (1 \times 2^7)$
$= 8 + 32 + 128$
$= 168$ as an unsigned integer value

b. 10101000 $= (1 \times 2^3) + (1 \times 2^5)$
$= 8 + 32$
$= 40$

This is the value of the magnitude portion of the number. The leftmost bit represents the sign bit. In this example it is a 1, which is a negative sign.

$= -40$ as a signed integer value

2. To answer this question, you need to represent the decimal value as a sum of powers of 2 and then convert that representation to binary.

$99 = 64 + 32 + 2 + 1$
$= 2^6 + 2^5 + 2^1 + 2^0$
$= 1100011$

However, this is only 7 bits and we need 8, so we must add one leading 0 to fill out the answer.

$= 01100011$

3. The 10 bits would be represented as 9 bits for the magnitude and the leftmost bit for the sign. To represent the magnitude, we must rewrite 300 as the sum of powers of 2, as we did in the previous question.

$$300 = 256 + 32 + 8 + 4$$
$$= 2^8 + 2^5 + 2^3 + 2^2$$
$$= 100101100 \text{ in 9 bits}$$

To make it a negative value, we must add a 1 bit (the negative sign) to the leftmost position of the number.

$$-300 = 1100101100$$
$$254 = 128 + 64 + 32 + 16 + 8 + 4 + 2$$
$$= 2^7 + 2^6 + 2^5 + 2^4 + 2^3 + 2^2 + 2^1$$
$$= 011111110 \text{ to 9 bits of accuracy for the magnitude}$$

To make it a +254, we must add a 0 (the + sign) to the leftmost position of the number.

$$+254 = 0011111110$$

4. a. To see what this value would look like in ASCII, we first look up the characters "X," "+," and "Y" in the ASCII conversion table to see what their internal representation is in decimal.

"X" = 88
"+" = 43
"Y" = 89

We then convert these decimal values to unsigned 8-bit binary values.

"X" = 88 = 01011000
"+" = 43 = 00101011
"Y" = 89 = 01011001

The internal representation of the three-character string 'X + Y' is formed by putting together all three of the preceding values, producing the following 24-bit string:

010110000010101101011001

which is how a computer stores 'X + Y' using ASCII encoding.

b. From the Unicode tables,

"X" = 0058
"+" = 002B
"Y" = 0059

where these representations are in hexidecimal (base 16) form. In base 16, digits run from 0–F rather than 0–9 as in the decimal system. Translating these representations into decimal, we get

"X" $= 0 \times 16^3 + 0 \times 16^2 + 5 \times 16^1 + 8 \times 16^0$
$= 80 + 8$
$= 88$
"+" $= 0 \times 16^3 + 0 \times 16^2 + 2 \times 16^1 + 11 \times 16^0$
$= 32 + 11$
$= 43$
"Y" $= 0 \times 16^3 + 0 \times 16^2 + 5 \times 16^1 + 9 \times 16^0$
$= 80 + 9$
$= 89$

These are the same decimal values as under ASCII encoding (Unicode for common characters agrees with ASCII encoding) but will be written in 16-bit binary form, with extra spaces for readability.

"X" = 88 = 0000 0000 0101 1000
"+" = 43 = 0000 0000 0010 1011

"Y" = 89 = 0000 0000 0101 1001

Putting these together produces the following 48-bit string for 'X+Y':

0000 0000 0101 1000 0000 0000 0010 1011 0000 0000 0101 1001

5. a. $+0.25 = 0.01$ in binary
$= 0.1 \times 2^{-1}$ in scientific notation
so the mantissa is $+0.1$ and the exponent is -1.
$= \underbrace{0\ 100000000}_{\text{mantissa}} \quad \underbrace{1\ 00001}_{\text{exponent}}$

b. $-32\ 1/16 = -100000.0001$
$= -0.1000000001 \times 2^6$
$= \underbrace{1\ 100000000}_{\text{mantissa}} \quad \underbrace{0\ 00110}_{\text{exponent}}$

Note that the last 1 in the mantissa was not stored because there was not enough room. The loss of accuracy that results from limiting the number of digits available is called *truncation error*.

Section 4.2.2   **1.** 44,100 samples/second $\times$ 16 bits/sample $\times$ 3 minutes $\times$ 60 sec/minute = 127 million bits

Compressed at a ratio of 4:1, this becomes about 32 million bits.

2. 2,100,000 pixels $\times$ 24 bits/pixel = 50,400,000 bits or 6,300,000 bytes

3. To reduce 6,300,000 bytes to 1,000,000 bytes requires a compression ratio of almost 7:1.
To reduce 6,300,000 bytes to 256,000 bytes requires a compression ratio of almost 25:1.

Section 4.3.1   **1. a.** $(x = 1)$ AND $(y = 3)$
True AND False
False   The final answer is False.

b. $(x < y)$ OR $(x > 1)$
True OR False
True   The final answer is True.

c. NOT $[(x = 1)$ AND $(y = 2)]$
NOT [True AND True]
NOT [True]
False   The final answer is False.

2. $(x = 5)$ AND $(y = 11)$ OR $([x + y] = z)$
True AND False OR True

We now must make an assumption about which of the two logical operations to do first, the AND or the OR. If we assume the AND goes first, then we get

False OR True
True

If we assume that the OR goes first, then the expression would be evaluated as follows:

True AND True
True

In this case the answer is the same, but we arrive at the answer in different ways.

3. $(0 \le x \le 100)$ AND $(0 \le y \le 100)$ AND (NOT $(x = y)$)

Section 4.4.2 **1.** The four separate cases are

$$\bar{a} \cdot \bar{b} \cdot \bar{c} \quad \bar{a} \cdot b \cdot \bar{c} \quad \bar{a} \cdot b \cdot c \quad a \cdot b \cdot \bar{c}$$

Combining them by using the OR operator produces the following Boolean expression:

$$\bar{a} \cdot \bar{b} \cdot \bar{c} + \bar{a} \cdot b \cdot \bar{c} + \bar{a} \cdot b \cdot c + a \cdot b \cdot \bar{c}$$

When this Boolean expression is represented as a Boolean diagram, it appears as follows:

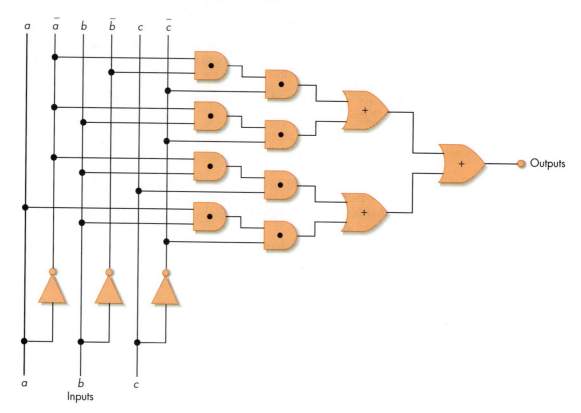

2. The Boolean expressions for the two cases are

$$\bar{a} \cdot b$$

$$a \cdot \bar{b}$$

Combining these two by using the OR operator produces

$$\bar{a} \cdot b + a \cdot \bar{b}$$

Pictorially, the corresponding circuit diagram is

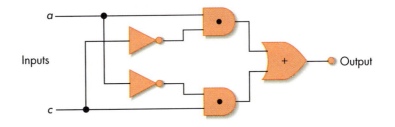

3. The Boolean expression for this is

$$\overline{a} \cdot \overline{b} \cdot \overline{c} + a \cdot b \cdot c$$

Pictorially, the corresponding circuit diagram is

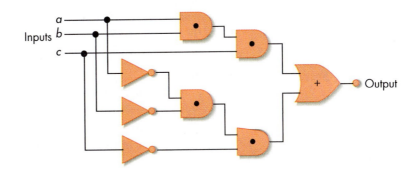

Section 4.4.3 **1.** Bit-compare $a > b$, where both a and b are one bit in length.

The truth table for this circuit would be as follows:

a	b	Output	
0	0	0	
0	1	0	
1	0	1	(because a is greater than b)
1	1	0	

There is only one case where there is a 1 bit in the output. It is in the third row and corresponds to the following Boolean expression:

$$a \cdot \overline{b}$$

We can skip step 3 because with only one case, there is no combining of Boolean expressions. Thus, the circuit diagram for this circuit is

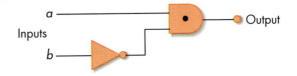

2. The truth table is already given, and again there is only one case with a 1 bit in the output. This occurs in the first row and corresponds to the Boolean expression

$$\overline{a} \cdot \overline{b}$$

Given this single subexpression, we can proceed immediately to draw the circuit diagram

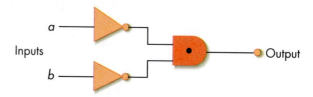

CHAPTER 5

Section 5.2.1

1. If the memory unit is a two-dimensional grid 1024 (2^{10}) by 1024 (2^{10}), then it contains a total of 1,048,576 (2^{20}) memory cells. We need a total of 20 bits to represent all the possible memory addresses, which range from 0 to $2^{20} - 1$.

2. Because there are $2^{10} = 1024$ row and column lines, we would need to send 10 (of the 20) bits in the MAR to the row decoder and 10 bits to the column decoder.

3. Average access time $= (0.9 \times 10) + 0.10 \times (10 + 25) = 12.5$ nsec.

Section 5.2.2

1. The total number of characters (ch) is
2 surfaces/disk $\times$ 50 tracks/surface $\times$ 20 sectors/track $\times$ 1024 ch/sector

which is 2,048,000 characters on a single disk. This is approximately what you might find on a typical diskette.

2. The seek time could range from 0, if the arm does not need to move, to a worst case of the arm having to move from the far inside track to the far outside track, a total of 49 tracks. The average, as stated in the problem, is a move across 20 tracks. The best-case rotational delay is 0, whereas the worst case is one complete revolution. On the average we will wait about 1/2 a revolution. Finally, the transfer time is the same in all cases, the time it takes for one sector (1/20 of a track) to rotate under the read/write head. Putting all this together in a table produces the following values:

	Best Case	Average Case	Worst Case
Seek time	0.0 msec	20 * 0.4 = 8.0 msec	49 * 0.4 = 19.6 msec
Latency	0.0	0.5 rev = 12.5	1 rev = 25.0
Transfer	1.25	1.25	1.25
Total	1.25	21.75	45.85

21.75 milliseconds is a fairly typical access time for a diskette.

Section 5.2.4

Assuming that   *A* is memory location 100
                B is memory location 101
                C is memory location 102
                D is memory location 103

1.

Memory Location	Op Code	Address Field	Comment
50	LOAD	101	Register *R* contains the value *B*
51	ADD	102	*R* now contains the sum *B* + *C*
52	ADD	103	*R* now contains the sum *B* + *C* + *D*
53	STORE	100	And we store that sum into *A*

There are many other possible solutions to this and the following problems, depending on which instructions you choose to use. This solution uses the one-address format. The two- and three-address formats will lead to different sequences.

2.

Memory Location	Op Code	Address Field	Comment
50	COMPARE	100, 101	Compare the values of A and B
51	JUMPNEQ	54	If they are not equal go to address 54
52	LOAD	103	Otherwise load R with the value D
53	STORE	102	And store it into C
54			The next instruction begins here

3.

Memory Location	Op Code	Address Field	Comment
50	COMPARE	100, 101	Compare A and B and set condition codes
51	JUMPGT	55	Jump to address 55 if $A > B$
52	LOAD	103	Load R with the value of D
53	STORE	102	And store it into C
54	JUMP	58	Jump to address 58
55	LOAD	103	Load R with the value D
56	ADD	103	R now contains 2D
57	STORE	102	And store that result into C
58			The next instruction begins here

4.

Memory Location	Op Code	Address Field	Comment
50	LOAD	103	R contains the value D
51	STORE	100	And store it into A
52	LOAD	100	R now contains the value A
53	ADD	101	R now contains the value $A + B$
54	STORE	100	And store that sum into A
55	COMPARE	100, 102	Compare A and C, set condition codes
56	JUMPLE	52	Jump back and do the loop again if $A \leq C$
57			The next instruction begins here

As with part (a), there are many different solutions to parts (b), (c), and (d), depending on which instructions you choose to use.

CHAPTER 6

Section 6.3.1

1. Initial values $R = 20$ memory location $80 = 43$
memory location $81 = 97$

	Operation	Final Contents of Register R	Final Contents of Mem Loc 80	Final Contents of Mem Loc 81
a.	LOAD 80	43	43	97
b.	STORE 81	20	43	20
c.	COMPARE 80	20	43	97

(and the GT indicator goes ON)

d.	ADD 81	117	43	97
e.	IN 80	20	Whatever value is entered by the user	97
f.	OUT 81	20	43	97

2. Initial value   memory location 50 = 4

Operation	Final Contents of Register R
a. LOAD 50	4
b. LOAD 4	A copy of the contents of memory cell 4
c. LOAD L	Because L is equivalent to 50, this operation is equivalent to LOAD 50, which is the same as part (a).
d. LOAD L + 1	A copy of the contents of memory cell 51. This operation means LOAD (L + 1), which is equivalent to LOAD 51. LOAD L + 1 does arithmetic on addresses, not contents.

Section 6.3.2   **1.**   a.

```
          INCREMENT X
              .
              .
              .
X:    .DATA    0
```

Another way to do the same thing is

```
          LOAD X
          ADD     ONE
          STORE   X
              .
              .
              .
ONE:  .DATA    1
X:    .DATA    0
```

However, the first way is much more efficient. It takes two fewer instructions and one fewer DATA pseudo-op.

b.

```
          LOAD X
          ADD FIFTY
          STORE X
              .
              .
              .
FIFTY: .DATA   50
X:     .DATA    0
```

c.

```
          LOAD      Y        --R holds a copy of contents of mem loc Y
          ADD       Z        --R now holds sum of CON(Y) + CON(Z)
          SUBTRACT  TWO      --R now holds CON(Y) + CON (Z) − 2
          STORE     X
              .
              .
              .
X:    .DATA    0
Y:    .DATA    0
Z:    .DATA    0
TWO:  .DATA    2
```

```
              d.         LOAD       FIFTY              --R holds the constant 50
                         COMPARE    X
                         JUMPGT     THEN    --if X > 50 go to label THEN
                         IN         X       --input a new value
                         JUMP       DONE    --and jump to done because we are all
                                                 finished
                 THEN:   OUT        X
                 DONE:                      --the next statement starts here
                           .
                           .
                           .
                 X:      .DATA      0
                 FIFTY:  .DATA      50


          2.             .BEGIN
                 LOOP:   IN         NUMBER
                         LOAD       ZERO
                         COMPARE    NUMBER  --see whether number > 0
                         JUMPLT     DONE    --the number is negative so go to done
                         INCREMENT  COUNT   --it is positive so increment count
                         JUMP       LOOP    --and repeat the loop
                 DONE:   OUT        COUNT   --print out the final count
                         HALT
                 COUNT:  .DATA      0       --count of number of positive values
                 ZERO:   .DATA      0       --the constant 0 used for comparison
                 NUMBER: .DATA      0       --place to store the input value
                         .END

Section 6.3.3   1.               .BEGIN
                         CLEAR      NEGCOUNT--Step 1. Not really necessary
                                            --because
                                                --negcount is already set to 0
                         LOAD       ONE     --Step 2. Set i to 1. Also not really
                         STORE      I       --necessary because I is initialized -
                                            -to 1
                 LOOP:   LOAD       FIFTY   --Step 3. Check whether i > 50,
                                            --and if so
                                            --terminate the loop

                         COMPARE    I
                         JUMPGT     ENDLOOP
                         IN         N       --Step 4. Read a value
                         LOAD       ZERO    --Step 5. Increment negcount if
                         COMPARE    N       --N is less than zero
                         JUMPGE     SKIP
                         INCREMENT  NEGCOUNT
                 SKIP:   INCREMENT  I       --Step 6. Count one more loop
                                            --iteration
                         JUMP       LOOP    --Step 7. and start the loop over
                 ENDLOOP: OUT       NEGCOUNT--Step 8. Produce the final answer
                         HALT               --Step 9. and halt
                 NEGCOUNT: .DATA    0
                 I:      .DATA      1
                 N:      .DATA      0
                 ONE:    .DATA      1
                 FIFTY:  .DATA      50
                 ZERO:   .DATA      0
                         .END
```

2. a.
    COMPARE = 0111   Y = decimal 10 = 0000 0000 1010
    instruction = 0111 0000 0000 1010
    b.
    JUMPNEQ = 1100   DONE = decimal 7 = 0000 0000 0111 =
    instruction = 1100 0000 0000 0111
    c.
    DECREMENT = 0110   LOOP = decimal 0 = 0000 0000 0000
    instruction = 0110 0000 0000 0000

3. LOOP is the address of an instruction (IN X), but decrement is treating it as though it were a piece of data and subtracting 1 from it. Thus, what this instruction is doing is "computing" (IN X) − 1, which is meaningless. However, the computer will be very happy to carry out this meaningless operation.

4. The address values that you come up with will depend entirely on your solution. The symbol table for the program in Problem 1 would look like the following. (*Note:* The solution assumes that each instruction occupies one memory location.)

Symbol	Address
LOOP	3
SKIP	11
ENDLOOP	13
NEGCOUNT	15
I	16
N	17
ONE	18
FIFTY	19
ZERO	20

Section 6.4.1

If there is 1 chance in 4 that a program is blocked waiting for input/output, then there is a $(1/4) \times (1/4) = 1$ chance in 16 that both of the two programs in memory are simultaneously blocked waiting for I/O. Therefore, the processor will be busy 15/16, or about 94%, of the time. This is the processor utilization. If we increase the number of programs in memory to 4, then the probability that all 4 of these programs are blocked at the same time waiting for I/O is $(1/4) \times (1/4) \times (1/4) \times (1/4) = 1$ chance in 256. Now the utilization of the processor is 255/256, or about 99.6%. We can see clearly now why in a multiprocessor system it is helpful to have more programs in memory. It increases the likelihood that at least one program will always be ready to run.

CHAPTER 7

Section 7.2.1

1. The figure shows the representation of a binary signal using frequency modulation of a carrier wave.

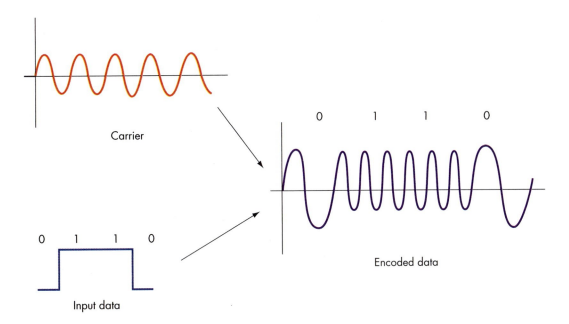

Carrier

0   1   1   0

Encoded data

0   1   1   0

Input data

2. The number of bits in the image is $1200 \times 780 \times 8 = 7{,}488{,}000$. To transmit this in 1 second requires a transmission speed of 7,488,000 bps, or nearly 7.5 Mbps.

Section 7.2.2   **1.** Collisions can occur in a ring topology because all nodes share the ring and a node may wish to send a message just as a message from another node is passing by. In a star topology, collisions are avoided because each node has a direct line (via the hub node) to any other node.

2. Because the message is to be broadcast, there is no need to include a destination address. Each node reads the message.

3. Node A sends the message on LAN1, where every node receives it, but only bridge B1 keeps it. All other nodes discard it because it is not addressed to them. Bridge B1 removes the message from LAN1 and rebroadcasts it out on LAN2. Every node on LAN2 receives the message, but again, only bridge B2 keeps it. All others discard it. Bridge B2 knows that node B is located on LAN3, so it rebroadcasts the message on LAN3, where node B receives it, recognizes its own address, and removes the message from the network. The message has arrived at its intended destination.

Section 7.3.2   a. A has resent M(3), presumably because B's ACK(3) message never reached A. When B receives the second copy of M(3), it should again send the ACK(3) to A but discard the message because it is a duplicate.

b. B should disassemble M(4) and check that it was correctly transmitted. If so, B should send an ACK(4) message to A; if not, B should discard the faulty message and wait for A to resend it.

c. B should disassemble M(5) and check that it was correctly transmitted. If so, B should send an ACK(5) message to A; if not, B should discard the faulty message and wait for A to resend it. Although this message has been received out of sequence (presumably because M(4) was lost), no special action is required at this time; B did not send an ACK(4) so A should in time resend M(4).

Section 7.3.3   **1.**   There are four distinct paths from node A to node D, and their total weights are

ABCD	Weight = 16
ABFD	Weight = 14
AEFBCD	Weight = 25
AEFD	Weight = 15

So the shortest path is ABFD, found by computing the weight of every possible path and then picking the smallest. This is essentially a "brute force" approach to the problem.

2.   This approach would not work with larger graphs such as one with 26 nodes and 50 links. The number of possible paths would grow much too large for us to enumerate and evaluate them all in a reasonable amount of time. We must use a more clever algorithm.

3.   If the link connecting node F to node D fails, then the paths ABFD and AEFD will not work and their weight becomes "infinite." Of the two paths remaining, path ABCD with weight 16 now becomes the shortest path. No one link in the network will disconnect nodes A and D. We can see that clearly by noting that the two paths ABCD and AEFD do not share any links in common. Therefore, if a link along one of these paths fails, we can use the other path.

CHAPTER 8

Section 8.4   **1.**   the first three

                2.   `int Number;`

                3.   12; 12*4 = 48

                4.   `Box[0][0]`

Section 8.5.1   `quantity = Console.readInt("Enter quantity " + "(an integer): ");`

Section 8.5.2   **1.**   `System.out.println("The average high temperature " + "in San Diego for the month of May is " + average);`

                2.   `This isgoodbye, Steve`

Section 8.5.3   **1.**   `Next = NewNumber;`

                2.   55.0

Section 8.5.4   **1.**   30

                2.   3
                      5
                      7
                      9
                      11
                      13
                      15
                      17
                      19
                      21

                3.   Yes

                4.   6

5.  ```
    if (night == day)
        System.out.println("Equal");
    ```

Section 8.5.5   1.
```
//program to read in and write out
//user's initials

public class Initials
{
  public static void main(String[] args)
  {
    char firstInitial, lastInitial;

    firstInitial = Console.readChar("Enter "
        + "your first initial: ");
    lastInitial = Console.readChar("Enter "
        + "your last initial: ");
    System.out.println("Your initials are "
        + firstInitial + lastInitial);

  }
}
```

2.
```
//program to compute cost based on price per item
//and quantity purchased

public class Cost
{
  public static void main(String[] args)
  {
    double price = 0.0, cost = 0.0;
    int quantity = 0;

    price = Console.readDouble("What is
        the price of the item? ");
    quantity = Console.readInt("How many of
        this item are being" + " purchased? ");
    cost = price * quantity;
    System.out.println("The total cost for this
        item is $" + cost);

  }
}
```

3.
```
//program to test a number relative to 5
//and write out the number or its double

public class FiveTester
{
```
```

```
        public static void main(String[] args)
        {
            int number = 0;

            number = Console.readInt("Enter a "
                + "number: ");
            if (number < 5)
                System.out.println(number);
            else
                System.out.println(2 * number);
        }
    }
```

4.
```
    //program to collect a number, then write all
    //the values from 1 to that number
    public class Counter
    {
        public static void main(String[] args)
        {
            int number = 0;          //number user enters
            int counter = 1;   //counter to control loop

            number = Console.readInt("Enter a positive "
                + "number: ");
            while (counter <= number)
            {
                System.out.println(counter);
                counter = counter + 1;
            }
        }
    }
```

Section 8.7.3 1. 20

2. 20

3. 7
    14
    10 (*number* was passed by value, it cannot be permanently changed by *doIt*)

4. a. `public static double tax(double subtotal)`
   b. `return subtotal * 0.55;`
   c. `System.out.println("The tax is "`
      `+ Sales.tax(subtotal));`

Section 8.8.4 1. `The area of a square with side 10 is 100`

2. Height and Base

Section 8.9.2 `g.drawRect(150, 150, 250, 200);`

`g.drawRect(170, 170, 40, 40);`

```
g.drawRect(340, 170, 40, 40);
g.drawRect(250, 270, 50, 80);
g.drawLine(150, 150, 275, 75);
g.drawLine(275, 75, 400, 150);
g.fillOval(290, 310, 5, 5);
```

CHAPTER 9

Section 9.2.1 `ITIME .LE. 7`

Section 9.2.2
```
outputNumber = inputNumber;
sumOfValues = sumOfValues + inputNumber;
```

Section 9.2.3
1. *Rate* refers to the contents of the memory cell called *Rate*; *&Rate* refers to the address of that cell.

2. 10

Section 9.2.4 Prints the numbers from 1 through 10 on a single line with a blank space between them.

Section 9.2.5 The name entered in the text box will be displayed in the label.

Section 9.3.3
1. Results in the names of all vendors from Chicago.

2. These are the *times* that try **men's souls**.

3. A message box pops up that says "You must enter a name."
A message box pops up that warns that the form is going to be emailed and that the form data will be sent unencrypted; user can cancel or go ahead. If you say OK, then you should get an email message that says Name = whatever you typed in the textbox.

Section 9.4.1
1. a. (2 3 4)
   b. 5

2. (define (threeplus x)
        (+ 3 x))

Section 9.4.2
1. No

2. X = jefferson

3. X = lincoln
   X = fdr
   X = kennedy
   X = nixon

Section 9.4.3 One processor could compute A + B while another computes C + D. A third processor could then take the two quantities A + B and C + D and compute their sum. Parallel processing uses a total of two time slots: one to simultaneously do the two additions A + B and C + D, then one to do the addition (A + B) + (C + D).
Sequential processing would require a total of three time slots: (A + B), then (A + B) + C, then ((A + B) + C) + D.

CHAPTER 10

Section 10.2.1

a.

Token	Classification
x	1
=	3
x	1
+	4
1	2
;	6

b.

Token	Classification
if	8
(	10
a	1
+	4
b42	1
==	7
0	2
)	11
a	1
=	3
z	1
—	5
12	2
;	6

Section 10.2.2 (Set 1)

1. <Boolean operator> ::= AND | OR | NOT

2. <identifier> ::= <first> <second>
   <first> ::= i | j
   <second> ::= <letter> | <digit> | Λ
   <letter> ::= A | B | C | D | . . . | Z
   <digit> :: = 0 | 1 | 2 | . . . | 9

   <identifier> is the goal symbol

3. <expression> ::= (<var> <op> <var>)
   <var> ::= x | y | z
   <op> ::= < | == | >

4.

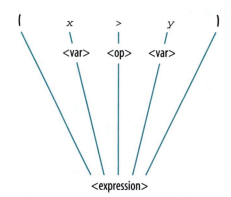

5. You eventually reach the point in the parse where you have the follow-ing sequence:

   (<var> <op>)

   which does not match the right-hand side of any rule, and the parse fails.

6. The first rule of Problem 3 could be changed to

   <expression> ::= (<var> <op> <var>) | <var> <op> <var>

Section 10.2.2 (Set 2) 1.

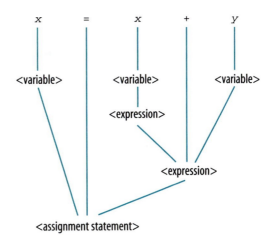

2.

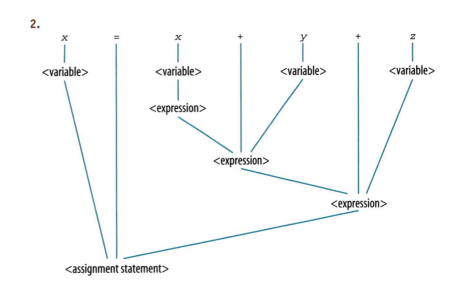

3.

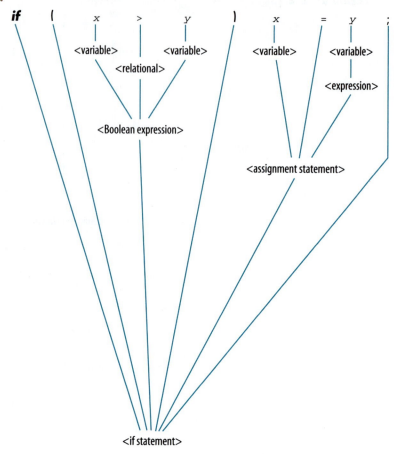

4. The language consists of all strings containing an arbitrary sequence of *a*'s and *b*'s of length 1 or more.

5. <goal> ::= <pair> | <pair> <goal>

<pair> ::= AB

Section 10.2.3 The parse tree for this expression is

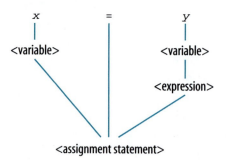

During the construction of this parse tree, you will build four semantic records, two for <variable>, one for <expression>, and one for <assignment statement>.

The code generated is

```
          LOAD      Y
          STORE     TEMP
          LOAD      TEMP
          STORE     X

                .

                .

                .

X:        .DATA     0
Y:        .DATA     0
TEMP:     .DATA     0
```

CHAPTER 11

Section 11.2

1. Piloting a boat, performing an operation, fighting a fire

2. Soil conditions, water supply, types of industrial waste. It could illustrate long-term effects of various waste disposal policies. If it were inaccurate, policies based on the model could be pursued that would result in environmental damage.

Section 11.3

1. a. $b\,1\,0\,1\,b$
$\uparrow$
2

b. $b\,1\,1\,1\,b$
$\uparrow$
2

c. $b\,1\,1\,1\,b$
$\uparrow$
2

d. $b\,0\,1\,1\,1\,b$
$\uparrow$
1

2. $b\,0\,1\,0\,b$

Section 11.5

1. a. $b\,1\,1\,0\,1\,0\,b$

2. $b\,1\,1\,1\,1\,b\,1\,1\,1\,1\,1\,b$ becomes
$b\,b\,b\,1\,1\,1\,1\,1\,1\,1\,1\,1\,b$

3. $(1,1,1,1,R)$
$(1,0,0,1,R)$
$(1,b,1,2,R)$

Section 11.7

1. To prove that something is not true, assume that it is and arrive at a contradiction. The assumption must then be wrong.

CHAPTER 13

Section 13.2.5

1. For example,
www.webmd.com
www.eco-portal.com
www.thebasketballportal.com
www.petersons.com
www.steelonthenet.com

Section 13.3.3

1. 149   12.35

2.

```
SELECT LastName, FirstName, MonthlyCost
FROM Employees, InsurancePlans, InsurancePolicies
WHERE LastName = 'Takasano'
AND ID = EmployeeID
AND InsurancePolicies.PlanType   =
InsurancePlans.PlanType;
```

3.

```
SELECT EmployeeID
FROM InsurancePolicies
WHERE PlanType = 'B2';
```

Section 13.4.2

1. STB NX YMJ MTZW

2. Because there are 26 letters in the alphabet, a shift of $s = 26$ encrypts each character as itself, so you should not trust the messenger.

CHAPTER 14

Section 14.3

For example, a hamburger is a kind of sandwich. As such, it comes between two pieces of bread, but it is hot. It may have various condiments, such as mustard, ketchup, and a pickle.

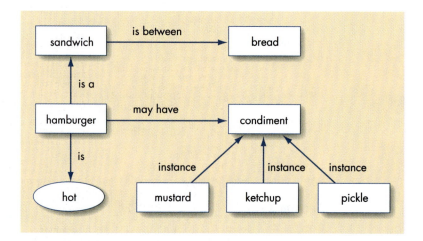

Section 14.4 No. N1 and N4 fire, but N2 and N3 do not, so N5 does not.

Section 14.5

1. Frank is tall. Knowing that Frank is tall does not imply that he is bald.

2. No conclusion can be inferred. Frank may or may not be tall.

comparison operators, 360
compiler, 377–378
concatenation operator,
 353–354
conditional flow of control,
 358–365
Console class, 351
control statements, 358–359
data types, 346
definition, 388
divide and conquer, 379–380
example program, 352, 371–373
expectations of high-level programming languages,
 374–378
free format, 347
graphical programming,
 404–416. *See also* Graphical
 programming
identifiers, 345
if-else statement, 360–365
initializing variables, 357
input statements, 350–352
Java bytecode interpreter, 377
JVM, 377–378
laboratory experience, 374, 388
literal strings, 353
looping, 365–369
Math class, 372
methods, 344, 380–388
modularization, 387
OOP, 393–398
origin, 343
output statements, 353–354
prologue comment, 343
sequential flow of control, 358,
 359
type casting, 357
variable declarations, 346
virtual data storage, 345–349
while statement, 365–369
Java Boolean operators, 360
Java bytecode interpreter, 377
Java comparison operators, 360
Java compiler, 377–378
Java Virtual Machine (JVM), 377
JavaScript, 451–454
JIT compiler, 446, 447
Job control language, 272
Johnniac, 25
JPEG, 141, 142
JUMP X, 211, 217, 244
JUMPEQ, 211
JUMPEQ X, 217
JUMPGE X, 211
JUMPGT X, 211, 217, 244
JUMPLE, 211
JUMPLT, 211
JUMPLT X, 217
JUMPNEQ, 211
JUMPNEQ X, 217, 244
Junk email (spam), 320
Just in time (JIT) compiler, 446,
 447
JVM, 377

K

Kaczinsky, Ted (Unabomber), 671
Kahn, Robert, 324
Kant, Immanuel, 673
Karmarkar, N., 122
Kasparov, Garry, 644
Kazaa, 662
Kemeny, John, 446
Key-punch, 21
Keywords, 345
Killer apps, 316
Kilobyte, 191
Kitab al jabr w'al mugabala
 (Al-Khowarizmi), 7
Kleinrock, Leonard, 323
Knowledge base, 465
Knowledge-based systems, 647
Knowledge engineering, 649
Knowledge representation,
 632–635

L

Label, 245
Laboratory experiences
 algorithm animation, 58
 assembly language programming, 252
 binary search algorithm, 111
 compiler, 509
 data cleanup algorithms, 111
 drawing routines, 416
 encryption, 619
 find largest algorithm, 63
 functional programming, 460
 HTML programming, 451
 introductory laboratory (glossary of terms), 34
 Java, 374, 388
 logic circuit construction, 164
 neural network, 641
 sequential search algorithm, 58
 simulation model, 581
 sorting algorithms, 97, 117
 SQL queries, 614
 sum of products algorithm, 172
 Turing machines, 548, 557
 Von Neumann computer, 221
 WAN simulation, 318
LAN, 294–297
LAN topologies, 295
Language, 489
Language services, 239
Language translation, 477–521.
  See also Compilation process
Large-scale software development.
  See Software engineering
Latency, 200
Left-hand side, 487
Leibnitz, Gottfried, 17
Leibnitz's wheel, 17
Level of abstraction, 184
Lex, 520
Lexical analysis, 482–485
Lexical analyzer, 482
lg *n*, 108
Library, 59
Licklider, J. C. R., 323
Linear programming, 122
Link, 327
Linked list, 121
Linker, 341
Linux, 675
LISP, 455
Listeners, 407
Literal string, 353
LOAD X, 210, 217, 244
Loader, 260
Local area network (LAN), 277,
 294–297
Local name server, 310
Local optimization, 513–514
Local variable, 386
Location counter, 256
Loebner, Hugh, 629
Loebner Prize, 629
Log-on password, 615
Logarithm of *n* to the base 2 (lg
 n), 108
Logic design, 128
Logic errors, 422
Logic programming, 461–466
Logical implication, 180
Logical link control, 305
Logical link control protocols, 306
Logo, 460
Look-ahead parsing algorithms,
 495
Loop, 49
Loop body, 50, 365
Looping, 50, 250, 365–369
Lossless compression, 144
Lossy compression, 144
Lossy JPEG, 144–145
Lovelace, Lady Ada, 20, 445
Low-level programming languages,
 242
LT, 211

Ludd, Ned, 19
Luddites, 19

M

Machine language instructions,
 207–212
 arithmetic, 210–211
 branch, 211
 compare, 211
 data transfer, 210
Macintosh, 264
Magnetic tape, 201
Mail filters, 320
Main method, 344
Maintainability, 245
Maintenance, 423–424
Majority-rules circuit, 180
Mantissa, 133
MAR, 191
Mark I, 22
Mask, 149
Mass storage devices, 198–203
Massively parallel processors, 227
Math class, 372
Matrix, 617
Mauchly, John, 22, 24
Maximum memory size, 189
McCarthy, John, 455
MDR, 191
Medium access control, 305
Medium access control protocols,
 305
Megabyte, 191
Megaflop, 96, 226
Megahertz (MHz), 220
Memory, 188–195
Memory access time, 190
Memory address register (MAR),
 191
Memory bytes, 189
Memory data register (MDR), 191
Memory location, 346
Memory managers, 240
Memory operations, 190
Memory registers, 191
Memory width, 188
Metasymbols, 490
Method header, 383
Methods, 344, 380–388
MFENet, 323
MFLOPS, 220
MHz, 220
μsec, 202
Microsoft, 28, 600
Microsoft Intermediate Language
 (MSIL), 446
Microsoft .NET Framework,
 446–448
Microsoft Windows, 419
Middleware, 605
MIMD parallel processing,
 225–227, 467–469
MIPS, 220
MIT turtle, 460
Mixed mode, 519
Mobile computing, 293
Model, 525–526, 568. *See also*
 Models of computation; Sim-
 ulation and modeling
Models of computation, 523–563
 Church-Turing thesis, 549
 computing agent, 526–527
 halting problem, 553, 562
 proof by contradiction, 553
 Turing machine. *See* Turing ma-
  chine
 unsolvable problems, 551–557
Modem, 289–290
Modularization, 387
Modulation, 289
Modus ponens, 649
Mosaic, 328
MOVE X, Y, 210
MP3, 139–140, 660–666
msec, 202
MSIL, 446
Multimedia user interfaces, 279